GOPSALL

A Millennium
of
Influence

John Matthews
&
Mike Foley

Supported by a National Lottery Heritage Fund
grant entitled: *"St Mary the Virgin Congerstone:
Restoring and sharing our heritage"*

All proceeds to St Mary's Church

Please direct all enquiries to John Matthews:

Email: oldpopublications@gmail.com
The Old Post Office, Main St, Congerstone, CV13 6LZ

ISBN 978-1-80068-316-7

Published by the Independent Publishing Network

First published December 2021

GOPSALL

A Millennium of Influence

John Matthews
&
Mike Foley

Supported by a National Lottery Heritage Fund
grant entitled: *"St Mary the Virgin Congerstone:
Restoring and sharing our heritage"*

All proceeds to St Mary's Church

Please direct all enquiries to John Matthews:

Email: oldpopublications@gmail.com
The Old Post Office, Main St, Congerstone, CV13 6LZ

ISBN 978-1-80068-316-7

Published by the Independent Publishing Network

First published December 2021

CONTENTS

The Earl and Countess Howe

Foreword by The Rt Hon the Earl Howe GBE PC

Were it to exist today, complete with its contents of fine art and furniture and surrounded by its magnificent gardens, Gopsall Hall would certainly be thought of as one this country's foremost grand houses. Designed and built to standards reflecting the height of eighteenth-century refinement, and greatly enlarged in the century that followed, Gopsall embodied the sophistication and confidence of the age.

But the story of Gopsall is not simply that of an important house: it is above all a story about people – those who lived in it and those whose lives were closely tied to it. For the majority of its existence, Gopsall was home to successive generations of my family, around whom were the many individuals and families who in various ways served and supported them. On the great landed estates of the nineteenth century, the relationship between a landlord, his workforce and his tenantry, though in an obvious sense unequal, was nevertheless one of mutual dependence. A benign and sympathetic landowner could expect to have around him a loyal and respectful community. One of the most vivid chapters of this book is the one which contains the personal testimonies of those who, in their various ways, worked for the good of Gopsall and took an evident pride in doing so.

In the pages that follow it is possible to appreciate the full depth and extent of that community. In the service of Lord Howe there were house staff, gardeners, groundsmen, gamekeepers, woodmen, coachmen, carpenters and lodgekeepers. The wider estate population numbered a host of tenant farmers, farm labourers, saw mill employees, publicans, alms house residents, schoolteachers and, importantly, clergy. For all these individuals and their families, their sense of identity would have been defined, to a greater or lesser degree, by their association with Gopsall Hall and its aristocratic residents.

Gopsall's slow demise can be mapped from the time of its sale to Samuel Waring in 1918. In the absence of supporting records, the reasons for my predecessor's decision to take such a drastic step can only be surmised; but in truth they are not hard to find. At the start of the First World War, farm rents per acre had fallen by nearly a third since their peak in the early 1870s. By the end of the War, not only had inflation more-than-halved the value of money in the space of four years but the marginal rate of income tax had also rocketed. Dependent as he was on an income from land holdings, Lord Howe's ability to maintain his pre-war way of life would have been drastically compromised. It was, in any case, a way of life which, with the changed mood of the times, he might have not had the energy or enthusiasm to replicate. Indeed Gopsall, as a rural estate, was by no means unique: between the Armistice and 1922, a quarter of all the land in Britain had changed hands.

It is difficult not to regret that a house created with such care and taste by Charles Jennens – its plasterwork, panelling, carvings and marble mantelpieces – should have vanished so completely. However, the soul of Gopsall, and the social order it represented, belong to an era that is now long-gone. It is left to us, in the twenty-first century, to reflect upon this microcosm of our collective history with an appreciation of its virtues as well as its failings. This book enables us to do so.

Penn, September 2021

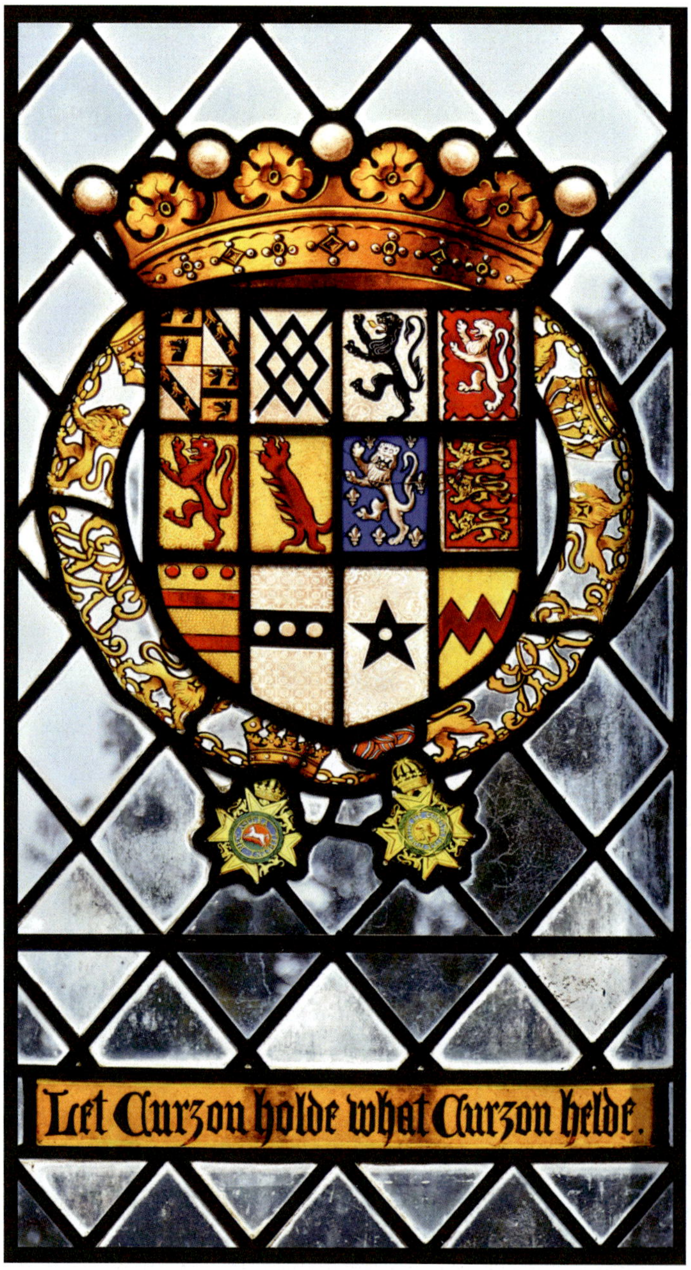

The Curzon window,
St James' Church, Twycross

Preface

This book has been twenty-five years in the making. As indicated in the book cover notes, its genesis was in the Horse and Jockey, Congerstone in the mid-1990s. Some five years later, having not written a word about Gopsall, we had another brilliant idea in 'the Jockey' - *"Why don't we learn to ring the church bells for the Millennium celebrations"*. Well, we did learn to ring tower bells and did 'ring in' the millennium, but still did nothing about a Gopsall book, except that we started to collect information and photographs about Gopsall Hall and the wider Gopsall Estate. Over the intervening years, people generously gave us photos, to keep or copy, and various bits and pieces of information. Some of the latter were available from newspapers and county directories etc, but precious information came from villagers who had memories of Gopsall during the early years of the 20th century. This book is an attempt to piece together what is known about the nearly one-thousand-year history of Gopsall and to preserve those last remembered years prior to Gopsall's decline after the estate was sold by the 4th Earl Howe. Over the years, the Lords of Gopsall had a significant influence over their villages and inhabitants, especially during the 19th century; providing work, housing and education. Today the Gopsall Estate no longer exists but, the Gopsall village churches, churchyards, almshouses and local schools (whether still functioning, as in Congerstone and Heather, or converted to houses) are tangible reminders of the past.

John Matthews & Mike Foley, Congerstone, November 2021

Acknowledgments

This book would not have been possible without the help and encouragement of a large number of people and several organisations over the last twenty-five years. The following is a list of those who have contributed in their various ways: unfortunately, some are no longer with us. While we hope the list is accurate, both time and our ever-declining memories may mean that some have been omitted, and for that we apologise now.

Pauline Bee, Margaret Braybrooks, John Burns, J.E. Cudmore, John Dexter, Russ Elliott (gwr.org.uk), Keith Farrell, Shirley Foley, Ray Green (Monza Ltd, NZ), David Grimmer, Ray Hale, Cecil Hart, Fred Hartley, Jane Harvey, Jean Headley, Norman Headley, Sid Hobbs, Reg Ison, Natalie Jones (Reach Licensing), John & Liz Lain, Peter Liddle, Jonathan Makepeace (RIBA.org), Stephanie Mallas (nee Headley), Brian McCullam, Glynis Oakley, Linda Plummer, Audrey Pearce, John Ramsbottom & Family, Rita Reading, Zoe Schafer (motorsportimages.com), Jean Sedgley, Chris Simmons, Lynn Stoney, Brian Sutton, Richard Trivett, Felicity Vero, John & Mary Waltho, Caroline White (Dept. Special Collections & University Archives, W.E.B. Du Bois Library, UMass Amherst, USA), Nigel Wilkins (Historic England Archives), David Wright, Olga Wright.

In addition, although inadvisable to highlight specific individuals for special thanks, four people have made very significant contributions to the book and its final completion:

Lord Howe has generously allowed us free access to his archive, spent hours proofreading the draft chapters, made suggestions to improve the script, contributed small sections on some Classical topics and encouraged us over the last two years.

Brenda Sumner's thesis is a mine of information on Charles Jennens, Handel and Gopsall and has greatly assisted our research. In addition, Brenda has allowed us to reproduce her transcript of John Grundy's description of Gopsall in 1750.

Geoff Frisby has contributed to a chapter in the book, proofread all the chapters, and has been a conduit to his many friends in the area who have provided valuable information and photographs.

Without the endeavours of Gill Lawrence in obtaining various grants to replace the lead roof of St Mary's Church stolen in 2015, this book might never have existed. The support of the grant obtained from the National Lottery Heritage Fund has meant that the size, scope and quality of the book has not been constrained. Gill has helped with our research, proofread several versions of the whole text and always constructively criticised and encouraged our efforts.

Gopsall Manor and its Lords

Today, Gopsall is generally known and remembered for a relatively small number of reasons. These include Handel reputedly being a regular visitor to Gopsall, Charles Jennens Jnr building 'the grandest country house in Leicestershire' at the cost of £100,000 (about £22.8 million in 2021), the ownership of the estate by the Curzon-Howe family throughout the 19th and early 20th centuries and the final demolition of the hall in 1951. This is not surprising as information about Gopsall prior to it being inherited by Charles Jennens Jnr in 1747 is very limited and confused.

There are two proposed meanings for the name Gopsall.[1] Either 'The servant's hill' or 'Gop's hill' from the old English 'Gop', meaning 'servant or serf' or Gop used as a proper name of a man. However, the spelling of Gopsall in manuscripts, rent rolls, deeds etc has varied throughout the years since it was first recorded as Gopeshille in the Domesday Book in 1086. Both Gopsal and Gopsall were used throughout the 19th century, but the double 'll' spelling became standard in the 20th century.

Year*	Name
1086	Gopeshille
1243	Gopeshull(e) & Gopshull(e)
1285	Gopeshill & Gopshill(e)
1410	Gopusyll
1415	Goppeshill
1461	Goppeshull
1502	Gopsell
1541	Goppyssell
1601	Goppshill & Gopsull
1795	Gopsal & Gopsall

* year first recorded

There do not appear to be any references to Gopsall prior to the Norman Conquest. Shortly after 1066, William the Conqueror (William I) gave Gopsall to Hugh d'Avaranches along with other lands including Tutbury Castle and its environs because his family had provided ships for the invasion of England.[2,3] Hugh had also been one of the trusted men left at home to assist William's wife, Duchess Matilda, to administer Normandy while he was away.[3] A few years later, in 1071, King William promoted Hugh to the Earldom of Chester and gave Hugh's lands around Tutbury and Gopsall to the Norman Knight, Henry de Ferrers (Ferrières).[4] Henry was a major landholder, having been granted some 210 manors throughout England and Wales, including Gopsall.[5,6] It is widely assumed that Henry was granted such a large number of manors because he fought alongside William at the Battle of Hastings in 1066, but there is no firm evidence to confirm this assumption. In 1086 Henry was put in charge of the West Midlands part of the survey that resulted in the Domesday Book. Interestingly, Henry brought several of his underlords from Normandy to hold his English lands. One of these families was the Curzons,[7] the name derived from Notre-Dame-de-Courson, who had subsequently settled in the Kedleston area by 1295. It was by the marriage of Charles Jennens' niece, Esther Hanmer, to Assheton Curzon that their son, Penn Assheton Curzon, inherited Gopsall in 1773.

de Ferrers coat of arms

The Domesday Book lists Henry de Ferrers as being the Tenant in Chief (i.e. the person holding land directly from the Crown) of Gopsall with the land leased to Roald 'of Gopsall'. Local to Gopsall, Henry is also said to hold Twycross, Orton-on-the-Hill, Sheepy Magna, Appleby Parva, Newton Burgoland, Swepstone, 120 acres of 'waste' land in Snarestone and the majority of Congerstone. At this time Gopsall was a settlement consisting of 13 households and covering about 360 acres of arable land. By comparison the whole of Congerstone had 18 households, 240 acres of arable land, 3 acres of meadow and a mill. Thus, Gopsall at this time was a not insignificant agricultural settlement. Furthermore, Gopsall had a chapel in the early 12th century which, together with some adjacent land, was given to Merevale Abbey by Robert de Ferrers Jnr (1100-

1162; variously referred to as the Earl of Ferrers, Earl of Derby and Earl of Nottingham), Henry's grandson, when he established the Abbey in 1148.[8] This again suggests that Gopsall was a significant settlement as the first evidence of a church at Congerstone dates from 1186 when William de Congerstone was priest.

Nothing visible remains of the settlement or the chapel at Gopsall today and there have been no archaeological investigations of the site. It is likely that the settlement was situated in the area that was subsequently the site of the post-medieval Gopsall homestead, but was probably long gone by then. This site, at the top of a hill within the 115m/377ft contour reflects the name, Servant's or Gop's Hill, and it is thought that the adjacent south facing slopes may have encouraged settlement and agriculture from as early as the prehistoric era. Gopsall is one of the deserted villages in this part of Leicestershire along with Wellsborough, Weston, Atterton, Ambion, Naneby and Brascote.[9]

de Grendon coat of arms

Shortly after setting up Merevale Abbey in 1148, Robert de Ferrers relinquished ownership of Gopsall and transferred all rights of ownership to Roger de Grendon and his heirs. The de Grendons were lords of Gopsall for seven generations until Robert de Grendon (born about 1295) died of the Black Death in 1349. Soon after, Gopsall was apparently purchased by the Langham family who had had land holdings in Gopsall since 1296.[10]

Langham coat of arms

The Hundred Rolls survey of Edward I in 1279 indicated that there were 9 inhabitants of Gopsall for tax purposes. A hundred years later, Poll tax records show that there were 17 and 15 adults over 14 years of age living in Gopsall in 1377 and 1379 respectively.[9,11]

Robert (de) Langham was known to be in possession of the manor of Gopsall in 1393. However, Langham's title to the manor seems to have been under dispute in 1395 for when he and his son Reginald (Reynold) conveyed land in Lindley to Thomas Bosevile of Nuneaton it was on condition that, if they should lose Gopsall by judgement or claim in the lawcourts, they could repossess the land. It would appear that Robert's title to Gopsall was confirmed by the courts as the manor was held by the Langham family for seven generations until it was eventually sold by George Langham to Sir George Hastings some 165 years later in 1564.[10,12,13] The sale document (Feet of Fines, co. Leicester, Easter) gives the details of this sale as the Manor of Gopsall, 10 messuages,[14] and 6,500 acres of land in Gopsall and Twycross, besides cottages, gardens etc.[12]

Sir George Hastings (1540-1604)
and his son Francis
(Leicester Arts & Museum Services)

George Hastings (1540-1604) was apppointed Knight in 1565 and became High Sheriff of Leicestershire in 1571. After the death of his brother Henry in 1595, he became the 4th Earl of Huntingdon. He initially lived at Gopsall but moved to Loughborough before he died in 1604. Gopsall and the title of Earl of Huntingdon were inherited by his grandson, Henry Hastings (1586-1643; 5th Earl), who finally sold Gopsall to Sir Thomas Merry (Merrye) in 1618.[10,15]

In addition to Gopsall, Sir Thomas held lands in Twycross and Norton, as well as large grants of lands from James I, which ranged from Somerset to Northumberland.[10] Whether he ever lived at Gopsall is unknown. However, it

North elevation of the Elizabethan House

is possible that his son Thomas, born in 1605, lived there for part of his life as he was returned unopposed as one of the Knights of Leicestershire (ie. as a Member of Parliament) in 1660.[16]

It was during Merry's ownership of Gopsall that a map of the manor was produced around 1650.[17] The map clearly shows the position of the manor house, a drawing of its north facade and the division of the manor into fields. Thus, the manor had already been enclosed (inclosed) by this time, as had Twycross and Bilstone, whereas enclosure did not occur in nearby Shackerstone and Congerstone until c.1774 and 1823-1826 respectively. The site of the manor house is on the same site as the extravagant hall built by Charles Jennens 100 years later, but when it was built and who built it is unknown. The fact that the house is the only building marked on the map suggests that all traces of the 'village' of Gopsall had been lost by this time. Indeed, the Hearth Tax records of 1670 only record one household where tax was payable, presumably the manor house.[9]

The 1650 map indicates that the access 'drive' to the manor house was almost due south, traversing Bilstone Hill presumably aiming for Bilstone (Bilson on the map). At this time the 'straight mile' between Bilstone and Twycross did not exist (the road was built in 1844 by the then

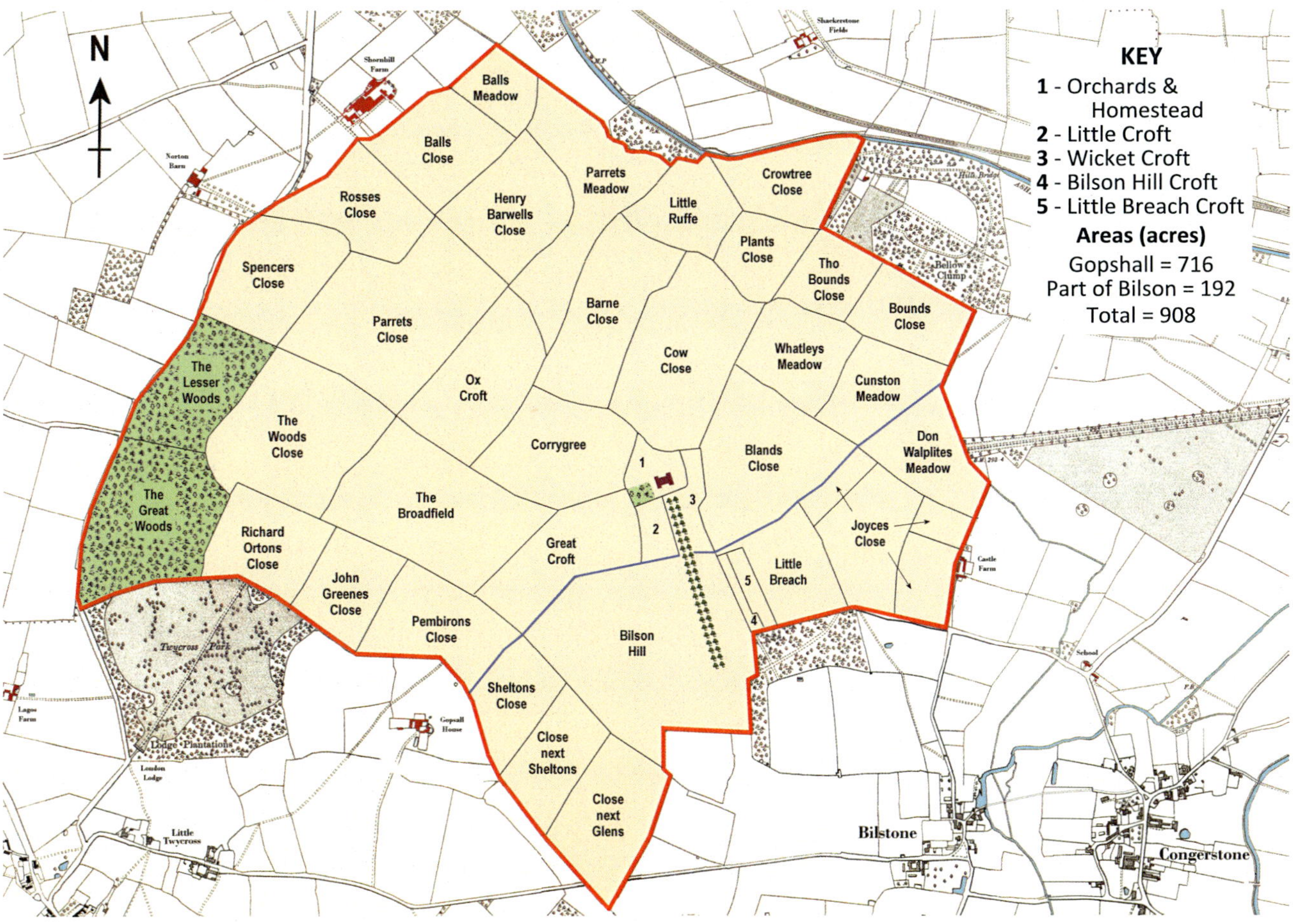

The 1650 map of Gopsall Manor, with field names and entrance drive to the house, overlaid onto the 1903 Ordnance Survey map.[18] The land north of the blue line is labelled 'Gopshall' and south, 'Part of Bilson'.

Lord of Gopsall - Richard Curzon-Howe, 1st Earl Howe).[19] Most of the land included in Gopsall Manor south and east of the house is labeled 'Part of Bilson', which may indicate that the house was originally built close to the southern border of the manor with those areas in Bilstone being acquired later.

Gopsall Parish outlined in red as shown on the 1835 (*top*) and 1899 (*bottom*) 1 inch Ordnance Survey maps.[21] The 1835 map shows a southern entrance to the hall and absence of the Bilstone-Little Twycross road, known as the 'Straight Mile'.

Interestingly, around the time the Gopsall Manor map was produced, Bilstone was purchased by Lord Henry Hastings (1610-1666/7; 1st and last Baron Loughborough of Loughborough). He was the second son of the 5th Earl of Huntingdon who had sold Gopsall to John Merry in 1618. In 1643, Lord Henry sold Bilstone Manor and some adjacent land to John Butler who was married to Joyce Hastings, his second cousin, once removed.[10,15] Some of the land marked 'Part of Bilson' on the Gopsall map is called 'Joyce's Close' presumably reflecting this. Although there is no documentary evidence, assuming that the map date of 1650 is correct, it is possible that some of the Bilstone land was passed to Thomas Merry by Butler to become part of the Gopsall Manor at this time, before Charles Jennens Snr purchased Bilstone Manor in 1692 (see later).

As far as can be found, the land south of Gopsall manor house shown within Gopsall but labelled 'Part of Bilson' has never been included within the Gopsall Parish boundary in its entirety. The parish boundary map dated 1835 only included part of this land whereas maps from the late 19th century up to the present day clearly show the southern parish boundary (civil and ecclesiastical) of Gopsall exclude 'Part of Bilson' from the Parish of Gopsall. The boundaries of the 1899 parish of Gopsall are identical to the 1650 plan of the manor without 'Part of Bilson'. Gopsall is now part of the ecclesiastical parish of Sheepy with Ratcliffe Culey, Sibson, Orton-on-the-Hill, Twycross and Shenton and the civil parish of Twycross.[20]

Comparing the 1650 plan with the early Ordnance Survey (OS) maps of Gopsall, it can be seen that most of the manor field boundaries are surprisingly accurate as they line up with field boundaries, streams and paths mapped at the end of the 19th century. Aerial surveys performed in the last half of the 20th century have also demonstrated evidence of ridge and furrow over almost the entire site confirming that that most of the manor was originally used as arable land.[22]

Viscount Lonsdale (1655-1700) by Hyacinthe Rigaud (Public Domain).

After 1660, Thomas Merry never stood for Parliament again and vacated Gopsall selling his lands in Norton and Twycross along with Gopsall to Sir John Lowther of Lowther Hall in 1677.[10] This appears to have been the 1st Viscount Lonsdale and 1st Baron Lowther of Lowther, previously known as Sir John Lowther, 2nd Baronet Lowther of Lowther from 1675 to 1696.[15] He became Member of

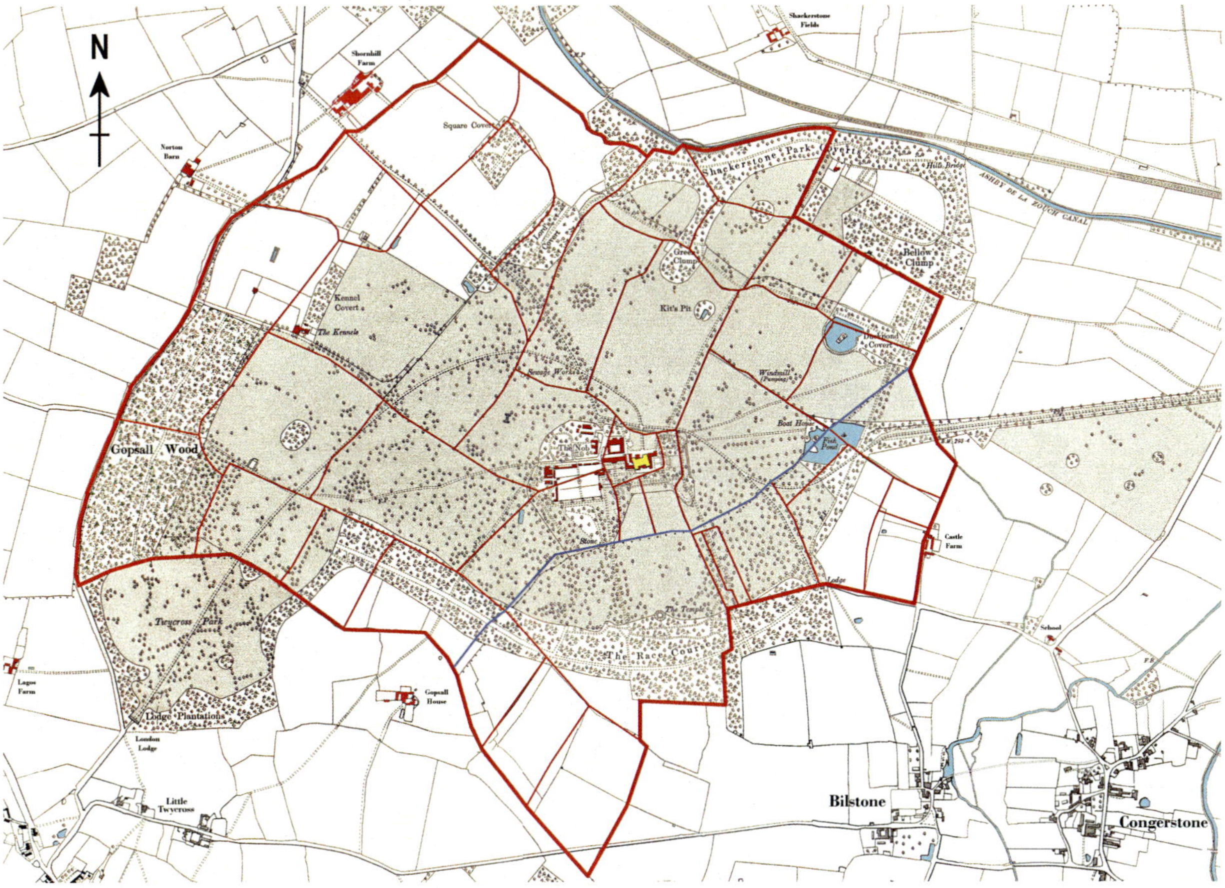

Perimeter and field boundaries shown on the 1650 Gopsall Manor map overlaid onto the 1903 Ordnance Survey map.[18]

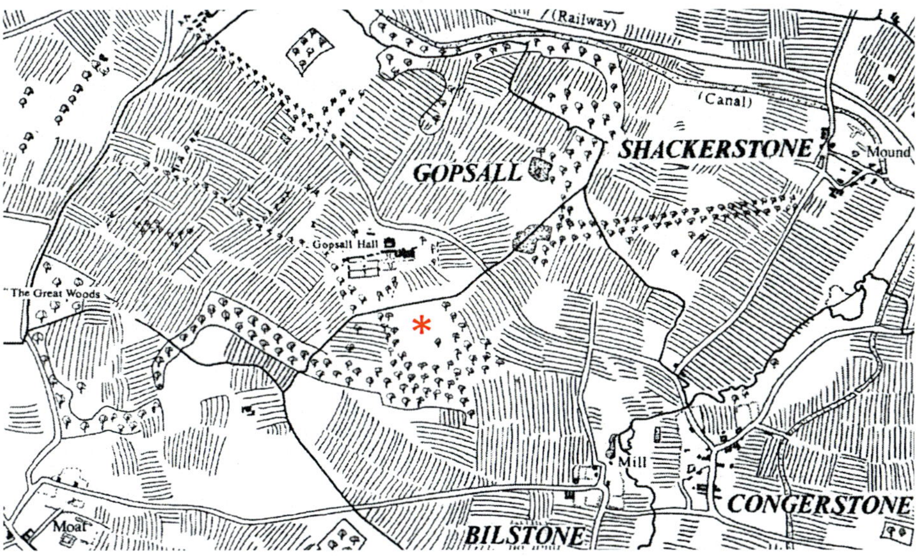

Map showing the ridge and furrow patterns in Gopsall Park and adjacent areas.

These maps were derived from photographs taken by 'aerial archaeologist', James Pickering.[22]

* = area occupied by the 'Great Pond' in the latter half of the 18th century (Chapter 4).

(Image courtesy of Robert F. Hartley)

Parliament for Westmorland in the year he purchased Gopsall and was politically active until his death in 1700.[23,24] In addition to his family seat at Lowther Hall in Westmorland, he had extensive land holdings in the north of England, and it is likely that he never lived at, or even visited, Gopsall. Indeed, his lordship of Gopsall only lasted 6 years and sale documents, dated 28th January 1684, were drawn up between Morgan Powell (on behalf of Sir John Lowther) and Humphrey Jennens. Jennens agreed to purchase Gopsall and other land in the area and elsewhere in the County of Leicester at a cost of £16,400. The area of land was not specified in this agreement but was referred to as being in Gopsall, Twycross, Norton-juxta-Twycross, Orton-on-the-Hill and Bilstone. However, in May 1685, an indenture between Sir John Lowther and Humphrey Jennens, identified the land involved by giving the names of fields and tenants.[25]

Humphrey Jennens was a rich industrialist (iron-master) from Birmingham who had extensive forges at Upper Whitacre (Furnace End), Weeford, Bromford, Aston, Halesowen and Whitwick. To keep his furnaces burning he aquired huge amounts of timber from the Forest of Arden and Sherwood and Charnwood Forests. In addition to his commercial properties, Humphrey Jennens owned a town house in High Street Birmingham, a country house in Warwickshire (Erdington Hall) and the manor of Nether Whitacre, which he purchased in 1681.[10,26] When he died in 1690, never having lived at Gopsall, the estate was inherited by his eldest son, Charles Jennens, who became the first of the family to take up residence. Little is known about Charles Jennens Snr (1662-1747). He studied at the Middle Temple (one of the four Inns of Court which served as colleges for the education of lawyers) and was a justice of the peace.[10] Throughout his life as Lord of Gopsall Manor he expanded his holdings of land local to the estate purchasing the manor of Bilstone (1692), land in Twycross (1697), land in, and finally the manor of, Congerstone (1698, 1708, 1712 & 1715) and land in Orton-on-the-Hill (1726 & 1743).[27] Upon his death in 1747, only two of his seven children from his two marriages were still alive, Charles and Elizabeth.

Portrait of Charles Jennens Jnr (c.1745) by Thomas Hudson (1701-1779) (Public Domain).

Charles Jennens Jnr (1700-1773) inherited the family estates including 34 properties scattered over six counties together with Gopsall. It is not known where Charles was born but he was brought up at Gopsall and during adult life divided his time between living at Gopsall and in London. He went to Balliol College, Oxford in 1715 but did not graduate. It was in that year that he met Edward Holdsworth, an English classical scholar, who refused to swear allegiance to George I believing that Bonnie Prince Charlie was the rightful heir to the throne (ie. he was a non-juror). Holdsworth had to resign his position at Oxford, but became a life-long friend of Charles Jennens, who also became a non-juror and was therefore not able to graduate. Jennens was a devout Christian but, as a non-juror, he could not hold any public appointment and devoted his time to the arts, as a collector of fine art and as a music patron. He became a friend, collaborator and patron of Handel, writing the words for many of his musical compositions, including Saul, Messiah and Belshazzar (1735-1745).[10,28,29] During this time there is some evidence that Handel visited Gopsall on several occasions.[30-32] However, Charles spent most of the winter months in London and, from letters written to Holdsworth, Jennens was not particularly happy living at Gopsall "*under his father's authority*" hinting that family life was unsatisfactory, even uncivilized.[28]

The frontispiece to Charles Jennens' edition of Shakespeare's Hamlet, Prince of Denmark; a Tragedy' (1773). Etching and engraving of the 'Closet Scene'; act 3, scene 4 (Public Domain).

In his last years, Jennens produced critical editions of Shakespeare's plays, to be published separately (unheard of at this time),[10,33] which drew ridicule from George Steevens, a rival Shakespearean commentator and editor. Several modern Shakespeare scholars do not share Steevens' view.[28]

In the same year that Charles Jennens Jnr inherited Gopsall, Norton was enclosed by Act of Parliament. The Jennens' holding of land in Norton was confirmed as 195 acres, 1 rood and 4 perches. This land included an extra 20 acres at Shornells or Shirnells (later Home Farm and now Shornhill Farm) as a reward for Charles Jennens Snr having agreed to the Inclosure.[34] Although Charles Jnr increased his holding of land in Bilstone by purchase and exchange in 1756 and 1768,[27] his main focus was the building of a grand hall set in fine gardens and parkland that befitted a man of his wealth.

The south and east fronts of Gopsall Hall

Almost immediately after his father's death, Charles set about building a new hall at Gopsall. The precise details of what was built, who designed and built it and whether it was a completely new build or an expansion of the existing house are not clear. Certainly the documents held by the Royal Institute of British Architects (RIBA) show a variety of plans for both the 'new' hall and for a variety of garden buildings. However, detailed analysis of the surviving plans strongly indicate that the new hall was centred on the old, Elizabethan house (Chapter 2). It is probable that the total cost of building the hall and laying out the park and gardens was £100,000, rather than the often quoted £180,000.[35]

Memorial to Charles Jennens (d. 1773) in St Giles' Church, Nether Whitacre (by Richard Hayward).

According to the description of the hall in 1750 by John Grundy, much of the building work on the hall had been completed, although the portico with Corinthian columns on the south front had not been erected.[36] How far the layout of the gardens around the hall had progressed by then is difficult to know, except that the layout of the gardens and parkland did take place at the same time as building the hall. Many of the plans for garden buildings held by RIBA are dated between 1754 and 1756. The best estimates for the building of the 'famous' Ionic temple on the northern edge of Bilstone Hill immediately to the south of the hall are between 1755 and 1760.[37] This being the case, although Handel may have seen the new hall, he could never have seen the temple as he was completely blind by 1753 and died in 1759.[38]

Charles Jennens died in 1773 and a funeral sermon was preached at St James' Church, Twycross on 4th January 1774 by the Rev. George Kelly Jnr.[10] Charles was buried in the family vault in Nether Whitacre, where a large marble memorial was erected in 1775 which records some of his charitable and Christian activities.[39] He never married and, on his death, all his manors and lands in Gopsall, Orton-on-the-Hill, Twycross, Norton-juxta-Twycross, Bilstone, Congerstone (ie. Gopsall and what is later known as the outlying parts of the Gopsall Estate and estate villages) and places in Warwickshire were inherited by his grandnephew, Penn Assheton Curzon. Penn Assheton Curzon was only 16 at this time and his inheritance was kept in trust until he came of age.[40]

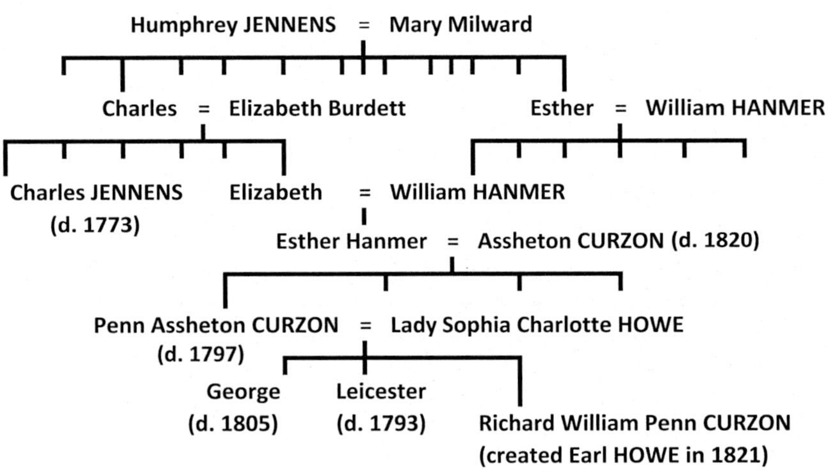

Simplified pedigree showing link between Jennens, Howe and Curzon families.

Penn Assheton Curzon married Sophia Charlotte Howe (the Baroness Howe from 1799), the eldest daughter of Richard Howe, 1st Earl Howe (of the 1st creation).[41] During his life, Penn Assheton Curzon added to the local estate holdings by purchasing land in Shackerstone and buildings and land in Twycross.[27] He is also said to have aquired a considerable collection of paintings for the hall and adorned the pleasure grounds with statues and ornamental temples.[42] Penn Assheton Curzon died in 1797 and, although 'of Gopsall' was buried in a specially extended family vault in Holy Trinity, Penn. His wife, as guardian for their eldest son George (age 9), purchased more land in Shackerstone (1798) and property and land in Twycross (1804). According to a survey in 1803, the Gopsall Estate covered 3,095 acres and yielded about £3,000 annual rental income.[43] After George's death in 1805 (age 16), Baroness Howe managed the Gopsall and other estates on behalf of her surviving son, Richard William Penn Curzon (whom she called Penn)[44] and purchased further property in Twycross.

In 1812, Baroness Howe married her second husband, Jonathan Phipps ('Phippy') and immediately transferred her property in Twickenham to him. Phippy was an oculist (albeit the King's oculist) and a mere commoner. The marriage was somewhat frowned upon in societal circles, including by Lord Curzon, Sophia's ex-father-in-law, who saw Phippy as a man on the make. Lord Curzon's anxiety about Sophia's marriage and rapid property transfer to her husband prompted him to obtain a writ in Chancery (dated 25th November 1812) to protect his grandson's interest in the Gopsall Estate and other properties being managed by Baroness Howe.[44,45] Following the writ, Baroness Howe and her husband took legal advice and issued a formal response in March 1813.[45] After this, the case does not seem to have progressed further and Richard Curzon came into his estates in 1817 on reaching the age of 21. Interestingly, the March 1813 response to the writ included a schedule of the towns, tenants, estates and rents being managed by Baroness Howe; total rents were £5,828, of which £1,692 came from the Gopsall Estate (see Appendix).

Assheton Curzon, 1st Viscount Curzon (1730 - 1820). Portrait dated 13th February 1813, when he was 84 years old.

Richard Curzon (1796-1870) was educated at Eton and Oxford and inherited the Curzon viscountcy, taking his seat in the House of Lords on the death of his grandfather in 1820. He then took the additional name of Howe by Royal licence a year later and was created Earl Howe that same year (Richard William Penn Curzon-Howe, 1st Earl Howe of the 2nd creation). Between 1829 and 1830 he was Lord of the Bedchamber to King George IV and acted as Lord Chamberlain to Queen Adelaide (1830-31 and 1834-37).[15,42,46,47] As a member of the Royal Household during this period, he would have spent a lot of his time away from Gopsall.

Richard William Penn Curzon-Howe, 1st Earl Howe (c1860).

Royal Collection Trust / © Her Majesty Queen Elizabeth II 2021

Prior to receiving the title of Earl, Richard Curzon married Lady Harriet Georgiana Brudenell in 1820, with whom he had ten children; the two eldest subsequently became the 2nd (George Augustus Frederick Louis Curzon-Howe) and 3rd (Richard William Penn Curzon-Howe) Earl Howe. Harriet died in 1836 shortly after giving birth to her tenth child. Nine years later, the Earl married Anne Gore, a union resulting in a further three children. Five of the Earl's nine sons joined the armed forces and attained senior ranks, including general (Richard William Penn Curzon-Howe, 3rd Earl Howe; Hon. Sir Leicester Smyth, originally Curzon) and admiral commander-in-chief, Portsmouth (Hon. Sir Assheton Gore Curzon-Howe).[15,46]

After Richard took possession of his estates, the enclosure map for Congerstone (1825) indicates that he purchased significant amounts of land in Congerstone from Lady Byron who, for a time, lived in Kirkby Mallory. Congerstone was the last area in this part of Leicestershire to be enclosed and the enclosure map shows that Earl Howe was by far the major land owner.[48] He also purchased Odstone Manor in 1826. The Survey of Land in Leicestershire dated 1826 indicates that Richard's total land holding in the county was 6,378 acres with 1,204 acres in hand.[49] Area measurements on the 1 inch First Series OS maps of Gopsall (1803 and 1838) demonstrate that the hall, gardens and parkland covered about 875 acres (1.37 sq miles). At this time, Earl Howe

Harriet Georgiana Countess Howe (1799-1836) by Margaret Sarah Carpenter (Public Domain).

Queen Adelaide (Princess Adelaide of Saxe-Meiningen) by Sir William Beechey (c.1831) (NPG 1533).

was Lord of the manors of Bilstone, Barton in the Beans, Congerstone, Nailstone, Newton Burgoland, Norton, Odstone, Shackerstone and Twycross, in addition to Gopsall. He also claimed the lordship of Ibstock, even though most of the land was owned by freeholders, who disputed his manorial rights. He was the major landowner in most of these manors and also had land in Orton-on-the-Hill.[42] Thus, most of the inhabitants of these villages worked directly or indirectly for Earl Howe and the wider 'Gopsall Estate', which was now approaching its maximum size.

Richard, 1st Earl Howe was known for his benevolence to the poor and the promotion of education and religion.[42,50] In the 20-year period 1825 to 1845, Earl Howe paid to refurbish/remodel the churches in Congerstone, Norton, Shackerstone and Twycross. Two years later, in 1847, he paid £500 towards the £1,200 cost of rebuilding the chancel of St John's Church, Heather. Amongst other things, he built schools in Twycross (1822), Congerstone (1825), Nailstone (1828), Norton (1839) and Shackerstone (1844), as well as almshouses in these villages (Chapter 13). He also maintained the property he owned in the villages. For example, in about 1830 he "*rebuilt in a uniform, neat and substantial manner*" most of the houses he owned in Twycross.[42]

Richard made a number of changes to the hall but their extent and details are obscure (Chapter 2). He made significant changes to the offices (service areas) at Gopsall and added the single-storey picture gallery and, probably, the billiard room. In the park, he had the Constantine Arch built at the Twycross entrance (variously known as Twycross lodge or, on Ordnance Survey maps, London lodge; Chapter 2), and added more statues and ornaments to the garden, including Pope's obelisk. He also planted thirteen *Wellingtonia gigantea* that are still standing today (Chapter 4).

Richard was a member of the Royal Household until 1837 when King William IV died. Thereafter, he maintained a friendship with William's widow, the dowager Queen Adelaide, who visited Gopsall each autumn from 1839 to 1844. Her Coat of Arms is depicted in a small window in St

Richard, 1st Earl Howe surrounded by his family at Gopsall (1863)

Standing (*L-R*): Col. the Hon Richard William Penn Curzon (3rd Earl in 1876), The Hon Mrs Richard Curzon (Isabella Maria Katherine Anson), Capt. the Hon Frederick Curzon, The Hon Montagu Curzon, Lady Howe (Lord Howe's second wife Anne Gore; m. 1845), Lady Westmorland (Lady Adelaide Curzon), The Hon Assheton Gore Curzon-Howe (Admiral later) & Lord Westmorland (Col. Francis William Henry Fane, 12th Earl). **Sitting** (*L-R*): The Hon Henry Dugdale Curzon, The Hon Mrs Henry Curzon (Eleanor Young Swinburne), The Hon Matthew Henry Moreton*, Lady Mary Anna Curzon & Col the Hon Leicester Curzon (Smyth from 1866). * Tenth son of the 2nd Earl of Ducie (b. 1847); friend of Montagu Curzon.

James' Church, Twycross and some of the church plate of St Mary's, Congerstone was a gift from Queen Adelaide in 1840 (Chapter 13).

George, Viscount Curzon (2nd Earl Howe in 1870).

Richard, 1st Earl Howe, died in 1870 and, unusually for this family, was buried in a vault at St James' Church, Twycross. The title and Gopsall passed to his son George Augustus Frederick Louis Curzon-Howe (2nd Earl Howe; 1821-1876). As 2nd Earl Howe, he gave up the south Leicestershire parliamentary seat that he had held since 1857 and was promoted to lieutenant-colonel commandant of the Leicestershire Yeomanry Cavalry.[15,46] He lived at Penn House, Buckinghamshire and used Gopsall as his country residence. Like his predecessor, the 2nd Earl was a keen huntsman, being master of the Atherstone hunt for the 11 years prior to inheriting his title.[51] He took responsibility for improving the health of the Atherstone pack and the building of the new hunt kennels. In addition, he was interested in exhibiting dogs and was president of the Birmingham Dog Show Society for seven of the years between 1860 and 1875.[52]

George died in 1876 and his lands and titles were inherited by his younger brother, Richard William Penn Curzon-Howe (1822-1900) who became the 3rd Earl Howe. He was a professional soldier and, after joining the army in 1838, he rose to become major general in 1869 prior to becoming a general in 1880. In addition to holding honorary ranks in the Leicestershire Yeomanry Cavalry and Grenadier Guards, Richard gained the rank of colonel in the service of the 2nd Life Guards and served as Gold Stick (Chapter 8). He was Lord-Lieutenant of Leicestershire from 1888 until his death in 1900, and was invested as Knight Grand Cross, Royal Victorian Order in 1897.[15,46]

Richard, 3rd Earl Howe continued to use Gopsall for sporting activities and is said to have engaged David Brandon (architect) to perform works at Gopsall spanning 1877-1880 that may have included the building of a single storey billiard room and an underground passage (Chapter 2). During the shooting season, members of the royal family were relatively frequent guests at Gopsall in the late 1880s and 1890s.[53] In his later years the 3rd Earl funded, in whole or in part, a variety of rebuilding and refurbishment projects in the 'Gopsall' villages including the re-roofing of St Mary's Church, Congerstone in 1897 (Chapter 13).

Above: Painting of Richard, 3rd Earl Howe, which hangs in the Officers' Mess of Knightsbridge Barracks, London.

Left: Colonel Richard Curzon prior to becoming Viscount Curzon in 1870 and 3rd Earl Howe in 1876.

On the death of the 3rd Earl in 1900, Richard George Penn Curzon-Howe (1861-1929), his eldest son became 4th Earl Howe. The 4th Earl was known as George throughout his life,[44] perhaps preventing confusion with his father. As with many of his forebears, the 4th Earl was educated at Eton and Oxford and had close associations with the royal household. He was

Treasurer of the Household from 1896 until 1900 when he became Earl Howe, Lord-in-waiting from 1900 to 1903 and finally Lord Chamberlain to Queen Alexandra between 1903 and 1925.[15,46]

The 4th Earl Howe and his Coat of Arms bearing the Curzon family motto: 'Let Curzon holde what Curzon helde'.

The 4th Earl was a friend of King Edward VII, who visited both the Penn and Gopsall estates during the shooting season. He made a number of improvements to the hall for the well publicised royal visit to Gopsall in December 1902. These included its complete redecoration, fitting of the 'famous' silver bath and the installation of an electricity supply (Chapter 8).

In 1905, on the coming of age of his only son, Francis Richard Henry Penn Curzon (Viscount Curzon, later 5th Earl Howe), several days of celebrations were held at Gopsall. These included donations to the poor of all the estate villages, ringing of the church bells, dinners and parties for the nobility, principal gentry and clergy of the neighbourhood, and dinners and luncheons for his Lordship's troop of cavalry and for the tenants and servants from all his estates (Chapter 9).

Earl Howe, when Viscount Curzon, had married Lady Georgiana Spencer-Churchill (the daughter of the Duke of Marlborough) in 1883 and, by this marriage, became Winston Churchill's uncle. However, tragedy struck in February 1906 when, after a long illness, Lady Georgiana died at Curzon House in London. After transferring Georgiana's body to Gopsall by train the day before the funeral, her coffin was placed in the hall's cedar chapel and watched overnight. The funeral service was held the following afternoon at St Mary's Church, Congerstone and Georgiana's body was buried in a newly built vault in St Mary's churchyard (Chapter 9).

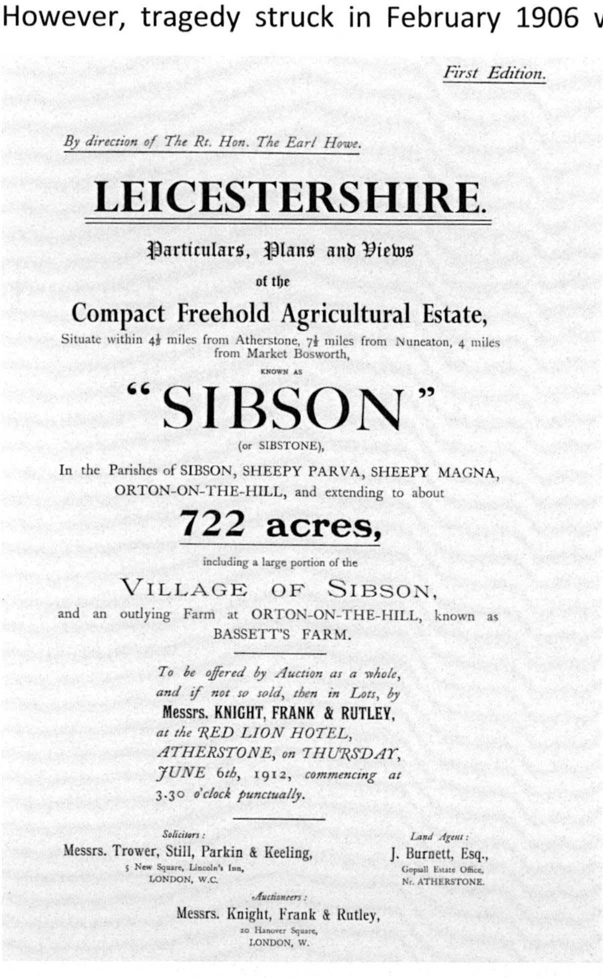

First Edition.

By direction of The Rt. Hon. The Earl Howe.

LEICESTERSHIRE.

Particulars, Plans and Views
of the
Compact Freehold Agricultural Estate,
Situate within 4½ miles from Atherstone, 7½ miles from Nuneaton, 4 miles from Market Bosworth,
KNOWN AS

"SIBSON"
(or SIBSTONE),
In the Parishes of SIBSON, SHEEPY PARVA, SHEEPY MAGNA, ORTON-ON-THE-HILL, and extending to about

722 acres,
including a large portion of the
VILLAGE OF SIBSON,
and an outlying Farm at ORTON-ON-THE-HILL, known as BASSETT'S FARM.

To be offered by Auction as a whole, and if not so sold, then in Lots, by
Messrs. KNIGHT, FRANK & RUTLEY,
at the RED LION HOTEL, ATHERSTONE, on THURSDAY, JUNE 6th, 1912, commencing at 3.30 o'clock punctually.

Solicitors:
Messrs. Trower, Still, Parkin & Keeling,
5 New Square, Lincoln's Inn,
LONDON, W.C.

Land Agent:
J. Burnett, Esq.,
Gopsall Estate Office,
Nr. ATHERSTONE.

Auctioneers:
Messrs. Knight, Frank & Rutley,
20 Hanover Square,
LONDON, W.

In June 1912 the Earl sold his Curzon Park Estate (71 acres containing private houses, licenced premises and cottages) on the outskirts of Chester.[54] Earlier that month, the Sibson Estate and Bassett's Farm (Orton-on-the-Hill), both parts of the outlying Gopsall Estate, were auctioned at the Red Lion Hotel in Atherstone. The Sibson Estate, said to have "*excellent shooting*", included most of the village of Sibson, four farms, three small holdings and about 38 acres of pasture.

Seven years after the death of his wife, tragedy struck the Earl again when in 1913 his sister, Evelyn Alice Eyre, died from injuries sustained in an accident with her pony and trap in Penn.[55] No one witnessed the accident, but while lying in hospital Lady Evelyn said that she had dismounted from her trap to brush off a horse fly

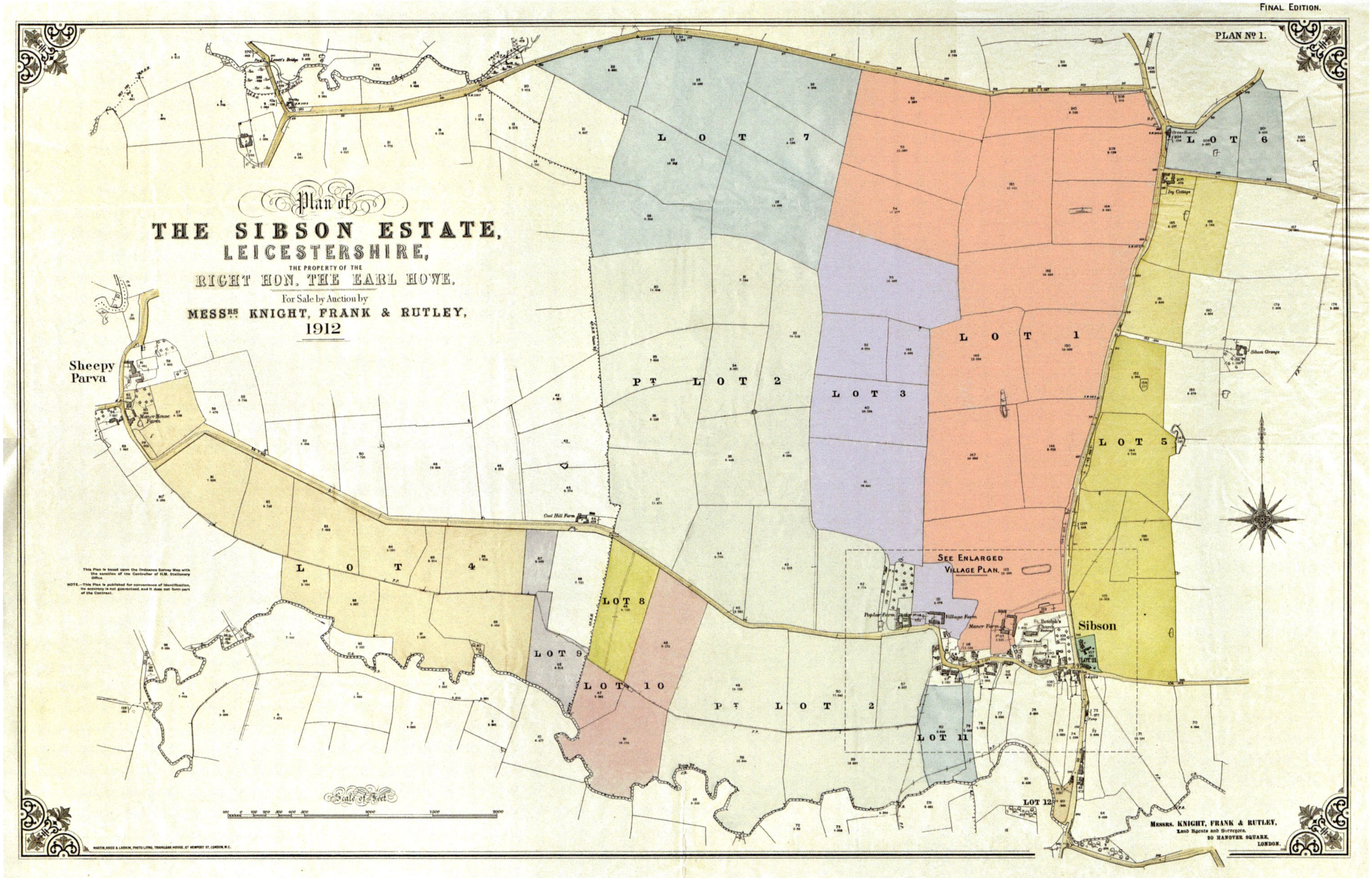

The Sibson Estate sale included: Manor Farm (Lot 1, pink); Poplars Farm (Lot 2, green); Village Farm (Lot 3, mauve); Manor House Farm (Lot 4, brown) & Ivy Cottage Smallholding (Lot 5, yellow; sold for £1,760).

from her pony's neck but, when she turned back to remount the trap, the pony turned and knocked her down. A wheel went over her, her foot caught in the spring of the carriage and she was dragged a considerable distance. She was buried in Penn Street churchyard four days after her death. It seems likely that the death of his sister, in part, prompted the Earl's decision to sell the Gopsall Estate in 1918 and move to his Penn Estate in Buckinghamshire. That his sister's death affected the Earl greatly is evident from a letter written by Elizabeth Battey (Earl Howe's housekeeper; Chapter 6) in January 1914:

"I am sorry to say that his Lordship is very poorly. The Doctor has ordered him to Cornwall for a little change. I do so hope it will do him good. He cannot shake off the death of his favourite sister, they were so devoted to each other, now his wife is dead. Poor Lady Evelyn and he were together so much and she always came here with him, and we all loved her so, and can therefore feel what the loss must be to her own dear ones".[56]

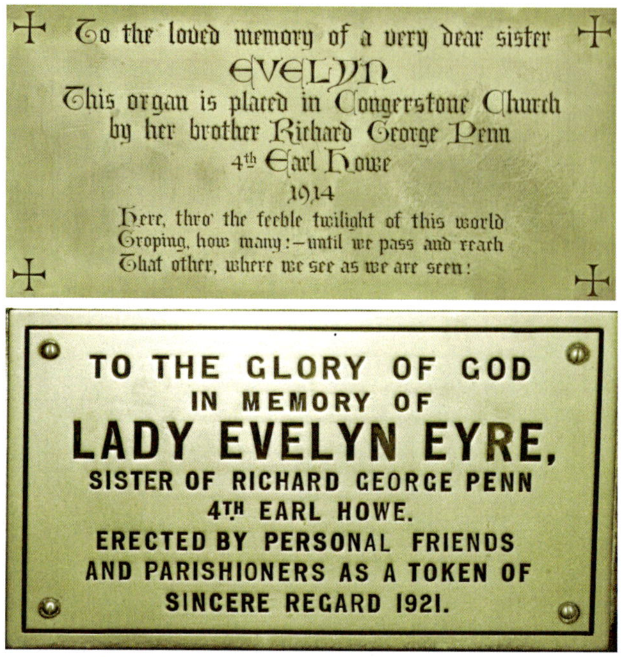

Brass plaques in memory of Lady Evelyn on the organ and pulpit in St Mary's Church, Congerstone.

The 4th Earl married twice more before his death in 1929. His second wife was Florence Davis (married in 1919), an American heiress and singer, who had been previously married to the 2nd Marquess of Dufferin and Ava. Florence died in 1925 and, in 1927, he married Lorna (nee Curzon), the widow of Captain Quintin Dick and his first cousin once removed.[15,46] In 1932, Lorna Howe was the first female owner of the Crufts 'Best in Show' with Labrador retriever, Bramshaw Bob. She won the title twice more in 1933, with the same dog, and in 1936 with another Labrador retriever, Cheverall Ben of Banchory.[57] Her interest in showing dogs echoes that of the 2nd Earl, who was president of the Birmingham Dog Show Society.[52]

Above: Curzon Coat of Arms from the front of a Sibson Manor purchase document (1912).

Left: Richard George Penn Curzon, 4th Earl Howe by Walter Stoneman in 1927 (NPG x162737).

Right: Lorna Katherine Dick (nee Curzon) (later Countess Howe) by Bassano Ltd, 1909 (NPG Ax161346).

Preparations for the sale of the entire Gopsall Estate including the hall and much of its contents were made in 1918. Many of the items that Earl Howe did not wish to keep were sold by George Trollope & Sons in a dispersal sale at the hall in October 1918 and in a later sale, of mainly 17th and 18th century furnishings, in London in 1920 (Chapter 12). The sale of the Gopsall Estate, totalling 10,765 acres, to Sir Samuel Waring (later Baron Waring of Foots Cray Place) for £407,500 was legally completed in August 1919, although the sale had been announced in the newspapers a year earlier. In the title, the Gopsall Estate is described as *"the mansion house and domain of Gopsall and other messuages and land in the parishes of Barton in the Beans, Bilstone, Congerstone, Ibstock, Nailstone, Odstone, Shackerstone, Twycross, Swepstone, Carlton, Appleby Magna, Snarestone, Orton-on-the-Hill, Sibson, Sheepy Magna, Norton-juxta-Twycross and Heather"*.[58] The price paid by Sir Samuel Waring for all this is equivalent to £23.75 million today, which is not too dissimilar to the amount paid by Charles Jennens Jnr to build his hall and park in 1750 (£100,000, about £22.8 million now). Sir Samuel may have thought that he had secured a bargain, but immediate postwar agricultural land values were high, with guaranteed minimum prices for wheat and oats. However, by 1921 the price of wheat had halved, the Corn Production Act was repealed and land prices had dropped.[59]

With the sale of Gopsall to Samuel Waring the estate became owned again by a businessman and industrialist rather than a peer of the realm and friend of the royal household. Prior to the First World War (WWI), Waring was involved in several Waring & Gillow-associated companies which failed and, in 1910, creditors of Waring and Gillow itself were losing patience and a receiver was appointed. The company was restructured, Waring stepped down as chairman and a smaller Waring and Gillow emerged in 1911. This led to the winding up of another company (Waring and White) that depended upon Waring and Gillow. Many shareholders and directors lost money, but Waring survived and managed to retain his Kent estate, Foots Cray Place. While Waring managed to secure some lucrative contracts with the German royal family and a German shipping company, it was the outbreak of WWI that secured his finances and his position back as the head of the company. Waring and Gillow manufactured thousands of tents and other equipment for the war effort, including aircraft wings and, by a subsidary company, complete aircraft (Alliance Aeroplane Company). Thus, by the end of WWI in 1918, Waring would have been a very rich man. In 1922 he was raised to the peerage as the 1st Baron Waring of Foots Cray Place.[60]

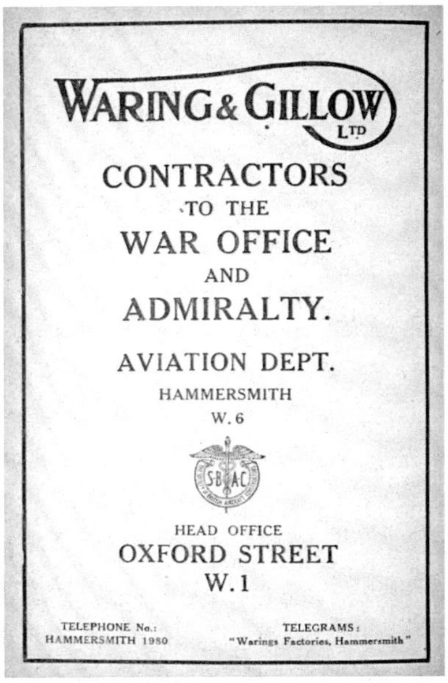

Waring & Gillow diversified in WWI and took full advantage of the need to produce military equipment. The Airco DH9 bomber, designed by Geoffrey de Havilland, was built by the Alliance Aeroplane Co. in Acton, West London.

(Grace's Guide to British Industrial History)

Waring never lived in Gopsall Hall and he probably viewed the purchase of the estate as a relatively short-term speculative investment, similar to his 1917 purchase and 1918/19 re-sale of the bulk of the Duke of Buccleuch's Dunchurch Estate (Chapter 12). Indeed, some of the outlying portions of the Gopsall Estate, including 30 farms and 134 cottages extending to some 5,600 acres, were put up for sale in June 1919.[61] In explanation to his tenants, Waring said that he had been forced to buy the whole estate when he only wanted Gopsall Hall and park. However, this sale was cancelled soon after being announced because Waring's agents had not given the tenants prior chance to purchase their farms and cottages.[62] That Gopsall was a short-term project is supported by a number of other factors. Firstly, Waring already owned a country estate in Kent and, when he was raised to the peerage in 1922, he chose Foots Cray Place, not Gopsall, as his baronial title. Secondly, he had already spent considerable amounts of money on his Kent estate by 1919 and, although a rich man, he purchased Gopsall via a huge mortgage (£340,000; 83% of the cost) secured by the freehold.[58] Despite this, in 1922 Lord Waring purchased the 32-metre yacht 'White Heather II' and lavished more money on Foots Cray Place by improving the gardens and providing better access routes and a new lodge.[60] Although the large sell-off of Gopsall farmland and property was cancelled in 1919, 23 farms and various properties were eventually sold during the following 4 years (Chapter 5), to reduce his mortgage debt.

As far as is known, Waring only hosted one large family event at Gopsall and that was on 13th October 1923 for his daughter, the Honourable Eleanor Gladys Waring and her husband, Captain Arthur Cunliffe Bernard Critchley DSO. The couple were married in St Margaret's Church Westminster[63] on the 3rd October and, after their honeymoon, made their way to Gopsall for 'The Presentations'. According to the report in the Nottingham Journal,[64] *"The villagers, tenant farmers and schoolchildren of the Gopsall Estate gave the couple a very splendid reception"* and *"It was a great day for those living in the vicinity of Lord Waring's mansion"*.

Top: Some of the tenant farmers and villagers photographed in front of the hall.
Bottom: The wedding gifts displayed at 'The Presentations'.

The couple were given many gifts by the tenant farmers, the estate staff, Gopsall tradesmen and the villagers of Congerstone, Twycross, Odstone and Shackerstone. The farmers gave a silver fruit dish and the villagers gave two Persian carpets. After the presentations of gifts the children, their mothers and the tenant farmers were entertained.

Although Lord Waring and his family appear not to have spent much time at Gopsall, he did allow both the hall and park to be used by others. For example, speed trials were held on Shackerstone Drive by a variety of Midlands car and motorcycle clubs between 1923 and 1934 (Chapter 10), fetes on behalf of the Conservative and Unionist Party, the Liberals (with Lloyd George in attendance) and Shackerstone village were held at Gopsall between 1921 and 1926,[65] and the North Atherstone Hunt held their annual Ball in the hall in 1922, 1924, 1935 and 1939.[66] The hall had been empty for nearly 10 years prior to the holding of the hunt ball on 7th February 1939. Lord Waring had transformed the empty rooms with furnishings specially sent down from London; each room was adorned with plants and flowers from Thorpe Hall and huge fires burned in the fireplaces, recapturing some of the hall's former glory. The reported 530 guests, including farmers and supporters, as well as hunt members and their guests, paid 7/- (35p) and 10/6 (52.5p) respectively, and were the last people to see and experience Gopsall Hall as it was meant to be. Interestingly, all the activity at the hall in 1939 caused Twycross to be "*alive with rumours*" that the hall was "*to be the home of the Duke and Duchess of Windsor*" or "*to be used as the residence of the King and Queen and the Princesses in the event of war*".[67]

Major Miles was Waring's agent for Gopsall Hall and Park from 1919 until the outbreak of the Second World War (WWII). He was a keen sportsman and organised and participated in shoots at Gopsall and sporting events in the local area, as well as being councillor for the Gopsall Ward of Twycross.[68] During the 1930s Major Miles was involved in some of the local arrangements for the planned Gopsall Club (Chapter 10) and supporting activities to generate income from Gopsall Park, including opening it to the public[69] and unsuccessfully promoting the use of part of the park as an aerodrome for a flying school instead of Desford.[70]

Guns at the Gopsall covert shoot in December 1929; Major Miles and Capt Critchley-Waring are standing 1st & 2nd from the left.

In 1927, Lord Waring again attempted to sell all the remaining outlying parts of the Gopsall Estate, essentially only retaining possession of the hall, park and the Shornhill and Norton Barn farms. The outlying freehold agricultural portions of the estate and village properties were offered for sale by auction, as a whole or in blocks or lots, by Knight Frank & Rutley at the Bell Hotel, Leicester. A few tenants purchased their cottages and land privately, before the

Mr Donisthorpe's shoot at Gopsall in December 1930; Mr Donisthorpe is standing 3rd from the left. He is also at the 1929 shoot and sitting 2nd from the left.

By Direction of the Right Honourable LORD WARING.

LEICESTERSHIRE

Shackerstone Station (L.M.S.) on the Estate.

Seven miles from Atherstone and Ashby-de-la-Zouch, 12 miles from Nuneaton and 16 miles from Leicester.

Illustrated Particulars with Plans and Special Conditions of Sale

OF THE

OUTLYING FREEHOLD AGRICULTURAL PORTIONS OF THE

GOPSALL ESTATE

situate in the Parishes of Snarestone, Swepstone, Norton-juxta-Twycross, Shackerstone, Odstone, Nailstone, Gopsall, Bilstone, Barton-in-the-Beans, Orton-on-the-Hill, Twycross, Congerstone, Carlton, Sheepy Magna, and Sibson.

INCLUDING

THIRTY WELL EQUIPPED FARMS,

principally Grass, with Superior Homesteads

SMALL HOLDINGS & ALLOTMENTS

THREE LICENSED HOUSES

PRIVATE RESIDENCES TWO HUNTING BOXES

NUMEROUS COTTAGES AND MATURED WOODLANDS

in all about

6230 acres.

To be offered for Sale by Auction, as a whole or in blocks or Lots, by Messrs.

KNIGHT, FRANK & RUTLEY

(Sir Howard Frank, Bart., G.B.E., K.C.B.; Alfred J. Burrows, F.S.I.; Arthur H. Knight, F.A.I.; Charles Phillips, F.A.I.)

At THE BELL HOTEL, LEICESTER,

On Wednesday and Thursday, the 23rd and 24th of February, 1927

commencing at 2.30 p.m. on the 1st day and 10.30 a.m. and 2 p.m. on the 2nd day

(unless previously disposed of privately).

Solicitor:—H. R. LAMONBY, Esq., 6, Portland Place, London, W. 1.

Auctioneers:—Messrs. KNIGHT, FRANK & RUTLEY, 20, Hanover Square, London, W.1., and at Edinburgh, Glasgow and Ashford, Kent.

Key to the 1927 Gopsall Sale Map

GOPSALL FARMS			
1	Culloden	17	Bates
2	Beanfield	18	Dawkins
3	Shackerstone Fields	19	Church
4	Tivey's	20	Hoo Hills
5	Oaklands	21	Bilstone Hill
6	Odstone Hall	22	Temple Mill
7	Walker's	23	Temple
8	Odstone Barn	24	Gopsall House
9	Hollow	25	Panter's
10	Arnold's	26	Gardener's
11	Cattow's	27	Harris Bridge
12	Wharf	28	Manor
13	Bridge	29	Clares Barn
14	Castle	30	Lagos
15	Glebe	31	Lea Grange
16	Dean's	32	Shaw House
NBF	Norton Barn	SF	Shornhill

Other LAND	
A	Shackerstone Barn (inc. land)
B	Site of Orange Hill Plantation
C	Gamekeeper's cottage & paddock
D	Parkland
E	Smallholding (Congerstone)
F	Horse & Jockey
G	Smallholding (Little Twycross)
H	Smallholding (Twycross)

Odstone Hall Farm, Odstone (190 acres). A well known mixed farm with picturesque Manor House suitable for a Gentleman Farmer or use as a Hunting Box. It is of historical interest, having been once occupied by Bradshaw, President of the Council, who signed King Charles' death warrant.

Oaklands Farm (or Oxhay Farm; 63 acres), Shackerstone. A well known Cheese Making holding, excellently placed adjoining the village and station. The attractive farmhouse has been modernised and enjoys pleasant views. There is a good garden with tennis lawn.

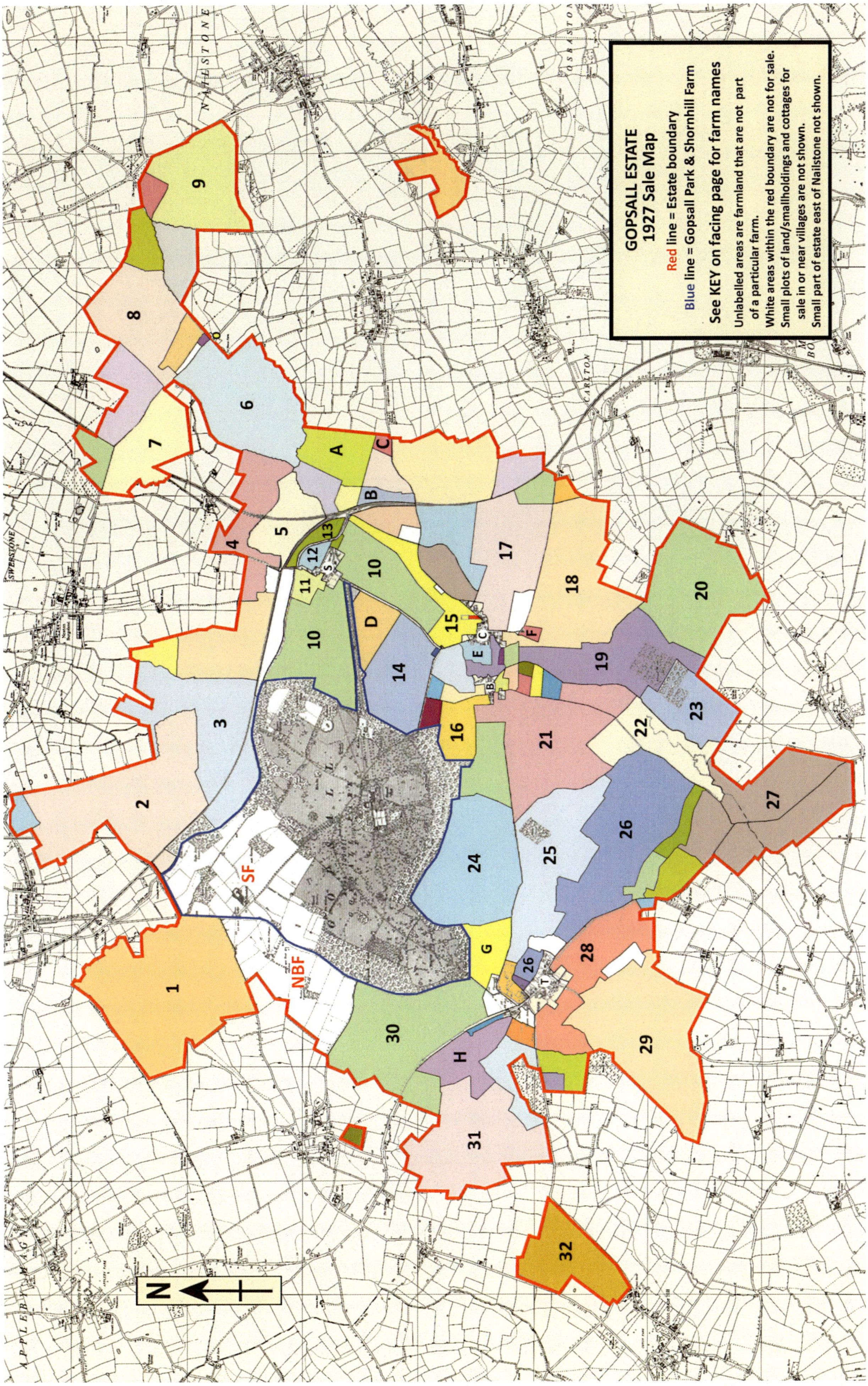
GOPSALL ESTATE
1927 Sale Map
Red line = Estate boundary
Blue line = Gopsall Park & Shornhill Farm
See KEY on facing page for farm names
Unlabelled areas are farmland that are not part of a particular farm.
White areas within the red boundary are not for sale.
Small plots of land/smallholdings and cottages for sale in or near villages are not shown.
Small part of estate east of Nailstone not shown.
NAILSTONE
SWEPSTONE
CARLTON
SF
NBF
N

See note 18.

Manor or Haywood's Farm, Twycross (128 acres). An excellent village farm with a 'Georgian-style' residence just off the road (the A444) and sheltered by a high brick wall. The land is fertile grass and arable, level and easy working.

auction, but most did not. The sale was over two days and, with no buyers interested in the whole or large parts of the land and property on offer, attempts were made to sell the estate as 239 individual lots. According to newspaper reports at the time only 6 lots were sold over the two days (£2,760 total value), two of which were the Horse & Jockey Inn, Congerstone and some adjoining land (£2,350).[71]

Waring and Gillow, with Lord Waring as chairman, appeared to be doing well until the summer of 1930, when rumours circulated that the company dividends would be deferred. In the autumn, Waring was removed as chairman and eventually the company was restructured in 1932. This third company had nothing to do with Waring.[60] It is against this background, and the start of the 'Great Depression' triggered by the crash of the USA stock market in October 1929, that Waring's Gopsall mortgage was called in and a receiver appointed out of Court in 1930. Late in 1931 the mortgagees (John Eyre and others; Howe family trustees) agreed to sell 6,107 acres of Gopsall land, including 42 farms and small holdings, 143 houses and cottages and 153 acres of woodland, to the Commissioners for Crown Lands. The sale proceeded in 1932[72] after a failed attempt by Lord Waring to obtain an injunction to prevent the sale.[73] The estate had suffered in the 14 years of Lord Waring's ownership with the farmhouses, farm buildings and cottages being allowed to deteriorate. The Crown Commissioners bought the estate lands for £128,000 (equivalent to £21 per acre, not the often stated, £1 per acre) but had to spend a further £90,000 on repairs and improvements in the following 14 years.[74]

In 1932, plans were proposed to build a racing circuit within Gopsall Park, which was still owned by Lord Waring but with a mortgage outstanding to the Howe family trustees. The plans included building an aerodrome and using the hall as the clubhouse (Chapter 10). These plans came to nothing and, shortly before the outbreak of WWII, the hall, gardens and park were requisitioned by the army. The park was used as an army vehicle supply depot from 1940 and the hall as No. 2 Radio Mechanics School from 1942 (Chapter 11).

Lord Waring died in 1940, with an estate valued at £0.[75] Following his wife's death in April 1941, Panton Investments Ltd purchased 1,233 acres from Lady Waring's administrators for £33,500. This sale included the hall, gardens and park that were, at that time, being used by the army, as well as, Shornhill and Norton Barn farms. The two farms purchased in this sale were then acquired by the Crown Commissioners in 1943, who had purchased Orton House Farm from a private seller the previous year.[76] When Panton Investments Ltd were bankrupt in 1951 the Crown Commissioners purchased Gopsall Park, including the gardens and hall site, in the July,[77] effectively becoming 'Lords' of the entire Gopsall Estate, which now extended to about 8,500 acres.

The liquidators of Panton Investments Ltd had already decided to demolish the hall and, in 1951, sold the structure of the hall to a demolition company (Thomas Oakley Ltd, Luton) before selling the site, gardens and park to the Crown Commissioners. Thomas Oakley Ltd, a firm specialising in demolishing 'unwanted' stately homes, purchased and demolished Hadlow Castle in Kent in the same year as Gopsall Hall. An interior and exterior fixtures and fittings sale, which included the 'famous' silver bath reputedly used by Edward VII in 1902, was held on site in May 1951 prior to

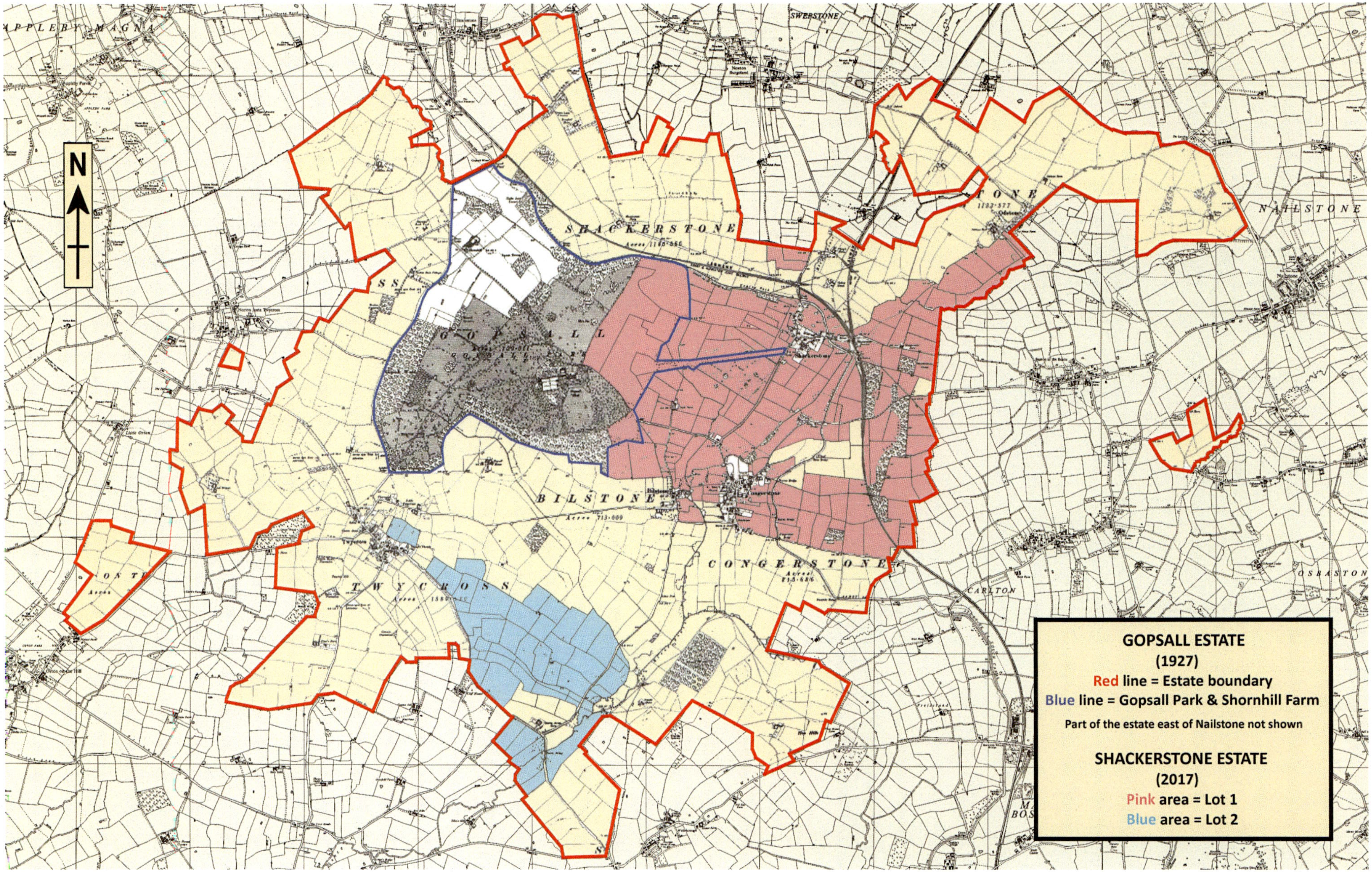
GOPSALL ESTATE
(1927)
Red line = Estate boundary
Blue line = Gopsall Park & Shornhill Farm
Part of the estate east of Nailstone not shown
SHACKERSTONE ESTATE
(2017)
Pink area = Lot 1
Blue area = Lot 2
N
SHACKERSTONE
NAILSTONE
BILSTONE
CONGERSTONE
TWYCROSS
GOPSALL
SWEPSTONE
CARLTON
OSBASTON

See note 18.

the complete demolition of the building, two further sales of the reusable building materials and the final clearing of the site (Chapter 12).

The Crown Commissioners were not interested in parkland and put all the land to agricultural use. Gopsall park became Gopsall Hall Farm with the house previously used by the head gardener, the steward and later, the bailiff, becoming the farmhouse. All the Gopsall lands and properties were tenanted, their rents providing the income sought by the Crown Commissioners (Chapter 5). Various properties in the villages were sold off piecemeal over the succeeding years. For example, in Congerstone, Dovecote farmhouse (now demolished) and the two cottages now known as the Old Forge where sold in 1976.[78] Over the years, small parcels of land were sold by the Crown for housing developments (e.g. St Peter's Place in Shackerstone and Crown Meadow in Congerstone). While often opposed by villagers, these developments were closely controlled by the Crown Commissioners, and sites were not allowed to be used for maximum profit to the builder.

Tim and Chris Stamper in 2015
(MrIanReynolds; CC BY-SA 3.0)

By 2017, the Crown Commissioners had decided to dispose of the Gopsall Estate as it no longer fitted in with their business plan. The vast majority of the 2017 estate was composed of farms and their associated farmhouses and farm buildings, with only 10 village homes. Before putting the estate up for sale, the tenants of the farms were given the opportunity to buy their farms at favourable cost but with conditions about any resale profits. Fifteen of the 17 long-standing tenants did purchase their farms including John Lain, the tenant of Gopsall Hall Farm. The remaining land and properties from the Gopsall Estate, consisting of about 1,738 acres and said to yield over £250,000 income per year, were re-named as the Shackerstone Estate and put up for sale for £13.5 million.[79] The estate was purchased by Chris Stamper, one of the two brothers who founded the computer games company, Rare Ltd in Twycross. In 2002, Microsoft acquired Rare Ltd, which retained the original brand, logo and most intellectual properties. The Stamper brothers finally left Rare Ltd in 2007.

So, although Chris Stamper is 'Lord' of the Shackerstone Estate, being the owner of the largest area of what was the Gopsall Estate, the new 'Lord' of Gopsall must be John Lain, the present owner of Gopsall Hall Farm, which comprises the largest proportion of the land within the 1650 Gopsall Manor.

Gopsall Hall Farmhouse (c.1951)

Originally the head gardener's house when built (c.1850), it was the steward's house in the 1920s. It was renovated after Gopsall was purchased by the Crown Commissioners in 1951 and became the home of Mr C.D. Fitt, Bailiff of Gopsall Hall Farm. Since that time the house has been significantly enlarged and the unusual 'dormer' windows no longer exist because the whole roof has been raised (see current image in Chapter 14).

Notes and References

Unattributed images of the Curzon-Howe family are courtesy of the Rt Hon Frederick Richard Penn Curzon, 7th Earl Howe, GBE, PC. Digital copies of the original photographs have been processed using Corel PaintShop Pro 2019.

1 *The Place Names of Leicestershire* (The Survey of English Place Names Volume XC, Part 6, Sparkenhoe Hundred). Barrie Cox. Nottingham: English Place Name Society, 2014, p.311.

2 *William the Conqueror*. F.M. Stenton. Prahbat Prakashan (eBook), 2019.

3 *William the Conqueror - The Norman Impact upon England*. David C. Douglas. University of California Press, 1964.

4 *Ferrers, Henry de (d. 1093x1100)*. Marios Costambeys. Oxford Dictionary of National Biography (online ed.) Oxford University Press, 2004. Accessed 3rd February 2021; library card number required.

(https://www.oxforddnb.com/view/10.1093/ref:odnb/9780198614128.001.0001/odnb-9780198614128-e-9361)

5 *'Henry 6 Henry de Ferrers'*, Prosopography of Anglo-Saxon England (http://www.pase.ac.uk). Accessed 3rd February, 2021. Gives a list of the properties and lordships of Henry de Ferrers; includes Gopsall.

6 *Domesday Book: A Complete Translation*. London: Penguin, 2003, pp. 656-657.

7 *The Origins of some Anglo-Norman Families*. Lewis Christopher Loyd. Genealogical Publishing Company, 1951.

8 *Houses of Cistercian monks: Abbey of Merevale. A History of the County of Warwick: Volume 2* . Edited by William Page. A part-volume, covering the religious houses of Warwickshire. Victoria County History, London, 1908. Note: Two areas within the civil parish of Twycross are part of the ecclesiastical parish of Merevale with Bentley. This presumably has its origins in the establishment of Merevale Abbey and gift of land by Robert de Ferrers when Lord of Gopsall. Robert de Ferrers, 2nd Earl of Derby was buried at Merevale Abbey, as were several of the de Ferrers family, prior to it being dissolved in 1385 and falling into ruin.

9 *Provisional List of Deserted Medieval Villages in Leicestershire*. Deserted Medieval Village Research Group. Transactions of the Leicestershire Archaeological and Historical Society 39, 1963-4, pp. 24-33

10 *Gopsal. History and Antiquities of the County of Leicester. Volume IV. Part II. containing the Sparkenhoe Hundred.* John Nichols. London, 1811, pp. 854-859.

11 *Gopsall (Leicestershire). Beresford's Lost Villages*. Department of History, University of Hull. Accessed 5th February 2021 . (https://dmv.hull.ac.uk/dmvDetail.cfm?dbkey=3613&search=Gopsall)

12 *Quorndon Records*. George F. Farnham. London: Mitchell, Highes & Clarke, 1912, p. 175.

13 Both Nichols and the Quorndon Records state that the Langham family owned Gopsall manor from at least 1393 to 1564, when it was sold by George Langham to George Hastings. However, there is a 'Feet of Fines' (co. Leicester), dated 1505 which conveys the manor of Goppeshill from Robert Langham of Goppeshill (son of John Langham; great, great grandson of Robert Langham of Gopsall - 1396) to "*Thomas Loweth, Robert Loweth and Thomas Haruye and the heirs of Robert Loweth for ever*". The description of the property conveyed is: "*The manor of Goppeshill' called Langhams Maner and the manor of Goppeshill' called Goppeshill' and 1 messuage, 10 tofts, 200 acres of land, 100 acres of meadow, 400 acres of pasture and 100 acres of heath in Goppeshill*". (http://www.medievalgenealogy.org.uk/fines/abstracts/CP_25_1_126_80.shtml; No. 38) Accessed 5th Feb. 2021.

14 Messuage: A dwelling house together with its outbuildings, curtilage, and the adjacent land appropriate to its use.

15 *The Peerage*. A genealogical survey of the peerage of Britain as well as the royal families of Europe. Compiled by Daryl Lundy (http://thepeerage.com/). Accessed 5th February 2021. Similar information can be obtained from Burke's Peerage, Baronetage and Knightage, only available online since 2003 and requiring a subscription: https://www.burkespeerage.com/search.php.

16 *Merry, Thomas (c.1605-82), of Gopsall, Leics. The History of Parliament: the House of Commons 1660-1690*. ed. B.D. Henning. London: Boydell & Brewer, 1983. Available online and accessed 5th February 2021 (https://www.historyofparliamentonline.org/volume/1660-1690/member/merry-thomas-1605-82).

17 *Map of the Lordship and manor of Gopshall with part of Bilson, with elevation drawing of Gopsal Hall* The Record Office for Leicestershire & Rutland. Document Ref: 35'29/317.

18 *1650 Gopsall Manor Maps*: The Gopsall Manor maps were overlaid onto OS maps produced from scans of 6 inch to the mile maps of Gopsall Hall and Park (1903; sheets XXVIII NE & XXIX NW) combined with the field boundaries, villages roads, etc south of Gopsall Park from 6 inch to the mile OS maps dated 1955 (SK30 NW & NE; Reproduced with the permission of the National Library of Scotland under the Creative Commons CC BY 4.0 licence). Field boundaries are virtually unchanged between 1886 and 1955.

1927 sale map: The 1927 sale map was overlaid onto the 1966 6 inch to the mile OS map, which includes parts of sheet numbers: SK30NW, SW, NE, SE and SE40NW & SW (Reproduced with the permission of the National Library of Scotland under the Creative Commons CC BY 4.0 licence).

2017 sale map: The 1927 Gopsall Estate outline, showing the 1903 field boundaries within, and the 2017 Lots 1 and 2 were overlaid onto the 1966 6 inch to the mile map as described above (Reproduced with the permission of the National Library of Scotland under the Creative Commons CC BY 4.0 licence). Note that the 1903 field boundaries within the Gopsall estate line up with those shown on the 1966 OS map (ie. the areas outside the estate boundary). Map images can be viewed online at the National Library of Scotland website (https://maps.nls.uk/index.html).

19 *A History of Gopsall*. G. Oakley, Private publication. Barncraft Printing, Sheepy Magna, 1995; reprinted 1996.

20 Church of England Ecclesiastical Parish and Hinckley & Bosworth Civil Parish Maps can be viewed at: https://www.churchofengland.org/sites/default/files/2018-01/ParishMapsArcGIS Userguide_Jan2018_1.pdf

https://www.hinckley-bosworth.gov.uk/download/downloads/id/2816/twycross.pdf. Accessed 5th February 2021.

21 This work incorporates historical material provided by the Great Britain Historical GIS Project and the University of Portsmouth via their web site *A Vision of Britain through Time* (http://www.VisionofBritain.org.uk) under Creative Commons Licence CC BY 4.0 (http://creativecommons.org/licenses/by/4.0/). Accessed 5th February 2021.

22 *The Medieval Earthworks of South-West Leicestershire, Hinckley & Bosworth*. Robert F. Hartley. Leicestershire Museums Archaeological Fieldwork Group, Monograph 2, 2008, Landscape Map 4, p. 72.

23 *Lowther, Sir John II, 2nd Bt. (1655-1700), of Lowther Hall, Westmorland. The History of Parliament: the House of Commons 1690-1715*. ed. D. Hayton, E. Cruickshanks & S. Handley. London: Boydell & Brewer, 2002. Available online: (https://www.historyofparliamentonline.org/volume/1690-1715/member/lowther-sir-john-1655-1700). Accessed 7th February 2021.

24 *Lowther, John, first Viscount Lonsdale (1655–1700)*. J. V. Beckett. Oxford Dictionary of National Biography (online ed.) Oxford University Press 2004. Accessed 7th February 2021; library card number required. (https://www.oxforddnb.com/view/10.1093/ref:odnb/9780198614128.001.0001/odnb-9780198614128-e-17111).

25 *Articles of Agreement between M. Powell & H. Jennens relating to payment for land in Gopsall, Leicestershire, 28th January 1684*. Doc. Ref: AR/94/80/232; *Deeds of Property in Gopsall, 1677-1689*. Doc. Ref: AR/94/80/354. *Papers of Earl Howe*. Buckinghamshire Records Office. The details in these documents have been obtained from: *Gopsall Hall: 'Look on my works, ye Mighty, and despair'*. Brenda Sumner. MA thesis, University of Leicester, 2009.

26 *Parishes: Nether Whitacre. A History of the County of Warwick: Volume 4, Hemlingford Hundred*, ed. L F Salzman (London, 1947), pp. 251-255 (British History Online http://www.british-history.ac.uk/vch/warks/vol4/pp251-255). Accessed 8th February 2021.

27 *Folio volume describing the estates of the Earls Howe, of Gopsall*. The Record Office for Leicestershire & Rutland. Document Ref: T198 - 3 - DE3541 (DG23).

28 *The Achievements of Charles Jennens 1700-1773*. Ruth Smith. Music & Letters 70 (2) May 1989, pp. 161-190.

29 *Charles Jennens: The Man Behind Handel's Messiah*. Ruth Smith. The Gerald Coke Handel Foundation, 2012.

30 In his early youth, Joseph Cradock (1742-1826; a hosier & draper) of Gumley Hall, Leicestershire, attended 'musical treats' at Gopsall Hall "where Handel himself had frequently presided, when the words of the Messiah were first selected". Literary and Miscellaneous Memoirs (2nd Ed.). J. Cradock. London: J. Nichols & Son, 1826, p. 124.

31 William Gardiner (1770-1853) visited Gopsall Hall in 1792 and met Jennens' old gardener, who remembered Handel visiting every year: Music & Friends or Pleasant Recollections of A Dilettante (Vol. 2). William Gardiner. London: Longman, Orme, Brown & Longman, 1838, p. 229. Gardiner owned a stocking manufacturing business in Leicester and was an English composer, thought to be the first to cause the music of Beethoven to be heard in England: William Gardiner, of Leicester. The Musical Times 67 (1004) Oct 1926, pp. 900-902.

32 *Letter from Handel to Charles Jennens, dated 9th September 1742*. The Handel Reference Database, Accessed 10th February 2021 (https://web.stanford.edu/~ichriss/HRD/1742.htm). This letter indicates that Handel called at Gopsall on his way back to London from Dublin because the opening sentence of the letter only makes sense if he is responding to a letter from Jennens asking "*Was it you that called ...*" (Dr Ruth Smith, Independent scholar, Cambridge / The Handel Institute).

33 Jennens had planned to produce new editions of all of Shakespeare's plays and publish them as individual volumes. He finished five plays before his death on 20th November 1773: King Lear (1770), Macbeth, Hamlet and Othello (1773) and Julius Caesar (published 1774).

34 *Norton. History and Antiquities of the County of Leicester. Volume IV. Part II. containing the Sparkenhoe Hundred*. John Nichols. London, 1811, p. 850.

35 These two figures for building the hall and laying out the pleasure grounds are often quoted in late 19th century and later accounts of Gopsall. £100k for building the hall is stated in *A Topographical History of the County of Leicester* by the Rev. J. Curtis. Ashby-de-la-Zouche: W. Hextall, 1831, p. 66. £80k for laying out the pleasure grounds is stated in Nichols 1811 (see ref. 10), with no comment about the cost of building the hall. However, according to two earlier accounts, the hall was built and the grounds laid out for a total cost of £100k: *Select Views in Leicestershire from Original Drawings: containing Seats of the Nobility and Gentry, Town Views and Ruins*. J. Throsby. Leicester, 1789, p. 283; *A Topographical and Historical Description of the County of Leicester*. John Britton. London: Sherwood, Neely & Jones, 1807, p. 485.

36 A transcript of John Grundy's visit to Gopsall in 1750 can be found at the end of Chapter 2.

37 *A Temple at Gopsall Park*. TV Parry. BA Dissertation, University of Manchester, 1981. Available at The Record Office for Leicestershire & Rutland. Document Ref: DE10125/6.

38 *Handel, George Frideric*. Oxford Music Online (includes Grove Music Online), 2001. Library card number required (https://www.oxfordmusiconline.com/grovemusic/view/10.1093/gmo/9781561592630.001.0001/omo-9781561592630-e-0000040060?mediaType=Article). Accessed 9th February 2021.

39 Charles Jennens' memorial in St Giles Church, Nether Whitacre, was made by Richard Hayward, who also executed the cenotaph inside the temple that Jennens had built (Chapter 4). The inscription on the memorial reads:

Here lie interred the remains of Charles Jennens, esq. of Gopsal in the county of Leicester, who died Nov 30, 1773 age 75; the last male heir, in a direct line, of an antient and most respectable Family; a gentleman of sound piety, and strict adherence to the principles and practice of the Christian faith. He was learned, and an admirer of learned men; fond of the Arts, and a great encourager of them among the Professors; of a liberal nature; very charitable in his life-time, and in his bequests, he shewed the same disposition of benevolence. He was never married; having, therefore, no children of his own, he endeavour'd to become as general as possible a Parent and Benefactor to Mankind as possible. By his will, he provided for his Relations, remember'd his Friends, and distributed amply to those Charities which are most beneficial to Society. For the propagation of the Gospel abroad he bequeathed 500; to six Hospitals in London 500 each; to two others, each 200; to the Widows of Clergymen in Leicestershire 200; for Lectures on the Catechism 1000; to schools round Gopsal 1000; and 200 to adjacent townships: And to this parish of Nether Whitacre, he left ample marks of his bounty; for having given in his lifetime the great tythes, a glebe to the curacy and 100 towards rebuilding the church: he bequeath'd at his death to the poor 100, and endow'd a school for the instruction of their children.

This token of gratitude was plac'd here, by his nephew and executors. 1775.

40 *Attested Copy of Will of Charles Jennens of Gopsall, esq. Dated 30th April 1765; Codicil 7th Aug. 1766.* The Record Office for Leicestershire & Rutland. Document Ref: DG22/5/8.

41 Admiral Richard Howe, 1st Earl Howe (b. 1726), never owned or lived at Gopsall and his title became extinct on his death in 1799, as he had no male children. For further information on Admiral Howe see: *Howe, Richard.* H.C.G. Matthews & Brian Harrison eds. Oxford Dictionary of National Biography 28, 2004, pp. 480-488.

42 *Gopsall Hall, Sparkenhoe Hundred. History, Gazetteer and Directory of Leicestershire and the small county of Rutland.* William White. Sheffield: Robt Leader, 1846, p. 547. Other parts of this Directory give information about Richard William Penn Curzon, 1st Earl Howe's charitable works, positions held, land owned and lordships claimed.

The 1st Earl's acts of benevolence also extended to his other estates. For example, he endowed a school in Gotham (Nottinghamshire), as well as (in 1862) a piped water supply to that village

43 *Valuation and Survey of the Estate of Gopsall. Papers of Earl Howe.* Buckinghamshire Records Office; Document Ref: AR/94/80/29.

44 Personal communication. The Rt Hon Frederick Richard Penn Curzon, 7th Earl Howe, GBE, PC.

45 *Bill of Complaint to the Rt Hon John Lord Eldon, Lord High Chancellor of Great Britain (25th November 1812)* by Lord Curzon and *The joint and several Answer of the Rt Hon Sophia Charlotte Baroness Howe and Jonathan Wathen Phipps to the Bill of Complaint (12th March 1813)* by Baroness Howe and JW Phipps. Documents kindly provided by Lord Howe but are available from The National Archives, Kew (*Curzon v Phipps* in Chancery Masters' Account Books. Document Ref: C 101/1036).

Jonathan Phipps assumed the name Waller in 1814 to inherit his maternal grand-father's estates. In the same year, George III created him a baronet, and he received a knighthood from King William IV in 1832.

The schedule of estate rents being managed by Baroness Howe in 1813 (see Appendix for full details) were listed as follows: Gopsall, including Bilstone, Congerstone, Twycross, Norton, Orton & Shackerstone - £1692; Gotham - £547; Birmingham, including Erdington, Edgbaston & Halesowen - £287; Warwickshire, including Whitacre & Weethley - £611 and Lancashire - £2690. The quoted rent yield from Gopsall was considerably less than that reported in the 1803 survey of the estate (ref 43; about £3000).

Weethley manor was purchased by Humphrey Jennens in 1695. Charles Jennens Jnr held half the manor in 1765, which passed to Richard Curzon, 1st Earl Howe via Elizabeth Jennens and Penn Assheton Curzon. The Weethley estate came into the possession of the 5th Marquis of Hertford between 1872 and 1877. *'Parishes: Weethley'*, in *A History of the County of Warwick: Volume 3, Barlichway Hundred*, ed. Philip Styles (London, 1945), pp. 187-188. British History Online http://www.british-history.ac.uk/vch/warks/vol3/pp187-188 [Accessed on 20th July 2021].

46 *Earl Howe (UK, 1821).* Cracrofts' Peerage. The Complete Guide to the British Peerage and Baronetage. Patrick Cracroft_Brennan (ed.). Accessed 5th February 2021. Similar information can be obtained from Burke's Peerage, only available online since 2003 and requiring a subscription (https://www.burkespeerage.com/search.php).

47 *William IV Cassel Biographies.* Philip Zeigler. London: Cassell, 1971.

48 *Congerstone - Unsealed Copy of Deed of Award with Map (probably deposited for enrolment).* The Record Office for Leicestershire & Rutland. Document Ref: QS47/2/5.

49 *Survey of Land in Leicestershire 1826. Papers of Earl Howe.* Buckinghamshire Records Office. Document Ref: AR/94/80/28.

50 *History, Gazetteer and Directory of the Counties of Leicester and Rutland.* William White. London: Simkin, Marshall & Co., 1863. Contains information about Richard William Penn Curzon, 1st Earl Howe's charitable works, positions held, land owned and lordships claimed.

51 *British Hunts and Huntsmen (The south-east, east, and eastern midlands of England).* Compiled in conjunction with The Sporting Life. The Biographical Press: London, 1909, p. 199.

52 *From Little Acorns: The History of the Birmingham Dog Show Society.* Annette Oliver. Birmingham, 1998, pp. 10-11.

53 *Visit of the Prince of Wales to Gopsall and Leicester.* Leicester Daily Post, Thursday 4th April 1889; *The Prince of Wales at Gopsall.* Melton Mowbray Mercury and Oakham and Uppingham News, Thursday 4th January 1894.

54 *Auction announcements of Messrs. KNIGHT, FRANK and RUTLEY, landed estates extending to 208,525 acres.* The Times, Tuesday 23rd April, 1912. Adverts for the sale of the Sibson and Curzon park estates appeared on the same page with the particulars of 28 other estates up for auction.

55 *Lady E. Eyre's Death. Fatal injuries received through kind act to pony.* Cheltenham Chronicle & Gloucester Graphic, Saturday 11th October 1913.

56 *Battey, Elizabeth. Letter from Elizabeth Battey to Elizabeth E. McCulloch, January 4, 1914.* Elizabeth Battey Papers (MS 947). Special Collections and University Archives, University of Massachusetts Amherst Libraries. Accessed on 12th February 2021 at: http://credo.library.umass.edu/view/full/mums947-b01-f11-i001 (view the enclosure).

57 *Crufts - Past and present winners: Best in show winners.* https://www.crufts.org.uk/about-us/past-and-present-winners/ Accessed on 12th February 2021.

Lorna, Countess Howe became one of the foremost authorities on the breeding of Labradors and published a book on the subject: *The Labrador Retriever* by Lorna, Countess Howe. Popular Dogs Publishing, 1st January 1957.

58 *Abstract of Title detailing an Indenture dated 13th August 1919 between the Earl and Countess Howe, the Trustees*

and Samuel Waring. The National Archives, Kew, Richmond TW9 4DU. Within document Ref: CRES 38/1002.

59 *How farming suffered post-WW1 from government's 'great betrayal'*. Richard Munday. Farmers Weekly, Friday 10th November 2018.

60 *What became of Waring? Fortunes of an entrepreneur in furnishing, shopkeeping and construction*. Construction History 29 (1) 2014, pp. 75-97.

61 *The Outlying Portions of the Gopsall Estate*. Rugby Advertiser, Friday 2nd May 1919; Pall Mall Gazette, Wednesday 7th May 1919.

62 *Gopsall Estate Rent Audit*. Leicester Journal, Friday 12th December 1919; *Gopsall Estate Sale, Sir Samuel Waring explains his position*. Nottingham Evening Post, Friday 5th December 1919.

63 *Yesterday's weddings: Captain A.C.B. Critchley and the Hon. Gladys Waring*. Yorkshire Post and Leeds Intelligencer, Thursday 4th October 1923.

64 *Villagers' Gifts. Lord Waring's Daughter's Homecoming*. Nottingham Journal, Monday 15th October 1923.

65 *Conservative Fete at Gopsall. Numerous Thrills for the Bosworth Division Crowd. Speech by the Colonial Secretary*. Times and Guardian, Friday 2nd July 1926; *Liberal Fete at Gopsall*. Midland Counties Tribune, Friday 25th July 1924; *Fete at Gopsall Park*. Nottingham Journal, Monday 18th July 1921.

66 *Atherstone Hunt. Annual Ball at Gopsall*. Coventry Evening Telegraph, Friday 22nd December 1922; *Brilliant Scene at Annual Ball at Gopsall*. Tamworth Herald, Saturday 29th January 1924; *M.F.H.'s Dinner to Atherstone Hunt Farmers. 550 Entertained at Gopsall Hall*. Leicester Evening Mail, 7th October 1935; *Farmers' Hunt Ball - One night stolen from Silent Splendour*. Atherstone News, 10th February 1939.

67 *Gopsall Hall: A Canard. Twycross Village Rumours Denied*. Tamworth Herald, Saturday 26th August 1939.

68 *Atherstone Boxer's Success*. Nottingham Evening Post, Monday 2nd December 1935; *Urban & Rural Councils - Market Bosworth*. Nottingham Evening Post, Wednesday 3rd April 1935.

69 *'Silent Knight' Motor Tours*. Lichfield Mercury, Friday 25th June 1937; *Cycling Notes. Kilburn Wheelers' CC*. Ripley & Heanor & Ilkeston Division Free Press, Friday 11th June 1937.

70 *Flying School for Desford: Council Critic*. Leicester Evening Mail, 15th August 1935.

71 *The Gopsall Estate Sale*. Tamworth Herald, Saturday 26th February 1927.

72 Details of the conveyance of the Gopsall Estate (excluding Gopsall Hall and Park, Shornhill Farm & Norton Barn Farm) from John Eyre and others to the Crown Estate are held by The National Archives, Kew, Richmond TW9 4DU. Doc. Refs: CRES 38/980, 986, 987, 988, 989, 990 dated 15th June 1932.

73 *Gopsall Estate to be Sold. No injunction for Lord Waring*. Leicester Mercury, Friday 11th December 1931.

74 *Gopsall Hall: 'Look on my works, ye Mighty, and despair'*. Brenda Sumner. MA thesis, University of Leicester, 2009.

75 *Gentrification and the Enterprise Culture,* Britain 1780-1980. F.M.L. Thompson. Oxford: 2001. Appendix 4, p. 193.

76 *Panton Investments Ltd. Crown 1943, Dec. 1 Gopsall: conveyance of Shornhill and Norton Barn Farms*. The National Archives, Kew, Richmond TW9 4DU. Doc. Ref: CRES 38/998; *Mrs F.M. Parkes and another Crown 1942, July 10 Gopsall: conveyance of Orton House Farm, Twycross*. The National Archives Doc. Ref: CRES 38/996.

77 *Panton Investments Ltd. Crown 1951, July 11 Gopsall: conveyance of Gopsall Park*. The National Archives, Kew, Richmond TW9 4DU. Document Ref: CRES 38/1002 dated 11th July 1951.

78 *Congerstone & Shackerstone - Auction Sale 18th May 1976*. Coventry Evening Telegraph, Friday 7th May 1976.

79 *The Shackerstone Estate Leicestershire 2017*. Carter Jonas, 12 Waterside Way, Bedford Rd, Northampton NN4 7XD.

APPENDIX

The Schedule of property and rents produced by Baroness Sophia Howe & JW Phipps in answer to the writ (see page 8)

Summary totals of rents

AREA		Rents		
		£	s	d
Lancashire		2690	3	4½
Gopsall		1692	5	2
Gotham		547	7	3
Warks	**Whitacre**	380	13	0
	Weethley	230	14	0
Birmingham		287	0	0
All properties		5828	2	9½

Full details of properties etc are on the following pages:

Page 1:
Lancashire

Page 2:
Leicestershire
Nottinghamshire
Warwickshire
Birmingham area

Winter 12 Mar 1813

The Schedule to which the foregoing Answer refers.

Townships	Tenants Names & Estates	Yearly Rents £	s	d
	Tythes of the Parish of Whalley			
Burnley with Habergham				
Eaves Hapton, Chiriger & Worsthorne	Charles Townley esq.	200	0	0
Briarcliffe with Entwistle	Mr William Kitchen	30	0	0
Clayton	John Butterworth	6	0	0
Clitheroe	not let; collected by Martin Richardson	44	10	9½
dº.	Thomas Alhrain 6 tythe pigs and Robert Farrar one tythe pig for 1796	7	7	0
dº.	John Taylor for the Tythe barn	1	11	6
Colne & Foulbridge	James Hargreaves & John Pollards	70	0	0
Heyhouses	William Green	4	0	0
Huncoat	John Grime	10	10	0
Haslington & Rosendale	Thomas Altham	70	0	0
Ightenhill Parks	John Whitaker & John Platt	11	11	0
Marsden	Mr Richard Hartley & Mr John Ridehalgh	45	0	0
Padiham	Richard Robinson & John Sellars	12	0	0
Trawden	Mr Midgley	33	0	0
Whalley	John & Roger Green	4	15	0
	Glebe Lands in the Parish of Whalley			
Whalley Glebe	James Whalley esq. for Clark Hill late Hammond late Slaters	23	0	0
	Ellen and Bernard Hartley late Thomas Drinkwater	21	0	0
	Ellen Hartley	5	5	0
	Mary Ramsbottom	2	2	0
	Elizabeth Lamb	1	5	0
	John Dean for Boltons Cottage	1	5	0
	Robert Parker and William Dugdale for Clarks Cottage and Land	6	15	0
	Francis Parkinson for 10 cottages, Gardens & Pool Stable all adjoining the churchyard	10	10	0
	John & Roger Green for an Allotment on Whalley Moor	9	9	0
Clitheroe Glebe	Mr Henry Eccles late Mrs Haworth	2	10	0
	Mr Richardson for part of Wm Heys	21	0	0
	Glebe farm & Cliff's farm & part of the common allotted to the glebe			
	The Rev'd Tho. Wilson for other pt of Cliff's farm	8	0	0
	Jonathan Wilson late Mr John Parker for Greenleach Meadows	16	10	0
	James Cammel (late Jonathan Wilson) for Salthill Side	5	10	0
Burnley Glebe	James Fletcher Parrock late Nich.ˢ Lacy's	3	3	0
	Joseph Sutcliffe, Bean Meadow & Tattersalls Meadow	11	11	0
	Banastre Halsteads, a close late part of Thomas Whitaker's	2	5	0
	Margaret Chaffer widow & sons	25	13	0
	James Read, a close late Halliwell's, now divided into two closes called Ball Field Nicholas Lacy	3	15	0
	Thomas Whitaker	6	10	0
NB - This rent was not then settled as it was not known how much of the glebe would be taken into the Leeds & Liverpool Canal which was then cutting.				
	John Riding	8	8	0
	Mr Grimshaw	5	0	0
	Mr John Whittam & Thomas Whitaker			
NB - these rents were not then settled it notbeing known how much of the glebe land would be taken in the above mentioned canal				
	The Churchwardens of Burnley for Land taken into the church yard	1	15	0
	The proprietors of the Leeds & Liverpool canal for part of Jonathan Meadow, Cross Field & Bradyll Meadow taken into the canal, the quantity or value of which was not then known			
	Also part of Haddocks			
	Miss Haddock			
NB - This also was not settled as it was not known how much of the glebe would be taken into the canal				

Townships	Tenants Names & Estates	Yearly Rents £	s	d
	Henry Rawlinson	2	2	0
	Mr Henry Greenwood late Jonathan Ingham		10	6
	Mr Holden or Mr Hammerton		5	0
	John Holt late Joshua Nuttall		5	0
	Mr Nicholas Halstead		5	0
	Mr Holden for a garden			
	Joshua Nuttalls garden to Mr Parker's House			
Coln Glebe	Catherine Hargreaves, widow for part of Farras late Slaters	22	0	0
	Mr Joseph Morrell for other part thereof	17	0	0
	The Rev'd John Hartley, late Wm. Hartley for dº.	17	0	0
	Mr Skelton, a Barn	2	0	0
	late Christ' Higgins for a passage		2	6
	Mr James Wilson late John Yates for Lonsdales & slate Quarry	9	10	0
	Mr John Starkill for making the cut to his factory	5	5	0
	Whalley			
	Thomas Green and others for Lambro & Tan Yard & part of Brookhouses	58	12	0
	dº. for part of Whalley Moor	43	1	0
	George Horner for late John Birch - for Deans also for abbey Bank End, Halls, Roberts & Mill & for a Garden for late George Reads	388	0	0
	John Eatough for late John Brown's	2	10	0
	James Clegg for Horrobins Grange & Grass Yard & four cottages Nº. 1, 3, 31 & 32	17	0	0
	John & widow Dean for late Eliz. Dean's & Clark's croft	16	10	0
	Michael dean for the Late widow Dean	10	0	0
	Thomas Dean for late Ramsbottoms	7	0	0
	Ellen Hartley widow late Rob't Hargreave's for late Grundy's	35	0	0
	dº. for Shayhouses & for late Francis Parkinson			
	Robert Hargreaves for a barn late John Eatough's		5	0
	dº. for late Robert Loftus	2	0	0
	John Wittam late James Kempon for late widow Drinkwater late Michael Rhodes & for three Smithfields late Mr George Horner	28	0	0
	Robert Eastwood for Cross House	3	13	6
	Mary & Ann Grundy for late Robert Grundys widow	9	9	0
	John Grundy clockmaker for late Edward Wright's daughter	1	10	0
	John & widow Chew	1	6	0
	John Grundy Taylor for Aspinall's part of grange		15	0
	James Loftus	2	0	0
	John Birch late Mrs Matthew's for Halls	4	4	0
	The Overseers of the Poor for Hills		7	6
	dº. for late George Read's		7	6
	Lawrence & Joseph Hartley for Brookhouses & part of Lambro	41	0	0
	dº. & Thomas Dean for part of Whalley Moor	11	0	0
	The widow of Henry Ingham for a house & close received in exchange from Mr Whalley	9	9	0
	Widow Rhodes for Eastwoods	3	3	0
	James Redhead	1	15	0
	Widow Yates	4	10	0
	Tythes of own Tenants- abbey & Lambro' excepted	4	0	0
	The Revrd Mr Baldwin for the Waste Lands			1
	Miss Millicent Johnson - for the new houses	8	8	0
Billington	Thomas Green for parts of Elker & Dugdales	40	0	0
	John Mayo for Alstons, widow Chew's & part of Elker and part of Billington Moor	50	0	0
	Richard Dugdale for Cravens & pt of Dewhursts	69	0	0
	Wm Eastwood for Buckfoot, part of Elker & Dewhursts	52	0	0
	James Proctor Jnr for part of Billington Moor	3	3	0
Harwood	James Proctor	3	3	0
	Tho. Aspden late Richᵈ. Seedal for Harwood Common	8	8	0
Oswaldtwistle	John Roscow & Ellis Ratcliffe late John Ramsbottom	40	0	0
	dº. for coal mines	20	0	0
Rossendale	James Lord	15	0	0

Townships	Tenants Names & Estates	Yearly Rents £	s	d
	James Whitaker & John Whitaker	10	0	0
	Lawrence Sutcliffe	11	5	0
	Mrs Alice Lord	12	0	0
Oldham	Mrs Taylor		5	0
	Widow Winterbottom	9	0	0
	for late Chadwick house & land			
Marsden	Mr John Ridehalgh & John Rigby late George Hartley for the Town	12	12	0
Sharples	James Mason late John Yates for Wields	10	10	0
Worston	Thomas Badger	36	0	0
Horrocksford	George Hayhurst for lands lately occupied by him & Jonathan Hargreaves & also late Robert Hopwoods	280	0	0
	Thomas Geldard for parts of Horrocksford Hall	3	3	0
	John Hayhurst for another part thereof	2	2	0
	James Embley and son for other part thereof	3	3	0
	James Embley for Ridinhey .	46	0	0
	Ralph Whitaker late Ellil for Kempstones in Chatburn	22	0	0
	Thomas Taylor for Bradford Mill	10	0	0
Hardhill	Thomas Waltom	94	10	0
	Lime Kilns			
	John Place, James Embley, William Thornber, James Cammel, Thomas Parkinson & James Cook (£8 8s 0d each)	50	8	0
	Clitheroe			
	Overseers of the Poor of Clitheroe late Christʳ. Heaps	1	10	0
	dº. for John Clark	1	10	0
	James Sellars late Walter Moren	3	0	0
	William Bullock late James Pilling	2	0	0
	James Fielding late John Riding late Thoˢ. Simpson	1	15	0
	Ann Sellars & Robert Kitchen late Wᵐ. Cottam	3	3	0
	Jonathan Watson, two meadows adjoining the Low Moor, with an allotment of common laid to & inclosed with the said two meadows	12	12	0
	Joseph Wood for a house in the market place	4	10	0
	dº. for a close called Wing	3	3	0
	Thomas Holt for Dulop of Dun Meadows, two fields part of Eashams late Mr Wilson with an allotment of common laid to a parcel of 1 of the last mentᵈ. fields	10	10	0
	dº. for two cottages at Dulop of Dun	1	0	0
	The Rev Thomas Wilson for a croft late Eastham's	5	5	0
	John Taylor, 4 closes called Nuncknols, 2 closes adjoining the back common & a Barn late Richᵈ. Wood & 4 fields called the Withins, all part of Eastham's with an allotment of common adjoining thereto	42	5	0
	dº. Jonathan Bowker for late Thº. Swindlehurst	1	5	0
	James Cammel late Peter Veitch 2 Salthill side meadˢ. with an allotment of common adjoining thereto	7	10	0
	Richard Parkinson for the Allotment on the low Moor	15	15	0
	Mr Thomas Baldwin for a close called Headings	1	16	0
	John Nowell	2	12	6
	Mr John Parker late Wm' Tomlinson	10	17	6
	John Robinson for Fairy Banks and Pimlico mean Lands	4	10	0
	Messrs Barry Lloyd for Cob Croft late part of Holgates	10	0	0
	Mr Lister a piece of land in Doctor's Croft		15	0
	Jonathan Wilson late Robert Wood for a close late part of Easthams called Coat Meadow	9	5	0
	dº. for 2 small allotments of common adjoining	3	3	0
	dº. for a field called Ivers late James Croasdale & for another field called Ribble Hill late John Taylor	5	15	6
	dº. for a croft late Rich' Parkinson late Mr Haworth	2	0	0
	Mr Addy late John Harris for pt of Fieldings wheatcroft	5	5	0
	John Illingworth late Mr Addy, Little Croft late Fieldings		10	0
	John Leach late Catheral Leach for two allotments on the High Moor	15	0	0
	John Strickland for other allotment on the High Moor	31	0	0
	dº. for Poor Bones adjoining ditto	4	0	0
	dº. & Thomas Warner late Gent Rigby & others for the Dog Kennell	2	2	0

Winter 12 Mar 1813

Tenants Names	Yearly rents £	s	d
GOPSAL			
William Dickinson	49	16	0
John Peggs Executors	25	12	0
ditto for Underwoods	6	10	0
James & William Winters Executors	81	4	6
William Worthingtons Executors	61	8	0
Bilston			
The Overseer		7	0
William Dickinson	27	18	0
William Glenn	55	0	0
ditto for Kellys Land	45	0	0
William Lilley	2	2	0
John Lilley	2	2	0
Thomas Taylor	2	2	0
Ann Green by the Overseer		8	0
Elizabeth Beadman	1	10	0
Edward Hollis	2	0	0
William & Joseoh Kuch	40	0	0
John Peggs Executors	49	5	0
Chief Rents			
Mr Glenn for Mr Jennens		18	8
ditto late his own		9	2
ditto....and Bennett			4
Congeston			
Widow Farmer		4	0
William Haddon		5	0
Edward Hollis	44	15	8
Norton			
Thomas Cowley		10	0
John Robinson	1	0	0
ditto late Whettons		15	0
John Taylor	2	5	0
Widow Martind & Hwicks		5	0
James & William Winters Executors	16	9	0
Qwilliam Worthingtons Executors	74	1	4
George Whight	1	1	0
Edward Townsend, a garden on the waste		1	0
William Worthington Executors ditto		1	0
John Miller ditto		1	0
Richard Miller ditto		1	0
William Smith ditto		1	0
Chief Rents			
George Moor esq			7
Mr Spencer			6
George Moor essq		2	8
Thomas Elton his own			4
Abraham Harding for Hastings			6
ditto for more Hastings			1½
for Curzons			1
William Hart for Hastings			¾
Joseph Smith ditto			1
Freeson for Worthington			¾
Tavernor for Pierson and Copsan			11
Orton			
Joseph Peggs Executors	28	17	0
Orton Tithes			
Thomas Parker	74	5	0
Joseph Peggs Executors	45	0	0
William Wheatley	19	10	0
Shackerston			
Samuel Watts Executors & William Lakin	90	0	0
ditto for tithes	4	10	0
William Clarkson	130	0	0

Tenants Names	Yearly rents		
ditto Chapel Hall and Derby Street	66	4	0
John Adie	20	0	0
Joseph Earp	56	10	0
Twycross			
William Smalley senior	2	0	0
William Glenn	2	0	0
William Wheatley	58	10	10
William Dickinson	36	19	10
ditto late his own	30	0	0
William Dickinson Junior	81	13	8
Thomas Ensor	85	12	10
Widow Hincks Executor	4	17	6
Mary Harriman		1	0
Edward Hollis	6	10	0
John Leedham		4	0
Henry Farmer	5	0	0
Widows Ward & Sanders		3	0
William Smalley junior	1	10	0
Joseph Herod		5	0
Eleanor Boon		5	0
Anthony Huggs		2	0
Eleanor Choyce		5	0
William Thomas		1	0
Thomas Lees a Garden Plech		3	0
ditto late Grundys	9	11	0
Edward Hartin	30	0	0
George Knight	4	4	0
William Hassell		8	0
Robert Faux	63	0	0
John Farrini	84	0	0
Twycross Tithes			
Mr Thomas Clare Farm	7	9	0
ditto for Kennels		14	0
ditto Mr John Harcourts		14	0
ditto a meadow		14	1
William King	2	3	2½
William Wheatley	4	4	0
ditto for Lakuis		7	6
ditto for Huichs's		18	6
William Dickinson	1	3	1
William Farrins Jones		5	4
William Dickinson junior	6	0	0
Thomas Ensor		3	0
John Farrini	3	0	3
ditto for Balls		3	6
ditto for Needhams	1	15	0
William Roulston	3	10	4
Edward Hartin	1	7	2
Francis skelton 1/3rd of Bartletts		4	5
ditto a meadow		5	0
John Harrison junior		4	3
John Farrini		2	2
William Dickinson	1	1	8
John Farrini's School Land		17	0
George Knight		1	3
Joseph Joyce for Hastings		7	6
ditto for part of		2	3
Farrinis for more late Farrinis		4	6
ditto late Thomas Ortons			6
ditto for Baxters		19	3
Thomas Lees		10	5
Mr Faux	5	6	6

Tenants Names	Yearly rents		
ditto for Curzons	3	0	3
John Farrini Curzons	4	1	10½
James Okey	1	14	0
Mr Glenn		3	4
Thomas King			6
John Booton		3	9
Chief Rents			
Mr Thomas Clare Farm		1	0
John Farrini			3
William Roulston		1	9
Edward Hartini			7
John Hamson junior			2
William Dickinson			2
John Farrini School Land			2
George Knight			1
Joseph Joyce for Hastings			½
Mr Faux			2½
John Farrini Curzons		1	2
GOTHAM			
John Hansley	103	3	0
Thomas Oliver	2	10	0
William Spencer	40	18	6
Henry Windley	79	14	8
Samuel Pepper		15	0
William Bowley	1	1	0
William Sharp		15	0
William Holland	1	0	0
William Smith		1	0
Thomas Redfern a small house	4	10	0
Thomas Bowley	1	3	0
Thomas Woolley	1	19	0
Widow Ellis		1	0
Thomas Redfern a chief rent			1
Keyworth Chiefs		5	0
Thomas Carver		4	0
Jonas Maltby		2	0
William Belton		5	0
Joseph Bexon		1	0
Thomas Smith	1	12	0
Widow Bexon & John her son	1	2	0
William Smith		10	0
Richard Julians Executors	29	5	0
Thomas Redfern	2	5	0
Charles Houghton		5	0
Sarah Holland widow	3	5	0
George Hives	3	0	0
George Pares		10	0
Willoughby Harrison	1	5	0
Joseph Hogg	2	5	0
Widow Haniswowrth		1	0
Widow Smith		1	0
Widow Collington		1	0
William Hallam	1	12	0
John Chalby	1	7	0
Widow Price & Henry		10	0
William Redfern	114	7	0
William Redfern Junior	98	10	0
Stephen Sharpe	46	11	0
John Marshall		1	0
Joseph Ellis		4	0
Daniel Harrison		5	0
Thomas Smith junior		1	0
William Rivington		1	0
Thomas Wilson		2	0
John Price		1	0

Tenants Names	Yearly rents		
BIRMINGHAM			
John Ryland Mander Esq	12	0	0
Erdington			
Thomas Greensall	4	10	0
Widow Thomas	5	5	0
Mr Twist	22	10	0
ditto	1	10	0
John James	4	0	0
William Fowler	8	8	0
Sarah Nichols	6	0	0
John Moss	39	8	0
ditto		12	0
Mr Holden		7	0
Mr Spooner		10	0
Edgbaston			
John Harrison	176	0	0
Hales Owen			
Samuel Harris	6	0	0

NB Of these rents in Erdington, Edgbaston and Hales Owen the Honorable Penn Assheton Curzon deceased was entitled to two third parts only and the other third part thereof belonged to William Jennens Esquire.

Tenants Names	Yearly rents		
WARWICKSHIRE			
Whitacre			
James Butler	150	10	0
ditto the Church Yard	1	10	0
Joseph Shilton	1	5	0
John Silk	19	7	6
Thomas Hasterlys Executors	20	3	6
Richard Newton	22	17	10
Charles Rotheram	35	8	8
Charles Rotheram's Executos	49	18	6
Isaac Clarke	75	7	10
Waste Rents			
Edward Briscoe		10	0
William Coulson		15	0
Widow & Joseph Capeulwest		2	6
Widow Harsthill		1	0
Mary Dixon widow		2	0
Joseph White		2	0
Thomas Arnold		2	0
William Huiton		1	0
Isaac Dixon		5	0
George Hall		1	0
Thomas Pickford		2	0
Henry Leak		1	0
Chief Rentals			
Mr Butler	1	19	8
Weethley Rents			
Thomas Morris & Mary Burstone	56	10	0
Harry Harvey	168	0	0
Thomas Frier	6	0	0
Waste Rents			
Thomas Harris		1	0
James Hubbard		1	0
Thomas Sampis		1	0
John Thornbury		1	0

NB Of these rents and waste rents in Weethley The Honorable Penn Assheton Curzon was entitled to one Moiety only the other Moiety belonged to the said William Jennens.

A House in Saint James Square in the county of Middlesex in which the Honorable Penn Assheton Curzon resided.

Howe JW Phipps

Gopsall Hall

The planning, building and 19th century alterations

The first known record of a manor at Gopsall was shortly after the Norman Conquest, when in 1068, William the Conqueror (William I) gave Gopsall to Hugh d'Avaranches along with other estates including Tutbury and much of the surrounding land. Soon afterwards Gopsall was transferred to Henry de Ferrers (Chapter 1). No buildings are recorded in the Domesday census of 1086, which states that Gopsall consisted of about 360 acres of farmland, inhabited by 8 villagers and 5 small holders. In about 1245, during the de Grendon's lordship, that part of Gopsall held by the abbot and convent of Merevale (about 90 acres) is said to have had a settlement consisting of an unspecified number of 'tofts' (homesteads, consisting of a house and associated farm buildings) and crofts, enclosed arable land and a 'capital house'.[1] This appears to be the first indication of a manor house at Gopsall.

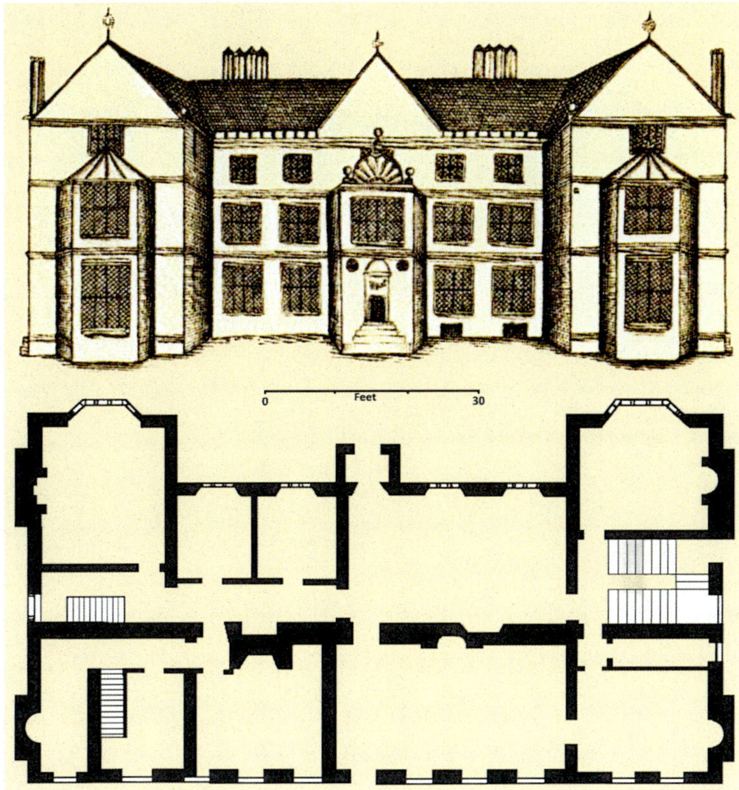

Figure 1a. North elevation and proposed ground floor plan of the original Gopsall Manor house. The plan is derived from that shown below and the drawing of the north elevation. The position of the south wall has been drawn assuming that north and south walls of the house were equidistant from the central wall.

The only other information about a manor house at Gopsall, prior to the building of Charles Jennens' hall in 1750, is contained in an undated map held at the Leicestershire Records Office[2] and a partial plan of the ground floor held by the Royal Institute of British Architects (RIBA).[3] The map, thought to have been made in about 1650, shows the north front of a 7-bay Elizabethan house (Fig. 1a). This was the house purchased by Humphrey Jennens and the home of his grandson Charles Jennens junior for all his life until he replaced it with his new hall. The RIBA plan, attributed to John Westley of Leicester, was produced in about 1745 to illustrate a possible way to extend and remodel the house while retaining the principal entrance and north front (Fig. 1b).

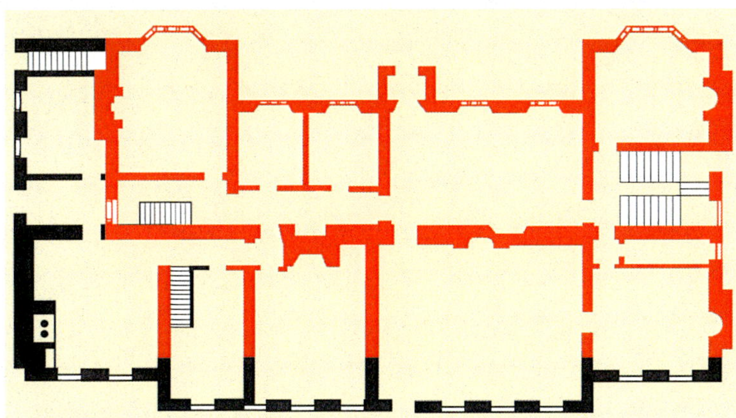

Figure 1b. Plan for remodelling the existing manor house attributed to John Westley (c1745)[3]; north front at the top. Walls in red show the retained walls of the original house. The proposed extension and new, repositioned and refaced south wall are shown in black. The frontages of the original and remodelled house were 100ft and 113ft respectively.

This plan for remodelling the house would have resulted in only a modest increase in floor area of 1200sq ft and, although none of the rooms were labelled, suggests that the main extension of the building on its west side was probably to provide larger service areas and servant quarters. Changes to the principal rooms within the house would have been relatively small, even if the south wall had been repositioned as proposed in this interpretation of the plans. Interestingly, the two largest rooms in the original manor house are the entrance hall (30.5ft long) and probable dining room (32ft long), the lengths of which are almost identical to those of the same rooms in the hall that was finally demolished in 1951.

It is impossible to be certain about the planning and building of Gopsall Hall. There are no descriptions about its erection and all the available plans for the main building, held by the RIBA, are undated and unsigned. Furthermore, confusion arises because there are three distinct aspects to consider, namely the planning and execution of the hall itself, the service blocks and the internal fittings for, and decoration of, the hall. The whole project probably spanned well over a decade and, according to the RIBA, involved John Westley, William and David Hiorn, James Paine and other unidentified 18th century architects/designers. In addition to those architects known to be directly involved in submitting designs for Gopsall, a number of the floor plans and façades proposed for the hall and outbuildings reflect the influence of James Gibbs' 'A Book of Architecture' (1728).[4] Charles Jennens subscribed to this book, which was used as a 'pattern book' for many provincial architects of the time, and it is likely that he played an influential part in the ultimate designs for the hall, its interior decoration and the service and garden buildings. However, if each aspect of the design of Gopsall is considered separately, the evolution of Charles Jennens' hall becomes clearer.

All the detailed floor plans bar one for the possible remodelling of the original house and building of the hall are attributed to John Westley.[3] The one relatively small-scale plan attributed to the Hiorn brothers,[5] shows the hall plus the proposed two service wings, but the details of the hall are identical to the final design of Westley's apart from the position of three internal doors. This plan was almost certainly produced to illustrate the relative positions of the service wings to the main hall, as was a drawing of the resulting elevation of the north front (see Fig. 8 later).

Although none of the plans are dated, it is very likely that some, if not all of the Westley plans were produced before Charles Jennens senior's death in March 1747. This is based upon the fact that, according to John Grundy who visited Gopsall in July or August of 1750, the new hall, except for the south portico and carved pediment, was built and partially decorated and furnished (Appendix I).[6] Grundy's account describes the music room and library in some detail and even gives costs of some of the furnishings, fittings and plasterwork. If the initial plans for remodelling/rebuilding the house had not been drawn up until after the death of Charles Jennens' father in 1747, it is extremely unlikely that the new hall would have been at the stage of completion reported by Grundy in 1750.

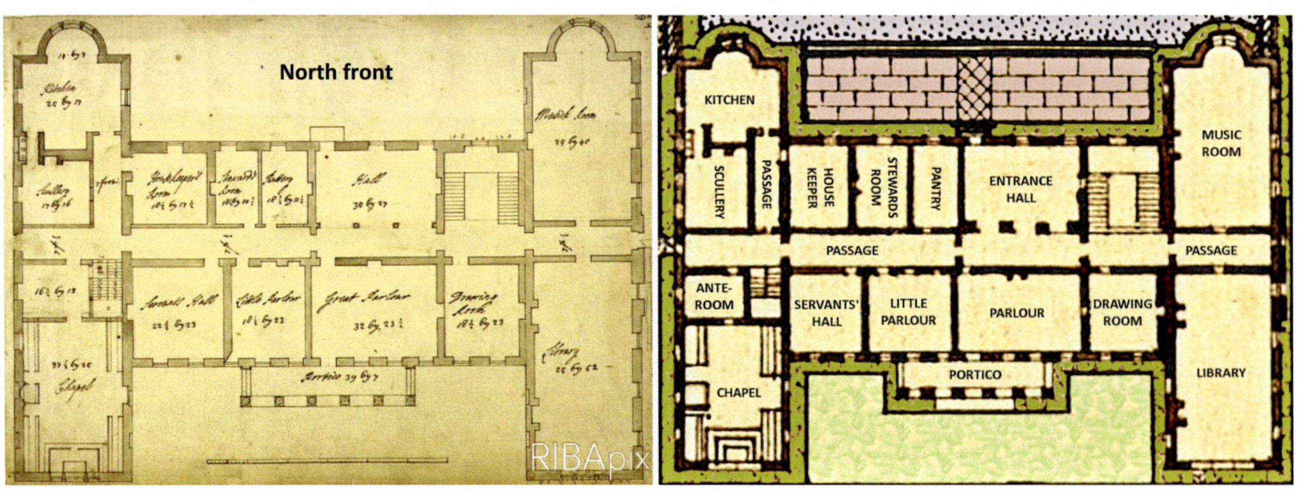

Figure 2.

Left: Westley ground floor plan of the hall showing a 6-column portico/arcade and room names.[7] The earlier 4-column arcade plan[8] showed the kitchen and servants' hall on the south front and a billiard room rather than the housekeeper's room (RIBA Collections).

Right: The hall as illustrated on the plan of the gardens[9] drawn by John Grundy in 1749 showing an identical design and room names.

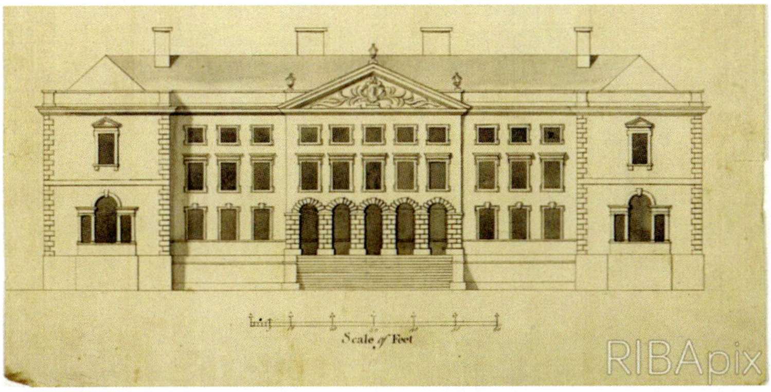

RIBA Collections

Figure 3.

Elevation of the south front of the hall designed by John Westley[10] (top left), showing a central projection with a ground floor arcade and surmounted by a carved pediment. The Hiorns' design[11] is shown beneath and features a 6-columned portico with receding carved pediment. The Westley alternative for the central part of the south front[12] is shown on the right and is very similar to that shown in the Hiorns' drawing but lacks the ballustraded flat top to the portico that was actually built. The photograph shows the south front of the hall as it appeared in the early 20th century. Note that the hipped slate roofs, clearly seen in the architectural drawings, are not visible in the photograph because of the change in roof design when the hall was built.

The plan for the gardens, made by John Grundy and dated 1749,[9] provides additional evidence that the design adopted for the new hall was as drawn by Westley. The hall is shown exactly as on Westley's 6-columned, south portico floor plan, including the room names (Fig. 2). The original drawing of the south elevation associated with this plan included a central, 6-pillared entrance arcade supporting the rooms above and surmounted by a carved pediment (Fig. 3). However, a further drawing by Westley shows an alternative south front dominated by a 6-columned portico and receding pediment (ie. part of the hall wall, not placed on top of the portico), similar to, but slightly different from, that actually built. A later drawing attributed to the Hiorns depicts the south front and portico as executed, apart from the design of the relief sculpture within the pediment. This indicates that they influenced the final appearance of this part of the building in 1750 when the design of the portico was still under discussion.[6]

There was one other change to the finished building not shown in the hall elevations drawn by Westley and the Hiorn brothers, namely a reduction in apex height of the hipped roof by 4 feet and an increase in the height of the surrounding parapet wall by 1 foot (Fig. 3).[13] This alteration meant that the roof could not be seen unless the hall was viewed from some distance.

Measurements[13] made from the floor plans attributed to John Westley show a logical chronology for the designs (Table 1):

- minor extension and remodelling of the original house.
- two different designs showing houses about double the size of the original but not retaining any or much of the original structure (U-shaped and stunted H-block plans).
- a sequence of H-plan designs retaining most of the original manor house but with floor areas over 2.5 times that of the original.

This proposal is also supported by overlaying the scaled plans from the original manor house onto those drawn by Westley (Fig. 4). Essentially all the designs except the 'new build', U-shaped and stunted H-block plans, are based upon retaining much of the original house except its south wall and part of the north wall. Indeed, all the H-plan designs add large east and west wings and a new decorative south front to the original house. Apart from the northwest part of the west wing, which contained the kitchen and scullery, the rest of the wing space was devoted to 3 large rooms linked to Charles Jennens' interests; religion, literature and music (Fig. 2). Interestingly, the servants' hall, housekeeper's and steward's rooms and a pantry are not segregated from the principal rooms of the ground floor. This layout, mixing service rooms with the principal rooms on one floor, reflects the apparent desire to retain as much of the old house fabric as possible. This layout is not in keeping with the normal practice, at that time, of a hierarchical arrangement of rooms with service rooms on the ground floor (usually a partial basement floor) and principal rooms on the floor above (known as the *piano nobile* or noble level/floor). That the 'new' hall retained much of the original house is also supported by John Grundy's comment about the windows on the south front[6]: "*the piers betwixt the windows are small on account of keeping the place of the old one*".

Table 1. Areas and dimensions of the ground floor plans (feet & square feet[13])

Ground floor plan	Area	Perimeter	Full width of house	Between wings (S)	Between wings (N)	Depth of central part	Depth of wing
	Inc. south portico		*E - W*	*E - W*	*E - W*	*N - S*	*N - S*
17th century house	**4652**	**347**	100	N/A	54	42	54
Remodelled house[3]	**5923**	**384**	113	N/A	54	49	56
Stunted H-block[14]	**8512**	**440**	121	70	70	65	78
U-shaped plan[15]*	**9609**	**489**	113	48	N/A	70	92
Offset-H plan[16]	**12210**	**741**	162 / 152⁺	106	96	56	120
H-plan plan (4-column)[17]	**12511**	**676**	158	100	100	59	114
H-plan plan (6-column)[18]	**12532**	**684**	157	98	98	56	115
Hiorns' plan[5]**	**12861**	**682**	158	99	99	59	117
Grundy plan (1749)[9++]	**13396**	**676**	160	98	98	60	117
20th century plan	**35333**	**2211**	160	98	99	65	179

* = plan has no scale; width of house assumed to be 113 feet; ⁺ = width of south front greater than the north front; ** = smaller scale plan which includes the service wings; ⁺⁺ = *very* small scale plan; presence of the hall is incidental in this plan for the layout of the garden, so the measurements will be less accurate than for the larger scale plans.

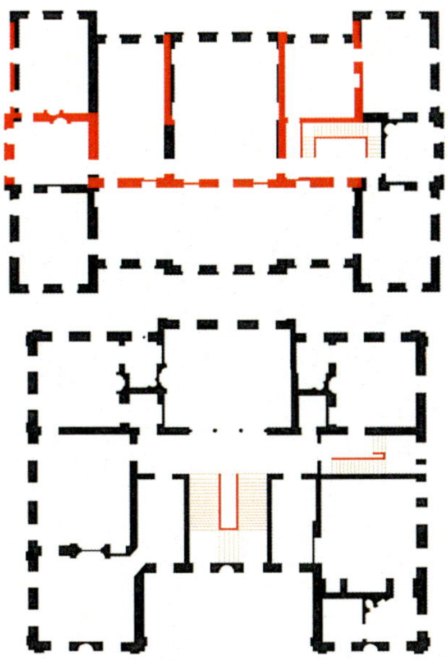

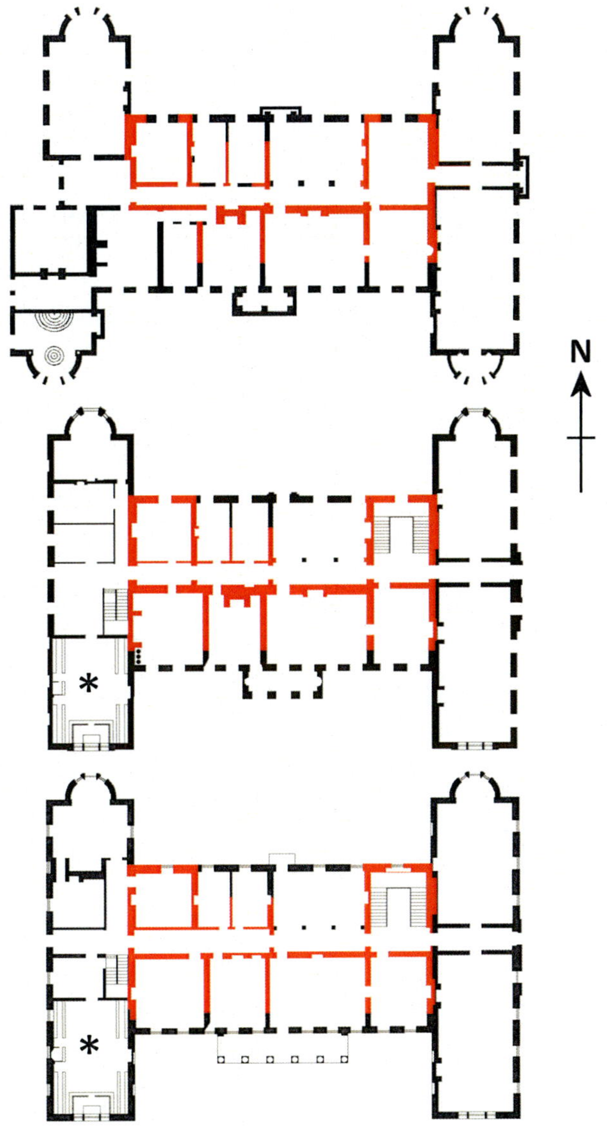

Figure 4.

Ground floor plans held by the RIBA attributed to John Westley for the remodelling/rebuilding of Gopsall Hall. Parts of the plan shown in red correspond to walls retained from the original Elizabethan house.

Above: Stunted H-block[14] (top) and U-shaped house plans[15] (bottom). While some of the old house walls could be incorporated into the new design for the stunted-H plan hall, this is not true for the more traditional U-shaped design incorporating a central entrance hall and staircase.

Right: Offset-H and H-plan designs. The southwest wing of the offset-H design[16] appears to be a 'spa' rather than a chapel as shown in the H-plan designs of both Westley and the Hiorns. The main difference between the 4-[17] and 6-pier[18] arcade H-plan designs is in the layout of the northwest wing and chapel ante-room. ∗ = chapel

Although the overall design of the layout and elevations of the hall constructed in 1750 is reflected in plans and photographs of the hall dating from the late 19th/early 20th century, the original outside appearance of the hall seems to have been very different (Fig. 5). In 1750, when the hall was nearing completion, Grundy says *"The outside case of the fronts is of a beautiful red brick"* and that *"breaks in the centre and corners are bounded by large quoin stones"*.[6] Furthermore, *"the windows* (of the north front) *are of rustic stone"* whereas the windows of the south front are *"plain stone work"*, clearly differing from the elevations drawn by both Westley and the Hiorns. This description of a distinctive red-brick building with contrasting stone quoins is clearly shown in a painting of the hall by an unknown artist sometime after the hall, service blocks (known as 'offices'), Ionic rotunda south of the hall and other park buildings were built (c.1764).[19] In his description, Grundy uses the phrases *"dress of brick and stone"* and *"dressed brick/bricks"* to describe the finish of the exterior walls of the hall. This could be interpreted to mean that the bricks were dressed or faced with stone to produce a building appearing to be built of stone. However, if this was the case, it is difficult to see why Grundy comments on the beauty of the bricks or why a painting was produced showing a red-brick hall. That the hall was eventually faced with stone, or more likely rendered, is borne out by engravings published in 1791[20] and 1829[21], not to mention the many photographs of the building that exist today (Figs. 3 & 5). An earlier engraving of the hall published in 1767[22] is essentially a copy of the Hiorns' drawing of the south front and does not represent a work based on direct personal observation of the hall by the artist. It shows a projecting west wing, flat east wing, a high roof apex and small chimneys as in the architectural drawing rather than as built (Fig. 6).

Figure 5.

Top: Painting dated to after 1764 showing red brick façades with lake and summerhouse, viewed from the south.
Middle: 1791 engraving[20] showing a similar view to the painting but no evidence of brick façades or quoin stones.
Bottom: 1829 engraving[21] of the hall showing the south and east garden fronts; no evidence of brick façades or quoin stones. The hipped slate roofs are not visible, as expected unless viewing the hall from a distance.

The 1767 Woolfe and Gandon engraving of the south front[22] (Fig. 6) clearly shows the receding pediment with a relief sculpture containing many elements similar to those in Neale's 1829 engraving[21] (Fig. 5) and as mentioned in the first written description of the south front of the hall by the Rev. J. Curtis in 1831[23]: "*...there is a receding pediment having a ship in a storm carved in white stone, with a haven in the foreground, and an inscription over the entrance, 'FORTITER OCCUPA PORTUM'*". Surprisingly, the 1791 Throsby engraving (Fig. 5), described as *"a slight picturesque view"* by Nichols, but created after he and Mr Throsby visited Gopsall, does not show a maritime themed pediment.[23,24] However, it is clear that a maritime design for the pediment on the south front existed 6 years prior to the death of Charles Jennens. Furthermore, the inclusion of the Latin inscription taken from Horace's Odes 1.14 (widely interpreted as representing the 'Ship of State' in troubled waters) probably reflected Jennens' position as a non-juror. Taken together, it seems likely that the maritime themed pediment on the south front was one of Charles Jennens' final additions to the hall prior to his death in 1773.

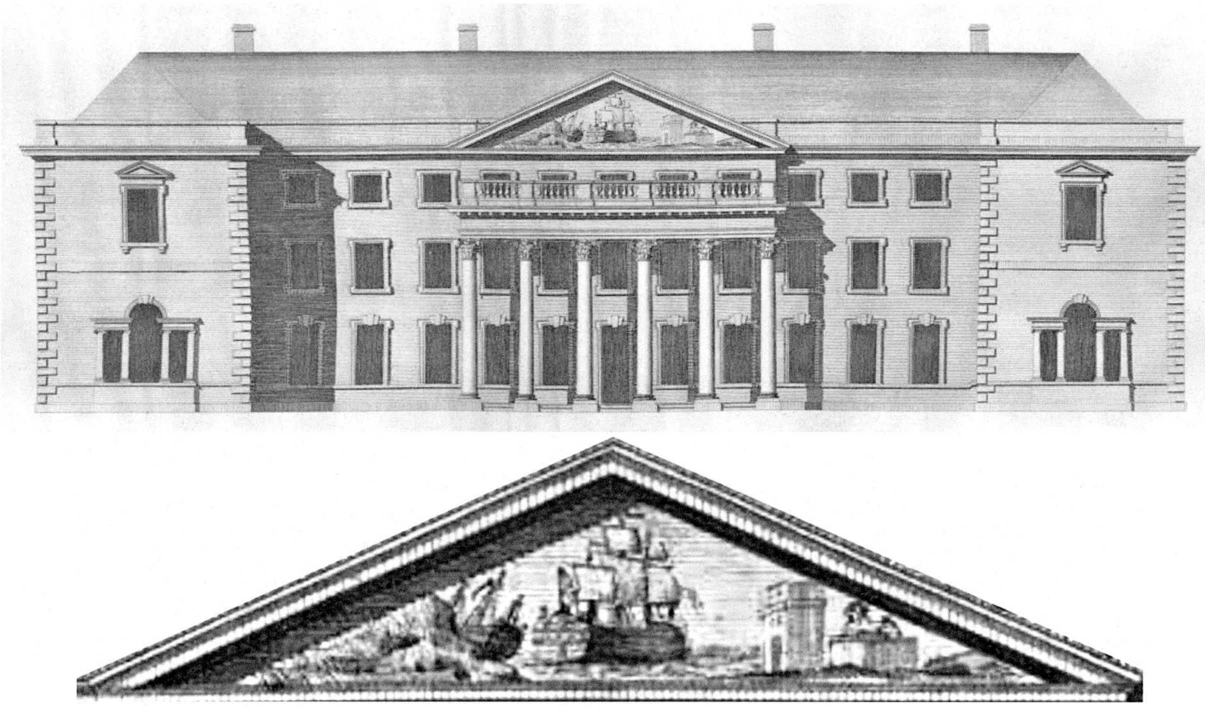

Figure 6.

Above: 1767 engraving[22] of the south front of Gopsall Hall showing the receding pediment containing a relief sculpture similar to that seen in 19th and 20th century photographs of the hall.

Below: Photographic detail of the pediments on the south (*top*) and north (*bottom*) fronts of Gopsall Hall. The pediment on the north front would have been added sometime after Charles Jennens' death, as it includes a coat of arms containing elements from the Curzon and Howe families together with the motto: Let Curzon holde what Curzon helde.

Figure 6 (cont).
Detail of pediment on the east front of Gopsall Hall.

No descriptions of the pediment on the east front of the hall exist and most images do not show any detail of the relief sculpture within. However, one photograph from Lord Howe's archive clearly shows a tempestuous sea, a woman looking right towards a character also looking right who is wearing a cap and holding a shield and a weapon raised above his body directed at a sea monster. The cap and the shield are characteristic accoutrements of Perseus and the sculpture probably represents Perseus killing the sea monster (Cetus) and rescuing Andromeda who had been chained to a rock as a sacrifice. Lord Howe observed: *"the point of the sculpture is to be a counterpoint to that on the other Gopsall pediment* (on the south front). *It is metaphorically guarding the house against all threats by showing the sea monster being overcome*". It is likely that this classical relief sculpture was commissioned by Charles Jennens.

While the designing of the hall appears relatively clear, there are no firm data on the actual builders. John Westley was, by his own description, a master builder,[25] so it is logical to assume that he played a large part in the construction of the hall to his plans. However, it seems possible that final completion of the hall fabric, including the south portico, was overseen by the Hiorn brothers, who were the main architects and contractors for completing the interior decoration of the hall and the subsequent building of the service blocks and garden and park buildings. This change was noted by Throsby in 1791[20] who wrote: "....*Westley of Leicester, architect. I believe, the offices* (service blocks)*, through a misunderstanding, were built by Mr Hiorn of Warwick*". By 1750, William and David Hiorn were well established architects and builders in their own right having taken over a very successful firm previously run by the architect and master builder, William Smith of Warwick for whom they had worked. William had been a mason and David a carpenter.[26]

From the account of Grundy's visit to Gopsall in 1750,[6] decoration and furnishing of the library and the music room on the ground floor, and the bedrooms in the east and west wings on the first floor, were essentially complete. For the music room this included the presence of a harpsicord and piano (imported from Italy and one of the first in Britain), but the room was still awaiting the installation of the organ being built in London to Handel's specification. The entrance hall with its gallery had been completed and the floor laid. Nothing is said about the dining and drawing rooms, but the ceiling and stucco work in the chapel had been finished although work on the interior had not begun.

The RIBA has 27 plans for the design of various ground floor rooms in the hall, which are believed to cover a period between 1745-1755 at least. The majority of the plans (22) are thought to date to before 1749 and 17 of these are by unidentified English architects. The remaining five early designs for the library, dining room, drawing room, an unidentified room and a ceiling were produced by the established London-based architect, James Paine.[27] By cross-referencing the RIBA plans with various descriptions of the interior of the hall and photographs of the interiors it is possible to confirm that some of the designs by unidentified architects were executed, specifically the ceiling[28] and fireplace[29] in the dining room (Fig. 7 and see Chapter 3) and the designs for the library[30] and music room[31]. Surprisingly, none of the designs submitted by Paine appear to have been used.

Of the five later interior designs by the Hiorn brothers for the dining room, drawing room, chapel and 'Eagle' reading desk, it is only those for the chapel[32] and reading desk[33] that appear to have been executed (Fig. 7). However, much of the interior decoration of the hall is rococo in

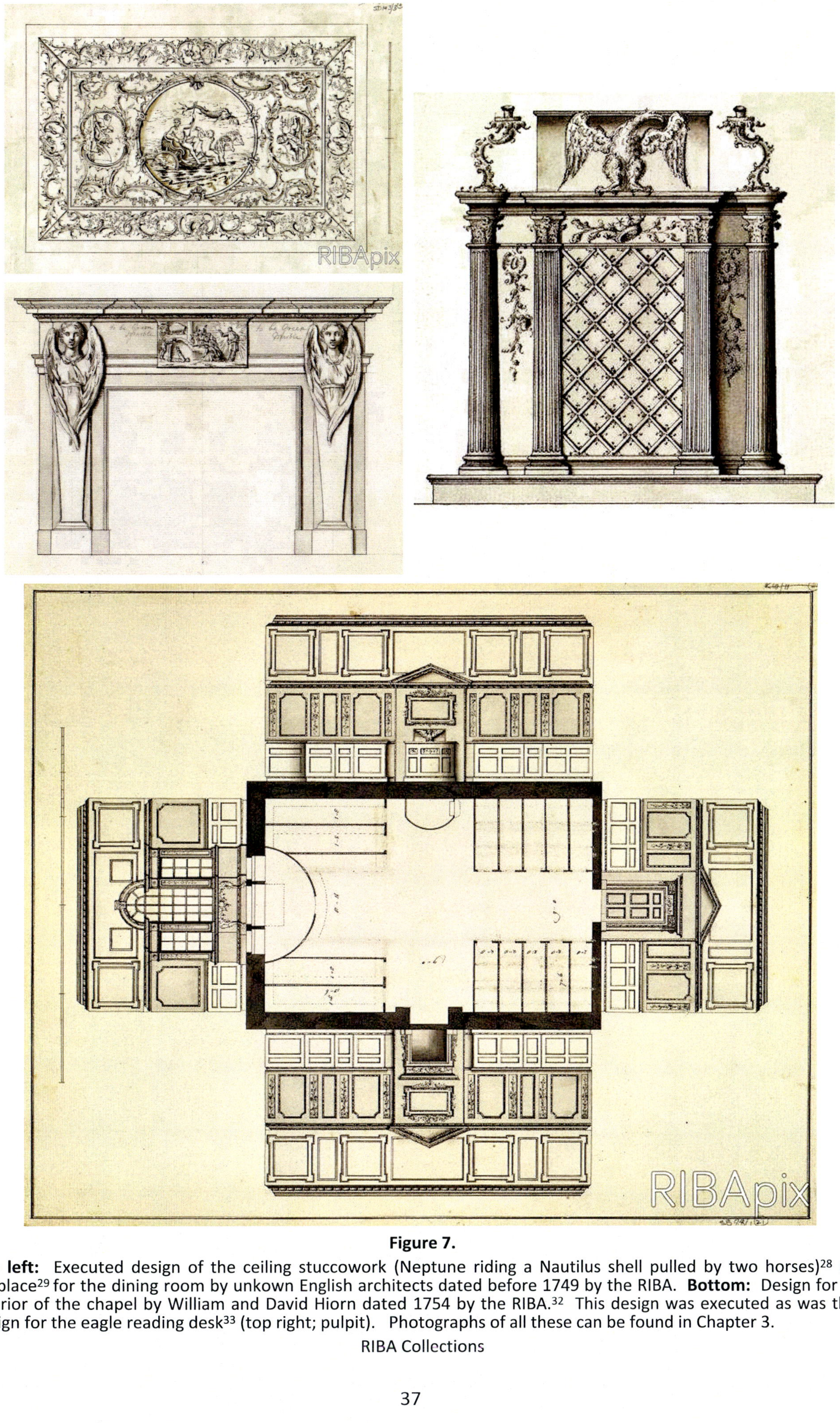

Figure 7.

Top left: Executed design of the ceiling stuccowork (Neptune riding a Nautilus shell pulled by two horses)[28] and fireplace[29] for the dining room by unkown English architects dated before 1749 by the RIBA. **Bottom:** Design for the interior of the chapel by William and David Hiorn dated 1754 by the RIBA.[32] This design was executed as was their design for the eagle reading desk[33] (top right; pulpit). Photographs of all these can be found in Chapter 3.

RIBA Collections

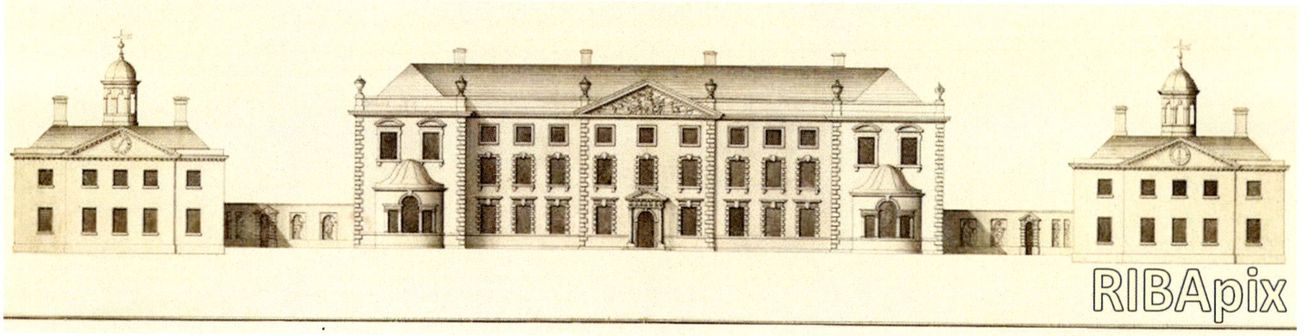

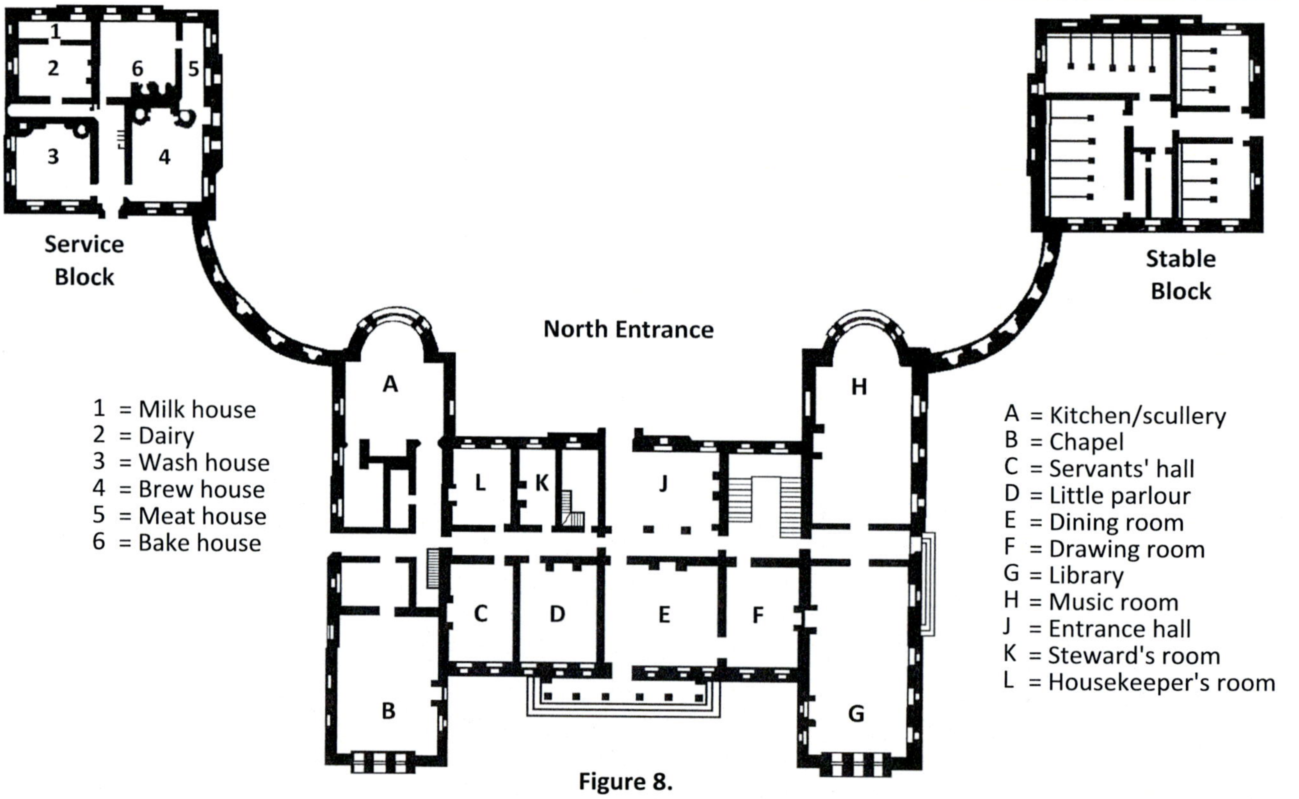

Figure 8.

Top: North elevation of the hall and service blocks as drawn by the Hiorns (RIBA Collections).
Bottom: Floor plan of the hall and service wings as shown in Nichols[24] and plans held by the RIBA[5].

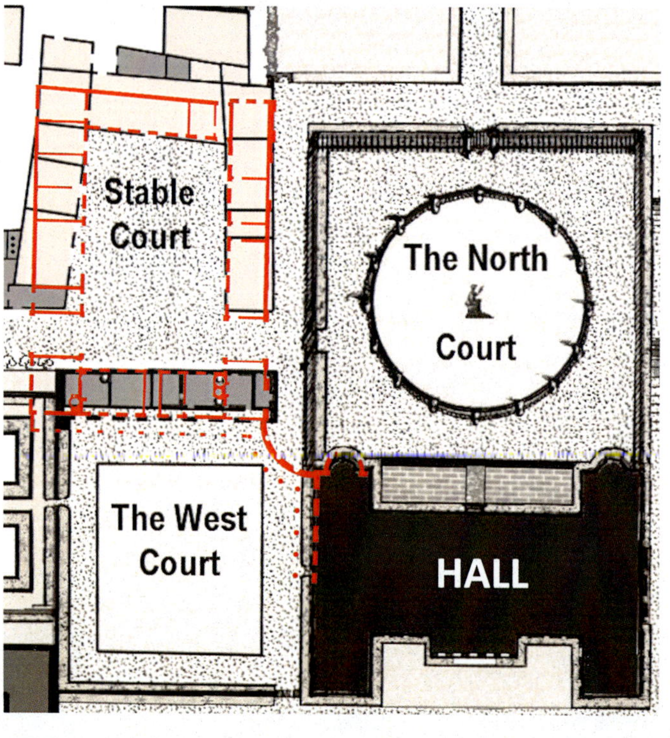

Figure 9.

Part of the Grundy plan (1749)[9] for the gardens at Gopsall showing the hall, the West Court and, to the north, the old 'offices' (service block) and stables.

Overlaid in **red** is the Hiorns' initial plan for remodelling and rebuilding of the offices and stables[34]; an option not requiring the building of the service and stable wings shown in Figure 8.

Note about Figures 9 and 10:

The Hiorns' plans were converted to the same scale as the Grundy plan before overlaying. The **red** overlay was then located by matching the position of the northwest wing of the hall in both plans.

In Figure 10, the second, **blue** overlay for the refurbishing of the west wing of the old stables was located by matching the position of the northwest service block.

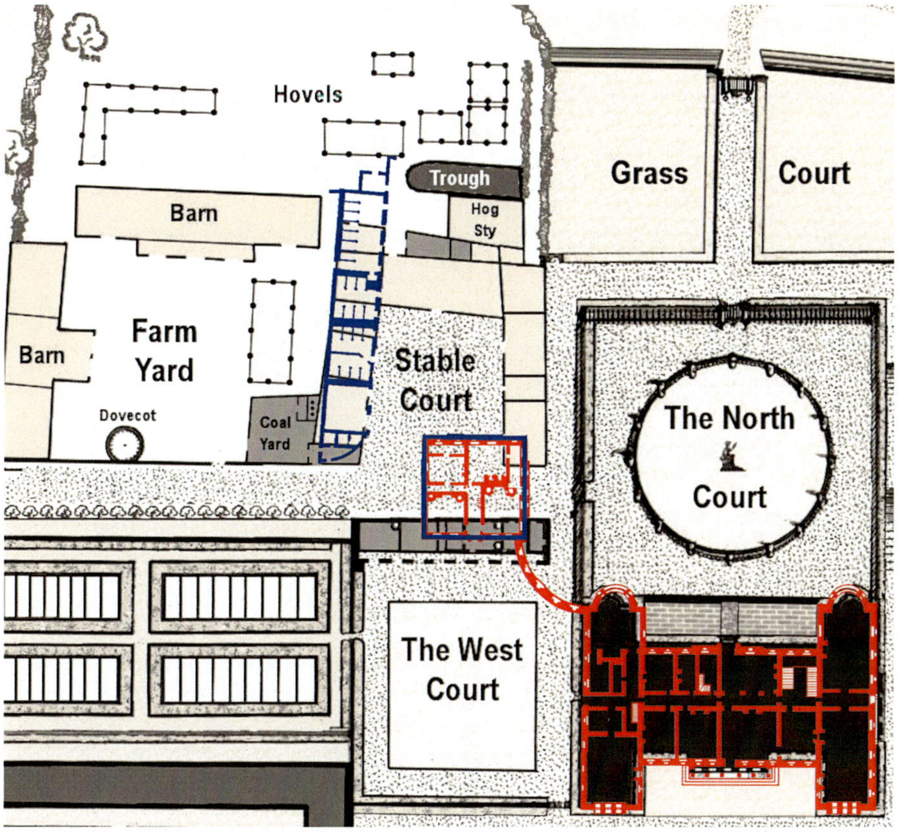

Figure 10.

Part of the 1749 Grundy plan[9] showing the hall, farmyard, old service block and stables. The Hiorns' plan for the west service wing containing the dairy and the brew, bake, milk, meat and wash houses, is overlaid in **red**[5]. Overlaid in **blue** is the Hiorns' plan for refacing / refurbishing the west wing of the old stables.[35]

Figure 11.

Top: East front of the remodelled stables proposed by the Hiorns[35] (RIBA Collections). **Bottom:** East front of the stable block (c.1920) (Historic England Archive).

character, consistent with it being work designed and/or supervised by the Hiorns as architect builders working with the owner.

The one part of the original building of Charles Jennens' Gopsall that appears certain, is that William and David Hiorn designed the 'office' blocks, consisting of the stables, coach house, dairy and the brew, bake, meat, milk and wash 'houses'. What is more difficult to determine is what was actually built. The RIBA has a number of plans showing east and west service blocks attached to the northeast/ northwest corners of the hall by curved walls (Fig. 8). Although none are dated, it seems likely that the first proposal was to renovate/ rebuild the existing stables, coach house and service block that were located to the northwest of the hall (Fig. 9).[34] This design, probably retaining much of the existing structures, would have resulted in an unbalanced façade of the hall complex that was probably unacceptable to Charles Jennens, who was not constrained by cost.

From looking at the painting dated after 1764 and the engraving of the hall dated 1791 (Fig. 5), the Hiorns' plans for service wings sited to the northwest and northeast of the hall appear to have been executed (Fig. 8). The northwest block contained service facilities, such as the bakery, laundry and brew house, whereas that in the northeast was the stables with an attached coach house (not shown in Fig. 8). Building of the northwest service block

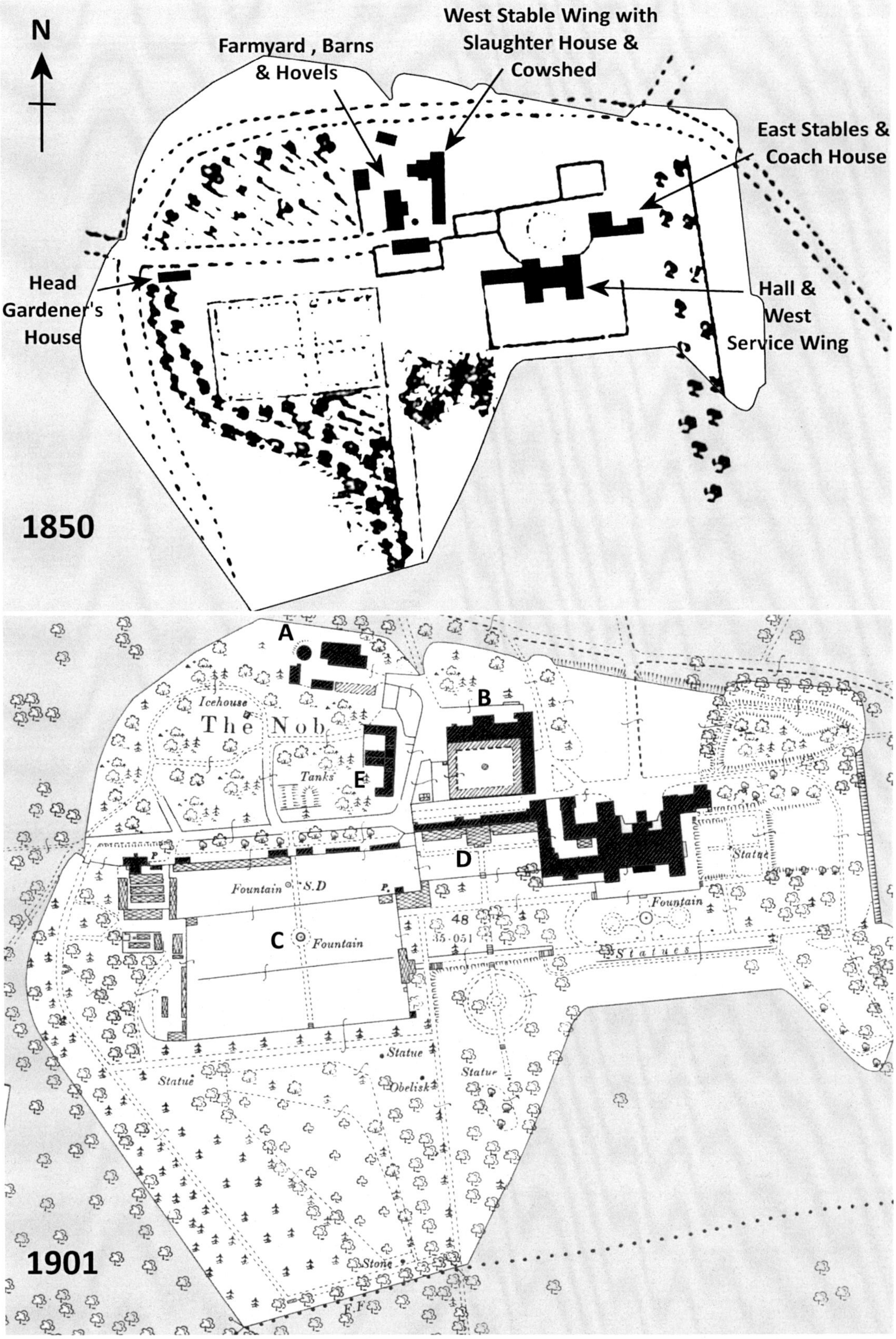

Figure 12.

Top: Detail from the 1850 tithe map of Gopsall[36] showing the extent of the buildings present. The area in white approximates to the extent of the gardens and outbuildings in 1901. No details are known about the building and enclosure south of the stables and farmyard; it may have been a large glasshouse and pleasure garden.

Bottom: Gopsall Hall and gardens as shown on the Ordnance Survey map surveyed in 1901. A gasometer and new power house (**A**) are shown northwest of the refurbished and extended, rectangular stable block (**B**). The existing kitchen garden (**C**) has been extended north, walls built and many glasshouses erected. Formal gardens have been laid out south and east of the hall and a large showhouse (**D**) backs on to the gardeners' bothies south of the stables. The hall shows the two west service extensions, the 'billiard' room, vestibule and carriage porch, picture gallery and 'smoking' room. The building 'E', used for keeping pigs and ferrets in c.1870, was converted to two cottages in 1901.

would have meant the demolition of the old 'offices' (building to the north of the West Court) and at least part of the east wing of the old stables (Fig. 10). The only evidence that the northwest service block was actually built are the painting and engraving referred to above (Fig. 5). However, this northwest block does not appear on the 1850 tithe map for Gopsall (Fig. 12), suggesting that it had already been demolished by this time. By contrast, the northeastern stable block and coach house are shown on the 1850 map, indicating that they were erected and used for about 100 years or more.

A further complication with respect to the stables arises because the Hiorns also put forward a plan and elevation for the refacing and renovation of the west wing of the old stables (Figs. 10 & 11).[35] As demolition of some of the eastern part of the old stables was required to make way for the northwest service block, demolition of this whole east wing, and re-siting some of the animal hovels that were part of the farm, was probably considered very desirable because they would have been an unwelcome intrusion to the view when approaching and leaving the main entrance of the hall via the north court.

Several factors indicate that this second stable plan was implemented. The position of the west wing of the old stable block, including its odd angle compared to the other buildings (Fig. 12), and the proposed new façade in the Hiorns' plan are all identical to those of the east wing of the stable block present in the latter part of the 19th century and demolished in 1951 (Fig. 11). In addition, this stable wing is shown on the 1850 tithe map for Gopsall (Fig. 12).[36] Whether the functions of the various parts of this refurbished stable wing were as proposed in the Hiorns' plan is unknown. It seems doubtful that a section for a coach house was required as one existed adjacent to the northeast stables. However, extra stabling for horses and storage of grain might have been necessary, as Gopsall farm accounts indicate that Jennens had an average of 26 horses at any one time.[37]

When Charles Jennens died in 1773, the Gopsall estate was inherited by his grandnephew, Penn Assheton Curzon. After his death, the Gopsall Estate was administered by his wife, Baroness Sophia Howe until Richard William Penn Curzon, the eldest surviving son of Penn Assheton Curzon, came of age in 1817. Nothing is known about whether any changes were made to the hall between 1773 and Richard formally taking charge of the estate. However, it is known that Penn Assheton Curzon added sculptures to the gardens and artwork to the contents of the hall, as well as purchasing land to add to the estate (Chapter 1). His wife painted the glass in the south-facing venetian window of the library[23] and, after her husband's death in 1797, also added land to the estate prior to 1817. A major change that probably occurred during this time was the draining of the large ornamental lake, Grundy's Great Pond, south of the hall (Fig. 5). Whether this was by design or simply due to failure of the dam is not known, but the lake is not mentioned in any of the descriptions of Gopsall written in the 19th century and the last known image of the lake is the engraving published in 1791 (Fig. 5). By contrast, Richard Curzon (created 1st Earl Howe in 1821) and his successors made huge changes to the hall and service buildings during the rest of the 19th century.

While details about the original design, building and decoration of the hall and erection of the service blocks are far from clear, the precise evolution of Gopsall in the 19th century is even more uncertain. During this period the hall footprint almost tripled in size (Table 1); the original service blocks were demolished; the west stable wing was extended; a number of service-related buildings were erected, as were the walled kitchen gardens, the head gardener's house, workers' cottages and bothies, many glasshouses and a gas works. Despite these extensive changes there appear to be virtually no surviving records or plans specifying what was done, when it was done and who was involved. Thus, the suggested timeline of events shown in Table 2 is a 'best guess' based upon information gleaned from descriptions of the hall from various sources, 19th century maps, two architectural plans dated 1871[38,39] and floor plans of the hall[40] as it existed in the early 20th century. These floor plans showed the cellars, the principal floor and first floor of the hall and its west service extensions.

Unlike Charles Jennens, who used local architect builders to design, build and decorate his hall, the Earls Howe appear to have commissioned well-known architects for the work performed at

Table 2. 19th Century alterations to Gopsall Hall and associated buildings

Date/period	Architect	Alterations
1819	Jeffry Wyatt (Wyatville from 1824; knighted 1828)	• **Construction of Constantine Arch Lodge at Twycross entrance** • *Filling in between the south wings and extending the north wings* • *New porticos to the south & east garden fronts* • *Addition of one or more service wings*
Before 1831	Unknown	• **Music room made smaller forming an ante-room between it and the library; folding doors fitted allowing the 3 rooms to be used as one** • Other unspecified internal alterations to the hall
April 1835 - August 1837	Edward Blore	• **Works on offices; work over 3 years** • Probable demolition of the west service block of the Hiorn brothers & construction of the west service wings*
1850 - c1865	Unknown	• Building of the walled kitchen garden, head gardener's house, bothies, glasshouses including the Cooke Show House • Extension of the west stable wing to form rectangular building with cobbled stable yard and integral coach house, smithy, game and gun rooms, storerooms, butcher's and carpenters' shops • Demolition of the east stable block and coach house • Building of gas works and installation of gas supply to the hall
1862 - 1863	Unknown	• **Picture gallery extension of the NE wing of the hall** • Billiard room extension of NW wing of the hall (see Brandon)?
1871	John Macvicar Anderson	• **New vestibule and carriage porch** • **Alterations to servant access to the west end of the hall corridor and the installation of a new window**
1871 - 1900	Unknown	• Building of the underground corridor between NW & NE wings via the vestibule and cellar beneath the picture gallery & smoking room • Installation of furnaces beneath the smoking room
1877 - 1880	David Brandon	• Billiard room extension of NW wing of the hall?+
Between 1885 & 1901	Unknown	• **Addition of a single-storey room to the east end of the gallery/salon; used as a smoking room until 1918 and billiard room thereafter** • **Changes to the picture gallery skylights** • **Erection of Shackerstone Lodge**
1901 - 1902	Unknown	• **Erection of power house and installation of an electricity supply** • **Redecoration of the hall & installation of a lift** • **Installation of an organ into the hall chapel** • **Alterations to the King's suite and staircase access** • **Remodelling of part of livestock building into a pair of cottages** • **Building of a new pantry for hanging and dressing game**

Bold = work definitely known to have been done at the date or in the period stated; ***Italics*** = work listed in Pevsner but thought not to have taken place according to several sources; **Plain text** = work known to have been done but dates deduced from descriptions in books, directories, newspapers, the gardener's journal, available plans, 19th century maps and length of contract.
* = this would have been accompanied by remodelling the rooms within the hall whose functions had been moved into the new extension. The north wings were probably extended at this time, resulting in loss of the bay windows, as in the Jeffry Wyatt plan.
\+ = no evidence for Brandon working on Gopsall Hall except for a comment in Pevsner[42].

Gopsall during the 19th century. For example, the four architects reported to have worked on Gopsall also worked on prestigious buildings such as Windsor Castle, Chatsworth House and Longleat (Wyatville); Buckingham, Lambeth, Hampton Court and St James' Palaces (Blore; special architect to William IV and Queen Victoria); Christie's Galleries, Lloyds, Coutts and British Linen Banks in the City of London (Anderson; president of the RIBA) and Badminton House, Fonthill Abbey and Chilham Castle (Brandon; vice-president of the RIBA).

Soon after Richard Curzon came of age he sought designs from Jeffry Wyatt (afterwards Sir Jeffry Wyatville)[41] for changes to the hall and the erection of an archway at the Twycross entrance to the park. Unfortunately, other than the works listed in Pevsner[42] (Table 2), no details of Wyatt's planned alterations for the hall appear to be available and most commentators consider that none were executed. However, the 'Constantine Arch', entrance lodge, known as London Lodge on Ordnance Survey (OS) maps, was built (Fig. 13). Wyatt obviously considered the design of the archway significant as he entered the plans into the Academy of Arts Exhibition in 1819.

Although there is no firm record that any of Wyatt's alterations to the hall were executed, the hall had "*recently undergone many internal alterations by the present noble owner*" by 1829 according

Figure 13.

The entrance lodge at Twycross, erected c.1819. The living accommodation in the lodge was located on either side of the entrance gate, hidden by the bushes and trees.

Figure 14.

Top: North front of Gopsall Hall in c.1905. The single story additions to the hall from left to right: smoking room (A), picture gallery (B), carriage porch and vestibule (C) and billiard room (D).

Bottom: Group photograph of guests attending Viscount Curzon's Coming of Age celebrations outside the picture gallery in 1905. The three small windows in the gallery wall are false, included to give a 'pleasing' façade. False windows were in the west and south walls of the gallery; east and west walls of the chapel and west walls of the red drawing room and the library.

to Neale[21] and, sometime before 1831, an ante-room had been formed between the library and music room, making the latter about 18 feet shorter.[23] This ante-room (later called the green drawing room) had folding doors enabling all three rooms to be made into one for large concerts; music being one of the 1st Earl Howe's major interests. No known architect or plans exist for these alterations, which may have been performed to some of the designs originally submitted by Jeffry Wyatt.

Edward Blore undertook extensive buildings works at Gopsall, vaguely described as alterations to offices by Pevsner[42], that lasted from April 1835 to August 1837.[43] Despite the hundreds of plans produced by Blore that can be found in collections at the RIBA, the Victoria & Albert Museum and the British Library, searches have found none describing the work carried out at Gopsall over this three-year period. However, we know that by the time the tithe map of Gopsall was produced in 1850, the west service block had been demolished and a single, new west extension had been added to the hall (Fig. 12). The time taken to do these alterations is excessive and it seems likely that other works were undertaken, such as the building of the head gardener's house and remodelling or rebuilding of some of the farmyard buildings to serve other functions (e.g. Blacksmith's and carpenters' shops, storerooms etc). The 1st Earl had enlarged the parkland from about 300 to 580 acres by 1831[23], so it is likely that the base for farming activities at Gopsall had already moved to Shornhill Farm (Home Farm), with the barns and animal hovels associated with the old farmyard becoming redundant and an unappealing blot on the landscape. However, as the 'royal architect'[43] Blore would probably not have involved himself with such mundane work. It therefore seems likely that the 1850 tithe map is inaccurate and that Blore built both west service extensions to the hall between 1835 and 1837, doubling the size of the hall (Fig. 12).

There do not appear to be any 'official' records of what happened at Gopsall in the 30 years after 1837 apart from the tithe map. However, Arthur Sage, one of the sons of Emmanuel Sage, head gardener at Gopsall from 1855 to 1870, wrote a journal about his life at Gopsall (Chapter 4). Arthur was born in 1862 and his family left Gopsall in 1870-71, shortly after the death of the 1st Earl, so his recollections probably date from the latter part of the 1860s. In his journal he does not mention any significant building works but he does write *"The western side of the hall is the servants' domestic part"*, presumably referring to the west service extensions to the main hall. Arthur also recalls a variety of buildings and structures not featured on the tithe map, indicating that they were built after 1850. These included the presence of the stables and stable yard on the north side of the Lime Walk incorporating the coach house; game and gun rooms; storerooms; smithy; butcher's and carpenters' shops; the gasworks to the northwest of the stables; a pig-yard (for stable refuse); a ferret house; the walled kitchen gardens and many glasshouses (Fig. 12). His description of the grounds immediately to the east of the hall does not include the presence of the stable block and coach house present on the 1850 map, indicating that it had already been demolished, presumably after the west stable block had been extended.

Addition of the single storey picture gallery to the north end of the east wing of the hall (Figs. 14, 15 & 16b) occurred in 1862-1863, a date derived from descriptions of the hall in White's Directory[44,45] and a very poor photograph of the north elevation of the hall in Lord Howe's archive (Appendix II). At this time, it seems likely that the cellars were extended (to run beneath the picture gallery; Fig. 16a) and the single story billiard room[46] was added to the north end of the west wing of the hall. The latter would have been required to balance the north façade of the hall and it seems unlikely that its building would have been delayed until 1877 (Table 2). The architect is unknown and no plans for the extensions can be found. However, the date suggested is supported by the fact that the Leicestershire Architectural and Archaeological Society visited Gopsall on 20th July 1864 and were shown many of the 1st Earl's book and art treasures in the picture gallery.[48] Thus, the assertion in Pevsner that the gallery (and possibly the billiard room) date from 1877 is incorrect, as is the stated location of the rooms being on the south front.[42]

Two plans dated 1871, showing a design for a carriage porch and vestibule[38] and alterations to the west end of the main hall corridor[39] are held by Historic England. The plans are not signed, but the address is given as 6, Stratton Street, which was the London address of John Macvicar Anderson,[49] a Scottish architect who had just taken over William Burn's architectural practice and house in Stratton Street, London. Photographs (Fig. 14) and later plans of the hall (Fig. 16) demonstrate that both of these plans were executed. The plan for the corridor alterations modified the access route from the cellars and principal floor of the hall to the kitchen, which is shown to be present in a west extension of the building adjacent to the chapel on the south front. The plan also shows the position of the west extension on the north front (i.e. the extension shown on the 1850 map), 43 feet north of the kitchen extension, exactly as shown on the architectural plans of the hall in the early 20th century (Fig. 16b).[40] Unfortunately, the 'corridor alteration' plan[39] is extremely limited in scope and gives no information about these service wings, but is evidence that both service wings were present in 1871, as expected from viewing photographs of the hall dated 1863 and 1865 (Appendix II).

The building of the service wings had a significant effect upon the use of some of the rooms on the ground floor in the body of the hall, as well as in the northwest 'kitchen' wing of the hall. The north service wing attached to the kitchen allowed the servants' hall, on the south front, and the steward's room, on the north front, to be moved out of the body of the hall. Similarly, the south service wing, attached to the chapel, provided a private suite of rooms (the Queen's, King's or Royal suite) in addition to a laundry, bakery, new kitchens, scullery, housekeeper's room and pantries allowing remodelling and refurbishment of two ground floor rooms on the north front of the hall and the whole of the old kitchen wing (Figs. 2, 8, 16b & 16c). The 1st floor of this large service wing also provided extensive accommodation (known as 'the Barracks'[47]) for the staff who, it is assumed, previously lived in rooms on the attic floor of the hall.

Figure 15.

Top: South and east fronts of Gopsall Hall (dated 1865) showing the single storey picture gallery extension built in 1862-1863. All three picture gallery windows are blank and the roof light is very large.

Bottom: A similar view showing part of the single storey, 'smoking room', extension to the right (east) of the picture gallery. Note that now only the middle window of the three in the picture gallery wall is blank, the roof light has a lower profile and chimneys are present on the corner of the NE wing and on the picture gallery-smoking room roof.

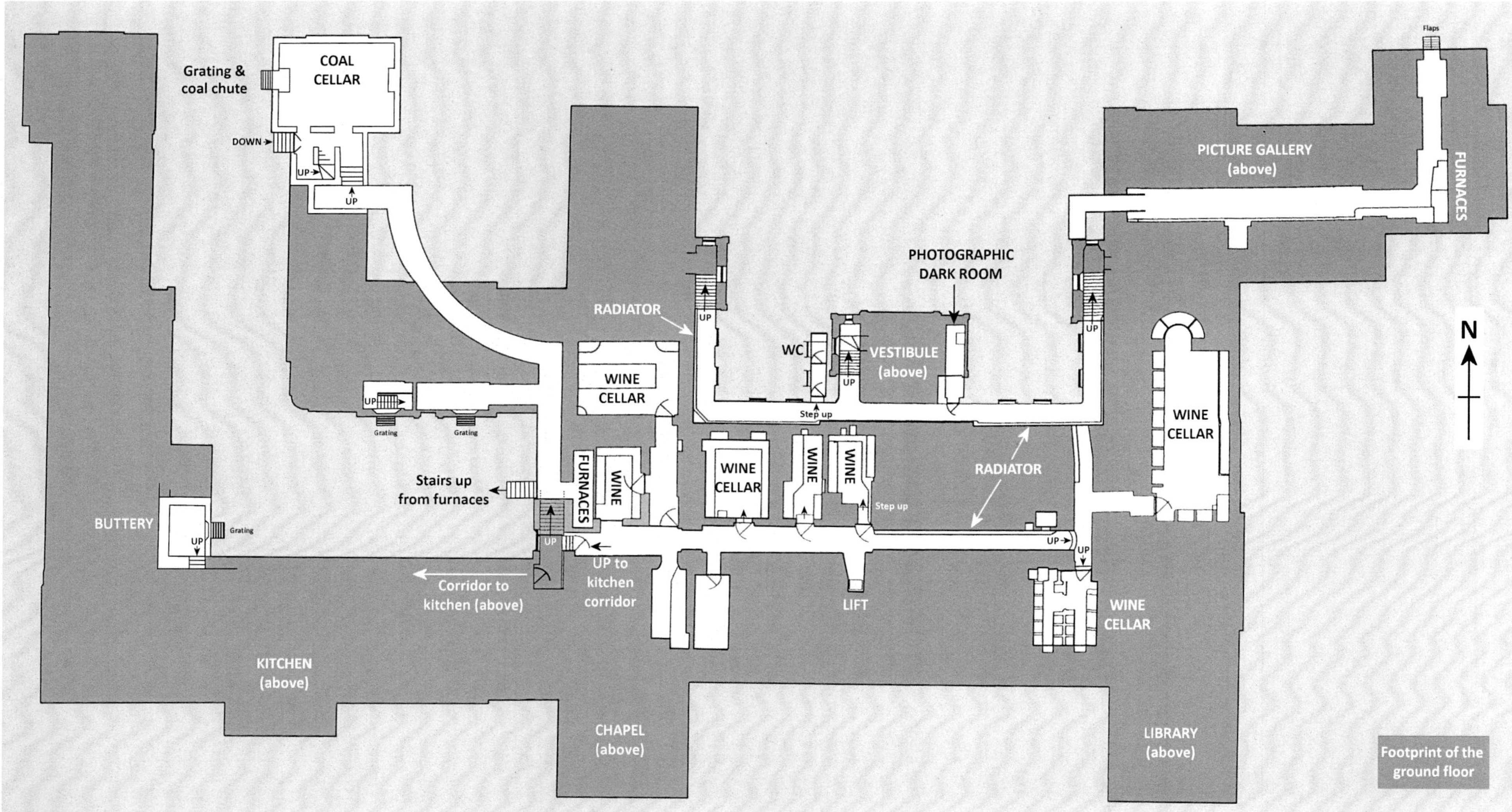

Figure 16a.

Early 20th century plan of the hall cellars. There were four distinct cellar areas. The main cellar, containing two store rooms and seven wine cellars, was accessed from the entrance at the east end of the kitchen corridor or by the lift. An underground corridor linked the northeast and northwest wings of the hall with the vestibule and contained a photographic dark room. The two other cellar areas were concerned with the furnaces at the west end of the main hall and beneath the smoking/billiard room extension at the far east end of the hall. The main coal cellar was beneath the steward's room, close to the courtyard gates. The cellars still exist but no longer contain large quantities of wine!

Excavated cellars of Gopsall Hall as revealed by Google Earth (2020)

All the main features of the cellars shown in the plan can be clearly seen. However two areas of the cellars are not excavated (or are no longer present): the coal cellar beneath the steward's room (north of B) and the cellar extending from point X beneath the picture gallery/salon and the smoking/billiard room. Except for D, white dotted lines mark parts of the pre-1862/63 hall foundations visible in the image.

A - position of the billiard room extension built in 1862-1863
B - servants' wing containing servants' hall and secretaries office
C - position of the bowed Venetian windows in the 1750 hall, lost when the north wings were extended

D - position of the curved walling at the north entrance
E - kitchens & housekeeper's room; half a storey below ground level
F - south front of the chapel
G - south front of the library

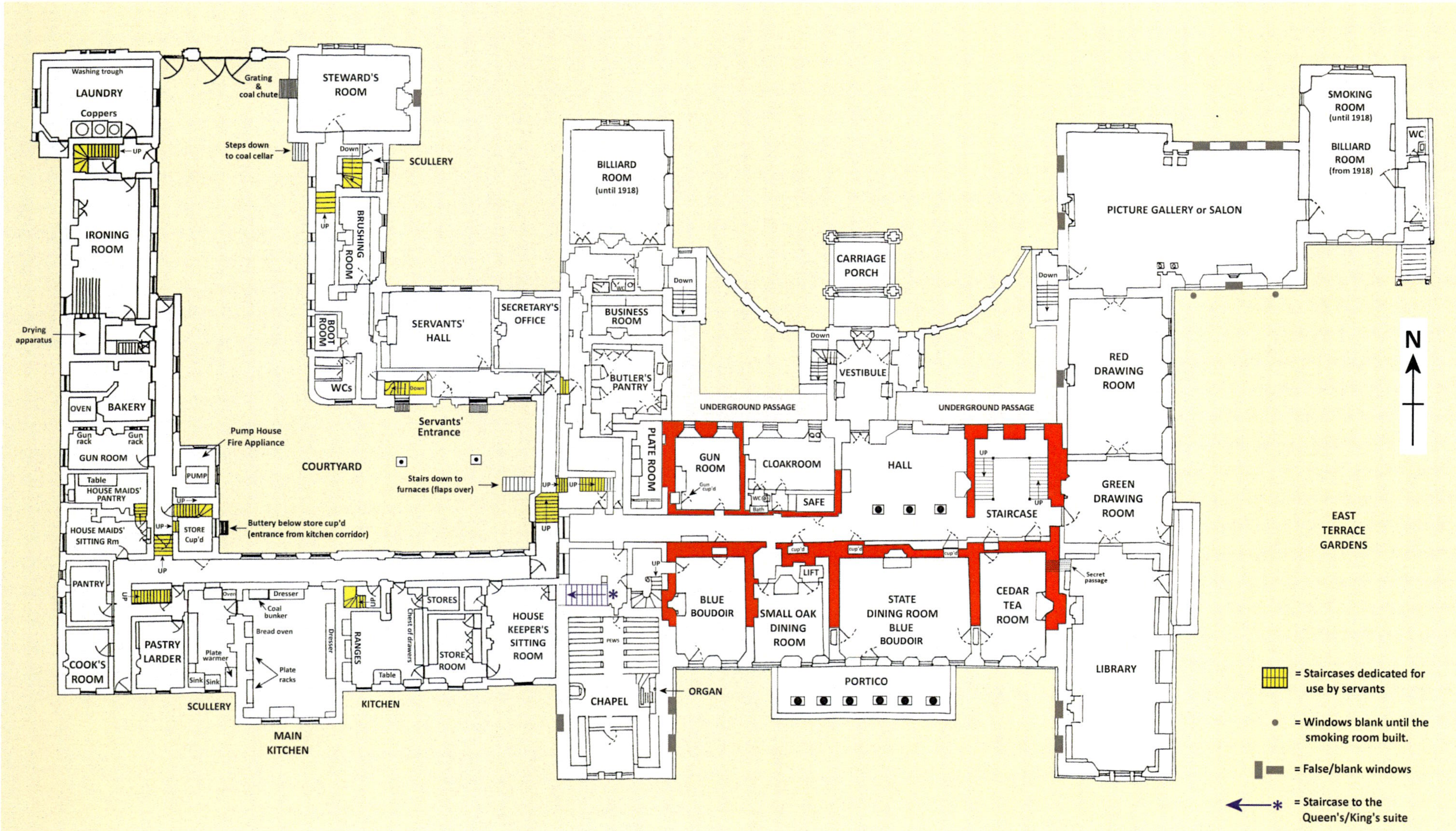

Figure 16b.

Early 20th century plan of the ground floor of the hall and both west extensions. Note that the level of the ground floor of the south front of the kitchen extension is about half a floor below the ground floor of the hall, the north extension to the kitchen wing and the northwest wing containing the servants' hall etc. The doorway between the Blue Boudoir and the staircase is believed to have been created in 1901-1902. The parts of the plan in red correspond to walls retained from the original Elizabethan house.

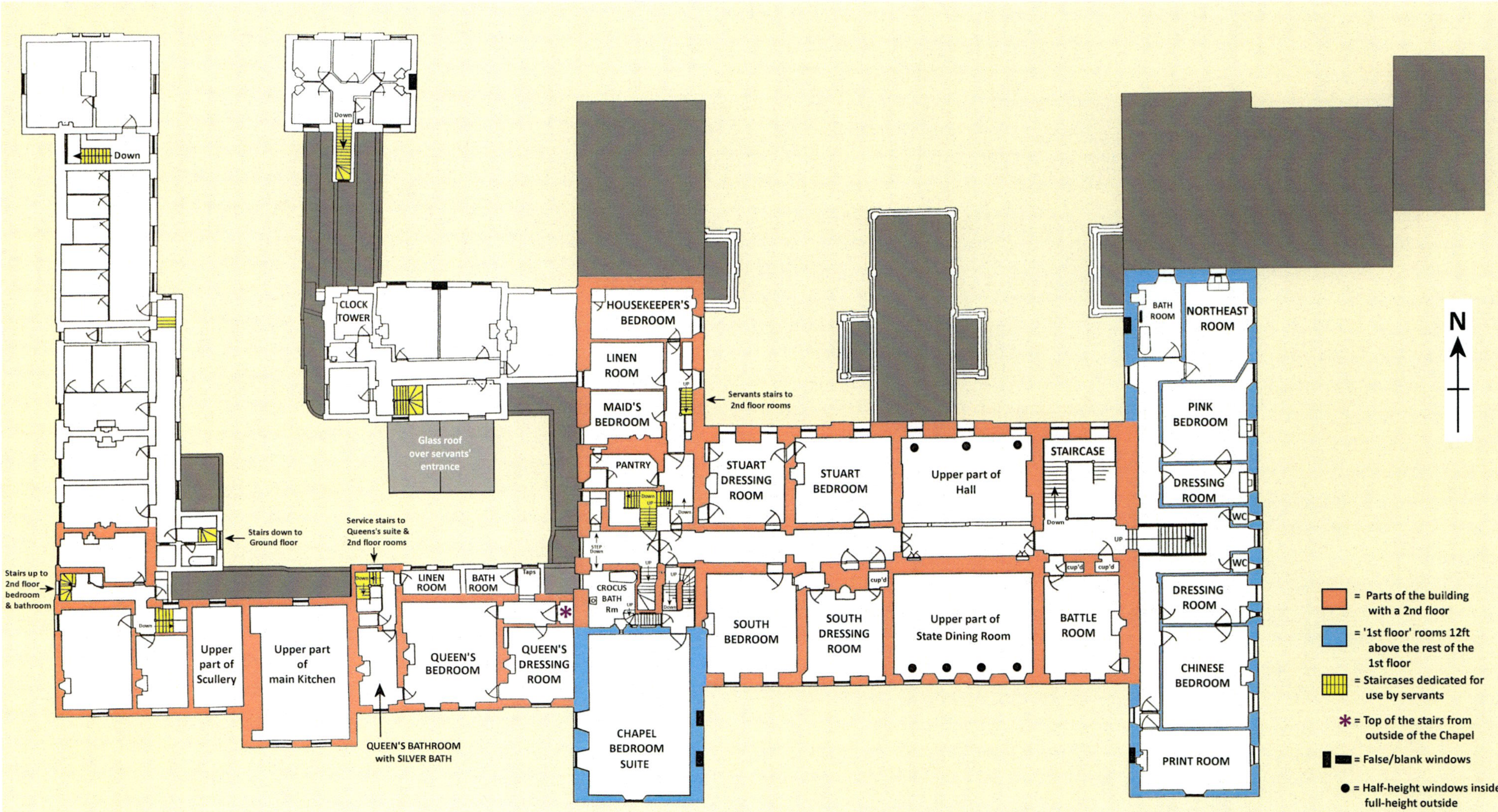

Figure 16c.

Early 20th century plan of the first floor of hall and west extensions. The first floor of the south front of the kitchen/Queen's suite extension is between the ground and first floor of the hall. Areas in dark grey are single story parts of the building. The main body of the hall, its northwest wing and the kitchen/Queen's suite extension on the south front had second floor rooms. Unlabelled rooms were mainly bedrooms for the staff. The north extension of the kitchen/Queen's suite wing containing servants' rooms was known as 'the Barracks'.[47] The two rooms at the far northwest had their own access from the courtyard.

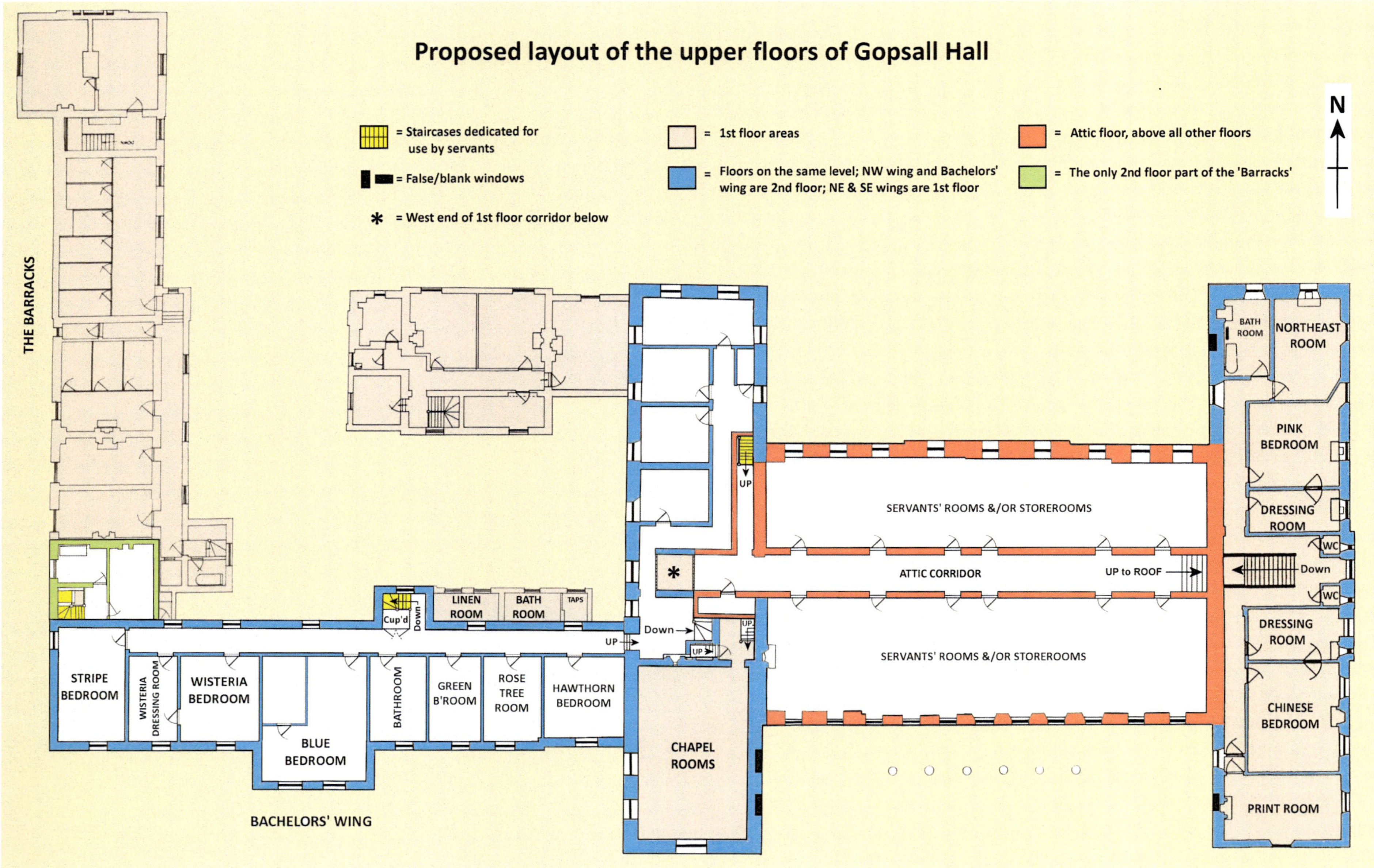

Figure 16d. There are no known plans of the upper floors of the hall. However, it is possible to determine the number of floors present in different parts of the building from studying the available architectural plans, elevations and sections of the hall (Figs. 16 a-c & e; Appendix III). The plan shown is a 'best guess' at the layout of the upper floors based upon the architectural drawings and information given in the 1918 sale catalogue of the contents.[40,47] The latter provided the room names for the Bachelors' wing.

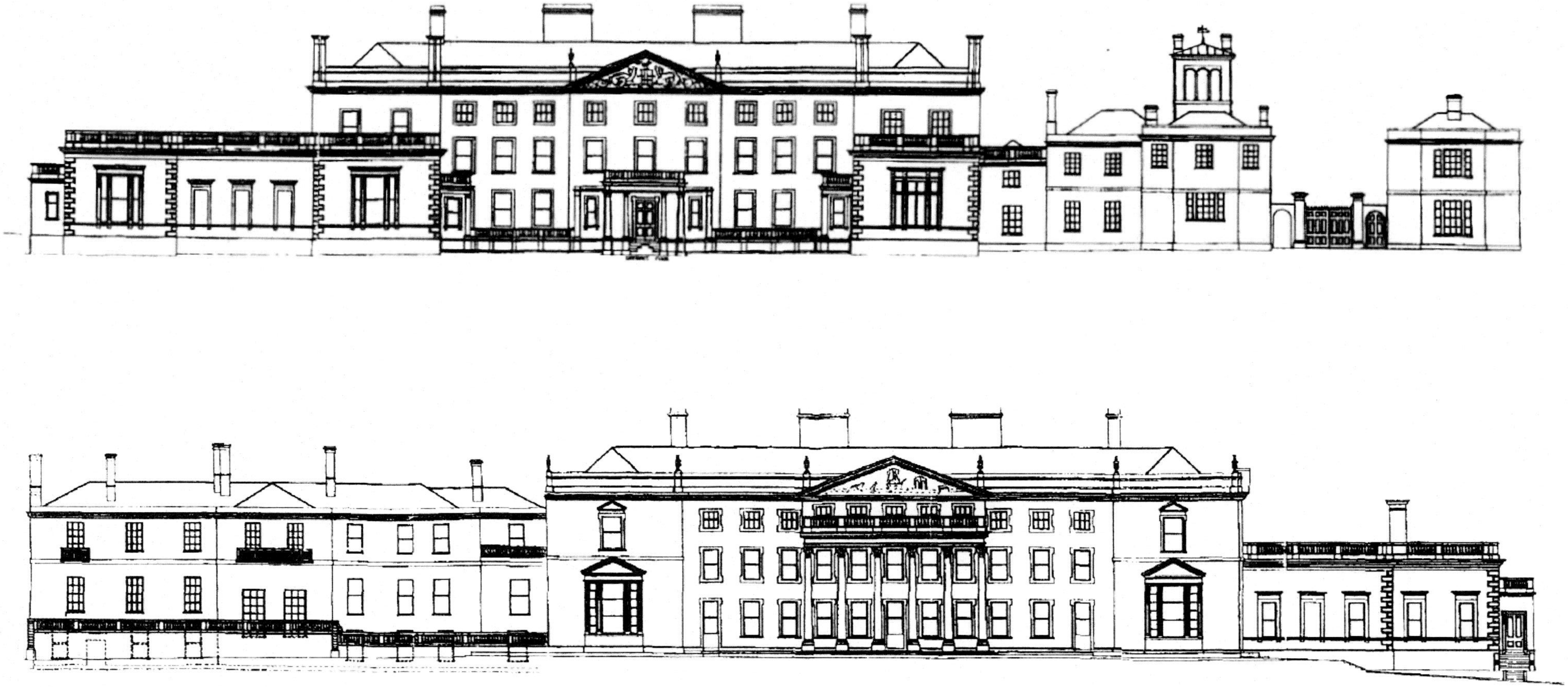

Figure 16e. North (top) and south (bottom) elevations of Gopsall Hall in the early 20th century.

The only reference to David Brandon working on the hall comes from Pevsner, who states "*D Brandon extended the house in 1877-1880 presumably by the one-storey billiard room and picture-gallery extensions on the south front*".[42] However, we know that the picture gallery was built in 1862-1863 (Appendix II).[44,45,48] Therefore, if Brandon did work at Gopsall, it is possible that he was responsible for the addition of the billiard room extension to the northwest wing, assuming that it had not been built at the same time as the picture gallery. If this was the case, the construction of the underground passage, linking the northwest and northeast wings via the vestibule and photographic dark room (Fig. 16a), was probably done at the same time. Coincidentally, Brandon was working for the 3rd Earl on alterations to Penn House around this time.[50]

Study of the OS maps surveyed in 1885 and 1901 demonstrates that the hall was extended during this period in the form of a single story extension built onto the east side of the picture gallery (Figs. 14, 16b & 15). This new room has normally been referred to as the smoking room, however an interior photograph of the room (Chapter 3), when viewed in the light of the known floor plan, shows that this room was eventually used as a billiard room.

Other relatively minor works known to have been undertaken between 1886 and 1902 are supported by examination of OS maps, newspaper articles and contemporary photos. The Shackerstone Drive entrance to the estate was developed after the opening of the Moira West to Nuneaton railway line in 1873 and the building of Shackerstone Station (Fig. 17). This route into the estate eventually became the principal entrance, necessitating the building of the lodge at the Shackerstone end of the drive sometime after 1885.[51] In 1901, a pair of workers' cottages were erected after partial demolition and remodelling of the old pig-yard (Fig. 18; labelled E in Fig. 12) and an electricity supply to the hall was installed with the generator building being sited at the old gas works (Chapter 14). It is likely that the lift between the cellar and small oak dining room was installed at the same time as the electricity supply. The other, more cosmetic, changes within the hall were in preparation for the King's visit in December 1902 (Chapter 8).

Figure 17.

Gates and lodge at the end of Shackerstone Drive, erected c.1890.

While there appear to be virtually no information or plans for the 19th century building works at Gopsall Hall, three architectural illustrations in the possession of the 7th Earl Howe envisage extensive changes to, and enlargement of, the hall that were not executed. None appeared to be dated or signed, but the two illustrations of the exterior of the hall (Fig. 19) show that plans were being considered to fill in between the east and west wings of the south front; erect new porticos

Figure 18. Pair of estate workers' cottages built in 1901 by remodelling the south end of a livestock building dating from the mid-19th century. The cottages still stand but are now separated from the original farm building (Chapter 14).

on the south and east fronts; add attic floors to the east and west wings; remodel the north ends of the east and west wings plus build a new 'office' wing (or wings) on the west front.[54] These remodelled views of the hall do not include the carriage porch and vestibule that were added in 1871, so must date from before then. Interestingly, all of these projected alterations to the hall, apart from adding the attic floors, are those said to have been planned by Jeffry Wyatt in 1819 (Table 2), indicating that they are the work of this architect (see legend to Fig. 19).

The third illustration (Fig. 20) shows interior sections of a picture gallery, two storeys high with, at one end, an organ in a gallery supported by two columns. The wall in the illustration is adjacent to the dining room, which means that this proposed gallery must have been within the body of the hall rather than a planned addition to the end of one of the hall's wings. The picture gallery addition to the north end of the east wing was built in 1862-1863, suggesting that this plan for a two-storey gallery pre-dated this. The illustration also indicates that there are rooms on the first floor above the dining room when it is known that this room (the State Dining room) has always been two storeys in height. Thus, this interior design is consistent with extending the hall to form new rooms between the south wings of the hall, as suggested by the drawings we attribute to Wyatt (Fig. 19). This picture gallery, lit by roof lights because it would not have had any external windows/walls, would replace the original two-storey dining room and a new, single-storey dining room would be accommodated centrally in the newly created interior space resulting from repositioning the south front. Why these proposals were not carried out is unknown.

North Entrance and East Garden front of Gopsal

Design A __ The Porticos _ Attic Stores _ and two ends
with Venetian windows are additions

South and East Garden fronts of Gopsal

The Centre part is brought forward to form new Rooms ____ The Porticos, Attics and Offices are new

Figure 19. Projected, unexecuted designs for the expansion of the hall, thought to have been submitted by Jeffry Wyatt in 1819.

Top: East and west wings of the hall showing attic floors, portico on the east front, remodelled north ends to the east and west wings, absence of the vestibule and carriage porch and presence of a west service wing ('Offices').

Bottom: South and east fronts showing centre part of south front brought forward to form new rooms on two floors, new porticos on the south and east fronts, new pediment on top of the south portico (not part of the hall wall as originally built) and a new west service wing.

In August 2021, Peter Flory of Christie's discovered a signature and date on the two watercolours depicting the proposed re-designs of Gopsall Hall: James Wyatt and 1819.[52]

James Wyatt died in 1813 and his nephew, Jeffry Wyatt, is known to have inherited some of his commissions (e.g. Bretby and Ashridge) and became the principal representative of the Wyatt family of architects[53]. The signature and date do not match, which suggests that James Wyatt may have had the original commission (from Baroness Howe), which was inherited by Jeffry Wyatt, who eventually submitted James' plans, plus his own for Twycross Gate, to Richard Curzon in 1819.

King George IV persuaded parliament to restore Windsor Castle, which had become unfit for the residence of the Sovereign. Jeffry Wyatt's designs for the building works were selected and, on 12th August 1824 the first stone was laid by George IV, who on the same day authorised the architect to call himself 'Wyatville' and to adopt the word 'Windsor' as his motto. On completion of the royal apartments, Wyatville was knighted and granted a residence in the Winchester Tower, a privilege afterwards confirmed by King William IV and Queen Victoria.[53]

Figure 20. Sections of the proposed picture gallery, attributed to Jeffry Wyatt (c. 1819).

Top: "*Side next the dining room*" showing the roof light, gallery with rooms above dining room and organ gallery at the west end supported by columns.

Bottom left: "*End next the staircase*" showing the roof light and, through the gallery arches, landings with rooms off to the right (south).

Bottom right: "*Organ gallery*" supported by columns and showing the position of the organ and roof light.

Note: the text in italics is taken directly from the architectural drawings.

Notes and References

The images of the hall (Fig. 15, bottom and Appendix II) and the coloured architectural drawings (Figs. 19 & 20) are courtesy of The Rt Hon Frederick Richard Penn Curzon, 7th Earl Howe, GBE, PC. Digital copies of the original drawings and photograph have been processed using Corel PaintShop Pro 2019.

1 *Miscellaneous Early Deeds - Gopsull.* Ref: D1798/H.M. Chetwynd/9. Staffordshire County Records Office.

2 *A mapp of the Lordship and Mannor of Gopshall with part of Bilson in Leicestershire.* Record Office for Leicestershire, Leicester & Rutland. Ref: 35'29/317.

3 *Design for Gopsall Hall: survey plan of the principal floor of the existing house and proposed refacing.* John Westley. RIBA Collection, library ref: SD141/1(1); RIBApix Ref. RIBA65834. "*The small enclosed porch leading into the short end of the hall and the shallow, polygonal windows represent the existing Elizabethan (?) house. The 12-bay regularized façade of the opposite elevation presumably represents the first intention for remodelling*" - T.F. Friedman in *Catalogue of the Drawings Collection of the Royal Institute of British Architects T-Z* (ed. Lever, Gill) Amersham: Gregg, 1984, p. 212.

4 *A book of Architecture containing Designs of Buildings and Ornaments.* James Gibbs. London 1748.

5 *Designs for the 3rd scheme for rebuilding Gopsall Hall, Gopsall, Leicestershire: ground floor plan of the house, quadrants and service blocks.* David & William Hiorn. RIBA Collection, library Ref: SB88/1(1); RIBApix Ref: RIBA96055.

6 *A Book of Minutes taken in a Journey to and from Chester and Liverpool.* John Grundy 1750. See Appendix I.

7 *Designs for 2nd scheme for rebuilding Gopsall Hall, Gopsall, Leicestershire (Group IV): principal floor plan.* John Westley. RIBA Collection, library Ref: SD141/5(1); RIBApix Ref: RIBA65848.

8 *Designs for 2nd scheme for rebuilding Gopsall Hall, Gopsall, Leicestershire (Group II): principal floor plan.* John Westley. RIBA Collection, library Ref: SD141/3(1); RIBApix Ref: RIBA65842.

9 *Survey plan of the house and gardens, Gopsall, Leicestershire.* John Grundy Jnr (1749). RIBA Collection, library Ref: SB53/5; RIBApix Ref: RIBA67899. See Chapter 4.

10 *Designs for 2nd scheme for rebuilding Gopsall Hall, Gopsall, Leicestershire (Group III): the south front.* John Westley. RIBA Collection, library Ref: SD141/4(1); RIBApix Ref: RIBA65845.

11 *Designs for the 3rd scheme for rebuilding Gopsall Hall, Gopsall, Leicestershire: the south front.* David & William Hiorn. RIBA Collection, library Ref: SB88/1(3); RIBApix Ref: RIBA29782.

12 *Designs for 2nd scheme for rebuilding Gopsall Hall, Gopsall, Leicestershire (Group IV): elevation and plan of the entrance portico.* John Westley. RIBA Collection, library Ref: SD141/5(3); RIBApix Ref: RIBA29746.

13 Roof and parapet heights, building and room dimensions and distances were determined using image analysis software (ImageJ open source software developed by Wayne Rasband at the National Institutes of Health, USA) and high resolution (1200dpi) images of the original plans, photographs and scale drawings. For a comment about lowering the hall roof profile, see: http://www.lostheritage.org.uk/houses/lh_leicestershire_gopsallhall.

14 *Designs for Gopsall Hall, Gopsall, Leicestershire: floor plan.* John Westley. RIBA Collection, library ref: SD141/1(3); RIBApix ref: RIBA65836.

15 *Designs for Gopsall Hall, Gopsall, Leicestershire: floor plan.* John Westley. RIBA Collection, library Ref: SD141/1(2); RIBApix Ref: RIBA65835.

16 *Designs for 2nd scheme for rebuilding Gopsall Hall, Gopsall, Leicestershire (Group I): principal floor plan.* John Westley. RIBA Collection, library Ref: SD141/2(2); RIBApix Ref: RIBA65839.

17 *Designs for 2nd scheme for rebuilding Gopsall Hall, Gopsall, Leicestershire (Group II): principal floor plan.* John Westley. RIBA Collection, library Ref: SD141/3(1); RIBApix Ref: RIBA65842.

18 *Designs for 2nd scheme for rebuilding Gopsall Hall, Gopsall, Leicestershire (Group IV): principal floor plan.* John Westley. RIBA Collection, library Ref: SD141/5(1); RIBApix Ref: RIBA65848.

19 See: *Charles Jennens: The Man behind Handel's Messiah.* Ruth Smith. London: Gerald Coke Handel Foundation, 2012, p. 32.

20 *Select Views in Leicestershire from Original Drawings: containing Seats of the Nobility and Gentry, Town Views and Ruins.* J. Throsby. Leicester, 1789 (engraving published 1791).

21 *Views of The Seats of Noblemen and Gentlemen, in England, Wales, Scotland & Ireland.* 2nd series, Vol. 5. J.P. Neale. London: Sherwood, Gilbert & Piper, 1829.

22 *Vitruvius Britannicus, or The British Architect. (Engravings from the buildings and original designs by Woolfe & Gandon Architects)* Vol. IV. London, 1767, plate 66.

23 *A Topographical History of the County of Leicester.* The Rev. J. Curtis. Ashby-de-la-Zouche: W. Hextall, 1831, p. 66.

The inscription over the entrance to the harbour depicted in the relief sculpture of the receding pediment: 'Fortiter occupa portum', is a quote from Horace's Odes Book I XIV, usually interpreted as 'Defend your harbours bravely'. Quintilian (c.35 - c.100 AD), a Roman educator and rhetorician, considered this ode to be a political allegory on the Ship of State. This was probably the accepted view of the poem in Charles Jennens' day and remains widely favoured today, although other interpretations have been suggested. See: *Horace's Ship Ode (Odes 1.14) in Context: A Metaphorical Love-Triangle.* Ortwin Knorr. Transactions of the American Philological Association 2006, 136(1):149-169. *Unity and Design in Horace's Odes.* Matthew S. Santirocco. University of North Carolina Press, 1986, pp. 46-49.

24 *Gopsal. The History and Antiquities of the County of Leicester. Vol. IV. Part II. containing the Sparkenhoe*

Hundred. John Nichols. London, 1811, pp. 854-859. The engraving of the hall and floor plan (Plate CXXVII) is dedicated to The Hon. Penn Assheton Curzon. It is dated 1793 and signed J. Nichols.

25 *A Biographical Dictionary of British Architects 1600-1840 (4th Ed.)*. Howard Colvin. Yale University Press, 2008, p. 1106.

26 *Ibid.*, p. 520-523.

27 *Ibid.*, p. 766-772.

28 *Designs for interior decoration related to the 2nd scheme for rebuilding Gopsall Hall, Gopsall, Leicestershire: a fireplace design*. Unknown 18th century British architect. RIBA Collection, library ref: SD143/3(11); RIBApix Ref: RIBA20347.

29 *Designs for interior decoration related to the 2nd scheme for rebuilding Gopsall Hall, Gopsall, Leicestershire: a ceiling or panel design*. Unknown 18th century British architect. RIBA Collection, library Ref: SD143/3(6); RIBApix Ref: RIBA20343.

30 *Designs for interior decoration related to the 2nd scheme for rebuilding Gopsall Hall, Gopsall, Leicestershire: the library*. Unknown 18th century British architect. RIBA Collection, library Ref: SD141/7(2) & SD141/7(4); RIBApix Ref: RIBA12279 & RIBA12280.

31 *Designs for interior decoration related to the 2nd scheme for rebuilding Gopsall Hall, Gopsall, Leicestershire: the music room*. Unknown 18th century British architect. RIBA Collection, library Ref: SD143/1(1) & SD143/1(2); RIBApix Ref: RIBA65864 & RIBA65865.

32 *Designs for interior decoration related to the 3rd scheme for rebuilding Gopsall Hall, Gopsall, Leicestershire:plan and interior elevations of the chapel*. David & William Hiorn. RIBA Collection, library Ref: SB88/1(21); RIBApix Ref: RIBA29743.

33 *Designs for interior decoration related to the 3rd scheme for rebuilding Gopsall Hall, Gopsall, Leicestershire: design for the reading desk for the chapel*. David & William Hiorn. RIBA Collection, library Ref: SB88/1(22); RIBApix Ref: RIBA29737.

34 *Designs for the 3rd scheme for rebuilding Gopsall Hall, Gopsall, Leicestershire: ground floor plan of part of the house and the stable court*. David & William Hiorn. RIBA Collection, library Ref: SB88/1(11); RIBApix Ref: RIBA96063.

35 *Designs for the third scheme for rebuilding Gopsall Hall, Gopsall, Leicestershire: plan and elevation of the stable block*. David & William Hiorn. RIBA Collection, library Ref: SB88/1(16); RIBApix Ref: RIBA29778.

36 *Tithe map of Gopsall Hall [Gopsall Hall Farm] (extra-parochial place), Leicestershire*. The National Archives. File Ref: IR 30/19/65.

37 Accounts for the farm at Gopsall dated 1753 record 6 coach horses, 7 saddle horses, one past business and 6 wagon mares. In addition 2 asses and a foal. Buckinghamshire Record Office. From: *Gopsall Hall: 'Look on my works, ye Mighty, and despair'*. Brenda Sumner. MA thesis, University of Leicester, 2009.

38 *Gopsall Hall: New Carriage Porch and Vestibule*. Historic England Archives, Neg. No. BB69/2532; card no. 2732_187.

39 *Gopsall Hall: Alteration at the end of West Corridor Main Building*. Historic England Archives, Neg. No. BB69/2531; card no. 2732_193.

40 *Plans of Gopsall Hall, Leicestershire*. The Record Office for Leicestershire, Leicester & Rutland. Ref: M10.

41 *A Biographical Dictionary of British Architects 1600-1840 (4th Ed.)*. Howard Colvin. Yale University Press, 2008. pp. 1197-1203.

42 *The Buildings of England: Leicestershire & Rutland. 2nd Edition*. Nikolaus Pevsner, Penguin Books, 1984, pp. 164-165.

43 *Edward Blore papers: MS.Add.3944: Gopsall Hall Leicestershire: account of wages and workman's time on building projects*, 13 April 1835 - 5 August 1837. Cambridge University Library.

Blore held the appointment of 'special architect' to King William IV and to Queen Victoria in the early part of her reign. *Blore, Edward (1787-1879) in Catalogue of the Drawings of the RIBA- B*. Gregg International Publishers Ltd, 1972, pp. 90-94.

44 *History, Gazetteer, and Directory of the Counties of Leicester and Rutland*. William White. Sheffield, 1863, p. 659.

45 *History, Gazetteer, and Directory of the Counties of Leicester and Rutland*. William White. Sheffield, 1877, p. 223.

46 Billiards appears to have been a popular game for both Charles Jennens and the Earls Howe. One of the original floor plans of the house by John Westley (see reference 17) included a billiard room which, in later plans, and the hall as built, became the housekeeper's room. Jennens never had a billiard room but one was added to the northwest wing by the 1st Earl Howe. Later, the 3rd Earl had a single storey 'smoking room' added to the east end of the picture gallery (salon). After the sale of Gopsall to Samuel Waring in 1918, this room was used as the billiard room.

47 *Gopsall Leicestershire. Catalogue of the Fine Antique and Modern Furniture in the Mansion*. Messrs. Trollope. 14th October 1918 and following days. Record Office for Leicestershire, Leicester & Rutland. Ref: L333 (LSP 7-G-13).

48 *The Excursion: Gopsall*. Transactions of the Leicestershire Architechtural and Archaeological Society (1866) 2 (pt. 1), pp. 344-345.

49 *Dictionary of Scottish Architects 1660-1980*. http://www.scottisharchitects.org.uk/architect_list.php, search John Macvicar Anderson.

50 David Brandon was the architect for St Margaret's, Tylers Green (built in 1854; a subsidiary church to Holy Trinity,

Penn), principally funded by Sir Philip Rose but supported by the 1st Earl Howe who donated land and £150 towards the cost (https://tylersgreenchurch.uk/history-of-st-margarets/).

In 1868-69, Brandon extended Rayners House in Penn for Sir Philip Rose (*Understanding Historic Parks & Gardens in Buckinghamshire: Rayners*. The Buckinghamshire Gardens Trust Research & Recording Project: https://www.bucksgardenstrust.org.uk/wp-content/uploads/2016/02/Rayners-Penn_School.pdf).

In the late 1870s, early 1880s, Brandon was architect working on the redesign of Penn House and its stables and coach house for the 3rd Earl Howe (*Understanding Historic Parks & Gardens in Buckinghamshire: Penn House*. The Buckinghamshire Gardens Trust Research & Recording Project: https://bucksgardenstrust.org.uk/wp-content/uploads/2021/02/Penn-House-BGT-RR-dossier-FINAL-18-Feb-21.pdf - accessed 25th May 2021).

It is possible that Brandon's advice on changes at Gopsall may have been sought by the 3rd Earl and gave rise to Pevsner's comments about his role at Gopsall in 1877-1880 (i.e. he may not have worked at Gopsall at all).

51 Shackerstone Drive is shown on OS maps drawn after surveys in 1885 and 1901 whereas the lodge only features after the 1901 survey. See: https://maps.nls.uk/os/25inch-england-and-wales/.

52 Personal communication. The Rt Hon Frederick Richard Penn Curzon, 7th Earl Howe, GBE, PC.

53 *A Biographical Dictionary of British Architects 1600-1840 [4th Ed.]*. Howard Colvin. Yale University Press, 2008, p. 1198.

54 We believe that construction of the new 'offices' and the remodelling/extension of the east and west north wings of the hall, as proposed by Wyatt, were performed by Blore when working at Gopsall between 1835 and 1837.

APPENDIX I

Description of Gopsall Hall and grounds by John Grundy in 1750

John Grundy Jnr (1719-1783) kept detailed accounts of his activities in a series of 17 notebooks. The majority of these are in the Brotherton Collection of the University of Leeds (volumes I, III-XVII); volume II is in the library of the Institute of Civil Engineers, London. The notebooks are written in several hands and some are signed by John Grundy. Volume IV contains an account of Grundy's journey to Chester in 1750 and includes a detailed description of Gopsall Hall. This description was painstakingly transcribed from the original handwritten notebook by Brenda Sumner for her Master of Arts thesis at the University of Leicester in 2001.[1] With her permission, the transcript, including some explanatory notes, is reproduced below.

John Grundy:
A Book of Minutes taken in a Journey to and from Chester and Liverpool

July 12th - August 12th, 1750

Gopsall is the seat of Charles Jennens Esq, situated upon a very pretty eminence, so as to command the Sherwood Forest Hills, several pleasant villages and a beautiful country about 9 or 10 miles in extent, very agreeably interspersed with wood, fields and meadows. Towards the east you have a most charming view of Market Bosworth & Sir Wolston Dixie's beautiful house and park with several villages from Congerstone, Carlton, Barton & Shenstone all with stand in a pleasant vale through which [*illeg.*] called in Burton's Antiquities,[2] the River Sence from the vale the country have a steep [*illeg.*] up to Bosworth and [*illeg.*] the church of which latter place terminates a visit through the Galaryes (*?*) and [*illeg.*] in the centre (*?*) of the Mease. On the south are the gardens or rather pleasure grounds.

Round the Portico there is a long gravel walk, round the house is an area of gravel walk parallel to the said front and extending round the east Front. From this gravel walk you descend down a large grass slope into a Terrace 150 yards in length & 50 feet in breadth. At one end of which is proposed to be erected a bath house. The other (*end*) a summer house both which buildings are to be of the same highness and design of brick with capitals, cornish (*cornice*) and windows all of stones from the terrace. You go down another grass slope of the same length as the terrace with a large bowling green from which you have another slope into a lawn at the bottom of which is the Great Pond containing 7 acres the area of which forms a serpentine terrace with rockwork cascade in the middle of the far side of this pond is an adjoining hill over which you don't see. 'Tis therefore proposed (as an Entertainment to the Eye) to fix a Gothick (*Gothic*) Temple or Triumphale Arch of stonework on the top of that hill but the design is not fully fixed upon. The water of the Great Pond when over full falls over a rockwork cascade into a serpentine stew which meanders into a plantation 'till it disappears. In this plantation are serpentine walks planted with evergreen and flowering shrubs - there is also another plantation with walks at the side of the Great Pond.

On the west side of the house are the kitchen gardens, which as they lie on the side of a hill are made in their plains one above another so that the south walls which bound them are 9 and 10 feet high on the Lower Side and but one foot on the upper, by which scheme you (from the house) look over all these gardens at once, and yet have the benefit of a fine south aspect for [*illeg.*] and are also screened from the northern windows. In these kitchen gardens are [illeg.] and pond for fish, greenhouse, melon ground and a very beautiful sundial, richly caved in Stone. On the west side you command a very pretty village called Twycross & Gopsal (*spelled with one 'l.'*) wood etc.

On the north side of the house are the present old stables which form two sides of a square. One other side of which is proposed to be completed by a new additional stable, coach house and the other side which completes the square by new offices of brick and stone, windows and doors cornishes, facias, columns with — all in a grand [*illeg.*] according to a design given in. This square of buildings [*illeg.*] that the whole north front is open and before which is prepared a large square or rather oblong entry, in the centre an oval grass court bounded by low octagonal and chains around which coaches pass on gravel to the door. This oblong is to be bound by iron palisades and iron gates in the centre. About half a mile distant is to stand the engine house which will be just [*illeg.*] the centre of the house and will terminate a vista through the same. This engine house is to be between 70 and 80 feet high and to be built of brick with rustic coins, door cases and window frames - according to the design of Mr Sands of Spalding and which in my opinion, a very elegant one. On this north side you command a tolerable good prospect of some distant villages and open fields.

The great ill conveniency of this situation (*i.e. of Gopsall Hall*) is that there is no water, but what falls by rain, nearer than about 3/4 of a mile where there is a fine spring which from experiments made by my father and we found produces [*illeg.*] in winter [*illeg.*] in summer when at the lowest. Now this Spring we also found to be 72 feet lower than the house by levels taken by both of us and which very accurately agree. My father therefore made a model of an engine from Jervis's (*Gerves's*) principle but with many improvements. Two of which, from his calculations, will rise a half hogshead of water to the house in an hour. Since his decease I have also made a model of another engine exactly agreeable to his improvements both to work within the same building and one above another which I am of opinion will move more water to the house than two single ones, separately fixed because the great bucket of the upper engine falls into the same well as that of the lower and thereby obtain a greater fall and therefore less water will be wasted since the whole of the proportions of this engine are formed from the fall we can get for the great bucket - the proportionate quantity of water to be raised, for instance of your spring produces 10 hogsheads of water per hour and you want to raise it 10 feet high I have only 5 feet fall for your great bucket, this bucket must be twice as big as your small one and you'll raise only one third of water viz 3.3 Hogsheads in proportion for any greater or lesser fall and [*illeg.*] drawing description and remarks with proper calculations of this engine hereto annexed.

I shall now give a short description of the house as far as it is already finished as also of the designs for the part not yet done.

The outside case of the fronts is of a beautiful red brick with ornaments of stone in the form of an H, the two wings projecting from the body of the same. More on the south than the north side. The north front has two full and one attic storey, the windows of which are of rustic stonework, the breaks in the centre and comers are bounded by large coin stones, the water table fascia and cornish which are very large and also of stone. In the centre of this front is a Doric door case, with pediment, columns and full entablature all of stone, very neatly finished. Over the break is a pediment with a cornish of stone and in the lower storey of each end of the wings is a very large bow Venetian window of stone covered with a half dome of lead. One which lights their kitchen, the other the musick (*music*) room.

The south front is of the same dress of brick and stone - fascia, cornish and pediment as on the north. The windows - plain stonework, two full and one attic storey, the piers betwixt the windows but small on account of keeping the place of the old one. A very large Venetian window of stone with Ionic pilasters and capitals in the lower storey of each wing. One of which is at the end of the library, the other of the chapel, in the centre of this front is proposed a portico with Corinthian columns and capitals of stone and a full entablature of design. This at present debated amongst the connoisseurs whether there should be a pediment over this portico or whether it should be a flat roof and are not yet determined.

The east front is also of dressed brick [*illeg.*] fascias, cornish, and, as the others, of stone, here is only two full storeys and very large windows with pediments semi-curved of same angular all full entablatures -

architraves and cornish; here is also a break with coin stones and two rustic door cases [*illeg.*].

The west front which is next the office and kitchen garden is the plainest and I think the worst; here is no break but a plain full storey at bottom. An attic storey in the middle and another full storey at the top. The windows of which upper storey are larger and more ornamented than those at the bottom, which I think would be inexcusable had not the designers been cramped by some old offices which stand on this site which hide the lower and attic storeys. The windows, cornish, fascia and coins of this front are also of stone though plain and dressed bricks as in the other fronts, here are also a rustic door case and blank window as a door case to keep the uniformity as the passage through the house is not in the centre.

In the body of this house is first on the north entrance a large hall, pantries, steward's room and housekeeper's room on the right hand of it and a very good staircase on the left. On the south entrance is a large dining room with a drawing room at each end. The east wing comprises a library and musick room with a passage betwixt them and the west wing, a chapel and anti-chapel, back staircase and kitchen, sculleries etc. In the second storey are a great number of large and grand lodging rooms very elegantly carved and furnished etc.

The hall is not very large but well proportioned, being not far from a [*illeg.*] the floor is proposed to be a Ketton stone with black marble dots.[3] The ceiling is very richly ornamented with stucco enrichments. The sides are wainscoted dado high from thence to the entablature stuccoed by tabernacle panelling or frames[4] and a full Corinthian entablature, its height takes in two storeys, but as there would not have been room for a full entablature without the upper were masked (*?*) Alas which I think have a better effect than if they had been whole. There is in this hall a gallery supported by Corinthian fluted columns with their capitals and the side of the said gallery is made of carved bannisters supported by a full Corinthian cornish which falls on the head of the capitals.

The staircase is small but very elegant; the steps, risers, bannisters and every part being of mahogany and the steps and landings are well inlaid with the same, picked and laid to form various figures, the pieces are stuccoed in tabernacle frame work a single cornish. The ceiling is richly decorated with a broken oval compartment in the centre (*which is*) of the Four Seasons on the four cardinal points [*illeg.*] The floor of the staircase is also to be of Ketton stone and black marble dots.

The library, which is the south end of the east wing is supposed to hold 10,000 books, being 52 feet long, 25 feet wide and 18 feet high with four windows on the sides and a grand Venetian window at the end. The floor of this room is of Norway oak as are all the other floors. The bookcases which are all round the room are about 12 feet high to the bottom of the cornish which is an Ionic full intablature (*entablature*[5]) of stucco painted and veined as mahogany to match the cases, which are all of that wood, glazed with crown glass from the base to the cornish. Betwixt each case is an Ionic fluted pilaster with capitals, the front of which open to receive books, as does the base. In each case is two sash doors below and two above in which lower part all the large folio volumes stand and the smaller volumes at top, as most of the books which fill this library are gilt they make a splendid appearance through the sashes. The (*library*) door is of mahogany as also the architrave, frieze and a pediment over, the same all richly carved as are the cases, panels, window shutters, soffeats (*soffits*), moldings etc. In the partition of the Venetian window is a lot of Ionic pilasters and capitals of mahogany and richly decorated with stucco enrichments of festoons[6], masks, etc. There are two fireplaces with very large marble chimney pieces carved at the top with festoons of oak leaves in one and of flowers and fruit in the other. Over them the chimney pieces are very beautifully tabernacle frames with very rich cartouches, plinths and other ornaments of carving. In these frames are to be pictures. The top of this room is coved on which cove as well as the ceiling are the richest compartments in stucco in the French taste. As it is proposed to set the bust of patron of the science, each perspective cove contains over the said cases, the compartments in the cove are made to those busts there is Shakespeare and Milton done in stucco. The carving of this room cost 120L (*£120*), the stucco near 200L, the joinery work and mahogany betwixt 300L and 400L besides the floor. Here is (*also*) a library table of beautiful workmanship and carved of mahogany. 'Tis about 7 feet long, 4½ feet wide and 3½ feet high with drawers and cases to the bottom, this table cost 100 guineas.

The musick room which is the north end of the east wing is about 51 feet long, 25 feet wide and l8 feet high and is wainscoted with deal richly carved, here is windows on the side and a very large bow window at the end and are very richly decorated with stucco work and casing in wood. Fluted pilasters etc. The door and floor case are of mahogany and furnished in the same manner as the library door. The cornish, cove and ceilings of stucco adorned with compartmented festoons etc and on the four corners of the ceiling are the heads of eminent musicians, two foreign and English in square frames. The chimney piece is of marble embellished with musick instruments on the frieze. Over this, a large tabernacle frame with very rich cartouches etc, in each is also proposed to be a picture, the Cornish over. This tabernacle frame is [*illeg.*]

by a pediment in which Mr Handel's bust is - as made by Roubiliac. The furniture of this room is very grand and expensive. On each side the fireplace stands a harpsicord of one of which is Tabercers (*?*) the other made in Italy by a native of Venice and is called Bartololmeo Cristofori[7]. Instead of quill jacks[8], the strings are struck by small hammers covered with leather which makes the tone infinitely softer and more melodious than the jacks and prevent the jar which the too long vibration of the strings occasions There is also small hammers covered with leather which falls on the strings to stop in due time the vibration thereof as well as to give due time to each note. This instrument is of very curious workmanship. It is said to be the first or second of the Inventor's making. It was sent from Italy by an acquaintance of Mr Jennens from his travels there. In the uppermost tier betwixt the windows is proposed to stand the organ which is now making by Bridge in London[9] and a book case in the other of the same make and size of the organ for musick books etc. One side of the Venetian bow (*window*) stands a musick desk of mahogany. This desk is made like a table standing on four feet richly carved, within this table are drawers that draw out on the sides and ends in which are stands for the books folded up and which are raised up to any height by the player. The faces of these drawers are also richly carved as are the mouldings and frieze, the above stands are for sitting players. Upon this table is a sort of desk of four sides supported with four carved feet, on this desk are laid the books of the standing performers supported by a carved moulding. On the top of this desk which is flat are sconces[10] for candles very richly made & double gilt with gold. This machine cost upwards of 75L [*or 95L*] and fourteen performers may play at once upon it. Answerable to this desk is a very large mahogany table very richly carved which serves on public days and at the upper end of the room an Italian marble slab, side table. The chairs are all mahogany, made in a new fashion and very richly carved they cost 2½ guineas per chair and the armed one 5 guineas.

The chapel which is in the south end of the west wing is about 36 feet long 25 feet wide and 18 feet high and takes in the lower end the attic storeys. It is only lighted by the Venetian window at the end, the other windows being all blanked off. 'Tis proposed to be wainscoted one storey high with cedar and carved, the seats and desk are also to be of cedar. The sides and ceilings against the attic storey are very richly ornamented with stucco work panelled and those panels filled with festoons, vases and other ornaments, it has a Corinthian cornish and very rich ceiling in the French taste. There is also proposed a marble chimneypiece which is in hand in London but under what design I can't know.

The chambers of the east end are very large and spacious and to each is a large dressing room all which have mahogany doors, are wainscoted with deal richly carved on the mouldings and painted stone colour. The architraves of the doors are all richly carved as are the frieze, cornish and pediments over all the doors. The beds and furniture very rich and mostly mahogany but are a good deal in the ancient taste, the feet of the beds being very large and full of carving etc.

The chambers of the west end and body of the house are very large and most of them with large dressing rooms and servants' rooms by them but are mostly plain wainscoting and cornishes without carving.

Notes

1 *Gopsall Hall: 'Look on my works, ye Mighty, and despair'*. Brenda Sumner. MA thesis, University of Leicester, 2009.

2 *The Description of Leicestershire: containing matters of Antiquity, History, Armoury and Genealogy*. William Burton, 1622.

3 Limestone named after the village of Ketton in Rutland; the small 'dots' were slate, see Chapter 12.

4 Tabernacle frame: an architectural picture frame consisting of a pair of columns or pilasters, flanking the picture space, supporting a frieze and pediment and resting on a base.

5 Entablature: the horizontal mouldings, bands and detailing of the upper part of a building supported by columns. Traditionally it contains (from top to bottom), the cornice, frieze and architrave.

6 Festoon: a chain or garland of flowers, leaves or ribbons hung in a curve as decoration.

7 The instrument is believed to be the first piano in England. It was sent from Italy in 1732 by Jennens' friend Edward Holdsworth and was made by Bartololmeo Cristofori who made pianos for the ruling Medici family in Florence. The piano may have previously been located in Jennens' London house where it is known that a piano was played by George Frideric Handel.

8 The strings of a harpsicord are plucked not struck, as in a piano. The jack is a long strip of wood that holds a small plectrum made of quill, which plucks the strings. Today the plectrum is often made from plastic.

9 Handel was a lifelong friend of Jennens and when Jennens decided to install an organ in his new mansion, it was to Handel that he turned to for advice. In response, Handel sent a very detailed specification which included the proposal to omit reed stops which require frequent tuning and which would be "*inconvenient out of the city*". The two-manual (keyboard) rosewood organ was eventually built in Holborn by Thomas Parker who was trained by Richard Bridge. Graffiti on the rear of the great key slip confirms Parker as builder.

10 Sconce - an old term used to describe a wall mounted candlestick or a group of candlesticks.

APPENDIX II

Gopsall Hall in 1863

An early 20th century photograph of the north front of the hall (bottom) shows a number of features not present in 1863 (top). These include:

1. The 4 chimneys at the corners of the NE and NW wings.
2. Staircase extensions (x) for the underground passage leading from the NE wing to the NW wing (picture gallery; A) via the vestibule (Fig. 16a).
3. The vestibule and carriage porch (B).
4. The billiard room (C).

The 1863 photograph also shows the absence of the smoking room (SR; built to the east/left of the single-storey picture gallery; not shown in the 20th century image) and the presence of very large skylights (SL) above the picture gallery [A], which are not present in photos dating from the late 19th century. Significantly, the 1863 image shows the west kitchen wing with its northern extension (arrows) behind the clock tower/steward's room wing (D), indicating that the two west service wings were constructed prior to 1863, probably by Blore between 1835 and 1837.[1]

The photograph of the south front dated 1865 (below) shows part of the picture gallery extension on the right and the west kitchen service wing (left), supporting the details seen in the 1863 image of the north front. These images clearly demonstrate that it was the 1st Earl (d. 1870) who was responsible for the majority of building works that increased the size of the hall (Tables I & II).

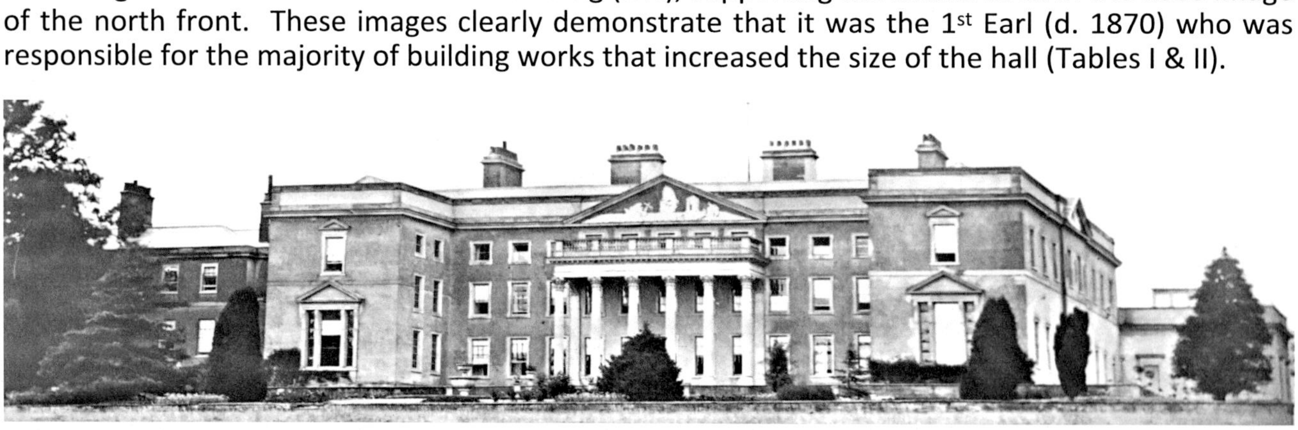

1 *Edward Blore papers: MS.Add.3944: Gopsall Hall Leicestershire: account of wages and workman's time on building projects*, 13 April 1835 - 5 August 1837. Cambridge University Library.

APPENDIX III

Architectural sections of Gopsall Hall

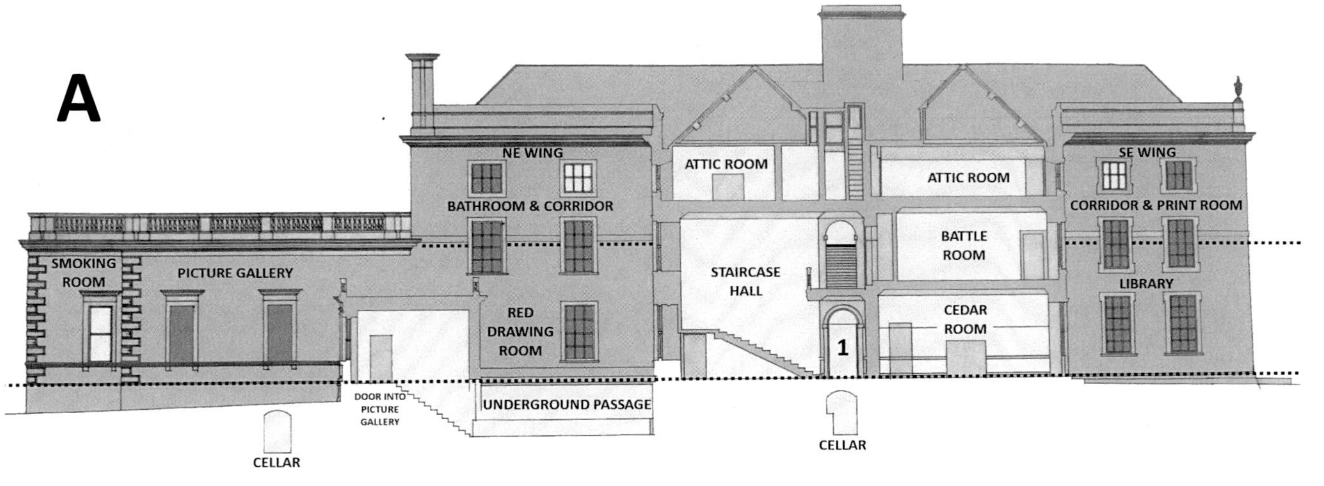

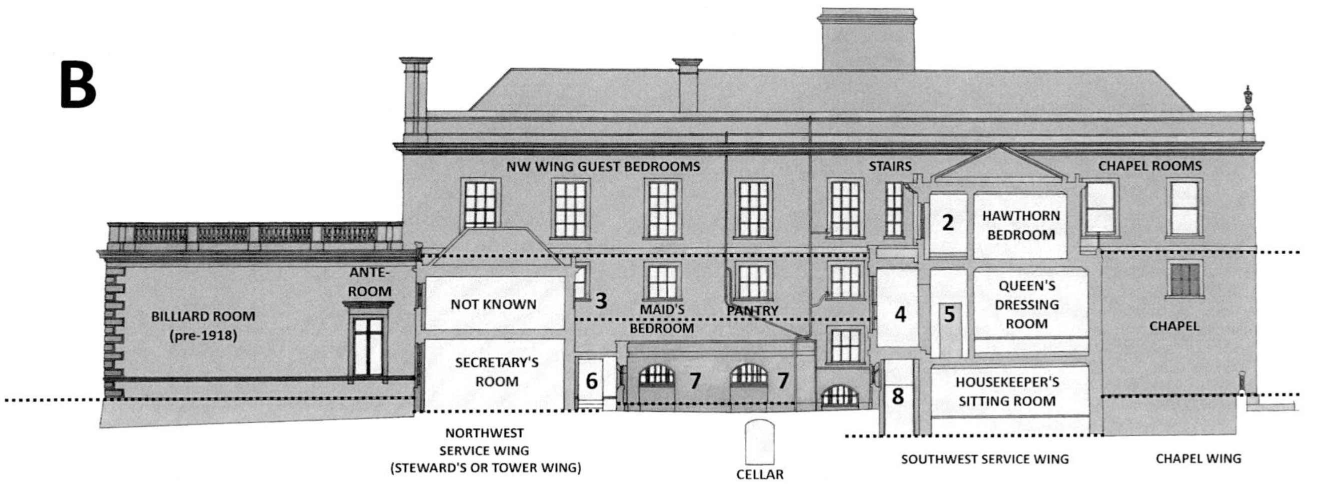

Above are north to south (*left to right*) sections through the staircase hall (A) and the courtyard (B) looking east. Floor levels for the areas of the building not sectioned are shown as dotted lines (e.g. the southwest chapel wing has two storeys whereas the northwest wing of the hall has three; B). Windows shaded grey are blank/false, visible on the exterior of the hall only.

1 Main ground floor corridor leading into the Green Drawing Room

2 Bachelors' corridor

3 Part of the Linen Room window

4 Tap Room

5 Top of stairs from Chapel Anteroom

6 Doorway into northwest wing of the hall (with access to the Butler's Pantry, Business & Billiard Rooms) and to the corridor to the southwest service wing (7) - from the northwest service wing.

7 Corridor leading via stairs down to the southwest wing and stairs up to the west end of the main hall corridor

8 Southwest service wing/Kitchen corridor

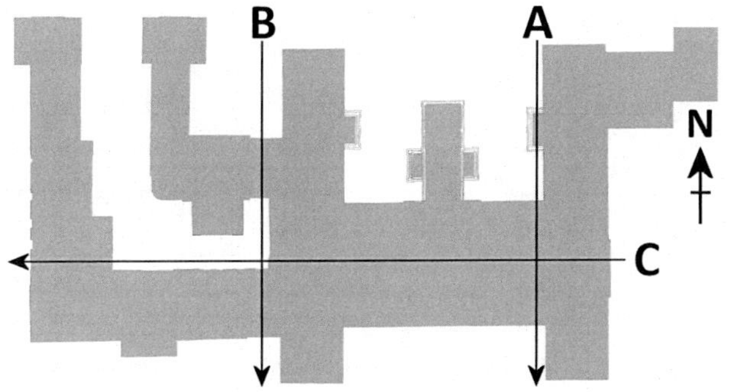

Position of the north-south (A & B) and east-west (C) sections of the hall.

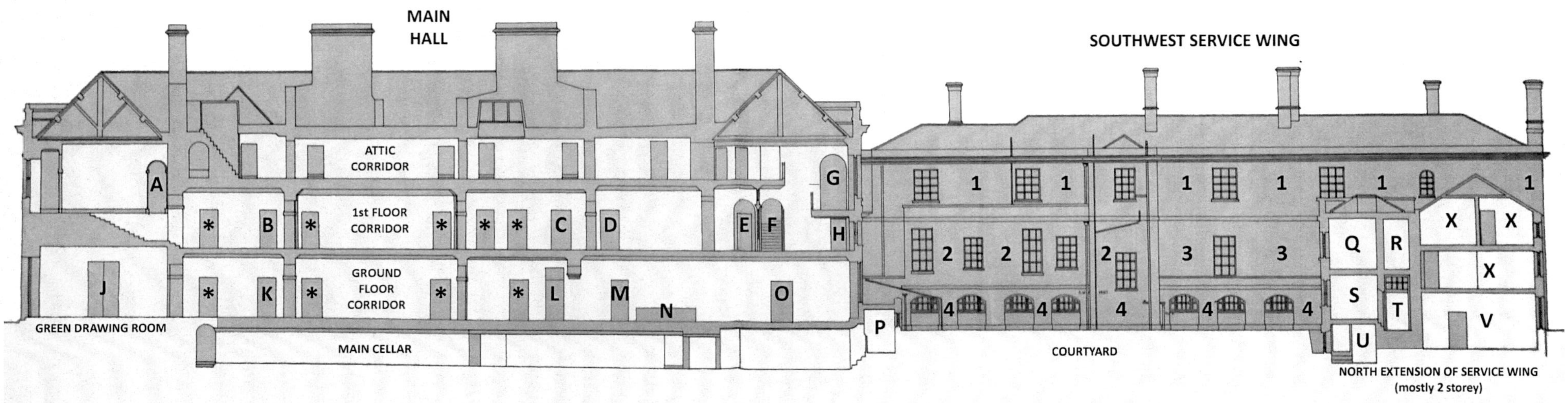

East to west (*left to right*) section of the hall (c) through the main hall corridor, the courtyard and the southern end of the north extension to the southwest service wing, looking south.

- A Passage to Chinese Bedroom and Print Room
- B Battle Room
- C South Dressing Room
- D South Bedroom
- E Stairs to Chapel Rooms
- F Stairs to Bachelors' wing and northwest wing (2nd floor)
- G Landing joining Bachelors' wing to the northwest wing
- H Crocus Bathroom
- J Library
- K Cedar (Tea) Room
- L Small Oak Dining Room
- M Stairs to 1st floor and Chapel Rooms
- N Radiator
- O Chapel Anteroom
- P Corridor to the lower floor of the southwest service wing (Kitchens etc)
- Q Small servants' Bathroom
- R 1st floor passage leading north to the Barracks (staff bedrooms)
- S Storeroom
- T Ground floor passage leading north to Gun Room, Bakery and Laundry
- U Buttery
- V Housemaids' Sitting Room
- X Unknown room
- * Cupboards
- 1 Bachelors' Corridor
- 2 Bathroom & Linen Room (Queen's suite is on the south side of the wing)
- 3 Upper parts of the Kitchen and Scullery
- 4 Service wing ground floor corridor with Housekeeper's Sitting Room, Stores, Kitchens and Scullery etc on the south side of the building (single storey where it passes the main Kitchen and Scullery)

Note: B-D, H-L and O refer to the rooms behind the marked doors.

Gopsall Hall in the early 20th century: A virtual tour

The mansion built by Charles Jennens in 1750 and altered by the Earls Howe, stood for 200 years, but was only used as a family home until 1918 when it was sold to Samuel Waring. Like our own homes, the hall changed over the decades, both in physical size and in internal fittings and decoration. The names of rooms also changed with modifications to the hall, use and fashion. Here we take a tour of the principal floor of the hall as it would have appeared in the first twenty years of the 20th century.

We are writing this in 2020, almost exactly 100 years from the 'beginning of the end' for Gopsall Hall. Earl Howe no longer owned Gopsall in 1918 and the Curzon family's collections of furniture, paintings, tapestries and ornaments were removed from the hall and either sold or moved to Penn House in Buckinghamshire. We have been able to source documents describing many of the details of the rooms and the fittings; these being the 1951 sale catalogues along with some comprehensive plans.[1] The latter have been painstakingly updated to show the clearest view of a very complex building (Chapter 2). In addition, photographs of the various principal rooms in the hall[2] have been instrumental in being able to take a tour of the hall at its zenith, when no further changes were undertaken until its use as No.2 Radio Mechanics School in World War II and demolition in 1951. However, in some instances, there are inconsistencies between our three sources of information, so our tour of the ground floor is not guaranteed to be totally accurate. It would probably help to get your bearings if you refer to the pull-out plan or the plan at the end of this chapter. You will need your imagination but, National Trust cards are not required. Please don't touch anything as you move around!

Carriage Porch and Vestibule

Arriving at the main entrance on the north front, you won't get wet on a rainy day visit as you step out of one of the Earl's motor vehicles, or step down from your horse drawn Brougham carriage driven by John McCullam (the 4th Earl's head coachman)[3], conveniently stopped beneath the large carriage porch.

Historic England Archive

Climb four steps and enter through the massive oak panelled entrance doors, 5ft wide and 9ft high, pass through the deep linings and carved porch sides and into the vestibule. Immediately you start to see the level of opulence. The ceiling and walls are covered in ornate plaster work. The wall panels surround 8ft high mirrors to both sides, in classic Georgian symmetry, above two intricately carved console tables. There are sash windows with deep linings and detailed carved oak frames on both sides. To your right, a half-glazed door leads to stairs down to an underground passage with toilets, a photographic dark room and access to the salon and the northwest service wing. On the left is a fully glazed door leading to a small anteroom with a window overlooking the north entrance gates. A panelled dado, 2ft 6in high, runs the length of the room and this is just the vestibule! Floorboards of oak, with a carpet runner, lead you into the entrance hall.

Entrance Hall

Walk on through the half glazed oak doors, again 5ft wide and 8ft high, into a two-storey entrance hall where you will find even more elaborate plaster panelling and another highly decorated plaster ceiling. The floor, all 690 square feet of it, is laid with Ketton limestone flags; each with an inset black slate diamond shaped corner. Every wall panel has a painting hung within, many of them being 'Old Masters'. A gallery, supported on 3 fluted columns with balustrading connecting the east and west upper rooms is directly in front of you. To your left, on the east wall, is a white marble fireplace and mantel, 7ft 10in wide. The supporting pilasters[4] bear carved patriarchal figures and the carved, central header is decorated with children kindling a fire. In front of the fire grate, there is a white painted fender with a mahogany top rail. An elegant desk sits in the middle of the hall, with a range of chairs throughout and a grandfather clock against the south wall, alongside a console table. Marble busts, each on 3ft mahogany pedestals, are next to the wall beneath the gallery, and potted plants and ferns, on various stands, stretch upward to the landing above.

Historic England Archive

The entrance hall fireplace (*above*) and the portrait of Admiral Earl Howe by Mather Brown[5] *(below)*.

Make your way to the exit door, in the far left-hand corner, and stop before you leave through the 7ft 3in high mahogany doors in the carved archway, to look back at the painting hanging near the door. It is a portrait of the 1st Earl Howe,[5] 'Black Dick', the famous naval ancestor keeping an eye on his Curzon descendants through the marriage of his eldest daughter, Sophia Charlotte Howe, to Penn Assheton Curzon. Also look along the 77ft-long passage that runs from the other side of the entrance hall to the west end of the building; the whole of the stone flagged floor matching that of the entrance hall. This is the main corridor, running east-west, which passes several principal rooms on the ground floor and leads to the chapel. Turning back, go through the door and come to the main staircase.

Main Staircase

The ceiling is again fine plasterwork and the area is well lit by the two 7ft 4in high sash windows with folding shutters. Mounted stags' heads adorn the plaster panels. High on the wall directly in front of the first stair flight is a large mirror, conveniently placed 'for the ladies to check their

The Entrance Hall

Views left (*top*) and right (*bottom*) as you enter the entrance hall.

Top: The main staircase and view west down the main hall corridor.
Bottom: The green drawing room with the red drawing room through the double doors on the right.

Historic England Archive

dresses as they descend from the bedrooms'. Standing on a chest of drawers, a flowering *Clivia miniata* (Natal lily) in a Chinese patterned flower pot is reflected in the mirror behind.

The staircase itself is mahogany, 5ft wide, rising 26 treads, with just one landing against the north wall. Again it is light and airy, being lit by 6ft 6in sash windows. The moulded handrail and carved balustrade are supported by 7 square mahogany newel posts. Unfortunately, the upper floors are out of bounds, so continue straight ahead and enter the green drawing room via the panelled mahogany door.

Green Drawing Room *(Part of the original Music Room)*

Looking up, there is another astonishing ceiling, this time with a deep dome at its centre which appears to rise into a room above, but is actually making use of the additional space created by a small 1st floor staircase. From the centre of the dome, as you might expect, hangs a huge, well-crafted light pendant suspended from chains, but it is not a chandelier, which might have detracted from the beauty of the dome. The plaster ceiling frieze and dome are picked out in gilt and it is no surprise that the wall coverings are green silk brocade. In front of you, the east wall of the room has a glazed door that leads out onto the east terrace with an oak-framed sash window to its left. To your left, is a fine white marble mantelpiece with carved scroll pilasters decorated with swags of grapes. The richly carved frieze, with festoons and garlands of flowers, has a centre panel with a dove in a shell scroll with bunches of fruit. Above hangs a large painting in a gilt frame. The room contains a range of chairs, a sewing box, a foot stool and a small writing desk facing towards the sash window in the east wall. The oak floor is covered in a large square patterned rug and several paintings adorn the silk brocade covered walls. To your right doors lead into the library, but to your left is a huge 11ft high pair of mahogany double doors which open into the red drawing room.

Green drawing room mantelpiece.
Historic England Archive

Red Drawing Room *(Music Room in Charles Jennens' lifetime)*

As you enter, on your left are maroon and gold tapestries hanging either side of yet another white marble mantelpiece, with a frieze bearing three carved panels depicting musical instruments. The tapestries are where, from the outside, there should be two large sash windows, but these are blanks, included to maintain a symmetrical appearance to the north front of the hall. Above the mantelpiece is fixed a gilt framed mirror partially covering the faded red damask silk wall covering, and to the left of the fireplace, sitting against the wall, is a 4ft 6in marble topped gilt console table. On the opposite wall are a pair of 10ft by 5ft gilt mirrors hung between three oak sash windows which look out over the east garden, where Holdsworth's cenotaph is centrally placed. In the distance the light shines on the lake at the end of Shackerstone drive, the other side of which is glimpsed the Viennese bridge. Looking up, the ceiling has highly decorated oval plasterwork, as you probably expected. Further on, in front of you, is another massive set of 11ft high doors, this time half glazed, which lead through to the salon. Between them and you is an array of comfy chairs and settees before the iron grate and hearthstone. Potted cordylines, 6ft high, grown in the greenhouses, stand on small tables and aspidistra and orchids take advantage of the light from the east windows. Walking through the half-glazed doors you enter the salon.

The Red Drawing Room

The red and green drawing rooms used to be one 52ft long room, which was originally Charles Jennens' music room. The room was divided into two in the 1820s by Richard William Penn Curzon, the 1st Earl Howe. This smaller music room contained "*a very large organ in a mahogany case*" in 1831,[6] details about which are unknown. The photograph shows the room as it existed in about 1920.

Historic England Archive

Salon or Picture Gallery

This is probably one of the most startling of all the rooms in the house, 60ft long and 40ft at its widest; a single storey extension built in 1862-1863.[7] Natural light floods into the room from two huge roof lights. The room was originally fitted to enhance the views of the family's collection of paintings; both 'Old Masters' and portraits of family ancestors. When built it was a picture gallery, but it now serves the purpose of a music room and is known as the salon. This space is really made up of two separate rooms, divided by 8 coloured marble columns (4 square and 4 round) placed at each side of the room supporting a massive, decorated structural beam. Immediately on your left, a discreet door leads to the underground passage to the vestibule and northwest wing. There is no lighting down there and the seven, now empty, wine cellars can't be accessed from the passage. So, without any light or any prospect of a drink, we won't be visiting!

The walls, as in many of the other principal rooms, are covered with silk damask, pink here, and the plasterwork is, again, highly decorative. There are two identical white marble mantelpieces, 7ft 6in wide, with panelled pilasters surmounted by carved brackets. The centre panels of the fireplace friezes are plain, but on either side are festoons of roses and other flowers. Large patterned rugs cover the expanse of oak floor boards and all sorts of chairs, occasional tables, settees, footstools, a chaise longue and a desk are scattered throughout the space. Potted Washingtonia ferns in jardinières, each on a stone pedestal, are placed around the room. In addition to the grand piano in front of you, there is an Aeolian pipe organ against the wall in the far right north east corner, which was installed at the same time as the chapel organ in c.1901. To the right of the organ, in the middle of the wall, a set of curtains is closed over a half-glazed oak door leading through to the billiard room.

Historic England Archive

The Salon

Top: The salon in c.1919 containing the Aeolian organ (installed in 1901). **Bottom:** The salon in c.1900. The 4th Earl is playing a small organ while Lady Howe listens. On the right, the doors to the billiard room (smoking room pre-1919) are open; they are covered with silk brocade and are hung with pictures. In later years the doors were hidden behind curtains.

Top: View of the billiard room (c.1919) looking towards the fireplace and the doors from the salon.
Bottom: View into the salon as you leave the billiard room. Above the fireplace is a portrait of the Duke of York by Pompeo Batoni, painted in Rome in 1764. A portrait of Mary Assheton by Charles Jervaise (1727) is on the right. Mary married Sir Nathaniel Curzon, 4th Baronet and their second son was Assheton Curzon.

Billiard room *(The Smoking Room before 1919)*

This large (40ft by 22ft), single-storey room was the last addition to the hall in the late 1880s or 1890s. In front of you, in the far wall, is an oak panelled door which leads into a hallway with a small WC and an exit door to steps down to the east gardens. To your right is an unremarkable (for Gopsall Hall) white marble mantelpiece with an oak framed sash window either side overlooking the east terrace and garden. A three-panelled oak sash window in the north wall at the far end of the room, to your left, has views over the north lawn and into the park. A dado and chair rail, 5ft 6in high, runs around the walls, broken by room height fluted columns with Ionic capitals seemingly supporting an elaborate, though very masculine, timber frieze. A few large paintings hang on the walls above the dado and one above the mantelpiece. The room is dominated by the billiard table, illuminated by 6 electroliers and the large roof light, which is surrounded by a collection of comfortable chairs and a small table in front of the fire.

Now retrace your steps through the salon and the red drawing room to the green drawing room and continue straight ahead into the library through the double doors.

The Red Drawing Room (c.1900)

The view as you you enter the room from the salon. The green drawing room is through the double doors ahead. To the left of the mirror is a portrait of Richard, future Admiral Howe, by Thomas Gainsborough (1763). The spinet in the left foreground is reputed to have belonged to George Frideric Handel.[8]

Library

This room contains a massive collection of books, housed in fitted, wall to ceiling mahogany bookcases, 12ft 6in high, each with glazed, sash doors. Between each bookcase is an Ionic fluted pilaster with capitals, the front of which opens to receive books. It is reputed to be one of the best private collections of books in England, numbering some 12,000 volumes and including some very rare and expensive items. Until 1907, it contained a fine set of 17th century Quartos of Shakespeare's plays, most of which were sold privately to Mr H.C. Folger of New York.[9]

On your right, the west wall has a pair of marble mantelpieces which have panelled pilasters surmounted by carved scrolls. The central panels are plain marble with carved festoons of flowers and fruit, or acorns and oak leaves, on either side. Above the mantels are carved timber chimney

The Library

Views looking towards the double doors and the green drawing room. These photographs were taken before the sale of Gopsall to Samuel Waring in 1918. A later image of the library can be seen in Chapter 10.

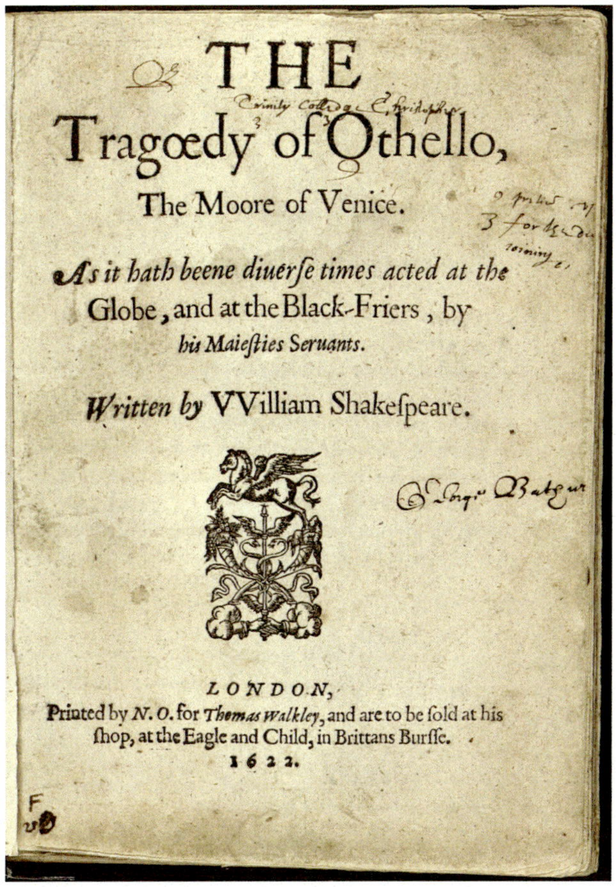

THE

Tragœdy of Othello,

The Moore of Venice.

As it hath beene diuerſe times acted at the Globe, and at the Black-Friers, by *his Maieſties Seruants.*

Written by VVilliam Shakeſpeare.

LONDON,

Printed by *N. O.* for *Thomas Walkley*, and are to be ſold at his ſhop, at the Eagle and Child, in Brittans Burſſe.

1622.

Above: One of the fireplaces in the library; the wooden fluted pilasters either side have handles and open to store books (Historic England Archive).

Right: The first page of the first edition Othello Quarto printed in 1622 and sold by the 4th Earl in 1907 (Folger Shakespearian Library; CC BY-SA).[9]

Historic England Archive

The Cedar Tea Room

The view when standing next to the state dining room door and looking towards the door leading from the staircase. The 'secret' passage to the library is disguised by the wood panelling to the left of the fireplace.

The secret door (1951)

pieces to match the bookcases. Not visible inside, there is a blank window on either side of the far mantelpiece, included to maintain the symmetry of the exterior appearance of the south front of the hall. Intriguingly, there is also a secret door leading from the library, via a short passage, into the cedar tea room. The door is disguised as a bookcase in the corner of the room to your right.[10]

At the far, south end, of the room is a large, 3-panelled window overlooking the south gardens which, in the early part of the 19th century, contained glass that had been painted by Baroness Sophia Howe. Unfortunately, the painting is no longer present for you to see today, but in 1831 it was described as being "*particularly beautiful, both from the excellence of the painting as well as from its situation*".[6] The east (left hand) wall of the library has three mahogany framed sash windows with views of the east terrace and gardens. Immediately on your left is a glazed door leading out onto the east terrace. By now you will know to look up, and yes, it is yet another fabulous ceiling, probably one of the best in the building; it cost nearly £200 in 1750.[11] The floor is Norwegian oak and covered with large rugs. Reading tables, desks and comfy chairs almost fill this enormous space (54ft long by 24ft wide and 18ft high). Pushed into one corner is a wheeled library ladder and platform with a handrail, again in mahogany.

Returning back into the green drawing room and turning left to the main staircase, turn left again through the first door under the carved frame and overdoor to enter the cedar tea room.

Cedar Tea Room

This little room (25ft by 11ft) is laid for tea; its oak floor covered by a single, large rug. An oval table draped in a linen cloth sits in the centre of the room, in front of yet another fine marble mantlepiece to its left. This has pilasters with carved trusses, festoons of fruit and a frieze of Sienna marble, with yellow veins running through it. A finely carved central panel in the frieze shows a man and an angel with lions. To the left of the mantlepiece is the concealed door leading to the secret passage to the library. On the wall on your right is a gilt

Above: Central carved panel of the fireplace representing Daniel in the Lions' Den or the martyrdom of St Ignatius in Antioch in 107AD.

Right: Detail taken from the view of the cedar tea room showing the outline of the secret door (*arrows*) leading to the library.

Historic England Archive

frame mirror, 7ft high, reflecting the mantlepiece and the mostly plain pine panelling, decorated with a few carvings of musical instruments and swags of flowers. Above the panelling, there is yet more silk damask and, of course, a stuccoed ceiling.

A half-glazed door and sash window give views of the south gardens and access to the south terrace. In the far-right corner of the room is a mahogany-panelled door leading to the state dining room.

State Dining Room

Walk into the state dining room and look through the three 8ft high sash windows or the glazed door on the left hand, south side of the room. The Corinthian columns of the portico are in front of you and beyond, are the south terrace and gardens. As your eyes pass the central fountain, they move on, across the valley, to The Race Course wood and the temple, white in the rays of the sun.

We have already established that Gopsall Hall has spectacular plasterwork ceilings; this one is the absolute pinnacle in terms of size and craftmanship. Above you, the ceiling curves upwards from the top of the 18ft walls creating an oblong panel in the centre, a full two storeys high. The curved borders are decorated with a forest of modelled tree work, with fruit, dogs and birds picked out. In the centre, the massive flat central panel shows Neptune riding a Nautilus shell. This ceiling and all the magnificent plaster panels and ceilings throughout the hall were created by Italian craftsmen engaged and brought to England by Charles Jennens.

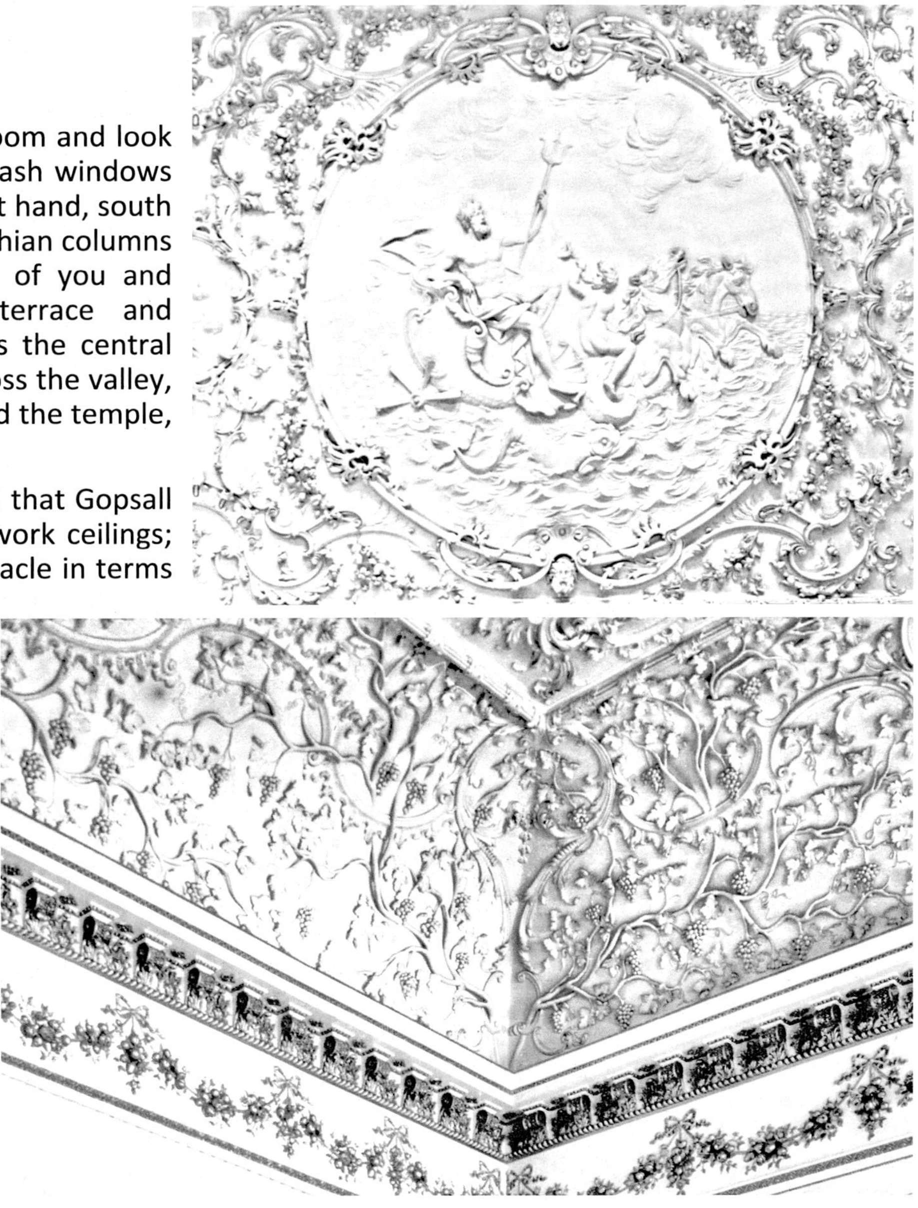

Plasterwork in the State Dining Room

Top: Centrepiece of the dining room ceiling: Neptune riding a Nautilus shell, drawn by two horses and accompanied by a small figure playing a conch.
Bottom: Curving plasterwork border of the ceiling with the dental carved cornice and painted border below (Historic England Archive).

Below the ceiling runs a dental carved cornice and, below that, a wide border painted with floral swags; another narrower frieze completes the ceiling area. The walls are decorated with painted plasterwork panels separated by vertical, heavily carved swags of flowers. Family portraits adorn the walls, flooded by light from the south facing windows at two levels; over each 8ft sash window and the glazed door there are smaller windows, which from outside appear to be full-sized 8ft tall windows to maintain the symmetry of the south front.

On the back, north, wall stands a fine statuary Parian marble mantlepiece, 8ft high. Tapered pilasters have large sized figures of angels, supporting the carved shelf, beneath which is a carved central panel showing biblical characters. The fireplace is often screened by curtains, as the three

6-column radiators[12] are considered to provide enough warmth when the room is filled with guests. Above the fireplace is a carved wood overmantel, surrounded by more fine flower carving with gilt ornamentation. A pine dado with chair rail and carved skirting run around all the walls and, above, a pair of 3-light electroliers stand by to augment the candelabra set for dinner; electricity was only installed in 1901; a recent and very modern addition.

Historic England Archive

The State Dining Room

A view from the southwest corner of the room. The door from the cedar tea room is on the right of the photograph.

For formal meals, a long table can be set for up to 28 diners using the family silver brought from the strong room by the butler, Mr Prince.[13] On such occasions, Mr Lee, the head gardener, would also be busy, providing floral arrangements to be strategically placed so as not to interfere with guests' views. Silver salvers, wine ewers and the other paraphernalia for service would be set on the round side table which, today, is set for just 4 diners. At 25ft by 32ft and double height, this room does not make for intimate dining so, on a quiet day when no guests are visiting, another room is often used.

Use the mahogany-panelled door, with the carved gilt wood framing in the south west corner of the room, to go through to the small oak dining room.

Small Oak Dining Room *(also called the Breakfast Room)*

This is a very, very much simpler arrangement for dining. A plain plastered ceiling, the walls covered in mostly plain timber panelling with the odd flower swag applied, and a simple moulding to the top. There is no gilding in this 18ft by 19ft room and it is almost stark in contrast with the other rooms you have visited. A rectangular table sits in the centre of the room, with several dining chairs, and the oak floor is covered by a patterned rug. A few small paintings are hung on the panelled walls which also boast wall-mounted, electric candlestick lights. To your left, through

The Small Oak Dining Room

A view of the room from the door from the state dining room showing the fireplace with doors to the main corridor (*left*) and the lift (*right*). In some 18th century plans of the hall this room was to be used as the servants' hall,[14] which may explain the presence of a plain plastered ceiling.

the windows, are views across the south terrace and gardens, and on the north wall, to your right, is a small moulded fireplace of dark marble with a white oval centre panel of cherubs and a sleeping child. On the hearthstone are a pair of ornate iron fire dogs. Above the mantelpiece is a carved timber-framed mirror. To either side of the mantelpiece are oak doors; the left one leads to the main hall corridor but the other is a disguised lift to the basement with its seven wine cellars and access to the kitchen corridor.

Leave the room by the left-hand oak door, through a small hallway into the main corridor and turn left and enter the blue boudoir by the first door on the left.

Blue Boudoir *(Originally planned as the Kitchen[14]; Servants' Hall in Charles Jennens' lifetime)*

This room picks up its name from the blue silk damask wall covering and was, for a time, Countess Howe's sitting room. The room has a simple pine 3ft high dado and chair rail, and a variety of small and large paintings hang on the wall. On the right, west wall is an unremarkable white marble fireplace, with carved trusses framing a 2-bar electric fire. Above the fireplace is an oval wall mirror with an ornate carved frame. Georgiana's writing desk is near the glazed door which leads to the south terrace and there is a scattering of small chairs and tables; the latter adorned with many photos of friends and family.

Turning back into the corridor, there is a huge radiator on the wall by which you can stand for a moment, to warm up. Throughout the ground floor and in some of the bedrooms there are radiators employed to try to warm the house. Now walk further down the corridor and enter the chapel anteroom through the second door on the left. The staircase ahead and to your right leads up to the 'Royal Suite'. You will have a quick look there, once you have seen the chapel which you enter through the door directly ahead.

Chapel

This is probably the most famous room in the hall. Immediately in front of you, above the altar, the large window in the south wall illuminates the whole chapel; heavy material drapery is pulled back beneath a deep valance. This is the only window in the chapel but, to maintain a pleasing external appearance, there are false windows in both the east and west walls.

Once over the surprise at the beauty of the chapel, take a deep breath; every inch of the fittings is cedar and, on a warm day, you can detect the scent, just like the smell of your school pencil case. Cedar trees have always featured heavily in Gopsall Park and it is thought that the chapel timber was harvested and processed into panels here on the estate.

Walk towards the altar between the rows of pews, 5 each side, their ends heavily carved giving the appearance of trellis. On your left is another of the famous Gopsall organs, installed in 1901, and opposite, the cedar pulpit, supporting a gold gilt eagle with wings partially unfurled. In the south west corner, to the right of the altar, is the family pew with its soft cushions, padded back rest, carpeting and wall-mounted electroliers above. It was this pew that was occupied by King Edward VII and Queen Alexandra during Sunday services when they visited Gopsall in 1902. Directly in front of it, in the window, sits the altar separated from the main area by a low knee-high Sanctuary Screen. The legs of the altar are reputed to have been made from oak taken from the Boscobel oak near Wolverhampton, where King Charles[15] spent a night hiding from his pursuers.

The Chapel
Views showing the organ, pulpit and pews. The family pew is on the right side, next to the altar.

A view of the Chapel from the family pew

All images: Historic England Archive

The 'Eagle' Pulpit

The interior of the chapel, including the pulpit, was designed for Charles Jennens by David and William Hiorn.

Decorative organ pipes

The organ was installed in the chapel fireplace opposite the pulpit in 1901.

18th century engraving of Gopsall Chapel[16]

Note that before the installation of the organ, there was a fireplace opposite the pulpit, above which was hung the Van Dyke painting of the Crucifixion.[6]

A large painting adorns the wall above the pulpit. As you would expect by now, this isn't just any painting, this is The Crucifixion by Van Dyke.

Unfortunately, the Chapel silver gilt cup and paten (c.1692) are not on display. The German-made cup is very beautiful and except for the lip, is covered with foliage repousse and chaste, studded all over with many different precious stones. On the bowl are three oval enamels, their subjects being, the Annunciation, the visit of the Virgin to Elizabeth, and the Nativity. Three futher oval enamels on the foot depict the Circumcision, Visit of the Wise Men, and Christ in the midst of doctors. In contrast to the highly decorated cup, the paten is plain.[17]

Before you leave look above your head, the Italian plasterers have been here too!

The Gopsall communion cup

The coat of arms engraved under the foot indicates that the cup formerly belonged to the Abbey of St Stephen, Wurzburg. The cup and paten were purchased by Richard William Penn Curzon, 1st Earl Howe[17].

Immediately after leaving the chapel, climb the stairs on your left to Lady Howe's suite, usually referred to as the Queen's suite, which consists of a dressing room, bedroom and two bathrooms.[18] There is a small, enclosed hallway at the top of the stairs; the door on your left is the dressing room, a couple of steps up on the right lead to a small bathroom. Open the door ahead and enter the bedroom.

Lady Howe's Bedroom *(also variously called the King's or the Queen's Bedroom)*

In the centre of the wall opposite is a carved white marble mantelpiece with a large mirror in an ornate, wood-carved surround. The cream-coloured plastered walls and ceiling are simply decorated by comparison to those in most of the other principal rooms. Some of the plasterwork wall panels are hung with paintings; others have wall-mounted electroliers. A huge, full length mirror is in the centre of the wall on your right. More intricately decorated plasterwork panels, depicting musical instruments are above the painted panel doors. The wood floor is covered with

Lady Howe's Bedroom
The room photographed from the northwest (*top*) and southeast (*bottom*) corners in the late 19th century.

Historic England Archive

The King's Bedroom

A photograph of Lady Howe's bedroom taken from the southwest corner in c.1921, after Gopsall was sold to Samuel Waring. This image is labelled as 'The King's Bedroom' by Historic England.

rugs and the room contains a variety of comfortable chairs, a settee and a chaise longue. A large double bed with heavy drapes and canopy over is against the wall opposite the fireplace. The two large windows have views south across the gardens and park. The door in the far corner leads to the large bathroom containing the famous 'silver' bath. Can you tell if it is tin or silver?

You won't leave via the servants' entrance in the bathroom, but will retrace your steps down the stairs into the chapel entrance. Through the door on the left, cross the main hall corridor and continue through the door opposite to enter a corridor in the northwest service wing. Wind your way along the corridor and go through the first door on the left and through a set of double doors. The secretary's office can be viewed through the door on the right.

Secretary's Office

A small, plain room with a pine wood floor and door; definitely a servant's room. There is a large oak sash window opposite in the north wall and, on the left, there is a small, 4ft 8in, white marble mantlepiece with shaped pilasters and carved central frieze. A desk and several chairs stand in the room, which has plain painted walls. The highlight in the room is a handsome mahogany two-door bookcase (4ft 6in wide and 8ft high) with glazed trellis panels in the top half. A little further down the corridor is the servants' hall.

Servants' Hall

This large room (26ft by 20ft), is where most of the servants have their meals and often spend their free time. There's plenty of space for the large pine table and chairs. Looking through the door you see 3 oak sash windows on the far wall and yet another white marble mantelpiece with shaped pilasters and carved central panel. The floor, skirting and doors are pine and there is a large mirror in a painted frame on the wall near the door; the servants are expected to look smart and be properly dressed when on duty. The usher (of the servants' hall) is responsible for this room; his duties include keeping the room clean, serving beer to those entitled to have it as well as ensuring that no person leaves intoxicated![19]

Retrace your steps past the secretary's office, through the double and single doors and turn left down the corridor, past the butler's pantry and business room on your right, to the large room at the north end of the wing. This single-storey extension, probably added in 1862-1863 (Chapter 2) was apparently originally used as a billiard room. Nothing is known about what this room was used for after the billiard table was moved to the other end of the hall after Gopsall was sold to Samuel Waring in 1918, but during World War II, it was used as the officers' dining room.

Old Billiard Room *(Officers' Dining Room in World War II)*

The room can be entered by either of the two pairs of oak panelled doors, each 2ft wide and 8ft 6in high, with carved framing and handsome carved wood overdoor. You immediately realise that this room, within the service part of the hall, was obviously not for the servants' use. There are three oak-framed windows. The large (9ft x 9ft) window in the north wall has four panels, folding shutters and carved oak wood framing; it overlooks the north lawns and into the park. The floor is oak, a 3ft 9in high oak dado with carved panels lines the walls and, surprisingly, there is an oak panelled mantelpiece (8ft by 5ft 9in) with carved pilasters and frieze and moulded marble linings.

Return to the main hall corridor past the business room and butler's pantry and turn left and enter the first room on the left, the gun room.

Entering the Entrance Hall from the hall corridor

Ahead, through the arched doors, are the staircase hall and green drawing room; the gallery is above. The door frame on the right is to a cupboard but, in previous times, it may have been one of two doors leading from the entrance hall into the state dining room.

Gun Room *(Housekeeper's Room in Charles Jennens' lifetime)*

This small oak floored room, with two windows overlooking the north entrance, boasts red silk damask covered walls and a small white marble mantelpiece. Each of the sash windows has mahogany writing table fitments below, presumably for the shooters to sign their weapons and ammunition in/out and to record their tally. A gun cupboard is to the left of the mantelpiece. Originally the room probably had rugs on the floor and some chairs, as it was likely used by the family and guests on shooting days. The main gunroom is on the ground floor of the north extension to the 'kitchen' service wing, the other side of the west courtyard (Chapter 2). No doubt the head gamekeeper would service the guns and then bring them to this room ready for the shoots. Back in the main corridor, the next room on the left is the cloakroom.

Cloakroom *(Steward's Room and Pantry in Charles Jennens' lifetime)*

Enter the room via the small hallway. To the right of this hallway is the strong room, accessed from the main corridor. Its slate shelving is used for storage of the valuable silver plate, jewellery and other valuables. To the left of the hallway is a very small bathroom, accessed from a door inside the cloakroom; only 6ft square it contains a bath, WC and towel rail! The main cloakroom has two large sash windows overlooking the north entrance; beneath the right hand window is a two-division marble washbasin with 4 plated taps. The floor is oak and pink silk damask covers the walls.

The portrait of Charlotte, Viscountess Howe (1703-1782; mother of Admiral Earl Howe) by Michael Dahl. It was temporarily moved to Assheton House in 1918[20] and is now in Penn House. The painting was recently cleaned and restored by Lord Howe.

Returning to the main corridor, continue left into the entrance hall and admire the stuccoed ceiling of the gallery above, and the view ahead of light streaming in through the glazed door leading to east garden terrace. Before you leave the entrance hall, look up to your left; a painting of Charlotte, Viscountess Howe is illuminated by light from one of the small second storey windows.

Finally, exit the building via the vestibule to end your tour and to be taken home in your transport, waiting under the carriage porch.

Other floors within the hall

The first floor and its bedrooms were out of bounds for the virtual tour as so little is known about them. As far as it is possible to ascertain, there are no surviving photographs of the first floor rooms. The plans of the hall dating from the early 20th century show that there were 8 principal bedrooms, 5 dressing rooms, and 4 bathrooms (including the Queen's suite). However, the sale of hall contents held in 1918 lists at least 12 other bedrooms on the 2nd floor of the hall for which plans do not exist (Chapter 2).[21]

A few details of the principal bedrooms are known. Thus, there were oak floors, carved wood door linings and some carved overdoors, a variety of mahogany and oak doors, not to mention the oak framed windows. Mantelpieces were a mix of marble, slate and carved wood, and the walls of most bedrooms and dressing rooms were covered with oak or pine panelling. The huge bedroom (or suite of rooms) above the chapel (39ft by 24ft), with views across the south gardens, was unremarkable except for the fact that it was heated by two 12-column radiators according to the 1951 sale catalogue of fixtures and fittings[1].

The second floors, present in some parts of the building (Chapter 2), were presumably for the servants and/or storage; although the two west extensions to the hall had many staff bedrooms. However, the 1918 sale of contents catalogue[21] lists several second floor rooms containing quite lavish furniture and fittings suggesting that at least some of the rooms were used as guest bedrooms. No information appears to exist for these areas as, is often the case, only the principal rooms of a mansion were considered worthy of record.

The hall plasterwork

As seen during your virtual tour of the hall, nearly every surface is decorated using ornate plasterwork. It is Rococo in style and developed out of an earlier form called Baroque. Both of these design types feature elaborate ornament and decoration, and were used in large buildings with a social or cultural status. Baroque architecture is serious, dramatic, and heavy in execution, whilst Rococo is light, airy, and decorative using detailed flowing curved lines, classical

The empty entrance hall (*left*; c.1918; Historic England Archive) and 18th century interior design for the north wall[22] (*right*; RIBA collections).

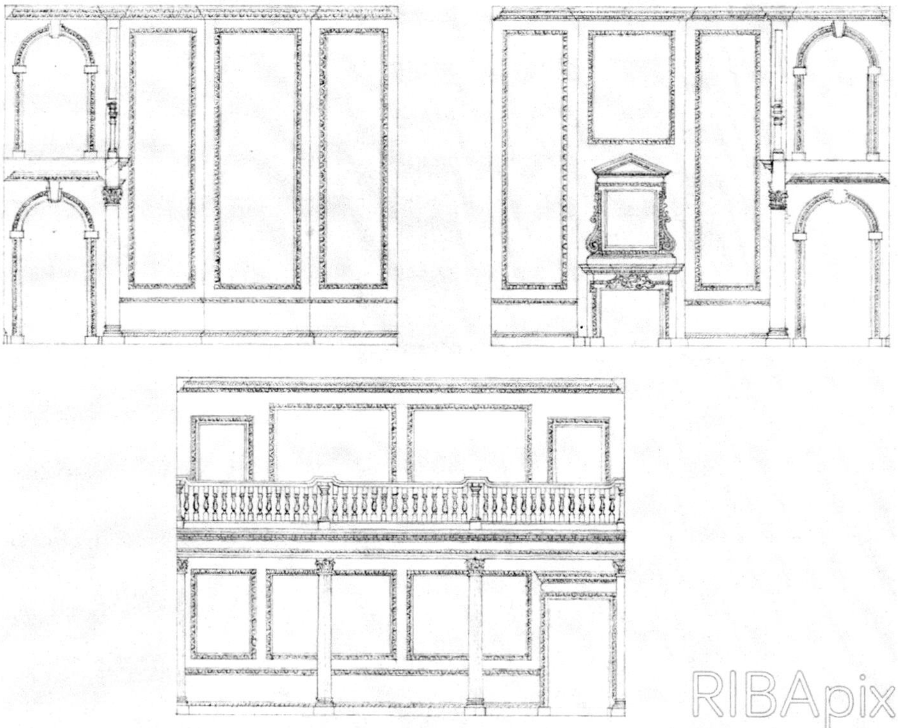

Designs for the west, east (with fireplace) and south (with gallery) walls of the entrance hall by an unknown 18th century English architect (RIBA Collections).[23]

motifs, themes of love, children and often myth and religion. Flowers and musical instruments sometimes feature. All of this was seen in the wall panels and ceilings at Gopsall.

The plaster is made from a mix of lime, gypsum and marble dust (added as a hardener), making it perfect for fine working. Cornice work is moulded in position using preformed timber templates and the 'enhancements' as the intricate additions are called, are produced as separate items before being applied to the ceiling or panel. Such was the value and appreciation for this work that many houses, as at Gopsall, were fitted out with timber dado and chair rails to ensure the fine plasterwork did not get damaged. Plasterwork is a very specialised trade and, in the mid-18th century, English craftsmen often travelled very long distances for their work. However, it is reputed that the the works at Gopsall were executed by even greater distance travellers, Italian craftsmen.

Entrance Hall ceiling

This would be the first original 18th century ceiling seen on entering the hall; its rectangular panels reflecting those on the walls designed to contain paintings.

Historic England Archive

The very nature of the way the plasterwork wall and ceiling panels were made meant that they were virtually impossible to easily remove and preserve during demolition. This, and the lack of interest in such things in 1951 (the year that the hall was demolished; Chapter 12) meant that no attempt was made to preserve the plasterwork masterpieces; the only surviving record

Cedar Tea Room ceiling
Top: The original design by an unknown 18th century English architect (RIBA Collections).[24] **Bottom:** Detail of the ceiling (Historic England Archive).

being some photographs and original plans held by the Royal Institute of British Architects (RIBA). It is ironic that Government legislation recognising the value of country houses and their interiors, came the year following the demolition of Gopsall Hall.

A number of designs for the interior wall and ceiling finishes were produced for Charles Jennens and can be seen on the RIBA Image Library website.[25] Many of these appear to have been discarded in favour of other designs, reflecting the personal preferences of Charles Jennens, whilst others, for the decoration of the entrance hall walls and the ceilings of the dining room and cedar tea room, were executed with only minor alterations.

Stripped of all furniture, paintings, floor coverings and other decoration, the photo of the empty entrance hall (p. 87) gives a clear picture of the quality and exquisite level of decoration produced by the plasterwork alone. All the walls were covered by panels, created by complex moulded borders, made to accommodate framed oil paintings. By contrast, the magnificent ceiling with its 'enhancements' stood as a piece of art on its own.

Each room had a different scheme but all conformed to an overall rococo feel favoured by the Hiorn brothers and, presumably, by Jennens. Geometric patterns characterised the plasterwork of the entrance hall walls and ceiling, and the capitals of the Corinthian columns supporting the

Green Drawing Room ceiling
The ceiling was much lower than those of the adjacent library and red drawing room. The 6ft gap to the floor above allowed the creation of the central dome with pendant light.
Historic England Archive

gallery were richly carved, with a plasterwork frieze above. The marble mantelpiece, seemingly supported by two figures with a central carved panel showing children kindling fire, was the focus of the space.

The design for the ceiling of the cedar tea room, showed birds flying into the centre through scroll work corner pieces and floral swags, towards central sunbursts. In contrast, the walls were covered in mainly plain timber panels, offsetting the richness of the ceiling detail.

In the 19th century, a number of rooms were added as extensions to the hall (vestibule, picture gallery, old billiard room and smoking room/new billiard room), or created within the existing hall structure (green drawing room). None of these rooms featured the extravagant plasterwork characteristic of those created in the 18th century. The walls were plain plastered or wood panelled. The picture gallery and smoking room had large roof lights and the curved plasterwork cornices had little stuccowork ornamentation. However, the green drawing room, created by combining part of the original music room and the hall corridor and occupying a strategic position within the hall, had a ceiling that was different but comparable with those created for Charles Jennens. The ceiling had painted stuccowork borders and corners with a ring outlining the base of a central, highly decorated dome, reminiscent of any church in Rome.

Notes and References

Unless stated otherwise, all images are courtesy of The Rt Hon Frederick Richard Penn Curzon, 7th Earl Howe, GBE, PC. Digital copies of the original photographs have been processed using Corel PaintShop Pro 2019.

1 *Gopsall Hall. Catalogue of the Interior & Exterior Fixtures and Fittings.* Perry & Phillips Ltd, Bridgenorth. Thursday 31st May 1951.

Plans of Gopsall Hall, Leicestershire. The Record Office for Leicestershire and Rutland. File Ref: M10.

2 Historic England has a collection of interior and exterior photographs of Gopsall Hall which can be viewed at: https://historicengland.org.uk/images-books/photos/; search for 'Gopsall Hall'.

3 More information about John McCullam can be found in Below Stairs (Chapters 6) and Memories of Gopsall (Chapter 7).

4 A pilaster is a rectangular column projecting from a wall. The term is used to describe the two upright parts of a fireplace/mantelpiece.

5 Richard Howe (1726-1799) joined the navy in 1739 and became Admiral in 1782 and Admiral of the Fleet in 1796. During his career he participated in the Seven Years War; the American War of Independence; the relief of Gibraltar and the French Revolutionary Wars during which he defeated the French force of Admiral Villaret-Joyeuse in June 1794 ('The Glorious 1st June', the first and largest fleet action of the conflict). Richard was created 1st Viscount Howe of Langar in 1782 and Earl Howe (1st Earl Howe of the first creation) in 1788. He never owned or lived at Gopsall and his title became extinct on his death in 1799, as he had no male children. However, his eldest daughter, Sophia Charlotte Howe, inherited her father's barony, becoming Baroness Howe. In 1787, Sophia married Penn Assheton Curzon, who had inherited Gopsall and other estates from Charles Jennens. Their third but only surviving son Richard (Richard William Penn Curzon-Howe) inherited Gopsall and other estates and was created Earl Howe in 1821 (1st Earl Howe of the 2nd creation).

6 *A Topographical History of the County of Leicester*. Rev. J. Curtis. Ashby-de-la-Zouche: W. Hextal, 1831, p. 66.

7 *History, Gazetteer, and Directory of the Counties of Leicester and Rutland*. William White. Sheffield, 1863, p. 659.

See discussion in Appendix II, Chapter 2.

8 The Rt Hon Frederick Richard Penn Curzon, 7th Earl Howe, GBE, PC. Personal communication.

9 Images of some Gopsall quartos can be viewed at: https://luna.folger.edu/luna/servlet - the Folger Digital Image Collection (LUNA). The quarto shown is one of only fourteen and was printed in 1622, around eighteen years after it was first written and performed. It was entered into the Stationers' Company Register on October 6, 1621 by Thomas Walkley, who then had it printed by Nicholas Okes. The text that appears in this quarto and the text that appears in the First Folio, printed only a year later, are vastly different. Scholars believe that this is a result of two different manuscripts being used for the typesetting. This quarto is the only Shakespeare quarto to have act divisions notated, and might have been set near to the time when it was first written. The quarto was acquired by Henry Folger from the Sotheby's sale of the Curzon-Howe family library in December 1907.

The Shakespearian quartos at Gopsall were originally the property of Charles Jennens.

10 Illustrated Leicester Chronicle, No. 1380 New Series. Saturday 12th May 1951, p. 2.

11 See: *Description of Gopsall Hall and grounds by John Grundy in 1750* (Appendix I, Chapter 2).

12 A number of the principal rooms and the corridors had radiators, often well disguised, that were heated by the two sets of furnaces in the cellars (see Chapter 2).

13 *A Royal Visit* (Chapter 8).

14 *Designs for second scheme for rebuilding Gopsall Hall, Gopsall, Leicestershire (Group II): principal floor plan.* Westley, John (1702-1769). RIBA Collection, library Ref: SD141/3(1); RIBApix Ref: RIBA65842.

15 This was the son of Charles I in 1651 before he became King Charles II in 1660.

16 *Inside View of Gopsall Chapel (plate 39). The History and Antiquities of the County of Leicester. Volume IV, part II containing the Sparkenhoe Hundred.* John Nichols. London, 1811.

17 *An Inventory of the Church Plate of Leicestershire with some account of The Doners - Vol. I.* The Rev. Andrew Trollope. Leicester: Clarke & Hodgson, 1890, pp. 397-398.

The current wherabouts of the Gopsall communion cup and paten are unknown.

18 This suite of rooms is next to, and half a storey above, the chapel in the west wing of the hall; nowadays usually referred to as the Queen's suite. We know little about these rooms except from what is shown in the plans of the hall (Chapter 2) and several photographs of the bedroom.

19 *The Usher of the Servants Hall. The Household Manager; being a practical treatise upon the various duties in large or small establishments, from the drawing room to the kitchen.* Charles Pierce. London: Simkin & Marshall, 1863.

20 See Appendix to Chapter 12.

21 *Gopsall, Leicestershire. Catalogue of the Fine Antique and Modern Furniture in the Mansion.* Messrs. Trollope, London. Monday 14th October and following days, 1918. The Record Office for Leicestershire and Rutland, File Ref: L333.

22 *Designs for interior decoration related to the second scheme for rebuilding Gopsall Hall, Gopsall, Leicestershire.* Unknown 18th century English architect. RIBA Collection, library Ref: SD143/2(2); RIBApix Ref: RIBA65866.

23 *Ibid.*, RIBA Collection, library Ref: SD143/2(1); RIBApix Ref: RIBA20137.

24 *Designs for interior decoration related to the second scheme for rebuilding Gopsall Hall, Gopsall, Leicestershire: a ceiling design.* Unknown 18th century English architect. RIBA Collection, library Ref: SD143/3(7); RIBApix Ref: RIBA20341.

25 RIBA Image Library: https://www.architecture.com/image-library/ - search for Gopsall Hall.

Engraving of the Morning of the Glorious 1st June 1794[5]

The engraving was one of the items not sold in the 1918 or 1920 sales of contents and was temporarily moved to Assheton House, Twycross in 1918 (see Chapter 12).

VIRTUAL TOUR MAP

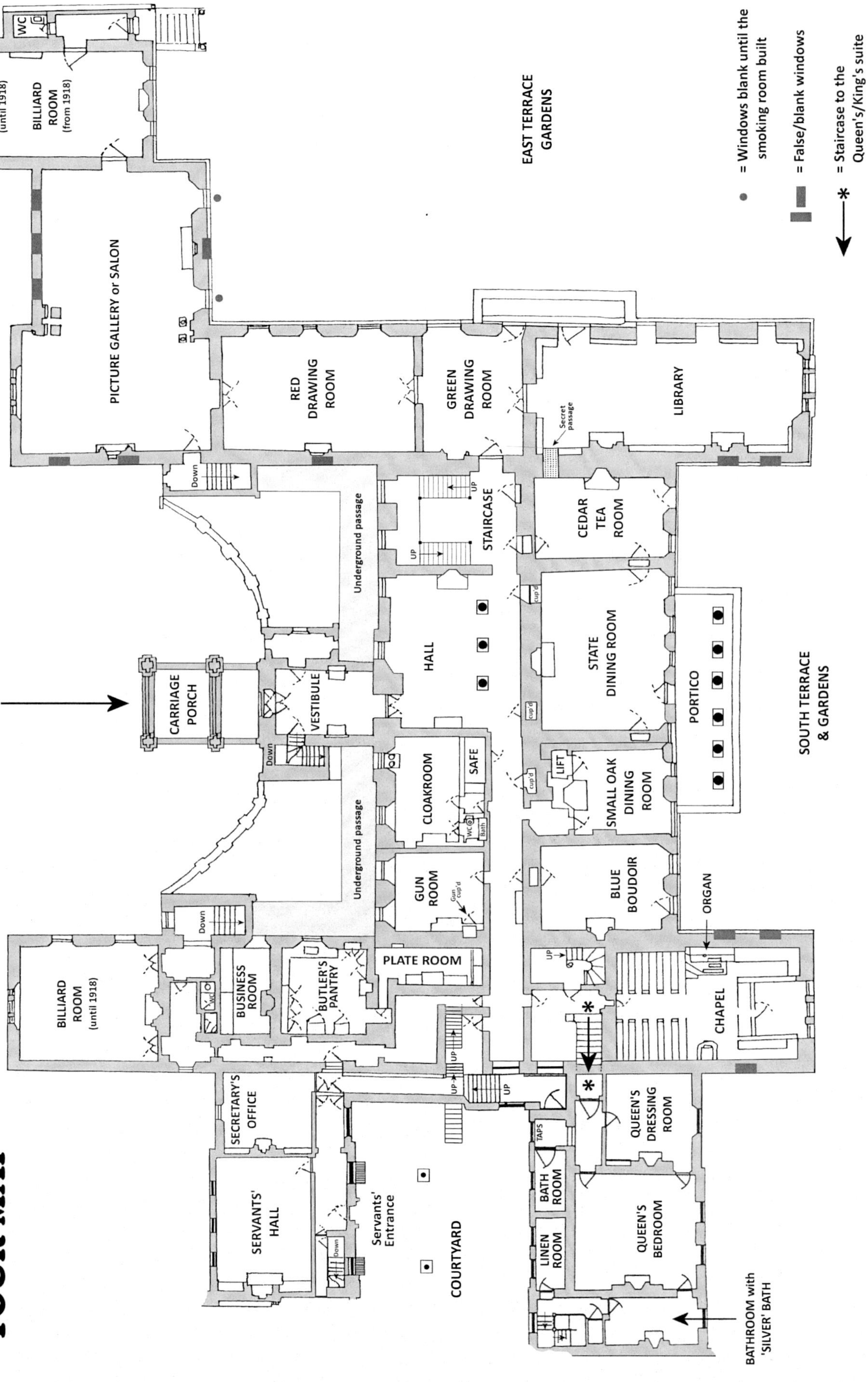

Gopsall Hall Gardens and Park

Tucked away in a quiet part of rural northwest Leicestershire in the centre of what was 940 acres of woods and deer park, lie the remains of a once highly regarded, 32-acre garden, lavishly executed and cared for since 1750. Initially built by Charles Jennens Jnr, the grandson of the wealthy Birmingham industrialist Humphrey Jennens, and subsequently passed into the care of the aristocratic Curzon family; the Gopsall gardens survived until recent memory. Despite being owned, loved and cared for by a family moving in fashionable high society circles, the gardens seem to have managed, through the years, to have avoided the attention of those who would wipe away formal gardens in favour of the Landscape movement in the manner of William Kent or Lancelot 'Capability' Brown. That said, the parkland around the gardens does show signs of some landscaping.

Although little is known about the original Gopsall manor house or the details of the building of the 18th century mansion (Chapter 2), far less is known about the planning and development of the Gopsall gardens and parkland. Around the time that Gopsall Manor was purchased by Humphrey Jennens in 1685, virtually all the land was used for small scale agriculture by a variety of tenants, and the manor house was sited within its own small orchard and croft (Chapter 1). The precise beginnings of the transformation of the land into gardens, park and woodlands is unknown, but it is certain that the major changes were initiated by Charles Jennens Jnr in about 1750, at the same time as the new hall was being constructed.

Early Developments

The father and son team of John Grundy senior and junior[1] are the only names that can be attached to any survey work at Gopsall or to the creation of possible designs and layouts for the gardens and park surrounding the manor house. In his early career and while living in Congerstone, John Grundy Snr was employed by Charles Jennens Snr to survey the Gopsall estate with a view to improving the water supply to the house. Subsequently, Grundy proposed the installation of his version of a 'multiplying wheel bucket engine', originally developed in Italy in 1616, but only introduced into England in about 1728 by George Gerves. More importantly, in terms of the layout of the garden and park, John Grundy Jnr produced a detailed plan for Charles Jennens Jnr in 1749.[1] This plan is said to have included the pioneering use of a cement-cored dam 300 yards long to hold back water for a large lake. Grundy Jnr also surveyed the estate, in terms of its water supply, and determined, as had his father previously, that the house was 72ft higher than the "*fine spring*" about half a mile from the house.[2] He subsequently suggested the use of a 'double engine', with significantly improved performance over his father's design, to provide enough water to supply the house and, possibly, his proposed lake and water garden features. This engine was to be housed in a tower, 70-80ft high, designed by Mr Sands of Spalding and built of brick with rustic quoins, door cases and window frames. It is not known whether the engine was ever installed and there is no evidence that a brick and stone tower ever existed at Gopsall.

John Grundy junior
(1719-1783)

Whether Jennens had any input into Grundy's plan is unknown, but it is almost certainly true that he had a significant influence on the gardens and associated buildings that were actually built. John Grundy Jnr kept meticulous notes about the surveying and engineering projects he oversaw, but none exist about Gopsall, suggesting that, apart from drawing up his plan, he played no part in the construction of the gardens or parkland features that were actually instituted by Jennens. Although no direct evidence exists, it has been suggested that David and William Hiorn supervised the construction of the gardens, as well as the building of the hall; both projects were known to have developed simultaneously.[2] Certainly, the Hiorn brothers did include aspects of Grundy's garden plan in their plans for the service blocks (e.g. The Canal is shown in their plans for the east stable block) and they also designed many of the garden buildings.

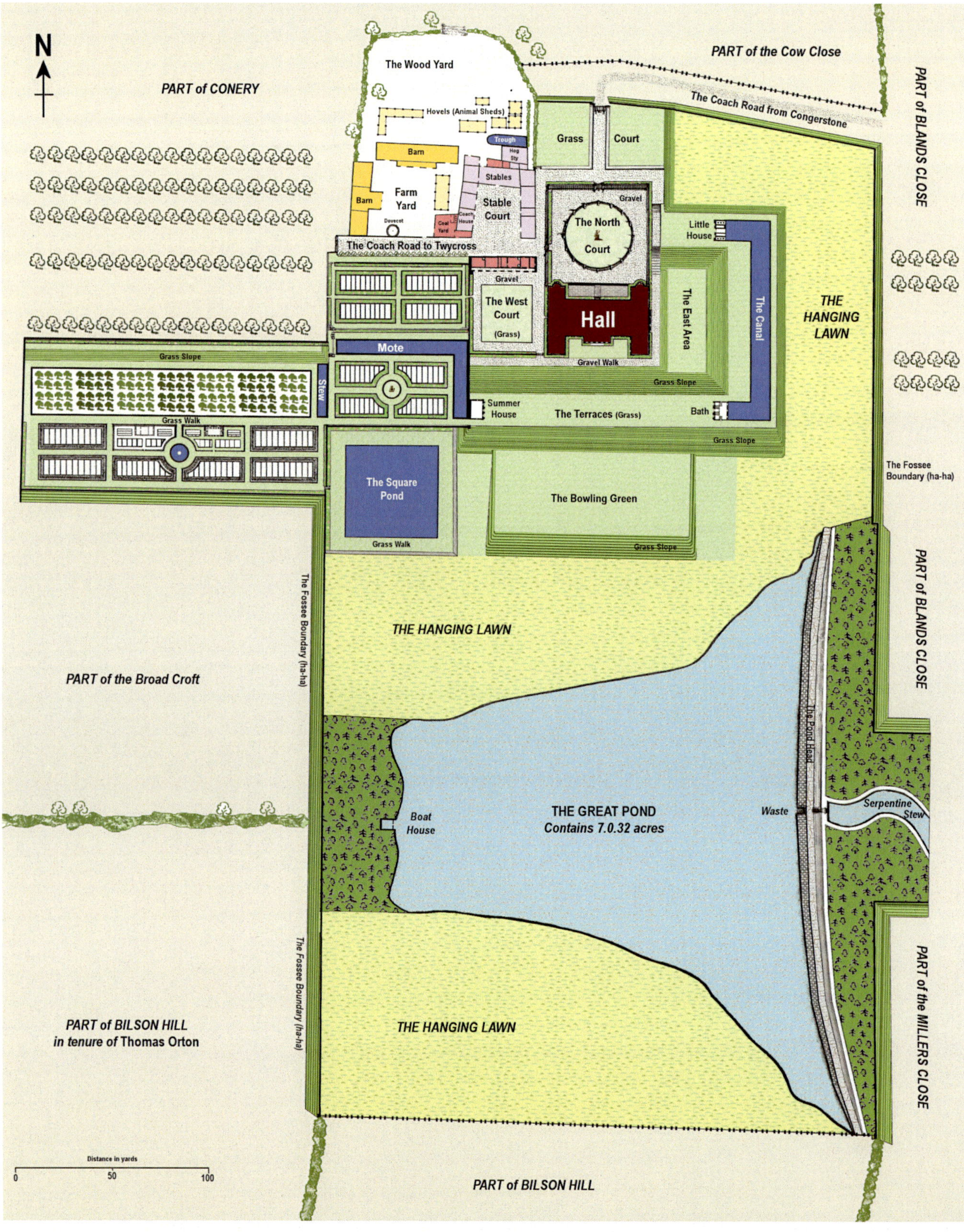

Survey plan of the house and grounds at Gopsall by John Grundy, dated 1749.[1]

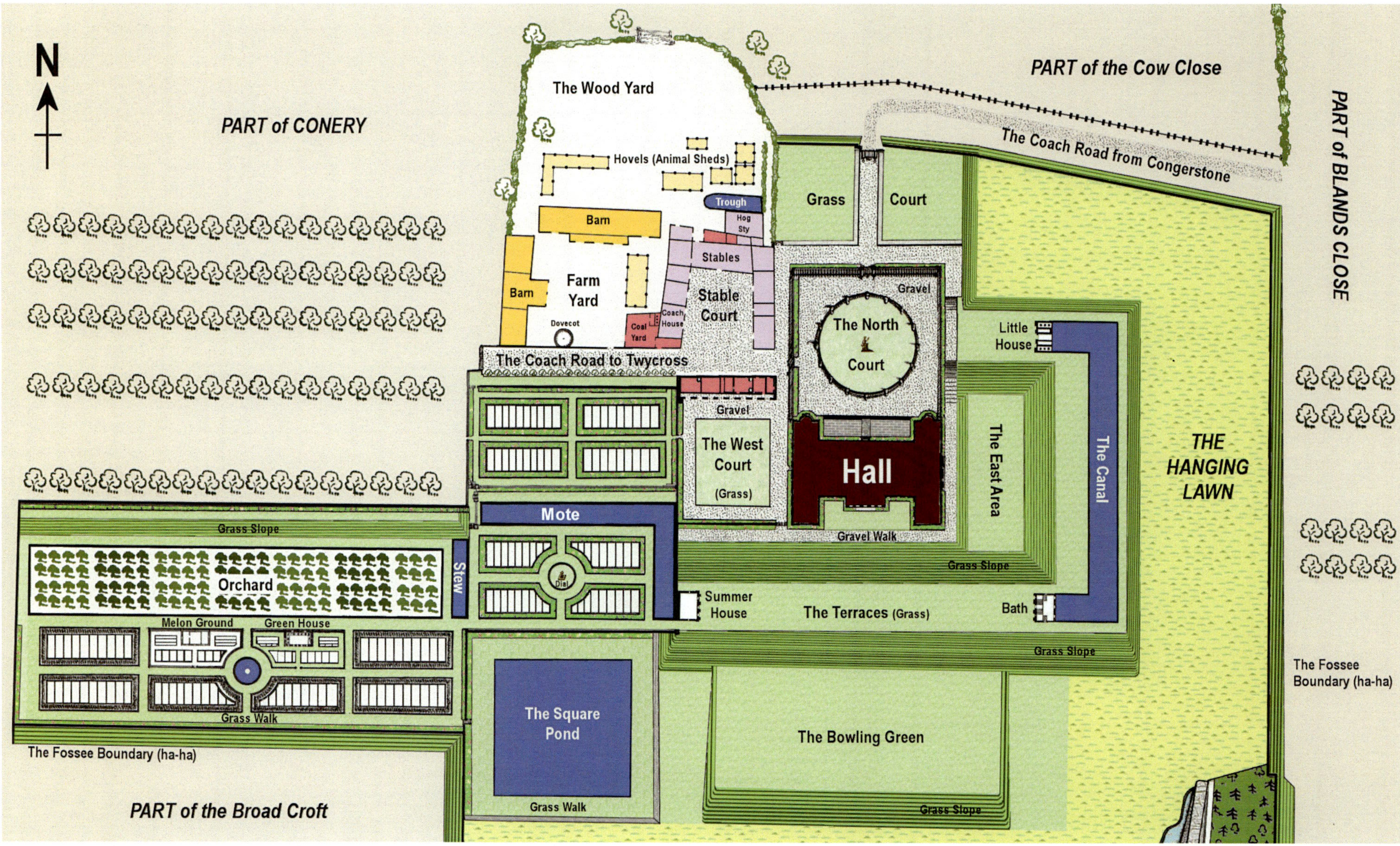

Detail from the 1749 plan showing the formal gardens and existing stables and farmyard.

Top: Painting (c.1765) by an unknown artist showing the hall, Great Pond, the dam, a summerhouse, a garden rotunda and the temple surmounted by the statue of Religion at the edge of The Race Course (Public Domain).
Bottom: Engraving by J. Walker (1791) showing a similar view and content to the painting.[3]

Today, virtually nothing remains to show where the gardens existed except for the very well-preserved walls of the 3.6 acre walled kitchen garden, a few ancient cedar trees and some elevation changes in the surrounding fields. However, thanks to photographs, some written memories from the last 100 years (Chapter 7), a saved memoir of a gardening family from the mid-1800s (see later) and John Grundy junior's 1749 plan[1] and his 1750 description of the hall and gardens,[2] we can rebuild the garden, even if only in our heads.

Gopsall gardens changed over the years, as do all great gardens with maturing planting and fashionable adjustments, but the basic layout can be seen in all versions. A grand house at its

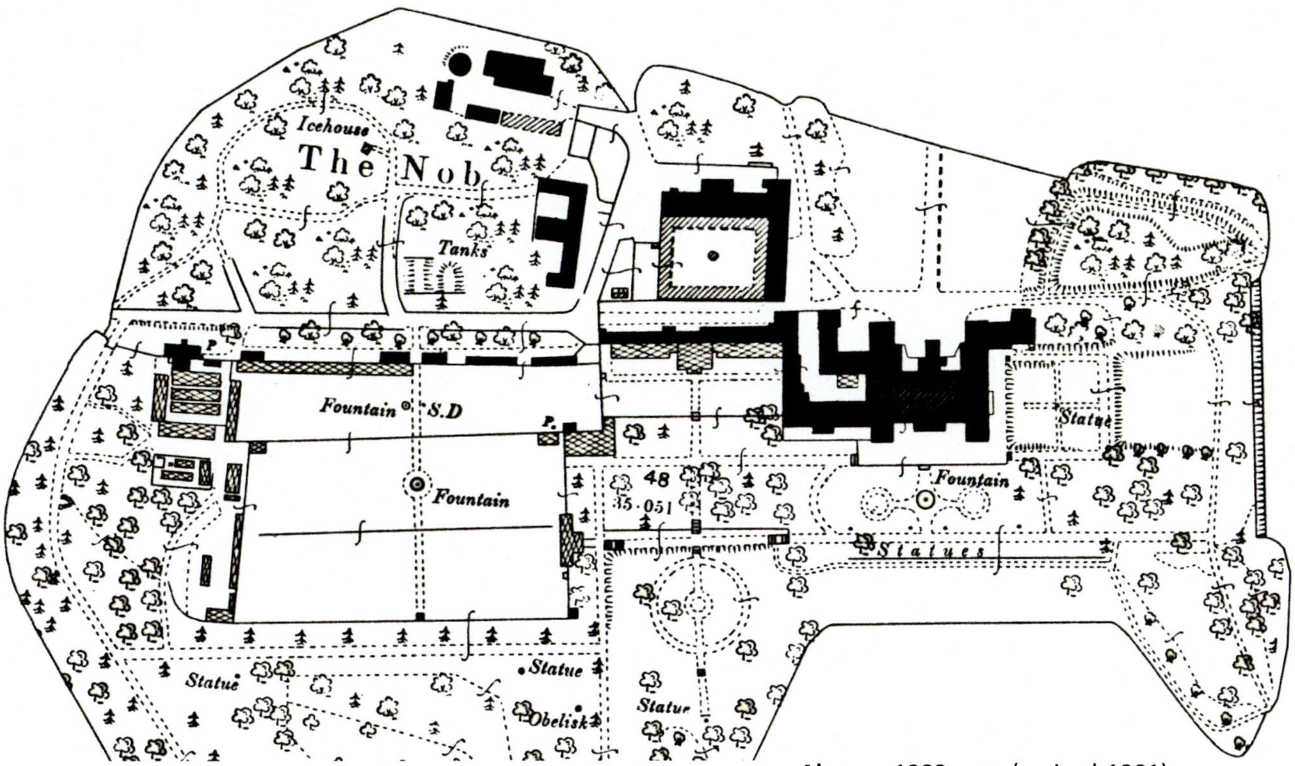

Above: 1903 map (revised 1901) of Gopsall Hall and gardens.
Below: 1903 map overlaid with outline of Grundy's 1749 garden plan showing overlap of many garden features and buildings.

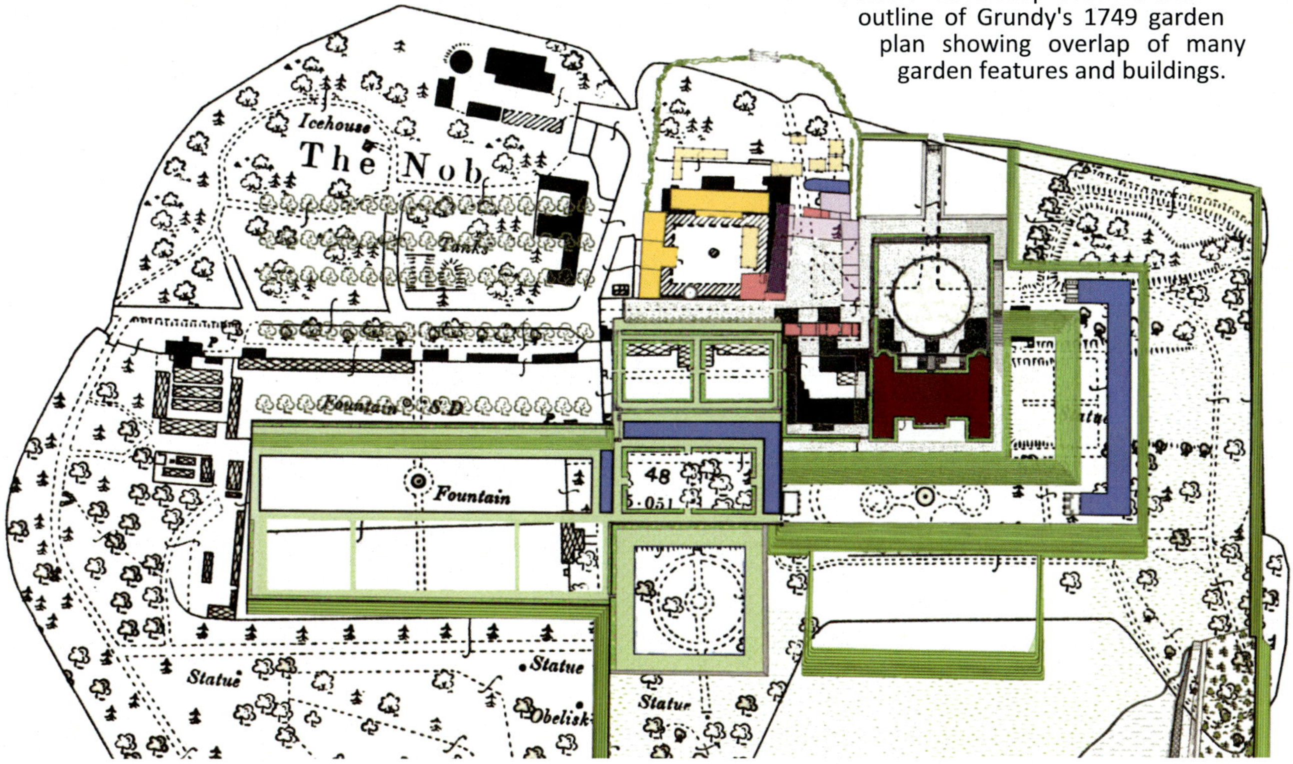

centre, formal flower beds laid out to its south and east, a kitchen garden west of the house and a range of sweeping lawns to the north, south and east. Stabling and service areas, providing daily requirements, nestled close to the north-western end of the house where there were open views out across the garden on three sides to the wider park and estate. It is unfortunate that we have no contemporary information about the construction of the gardens. However, when the Grundy plan is overlaid onto the 1886 and 1903 Ordnance Survey maps of Gopsall gardens, it is clear that the major levels and components of the plan were carried out. Thus, while John Grundy's design may not have been executed exactly as he planned, it did provide the basis for what was originally laid out by Charles Jennens and continued, in essence, until the last days of Gopsall's gardens.

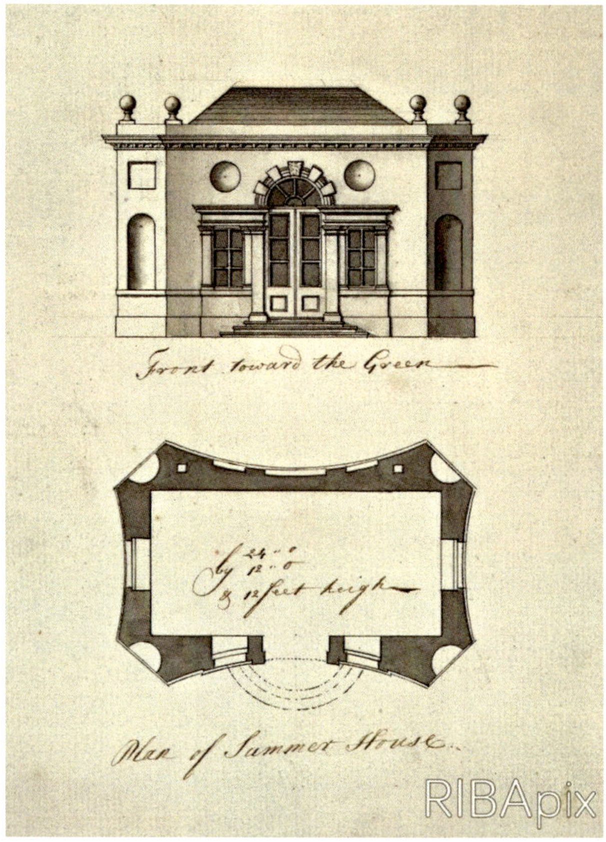

Plan and front elevation of a summerhouse by David and William Hiorn (24x12ft; 12ft high).
RIBA Collections

The broad sweep of grass (The Hanging Lawn) to the south of the hall sloped down to The Great Pond; a dam having been constructed across the end of the valley and the ground behind flooded. The clay puddling used as waterproofing for this still exists and was 'rediscovered' by the family now farming this piece of land in the early 2000s, when a planning application was made to reinstate the dam and Great Pond. The only other evidence that Grundy's pond existed is in an undated painting by an unidentified artist and an engraving produced in 1791 by John Throsby. On top of the dam was a track-way leading from The Race Course wood (Part of Bilson Hill on Grundy's map) towards the house. Both the painting, often incorrectly attributed to Pieter Tillemans, and the engraving show an ionic rotunda on the far bank close to the north end of the dam and a summerhouse to the left (west). The latter is similar in appearance to the plans for a summerhouse drawn up by the Hiorn brothers. No trace of these buildings exists today. By contrast, the rotunda or temple on the near bank in the painting, topped with a sculpted figure, represents the temple, the ruins of which can still be seen.

When the water level reached close to the top of the dam a spillway, created at the centre point, allowed it to overflow down a cascade into the Serpentine Stew. A contemporary description says it ran away to 'somewhere' near the woods (but see description by John Grundy[2]). It can only have been built by hand with shovels and spades. So, creating the dam and clay puddling the whole area to waterproof the 7-acre pond must have been a very large undertaking which agrees with the accepted estimate of the overall garden construction costs of between £80,000 and £100,000, a huge amount for the 1750s. Using an equivalence cost calculator, we arrive at a figure of between £18m - £23m in 2021 to produce the same garden. For comparison, in 2020 the Royal Horticultural Society's new 154-acre garden 'Bridgewater' in Salford was being built at a cost of £31m. Gopsall's gardens, as originally planned by John Grundy, including the Great Pond and surrounding lawns but excluding the hall, farmyard, stables and outbuildings, were just 36 acres, and funded by the one private owner.

Grundy's 1749 plan shows a formal layout close to the house with service yards crowded in upon them, as would have been the style at that time, with the house and garden sitting very much in a farming landscape; Cow Close, Broad Croft and The Conery[4]. Formal flower beds sat side by side with a large square pond, grass walks and, on the east side of the hall, a canal. One flower bed was surrounded on two sides by a 'Mote' and a third side was bordered by a stew pond, for supplying fish to the kitchen. Further west was proposed an orchard and the kitchen garden, including a melon ground and areas under glass. All these features were still present in the late 19th and early 20th centuries, though the square pond was a sunken garden, the north flower beds included a glass 'show house' and the orchard and kitchen gardens were now only part of a larger walled garden.

The hall, built on a flat platform, was surrounded by sloping grass and much was made of the elevation changes in the Grundy design. A large flat area to the south of the hall was designated a Bowling Green. In other areas hedged enclosures of grass were employed as ornament. It may seem to us today, that lawns are fairly uninteresting, but given that little or no mechanical cutting equipment was available at the time, it demonstrates once again the wealth and commitment of Charles Jennens to be able to employ enough manpower to upkeep such high maintenance areas; huge areas to cut with scythe and sickle. It wasn't until 1830, 80 years after Jennens' first garden was built, that Englishman Edwin Beard Budding invented the first mechanical lawnmower.

Perhaps the most famous garden/parkland structure built by Charles Jennens was the temple, which has been the subject of lots of interest for many years. George Frideric Handel, a regular visitor to Gopsall, is widely reported as having composed some of his music, including the 'Messiah', while sitting in the temple, admiring the view across the lake to the hall; sadly, this is a fallacy. Both 'Messiah' (1741) and 'Gopsal' (c.1744), the tune to the Charles Wesley hymn 'Rejoice the Lord is King', could only have been composed before the new hall, gardens, lake and temple were constructed and whilst the 17th century house was still standing. Furthermore, as the temple was not thought to have been built until the late 1750s,[5] it is almost certain that Handel never saw the temple or sat in it, as he became blind in 1753 and died in April 1759. Charles Jennens was a friend of Handel and wrote the libretto for 'Messiah' before starting the building of the new hall. It is possible that Handel composed some of his later music at the 'new' Gopsall Hall but he produced very little music after 1753.

Situated on a gentle eminence at the edge of The Race Course wood, the temple provided an

Design for a garden temple by James Paine.
RIBA Collections

An Ionic rotunda by David and William Hiorn.
RIBA Collections

important focal point in the view south across the ornamental lake (The Great Pond) from the hall and formal gardens. There were no temple structures in Grundy's original plans for the gardens and formal parkland but, in his account of a visit to Gopsall in the summer of 1750, he states that *"It is proposed, as an entertainment to the eye, to fix a Gothic temple or triumphal arch of stonework on the top of that hill* (i.e. Bilson Hill) *but the design is not fully fixed upon"*.[2] The original plans for the temple were drawn up in about 1750 by James Paine who also produced designs for the hall interiors, most of which were not executed. However, in about 1755, further plans were produced for Charles Jennens by William and David Hiorn depicting an open temple which appears to be a simplified version of the elaborate and decorative structure favoured by Paine. This simplified version conforms to the structure of the ruin in existence today and must have been constructed in the late 1750s, as the Hiorns finished work at Gopsall in 1759/60 (David Hiorn died in 1758).

The temple was erected as a memorial to a friend of Charles Jennens, the classical scholar Edward Holdsworth (1684-1746). It was octagonal externally but internally circular, with eight columns and surmounted with a domed roof. The whole structure was surrounded by a brick-built ha-ha and entered via steps on the south side. A statue of Religion (Roubiliac, c.1760; Chapter 12) adorned the domed roof and a cenotaph (Richard Hayward, 1764), with inscriptions in memory of Holdsworth, stood within. There was also a Greek inscription around the frieze of the temple just below the statue of Religion, translated it read as:

"Thanks be to God who gives us the victory through Our Lord Jesus Christ. A temple of victory"

(First Epistle to the Corinthians XV, 57)

The temple was partially collapsed by 1835. The statue of Religion was removed and donated to Leicestershire Museums and Art Galleries in 1857, but where it had been for the 22 years immediately after the collapse of the temple is unknown. It was gifted to the newly opened Leicester Museum by Richard Penn Curzon, 1st Earl Howe *"As a tribute of regard and goodwill towards the metropolis of his native county"*.[5] The movements of the Holdsworth cenotaph, sculpted by Richard Hayward (1728-1800), after the partial collapse of the temple are confused. Accounts in White's Directory (1863 and 1877) clearly state that the cenotaph was used as ornamentation in the flower gardens at the east front of the hall. However, at some time later it

Historic England Archive

Gopsall Temple ruins with the Holdsworth cenotaph within.

was placed in the centre of the sunken garden and in the early 1900s it had been returned to the ruined temple as shown in the photograph. It is likely that this move to the temple was temporary as most early 20th century photos of the cenotaph show it in the gardens at the east front, where it remained throughout World War II and until the hall was demolished in 1951.

Both the statue and cenotaph can now be seen at Belgrave Hall, Leicester. The temple ruin was listed by English Heritage in 1996 but is seldom visited, even though there is a permissive footpath to the temple which stands in the privately owned Race Course wood.

The parkland saw significant change in the early 1800s. The Great Pond and dam appear to have disappeared by 1830, as descriptions of the park fail to mention them, whereas the temple at the edge of The Race Course wood is invariably described. Whether loss of the dam and lake was an intentional change, or the result of failure of the dam and/or lack of sufficient water supply, is unknown. In addition, by 1830, the 1st Earl Howe had increased the size of the parkland from about 300 acres to 580 acres and *"it now contains the greater part of the liberty of Gopsall and about 100 acres in the parishes of Bilston, Twycross and Shackerstone"*.[6]

Top: The temple as it appeared for most of the 20th century. **Middle:** The cenotaph in the east front flower beds.[7] **Bottom:** The cenotaph in the sunken garden. **Bottom right:** Detail - Pope's obelisk, sited near the southeast corner of the walled garden, can just be seen in the distance behind the cenotaph.

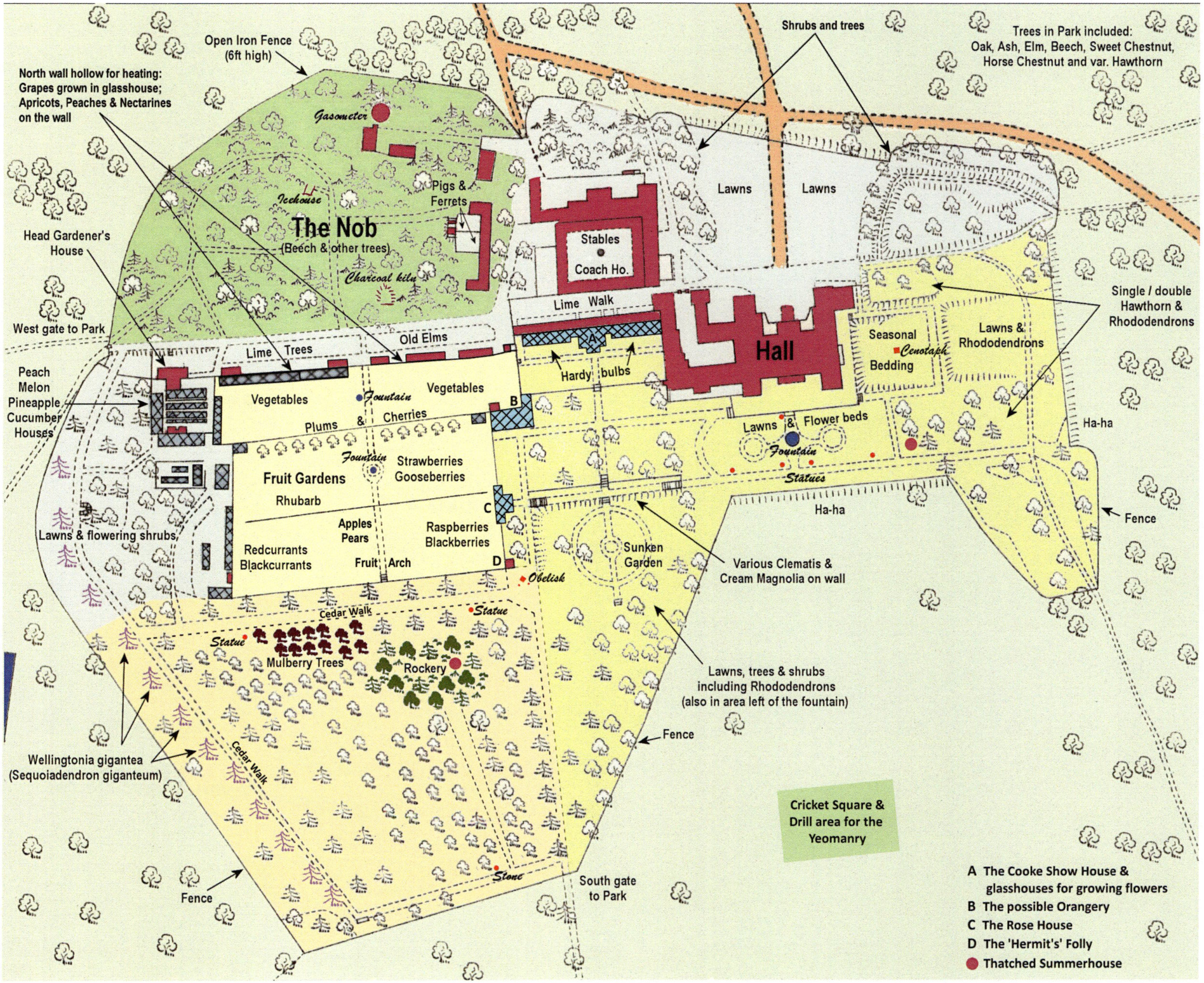

Gopsall Hall & Gardens

Details of the planting of the gardens in about 1868, as described by Arthur Sage, son of the Head Gardener, Emmanuel Sage.

Emmanuel was employed at Gopsall from the summer of 1855 until shortly after the death of the 1st Earl Howe in May 1870.

The map includes features from both 1886 & 1903 OS maps and those seen in photos of the gardens and park.

KEY

- Buildings
- Park
- Formal Gardens
- Cedar Walk
- Walled Gardens
- Glasshouses
- The Nob
- West and north Gardens including Front Lawns

Measurements of the parkland surrounding Gopsall Hall shown on the 1886 and 1903, 25-inch Ordnance Survey maps, confirm this and give an acreage of 553; 589 acres if the hall and gardens are included.[8]

Over the 100 or so years following Grundy's first design and the construction of Jennens' garden, much of the detail changed but, unfortunately there are virtually no records of when the developments took place. Several additional garden buildings were introduced and garden follies, stone urns in large numbers, elaborate steps and colonnaded walling were placed throughout. Items were acquired from far and wide, even an obelisk being brought from Alexander Pope's garden in Twickenham. Sophia Charlotte, Baroness Howe of Langar (widow of Penn Assheton Curzon and mother of Richard Penn Curzon, later 1st Earl Howe) acquired a property next to Pope's villa in 1803 and, to stop the hoi polloi visiting the dead poet's house and spoiling her views, purchased and demolished Pope's villa in 1807.[9]

Looking north along the path on the east side of the Cedar Walk area of the gardens.[7] The 'Hermit's Folly' at the southeast corner of the walled garden and Pope's obelisk can be seen straight ahead (see Chapter 12).

The Gardens

A major development in the 1850s was that the kitchen garden was extensively increased in size to 3.6 acres and enclosed in red brick walls. At the same time a large range of glasshouses was introduced. Walled gardens might be considered the period version of silicon valley. Newly discovered crops were brought into the country and, often being tender, had to be grown under cover in specially constructed heated glasshouses. Even the very walls of Gopsall's kitchen garden were heated to ensure the worst of our weather didn't interfere with growing such crops imported from the Empire. The north wall had a series of coal fired grates inserted into it and serpentine-like flues carried the hot fumes, through the wall to discharge smoke at the top from chimneys, thus heating the brickwork and keeping tender crops safe. Imagine being the Journeyman gardener tasked with keeping these and the glasshouse boilers alight all night through the winter or explaining to the head gardener (Emmanuel Sage from 1855 to 1870) why the crops had succumbed to the frost!

At this time of Empire, Britain and its gardening aristocracy could and did spend huge amounts to show off their wealth and ability to control the horticultural environment. The 1st Earl Howe was no exception and Gopsall's gardening and farming reputation was second to none (Chapter 5). Head gardeners from different estates, vied with each other to produce specimens their employers could boast about. Gopsall head gardeners (Chapter 6) proved to be very successful at this and some went on to open their own plant nurseries when they left Lord Howe's service. Peaches, nectarines, grapes, melons and cucumbers were recorded as having their dedicated houses at Gopsall and, in 1902, a total of over 40 glasshouses[10] were recorded under the care of head gardener Joseph Lee (Chapter 6). In addition to exotic products, the gardeners had to grow the staples, potatoes, brassicas, root vegetables and so on, but not just in season, so methods for forcing were introduced and again Gopsall garden produced these out of season crops.[11]

Today we are used to going to the supermarket and getting whatever we want whenever we want it, regardless of the season. However, if the Gopsall family required produce it had to be produced on site and the walled gardens were there to make a family and its retinue of scores of workers self-sufficient. But more than feeding the estate, head gardeners had to cater for less

A view of the Rose House. The 'Hermit's Folly' built into the southeast corner of the walled garden is on the left and the north part of the sunken garden is in the foreground. Historic England Archive.

prosaic needs; cut flowers for the hall were required when the family was in residence and this meant house plants and flowers needed to be available in large numbers. Gopsall had a dedicated rose house and, although we can all grow roses outside in our gardens, managing to extend the season at both ends with very early and end of the season late blooms was no easy matter, but Gopsall's head gardeners had the luxury of the rose house to do just that. It was of course the perfect place for the family to take a rainy-day stroll.

Stabling and service areas providing most daily requirements were nestled close to the western end of the house. Maps of the gardens in 1886 and 1903 show a much-developed range of buildings and consequently, an evolved arrangement to the earliest incarnation of the garden. The planting layout is based upon the recollections of Arthur Sage, dating from the late 1860s, showing what it was like at what might be considered its zenith. Much of the detail in the descriptions that follow is based upon the memoir written by Arthur, a son of the head gardener, Emmanuel Sage (see Appendix), and photographs of the gardens and park, mainly dating from the early years of the 20th century.

The Cooke Show House viewed from the south (*above*) and the fountain in the entrance (*right*).

On an inclement day you could take a walk in the show house, conveniently built near to the west end of the hall and facing south. This stunning structure housed a range of plants produced in the working garden for show when at their best. At Gopsall this house was a particularly fine and elaborate double barrel-vaulted conservatory style building manufactured by A. Cooke and Son, who are sadly no longer trading.

Records tell us that citrus was grown, mainly for orange blossom, which was very popular in ladies' posies and for household arrangements. These orange trees will have been overwintered inside, where frost could be kept at bay over the cold months. No mention of Gopsall having an orangery is made anywhere but, shown on the 1903 plan of the gardens, there is a large, south facing, 'L' shaped glasshouse built against the walls of the kitchen garden (labelled B). Although it is not specifically identified on any plan or referred to in any text, it is reasonable to suggest that this glasshouse was an orangery and supplied blossom to the house, as recounted by Arthur Sage.

Gopsall gardeners record a large range of ornamental plants being produced and planted out each year in the various beds, as well as much hardy planting ("...*all kinds of hardy bulbs*") near the house, and in front of the walls of the hall and show house. Fountains appear to have been *de rigueur* and at least four are known, with two in the walled kitchen garden, somewhere unlikely to have been visited regularly by the family.

In 1853 John Veitch[12] a well-known plant nurseryman had seed and cuttings of the Wellingtonia tree (*Sequoiadendron giganteum*) brought into the country for the first time by his plant hunting team, the brothers Lobb. Remarkably, less than ten years later a row of 13 Wellingtonia had been planted (one for each of the family's children) at Gopsall.[13] These were rare items so we can infer that either the garden, the head gardener (Emmanuel Sage) and/or Lord Howe were regarded highly enough to have been allocated some of this new introduction by Veitch.

The garden was also well planted with Lebanon cedar trees (*Cedrus libani*), which in 1870 were reported as being so large they needed to be chained against the forces of the wind. These trees grow to a height of 130ft at maturity so must have been fairly old when the report was made; they were introduced into England around 1650. Some of these cedars still survive today. They were planted in two walks, one running north to south and the other east to west, bordering the south wall of the kitchen gardens; the area was known as Cedar Walk. They must have been very early plantings in the life of the garden. Peppered all over the garden and wider estate, were species of rhododendron and a walk around the area today shows some of their descendants still growing. These will have been new species introductions and at the time, very exotic. It's ironic that today many large gardens and estates, including those of the National Trust, are busy trying to eradicate *Rhododendron ponticum* as it seeds and spreads itself, muscling out more delicate or local flora.

View southwest from the south terrace showing the fountain and The Race Course wood.

Standing on the terrace of the south front in the early 20th century you would look past the three-tiered fountain, across the gardens to the temple and The Race Course wood. Flower beds cut out of the lawns and rows of standard roses spread left and right of the fountain and at either end of the terrace elaborate colonnaded steps, book ended by stone urns, led down to a lower level. If you walked right (west) along the terrace you would pass the front of the west wing of the hall and be able to make your way to the show house (up steps on the right), the orangery (straight ahead) or rose house, on the left after passing the orangery. Following this path south, with the sunken flower garden on your left and the wall of the kitchen garden on your right, always moving downhill, you would have arrived at a Folly, built into the south-east corner of the kitchen garden walls. Some stories suggest that, in earlier times, one of the locals was employed as a 'Hermit' to sit inside and entertain visitors.

Paths met at this point and standing here you would have seen one of the Cedar Walks stretching away westwards and Pope's obelisk before you. Southwest from this junction, there was an area overhung with trees and planted with ferns where a rustic building and pergola, a small fountain and a rockery were constructed. There are several photos of the family taken here suggesting that the rockery was a favourite spot, perhaps because mulberries grew close by. A group from The Leicestershire Architectural Society, on an excursion to Gopsall in July 1864, made comment at the amount of fruit growing on the mulberry trees that were planted close to the rockery and the south gate to the walled gardens.[14] Looking west along the walk, tops of pergolas would have been visible over the kitchen garden wall on your right, perhaps planted with cordon apples or pears. At the end of the walk is the Wellingtonia Avenue, running north-south, decorative but also a wind break protecting the gardens from damage by the prevailing westerlies.

The Cedar Walk running east - west at the southern edge of the walled kitchen garden.
Top: Looking west with the walled garden on the right; a pergola is projecting above the walls.
Bottom: Looking east along the Walk with the walled garden on the left. Pope's obelisk can be seen on the right of the walk; at this time not close to the southeast corner of the walled garden.

The Rockery with a thatched summerhouse (*top*) and a family gathering (*bottom*).

Walking north up the Wellingtonia Avenue, you arrive at the top of the slope on the west side of the kitchen garden. Here, just outside the walled garden and beyond a host of glasshouses, is the head gardener's cottage (it became the Steward's house later). Living here the head gardener was able to watch all activity (or inactivity) at any time of the day or night. The glasshouses needed attention pretty much 24 hours a day from one of the live-in Bothy boys (journeymen gardeners or apprentices)[15] on duty to feed the boilers or wall fireplaces. Turning right (east) in

The cottage that was the Head Gardener's House in the mid-1800s.

It was known as the Steward's House in the early 1900s and is now Gopsall Hall Farm farmhouse (see Chapter 14).

The photo shows the house walls covered in trellis, which gives the appearance of diamond brickwork.

Historic England Archive

Above: View east along the Lime Walk towards the hall. The wall of the stableyard is on the left and the Bothies and top of the Cooke Show House are on the right.

Right: Detail of the double barrel roof of the Cooke Show House.

Historic England Archive

front of the head gardener's cottage you could walk back towards the hall, beneath lime and elm trees and past the potting sheds, boiler room and the north wall of the kitchen garden; smoke curling from the chimneys on top of the heated wall.

Further on towards the hall, pleached limes formed an avenue on both sides of a cobbled walk (Lime Walk); some of the cobbling and lime trees survive today. On the right were the lean-to, brick-built, garden bothies built against the north wall of the show house and attached glasshouses. The journeymen lived, ate and slept in these bothies as long as they held their positions at Gopsall. Sticking up above the bothies and the wall, the magnificent show house's

Above: View east towards the Fish Pond, Viennese Bridge and Shackerstone Drive.

Left: Detail of the view with Nailstone Church spire on the horizon.

double-barrelled vaults would be clearly visible. If you continue straight ahead, down the Lime Walk, you would pass the courtyard gates before ending up at the north front of the hall. However, a return to the south front and terrace could be made via a gate on the right. After passing in front of the Cooke show house, you would be back on the south terrace having walked around the outside of the 3.6 acres of walled garden. If you continued your walk past the fountain towards the east front, the land slopes down and Shackerstone Drive and the village would be seen in the distance.

On the east front itself, lay a range of seasonally planted beds with the Holdsworth cenotaph, once inside the temple, in centre place on a 3-stepped plinth. With your back to the east front, framed by 18 massive sash windows, the two central ones working as doors onto the east terrace, you would have urns to both sides supported by dolphins and a pair of lions guarding the entrance. The geometric beds around the cenotaph planted with low growing subjects would allow a clear view across to a white stripe of a gravel trackway leading, dead straight, to Shackerstone lodge. Nearer, a wide avenue of trees and grass led to, in the mid-distance, a lake and a Viennese bridge that cut the view in half. To your right a cedar tree, planted by Edward VII in 1902, would have been starting to make growth but it's gone today. On your left, a tree-planted grass slope leading to the north front was a shrub border filled with a mix of specimens including, single and double hawthorn and the ubiquitous rhododendron. Walking to the end of the planted beds you would come across a sudden drop onto the grass below, a ha-ha,[16] constructed from brick 4-5 feet high, and designed to prevent the deer, sheep and cattle from the park straying into the garden, but totally invisible from the house. Similar structures protected the garden immediately south and north of the hall, whereas the rest of the gardens were guarded by wrought iron fences, six feet high. The ha-has and remains of some of the iron fencing are still visible today.

The north front of the hall showing an expanse of lawn and the ha-ha. Historic England Archive

The north front was the main entrance to the hall and consisted mainly of large sweeps of lawn with no planting; offering a plain green supporting backdrop for the hall itself. There were probably a few climbers to soften the stonework, with low hedges, maybe yew or box against the frontage, but nothing to detract from the architecture. After arriving at the north entrance, imagine the surprise the first time a visitor viewed the gardens from the south or east fronts.

To the northwest of the hall, The Nob was a mass of large beech trees and other native species, that hid some of the service areas of the estate and gardens. The Nob was the site of a large rookery and annual shoots used to take place in order to control the number of birds. Little in the way of ornamentation was planted in this area of the gardens, which also contained the icehouse, water tanks and an area used for producing charcoal.

As for the rest of the gardens, no planting plan exists for the walled kitchen gardens. However, it has been possible to piece together the recollections of Arthur Sage (see Appendix), a brief description of a visit to the gardens by the Leicestershire Architectural Society in 1864[14] and a few photographs, to give an idea of the interior layout in the late 1860s.

Inside the walled gardens the land sloped downwards away from the heated north wall to the south, taking best advantage of the sun's course. It was divided into three, roughly equal, sections by two brick walls, each of these slightly lower than the perimeter walls. A central path led from the gate in the north wall, past a small fountain to the right, down the sloping path through an opening in the first interior wall to the central section containing a larger fountain, surrounded by the gardeners' circular dipping pool where they filled their watering cans. The pergola-covered path then led through an opening in the next interior wall to the lower garden and straight on to a gate at the bottom of the slope, which exited onto the Cedar Walk running along the south side of the walled garden. This central path effectively subdivided the garden into six roughly equal plots.

The Vine House.[7]

The most northerly, top section of garden had a range of lean-to glasshouses against its south facing north wall. These heated glasshouses were planted with grapevines and photographs show how extremely successful this was. One head gardener, Emmanuel Sage, must have had a particular interest in vines for he eventually left Gopsall to set up a successful nursery in Atherstone where he specialised in indoor grape culture. In front of the glasshouses were planted crocus, hyacinth, tulips and, according to Arthur Sage, *"vast numbers of others too numerous to mention"*. These will have been grown for cutting to decorate the hall. The other section of the northern-most wall had no glass structures, but using the heated wall and the southern facing aspect, peaches, nectarines and apricots were cultivated. The rest of this part of the walled garden was planted with a range of vegetables.

Interior of the walled garden looking northwards up the garden slope. The path is covered in a rustic pergola and bordered both sides by dense herbaceous planting. It passes the central fountain and dipping pool, and ends at the gate in the north, heated wall.[7]

The north side of the first dividing wall was planted with cherries. This would have been the Morello cherry, a dark fruit often used in cooking and very popular in the mid to late 19th century. It fruited best facing north, hence its planting here. In the central, second section of the garden the south facing side of this dividing wall was planted with more cherries, the sweet dessert types, and plums. All these would usually be fan-trained against the wall. This area was obviously the fruit garden as many beds of strawberries, blackcurrants, red-currants, gooseberries and raspberries were recalled as being planted here and in the lower, south section of the walled garden. The central large round dipping pool and fountain would have been essential for watering to maximise fruit crops and to maintain the dense hebaceous planting along the length of the path.

Through the final interior wall was the lower section, also believed to have been dedicated to producing fruit. Pictures show a pergola or fruit walk, no doubt with an herbaceous border on both sides, as seen in the central part of the gardens. No one chose to record what was planted here, but many contemporary gardens had pear and apple varieties trained on walls and pergolas, and these would have been likely crops at Gopsall.

Each of the internal walls of the garden was designed specifically to produce fruit from trained trees, espalier, cordon or fan.[17] In an experiment in the 1980s, at a similar walled garden (Chilton Estate, near Chilton Foliat, Berks), it was demonstrated by horticultural expert Peter Thoday[18] that the difference in temperature on a summer day, between the most northerly wall of a garden and the most southerly wall, could be the equivalent of planting a tree in the south of England, and another in the south of France. Gopsall walled garden was a vital part of the estate's life.

No record of cold frames or cloches has been found but there must have been great numbers of these to support the glasshouse ranges. Just to the west of the walled garden, near the head gardener's cottage, was a bigger range of glasshouses and sheds, which will have been dedicated to specific crops. Arthur Sage recalls melons, cucumbers, white mushrooms and even pineapples being grown amongst others. Each of these crops had specific growing requirements, so we know that somewhere in this area was a melon pit, a cucumber house and a pineapple pit, not to mention bothy-style forcing sheds for mushrooms. We may wonder what level of quality was produced, but we know that at least one of the head gardeners chose to show produce at horticultural shows quite far afield. If you wanted to stay employed you didn't embarrass your employer, so we can assume the produce was, as expected, of high quality.

Left to right: A gardener (possibly Sam Pegg), Rev Ottley Warner (Rector of St Mary's Church, Congerstone and Domestic Chaplin to Earl Howe) and a friend of Viscount Curzon in the walled gardens. Note the fruit trees trained against the walls. Photo probably taken in September 1905 by Viscount Curzon.

The Park

The hall and gardens were centrally placed within the park, which was separated from them by either a ha-ha or metal fence. Unlike many contemporary parks, Gopsall was not walled at any point of its perimeter but was surrounded on all sides by woods. The largest of these, The Race Course, lay to the south of the hall on an elevated piece of ground and stretched east to west. Early in its life, when the hall and gardens were first laid out, the wood overlooked the flooded 'valley', John Grundy's Great Pond. Views into the park from the surrounding villages and farmland were mainly blocked by trees, but vistas from the hall, particularly down the valley to the east were expansive. About a third of the way along The Race Course from its eastern end was placed the temple, with the cenotaph inside dedicated to Edward Holdsworth, Charles Jennens' close friend. The temple was topped by the statue of 'Religion' by Roubiliac (c.1760), which was probably hoisted into position sometime after 1761.[5] After its partial collapse in c.1835 no reconstruction was attempted and it has stood as a folly ever since; being visible from the hall and garden site, as well as from further east.

For much of the 19th century, a flat area, once at the bottom of The Great Pond south of the hall, was a parade ground for the Leicestershire Yeomanry (renamed the Prince Albert's Own Leicestershire Yeomanry Cavalry in 1844). This was a volunteer force, originally made up from smallholders and tenant farmers, with the officers being drawn from the nobility or the landed gentry. They were used to support the civil authorities but were in active service during the Boer War and later conflicts. The Earls Howe held both honorary and commissioned roles in the Yeomanry. The same area was also used for cricket and, in the late 1800s and first years of the 20th century, it was recorded as one of the finest cricket squares in the County. In between doing duty for both uses, it was also used by grazing cattle. Being a fielder must have been hazardous after the cattle had spent time there!

The cricket square, complete with grazing cattle.[7]
This photograph appeared in the prospectus for The Gopsall Club (Chapter 10).

Moving further east in the park, following the perimeter, is the Fish Pond. Again, man-made, probably at sometime after 1820, and used both for fishing and boating; the pond survives today. The pond straddles the direct line from Shackerstone Drive to the east front of the hall. On its east side the pond originally overflowed down a blue-brick spillway under an elaborate Viennese bridge, which led from nowhere to nowhere but was a magnificent garden folly. A boat house was on the northern side of the pond. In about 1997 the central section of the Viennese bridge was still in place with the spillway beneath (Chapter 14). The Commissioners for Crown Lands (who owned the estate at the time) decided to demolish the remnants of the bridge and, sadly, all that remains now are the bridge piers and part of the spillway. For a few years after its demolition, the keystone of the arch bearing the letter 'H' (for Howe) was placed nearby, on what the authors consider a sad looking red brick plinth.

In keeping with the high level of detail found all around the park, the east front of Gopsall Hall was framed perfectly by the arch of the Viennese bridge and, in return, a view from the east front shows the entire Viennese Bridge with the Fish Pond in front and Shackerstone Drive running dead straight away into the distance. Local tradition has it that vast amounts of crockery from the hall which remained unsold at the demolition sale in 1951 were unceremoniously dumped into the pond. Certainly, one local individual remembers that, as a child in the late 1950s, one of her favourite pastimes was collecting 'sparklers' (pieces of tile from the hall that sparkled like sequins) and dipping in the pond to find and break china dishes and bowls from the hall. Who knows?

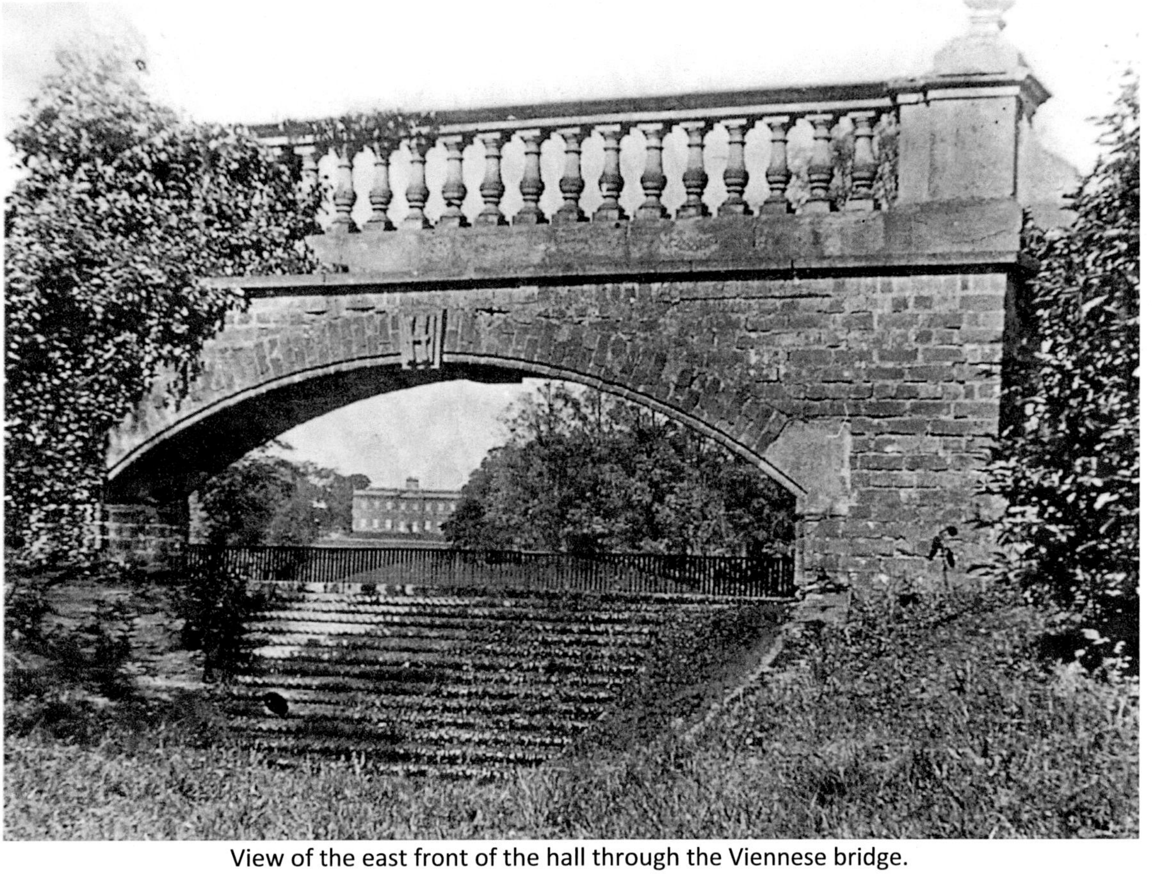

View of the east front of the hall through the Viennese bridge.

East of the Viennese bridge runs Shackerstone Drive or Avenue, which may have been called 'Fairmile' at one time and was planted on both sides with a range of lime trees and rhododendron. The surface of the drive was dressed in white gravel and was easily visible from the hall. It ended at Shackerstone lodge and the gates onto the road between Shackerstone and Congerstone. It was this drive that was used for speed trials in the 1920s and 1930s (Chapter 10). During World War II, a young Brian McCullam (Chapter 7), remembers helping Italian prisoners of war who were felling the mature pine and sycamore trees that lined Shackerstone Drive. The timber was sent to Walkers of Syston where it was made into pit props.

Following the perimeter of the park north from the Fish Pond, past the site of a windmill (no longer present) used for pumping water, are The Duckpond and associated woods; Duckpond Covert. Access to, and provision of, clean water at Gopsall was a significant problem. The "*great ill conveniency*" of Gopsall was, in John Grundy Jnr's view, its lack of water.[2] A windmill "*for pumping water*", shown on early OS maps, may have been in place in the 18th century. However, this was the site where John Grundy proposed the installation of his water lifting machine within an engine house some 70-80ft high. As this was the main on-site source of clean water for Gopsall, it became the subject of some discussion when the canal and, later, the railway were planned to cross the land close to the north of the park. When work commenced on building the canal, the canal company guaranteed that if any water was abstracted from the spring they would compensate the owners (Penn Assheton Curzon, at the time) by up to £50,000.[19]

Further to the north of Duckpond Covert, is the Ashby canal, hidden from the view from the hall by Bellows Clump, Square Spinney and the obviously planted screen of Shackerstone Park Coverts. A finger of Shackerstone Park Covert, called 'Green Clump', originally pointed back to the hall across the northern park, past Kit's Pit; possibly one of the clay pits used to puddle the lakes. Shooting was a big part of life on the estate and the many coverts were established for the breeding of pheasants. Members of the British Royal Family frequently came for the shooting season, along with German Royalty, British Aristocracy, members of parliament and the great and the good. Once again there appears to have been money enough to employ keepers, beaters, woodmen and victuallers (butchers) for dressing the game birds.

A gamekeeper, his hound and a deer carcass; pheasants were not the only game shot in Gopsall Park. A large number of Sika and Red deer roamed the park and were an important souce of meat. Sika deer, which are black in winter, were first introduced into Eire and England in 1860.

Following the park perimeter southwest from the canal, past Lord's and Kennel Coverts, are The Kennels (Kennel cottages today). Maps published in 1886 and 1903 clearly show 2 buildings, one of which is associated with animal pens and exercise areas. Records show that The Kennels at Gopsall existed in the late 1790s and, from about 1798 to 1812, they were often used to house Lord Vernon's hounds, of the Meynell Hunt.[20,21] The 2nd Earl, when Viscount Curzon, was master of the Atherstone hunt and owner of the pack and many horses, but the hounds were kennelled at Witherley. In fact, at that time he often stayed at Atherstone Hall. In the months before becoming the 2nd Earl Howe he made arrangements to dispose of the pack of hounds and the hunters.[22] During the latter part of the 19th century/early 20th century, The Kennels were occupied by gamekeepers and their families. The cottages now on The Kennels site are likely to incorporate parts of the original structures (Chapters 12 & 14).

The Kennels as shown on the 1886 OS Map. By 1903, the most westerly building was enlarged, encompassing the area marked with an asterisk; the number of runs reduced to three; the fences quartering the exercise area removed and an outbuilding erected at the southern edge of Kennel Covert.

South from The Kennels, the park perimeter is marked by Gopsall Wood which passes through an area called Twycross Park and on to London lodge (now demolished) within Lodge Plantation, the southernmost part of the park. Northeast from here is the western end of The Race Course, which stretches east to the temple and hall.

Gopsall Park had four entrance routes each with its own lodge - Shackerstone lodge, Farm or Snarestone lodge, Bilstone lodge

London or Twycross Lodge, sadly demolished along with the hall. It was the home of George (Bill) Smith (Head gamekeeper) and his family in c.1920.

Shackerstone Entrance & Lodge

The stone pillars, gates and fencing at the end of Shackerstone Drive. The gates are no longer present and the stone pillars now lack their original carved tops and ball ornaments.

Behind the stone pillars are two globe lights on cast iron pillars, which are no longer present. Today a modern 5-bar gate hangs from a pair of ornate cast iron pillars (Chapter 14).

The gates at the Twycross and Bilstone entrances were sold in the sale of fixtures and fittings in 1951 (Chapter 12) but the fate of the Shackerstone Drive gates is unkown.

The lodge at the end of the drive was built in about 1890, after the opening of the Moira West to Nuneaton railway line and building of Shackerstone station. It was at this time that Shackerstone Drive superseded Twycross Gate as the principal entrance to Gopsall.

After the sale of the Gopsall Estate by the Crown in 2017-18, the drive and the lodge became part of the so-called 'Shackerstone Estate'.

Bilstone Lodge stood at the eastern end of The Race Course wood and was the home of Tom Clarke and his family in c.1930.

and London or Twycross lodge. The latter, built in 1819 and originally the main entrance, was a very grand affair designed by Jeffry Wyatt. It was based on the arch of Constantine in Rome (commissioned in 315AD) which, although fifteen hundred years older, can still be visited today, unlike London lodge, which was demolished along with the hall. The other lodges were much simpler affairs and were just small cottages big enough to house the people required to manage the gates. Nothing remains of Bilstone, Snarestone and London lodges, although a few cobblestones and several large stone blocks (probably part of the gate foundations) can be seen at the site of the latter (Chapter 14). Bilstone lodge is said to have been dismantled brick by brick and transported to the USA. By contrast, Shackerstone lodge survives largely unchanged, next to the stone piers.

Mid-19th century memories of Gopsall Gardens and Park

In 1995, while the authors were researching for a village exhibition, extracts of a document, said to have been written by a Gopsall head gardener's son, appeared in a small book on the history of Gopsall by Glynis Oakley.[23] The account was unsigned and undated and gave few clues as to who the author might be. It did, however, name the author's brothers and their position in a family – 1st son, 2nd son etc. Using that, some knowledge of Gopsall, White's 1863 Directory and the UK census documents, together with the brothers' Christian names we were able to identify the Head Gardener in question as Emmanuel Sage, and the author as his son, Arthur Sage. Emmanuel had an interesting career, recalled in the chapter 'Below Stairs' (Chapter 6).

The memoir is a remarkable feat of memory being written fifty years after things occurred by a man in his late 70s and recalls Gopsall between about 1865-1870. It appears that Emmanuel Sage left Gopsall voluntarily after the death of the 1st Earl because, in Arthur's own words, "*whereas the old Earl and Countess lived for the hall and all the surroundings, the new Earl took very little interest*". Certainly, the 1st Earl was very keen on all aspects of farming and horticulture.

Arthur was born in 1862[24] and the Appendix is an unedited account of his life at Gopsall, which includes some minor factual and grammatical errors. It demonstrates a love for all things natural, and it makes for fascinating reading.

APPENDIX

Gopsall by Arthur Sage

Introduction

The following is the record of events that occurred during the author's experience in the theatre of life during a period of more than seventy four years.' It is the first twenty-seven years of his life that is mostly dealt with, such time being spent in England where he was born, the rest part of his life has been in Australia. Some of the records are just simple facts, some a little humorous, others historical; but all of them are what actually did occur but all that is written is from memory not any references or notes being used, a little allowance must be made for the correctness of actual dates, and perhaps in the details of some of the events, otherwise the records are true in the principle. Some of the records are those in which the Author took part himself on the Stage of Life while the other events are those which he viewed like millions of others as one of the audience in the Theatre of Life during a period of over seventy years. I shall divide all these memories of events recorded into specific parts, thus making the reading of such more easily understood.

Birth

More than seventy years ago I was born at Gopsall Hall, Leicestershire, an estate which was owned and occupied by Lord Howe whose family name was Curzon. This was a family which had been for many years very much associated in many ways with India, and in this nineteenth century, since the end of the Great War a member of that family, Lord Curzon, was viceroy of India[25]. Gopsall Hall was where Handel composed his great work 'The Messiah'. Many may have heard or read about 'The Jennings Millions' as it was called, an estate that was in 'Chancery'. Gopsall Hall was at one time part of the Jennings estate but with this difference that it was given to Lady Howe, who was a member of the Jennens family before the death of Mr. Jennings[26]. My father was head gardener to the Earl Howe of the time. Myself and three brothers were born there and spent all our childhood days in the beauties of its surroundings. Before going further I would like to ask any reader a rather strange question, "*what is the farthest back in your life that your memory can go to recall an event with any certainty?*" I will answer it myself in relating my own experience:

The Yeomanry on the north lawns at Gopsall Hall (early 1900s).

"*It was a Sunday morning, I had gone to the village Church with my father. I cannot remember my age but I do remember this: I had a half-grown pet kitten of which I was very fond and when I came back from Church my pet kitten was dead. Some of the young visiting nobleman at the hall had taken the terrier dogs from the stables out rabbit catching but my pet kitten was the victim.*"

Gopsall Hall and its surroundings

Gopsall Hall was a large and also a very ancient building. I cannot describe anything about the interior of the hall, my memory is more concerned with its exterior. The north front of the hall was the front and main entrance. A carriage drive led up to the front door, on each side of the drive was a stretch of beautiful grass with a background of beautiful shrubs inter-mingled with large specimens of the oak and many other varieties of trees. As one stood at the front of the hall a pretty view of that part of the park could be taken. A grassy stretch of land with magnificent trees of various ages, some of the oaks and elms very old indeed while wandering among them were the pretty deer of many kinds nibbling the grass in summertime, or when the ground was covered with snow, they could be seen turning it over in search of the acorns under the great oaks. Halfway across the park was a level flat that was used for cricket and many other games. At this spot the Yeomanry used to come to drill at various times. The Yeomanry, as they were called at that time, were the farmers or their sons who lived in the surrounding country, they had their own horses and equipment. No doubt they were the remains of the old custom from which the Lord or Duke of the district obtained his followers in their little wars among themselves. What are called the volunteers of the present day.

View of the south front of the hall showing the ha-ha and flower beds.[7]

On the east front of the hall again a vista of beauty although slightly different, for in this instance the flower beds of many designs and patterns were close to the hall, each year according to the seasons these beds were gay with the choicest of flowers. Then a lower level, with flower and green lawns spread out before the eye. Here and there were interspersed in the lawns, small beds of beautiful rhododendrons, and other small shrub on either side of this view were larger trees or shrubs, such as the many different coloured double and single hawthorne. Farther on was again a view of the park with its trees while in the far distance could be seen a large pond of water where the deer or any cattle in the park could drink. In the wintertime when frozen over this pond was used for skating. Also, a supply of ice was obtained to store in the Ice house for summer use.

On the south front of the hall again were the many flowerbeds of beautiful varieties but here the shrubs perhaps were the most conspicuous, especially the rhododendrons of which there were great masses. Again from this part a view of the park spread out before the eye with its big oaks or elms but the distance was very much shorter, and its background was the woods or plantations of big pine trees and many others, where the pheasant and other kinds of game were safely guarded for the pleasure of special shooting days, but there is more concerning the south front for it extended even farther. Its extension being really the south of the western side of the hall, in the same way as the northern side of the park has an extension west. This will be understood when reading about the western side of the hall.

Above: Looking west along The Lime Walk. The stables are on the right and gardeners' bothies on the left.

Left: Detail of the above showing two carriages and pair approaching the gates.

The western side of the hall is the servant's domestic part. A road from the hall going west. On the south side elms, trees of many years, then a row of magnificent limes, finally the head gardener's house (where I was born) ending at the park entrance. All on the south of this road. On the north of this road, as it leaves the hall, are the stables and coach-houses, store-rooms, carpenters' and blacksmith's shops, gun-rooms, and butcher's conveniences for attending to the game as required. Farther along by this road was a plantation of enormous beech and other trees, where hundreds of crows built their nest, and sportsmen came annually to shoot the young rooks. In this plantation was the gasworks to supply the hall. A pig yard for stable refuse. A place where a number of ferrets were kept. And an Ice House built underground. Also, the charcoal was made there to supply the hall. A fire is made then fairly thick logs are placed on it like the roof of a circular house then the whole is covered with dirt, it is really baked not burnt. On the south side of this road as it leaves the western side of the hall first are the potting sheds used by the gardeners, then a high wall extending along by the big lime trees up to the head gardener's house which is the western entrance to the park. On the south side of the potting sheds are the glasshouses where the grapes are grown nearly all the year round and other glasshouses where many choice flowers are grown, also a very large cool glasshouse where all the choicest and most beautiful flowers are placed when they are all in full bloom. Outside, in front of all these glass-houses were grown many of the most beautiful and hardy bulbs. Many beds of the English crocuses, hyacinths, tulips, and vast numbers of others too numerous to mention.

View east into the stable yard from the northwest corner; a car is parked in the opposite entrance (Historic England Archive). In Arthur's time, the stables included the coach house, carpenters' and blacksmith's shops, storerooms and facilities for butchering and hanging game.

View south down to the path on the east edge of Cedar Walk from near to the Rose House. The 'Hermit's Folly' is on the right. Steps lead left down to the Sunken Garden and the path opposite, on the right, to the Rose House.

On the south of this part you pass to a lower level, down wide stone steps. Here again are the green lawns and many kinds of shrubs also. On the left is a beautiful water-fountain, with its many varieties of aquatics, also fish and reptile life. On the right a path leads to a grotto and rockery many feet below the level of the surrounding garden. There again is a small fountain in the midst of many kinds of trailing plants, while there is also a mass of fern rockeries.

Continuing south down steps again to a still lower level, the higher ground being stayed up by a long stone wall on which are grown many kinds and colours of beautiful clematis, also on this wall are grown the beautiful cream magnolia (grows as a tree in Australia). South of this are more lawns and shrubs until they join the park. Now take your mind back to the high brick wall which extends as far as the head gardener's house at the west entrance to the park. This brick wall is rather peculiar from the fact that it is hollow. Chimney pots are at various distances on the top of this wall, at the base of the wall on the north side are fireplaces. A fire can be lit and the wall made moderately warm in the wintertime. On this wall are grown just like any climber all the choice peaches, apricots and nectarines. South of this is where all the vegetables are grown. Then another wall on both sides of which are grown plums, cherries and other kinds of fruit. On the south of this second wall are the many beds of strawberries, raspberries, gooseberries,

The Sunken Garden **A** - Rose House (*left*) and show house (*ahead right*). **B** - Central urn and south front of the hall (Historic England Archive). **C** - Steps leading to the Show House and no central ornament[7]. **D** - The cenotaph in the centre with the hall behind trees[7].

currants and many other things. Once again you come to a lower level, this time it is only by a few feet, but it is a most interesting part of the garden, for there could be seen beautiful specimens of the cedars of Lebanon.

There were two rows of them, one to the west, the other extending south. Great big giant trees, more than a dozen of them in the row leading to the south, underneath them was a wide gravel path which led to a park entrance. Their age I do not know but they must have been very old for some of them had great iron chains holding them up in the battle against the many storms and gales that they had lived through. This part of the garden was generally called the Cedar Walk. Now dealing with the final parts of the gardens, that part south of the head gardener's residence. Here were many glasshouses used for the production of early fruits such as: peaches, sweet melons, and special ones for the growing of early cucumbers, also pineapples, and many other things almost too numerous to mention. Continuing farther to the south, once again were the lawns, the flowering shrubs and many of the larger ornamental trees, also along the lawns which bordered the park at intervals were planted several of the *Wellingtonia giganteum*, at that time a few feet high. The *Wellingtonia* is spoken of under other names. It is a kind of cedar or pine; in America there are specimens of it that are claimed to be the largest of any kind of trees in the world.

South terrace gardens and ha-ha.[7]

Holdsworth's cenotaph on the east lawn in October 1934.[7] Note the avenue of trees, which no longer exist, running into the distance towards the Fish Pond and Shackerstone Drive.

The whole of the garden is enclosed by an open iron fence nearly six feet high, except that part directly in front of the hall at the east and the south, where there is an excavation in the ground something similar to the ancient moat around the castle. Thus, there is an unobstructed view across the park, also nothing can enter the garden grounds. There are many more things which I have not mentioned before such as the mushroom houses all dark to produce white mushrooms, also many conveniences for producing such things as beans, seakale, rhubarb, strawberries when the outside ground was covered by frost and snow. Even orange trees were grown under glass, just for the blossom alone.

Top: Summerhouse in the gardens to the southeast of the hall.[7]
Bottom: A similar summerhouse in The Rockery (labelled the Japanese Garden in the family photograph album).[7]

The Park

The hall, the gardens and all other conveniences are surrounded by the park. There are three main roads through the park: one leaving the front of the hall passing through the park to the lodge on the southeast; the second road joining the one at the front of the hall leads to the lodge on the western side of the park; then the third one which leads to the lodge on the northwest of the hall. At this point is the Home Farm where the supply of eggs, milk, poultry and all domestic requirements of that kind are produced. These three roads lead to the villages or towns wherever they may be. In those days the hall letters had to be fetched from the village Post Office. A special messenger on horseback from the hall being sent. It is not necessary to state the rise of the park, for what it contained will give you a much better idea. Its various kinds of trees: oaks, elms, beech, ash were perhaps the eldest and the largest; then great numbers of the beautiful varieties of the hawthorne; also, big trees of the sweet chestnut (edible) and many walnut trees were growing there almost wild. The beautiful horse chestnut trees with their

Historic England Archive

Golf at Gopsall[27]

Top: View southwest from the hall terrace showing the park, semi-cicular golf bunker around the green and the iron fence.

Middle: View from the golf bunker and green back to the hall.[7]

Bottom: Earl Howe playing the 8th hole with his male house guests at the Coming of Age Celebrations for Viscount Curzon (5th September, 1905).

magnificent spikes of flowers in the springtime, as well as their beauty as trees. In some part were great elms, that were close together. Here the crows had started a new colony, with their nests high up in the trees. In some parts of the park were clumps of trees fenced around where the rabbits used to make their homes in the ground, among the roots of the big trees.

The park has its share of animal life too. Beside ordinary cattle, at times I have seen herds of Scotch cattle. To those who are not used to them they would appear ferocious looking things, some of them brown others jet black, rather short-legged, with very long hair and great long horns, but they were, as a rule, quite harmless. There were herds of the ordinary deer, pretty and graceful looking things, but the bucks or males were rather different with their noble looking horns surmounting their heads when they stood and looked at you, then perhaps one might feel a little afraid them. As a boy I have often chased them myself just to see them jump. The young deer, such pretty little things, one would often find lying in the long grass as you walk through the park. There were sheep in the park, also sometimes there would be flocks of them. The Welsh sheep: they were smaller and had always long tails. The most noble animals and perhaps rarest animals in the park no doubt, the red deer. About the size of a donkey but graceful in their build, of a red-brown colour, the male being called a stag, the female being called a hind, while the young went by the name of calves. The hind had no horns and could be seen always in close watch to where the young calves often lay half-hidden in the grass. If anyone went near the calves they muck out for their own safety. The stag with its magnificent set of horns was very dangerous at certain seasons of the year. As the young stags grew up they fought desperate battles between themselves, so rarely no more than two stags were kept in the park at one time. Many times, when crossing the park I have been chased by a hind when passing near its young. The stags we always kept at a safe distance for they were really dangerous (A stag once attacked the letter-carrier on his pony with very serious results).

There are many other interesting things concerning the park which could be mentioned, for instance, what are called 'Fairy Rings' I have seen many in the park myself. A circle in the grass, just like the ring in a circus only about three or four feet in diameter, just the narrow track with green grass in the centre and of course on the outside. It is said that the Fairies form it by dancing around, that is why they are called 'Fairy Rings'. There were many other interesting things concerning the woods and the park such as the water fowl in the pond, the many varieties of birds; with their beautiful song or strange cries, the starling with its nest in the hollow trees or the nest of the hawk high up in a tree. The wood pigeon's nest in the pine trees, also the many interesting and pretty nests of the smaller birds, not forgetting the smallest of them all - the little historical English wren, with its quaint little call and peculiar little nest. In the nighttime the owl could be seen as it left its home in the hollow trees to prey upon the smaller birds or animals. Such is Nature, just as the cuckoo came each year with its cry to say that spring had come once again.

Around the Park

The hall and the park are surrounded by woods varying in their distance through them, being narrower at the lodge gates than at the other parts. Giant trees growing there of very many kinds too numerous to name. The whole, making a home for all kinds of game especially pheasants while rabbits and hares lived and thrived amidst the undergrowth, while in the big pine trees the wood pigeons would rear their young, all sport for the gun. In the woods lived pests also the fox, the stoat, the weasel and even the badger, all prey on the other animals or birds. But the woods had many things of beauty: the giant and stately trees where many of that pretty little animal the English squirrel could be seen as it jumped about in the branches of the trees or sat up in its pretty way eating nuts. Among the trees could be heard the singing of the blackbird or the thrush and many others too. The cooing of the wood pigeon, the call of the pheasant and even the cries of the young birds in their nests. Under the trees wild ferns grew, and at certain parts, the primrose and the cowslip grew in luxuriant wildness while great patches of the ground were covered here and there with the full beauty of the English bluebells. Also, hundreds of the other varieties of flowers just trusting to nature alone for their existence. At one part near the woods the gamekeepers lived. Anyone might have thought that this place was a poultry farm, by the number of hens and the various pens that were there but it was not ordinary chicks that were raised there. Young pheasants and partridges were the chicks raised. On account of the nuisance of the foxes, stoats, weasels, which either eat the eggs or kill the birds on their nests for they were always built on the ground. The eggs

Ivy-covered east front of the hall showing the landscaping of the lawns and flower beds at different levels.[7] Note the absence of the Holdsworth cenotaph at this time. The recumbent lions, either side of the entrance doors to the hall, are now in the grounds of Penn House (Chapter 12).

of many of the pheasants and partridges were collected and taken to head gamekeeper's house and there placed under any broody hen, hatched and reared just like the common chicken, and when they were big enough to take care of themselves, they were turned loose into the woods. Through the lodge gate on the western side of the hall the road led to a little village named Twycross. It was there that the last Earl Howe was buried in the family vault. The other title Lord Curzon remaining for the future generations[28]. However, that maybe I remember that I went into the family vault at the death of Earl Howe about the year 1870.

Tomb of the 1st Earl Howe (11th Dec 1796 - 12th May 1870) and his second wife, Anne Frances Countess Howe (8th Mar 1817 - 23rd July 1877) in St James' churchyard, Twycross.

The Author

I was unusually shy of girls or ladies, perhaps even in a senseless degree. I cannot say to exact age that my memory recalls the events of my life, but I do know that in my young days I was shy, speaking from memory I should say very shy, but also I was obstinate, at least that was what my parents said about me. I was unusually shy in the company of girls or ladies, perhaps even in a senseless degree but then I had no sisters of my own, that may partly account for my shyness, but even now I do recall the fact that in those very early years of my life I looked upon girls and ladies with a kind of awe, just thinking and feeling that they were something different, something above men or boys. With men and boys I was just normal, but always the happiest when I rambled the fields, the woods, amidst the birds, the flowers and the trees, perhaps it was Fairyland to me, for, I practically knew very little of big towns or crowds, also too young to know anything of the world.

I will give you an incident which no doubt illustrates both my shyness and obstinacy. One day several young girls were visiting my home and they wished me to join in their play, but I was too shy therefore I was looked upon by them as a senseless little boy, and they would not have anything to do with me, but I had my own way of amusing myself so I wandered across the park to a hawthorn tree where I knew that a starling had built its nest in a hollow branch. Soon I had wandered back home with the starling held in my hand, for I had caught the old bird on its nest. At once the girls left their play wishing to see the beautiful bird that I held in my hand, perhaps it was obstinacy but I just opened my hand and the bird flew away.

At that time I was going to the village school, a walk of about two miles. Schools were very different in those days. There were no state schools, they depended on the voluntary help given by the people of the district both in financial and other ways. Many of the school children came to the hall where they were given a Merry Christmas by the ladies and helpers. Also during the summer time they were treated to various amusements in the gardens and park of the hall. Personally, I can just remember at seeing the great Christmas Tree in the ballroom of the hall and in the summertime the gatherings of the school children under the big cedar trees in the hall gardens.

In my country school life, my brothers took part as they became old enough. Personally, I remember nothing of special interest concerning those school days, perhaps I was just normal, and yet I can remember hundreds of things that did occur apart from my school life, perhaps I was too interested in my natural and pleasant surroundings. Well I do remember shooting one of the pretty little squirrels with a 'Shangai' and although it bit me very severely, I carried it home and kept it in a cage for many months as a pet. Even at the of my writing this I can remember in my mind's eye a special bird nest that I found in a particular tree, in some cases where particular birds built their nest in successive years. Well do I remember how a starling would build its nest in the hollow part of a certain tree.

Well do I remember where the owls built in a great hollow branched elm tree and when the gardeners caught the old owl on its nest how they gave me one of the young ones, such a funny little thing, just like a downy duckling, but almost round in shape with its two little eyes and funny little beak half hidden in the downy mass. This funny little thing I reared until it was a full feathered owl and many funny things I used to do with it. Young as I was, I knew a great deal about bird's nests whether in trees or on the ground. Of course, I did not have it all my own way, for I had several nasty falls out of trees, and once I got caught by the leg and had to stop there until someone helped me out. All this must have been strange study for my very young days, for memory again paints an interesting and vivid picture of the many and beautiful forms of the nests of the wild birds - the pretty nests of the chaffinches on the branches of the trees; the bullfinches in the bushes so totally opposite in their structure; the pretty little nest of the robin built in the hollow of a branch or on the side of an old tree stump; then all the larger classes of birds up to those whose nests could be seen almost without looking for. What a strange lure it had for me, was it because, even at that age, I had the desire to seek into the unknown?

But there were other things besides the birds, for these were the primroses; bluebells; and daffodils all growing wild in the woods, and many bunches of which we used to gather, and they were sent to the big towns in England to the ladies from the hall. Then again there was that old English sport fox hunting. Many times, even though only a boy, I have been at the kill, that means where the fox is caught by the dogs. Then there were many other things which brought me more in contact with my elders. Many times, when finding the wild pheasants' or partridges' nests, we would show them to the gamekeepers who would gather the eggs to take to where young pheasants were raised. Perhaps the most interesting part is what I will call 'Shooting Days'. On the 1st September each year pheasant shooting began, of course other game as well. I remember as a boy going with the men who were called 'beaters'. The men would go into the woods driving the various kinds of game out, while the gentlemen with the guns would stay outside and shoot at the game as they either ran or flew out of the wood. I have seen the day after the 'shoot' when the result has been gathered in rows, all kinds of game laid out - hares; pheasants; and many others.

"Strange how early to Remember" *"Strange how early to Forget"*

Of course, all this time I was going to the village school about two miles away. What seems strange to me now as I write is that that I do not remember anything, only the fact that I did go with my brothers up to 10 or l2 years of age, and yet hundreds of other things during that time are vividly stamped on my memory.

I can remember going with my father to 'Alton Towers', the residence of Earl Shrewsbury in Derbyshire, also to several shows at which my father exhibited. One of the things I can remember is the staying at the home of Mr. Cox who was the editor of the The Leicester Advertiser.

Here I will speak of the bear that was kept in a cage in a corner of the stable yard. It was great fun I thought when we chucked green grass into the bear's mouth, but when we chucked a stone instead the bear would rush at the iron bars of his cage with a savage growl. Then we would be sent out of the stable yard very quickly.

Now I will speak of my memory of an English farm, being under 12 years of age at the time of my frequent visits. It was a place called Sibson, about five or six miles from Gopsall Hall. It was my grandfather's farm[24], distinctly different from anything Australian as it included nearly everything in the nature of what is called farming. A great number of cows in milk, the rearing of calves, also numbers of common fowls, also the rather quaint little Guinea fowls, all running freely about the farmyard. Turkeys, geese and ducks that would wander off to the water ponds or paddocks to return to the farmyard again in the evening, also the many pigs running more or less freely about. There was the regular butter and cheese making while enclosed around were the stacks of hay, also the stacks of wheat, barley or other kinds to be thrashed out, the straw to be used for the horses or cattle, finally to be used as manure on the various parts of the farm. Also there was an orchard the fruit trees growing almost wild, just like a grass paddock with sheep at times running under the trees feeding on the grass. In connection with this were the many fields or paddocks separated by the green hawthorn hedges, some of the fields were natural grass just for the cows, others for growing oats, barley, wheat, some for growing turnips, mangols, cabbages. All food for the cattle when the ground was covered with snow. In nearly all the various farms there would be a small river or creek running through it, thus giving a good water supply. The hay on those farms is made from the natural meadow grasses. It is cut when half-ripe, then turned over and over in the sun until sufficiently dry, then it is generally carted up to the farm and put up in stacks the same as in Australia. Many hours have I spent myself helping to make hay on my grandfather's farm, also many hunting for birds' nests in the hedges or catching fish in the creeks or water ponds. Of course, all this was the time spent during school holidays. Later on, came the death of my grandfather and he leaving no son to take on the farm, everything was sold and that part of my life was gone, even though the memory still lives.

So time passed and then came the death of Lord Howe, his oldest son succeeding to the title and estate. Then things became different in many ways, for whereas the old Earl and Countess lived for the hall and all the surroundings, the new Earl took very little interest in the district and soon there were many changes at the hall and my father left after nearly twenty years' service there (*actually 15 years from 1855 to 1870*[29]), and there ended my days in Fairyland, and a new life began, what me memory tells me was my first contact with the world.

At this point Arthur's life changed and he went with his family to live in Atherstone running a plant nursery (The Graperies[29]*) in Coleshill street. After his father's death in 1872 and the expiry of the nursery lease, Arthur followed his brothers to what he reports as a very happy life in Australia.*

Notes and References

1 John Grundy Snr was born in Bilstone in about 1696 and was the son of Benjamin and Mary Grundy. He died on 30th December 1748, aged 52 years. Little is known about John Grundy's life other than the surveying and engineering projects that he undertook; his autobiography having been unpublished and the manuscript lost. However, it is obvious that without any formal education he mastered various branches of mathematics and was one of the first people to apply mathematical principles to engineering, particularly water management and land drainage. John Grundy married Elizabeth Dalton in c.1719. They lived in Congerstone until 1738 and his first son, John Grundy Jnr was baptised in St Mary's Church in Congerstone on 1st July 1719 and followed in his father's footsteps as an engineer. John Grundy Jnr was probably the first person to be trained as a civil engineer and then to work as a consultant, purely in civil engineering for most of his life. John Grundy Snr is buried in St Mary's churchyard, Congerstone.

Further details about the John Grundys and building dams and lakes can be found in: *John Grundy of Spalding: His life and times*. Neil R. Wright. Lincolnshire County Council 1983; *The engineering works of John Grundy (1716-1783)*. A.W. Skempton. Leicestershire History & Archaeology (1984) 19, 1984; *'Well Temper'd Clay': Contructing water features in the landscaped park*. Judith Roberts. Garden History (2001) 29 (1) 12-28.

Survey plan of the house & gardens, Gopsall, Leics. RIBA Collection, library Ref: SB53/5; RIBApix Ref: RIBA67889.

2 See appendix to chapter 2 for John Grundy junior's description of the hall and gardens in 1750. Photos of the spring today are in Chapter 14.

3 *Select views in Leicestershire*. J. Throsby (1791), page following 280.

4 The old English word for rabbit was coney; the conery or rabbit warren would have been an important source of meat for Gopsall.

5 *A Temple at Gopsall Park*. T.V. Parry, BA thesis, University of Manchester (1981).

6 *A topographical history of the county of Leicester*. The Rev. J Curtis (1831), p.67.

7 Images courtesy of The Rt Hon Frederick Richard Penn Curzon, 7th Earl Howe, GBE, PC. Digital copies of the originals have been processed using Corel PaintShop Pro 2019.

8 Measurements on 1200dpi images of Ordnance Survey maps and plans were performed using ImageJ, a powerful, open source image analysis program, developed by Wayne Rasband at the National Institutes of Health, USA.

9 *Uvedale Price (1747-1829) Decoding the picturesque*. C. Watkins & B. Cowell, The Boydell Press (2012). See Chapter 12 for a contemporary image of the obelisk at Penn House and an explanation of how it came to be transferred from Gopsall in 1935.

10 Although 40 glasshouses are reported these will not have been 40 stand-alone buildings. A lean-to for example may have been divided internally into several sections, for varying reasons – climate, shading, crop type etc and therefore what appears to be one building will have been reported as several. That said, 40 glasshouses was still a

very large glasshouse range for the time.

11 Forcing: The art of raising plants, flowers, and fruits at an earlier season than the natural one, by the use of artificial heat in a glasshouse, cold frame or cloche, also making it possible to grow non-UK fruit and vegetables in the UK climate.

12 John Veitch was a nursery man who began trading c1880 in Chelsea, he was so successful in finding (using plant hunters like the Lobb brothers and Ernest Wilson) and growing newly discovered species that his business outgrew the Chelsea site and a second was created in Exeter. The Chelsea nursery closed in 1914 and the Exeter site was taken over by another nursery business in 1969.

13 *Gazatteer and Directory of the counties of Leicester and Rutland.* William White (1863), 658-61.

14 The Leicestershire Architectural Society was founded in 1855. It is interesting to note that even in 1864 a visit to a stately home was seen as a fine way to spend ones' time. A somewhat more genteel affair than we might expect today is recorded in a contemporary report of the visit: *"The company were led beneath the shade of some splendid cedars of Lebanon, and some richly laden mulberry trees, into the fruit gardens, of whose contents the noble lord kindly invited all who felt inclined to partake. On their return to the mansion, Countess Howe begged that the party would repair to the entrance hall, where iced wines and claret cups were prepared in abundance for the refreshment of the wearied, dusty, and thirsty travellers. This hospitality was extended to all in a manner truly characteristic of the noble possessors of Gopsall".* Transactions of the Leicestershire Architechtural and Archaeological Society (1866) 2 (pt. 1), 344-5.

15 Bothy Boys, Journeymen Gardeners. Walled gardens were very hierarchical places and climbing the career ladder involved time at various stages. After 2-3 years as an undergardener a young man (no ladies until the 1950s!) could move up to Journeyman Gardener where he would be expected to work without supervision. Further moves to Foreman, assistant Head and finally Head Gardener were possible. During their time as under-gardeners or Journeymen, employees were given on-site accommodations as part of their pay structure. These accommodations were not always very good quality and referred to as Bothies.

16 Ha-Ha. A ditch cut into the earth with a brick wall on one side no higher than the surrounding ground. Designed to keep grazing animals out of the more formal areas of a garden, the ha-ha does away with the need for a fence, enabling unbroken views from the house and garden to the parkland beyond.

17 Espalier, cordon and fan were training methods used for several species of tree fruits. They kept overall size of the plant manageable, allowing more varieties in a given space whilst making maintenance more achievable. Crop quantity was often enhanced by use of these methods.

18 Peter Thoday was a horticultural lecturer, and the presenter of the BBC Television series *The Victorian Kitchen Garden* and *The Victorian Flower Garden*.

19 *A topographical history of the county of Leicester.* The Rev. J. Curtis (1831), Introduction, xxix.

20 *A History of the Meynell hounds and country 1780-1901.* J.L. Randall (1901), p.9.

21 *Fox-hunting in the shires.* T.F. Dale, Grant Richards, London (1903), p.173.

22 Letter dated 8th January 1870 from Viscount (George) Curzon to Mr Oakeley (Hon. Sec. of the Atherstone Hounds) resigning his Mastership and outlining the disposal of the hounds and horses. Atherstone Hunt minutes book.

23 *A History of Gopsall.* Glynis Oakley, private publication printed by Barcraft Printing, Sheepy Magna, 1995.

24 Arthur's maternal grandfather was Edward Hopkins (1789-1870) who farmed a large acreage in Sibson and had three daughters with his wife Harriett (b. 1795) - Harriette, Emma (b.1826) and Elizabeth. Emma married Emmanuel Sage in 1858 and they had four boys while at Gopsall: Edward Merevale (b. 1861; called Merevale by parents and siblings), Arthur (b. 1862), Edward (b. 1863) and Charley (b. 1865). Emmanuel Sage was head gardener at Gopsall from sometime in the 1850s (after Neil Wilson) until soon after the death of the 1st Earl in May 1870. The family were living in Atherstone in 1871 and Emmanuel died in the following year.

After the death of her first husband (William Gilbert; 1821-1863), Emma's sister, Harriette, married William Dawkins in 1871. William was miller and farmer at Temple Mill (off Gibbet Lane) between Sibson and Bilstone/Congerstone. In a continuation of Arthur's journal (not included here), when writing about his life in Atherstone, he recalls frequent visits to his Uncle Dawkins' place "*at the Old Mills*" by Gibbet Lane. Besides the water mill, William had farmland, a herd of cows and made cheese and butter. Arthur writes : "*He, himself was a blunt and honest man*". This information was researched by Prof. John V. Dawkins and Carole Dawkins.

25 The Curzons associated with India are part of a separate family associated by marriage through Penn Assheton Curzon, son of 4th Baronet Curzon and were never involved at Gopsall. George Curzon (1859-1925), Marquess, Lord and Earl from Kedleston Hall Derbyshire was appointed Viceroy of India in 1899.

26 On the death of Charles Jennens in 1773, the Gopsall Estate and other land was inherited by his grand nephew, Penn Assheton Curzon (*Attested will of Charles Jennens [1766]*. Leicester Records Office, record DG/22/5/8). Penn Assheton Curzon married Lady Sophia Charlotte Howe (Baroness Howe from 1799). When Penn Assheton Curzon died in 1797, Sophia Howe ran their estates until their son, Richard William Penn Curzon (1st Earl Howe in 1821) came of age in 1817.

27 The 4th Earl enjoyed golf and Gopsall boasted a fine, 9-hole golf course, which provided an important entertainment for guests staying at the hall. Golf was popular with many of the house guests in December 1902 during the visit of King Edward VII and Queen Alexandra to Gopsall. The ninth hole provided a considerable challenge to players, as it was positioned on the lawn immediately in front of the main hall entrance. Newspapers recorded that the approach shot must negotiate "*a dip and the tall iron pallisadings and massive entrance gates which enclose the gounds in front of the hall*" (Birmingham Post, 12th December, 1902).

28 The title Viscount Curzon is given to the person who is next in line to inherit the title of Earl Howe.

29 *Obituary*. The Gardener's Chronicle, June 1872, p. 806.

Farming on the Gopsall Estate

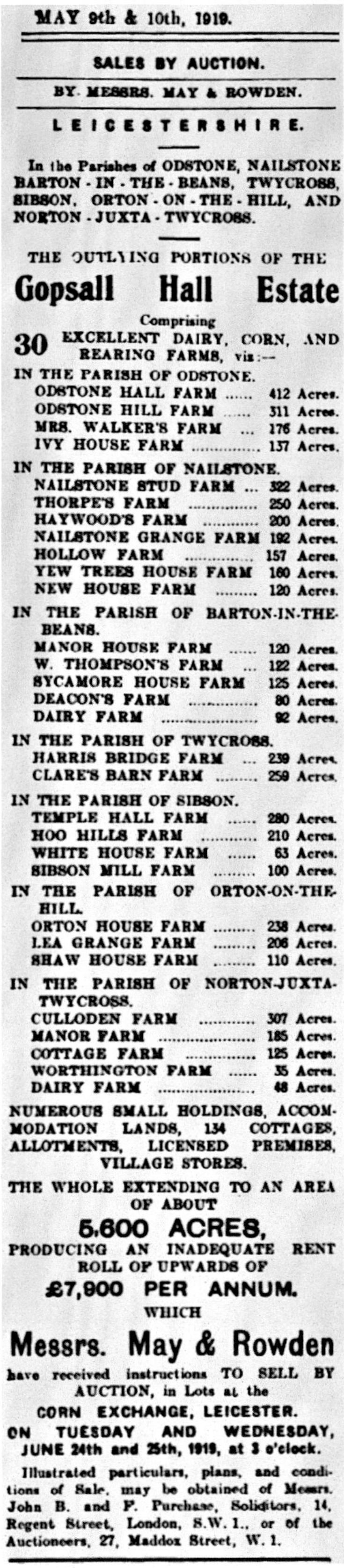

MAY 9th & 10th, 1919.

SALES BY AUCTION.

BY MESSRS. MAY & ROWDEN.

LEICESTERSHIRE.

In the Parishes of ODSTONE, NAILSTONE BARTON-IN-THE-BEANS, TWYCROSS, SIBSON, ORTON-ON-THE-HILL, AND NORTON-JUXTA-TWYCROSS.

THE OUTLYING PORTIONS OF THE

Gopsall Hall Estate

Comprising

30 EXCELLENT DAIRY, CORN, AND REARING FARMS, viz:—

IN THE PARISH OF ODSTONE.
- ODSTONE HALL FARM ...... 412 Acres.
- ODSTONE HILL FARM ...... 311 Acres.
- MRS. WALKER'S FARM ... 176 Acres.
- IVY HOUSE FARM .... 137 Acres.

IN THE PARISH OF NAILSTONE.
- NAILSTONE STUD FARM ... 322 Acres.
- THORPE'S FARM .... 250 Acres.
- HAYWOOD'S FARM .... 200 Acres.
- NAILSTONE GRANGE FARM 192 Acres.
- HOLLOW FARM .... 157 Acres.
- YEW TREES HOUSE FARM 160 Acres.
- NEW HOUSE FARM .... 120 Acres.

IN THE PARISH OF BARTON-IN-THE-BEANS.
- MANOR HOUSE FARM ...... 120 Acres.
- W. THOMPSON'S FARM ... 122 Acres.
- SYCAMORE HOUSE FARM 125 Acres.
- DEACON'S FARM .... 80 Acres.
- DAIRY FARM .... 92 Acres.

IN THE PARISH OF TWYCROSS.
- HARRIS BRIDGE FARM ... 239 Acres.
- CLARE'S BARN FARM .... 259 Acres.

IN THE PARISH OF SIBSON.
- TEMPLE HALL FARM ...... 280 Acres.
- HOO HILLS FARM .... 210 Acres.
- WHITE HOUSE FARM ...... 63 Acres.
- SIBSON MILL FARM .... 100 Acres.

IN THE PARISH OF ORTON-ON-THE-HILL.
- ORTON HOUSE FARM .... 238 Acres.
- LEA GRANGE FARM .... 206 Acres.
- SHAW HOUSE FARM .... 110 Acres.

IN THE PARISH OF NORTON-JUXTA-TWYCROSS.
- CULLODEN FARM .... 307 Acres.
- MANOR FARM .... 185 Acres.
- COTTAGE FARM .... 125 Acres.
- WORTHINGTON FARM ...... 35 Acres.
- DAIRY FARM .... 48 Acres.

NUMEROUS SMALL HOLDINGS, ACCOMMODATION LANDS, 134 COTTAGES, ALLOTMENTS, LICENSED PREMISES, VILLAGE STORES.

THE WHOLE EXTENDING TO AN AREA OF ABOUT

5,600 ACRES,

PRODUCING AN INADEQUATE RENT ROLL OF UPWARDS OF

£7,900 PER ANNUM.

WHICH

Messrs. May & Rowden

have received instructions TO SELL BY AUCTION, in Lots at the

CORN EXCHANGE, LEICESTER.

ON TUESDAY AND WEDNESDAY, JUNE 24th and 25th, 1919, at 3 o'clock.

Illustrated particulars, plans, and conditions of Sale, may be obtained of Messrs. John B. and F. Purchase, Solicitors, 14, Regent Street, London, S.W. 1., or of the Auctioneers, 27, Maddox Street, W. 1.

Proposed sale of the outlying parts of the Gopsall Estate: Coventry Herald 10th May, 1919.
Reach Licensing

Gopsall is mainly remembered because of the vast cost of building the hall and the laying out of its gardens by Charles Jennens Jnr; the friendship between Charles and Handel, who visited Gopsall a number of times (but didn't write 'Messiah' in the temple); the visit of King Edward VII in 1902; the death of Georgiana, the Countess Howe in 1906, and the cedar chapel and the many ornate rococo plasterwork ceilings within the hall itself. However, Gopsall was always primarily an agricultural estate. Prior to 1750 and the building of Charles Jennens' grand hall, the entire area of Gopsall manor and the surrounding countryside, much of which was part of the larger Gopsall Estate, was used for agricultural purposes. At that time, the pigsty and the rest of the Gopsall farmyard were only 240 feet from the main, north entrance of the newly constructed hall,[1] not as envisaged from reading present day descriptions of the hall and park.

Land acquisitions by the Jennens family and later by Penn Assheton Curzon, Baroness Howe and the 1st Earl Howe increased the size of the Gopsall Estate to about 7,500 acres by 1826 (Chapter 1). The 1st Earl Howe significantly increased the area of parkland surrounding the hall and, at its height, in the mid-1800s, Gopsall Hall, park and woods, occupied about 940 acres.[2] However, this only represented 12.5% of the estate area, with the bulk of the other 87.5% of the land being farmed 'directly' by the Earl (Home Farm, formerly Shornell's Farm and now Shornhill Farm), but mostly by tenant farmers. The 1st Earl Howe, in particular, had a keen interest in horticulture and farming, as indicated in a Bell's Weekly newspaper article describing a visit to Gopsall in 1860 (see later).

An interest in farming, for both economic and social reasons, seems to have been shared by the Earls Howe throughout the 19th century; with tenants on the estate apparently being very satisfied with their lot. This situation changed almost immediately when Samuel Waring purchased Gopsall from the 4th Earl in 1918. In May 1919, before the legal transfer of ownership of the estate in the August, Waring put the outlying parts of the estate up for sale, retaining only the hall and park. However, at a meeting with the tenants at the Curzon Arms, Twycross Waring said that he had cancelled the sale, so that tenants could be given the first opportunity of purchasing their farms and properties.[3] He explained the sale saying: *"Gopsall (Hall) had appealed to him as ideal, with its beautiful surroundings, but he had found that to obtain possession of it, it was necessary to purchase the whole estate and, rather than lose it, he did so. He did not wish to own so much land, and had no intention of retaining more than a portion of it."*

Having no interest in the farms, Samuel Waring sought other ways of earning income from the estate. In 1920, he commenced boring operations near to Shackerstone Station in a search for coal deposits with a view, if successful, to underpin *"considerable industrial developments in this part of the county."* The coal boring operations came to nothing[4] and between July 1920 and June 1923, Lord Waring

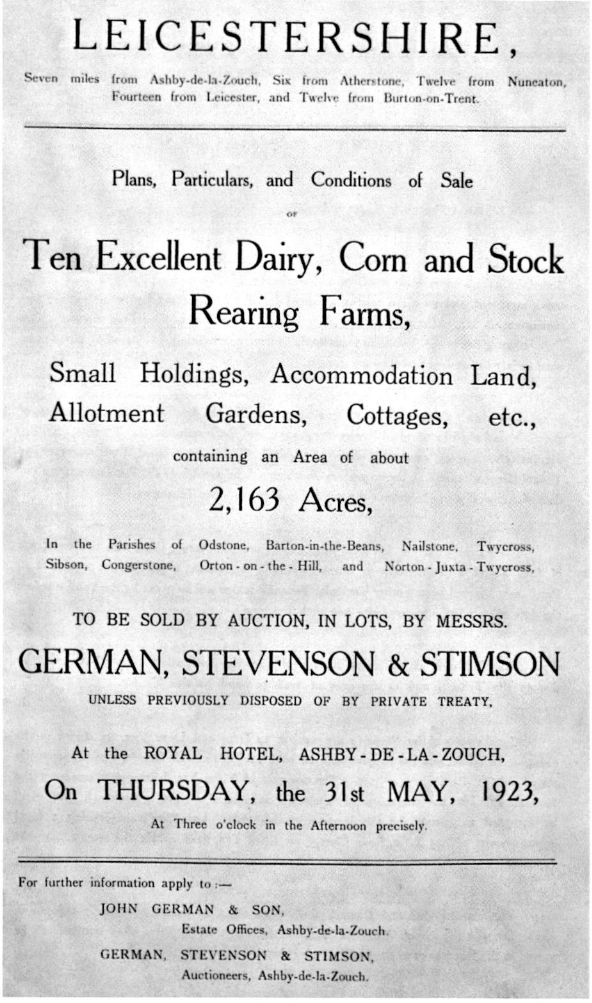

LEICESTERSHIRE,

Seven miles from Ashby-de-la-Zouch, Six from Atherstone, Twelve from Nuneaton, Fourteen from Leicester, and Twelve from Burton-on-Trent.

Plans, Particulars, and Conditions of Sale

OF

Ten Excellent Dairy, Corn and Stock Rearing Farms,

Small Holdings, Accommodation Land, Allotment Gardens, Cottages, etc.,

containing an Area of about

2,163 Acres,

In the Parishes of Odstone, Barton-in-the-Beans, Nailstone, Twycross, Sibson, Congerstone, Orton - on - the - Hill, and Norton - Juxta - Twycross,

TO BE SOLD BY AUCTION, IN LOTS, BY MESSRS.

GERMAN, STEVENSON & STIMSON

UNLESS PREVIOUSLY DISPOSED OF BY PRIVATE TREATY,

At the ROYAL HOTEL, ASHBY-DE-LA-ZOUCH,

On THURSDAY, the 31st MAY, 1923,

At Three o'clock in the Afternoon precisely.

For further information apply to :—

JOHN GERMAN & SON, Estate Offices, Ashby-de-la-Zouch.

GERMAN, STEVENSON & STIMSON, Auctioneers, Ashby-de-la-Zouch.

sold 23 farms, comprising over 3,000 acres, in addition to a number of small parcels of land and cottages. Most of the farms sold were in Nailstone, Barton in the Beans, Norton-juxta-Twycross and Sibson.[5] A further attempt to sell the rest of the outlying parts of the estate in 1927 failed and, in 1932, because of Lord Waring's financial situation, the bulk of the Gopsall Estate was sold to the Commissioners for Crown Lands (Chapter 12). The 6,107 acres purchased for £128,000, consisted of thirty two farms, ten small holdings, 143 cottages and 153 acres of woodland.

Subsequently, the Crown spent £90,000 on repairs and improvements,[6] as well as instituting some rationalisation of the agricultural land. After aquiring four further estate farms in 1942, 1943 and 1949, the Crown purchased the hall site and Gopsall Park in 1951.[7]

Gopsall Park was rapidly transformed into farmland and, in contrast to the other estate farms that were tenanted, the resulting Gopsall Hall Farm was farmed 'in hand' with the farm manager being a Mr Fitt. However, in 1961, the Crown sold the livestock and all the agricultural implements and machinery in two sales in readiness for the farm to become tenanted. The tenancies of a number of Gopsall farms changed in the early 1960s, including Home (Shornhill) and Gopsall House Farms in 1962. Mr Fitt was given the tenancy of Lea Grange Farm and the Lain family took on the lease to Gopsall Hall Farm. The Lains were tenants until they purchased the farm in 2017-18 when the Crown Commissioners disposed of the whole Gopsall Estate. At that time most of the farms were purchased by their long-standing tenants. However, three farms (Castle, Fox Covert and Wharf Farms) plus some additional land and village properties, were marketed by Carter Jonas, the Crown's property consultants, as the 'Shackerstone Estate', and purchased by Chris Stamper, one of the brothers who founded Rare Ltd in Twycross.

Gopsall Home Farm (c.1910)

Now known as Shornhill Farm, it was originally called Shornell's Farm when it was allocated to Charles Jennens Snr at the time of the Inclosure Act for Norton-juxta-Twycross (1748).[8] Snarestone or Farm Lodge was close to the farmhouse and stood where the farm track meets the main Twycross - Snarestone road. The lodge is gone, but the farmhouse and barns remain almost unchanged, except for the removal of the ivy (Chapter 14). Until recently, the main access to Gopsall Hall Farm was via the track to Shornhill Farm; it is now further south and passes Kennel Cottages.

Farms offered for sale in 1922 and by auction in 1923[5]

Top: Nailstone Stud Farm (*left*) and Pratt's Farm (Nailstone; *right*). **Bottom:** Hollow Farm (Nailstone; *left*) and Odstone Hall (*right*).
Photographs sent to Messrs. Shakespeare & McTurk by Major Miles (January 1922). Pratt's Farm was sold in 1922 and Nailstone Stud Farm in 1923.

Farms offered for sale in 1922 and by auction in 1923[5]

Top: Culloden Farm (*left*) and Manor Farm (Norton; *right*). **Bottom:** Clare's Barn Farm (Twycross; *left*) and Lea Grange Farm (Orton; *right*). Manor Farm sold in 1922 but the other farms were still part of the Gopsall Estate in 1927.

A visit to Gopsall Farm

Published in Bell's Weekly Messenger, Monday 29th October 1860[9]

Being in the neighbourhood of this justly renowned farm, during our recent tour through the middle and Northern Districts, we availed ourselves of the circumstance, and paid it a visit. We need scarcely remark that we were highly delighted by the visit, and that we derived both pleasure and profit through making it, if we even limit our views to agricultural affairs. But there are other equally interesting circumstances, connected with a visit to Gopsall Farm which are well deserving of notice as they not only furnish a striking illustration of industrial success, but present an example of how much moral good may be affected, if those who have the management of affairs strenuously and consistently direct their minds to the accomplishment of that end.

The Gopsall Farm is a portion of the Gopsall Estate belonging to Earl Howe, and is without any doubt one of the most splendid properties in the United Kingdom. A ride of several miles or so on the road from Atherstone to Gopsall, which is well worth taking, will bring you to the farm. It borders on the rich dairy districts of Leicestershire. The harvest, with the exception of here and there a field of beans, was pretty well in, and the crops were much the same as we had witnessed elsewhere – a fair average in quantity, but much below an average in quality. The wet weather was much against getting the seeds in, and the late sown turnips were mostly in a sad condition. The first object of importance is Gopsall Hall, the seat of Earl Howe.

" It lies embosomed in a happy valley,
Crowned by high woodlands, where the Druid Oak
Stood like Caractacus in act to rally
His host, with broad arms 'gainst the thunderstroke;
And from beneath whose arms were seen to sally
The dappled foresters, as day awoke
The branching stag swept down with all his herd,
To quaff a brook which murmured like a bird."

The main entrance to the park, which we really could not resist visiting, is through a noble gateway constructed of stone in the pure Doric order of architecture. A scene of transcendent beauty immediately presents itself, and the eye for a time, artistic as it may be, has some difficulty to fix itself on one object, their being such perplexingly picturesque panorama before it. There is food in that park for a thousand artists, vivid as may be their imaginative powers, and felicitous the touch of their pencil – but we must proceed to matters more germane to the purpose of our visit. Still, we cannot refrain from a glance at the mansion and gardens. The first is built after the Italian style, and is a convenient rather than an imposing structure; the last are laid out with exquisite taste and abound in fruit and flowers - in all that can possibly pleasure the eye or refresh the taste. The grand avenue of Cedars perhaps the finest in Europe, is alone worth a journey to look at – they appear so solemn and so majestic amidst their sylvan companions. At one end of this avenue our attention was arrested by a stone obelisk, which was flanked by a couple of urns; there was no peculiar character, or beauty in this structure, but on each of its four sides it bore a touching and tender inscription - commemorative of one who must have been endearing to those who felicitously express it:-

> Ah Editha; Matrum optima; muliorum amantisimi; vale.
>
> A gentlewoman, evidently, in every sense of that delicate and dignified term.

The mansion contains a considerable collection of beautiful and valuable paintings by Rubens, Rembrandt, Teniers, Cuyp, Vandyke, Murillo, Neefs, Gainsborough and other great masters. The death of Richard the Third, by Hayman, is there, and there are also several portraits of the Stuart family. In the grounds there is an appropriate temple, consecrated to the memory of Edward Holdsworth, author of 'Musulman' and 'Remarks and Dissertations on Virgil' who died in 1746. The beautiful chapel is 36 feet long and 24 broad, and its altar, seats and wainscoting are made of richly carved cedar, and the standards of the communion table of the oak in which Charles II concealed himself. Enough - to our especial task.

The management of the farm and the general estate, as we shall presently show, is fully equal to its quality and dimensions. The Gopsall Farm, which is a kind of pet of the noble Earl, being immediately adjoining his country mansion, has had the advantage of the most advanced experiments of agriculture, and no pains have been spared, during the last 20 or 30 years, to bring it to its present high condition. The noble owner of the farm is a good practical farmer himself, and takes great delight in that pursuit; so much so, indeed, is this the case, that his lordship ordinarily spends ten out of the twelve months of the year at his country mansion, busily and studiously occupied with rural affairs, and taking the greatest interest in promoting the success of his tenantry, and in carefully providing for the well-being of the labourers who they employ. The unobtrusive way, too, in which this work is got through furnishes a rare example of character, in which simplicity and unaffected goodness are the predominant traits. Our object is not to eulogy, but delineation of truth.

Let us furnish a few proofs in support of this asseveration.

The farmers of the Gopsall Estate are allowed to farm as they think proper, and there is no dictatorial covenants as regards rotation of crops. The only provision made by his Lordship, is against any actual abuse of his property; and if this were neglected, instead of eulogising the noble lord for being the instrument of affecting great good, we should become the censors, we apprehend, of his weakness and folly. Every encouragement, also, is given to successful farming on the estate; hedgerows are rooted up to make the fields better adapted for good cultivation; the fences kept down to a proper and healthy height; the ditches are cleaned out; the drainage is well secured; the farm buildings are made commodious; the roads are kept in good order; and every attention is made to the suggestions of the tenantry, and seldom, if ever, not complied with. The game, moreover is not preserved to any appreciable extent; indeed, it may be said to be at the mercy of the tenantry, for the few pheasants on the estate are thinned by foxes, much more so than they are by the gun, and a rabbit or a hare is rarely seen

Earl Howe is perfectly cognisant that the preservation of game is utterly incompatible with good cultivation. Other landlords are also beginning to see the subject in the same light, and the day is not far distant when the game laws in all probability will die a natural death.

This is not the only merit, as a landlord, to which his lordship is fairly and justly entitled. All the churches on the estate are in good repair; several of them, indeed, have been rebuilt and new ones added to them. Each parish is provided with a commodious school, in which the rudiments of education are taught to the humblest classes; and to the later clothing is given at suitable periods, besides other incentives to good behaviour. There are five schools on the estate, all of which have been erected at his lordships expense. But the most prominent feature of the noble lord's attentions to the comfort and convenience of the labouring classes on the estate, is to be found in the numerous cottages, which have been newly built. These humble structures are models of simplicity in rural architecture, and they are as convenient and comfortable within as they are simple without. Each labourer is provided with a cottage, containing five rooms, two lower and three sleeping rooms, a provision for cooking and other essential conveniences, all of which are built of good red brick, and are roofed with slates so that they are perfectly dry. In buildings like those, the labourer can preserve the decencies and proprieties of humble life, and the instincts of his moral nature receive no repulsive insults. One other remark, and we shall close our observations upon this part of the subject, although much more might be said with the utmost propriety, did space afford us sufficient indulgence. We said that the tenantry of Earl Howe were devotedly – we might have said affectionately - attached to his lordship, of which there are ample proofs besides mere lip expression. We have witnessed this feeling at several agricultural gatherings, at which it might easily be seen that there is a vast difference between the somewhat forced assent, which mere rank and wealth occasionally command, and the spontaneous recognition which is ever accorded to real goodness and unaffected integrity, especially if those be the attributes of one who occupies the same elevated position.

We have further witnessed this truth in the fact of the tenantry of Earl Howe voluntarily subscribing a handsome sum for presenting him with his portrait, as a hearty and respectful token of his conduct as a landlord; and those who may have the rare pleasure of visiting Gopsall House, will see a full length likeness of his lordship, admirably painted by Grant, and which will certainly form one of the many appropriate heir-looms which the House of Howe can lay claim to. We ought not, however, here to omit mention of his lordship's noble and intelligent bailiff, Mr John Savidge, under whose auspices, and through whose efficient assistance, the Gopsall Estate has been brought to its present state of perfection, and which is fully appreciated by those who know him. We had not the pleasure until our visit to the Gopsall Farm, and we thank him for the kindness and courtesy we received on that occasion.

The Farm

The Gopsall Farm comprises about 800 acres, 450 of which are tillage, the rest is in grass. A good portion of the tillage land is a stiff and tenacious clay, the remainder is of a light gravelly nature; the grassland is a good average quality, 60 acres of it being capable of fattening of beasts. The park, consisting of 500 acres, furnishes food for 300 head of deer, and a large number of breeding cattle. The tillage land is remarkably clean, and well drained throughout.

Course of Cropping

The lightest part of the farm is on the four-course system – namely, turnips, barley, seeds and wheat. The seed crop is substituted either by beans or peas, so that it only becomes seeds once in eight years. Another part of the farm is on the seven-course system – namely, turnips, barley, seeds, seeds, wheat, beans and wheat. This course, for heavy clay farming, answers remarkably well at Gopsall. The autumn cultivation is carried out on the farm, the land being prepared for roots in September, and manured in January for mangolds and swedes, one ploughing being sufficient for the root crop. Two hundredweight of Lawes phosphate, drilled by Chandler's (Reeve's) liquid manure drill, and two hundredweight of guano sown broadcast, are used for the green crops. We ought here to remark that one of Smith's (Woolston) cultivators was extensively and successfully used during the last autumn, and this year has again been brought into requisition, which affects a great saving in horse power.

We found the mangolds about two-thirds of a crop, and estimated at 16 tons per acre; the forward sown swedes are about 12 tons per acre, while the later sown swedes, and green round turnips are next to a total failure. The wheat and barley crops were this year under average; the oat crop was fair, and the bean crop exceedingly good and heavy. The wheat was set up in a number of small round cobs, each containing 8 - 10 quarters, on different fields, in order the wind might get to it, and make it dry enough for thrashing. The wheats were cut by a short scythe, and the stubble showed it had been a most excellent job. The reaping machine was not used, the season being too wet; indeed, one of the Burgess and Key's was standing under the shed in the farmstead without being even mounted.

The Cattle

The cattle consist of 160 head, the whole being Shorthorns, bred from the first herds in the kingdom. For instance, the 2nd Duke of Oxford was purchased by the Earl Howe, of Mr Bates,[10] and he has been much used in the herd; also bulls from Lord Ducie's, Lord Feversham's, Mr Langton's, Colonel Kingscote's, and Mr Rich's herds, have been used at Gopsall.[11] The cows are in fine healthy condition and look like filling the pail. Three bulls are used in the herd, and the tenants have free access to them without charge - a boon rarely granted elsewhere. We saw the beautiful roan cow, (*name not entered but space left*), which gained the first prize at Sparkenhoe, in September last, and which promises to cut a fair figure at the forthcoming Birmingham and Smithfield shows. Two Devon oxen, bred by Mr Turner, which looked remarkably handsome, and will be shown at Birmingham, were in the adjacent stalls. Forty calves are brought up annually on the farm, and fed off when they are three years old; and this, we think, must be a profitable plan, as it includes both the profit of the breeder and the feeder.

Sheep

The flock consists of about 800 head, 200 of which are Leicester breeding ewes, and 100 of Jonas Webb's Downs.[12] The Leicesters, in consequence of the heavy state of the land, are in a more thriving condition than the Downs. The flock is in a very healthy state, and a very few, indeed, are suffering from lameness, which is not the case in several flocks we have seen during our tour through the country. The mortality in the flock, during the late trying season, has been comparatively small, which may be attributed to the circumstances of corn and cake being freely but judiciously used.

Pigs

There are 30 pigs of the Berkshire breed, on the farm, which have sprung from Mr Watson's noted breed.

Horses

There are 16 Suffolk cart horses used on the farm, which appear to have been selected with great care, as they are remarkably fine animals. There is, perhaps, no finer team to be found in the United Kingdom.

Machinery and Implements

We need scarcely remark that the machinery and Implements on Gopsall Farm are of the first-class character. There we saw Howard's ploughs, Hornsby's drills, Corne's chaff-cutter, Crosskill's clod-crusher, Ransome's harrows, and Reeves' liquid manure drill. There is also a fixed steam engine of 7-horse power (by Dean, Birmingham); this is used for thrashing, for grinding, and for chaff cutting. In addition to these well-known implements, we remarked a very useful harvest carriage, which was made on the premises; and as it is desirable that farmers should become acquainted with its peculiar usefulness, we shall briefly describe its construction. Let the reader imagine a Crosskill's cart with the shafts removed; to the body of this cart is attached a fore-carriage with shafts; the fastening is effected by a hook, which connects the fore-carriage and the cart together. Here, then, the length of a wagon is attained; but to make it as roomy as the later, ravings are attached, which cover the whole length of the fore-carriage and the cart. By this simple means we have the advantage of the wagon, without its great weight, and the facility of the cart, which is a great desideratum where loose grain is to be carted. The weight of this wagonette, as it is appropriately termed, is about 14 cwt., while that of a wagon, capable of carrying the same quantity of corn, would be about 20 cwt. And as regards the price, the waggonette is about half that of the wagon. We shall, in all probability, favour our readers with a drawing of this waggonette.

We would in all sincerity, recommend a visit to this model establishment of first-class agriculture, as it cannot fail to repay anyone who may avail himself of the opportunity.

A selection of the farming machinery seen at Gopsall Farm in 1860

A

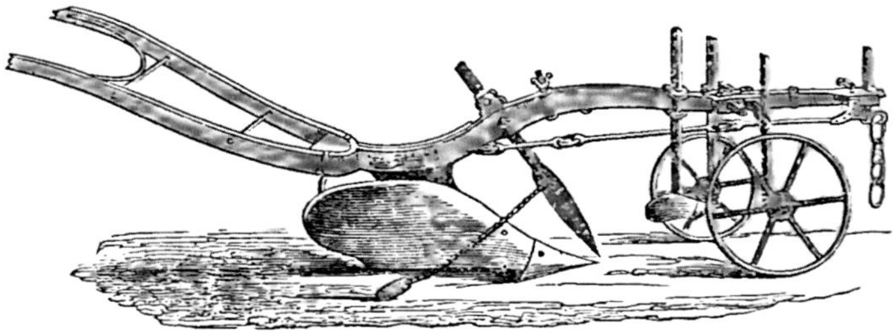

B

C

D

E

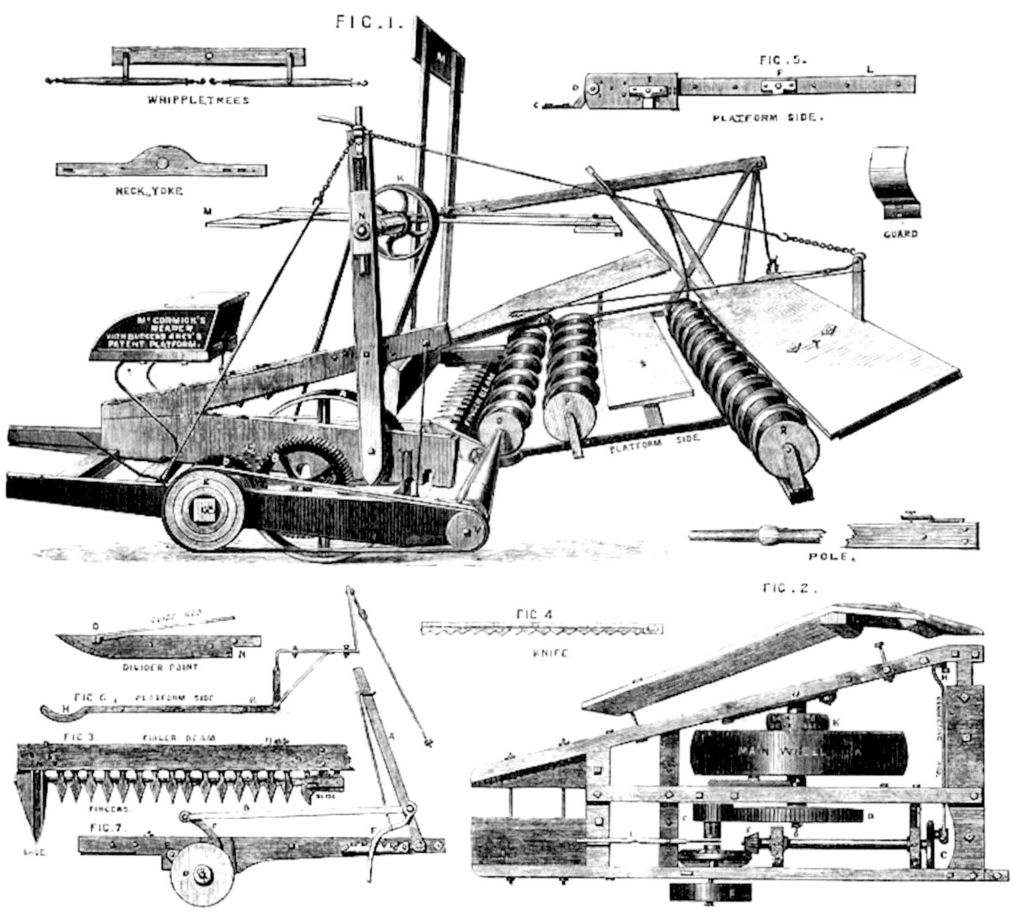

A: Howard's prize plough;[13] **B:** Crosskill's self-cleaning clod-crusher and roller;[14] **C:** Chandler's (Reeves) liquid manure and seed drill;[14] **D:** Corne's chaff-cutter;[14] **E:** Burgess & Key reaper.[14]

A personal account of farming life on and around the Gopsall Estate

Geoff Frisby[15]

KNIGHT, FRANK & RUTLEY,
20 Hanover Square, London, W.1.

By Direction of The Right Honourable Lord Waring.

LEICESTERSHIRE.

FORTHCOMING SALE OF THE OUTLYING PORTIONS OF THE

GOPSALL ESTATE,

Situated midway between Tamworth and Leicester and about 16 miles from the latter.

Extending to

6,230 ACRES;

divided into 239 LOTS of the best DAIRY FARMS & SMALL HOLDINGS in the district, with capital homesteads and some with Possession.
THE VILLAGES OF SHACKERSTONE, BILSTONE & CONGERSTONE.
TWO WELL-KNOWN HUNTING BOXES.
3 LICENSED HOUSES. VILLAGE PROPERTIES.
COUNTRY COTTAGES & WOODLANDS.
Amongst the Principal Lots are:—

FARMS.

Lot.		Acres.
12.	Bilstone Hill Farm	... 193
31.	Church Farm	... 211
78.	Arnoid's Farm	... 223
80.	Oaklands Farm	... 63
153.	Odstone Hall Farm	... 191
181.	Culloden Farm	... 318
214.	Lago's Farm	... 218
218.	Manor Farm	... 128
230.	Harris Bridge House	... 233
208.	Shaw House Farm, Orton	... 111
209.	Lea Grange Farm	... 195
221.	Gardner's Farm, Twycross	... 241
210.	Twycross, Small Holding	... 62

SMALL HOLDINGS.

Lot.		Acres.
1.	Congerstone, Small Holding	... 4
4.	Bilstone, Small Holding	... 3½
32.	Congerstone, Small Holding	... 11
58.	Congerstone, Small Holding	... 2½
82.	Wharf Farm, Shackerstone	... 9
83.	Bridge Farm, Shackerstone	... 14½
85.	Cattow's Farm, Shackerstone	... 14¼
189.	Norton, Small Holding	... 1½
215.	Twycross, Small Holding	... 7½
220.	Twycross, Small Holding	... 2½

LICENSED HOUSES.

33. "Horse and Jockey," Congerstone.
54. "Fox and Hounds," Congerstone.
84. "Rising Sun," Shackerstone.

VILLAGE PROPERTIES.

3. Bilstone Mill.
57. Butcher's Premises, Congerstone.
72. Congerstone Post Office.
105. Shackerstone Post Office.
107. "Elmside." Shackerstone.
223. "The Hollies," Twycross.

PARTICULARS ARE NOW READY.

Illustrated with Plans, 5s. each.
Abbreviated copies free

SALE BY AUCTION by Messrs.

KNIGHT, FRANK & RUTLEY,

at The Bell Hotel, Leicester, on

WEDNESDAY and THURSDAY, 23rd and 24th FEBRUARY, 1927

(unless previously sold privately).

Solicitor:—H. R. Lamonby, Esq., 6 Portland Place, London, W.1.

Auctioneers:—Messrs. Knight, Frank and Rutley, 20 Hanover Square, London, W.1, who will forward particulars (please state requirements).

The Herald, Saturday 29th January, 1927.

Reach Licensing

By some adverse coincidence, the Covid-19 pandemic struck in 2020, as did Spanish Flu one hundred years before in 1918-1920. The effect of World War I (WWI), followed by the Spanish Flu pandemic, and the imminent Great Depression of 1929 probably brought about the decision, by Lord Waring, to attempt to sell the Gopsall Estate in 1927. Lord Waring's financial problems and the liquidation of Waring in 1932 almost certainly led to the eventual sale of the outlying parts of the Gopsall Estate to the Crown Commissioners that same year.[16]

The 1927 auction catalogue listed thirty well equipped farms with superior homesteads, many smallholdings and allotments with other private residences and, of course, three pubs. Working the estate lands required a large number of tenants and workers, reflecting the amount of labour needed to farm the land on the estate, essentially by hand. In 1927 there were 202 tenants occupying the properties and land within the Gopsall Estate.

When I began in agriculture as a boy in the 1940s, on the edge of the Gopsall Estate, farming practices had changed little in the preceding 40-50 years. That being the case, I represent the last generation that experienced the hand and equine toil that was farming prior to the introduction of wholesale mechanisation and the amalgamation of land to form the large farms characteristic of today. The following is a description of farming mostly as it would have been undertaken during the first half of the 20th century and includes some 'stories', the truth of which is left up to the reader to judge! As may be appreciated, many of the things described will not be significantly different to how farming was performed when Gopsall Farm was visited in 1860.

Work horses, throughout the years, were the main source of power and, as indicated in the Gopsall sale catalogue, there was a blacksmith's shop in most villages. However, the blacksmith's shop in the stable block at Gopsall Hall, present in the 19th century, was almost certainly no longer present at this time. Apart from shoeing horses, the blacksmith, having a forge, was required to make and to repair all types of metal farm equipment. An opportunity for a social chat was always a good reason to wait for a horse to be shod, and one could always help by pumping the bellows to keep the forge up to heat. Memories remain of that red-hot burning forge and the strong, unique aroma when the hot shoe was placed on the horse's hoof, and the tip tap of the blacksmith's hammer that followed. There would also be a saddler nearby, who would make and repair saddles and the various harnesses used for riding and working horses.

Bilstone Hill Farm in 1927

Apart from walking, a pony and trap were then the main means of personal transport and the three Gopsall pubs (The Horse & Jockey, The Curzon Arms and The Rising Sun) were the social hubs of the community. Handily, when his master had had a heavy session, a horse knew its way home! Stories abound, my favourite one told to me, was when the youths of the day would untack the awaiting pony, take it from the trap, put the shafts through a five barred gate, and tack it up again. You can imagine the owner when he came out of the pub, scratching his head whilst exclaiming, *"How did you get like that you silly old bugger?"*

The horse stock had been somewhat depleted by the demands of the British Army during WWI but, even after WWII, we still had four horses in 1950; Bonny, Bess, Bill and Captain. Horsepower still prevailed at that time, along with manpower. We had a waggoner who looked after and worked the horses, and who taught us how to 'tack up', or harness a horse, a skill which took a little time to learn. Horses were harnessed to carry out most of the farm tasks, with either one, two or three to undertake the particular work. The first action was to put on the collar, with hames attached[17], upside down over the horse's head and then turn it upright and push it back onto its shoulders. The hames bore the load when attached, by means of a shaft or shafts and chains, to whatever implement was to be used. Then the horse was backed with the saddle and breeching which went over the horse's rear to act as a brake when a horse was travelling down a slope, and then the bridle with bit and reins (horse in tack).[17]

Work horses were essential for the running of the farm. Before cultivation of the fields, they would haul carts loaded with cow manure to a field, maybe a mile away, where the contents were piled into small heaps, in rows, throughout the field. Later the manure was spread from the heaps by three or four men laboriously working down the rows with four-tined forks. There were numerous horse-drawn implements, one being a mangold[18] or kale drill, which was constructed of two wooden seed boxes spaced above two sets of rollers. The drill planted seed along two ridges at a time which had been previously formed with a ridge plough. When mangolds reached seedling size, they were then 'singled', row by row, with hoes; the singling was to remove the excess plants which would allow a mangold to grow to an acceptable size at harvest. Mature mangolds, used for cattle fodder, were pulled out, the leaves chopped off with a mangold knife and then thrown into small heaps. The mangolds were then taken to a clamp[19] at the corner of a field by horse and cart. Once full, the clamp was covered with straw, and soiled over by hand to keep out winter frost. By contrast, some crops like kale were harvested daily, by cutting with a slash hook, then carted to the farmyard as cattle fodder.

Most land was ploughed first using a single furrow plough pulled by two horses and attached by chains to the hames which were coupled to swingletrees[17] and hitched to the plough. The ploughman walked behind to guide the plough, and as he came to the headland, he would turn the horses round to the next furrow, by using the terms, 'gee back' or 'come back', depending on whether he wanted them to turn left or right. By this means, the ploughing of 1-2 acres per 10-hour day, was a reasonable achievement, depending on soil type. After ploughing, scuffles or harrows pulled by a horse or horses, would then be used to cultivate the ploughed land into a seedbed, but always with a man to guide them. Following these preparations came the seed drill, which was a hefty piece of equipment when filled with grain (wheat, barley or oats) and was pulled by two or three horses; both autumn and spring crops were planted.

Bob Lampard hand ploughing at Dean's Farm, Bilstone.

Although horses were essential for many farming activities, other tasks were purely manual. During the growing season, before the advent of chemical treatments, crops were weeded by hand. Thistles, docks, wild oats and other weeds were pulled as we walked through the crop, thistle pulling being a somewhat painful task! Fertiliser was applied by hand. Initially bags of fertiliser were spaced out across the field. Workers would then fill breast hoppers and, with the hopper suspended around the neck, fertilizer was broadcast, by hand, as they walked through the crop. Similarly, sowing grass seed was a purely manual process using a seed barrow, which had a large wheel and carried a long seed box driven by the land wheel and shaft that rotated a line of brushes, which distributed the seed. I remember pushing the barrow up and down the field sowing seed, with my father walking along the previous wheel mark with an appropriate length of string to ensure that no area was missed. A seed fiddle could be used for the same purpose.[20] The shoulder mounted fiddle was held in front of the body and a bow was pushed backwards and forwards to operate a disk which threw out the seed, as you walked along the field. The maintenance of field boundaries was also a labour-intensive job. Chains (1 chain = 22 yards) of hedges had to be trimmed or 'brushed', by hand, with a 'slash hook', which had a curved blade attached to the end of a wooden shaft. The cutting and laying of hedges took time throughout the winter days. Post holes were dug by hand to set posts for fences to enclose livestock, as were ditches and furlongs of land drainage with what was called a 'grafting tool', to reset mainly horseshoe drains.

A Massey-Harris reaper-binder pulled by a tractor (John Poyser; CC BY-SA 2.0). Binders were horse-drawn from when they were invented in 1872 to well into the 1940s, despite diesel tractors being available from the early 1930s.

Once the grain crop reached maturity in late July or early August, the harvest was performed using a binder, which was powered by a large metal drive wheel, that ran along the ground.[21] The binder, pulled by two or three horses hitched to a pole extending from the machine, would cut and bind the ripened crop. The crop was cut by a reciprocating blade (5ft long) and pushed onto the bed of the machine by the revolving wooden 'sails'. Revolving canvas belts then carried the crop along the bed and up and over the machine to be tied with binder twine from balls of string, by a device on the binder, forming a sheaf that was then cast out by a three-pronged fork-type mechanism, onto the ground. After four passes of the binder, producing four rows of sheaves, pairs of sheaves would be picked up, one under each arm, stood up and pressed firmly together; three or four pairs of sheaves, pressed together would then form a stook ('shuck' or 'shook', locally). Normally, two pairs of men, probably starting at each end of the field would stook away to see who could complete their half first. As a very young boy, I remember stooking races and the hope of a rest before the next four rows of sheaves were ready.

Above: A stook. **Right:** Wheat at Harris Bridge Farm after reaping/binding (1941).[22]

The stooks were left in the field for maybe two weeks, or longer if the weather was poor, to dry out and ripen completely. When the time was right, the sheaves were loaded onto a horse-drawn dray; two men normally pitched onto the dray and a third one loaded on the dray. The loaded dray was then hauled by horses to the rick, where two men on the rick stacked and two others pitched up from the dray. Normally, while one dray was being unloaded at the rick, a second was being loaded in the field and work would be from dawn to dusk. When harvest was home and the ricks were finished in a gable shape, they were then thatched. With the use of a ladder, battens were carried onto the rick, spread over and secured with thatch pegs ('thack' pegs, locally) pushed into the rick. Each peg was spaced about two feet from the previous one, with binder twine tied between each to secure the thatch. This was very hard work for a one-man band, as I know from personal experience! The thatch pegs were sourced from hedgerows on the

Above: Loading the crop onto the dray (c.1905).
Below: Building a rick (c.1905).

Early 20th century advert for steam thrashing machinery.[14]

farm, often made from nutwood, cut into lengths of about two feet and sharpened at one end.

Sometime through winter and often well into spring, there would be several days of thrashing, when a contractor would visit with his thrashing set. This equipment, thrashed the grain from the ear, with the straw and the chaff being the separated products, combining what used to be two manual processes of threshing and winnowing. Thrashing machines were first recorded in about 1760, but became common in early 19th century England. Their introduction reduced the need for farm labour which, in part, led to the Swing Riots in 1830.[23] Thrashing machines were generally horse-powered well into the 20th century, although steam-power was introduced much earlier by the more progressive and rich landowners. Earl Howe, in 1860, had a steam engine at Home Farm that was used for threshing, grinding and chaff cutting.

Henton's steam thrashing set in the snow at Murray's Meadow, Orton-on-the-Hill (c.1917)

The 7 horse power steam engine photographed was built in August 1890 by Charles Burrell of Thetford (serial no, 1491; Regn. AY 9882). The people in the photo are (*from L to R*): May Fisher (Threshing drum feeder), George Yeomans (Father-in-law to Arthur Henton), Dan Hume (Engine driver), Harold North (in front of rear wheel; Steersman), Arthur A Henton (Owner), Vic and George Faulkner (Threshing hands/gang).

The Henton family have worked on, and from, farms within the Gopsall Estate for over 130 years. Originally at Lea Grange Farm (Orton), Arthur Albert Henton moved to Worthington Farm (Norton) and in 1903 started steam thrashing contracting, serving the local farming community. Athough no longer in the threshing business, A.A. Henton & Son (Steel Fabrications) Ltd still trades from Worthington Farm, purchased from Lord Waring between 1919 and 1922.[5]

(Original photo supplied by Peter Oakden and details by Arthur Henton)

In my day, the contractor would haul his thrashing set behind a single cylinder Field Marshall Diesel tractor and draw up alongside the rick to be thrashed. I can hear it coming now, chug-chug-chug. It was then 'set up', with the drum opposite the rick, the baler behind and the diesel tractor positioned some way back at the other end to drive the drum by means of a large belt around its flywheel; the belt being attached to a similar one on the drum. At 8am on the dot, two men manned the drum, one man cutting the string or band ('bont', locally) from the sheaf and the other feeding the sheaves into the drum. The sheaves were loaded onto the drum by one man on the rick; being fed with the sheaves by one or two others. We enjoyed the day as we had twenty-minute breaks at two-hour intervals, which was an opportunity for social gossip and banter. However, during work periods, as the thrashed grain came down from the drum, it was fed into two hundredweight sacks, hired from the London, Midland and Scottish Railway. The full sacks were then wound up on a sack lift then hoisted onto our backs and carried to the store. My first job, when a youth, was to rake out chaff, which was the thrashed husk from the grain, from under the drum and onto a large hessian sheet, which I then carried to the 'chaff place'. There was always excitement, when we reached the bottom of a rick, as rats tried to leave the scene. However, wire netting was erected to prevent them from fleeing and pitch forks would be flailing everywhere. The thrashed straw came out of the drum and through the baler, which was sited behind the drum. On the farm, the straw was tied as battens (or battins) for use in bedding livestock and for thatching the ricks. However, a different baler was used to form large wire bales to sell on away from the farm. Two men would stack the battens or bales into a rick close by.

A young Bob Lampard carrying sacks of grain from the threshing machine at Dean's Farm, Bilstone.

As described, the whole process from harvesting the crop from the fields to producing sacks of grain took some 3-5 months and a lot of man-hours and manpower. Combine harvesters 'combine' the harvesting operations (reaping, threshing and winnowing) and, in so doing, reduce the manual labour and time required for a successful harvest. The first combine harvesters, pulled by horses, oxen or mules, were developed in the 1830s for the vast wheat lands of America. However, their size and the smaller fields and damper conditions in Britain, made their use here impractical. It was only really after WWII that 'small', tractor-hauled and later self-propelled, combine harvesters began to be used in England. One of the first combines on the Gopsall Estate was that of Fred Sutton, tenant of Ivy House Farm in Congerstone.

Fred Sutton on his brand-new Massey-Harris combine (c.1948), purchased from Messrs. Holdrons in Ashby-de-la-Zouche.

Potatoes were hand planted in the spring. The soil was ridged by a ridge plough, which consisted of left and right hand mould boards which formed the ridges. A hessian sack, folded half size with string attached, was filled with seed potatoes and suspended round the neck. We would then walk along the formed ridge and drop potatoes, 12 inches apart, into the ridge, as we walked. The horse and ridge plough followed behind to 'split back' the ridges, in order to cover the planted potatoes. When the potato plants had emerged and grown to a reasonable size, we hoed through acres, row by row, to keep the weeds down. At harvest time, probably in early October, around twenty workers, mainly women, were employed to pick potatoes by hand, with their youngsters chipping in at half-term. The field was split into lengths marked with sticks, and as the potato spinner[24] spun out a row, the pickers picked them into buckets, which were then emptied into sacks. This was hard work, but great fun with lots of arguments about sticks being moved and loads of banter, some not repeatable! The sacks were collected and carted, to be emptied into a long clamp at the edge of the field. The clamp was then covered with straw as it was filled and later ploughed around so that the loosened soil could be used to cover the clamp before winter.

During the winter the clamp would be un-soiled and potatoes dressed (riddled) from the clamp. This took probably a group of five, with one loading from the clamp onto the riddle, two sorting and two weighing and loading the one hundredweight sacks of potatoes onto a trailer.

Given the great depression endured during the 1920s and 1930s, farmers were generally extremely cautious and, not wishing to 'put all your eggs in one basket', most had a mixed enterprise policy, which included a dairy herd. Throughout that time, most farms and smallholdings in the area kept cows, some with one or two, and thirty being about the maximum.

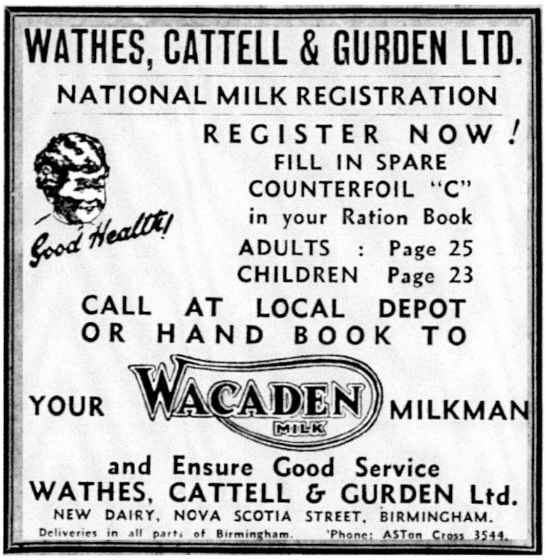

The Evening Despatch, 20th August 1941.
Reach Licensing

In Austrey, there were probably around thirty milk producers within the parish boundary and, as indicated in the newspaper adverts offering Gopsall farms for sale in 1919, 1923 and 1927, dairy farming made a up a significant portion of the agricultural activity on the Gopsall Estate. Until the late 1940s, cows were hand milked and, for our herd of 30, three or four men did the job. They sat on three-legged milking stools, peaks of their caps at the back of their heads and leaning into the cow's belly as they milked, two teats at a time! The milk was then cooled using a surface cooler, before loading into conical, 17-gallon churns, which were collected each day by lorry and taken directly to a dairy in Birmingham (Wacaden; Wathes, Cattell & Gurden Ltd).[25] However, by the late 1940s, the more familiar, 10-gallon cylindrical churns replaced the conical churns. This happened at our farm until the mid-1960s when tanker collections became the more normal standard.

In the early 20th century, milk from the Gopsall farms was taken to Shackerstone station by horse and cart for onward rail transport to the processing dairy in Birmingham. In the 1920s, there used to be great competition between the carters to see who could be the first to get their load of full milk churns to Shackerstone station to catch the 6am milk train. By the 1940s, lorries replaced the horse and cart and ended the 'milk races'. Percy 'Pip' Cowdell, from Shadows Lane, Congerstone had a lorry and collected the churns from many of the Gopsall Estate farms for transport to the station.

Milk in conical, 17-gallon churns awaiting the milk train at Highbridge station in 1928 (http://www.gwr.org.uk/nochurns).

Our herd, like many on Gopsall farms, was housed in part of a traditional rectangular farmyard, in a byre or cowshed, with cows in single row along the shed. When in their stalls, they were chained by the neck and released after milking back to the field to graze in summer. In wintertime they were put out for a short period during the daily 'mucking out', re-bedding and putting hay and feed in their mangers. When they came back into the byre, they knew which stall was theirs, and stood waiting to be chained up. When the cows were out in summer the byre was spruced up; the stalls thoroughly cleaned and walls lime washed.

Up until recent times, many farmsteads were centred in a village, with the farmland extending away from the stead, almost as a slice of cake. However, it was often the case that some grazing

Church Farm, Congerstone in 1927. Since about 1988-1989, the ex-farmhouse shares its 'farmyard' with 10 new houses and a large brick barn conversion.

land could be a distance away and many herds were driven along the country byways, to and from the stead, at milking times. Indeed, some small herds were driven out to graze the road verges and were tended ('tented', locally) by one man, for a few hours.

Grass was usually cut in June to make hay for winter use, by means of a horse drawn mower, which had a five-foot cutter bar with a reciprocating knife that was ground-wheel driven. The mown grass was left in swathes for a few days, then turned by a tedder[26] periodically in order to dry it out, and to make hay. Once dry, the hay was gathered by a pair of horses hitched to a sweep (rake), controlled by one man, and swept to the edge of the field where the hay was then stacked into a rick by two or three other labourers. The hay was heaved by hand, or by use of a hay pole, onto the rick, which was finished in a ridge and then thatched. During the period from building the rick in May until needing winter fodder in October, the hay rick would settle. Every few days throughout the winter period we would go with horse and cart to fetch sufficient hay for cows, young stock and horses. Two of us would use a hay knife[27] to cut a section from the rick and load it onto the cart.

Far more grassland existed before WWII than today. The advent of the war and the German blockade meant that home food production was paramount. The 'War Ag' as it was known (the War Agricultural Executive Committee), was formed and given power to serve orders on farmers, and could decide which crops should be planted in which fields. At that time, the ploughing out of grassland was paramount and quite an area was taken out of permanent pasture. However, the grassed parkland of Gopsall was spared as it was used for a Vehicle Reserve Depot by the army (Chapter 11). During those years the phrase, 'Dig for Victory', was on everyone's lips, and everyone was encouraged to grow more food, whether in gardens or field, to maximise production from home soil. However, many farm workers left the land for military service and in order to maintain production, the Women's Land Army was formed and many Land Girls 'manned' farms all over Britain, including those within the Gopsall Estate. Later in the war, Italian and German prisoners of war joined the Land Girls in the fields, watched over by armed guards. At this time, Italian prisoners were important members of the workforce at Gopsall Home Farm (Chapter 11).

As indicated in this account, farming up until well after WWII was predominantly manual in nature, requiring a significant labour force. The introduction of increasing amounts of mechanisation through later decades resulted in an associated reduction in the workforce and complete loss of the need for working animals. Today, highly mechanised farms are becoming increasingly computerised and, almost without human intervention, fields can be ploughed, planted and harvested thanks to global positioning technology. Dairy cows are no longer hand milked and systems exist for robotic milking. Furthermore, cows can be tagged, allowing the farmer to monitor the behaviour, health and nutrition of individual animals, all from a mobile phone; a 'Fitbit' for cows!

Although these changes have not had a great impact on the landscape of the area covered by the Gopsall Estate, they have forever changed the population and nature of the Gopsall villages. Now there are virtually no working farms in the villages; the farmhouses and farm buildings having been demolished for new housing developments, or barns converted to provide, in the words of some estate agents, "*stunning living accommodation with original character features*". The villages, once predominantly inhabited by estate workers on farms, in the park and at the hall, as tenants, are now populated by home owners who commute to work in the surrounding towns and cities. This is the inevitable consequence of the loss of the hall and the huge reduction in labour requirements to run the farms.

Notes and references

1 See Chapter 4 and the Grundy survey plan of the house and grounds at Gopsall (1749); RIBApix RIBA67889.

2 *Gazetteer and Directory of the counties of Leicester and Rutland.* William White (1863), pp. 658-661.

3 *Gopsall Estate Sale - Sir Samuel Waring explains his position*. Nottinghamshire evening Post, 5th Dec 1919.

4 *The Gopsall Estate - Proposed search for coal. Boring operations commenced.* Leics Daily Post 30th Jan 1920; *A Disappointment. No coal on the Gopsall Estate after all.* Nottingham Journal 23rd Sept 1920.

5 **Odstone Hall Farm, Odstone Barn Farm**, Odstone Hill Farm, **Walkers Farm**, Ivy House Farm (Odstone); Nailstone Stud Farm, Thorpe's Farm, Haywood's Farm, Nailstone Grange Farm, **Hollow Farm**, Yew Trees House Farm, New House Farm (Nailstone); Manor House Farm, W Thompson's Farm, Sycamore House Farm, Deacon's Farm, Dairy Farm (Barton-in-the-Beans); **Harris Bridge Farm**, **Clare's Barn Farm** (Twycross); Temple Hall Farm, **Hoo Hills Farm**, White House Farm, Sibson Mill Farm (Sibson); Orton House Farm, **Lea Grange Farm, Shaw House Farm** (Orton-on-the-Hill) and **Culloden Farm**, Manor Farm, Cottage Farm, Worthington Farm, Dairy Farm (Norton-Juxta-Twycross) were listed for sale in the 1919 sale advert. Ten of these farms (**in bold**) were still part of the Gopsall Estate when it was put up for sale in 1927.

Nailstone Stud Farm and Thorpe's Farm (Nailstone) and Manor Farm (Norton) were offered for sale in 1920: *Farms for sale with possession*. Atherstone News, Friday 30th July 1920. Thorpe's Farm was the only successful sale.

It is assumed that Odstone Hill Farm, Ivy House Farm (Odstone); Haywood's Farm, Nailstone Grange Farm, Yew Trees House Farm, New House Farm (Nailstone); Manor House Farm, W Thompson's Farm, Sycamore House Farm, Deacon's Farm, Dairy Farm (Barton-in-the-Beans); Temple Hall Farm, White House Farm, Sibson Mill Farm (Sibson); Orton House Farm (Orton-on-the-Hill) and Manor Farm, Cottage Farm, Worthington Farm, Dairy Farm (Norton-Juxta-Twycross) were sold in the period between 1919 and 1922 because their names do not appear in farm sale lists dated 1922, 1923 and 1927.

Manor Farm (Norton) and Pratt's Farm (Nailstone) were sold by Messrs. Shakespeare & McTurk in 1922 and Nailstone Stud Farm after the 1923 sale. The latter sale listed all but one of the farms shown in bold above.

Gopsall. Gopsall Estate. Bundle of letters, Sale particulars etc. The Record Office for Leicestershire, Leicester & Rutland, Document Ref: DE688/140.

6 *Gopsall Hall: 'Look on my works, ye Mighty, and despair'.* Brenda Sumner. MA thesis, University of Leicester, 2009.

7 *Mrs. F.M. Parkes and another Crown 1942, July 10 Gopsall: conveyance of Orton House Farm, Twycross.* The National Archives. Doc. Ref: CRES38/996; *Panton Investments Ltd. Crown 1943, Dec. 1 Gopsall: conveyance of Shornhill and Norton Barn Farms.* The National Archives. Doc. Ref: CRES 38/998; *G.A. Isaacson Crown 1949, Mar. 25 Gopsall: conveyance of Temple Hall Farm.* The National Archives. Doc. Ref: CRES 38/1001; *Panton Investments Ltd. Crown 1951, July 11 Gopsall: conveyance of Gopsall Park.* The National Archives. Doc. Ref: CRES 38/1002.

8 *Norton. History & Antiquities of the County of Leicester. Volume IV, Part II, containing the Sparkenhoe Hundred.* John Nichols. London, 1811, p. 850.

9 Bell's Weekly Messenger was a British Sunday newspaper that began publication on 1st May 1796. After 1832, it gave extensive coverage to agricultural affairs and was for many years the leading agricultural newspaper in the U.K. It ceased publication in 1896.

10 Thomas Bates (1775-1849) was a premier breeder of shorthorn cattle from 1810 until his death in 1849. He was recognised as producing consistency of type and, in choosing his animals for his herds, he stressed heavy milking qualities. Today's dairy shorthorns are direct bloodline descendants of Bates' cattle.

11 These are owners of well-regarded and prize-winning herds of shorthorn cattle.

12 Jonas Webb (1796-1862) was a leading breeder and developed a strain of Southdown sheep of larger size, earlier maturity and improved fleece quality.

13 Image obtained from: *Rudimentary treatise on Agricultural Engineering Vol III: Field machines & Implements*. GH Andrews, John Weale, London (1853).

14 Images obtained from: *Grace's Guide to British Industrial History* (https://gracesguide.co.uk/).

15 The Frisby family took on Warren Farm, Austrey in 1937. Geoff grew up and helped on the family farm throughout his youth and worked full time on leaving school in 1954. He took on its management in 1960 and retired in 2009.

16 *What became of Waring? Fortunes of an entrepreneur in furnishing, shopkeeping and construction.* Construction History 29 (1) 2014, pp.75-97.

17 Hames: two curved pieces of iron or wood forming or attached to the collar of a draught horse, to which the traces are attached; Breeching: a strap around the haunches of a draught horse and attached to the saddle. Breeching engages when an animal slows down or travels downhill and is used to brake or stabilize a load; Swingletree: a wooden or metal bar used to balance the pull of a draught horse when pulling a vehicle. See: http://www.equineheritagemuseum.com/additional-information/a-glossary-of-harness-parts-related-terms

18 Mangold, mangelwurzel or mangold wurzel is a cultivated root vegetable. Their large white, yellow or orange-yellow swollen roots were developed in the 18th century as a fodder crop for feeding livestock.

19 A storage clamp was used for temporary storage of root crops such as potato, turnip, mangold and sugar beet. Root crops were stacked in a rectangular area up to a height of about 5ft giving a triangular cross-section. When the clamp was full, the crop was covered with straw and then soil.

20 Hand-operated broadcast sowing machines were introduced from America from c1850. The 'Aero' brand of seed fiddle was manufactured in Scotland and sold for 27s 6d (£1 37.5p) in 1940.

21 The binder, or reaper-binder, was invented in 1872 by Charles Withington. It cuts the cereal crop a couple of

inches above the ground and ties the cut crop into sheaves, ready for 'stooking'.

22 Images from: *A geographical survey of an agricultural region in south-west Leicestershire*. Jean K Dexter, Advanced Geography Thesis, Goldsmith's College, University of London (1942). The Record Office for Leicestershire, Leicester & Rutland, Document Ref: DE10125/4.

23 Swing Riots – The Swing Riots were a widespread uprising in 1830 by agricultural workers in southern and eastern England, in protest at agricultural mechanisation and harsh working conditions. It began with the destruction of thrashing machines in the Elham Valley area of East Kent in the summer of 1830, and by early December had spread through the whole of southern England and East Anglia. The first thrashing machine was destroyed on Saturday night, 28th August 1830 and, by the third week of October, more than 100 thrashing machines had been destroyed in East Kent. As well as attacking the popularly hated thrashing machines which displaced workers, the protesters rioted over low wages and required tithes, destroying workhouses and tithe barns associated with their oppression. They also burned ricks and maimed cows.

The common people of Great Britain: a history from the Norman Conquest to the present (1st Midland book ed.). J.F.C. Harrison, Bloomington: Indiana University Press (1985), pp. 249–253.

1830 Agricultural 'Swing' Riots Hungerford Virtual Museum. 25th March 2018. Retrieved 22nd May 2020.

24 A potato spinner is pulled by a horse or tractor. A flat piece of metal runs horizontal to the ground and lifts the potatoes up and a large wheel with spokes on it, called a reel, pushes the soil and potatoes out to the side. The potatoes are then gathered by hand.

25 Wathes, Cattell & Gurden Ltd, dairymen, of Nova Scotia Street, Ladywood; their trade name, 'Wacaden'. As Wathes Brothers, the company began in the latter part of the 19th century and traded until about 1964.

26 A tedder is a horse or tractor drawn machine used to aerate the hay and speed up the drying process.

27 A hay knife is a long-bladed knife (24-34 inches) used for sawing off sections at the end of a stack.

Newspaper adverts were downloaded from www.britishnewspaperarchive.co.uk and reproduced courtesy of Reach Licensing / Mirropix.com.

Walker's Farm, Odstone (1922)

Described as "*A valuable mixed farm*", consisting of 176 acres 0 roods and 19 perches, with a reserve price of £6,500 according to the informal sale documents produced by Messrs. Shakespeare & Mc Turk in 1922. The brick and tiled 5-bedroom farmhouse had the benefit of 4 attics and a flower garden complete with brick and slated summerhouse. The lot also included a multitude of farm buildings, including a lean-to duck house, as well as two, 2-bedroom cottages (one tiled and one thatched).

The farm was put up for sale again in 1927, but divided into four lots: the farmhouse; the farm buildings and the brick and tile cottage (93 acres in total); the thatched cottage; 62 acres of grass and arable land including 3 cowsheds and two grass and arable fields (20.5 acres).

Below Stairs and In Service at Gopsall

It is an irony that although Gopsall was built by a wealthy industrialist, Charles Jennens, and later transferred into the hands of the wealthy aristocratic Curzon-Howe family, the people who spent most time in the house were the many members of the domestic staff. From its earliest days, Gopsall was home to a vast number of servants, both those who 'lived in' and those who lived in the estate villages and tied cottages. Indeed, until the 1930s only those who worked for the 'big house', either directly in service or through some other avenue such as farming, were allowed to live in the village cottages. The first outsider to move into Congerstone was a miner called Pare who was not made overly welcome and was treated with great suspicion for a long while. He lived in Congerstone in one of the eyebrow cottages (now demolished) on the corner of Main Street and Shadows Lane opposite Fox Covert Farm. He liked to tell people he was so strong, he could *"lift himself up in a basket"*.

Little if anything, is known of the lives of the many people who worked in service at Gopsall Hall, as is the case for most large or aristocratic houses. The only exception to this is Errdig Hall in Wrexham (now in the care of The National Trust), where *"for nearly 200 years, Erddig's servants were recorded in portraits, photographs or verse"*.[1] If only that had been the case at Gopsall.

The further back in the record one travels, the more difficult it is to find details of anyone who was in service anywhere. There is virtually no information on Gopsall's 'Below Stairs' staff in the 18th century when Gopsall was owned by Charles Jennens and then his grand-nephew, Penn Assheton Curzon (Chapter 1). There were no census records before 1801 and lists of names were not collected centrally until 1841, so most of the information available is anecdotal and names are often missing or inaccurate. However, the will of Charles Jennens (dated 30th April 1765; proved 4th December 1773),[2] lists some small bequests that provide insight into the number and importance attached to his servants. Ten pounds was left to each of his 'minor' servants, listed as the under butler, groom, under groom, postillion[3] and six maid servants. The butler, coachman, gardener, grounds keeper and housekeeper received £20 each, and Jennens' husbandman, John Mugglestone, who was in charge of the day to day running of Gopsall Farm (Home Farm or Shornhill farm), received £50. The largest bequest of £200 (equivalent to about £31,000 in 2020) went to Benjamin Sevem (or Severn) who was simply described as *"my servant"*; his role and why he was Jennens' most rewarded servant is unknown. Therefore, in 1765, Jennens had a permanent staff of 15 servants and a farm manager to run the hall, park and farm at Gopsall.

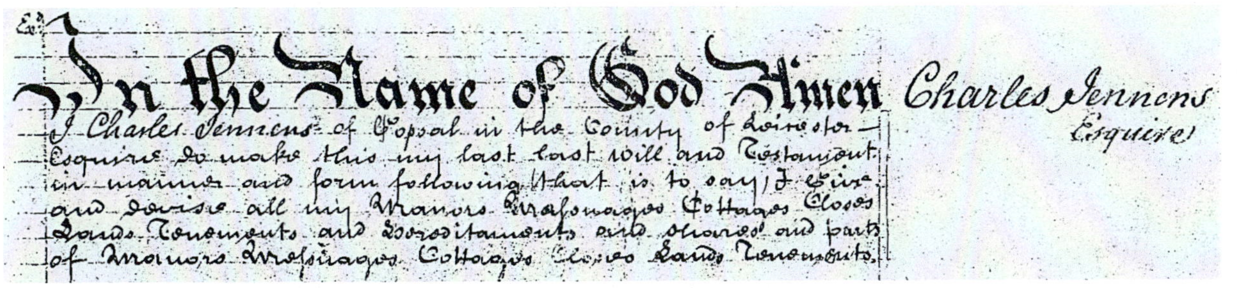

In the Name of God Amen Charles Jennens Esquire
I Charles Jennens of Gopsal in the County of Leicester Esquire do make this my last last will and Testament in manner and form following that is to say I give and devise all my Manors Messuages Cottages Closes Lands Tenements and Hereditaments and shares and parts of Manors Messuages Cottages Closes Lands Tenements.

Jennens' will also included one other 'staff' beneficiary, namely William Dickinson (1724-1808), who was bequeathed £200. Dickinson was described as steward in the will and, from the size of his legacy, must have been in post for some considerable time, possibly from the early 1750s.[4] A steward, in terms of the position held by William Dickinson, was today's equivalent of a Chief Executive Officer, a professional employee and should not be confused with a domestic steward, who was responsible for the day to day running of a house, hall or castle. William Dickinson had overall responsibility for running Jennens' estates and his duties included settling tenant disputes, overseeing the harvest and livestock, collecting rents, keeping the financial records, etc.[5] Land or estate stewards were well educated, had land and property of their own and reported directly to the owner. William was steward to Charles Jennens and, after Jennens' death in 1773, to Penn

The Grade II listed chest tomb of William and Mary Dickinson in St James' churchyard, Twycross. The tomb is in a prominent position close to the south entrance porch.

Assheton Curzon and finally to Baroness Howe. He died in 1808 and was buried in St James' churchyard, Twycross (see Appendix I for more information about William Dickinson).

Typically, information about Gopsall during the Victorian period, although full of references and pictorial evidence relating to the Curzon-Howe family, says very little about the staff. Virtually every family room is recorded in one or more photographs, but none appear to exist of the domestic or working rooms (kitchen, scullery, laundry etc).

For over 140 years, Gopsall was one of several Curzon-Howe family homes and, as was common practice for the wealthy at that time, used predominantly at particular times of the year. In the 19th century, the Curzon-Howe family had homes at 20 Curzon Street, Mayfair, London, Penn House near Amersham and Woodlands in Uxbridge, Middlesex as well as Gopsall Hall. Gopsall Hall was by far the grandest house with an enormous estate and garden that seems to have been especially used in the period around Christmas and for the shooting season. No doubt it was also used at other times and seems to have been a particular favourite with Georgiana, Countess Howe who was interred, at least temporarily, in the graveyard of St Mary's Church, Congerstone in 1906 (Chapter 9).

One of the most striking things about the domestic staff at Gopsall was how far many had been prepared to travel in order to take a position. Census records show that the staff came from every corner of the United Kingdom, which until 1921, included the entire island of Ireland. Many had been in service elsewhere before taking up Gopsall positions, some training at other big estates before securing higher positions here. Most of the women, if not all, appear to have been single, presumably being required to leave positions once married, something we would not countenance today. Indeed, being single would have been an attribute for those employed as personal servants who were required to travel with the family from home to home.

Although the majority of the staff at Gopsall were from the local area, an example of someone who travelled a considerable distance to work at Gopsall was John McCullam (1857-1944). He was born in County Monaghan, Ireland, moved to Scotland and then came to Gopsall as a groom, initially living above the stables!

'Irish Johnny', as he was known, eventually became head coachman. He married Elizabeth Jebbett from Newton Burgoland in

Gopsall coachmen photographed in the early 20th century. John McCullam is standing in the middle.

Coachmen and postillions were liveried and wore scarlet jackets with buttons carrying the Howe family crest. Dress shoes and bowler hats were worn by the men of the indoor staff. Even the beaters for the shoots were issued 'regulation' heavy thornproof 'cowgowns'.

1893 and settled in a rented estate cottage in Barton Lane, Congerstone. It was John who drove the coach to Shackerstone station to collect King Edward VII when he visited Gopsall in 1902 (Chapter 8) and, along with the estate tenants and cottagers, John and his family were invited to Viscount Curzon's 'Coming of Age' luncheon in 1905 (Chapter 9). John and Elizabeth eventually purchased their cottage in 1930, where they lived until they died in 1944; John having become a 'local' after living here for over 50 years. They had two sons and three daughters, one of whom, Beatrice, worked at Gopsall before she was married (Chapter 7).

A small number of memorial tablets in St Mary's Church and stones in estate village graveyards represent some of the few records we have of many of the Gopsall servants. One particularly intriguing inscription found above the retainers' (servants') box pew in St Mary's Church reads:

Sacred to the memory of Mrs Anne Hodson who was unfortunately
burnt to death December 16th 1824
She was 60 years of age, 30 of which
she spent in the service of the Curzon family
This small tribute of regard is erected by a grateful master to
the memory of an attached and faithful servant.

"*Unfortunately burnt to death*" would seem to be a classic piece of British understatement and one wonders what happened to Mrs Hodson so close to Christmas.

Below this there are two other memorial plaques, in remembrance of faithful servants who had long service careers with the family and lived to a good age. Francis Curzon was born in 1884, so Susan Dolby must have been working for the family for about 30 years when she died in 1914. Emily Chapple is not only described as a devoted nurse but also a faithful friend of the family of the 3rd Earl and Isabella, Countess Howe. She died aged 87 in 1915 and, if she had 46 years service, must have begun working for Richard William Penn Curzon in 1869, seven years before he became the 3rd Earl Howe.

IN
AFFECTIONATE REMEMBRANCE
OF
EDWARD IRWIN,
BORN AT FLORENCE COURT,
FEB 19, 1850,
DIED AT GOPSALL, OCT. 15, 1893.

A TRIBUTE OF RESPECT BY A FEW OF
HIS FRIENDS AND FELLOW SERVANTS
WHO VALUED HIS WORTH.

In St Mary's churchyard, an inscription on a gravestone refers to Edward Irwin. Irwin is an Irish surname and the only Florence Court we can trace at this time is Florence Court near Enniskillen. So, it looks as if Edward came here from Ireland. Florence Court is where the first ever Irish (fastigiate) yew tree was found and, unfortunately, we know more about the tree than we do about Edward.[6] He was working as a butler at Gopsall Hall between 1878 and 1893 and was married to Emma, a Yorkshire girl. The Irwins had four children, three of whom were born in Congerstone (Thomas, b. 1877 at Campsall, Yorkshire; Edward, b. 1878; Robert Henry, b. 1881 and George, b. 1882, all in Congerstone). The family lived in Congerstone whilst Edward 'lived in' at the Hall. When Emma died in 1883 the children lived with, and were brought up by, their aunt, Harriet Shillitoe, in Congerstone. So, Edward was widowed by the time he was 33 years old but remained in service at Gopsall until his death 10 years later.

Edward's inscription is surprising, as it suggests that his memorial was erected and paid for by "*his friends and fellow servants*" and not the 3rd Earl Howe. By contrast, several gravestones bearing witness to the long service of some of the servants were erected in St Mary's churchyard by the 1st Earl Howe:

Dear Lord, what helpless worms we are!
How weak and feeble is our frame!
We live exposed to every snare,
And life itself is but a dream.

IN
AFFECTIONATE REMEMBRANCE OF
Isaac Masser,
HE WAS IN THE SERVICE OF
THE EARL HOWE,
UPWARDS OF 37 YEARS,
and died much respected
FEBRUARY 17. 1856;
AGED 54 YEARS.

One wonders who chose the short verse inscribed at the bottom of Isaac's gravestone.

TO
the memory of
MILES THISTLEWHAITE,
who departed this life
the 2nd of July 1836:
in the 83rd YEAR of his AGE
Upwards of 60 years
in the service of
the NOBLE CURZON FAMILY,

ALSO, the body of
ELEANOR THISTLEWHAITE
his sister
who died Novr 19, 1829:
AGED 71 YEARS.

Both Isaac and Miles appear to have been happy to stay in their jobs at Gopsall for the best part of their lives. Sadly, although they were at Gopsall many years and Isaac *"died much respected"*, no record indicates what positions they held.

Apart from the domestic staff who travelled with the family (lady's maids, valets etc), there was also a core of staff who worked at one particular family house. Gopsall had a range of permanent skilled and unskilled people who were employed in the maintenance and working of the house and estate. These people are recorded in the various census documents of the time and it is surprising just how many staff were employed even at times when the family were in residence elsewhere. As Gopsall was the largest estate owned by the Curzon-Howe family, the kitchen gardens were put to full use supplying the family wherever they were domiciled. Hampers of fruit and vegetables were sent by train from the then busy Shackerstone railway station along with meat and cheeses from the farms and venison from the deer park.

The importance and extent of the kitchen and pleasure gardens at Gopsall required the employment of many gardeners, under the direction of a head gardener. Being head gardener at Gopsall was a significant position. The Curzon-Howes were closely associated with the Royal Family, they were widely known to treat their staff well (Chapter 7), Gopsall Park and gardens were nationally known and the 1st Earl Howe, in particular, was recognised as having expertise in, and knowledge, of farming and horticultural practices (Chapter 5). After about 1850, the added perk of a cottage for you and your family 'on site' would also have been an attractive prospect. The position of head gardener was one of the major appointments in any estate[7] and most 19th and early 20th century directories listed the name of the head gardener along with the bailiff or land agent, housekeeper and estate owner. Unlike for most of the Gopsall staff, information is available on the head gardeners at Gopsall from 1841 until the estate was sold by the 4th Earl Howe to Samuel Waring in 1918.

Neil Wilson was born about 1811 on the Isle of Bute; his father working for the Marquess of Bute as the forester. He served his apprenticeship at Mount Stuart House before getting a place at Chiswick gardens in London in 1828. Chiswick was the Horticultural Society's (not yet Royal) training garden for aspiring gardeners, and a position here was not easily attained.[8] After training at Chiswick, Neil was able to gain the position of head gardener at Gopsall, quite a step up in his career. In 1836 he married Sarah, also from Bute and by 1841 was listed on the census as 'Gardener' living in Congerstone. This was probably before the walled kitchen garden and adjoining head gardener's cottage were built and before the large numbers of glasshouses were erected (Chapters 2 & 4). He was apparently earning enough to employ Caroline Smith as a live-in domestic servant to assist Sarah when she had her first two children, Colin and Jane.

Ten years later, in 1851, Neil is recorded as living at Gopsall (in the newly built head gardener's cottage) with Sarah and a further group of offspring; Margaret, Isabella, Sarah, James and Mary. The servant Caroline seems to have moved on, but now a 13-year-old lodger lives with them. He is a scholar, William, from London. From what we know about the development of the hall site and associated garden buildings it is probable that Neil was intimately involved in establishing the walled kitchen gardens, glasshouses and the Cooke Show house (Chapter 4).

After being in charge of the park and gardens at Gopsall for around 20 years, in 1855, Neil decided to move on, and he and Sarah returned to Bute where he set up a nursery and seedsman business and was very successful.[9] One would think that Bute was a rather limited market for a nursery business, but there were a number of wealthy islanders at that time, not to mention the Marquise of Bute at Mount Stuart, where Neil had served his apprenticeship 30 years before.[8]

Emmanuel (sometimes Emanuel) Sage was born in 1827 in Colaton Raleigh, Devon and it is an account of the park and gardens at Gopsall, written by his son Arthur, that formed the basis for the descriptions of the park and gardens in Chapter 4. We know very little about Emmanuel until he appeared at Gopsall in September 1855 as head gardener,[10] taking over from Neil Wilson, now returned to Scotland. He cannot have suddenly become the head gardener at Gopsall and must have been through an apprenticeship and spent time as a journeyman gardener, working his way up the hierarchy. According to the Gardeners' Chronicle, a Mr Sage, gardener to Mr W.R. Robinson, Hill House, Acton won a number of prizes at horticultural shows from 1853 to June 1855.[11] Neither Mr Robinson nor his gardener are mentioned as prize winners during the following ten years, presumably because Mr Sage had moved to Gopsall.

An intricately designed wrought iron gate leading into the walled garden; probably through the east wall.

Emmanuel lived, in Colaton Raleigh, 2 miles from where Bicton Park is situated. At the time Bicton was a large country estate with a notable garden, so much so that today it is a botanical garden, with much of the planting and architecture contemporary with Emmanuel. The house itself is now Bicton College offering, by coincidence, training and apprenticeships to budding horticulturalists. As Emmanuel's home was within easy walking distance of Bicton, it is likely that he trained there before working his way up to his position as head gardener at Gopsall, a position he held from 1855 to 1870.

In 1858, Emmanuel married Emma Hopkins (b. 1826), whose parents farmed a large acreage at Sibson, and they had 4 sons: Emmanuel 'Merivale', Arthur, Edward and the youngest Charles. All were born at Gopsall where they lived in the gardener's cottage near the walled garden. In 1861, Emmanuel was recorded in the census as living in the cottage with Emma and first-born Emmanuel M. together with 15-year-old Eliza Henton, his domestic servant. Four young men are also listed as lodgers, all under-gardeners: Charles Tilley 22, Joseph Smith 18, James Laverner 18 and William Crosher 16. Usually, under-gardeners or journeymen would have lived in the bothies, so 'lodger', in this case, may mean living in the gardens' bothies. It would be very unusual for the staff to be living with the head man.

Emmanuel was obviously well regarded and The Gardeners' Chronicle and other sources record him showing produce at horticultural shows, both local to Gopsall and further afield. For example, in 1867, Emmanuel came second in two categories for growing grapes at the Crystal

In loving memory of Emmanuel Sage who died at Atherstone June 2nd 1872, aged 46 years.

Palace autumn show.[12] Despite being very successful at Gopsall and raising his family there, Emmanuel is shown in the 1871 census as having moved on. He is no longer head gardener to Earl Howe but is in business in Coleshill Street, Atherstone as a nurseryman and florist, employing 2 men and 1 boy. His sons also worked in the nursery when they were at home (2 sons went to boarding school, Emmanuel must have been making a good living). According to the memoir written by his son Arthur, Emmanuel left Gopsall after the death of the 1st Earl apparently because "*...the new Earl took very little interest in the district and soon there were changes at the hall...*" (Chapter 4). Much of the planting of the garden seen in photographs taken some 30 years after his departure is contemporary with Emmanuel's stewardship.

Emmanuel and Emma ran the nursery for several years specialising in early produce grown under glass; a major crop for the Sages being grapes. The family lived in a house on the nursery which had once been a 4-cottage terrace. They lived on the ground floor; the upper part having had its tiled roof removed and a glass structure replacing it, where grapes were grown. On 2nd June 1872, just two years after moving from Gopsall, Emmanuel died, aged 46 and was buried in St James' churchyard, Twycross. His wife Emma, continued to run the nursery until the lease on the property expired. We don't know what she did next, but over a period her sons emigrated to Australia where they continued their lives involved in farming and horticulture.

John Brown took over as head gardener at Gopsall on Emmanuel's departure. He served between 1871 and October 1875, living in the gardener's cottage with his wife Sarah, two daughters, Eleanor and Mary Ann, and his son John, who was himself employed as a gardener by his father. Judging from the produce he submitted to shows and articles written to the Gardeners' Chronicle, John's specialty was fruit of the *Prunus* genus; specifically apricots, peaches and nectarines. In October 1875, John has left Gopsall and appears to be at Kirby Hall Gardens, Fleetham, Bedale, Yorkshire.[13] He is advertising for a head gardener's position having been "*Gardener for the last five years to the Right Hon. Earl Howe.....*". However, he has not found a suitable position by March 1876 (the 2nd Earl Howe died in the February) when he again advertises his services: "*Gardener for the last five years to the late Earl Howe, Gopsall, is now disengaged and offers his services to any Nobleman or Gentleman requiring a first-class practical Man*".[14] Head gardeners usually moved to a better position at larger or more challenging gardens by choice, so one wonders if John moved of his own choosing.

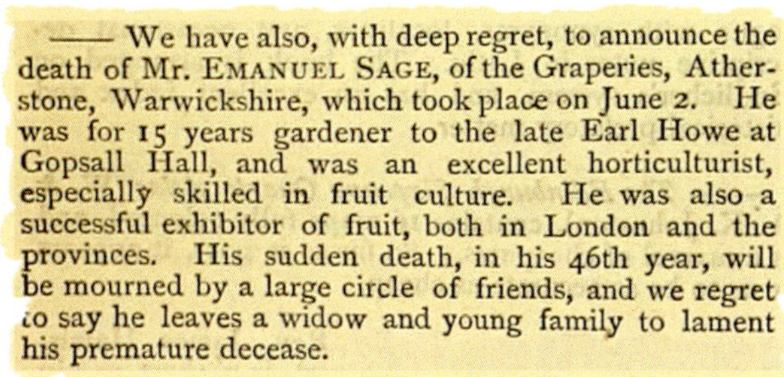

—— We have also, with deep regret, to announce the death of Mr. EMANUEL SAGE, of the Graperies, Atherstone, Warwickshire, which took place on June 2. He was for 15 years gardener to the late Earl Howe at Gopsall Hall, and was an excellent horticulturist, especially skilled in fruit culture. He was also a successful exhibitor of fruit, both in London and the provinces. His sudden death, in his 46th year, will be mourned by a large circle of friends, and we regret to say he leaves a widow and young family to lament his premature decease.

Emmanuel Sage's Obituary
(The Gardeners' Chronicle , June 1872)

A Mr H. David succeeded John Brown and stayed in post until 1878 or early 1879, during which time he reported the state of the potato and fruit crops at Gopsall to the Gardeners' Chronicle.[15] Presumably, he was initially appointed by the 2nd Earl Howe but must have spent most of his time working for the 3rd Earl.

Robert Williams was head gardener at Gopsall for the 3rd Earl Howe in August 1879. He had a team of 11 gardeners working for him, and lived with his wife Alice in the head gardener's cottage

Robert Williams of Gopsall, died June 10th, 1891, aged 42 years. Also Alice, his wife, died July 11th, 1889, aged 31 years.

along with their children Robert, Alice, Arthur and youngest son Francis. Robert Jnr was only 9 when he lost his mother in 1889 and 11 when his father died; his siblings even younger. We don't know what became of them. Robert Williams died 'in service' shortly after the census was taken in 1891 and is buried in St. Mary's churchyard with his wife.

The final head gardener at Gopsall was Joseph Lee, who worked for both the 3rd and 4th Earl Howe. Despite being the most recent head gardener, there is little information about Joseph or his family. We do know that some time before coming to Gopsall he worked in the gardens of Highbury Hall, Birmingham, the residence of the Rt Hon Joseph Chamberlain.[16] However, his life at Gopsall and what happened to Joseph after its sale is unknown.

After the sale of Gopsall in 1918, Edward Jones, an undergardener at the time, was kept on to try and maintain the garden, a seemingly impossible task for one man. He later took over as landlord at the Curzon Arms pub (now Turpin's Restaurant) in Twycross.

Garden produce, meats and cheeses were not the only things sent from Gopsall to the family when they were not in residence. Also making this journey on a weekly basis were mundane items of laundry

Mrs Hextall, second laundress (*left*) and the head laundress (*right*) in c.1900.

sent from Curzon Street to the many staff employed in the extensive laundry rooms at Gopsall, which included a large ironing room with an adjacent 'drying apparatus' (Chapter 2). Table linen, clothes and all other items of household furnishings were maintained and serviced by the permanent staff at Gopsall. One member of the laundry staff was Mrs Hextall of Congerstone (Chapter 7), who was employed as second laundress (1890-1901) along with her friend, who was the head laundress. She later became known as 'Granny Hextall' and lived in one of the pair of cottages overlooking the memorial green in Congerstone.

Gopsall footman (c.1895).

In 1851, a time when Gopsall was at its zenith in terms of family life and stature there were 34 servants (19 women and 15 men) classed as resident at Gopsall Hall for the terms of the census. This will not have included any staff resident at any of the other houses at the time or those who lived in estate property outside of Gopsall Park.

The butler, a Mr Speech, was apparently a bit of a stickler and was 48 years old; only the brewer-baker James Jaques being older at 52 years. The average age of staff at this time was 28 years.

According to the census document of 1851, the cook at Gopsall was a man, which must have been a very modern idea at the time. But were Martha Diaper (nursery maid) and Sopie Duck (laundry maid) having a bit of fun when they filled in the census form, or was this unintentional misspelling or their real names? Servants seem to have been made up of quite a transient population at this time as the next census in 1861 does not record any of the individuals listed in 1851.

In service at Gopsall Hall - 'living in' according to the 1851 census

Name	Position	Age	Name	Position	Age
Thomas Adcock	Outdoor servant	25	James Jaques	Brewer and baker	52
Ann Adcock	Kitchen maid	22	Eliza Jones	Housemaid	25
Edward Barbett	Footman	23	Elizabeth Martin	Coachman's wife	36
Ellen Bartlett	Housemaid	21	Isaac Massey	Groom	17
George Bloomfield	Postillion	18	Lydia Mice	Housemaid	24
Henry Briggs	Groom	19	Elizabeth Miller	Nursery maid	23
John Burdett	Outdoor servant	20	Louisa May Miller	Lady's maid	24
Rebecca Calder	House servant	26	Christiana O'Brien	Governess	42
William Deat	Usher	33	Jane Powell	Laundry maid	25
Martha Diaper	Nursery maid	17	Joshua Riley	Outdoor servant	22
Sopie Duck	Laundry maid	22	John Sian	Cook	29
Louis Eys	Footman	23	Margaret Smith	Laundry maid	19
Timothy Geeving	Under butler	38	Mr Speech	Butler	48
Catherine Gray	Kitchen maid	25	Catherine Tebbett	Housekeeper	41
Sarah Holliday	Housemaid	48	James Widdowson	Valet	23
Edward James	Keeper (out)	23	Neil Wilson	Head gardener	41
Hannah Jaques	House servant	23	Jane Wrighter	Laundry maid	34
Average age = 28					

Gopsall postillions[3]
Earnest Wormington from Shackerstone is on the left and his hat shown above.

Today, it seems hard to believe that being the coachman, postillion, usher, coalman or footman were full time occupations. When the coach wasn't required by the family, what did the coachman or the postillion do? The head coachman had various responsibilities, including overseeing the cleaning and maintenance of the vehicles in the 'carriage department' (e.g., gigs and four-in-hand) and the training of stable boys to serve as postillions. In addition, his position within the servants' hierarchy, equivalent to the under-butler, gave him other responsibilities in the management of the staff.[17] Similarly, the coalman had to ensure all the room coal scuttles were full and maintain the fires when lit, but what happened in the summer? Were fires required all year to combat the damp? No doubt he had several roles and was kept busy with other duties when fires were not required.

But what on earth were William Deat (1851) and John Jackson (1871) ushering? Well, an usher in a great house like Gopsall Hall in the 19th century that had a servants' hall (a large room serving as

In service at Gopsall Hall - 'living in' according to the 1871 census

Name	Position	Age	Name	Position	Age
Charlotte Bradley	Housemaid	29	William Heard	Helper	45
William Bradley	Butler	38	Susannah Holmes	Stillroom maid	21
John Brown	Head gardener	41	John Jackson	Usher of the Hall	42
Aluclia Chapman	Housemaid	23	Samuel Maidwell	Valet	26
Elizabeth Chapman	Cook	29	John Mould	Groom	17
George Henry Chiles	Underbutler	30	Mary Ann Paget	Kitchen maid	23
John Clarke	Footman	31	Elizabeth Pewitt	Housekeeper	40
Jane Collin	Laundry maid	23	John Rowell	Gardener	48
Samuel Collin	Helper	27	Sarah Sacombe	Housemaid	32
Henry Davis	Gardener	12	Charles Slurfit	Gardener	16
Eliza Evans	Laundry maid	30	Thomas Twigg	Gardener	27
John Forty	Helper	56	Caroline Villas	Lady's maid	37
Harriet Godfrey	Housemaid	23	George Wakefield	Coachman	57
Robert Harries	Footman	25	Jane Wilson	Housemaid	20
Ellen Hartwell	Scullery maid	20	Average age = 30.6		

In service at Gopsall Hall - 'living in' according to the 1881 census

Name	Position	Age	Name	Position	Age
Mary Adcock	Laundry maid	36	Maria Rowland	Housemaid	21
Bertha Ball	Housemaid	26	Nathaniel Stone	Gardener	23
John Cherrington	Gardener	24	James Tomlinson	Gardener	20
Frederick Cullen	Coachman	38	Ellen Whyte	Housemaid	18
Thomas Frost	Groom	25	Jane Williams	Housekeeper	35
George Jackson	Gardener	19	Robert Williams	Head gardener	31
Herbert Peach	Gamekeeper	15	Harriet Winter	Housemaid	22
William Peach	Gamekeeper	53	Laura Winterbourne	Laundry maid	31
Average age = 27					

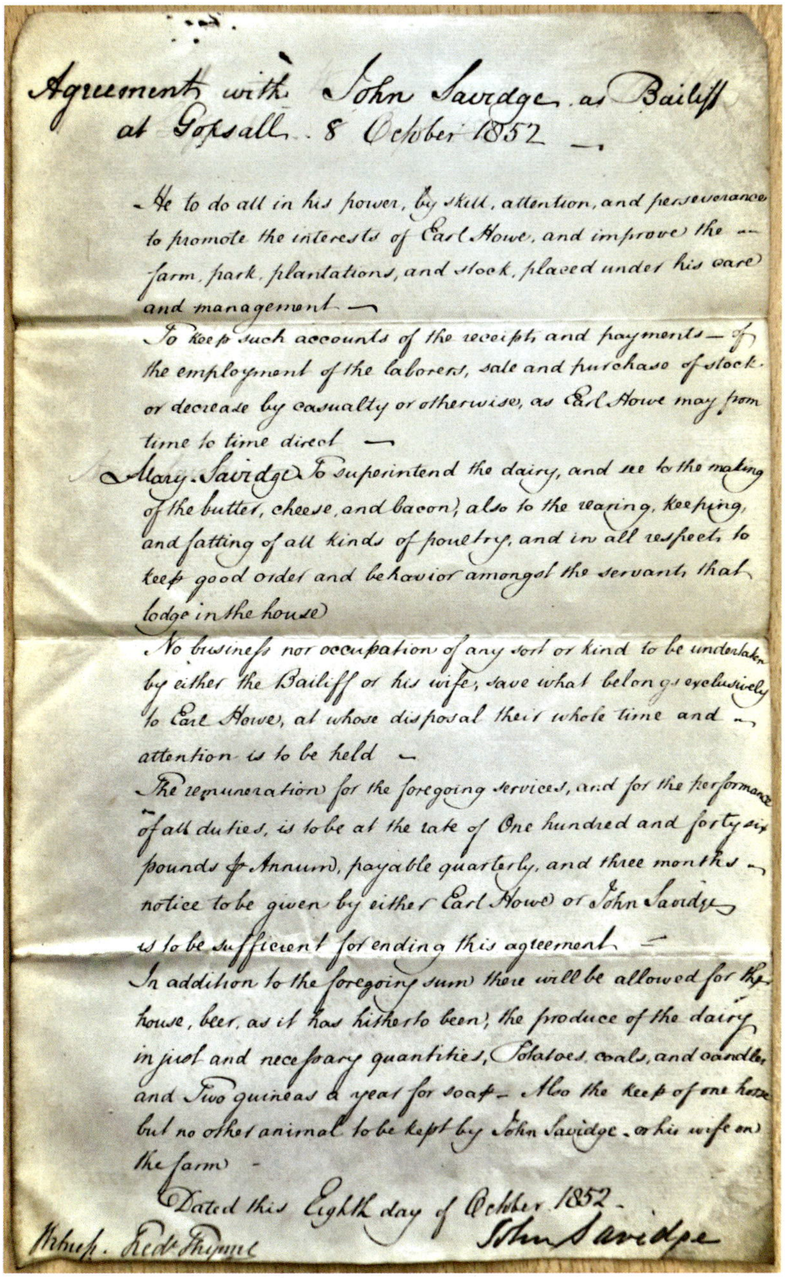

Agreement with John Savidge as Bailiff at Gopsall 8 October 1852 —

He to do all in his power, by skill, attention, and perseverance to promote the interests of Earl Howe, and improve the farm, park, plantations, and stock, placed under his care and management —

To keep such accounts of the receipts and payments — of the employment of the laborers, sale and purchase of stock, or decrease by casualty or otherwise, as Earl Howe may from time to time direct —

Mary Savidge To superintend the dairy, and see to the making of the butter, cheese, and bacon; also to the rearing, keeping, and fatting of all kinds of poultry, and in all respects to keep good order and behavior amongst the servants that lodge in the house

No business nor occupation of any sort or kind to be undertaken by either the Bailiff or his wife, save what belongs exclusively to Earl Howe, at whose disposal their whole time and attention is to be held —

The remuneration for the foregoing services, and for the performance of all duties, is to be at the rate of One hundred and forty six pounds p Annum, payable quarterly, and three months notice to be given by either Earl Howe or John Savidge is to be sufficient for ending this agreement —

In addition to the foregoing sum there will be allowed for the house, beer, as it has hitherto been; the produce of the dairy in just and necessary quantities, Potatoes, coals, and candles, and Two guineas a year for soap — Also the keep of one horse but no other animal to be kept by John Savidge or his wife on the farm —

Dated this Eighth day of October 1852 —

Witness. Richd Thynne — John Savidge

Bailiff's contract signed by John Savidge on the 8th October 1852.[18]

a dining and sitting room for the majority of servants), was essentially the master of that hall. Amongst other things, he would have to keep the servants' hall clean, lay the cloth for meals, bring refreshments or beer to those privileged to have it, keep the tankards and beer vessels clean and ensure that no person left the hall intoxicated! William Deat probably also had to assist James Jaques in brewing beer and baking bread. By contrast, as there were no brewers or bakers mentioned in the 1871 census, it is likely that John Jackson was wholly responsible for brewing and baking, as well as his servants' hall duties.[17]

Senior staff on the Gopsall Estate, such as the bailiff were employed after signing quite detailed and wide ranging agreements. John Savidge's contract stated that he should "*do all in his power, by skill, attention and perseverance to promote the interests of Earl Howe*" in terms of the farm (Shornhill), park, plantations and stock. In addition, he was to "*keep accounts of receipts and payments*" for employing labourers and the sale and purchase of all stock etc. The agreement also covered his wife Mary who was "*to superintend the dairy and see to the making of the butter, cheese and bacon, also the rearing, keeping and fattening of all kinds of poultry, and in all respects to keep good order and behaviour amongst the servants that lodge in the house*".

Neither were allowed to undertake other work as their whole time "*belongs exclusively to Earl Howe*". The salary was £146 per year (about £21,000 today) and also included accomodation in the farmhouse, allocation of "*necessary quantities*" of beer, dairy products, potatoes, coal and candles plus the keep of one horse and two guineas a year for soap!

From studying the floor plans of the hall (Chapter 2) it is clear that the hall servants were well provided for in terms of their personal and social space. There was a large servants' hall close to the servants' entrance. In addition, the housekeeper, a very important member of the domestic staff, had her own sitting room and a large first floor bedroom overlooking the north courtyard. Similarly, the house steward, butler and cook all had their own rooms and even the housemaids had their own sitting room.

Although there were a number of staff working at Gopsall in the early part of the 20th century whose names could be recalled by local villagers in the latter part of the century, few details were remembered (Chapter 7). However, one or two have left trails that we have been able to follow in a little more detail. John McCullam (head coachman), Joseph Lee (head gardener), Edward Jones (gardener) and Mrs Hextall (laundress), have already been spoken of. Another is Charlie Clarke who lived in the Old Forge in Congerstone, which was actually a carpenter's shop. Charlie was, at times, a gardener and gamekeeper at Gopsall, as well as being village constable. He died on the 10th October 1970, aged 89 years. We also have a little information about some of the 20th century gamekeepers and, the most important servant of all, Mrs Battey, the housekeeper.

Gopsall staff recorded in the first years of the 20th century[19]

Name	Position	Name	Position
Mrs Dunstan*	Housekeeper	Mr Burnett	Agent of the estate
Mrs Elizabeth Battey+	Housekeeper	Mr Saunders	Bailiff at Snarestone
Henry E Wise	Butler	(Thomas) Joseph Lee	Head gardener
Samuel Prince	Butler	Frank Bartlett	Gardener
Mr JG Lambdin	House steward	Henry Blakeway	Gardener
Thomas Blanchard++	Unknown	John Carrington	Gardener
Anastasia Murphy	Lady's maid	Henry Dunning	Gardener
Alice Pickett	Housemaid	Henry Grant	Gardener
Harriet Reece	Housemaid	Frederick Harrison	Gardener (pot boy)
Mary Townend	Housemaid	Frank Hough	Gardener
Mrs Hextall	Laundress	Edward Jones	Gardener
Annie Gosling	Laundry maid	Allen Ridgeway	Gardener
Harriet Moslin	Laundry maid	William Tuff	Gardener
Ms A Race	Laundry maid	Lewis Young	Gardener
Thomas Spare #	General servant	Charlie Clarke	Gardener/keeper
Mr Godfrey	Coalman	William Peach	Gamekeeper
Beatrice McCullam	Unknown	Herbert Peach	Gamekeeper
John McCullam	Head coachman	George (Bill) Smith**	Gamekeeper
Mr A Challis	Stud groom	Willie Wormington	Gamekeeper
John Alison	Groom	Mr H Wood	Golf professional
Mr Jakes	Carpenter	Jack Harris	Lawnman (golf links)
Mr Oliver	Carpenter	Mr Pear	Bricklayer
Mr Willeby	Carpenter	James Jones**	Farm labourer

+ In post from 1904; ++ Ex. Bearer Company of the Imperial Yeomanry Field Hospital in South Africa; * In post until 1904; ** Lived in Twycross lodge at different times; # Lived in Shackerstone lodge.

Charlie Clarke in his WWI uniform.

During the first decade of the 20th century, the names of eight gamekeepers are mentioned in newspaper cuttings about poaching on the Gopsall Estate (W. Peach, H. Peach, J. Carrington, A. Payne, R. Payne, A. Lees, G.W. Smith and W.R. Wormington). However, there is one gamekeeper, Woods, whose name only appears in the shooting records kept by the 4th Earl Howe (Chapter 8). He is mentioned repeatedly from December 1900 through to the 1909-1910 shooting season and was the keeper who accompanied the Earl and King Edward VII on the December shoots of 1902. It is possible that he was head keeper for the period between 1900 and 1904. We know that Herbert Peach called himself head keeper by 1905[20] and Woods together with Peach are mentioned in the shooting records from 1904 to 1910. We have, however, been unable to find any mention of Woods at Gopsall or Penn in census records or newspaper reports.

William Peach was head gamekeeper in the twenty year period up to the turn of the century and his son, Herbert Peach was head keeper in 1905[20]. Indeed, Herbert (aged 35) was living in the head keeper's cottage according to the 1901 census, so may have taken over as head keeper directly from his father at this time and would have been head keeper during the visit of King Edward VII in 1902 (Chapter 8). According to the Gopsall shooting records, Herbert was still a keeper at Gopsall during the 1917-1918 season but had moved on by 1919 to become keeper for Market Bosworth.[20]

Gopsall gamekeepers and beaters

This photograph was probably taken in the second decade of the 20th century. The five keepers are wearing their lovat green tweed jackets and knickerbockers for which they were measured annually by a firm of London tailors.[21]

The two older men on the right, not wearing beaters' smocks, are probably retired keepers, working part-time. One appears to be wearing his old lovat green uniform. The beaters from local villages were employed on an *ad hoc* basis.

WILLIAM PEACH, died July 4, 1909, Aged 83. Gamekeeper at Gopsall in the 1881 census and buried in St James' churchyard, Twycross.

George William (Bill) Smith appears to have been the next head keeper. He had started work at Gopsall as a gamekeeper's lad in 1878, when he was 16 years old and became assistant keeper in 1896. From the recollections of his daughter Daisy (b. 1904), the family were living in the head keeper's cottage in about 1914.[21] However, because of the isolation of the gamekeeper's cottage in the park, Bill and his family moved to Twycross lodge, where they lived until sometime after Samuel Waring purchased Gopsall in 1918. When Bill retired and vacated Twycross lodge is unknown, but by 1929, the lodge was occupied by James Jones, who at age 74, was awarded first prize for long service at the Ashby Show.[22] His 52 years at Gopsall appear to have been as a farm labourer, making him a surprising choice as the guest, representing the Gopsall Estate, at the London wedding of Eleanor, Lord Waring's daughter, to Captain Critchley in 1923.[23] Perhaps seniority in length of service for the estate was the deciding factor.

Waring rarely visited Gopsall, which was managed by Major Miles who participated in and encouraged shooting on the estate (Chapter 1). As far as we know, Willie Wormington took over from Bill Smith as head gamekeeper and was living in the keeper's cottage northeast of the hall on the edge of Shackerstone Fields Covert in the 1930s (see Brian McCullam, Chapter 7). He had been a keeper at Gopsall since the early 1900s (at least) and would have had extensive experience of formal game shoots, including those during the visit of King Edward VII in 1902 (Chapter 8). In the 1930s he organised informal 'corn cutting' shoots; spacing the men out with the guns to shoot the rabbits as they came out of the corn during harvesting. In addition, as head gamekeeper he was responsible for rearing partridge and pheasant; the rearing pens (pheasantry) were behind his cottage. When he retired, he went to live in Church Walk, Shackerstone with his wife, Mary Ann. whom he predeceased. Mary Ann died in 1951, aged 86; the couple had been married 64 years.[24]

Elizabeth Battey was born in 1855 at Cubbington, near Leamington Spa, Warwickshire and, in 1891 at the age of 36, she was working as a housemaid at Maiden Erlegh House, Earley, Buckinghamshire. Elizabeth was obviously a very capable and ambitious lady. In 1901 she was recorded in the census for Warwick St Mary as the housekeeper at Warwick Castle, employed by Frances Evelyn Greville, the Countess of Warwick, to manage the female staff, and from 1904 until 1914, she was the housekeeper to the 4th Earl Howe. Gopsall's last housekeeper had quite a reputation and was described by some as "*thinking herself the Countess*". It is said that she filed into St Mary's Church on Sundays into the second box pew (only second to the Howe family pew) with an entourage of lesser servants behind her (Chapter 7). She seems to have been a very strict woman, but given her place in the household, one would expect her to be so considered.

Mrs Battey had a friend, Elizabeth McCulloch, in America with whom she corresponded regularly by letter.[25] These letters are a fascinating record of what was happening with the Howe family and the many family homes, as Mrs Battey seems to have been the housekeeper at both Woodlands Park and Gopsall Hall, so must have moved as and when required with the family. Her letters show that she also accompanied the family when they were in their London home, Curzon House in Mayfair.

Elizabeth Battey's letters portray a woman proud of what she did as a career, and that she was well regarded by all her employers (summaries of the letters are reproduced in Appendix III of this chapter). They give a real insight into the daily comings and goings of a well-connected aristocratic family. They also rather contradict her staff's belief that she was haughty and "*above herself*", as she writes to her friend in a very down to earth manner (for the time) and specifically asks her friend, Elizabeth McCulloch, to call her by her first name and be less formal. At Gopsall, Mrs Battey was probably using an air which she felt was appropriate with staff of lower rank. That said, Mr McCullam, the head coachman clearly did not have a great relationship with Mrs Battey (Chapter 7). At one of their meetings, he is said to have told her, *"I hope that I die the same day as you, the devil will be that busy dealing with you, he'll never have time to deal with me!"*

At the end of her working career, sometime after 1914, Elizabeth Battey moved to Assheton House, Twycross where she died on 27th March 1920 and was buried in St James' churchyard. One of her letter's, dated 21st January 1912 is copied on the following two pages. It tells about the December 2011 shoot at Gopsall when King Manuel of Portugal was a guest; shoot photos are shown in Chapter 7.

Edward Jones, Gopsall's last gardener.

ELIZABETH BATTEY of Cubbington, Warwickshire.
Died March 27th 1920, Aged 65.

In 1951 when the hall was awaiting demolition, the staff at Gopsall consisted of two people, Edward Jones, left to look after the gardens and a woman left to look after the house. Many reasons are cited for the decline of the country house in the United Kingdom in the period around the 1950s including running costs, lack of empathy, death duties etc. One item often overlooked was the difficulty in finding staff during a period when two world wars saw hundreds of thousands of able-bodied men leave their positions never to return.

However, Gopsall Hall's fate was probably sealed when it was purchased by Samuel Waring in 1918. The hall was never again used as a family residence and after the failed sale in 1927 the building was left empty until it was requisitioned by the government for military use in the second World War (Chapter 11). Even so, it may have survived destruction had thieves not stolen much of the roof lead in December 1950, making renovation economically unviable. It is a cruel irony that the day before the first lead theft that December, the hall was surveyed by the Society for the Protection of Ancient Buildings and it was concluded that *"the main structure was sound, and that a few first-aid repairs of a comparatively minor nature would have made the building weatherproof for many years"*.[26]

Over time many people came and went, lived and died in service at Gopsall Hall and, like the hall, for most there is little trace left today.

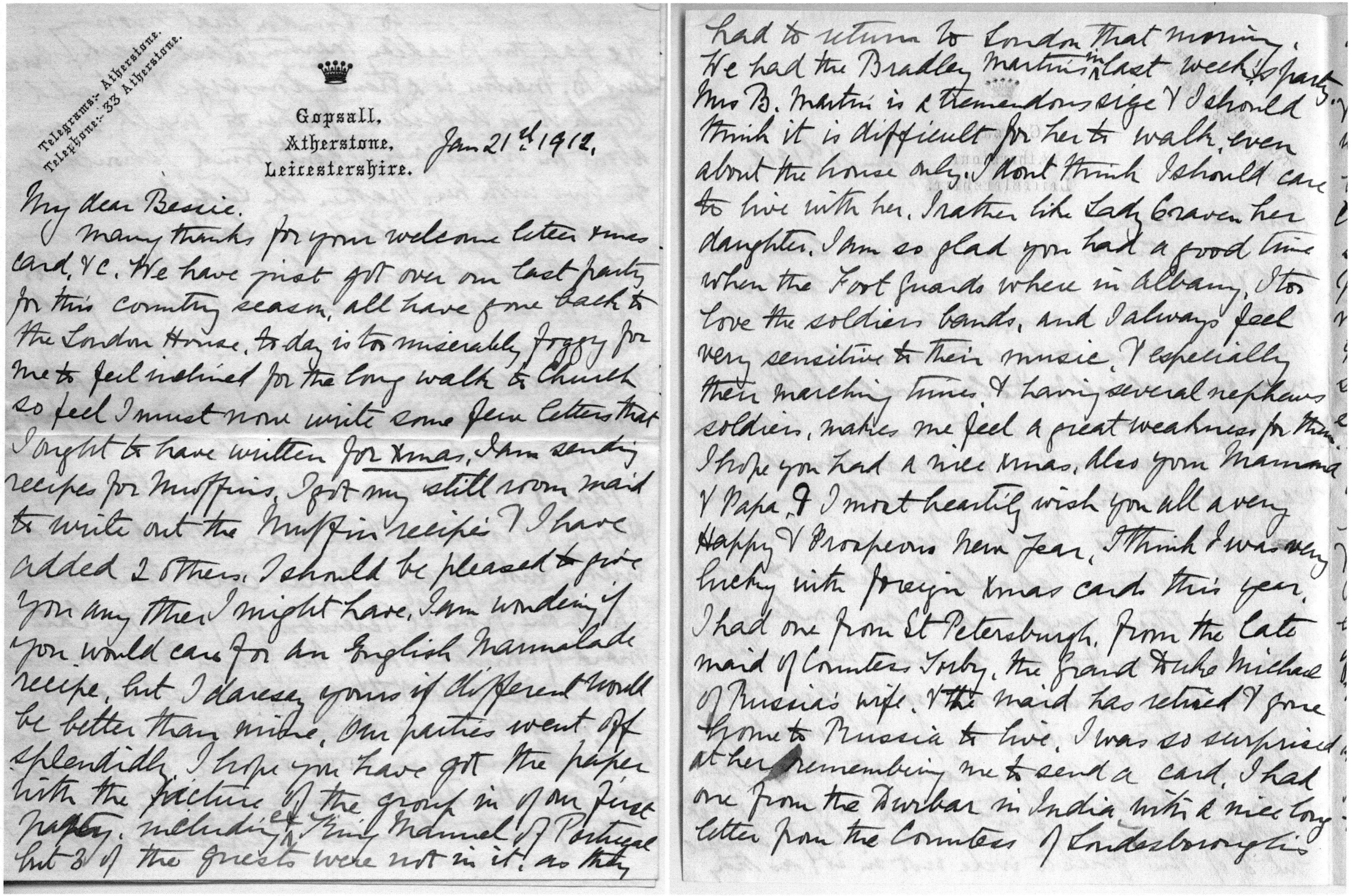

Telegrams:- Atherstone.
Telephone:- 33 Atherstone.

Gopsall,
Atherstone,
Leicestershire.

Jan 21st 1912.

My dear Bessie.

Many thanks for your welcome letter Xmas card, &c. We have just got over our last party for this country season, all have gone back to the London House. To-day is too miserably foggy for me to feel inclined for the long walk to Church so feel I must now write some few letters that I ought to have written for Xmas. I am sending recipes for Muffins. I got my still room maid to write out the Muffin recipe & I have added 2 others. I should be pleased to give you any other I might have. I am wondering if you would care for an English Marmalade recipe, but I daresay yours if different would be better than mine. Our parties went off splendidly. I hope you have got the paper with the picture of the group in of our first party, including King Manuel of Portugal but 3 of the guests were not in it, as they

had to return to London that morning. We had the Bradley Martins in last week's party. Mrs B. Martin is a tremendous size & I should think it is difficult for her to walk, even about the house only. I don't think I should care to live with her. I rather like Lady Craven her daughter. I am so glad you had a good time when the Foot Guards where in Albany. I too love the soldiers bands, and I always feel very sensitive to their music, & especially their marching tunes & having several nephews soldiers, makes me feel a great weakness for them. I hope you had a nice Xmas. Also your Mamma & Papa. & I most heartily wish you all a very Happy & Prosperous New Year. I think I was very lucky with foreign Xmas cards this year. I had one from St Petersburgh. from the late maid of Countess Torby, the Grand Duke Michael of Russia's wife. & the maid has retired & gone home to Russia to live. I was so surprised at her remembering me to send a card. I had one from the Durbar in India with a nice long letter from the Countess of Londesborough

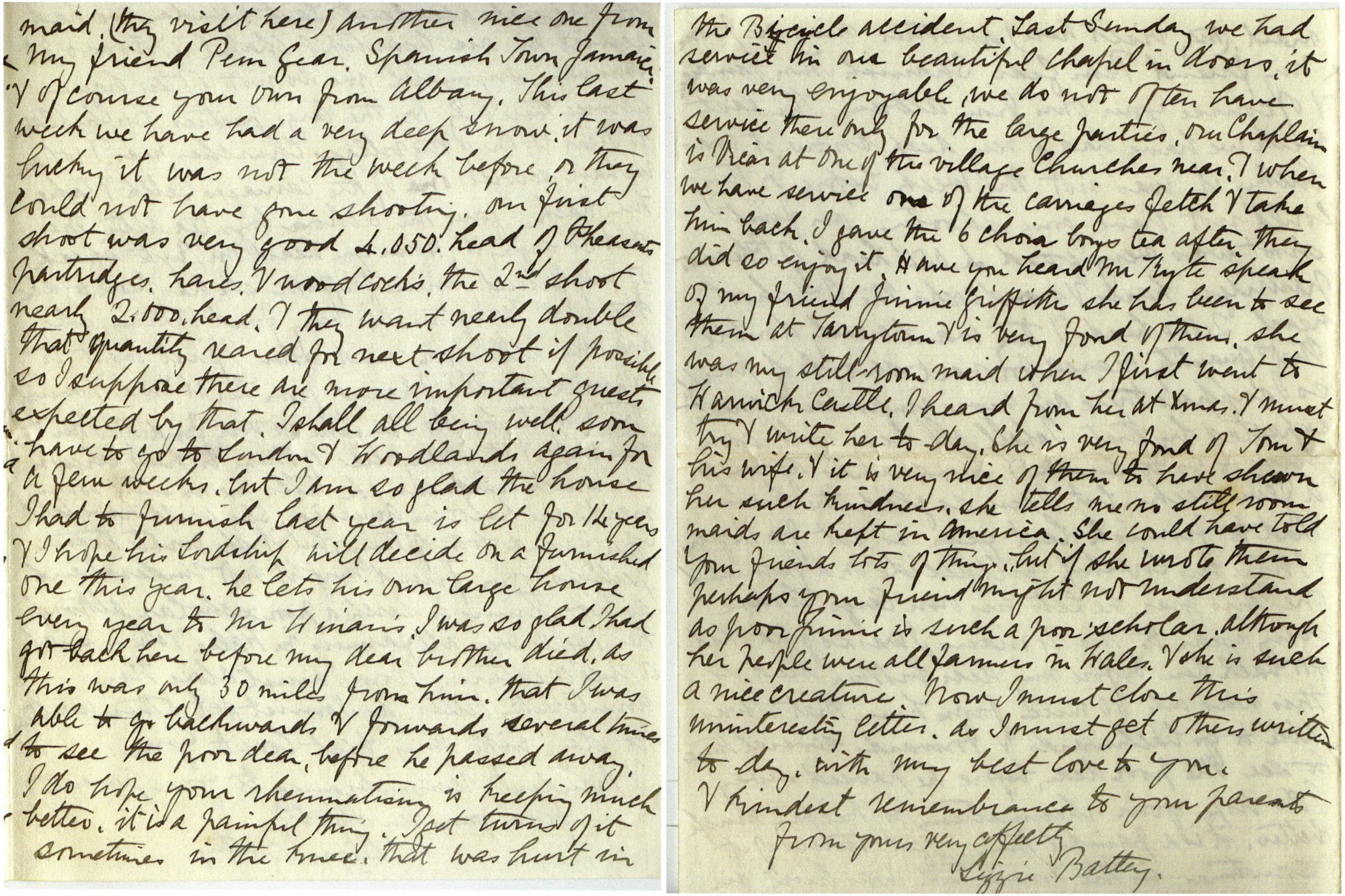
maid (they visit here) another nice one from
my friend Pem Gear. Spanish Town Jamaica
& of course your own from Albany. This last
week we have had a very deep snow. it was
lucky it was not the week before, or they
could not have gone shooting. our first
shoot was very good 4.050. head of Pheasants
partridges. hares. & woodcocks. the 2nd shoot
nearly 2.000. head. & they want nearly double
that quantity reared for next shoot if possible
so I suppose there are more important guests
expected by that. I shall all being well soon
have to go to London & Woodlands again for
a few weeks. but I am so glad the house
I had to furnish last year is let for 14 years
& I hope his Lordship will decide on a furnished
one this year. he lets his own large house
every year to Mr Winans. I was so glad I had
got back here before my dear brother died. as
this was only 30 miles from him. that I was
able to go backwards & forwards several times
to see the poor dear, before he passed away.
I do hope your rheumatism is keeping much
better. it is a painful thing. I get turns of it
sometimes in the knee. that was hurt in

the Bicycle accident. Last Sunday we had
service in our beautiful chapel in doors. it
was very enjoyable. we do not often have
service there only for the large parties. our Chaplain
is Vicar at one of the village Churches near. & when
we have service one of the carriages fetch & take
him back. I gave the 6 choir boys tea after. they
did so enjoy it. Have you heard Mr Tyte speak
of my friend Jinnie Griffiths she has been to see
them at Tarrytown & is very fond of them. she
was my still-room maid when I first went to
Warwick Castle. I heard from her at Xmas. & I must
try & write her to-day. She is very fond of Tom &
his wife. & it is very nice of them to have shewn
her such kindness. she tells me no still room
maids are kept in America. She could have told
your friends lots of things. but if she wrote them
perhaps your friend might not understand
as poor Jinnie is such a poor scholar. although
her people were all farmers in Wales. & she is such
a nice creature. Now I must close this
uninteresting letter. as I must get others written
to-day. with my best love to you.
& kindest remembrance to your parents
from yours very affectly
Lizzie Battey.

Reproduced by kind permission of the Department of Special Collections and University Archives, W.E.B. Du Bois Library, University of Massachusetts Amherst.

The carpenters at Gopsall; their workshop was in the stable block.

Major Albert Miles (*left*) was in charge of the Gopsall Estate for Lord Waring from 1919 to the outbreak of WWII. He also represented Gopsall Ward on the local rural council.

Sam Pegg (Gopsall gardener; *left*) with the Rev Leonard Ottley Warner, rector of Congerstone (c.1905).

The hundreds of tenants, estate workers and their families photographed outside the north front of Gopsall Hall in October 1923.

APPENDIX I

William Dickinson
Steward to Charles Jennens, Penn Assheton Curzon & Baroness Howe

The following is derived from 'No Ordinary Surgeon' by Dorothy Bentley Smith based upon source material from 'The Diaries and Estate Memoranda books of William Dickinson'.[4,5]

In 1752/3 William Dickinson was living in Congerstone as a Gopsall tenant with his wife Mary. William's schooling in Yorkshire had given him a clear understanding of accountancy, and from the age of 13 or 14 he was apprenticed to a gentleman farmer to learn farm and estate management. When William came of age, he claimed his inheritance; a small farm in Exilby, Yorkshire. The family also had some local land, as William and Mary's marriage agreement included a tenanted property; 10 acres near Belton with house, barns and stable.

It is not known whether William was in sole charge as steward in 1753 or whether he was an assistant or journeyman steward serving his apprenticeship before stepping into the main role. However, late in 1753, Mary gave birth to their first son, William, who was baptised in St Mary's Church, Congerstone on 9th December. Over the following 16 years, whilst William Snr worked as steward for Charles Jennens and developed his own farm, Mary industriously produced a further 6 children: Elizabeth, Robert, Stephen, Mary, another Robert and Ann.

William had sufficient money to have his own brewing arrangements in Witherley; not as a business but to provide beer for the household to drink, a safer bet than contaminated water. On a visit to the site, William's second son Robert was tragically killed, the death recorded as being "*scalded in a tub of wert*". A later son was christened Robert in his memory but, in a further tragedy, this Robert died, aged 8, after contracting smallpox whilst at school in Atherstone.

The death of Charles Jennens in 1773 complicated William Dickinson's job with the dividing up of the various estate holdings between several beneficiaries. His son, William Jnr, who had gained skills in accountancy and would have served as apprentice to his father for some years previously, helped his father and, over the years, took on more and more of the work. William Snr was now steward for Assheton Curzon, whose son Penn Assheton Curzon (1757-1797), would inherit Gopsall when he came of age in 1778. It was from just before this time until his death in 1808 that William Snr started to keep detailed notebooks of his duties as estate steward.[5]

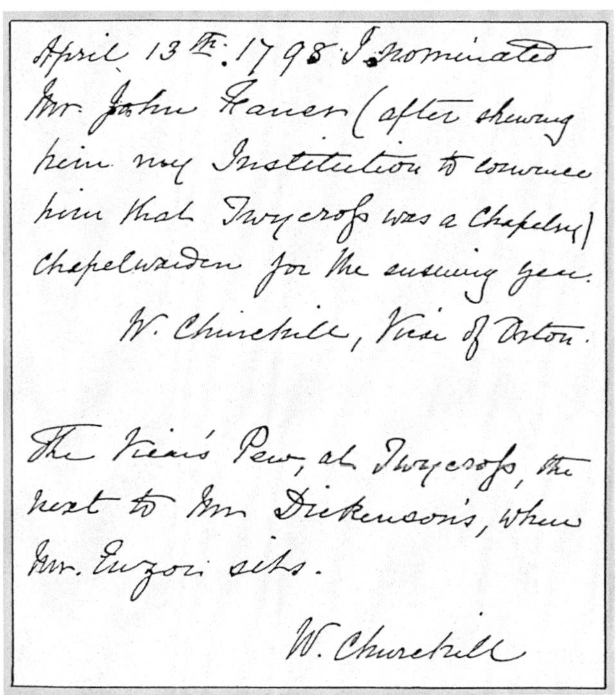
April 13th: 1798 I nominated Mr. John Hauer (after shewing him my Institution to convince him that Twycross was a Chapelry) Chapelwarden for the ensuing year.

W. Churchill, Vicar of Orton.

The Vicar's Pew, at Twycross, the next to Mr. Dickinson's, where Mr. Curzon sits.

W. Churchill

William Snr's duties became more arduous when plans for building the Ashby canal were put forward in 1792 and, in addition to William Jnr's help, he engaged his other son Stephen, a solicitor, to deal with the legal aspects of the case. Penn Curzon was initially against this development because the canal crossed the Gopsall Estate and may have affected the water supply to the estate and contravened a clause in Charles Jennens will[2] invalidating Penn Curzon's ownership of Gopsall. However, the bill to allow its construction was passed in 1794, with a guarantee that if the Gopsall water supply was affected the owner would receive £50,000 in compensation.[27] It was around this time that William Snr moved to a farm he had purchased in Witherley, but he continued to be steward, with increasing help from son William, to Penn Curzon and then, after his death in 1797, to his wife Baroness Howe.

The death of William Jennens, who died without children or a signed will in 1798, resulted in Court of Chancelry proceedings that may have involved all three of the Dickinsons. However, the great 'Jennens versus Jennens' lawsuit did not start until 1810, years after part of William Jennens' estate had been awarded to the young Richard William Penn Curzon-Howe (later 1st Earl Howe of the second creation) while under the guardianship of his mother, Baroness Howe.[28]

An extract from the writings of the Rev. William Churchill (vicar of Orton-on-the-Hill; inducted 24th October 1789, died 1804) in 1798 demonstrates the Dickinson family's position in society and relationship to the Curzons. Written at a time when the wealthy paid for a pew in church, Churchill writes: *"The vicar's pew at Twycross, the next to Mr Dickinson's, where Mr Curzon sits"*. William could obviously afford to pay for the same pew used by his employers. Interestingly, although living in Congerstone, William Snr christened 5 of his 7 children at St James', Twycross, which was the favoured church of both Charles Jennens and the Curzon family at this time.

In the Name of God Amen William
I William Dickinson of Witherley in the
County of Leicester Gentleman do make and
ordain this my last Will and Testament in manner
and form following that is to say I give and
bequeath to my Wife [illegible] Dickinson and
her assigns for and during the term of her
natural life one annuity or yearly sum of
one hundred pounds of lawful money of
Great Britain free of all taxes and deductions
Dickinson

William Dickinson Snr died in August 1808, with his son William Jnr as sole executor of his will.[29] The contents of the will revealed William Snr's considerable astuteness in amassing a small fortune. In addition to the inherited property in Yorkshire, the Belton holding from his marriage settlement and his Witherley farm, he had invested in properties just beyond the periphery of the Gopsall estate. These included 66 acres at 'Battle Flat' (with tenanted house and closes) between Ellistown and Stanton under Bardon and 75 acres at Wigston Parva (with 3 houses, buildings, closes and meadowland). Cash bequests to family members amounted to nearly £11,000 (equivalent to over £900k in 2020), emphasising the fact that he was a middle class professional and certainly not a servant. William Snr was buried in St James' churchyard, in an altar tomb close to the church entrance.

William Dickinson Jnr, continued to do the Gopsall estate accounts for Baroness Howe and then for Richard William Penn Curzon-Howe (later 1st Earl Howe in 1821) when he came of age in 1817. However, he did not take on the full stewardship. William Jnr died on 4th April 1825 and was buried in a vault in St James' churchyard, separate to, and the other side of the church from, his parents' chest tomb.

Stone top of William Dickinson Jnr's vault, which also contains the remains of his wife (Frances; d. 1831), his nephew (William Binley Dickinson; d. 1870) and his wife (Elizabeth; d. 1836) and two of their children (William; d. 1825 & Charlotte; d. 1827). As seen today, much of the lead lettering of the inscription has been lost.

APPENDIX II

James Widdowson
In service under four Earls Howe

HALF A CENTURY WITH THE HOWES.[31]

CHAT WITH MR. J. T. WIDDOWSON.

INTERESTING REMINISENCES OF THE ENCLOSURE RIOTS.

The South Bucks Standard, Friday 12th August 1910

"*Come any day you like and at any hour most convenient to yourself, I never leave the estate, and you will have no difficulty in finding me*." It was the way that Mr. J.T. Widdowson, the veteran agent of Lord Howe, at Penn; replied to my suggestion of a chat with him over his reminiscences of a long life. It will be remembered that he was 83 years of age only a few days ago.

The reply was, too, characteristic of the man, and the sentence with which we have opened this article embodies his sense of loyalty to duty. For some sixty-four years he has been in the service of the family of the Earls of Howe, and of that number he has spent no less than 52, as agent of the extensive estate at Penn. He has seen service under four Earl Howes, including of course, the present holder of the title (*the 4th Earl*), who, as Lord Curzon, represented the Wycombe (or South Bucks) Division in Parliament as the predecessor of Mr. Grenfell (now Lord Desborough).

When I arrived at Mr. Widdowson's residence, on the Penn Street Estate, I found him in his office amidst typical surroundings. Books relating to the affairs of the estate were piled around the room, and on the desk there was evidence of extensive correspondence. The 'other side' of the agent's life was to be found in the rack of guns and other weapons, and evidence of a love of English sport. *"For over half a century I have done their Lordships' business in this room, and from here a vast amount of correspondence has been carried on,"* said Mr. Widdowson noticing my glance of interest over the room.

To look at Mr. Widdowson - and let our portrait be the judge - it seemed almost incredible that he had passed well over the fourscore span. Upright, clear-featured, courteous and genial, the uninitiated would have credited him with much younger years.

It was soon made perfectly clear that Mr. Widdowson is not a man who likes to talk about himself, but, in the course of a frank informal chat, I gathered some interesting reminiscences of a faithful and strenuous career.

As a youth, Mr. Widdowson saw service with the First Earl of Howe, on the estate at Gopsall, Leicestershire; and was for some little time on the estate at Gotham, Northamptonshire. He said, *"I joined the family when I was 18 years of age and I have never since left it"*.

James Widdowson entered the 1st Earl's employment in 1845-46 and in 1851 he was valet at Gopsall. He gained promotion at Gopsall and then moved to the Penn Estate in 1858 as agent where he worked for four Earls Howe.

James died in March 1921 (aged 93) and was buried in Holy Trinity churchyard, Penn Street.

Mr. Widdowson, like his father before him, was in his younger days, an expert 'dog breaker'. That is to say, one who trains pointers and setters. And, there hangs in his office at the present time, a quant painting of a dog, 'pointing' at a pheasant in a tree. It is a pictorial conception which does credit to the artist's imagination. Mr. Widdowson's skill in the management of field dogs was so great that on the recommendation of a Leicestershire gentleman he was taken into Earl Howe's service. His conscientious attention to duty, coupled with his ability, made advancement rapid for him, and he eventually became House Steward at Gopsall.

Then came the great change and chance of his lifetime. The Earl Howe of that time *(1st Earl)* desired him to come into Buckinghamshire and take over the management of the Penn Estate. This was a momentous step. At that time, some 52 years ago (*c.1858*), the estate was in a condition of lawlessness. A considerable portion of the existing demesnes in those days was common land, and they were taken in under the Commons Enclosure Act.

This step raised the peasantry of the district to a condition of resentful fury. Fences were put round the enclosed land, and the next night, down they would come at the hands of the infuriated mob. Their daring increased, and the deeds done by night they did not hesitate thereafter to execute in broad daylight. More than this, emboldened by their disorderly license, the unruly country folks overran the farms, and yeomen complained that they could hardly call their lives or their property their own. In addition, poaching seemed to go on wholesale.

To meet these troubles, Earl Howe saw that a 'strong hand' was required, and Mr. Widdowson was the man to use it. Accordingly, Earl Howe called Mr. Widdowson to him; and bade him go down to Penn, and see what he could do. He came, not without some misgivings of failure, but, with the support of the Earl behind him, he determined to do his best.

The lawlessness had been going on three years when Mr. Widdowson, got to Penn. He at once grasped the situation, and saw that firmness, as well as tact, was what as required. He soon let the malcontents understand that he was to be master of the situation; and by degrees they comprehended the fact. Common sense argument and reasonable persuasion were first tried. and when these failed, recourse was had to the law. Persons detected in these acts of wilful destruction of property were hauled before the Justices and the sentence of the ringleaders to exemplary terms of imprisonment soon made a healthy impression on others.

"It took me seven years to completely stop these discreditable deeds of violence and mischief. But I meant to restore order. I did so and his Lordship lived to see it done," said Mr. Widdowson. So far as I could gather, the enclosures which caused the most trouble were those of Penn Wood (*c.1855*), and others at Hazlemere. The manner in which Mr. Widdowson restored order, and the many ways in which he improved the estate, deeply impressed Earl Howe with his value, and it is said that on his deathbed his Lordship made Mr. Widdowson promise that he would never leave the estate so long as he lives. This has been echoed by the three other holders of title. The active management of the estate now devolves on his eldest son, but he himself performs the duties of Consulting Agent.

It is interesting to note that of the 5,000 acres comprising the Penn estate, 2,000 are woodland. Most of the trees were 'self-grown', but Mr. Widdowson has, during the tenure of his agency, planted no less than 300,000 trees in Penn Wood alone, to fill up gaps. Beech and oak are principally grown. Much of this finds its way to Wycombe in connection with the staple trade of that town (*furniture making*), but the larch is chiefly used for fencing on Lord Rothschild's estate. Incidentally, I might mention that there are some thirty miles of rails and posts around the Penn Estate, erected primarily to protect the 'quicks' when planted.

Some of the land that is now arable and pasture was formerly woodland. It was grubbed up some few years ago, mainly for the purpose of giving employment to labour in the district - a most worthy cause.

The subject of this notice does not take a very great interest in public affairs outside of his own district. His chief concern has been to mind his own business, which is that of his employers'. He was however for thirteen years, Chairman of the Penn Parish Council, a position now held by his son. He was elected vice-chairman at the first meeting after the passing of the Local Government Act (*Came into force in December 1894*), Mr. Thomas Grove being appointed to the chair; and when that gentleman died, Mr. Widdowson was unanimously elected to the premier post on the Council. Mr. Widdowson still has the happy companionship of a devoted wife, and they have two daughters and six sons, and they are all doing well.

My closing observation shall be an expression of the wish that Mr. Widdowson may long be spared to continue to enjoy the confidence of the noble family he has served so long, as well as the genuine esteem of all with whom he comes into contact.

APPENDIX III

The Elizabeth Battey Letters
Housekeeper to the 4th Earl Howe

Elizabeth Battey was born on 27th May 1855 to Thomas and Elizabeth Battey in New Street, Cubbington near Leamington Spa where her father was a farm labourer. She lived there with three brothers George, William and Daniel together with her younger sister, Hannah. When old enough, Elizabeth went into service as a housemaid and spent the rest of her life working her way through the domestic service hierarchy. She eventually reached what would have been the pinnacle of her career, housekeeper at Warwick Castle for the Countess of Warwick before finally moving to Gopsall Hall as housekeeper to the Earl Howe.

Elizabeth 'lived in' at Gopsall having her own suite of rooms, managing the female staff and running the daily activity of the house. At the end of her career sometime after 1914 (she may have worked for Earl Howe until 1918 when Samuel Waring took ownership of Gopsall) she moved to Assheton House Twycross. This house, which was part of the Gopsall estate, was demolished in the mid-1970s; new houses were erected on the site now called Assheton Lane.

On 27th March 1920 at the age of 65 Elizabeth, a spinster, passed away while at Assheton House. In her will she left to a Hannah Pratt the sum of £1,194 3s 9d (about £53k in 2020).[30] It is probable that Hannah Pratt was her younger sister Hannah. Elizabeth now lies in St James' churchyard 200 yards from the site of Assheton House and 1.3 miles, as the crow flies, from where Gopsall Hall once stood.

'Mrs' Elizabeth Battey wrote to her friend Elizabeth McCulloch in America (Albany, New York) for a period of over 10 years. These letters are kept at the Department of Special Collections and University Archives, W.E.B. Du Bois Library, University of Massachusetts Amherst, USA and make somewhat one-sided stories as, unfortunately, Mrs McCulloch's replies do not form part of the collection. The letters are available to read, with some difficulty, in Elizabeth's florid handwriting[25]. They record her work and social life during her time as housekeeper to the 4th Earl Howe at Gopsall Hall, Woodlands and Curzon House. It has to be said that her work life seems to have been greater than her social life, but that does not reflect an unhappy woman.

Below is a brief summary of each of the letters, but fuller reading gives a bigger picture.

Elizabeth Battey to Elizabeth E. McCulloch - November 20th 1904

Mrs Battey was referred to as haughty and above herself by some of those who worked with her at Gopsall. One colleague saying she thought herself the Countess, another saying he hoped that he died the same day as her as the devil would then be preoccupied with Mrs Battey and not him. But her letters show a different side to Elizabeth.

She begins by addressing her friend as Bessie. In previous letters she has called her *"My Dear Miss McCulloch"* and goes on to ask her friend to call her Lizzie in her return correspondence. She says how much she dislikes formality between friends and relatives and offers some apologies for not ever replying quickly enough to Bessie's letters.

She finds the place (Gopsall Hall) dreadfully quiet and where she may not see another soul even on a walk of 2 or 3 miles. This suggests that, at this point, she is fairly new to Gopsall Hall, having left employment at Warwick Castle only recently. She rarely goes out except to attend church on Sunday and has an occasional friend to stay with her for a few days. There is much mention of her previous place at Warwick; an obviously much loved and familiar position. She discusses the Howes' trips and relationship to other aristocratic families. She says she is fearful of a war coming with Russia.

Elizabeth Battey to Elizabeth E. McCulloch - April 2nd 1905

As is often discussed, Lady Howe's health is not good. The family has been on a long stay in Egypt but is on the way home (another letter where, again, her job is uppermost in her thoughts). Due to the Lady Howe's health, the Viscount Curzon's 21st Birthday won't be celebrated. (This was not quite correct; Viscount Curzon's 'Coming of Age' party was not held on his birthday on 1st May because of his navy commitments, but it was celebrated in September; Chapter 9 and letter dated 22nd October).

She describes the size of Gopsall saying it accommodates more people than her previous employer's home, Warwick Castle, though again says it's a lonely place. The family has gone to stay at Curzon House in London *"even taking their little doggie"*, leaving her to manage things with a skeleton staff. Her previous employer (Lady Warwick) has told Countess Howe she hopes to get Mrs Battey back as soon as she starts the party season again, but Mrs Battey confides in her friend she would only consider going back *"If I was out of position"*. Mrs Battey goes on to say what lovely towns Warwick and nearby Leamington are, but also how beautiful the views from Gopsall windows are. One wonders what her motives for leaving Warwick Castle were, given her obvious fondness for the place.

The Howes are spending Christmas at Curzon House in London because if Countess Howe had a relapse it would take too long to get the doctors to see her. Once again, the Countess' health is a concern. Mrs Battey spent Christmas at Gopsall with a few of the maids whom she allowed to have a party (which ran till two o'clock in the morning when she had to draw it to a close). Her sister's daughter, from Birmingham, spent a few days with her over Christmas.

Elizabeth Battey to Elizabeth E. McCulloch - October 22nd 1905

Mrs Battey tells her friend Bessie of the Viscount Curzon's 'Coming of Age' party. His birthday had been in May but festivities waited till August due to other events. On day one 500 farmers and better tenants were entertained, on day two 1,100 other people from the surrounding villages were guests. The Earl suggests supplying a *"substantial lunch to all but no tea"* but his sister Evelyn is of the opinion they should supply tea. So, although all food has been prepared by Gopsall staff, because insufficient cakes would be available for the large numbers at tea, all the local towns are then visited and every cake available is purchased.

Viscount Curzon has gone to India with the Prince of Wales for 6 months. (He was actually aboard H.M.S. Terrible, the escort vessel for the Royal Yacht).

Lady Warwick, Mrs Battey's ex-employer, seems uninterested in her baby daughter, and has become involved in socialism and this takes her time. *"It is such a pity she goes to such great extremes and then tires of things"*. Lady Warwick does not seem to be overly high in Mrs Battey's regard. A grand pageant is planned at Warwick Castle to celebrate its age and position, apparently 1,000 Warwick people will play characters from the Castle's history.

Elizabeth Battey to Elizabeth E. McCulloch - April 24th 1906

Mrs Battey is at Woodlands having travelled from Curzon House; she obviously has housekeeping roles wherever required by the Howes. She will stay at Curzon House to produce an inventory of all the china, little cracks or chips etc and then return to Gopsall having settled the new maids into Curzon House. Woodlands is a very lovely little house; not much used for the last 5 years since the Earl took to Gopsall. The Earl is with the King and Queen on the Yacht (The Royal Yacht 'Osborne', Chapter 9).

Interestingly, although the Du Bois Library synopsis of this letter mentions the death of the Countess Howe on 9th February, there is no reference to it in the letter. This is surprising as the event happened only 10 weeks before the letter was written and would have been a major event in Mrs Battey's life and work. One might conclude, given the importance of the event, that a letter of which we are unaware is missing. She does comment *"How terrible that earthquake is, oh the sadness of it"* but does not identify which quake (there were several in the world that year) but, as the California earthquake of 1906 occurred just 6 days before she wrote this letter, it is probably a reference to that.

Elizabeth Battey to Elizabeth E. McCulloch - December 2nd 1906

Mrs Battey is back at Gopsall after seemingly spending much time at Woodlands and Curzon House. There is news that Viscount Curzon may be announcing nuptials, as Mrs Battey has been asked to ensure a daily supply of fresh pink roses are in his intended's rooms when he stays. In an aside she wonders whether any such announcement may be delayed *"until after the year of mourning"*; evidently a reference to the late Countess.

The Earl and Viscount have been asked to stay at Sandringham with the King and Queen for the Christmas period.

Apparently, friends of the Howes, the Duke and Duchess of Marlborough are *"living a separated life"*.

Elizabeth Battey to Elizabeth E. McCulloch - September 22nd 1907

Mrs. Battey again makes apology for being remiss in her replying to Bessie McColloch's letters, a repeated theme through all letters – *"Due to her busy life"*. Her friend, has just celebrated her 29th birthday and has apparently enquired about the Rhodes scholarships at Oxford University, we are not told why. Mrs Battey can recall little about it, but will investigate. Rhodes scholarships still support a two-year study course at Oxford, recent alumni include Bill Clinton.

Mrs Battey's brother Harry has suffered a stroke. He is 61 and lives in Lancashire. Currently he cannot speak. This leads Mrs Battey to mention the death of Colonel Curzon, Mary Curzon's father. Mary is Viscount Curzon's betrothed. Mrs. Battey thinks it will cause a lot of work for her, as she finds she has more to do since the death of the Countess.

Elizabeth Battey to Elizabeth E. McCulloch - September 29th 1908

This letter is almost impossible to read. Mrs Battey is much exercised that the Post Office has sent Bessie a parcel and letter with too little postage paid; very remiss of them and not Mrs. Battey's fault having given the Post Office two shillings and sixpence to properly stamp them.

She has apparently had a tooth removed and found it a very painful process.

Francis and Mary Curzon have had a son.

She encloses pictures from newspaper cuttings of "*some parts of England I have been to*" including Dover, Llandudno and Scarborough, but she does not say when exactly she visited.

Elizabeth Battey to Elizabeth E. McCulloch - April 30th 1910

Mrs. Battey has spent a lot more time working at Woodlands and also at Curzon House this year when the Earl has been in residence at those properties. This might suggest Gopsall is not the Earl's first choice now he is a widower. Bessie's mother has become an invalid and Mrs Battey sympathizes. She has been to Coombe Abbey (she does not say in what capacity) but it is not as nice as Gopsall, even though they try hard with the gardens.

There was a ball at the Duke of Connaught's where her friend Miss Murphy, previously the Countess Howe's lady's maid, was working, but there are too few gentlemen dancers, so it ended rather early at two thirty in the morning, rather earlier than those at Gopsall she says. Mrs Battey did not attend, despite being begged to, due to a cold caught in all the travelling to Woodlands.

Miss Murphy doesn't appear on the Gopsall census documents as a maid. Viscount Curzon and his wife now have a second child, a daughter.

Elizabeth Battey to Elizabeth E. McCulloch - January 21st 1912

The family has returned to Curzon House from Gopsall after the Christmas period. Mrs Battey sends Bessie an English muffin recipe and enquires whether she would like a marmalade one also. She lists all the cards she has had from people who have worked for her in the past and now have positions with other families all round the world: America, Jamaica, Russia and India amongst them. Again, this rather refutes the idea that she was at times an unpleasant person to work for.

The shooting party at Gopsall last week was a success, 4,050 pheasant, partridge, hares and woodcock being taken; the second shoot has 2,000. Not such a successful shoot for the wildlife! Important guests must be expected for a forthcoming shoot as double the number of pheasants have been ordered to be reared. Mrs Battey is to return to Curzon House soon.

She is glad to have been in the Midlands as she was able to visit her brother who has now sadly died.

Elizabeth Battey to Elizabeth E. McCulloch - January 4th 1914

Another of Mrs Battey's friends is travelling back home from America to retire, missing her home in Wales and writes that she will be in Albany, Bessie's home, shortly. More apologies for not writing sooner.

A visit from the daughter and son in law of President Wilson has, sadly, been rather spoiled by the actions of the Suffragette Movement. "*I wish you had put Mrs Pankhurst on some island and made her stay there forever*". Evidently, Mrs Battey was not a fan of women's suffrage.

Elizabeth Battey to Elizabeth E. McCulloch - April 13th 1914

Mrs Battey encloses a letter received from Lady Edith Franklin, one of the Earl's sisters regarding the death of her sister Lady Evelyn. Mrs Battey having written to her with condolences: "*some of our real aristocrats are very nice to servants……… rather serve them for half the money available from some of the millionaires*". Doctors have sent the Earl to Cornwall as he is struggling to come to terms with the death of his favourite sister, the Lady Evelyn, with whom he has been very close since the death of the Countess Howe. The Lady Evelyn had been driving a pony rig when a fly had settled on its neck, she stepped down to dislodge the fly. The pony turned, Lady Evelyn stumbled and her leg was caught in the springs. After being dragged some distance she incurred severe flesh wounds. These wounds developed into septicaemia and she died from heart failure.

This is the last of the letters from Mrs Battey to her friend Bessie in the Du Bois Library collection. We do not know whether her relationship with Bessie continued, but are grateful that these few precious letters survived.

Notes and References

Details about individuals have been derived from census returns, registers of births, deaths and marriages, and newspapers. In some cases, information and photos have been provided by their families.

1 *Erddig*. National Trust. https://www.nationaltrust.org.uk/erddig/features/unique-collection-of-portraits-at-erddig accessed on 27th February 2021.

2 *Attested Copy of Will of Charles Jennens of Gopsall, esq. Dated 30th April 1765; Codial 7th Aug. 1766*. The Record Office for Leicestershire, Leicester and Rutland. File Ref. DG22/5/8.

3 Postillion. A person who guides a horse-drawn coach while mounted on the horse, generally the leading nearside (left-hand side) horse of a team or pair, especially when there is no coachman. By contrast, a coachman controls the horses from the vehicle itself. The term is derived from mid-16th century French (postillon) – forerunner acting as a guide to the post-horse.

4 *No Ordinary Surgeon*. Dorothy Bentley Smith. Amberley Publishing: Stroud, 2017. This book includes a summary of the lives of William Dickinson Snr and Jnr and their relationship with the Gopsall Estate.

5 *Diaries and estate memoranda books of William Dickinson of Twycross (steward to Charles Jennens) 1777-1808*. The Record Office for Leicestershire, Leicester and Rutland. File Ref. DE1004.

6 Florence Court was a substantial country house and estate, indicating perhaps that Irwin was born to a family already in service.

The original Irish Yew Tree at Florence Court. National Trust. https://www.nationaltrust.org.uk/florence-court/features/the-original-irish-yew-tree-at-florence-court accessed on 28th February 2021.

7 *The Head Gardeners. Forgotten Heroes of Horticulture*. Toby Musgrave. London: Aurum Press Ltd, 2007.

8 *The Hidden Horticulturalist*. Fiona Davidson. London: Atlantic Books, 2019.

9 Neil Wilson's second youngest child Elizabeth was born at Gopsall in 1855. His youngest child John was born in 1857 at Kingarth, Bute. It is likely that he spent his first 12-18 months in Bute propagating stock for his nursery.

10 *Page & Co.'s Composition for the destruction of blight - Testimonials of 1855: From Mr E. Sage, Gr to the Right Hon. Earl Howe, Gopsall Hall, Sept 21 1855*. The Gardeners' Chronicle June 14 1856, p. 402. The Gardeners' Chronicle (1841-1925) is available at: https://onlinebooks.library.upenn.edu/webbin/serial?id=gardenerchron.

11 Prizes won by Mr Sage, gardener for W.R. Robinson include: The Gardeners Chronicle July 1953, p.450; May 1854, p. 316; June 1855, p. 418.

12 *Crystal Palace Autumn Flower Show*. The Morning Post, Wednesday 11th September 1867.

13 *Gardener (Head) JOHN BROWN*. The Gardeners' Chronicle (new series) Volume IV, October 1875, p. 571. Interestingly, Brown was still gardener to Earl Howe in the July issue, p. 87.

14 *Gardener (Head) JOHN BROWNE*. The Gardeners' Chronicle (*new series*) Volume V, March 1876, p. 383.

15 The Gardeners' Chronicle (*new series*) Volume V, July 1976, p. 147; Volume X, August 1878, p. 152 & p. 173.

16 *The crosses of Anthuriums at Highbury, Birmingham*. J. Lee. The Gardeners' Chronicle (*series 3*), Volume 15, Jan 13 1894, p. 48.

17 *The Household Manager being a Practical Treatise upon the various duties in large and small establishments*, from *the Drawing Room to the Kitchen*. Charles Pierce. London: Simkin & Marshall, 1857.

18 *Agreement Bailiff of Gopsall*. The Record Office for Leicestershire, Leicester and Rutland. File Ref. DG23/7 (DE323).

19 This list of staff is derived from the 1901 and 1911 census reports, interviews of people living at the time (Chapter 7) and written reports. Individuals would not necessarily have worked at Gopsall at the same time; housekeepers, and butlers are listed in the order they were in post. Samuel Prince was butler to W.E. Oakley (d. 1912) at Cliff House before working at Gopsall Hall. He and his wife ran Twycross post office for nearly 50 years. He died in 1957, aged 97 (Coventry Evening Telegraph, Friday 22nd March 1957).

20 *Night poaching on the Gopsall Estate. Atherstone men sent to prison*. Atherstone News and Herald, Friday 13th October 1905; *Petty Sessions - Market Bosworth*. Leicester Daily Post, Thursday 13th March 1919.

21 *A History of Gopsall Hall (chapter 7)*. Glynis Oakley. Sheepy Magna: Barncraft Printing, 1995, pp. 37-39.

22 *Long Service*. Leicester Chronicle, Saturday 21st September 1929.

23 *Yesterday's weddings: Captain A.C.B. Critchley and the Hon. Gladys Waring*. Yorkshire Post and Leeds Intelligencer, Thursday 4th October 1923.

24 *Shackerstone death*. Leicester Evening Mail, Tuesday 13th February 1951.

25 *Elizabeth Battey Papers, 1900-1914*. Department of Special Collections and University Archives, W.E.B. Du Bois Library, University of Massachusetts Amherst. https://credo.library.umass.edu/view/collection/mums947 accessed on 2nd March 2021.

26 *News and Notes. Departed Glory and Now Vulnerable*. Leicester Daily Mercury, Saturday 2nd December 1950.

27 *A topographical History of Leicester*. Rev. J. Curtis (1831), Introduction xxix.

28 *Stranger Than Fiction? The Jennens Inheritance in Fact and Fiction Part 1: The Jennens Fortune in the Courts*. Patrick Polden. Common Law World Review (2003) 32 (3), 211-247. See Chapter 7, note 2 for more details.

29 *Will of William Dickinson, Gentleman of Witherley, Leicestershire*. National Archives. File Ref. PROB 11/1486/169.

30 *Index to Wills and Probate 1858 - 1996*. Search Battey/1920 at https://probatesearch.service.gov.uk/#wills, accessed 4th March 2021.

31 Newspaper article title and text reproduced as printed, including spelling and grammatical errors.

Memories of Gopsall

The following memories are based on a series of interviews undertaken by Stephanie Headley, a member of a family who farmed Fox Covert Farm in Congerstone from 1942 to 2000. They were carried out 40 years ago between October 1981 and February 1982. Happily, Stephanie had the foresight to realise that the last direct contacts to Gopsall Hall and its people were going to disappear in the then, near future and she took the time to speak to those who worked with, or were familiar with, 'Gopsall People'.

Having amassed the information, Stephanie wrote it down and kept the hand-written accounts safe for years. The authors are grateful that she has allowed us to reproduce the transcripts of her conversations with local people, which have confirmed and added to our research and provided some interesting anecdotes which would otherwise have disappeared, along with Gopsall Hall.

The local people interviewed who lived near Gopsall are listed below, with their work background and ages (at the time of interview):

Mr and Mrs Jack Seekins: Farm labourer, Housemaid (both aged 72 years).

Mrs Edith Leek (nee Rock): Laundry girl (aged 91).

Mr and Mrs Charles Hayes: Collier, Hospital cleaner (aged 83 & 80).

Mr and Mrs Ernest Brown: Council worker, Factory worker (aged 78 & 86).

Mr Brian McCullam: Salesman for Dawkins of Congerstone (aged 52).

Mrs Elsie Bennett (nee Hextall): School teacher (aged 82).

At the time of writing, one interviewee, Mr Brian McCullam, is alive and well and living in Sheepy Magna with his wife.

As you would expect, knowledge seems to have been passed down in stories, from family members and friends, or relatives of those who worked or lived on or near the Gopsall Estate. Some dates are a little confused, as the events being recalled are 50 years in the past and being remembered by different people from different viewpoints. However, occasionally several stories come together as one but differ in some specific points. For example, the reported feud between the housekeeper, Mrs Battey and coachman John McCullam is recalled by more than one person but the remembered timing, during Lord Waring's tenure of Gopsall, is unlikely, as Mrs Battey had already left employment at Gopsall Hall at this time. Some stories are obviously false, such as the 2nd Earl dying in a motoring accident, before motor cars were invented! But often a grain of truth hints where the stories came from. The sister of the 4th Earl did die after a pony and trap accident in 1913 and the 5th Earl had several non-fatal motor racing accidents, so one can see how stories evolve.

The interviews confirm that the hall servants moved from one property to another, as required. Thus, Edith Leek recalls that when the hall was sold to Samuel Waring, she moved to the Earl's Uxbridge home 'Woodlands', after 8 years as laundry maid at Gopsall. It is probably true to say that these jobs were considered good enough positions to put up with that inconvenience. Perhaps a lot decided not to move and chose a different path. Certainly, a peripatetic core of servants, fully expected that as a condition of their employment, they would be living and working in different houses according to the family's needs.

Further stories show the Howes as rather caring 'employers' with meat from shoots being distributed to all staff and workers. Hampers of food were also delivered free to estate villagers at Christmas, including venison or rabbits, and the farmers could have a choice of the feathered birds. Everyone on the estate was invited to celebrate Viscount Curzon's coming of age birthday celebrations in 1905 (Chapter 9). Mr and Mrs Seekins state that, *"The Howes were good people to work for because they looked after the villagers well"* and then go on to describe the Howes' short lived successor, Lord Waring, but in rather less glowing terms.

The impact on the family, estate and villagers of the death of the Countess Georgiana in 1906 (Chapter 9) is clearly recalled in the interviews. The family tragedy resulted in the social life at Gopsall being scaled down, with the need for staff for day to day work, special events and seasonal celebrations at Gopsall virtually disappeared.

Various stories mention the elaborate and extensive interior decorations and fittings in the hall, often viewed when the family were away and access to all parts of the hall was possible. The tapestry hangings, silver bath, silver gilt dinner service (apparently second only to Queen Alexandra's) and the ornate plaster ceilings were recalled with no hint of envy or ill feeling for those with so much more than most. These interviews show a real sense of admiration and general good will to the Howe family.

Initially, we were going to edit and summarise the transcripts of the interviews conducted by Stephanie. However, attempts to do that resulted in the loss of much of the character of those interviewed and the significance of the memories told. Therefore, the interviews are reproduced below, mostly as recorded by Stephanie with, where appropriate, some explanatory comments in brackets.

The Stephanie Headley Interviews

Mr and Mrs Jack Seekins, Congerstone, October 1981

Where did you acquire your knowledge about the hall?

Edith's father, her uncle, my uncle, J. Pegg, Mr Lee, Mr Simons, Twiggy (Billy Twig), the knowledge passed down from person to person, but some of the people, such as Mr Pegg and Mr Simons, we actually knew.

Edith's father worked on the golf links at the hall and also acted as caddy, her uncle worked in the lawns, Mr Pegg worked at Home Farm, and as an engineer, looking after the saw mill, which was part of the hall. *(Home Farm is Shornhill Farm)*

Mr Simons, who lived at Shackerstone, was a bricklayer and labourer on the estate property and a bit of a carpenter as was Mr Lee, who lived at Norton village.

The whole estate was self-contained. The estate owned its own farms and grew its own corn and grain with which to feed the animals. A saw mill existed so that the estate could produce its own fencing. Gamekeepers looked after 1,000 head of deer in the park; the deer being both red and black. At Congerstone, Mr McCullam was employed to meet the trains at Shackerstone railway station with a horse and float. *(The woodlands on the estate were actively managed and, in the 19th and early 20th centuries, sales of Gopsall grown timber were an annual event. John McCullam was head coachman.)*

A local story about Mr McCullam, from a later year when Lord Waring owned the estate: Mr McCullam was sent to the station, and very often he would see Mrs Battey, the housekeeper. The two did not get on well together and one day Mr McCullam said to her, "*I hope that I die the same day as you, the devil will be that busy dealing with you, he'll never have time to deal with me.*"

What sort of people were on the estate?

The estate included the villages around the hall. The only people living in the villages were the farmers and the men who worked on the estate. When the first miner came into the village in 1920 there was a bit of a fuss, because formerly the only people to live in the village were from local families. The farm labourer was seen then as the most important person and the miner as some mere unskilled labourer.

Who lived at the hall?

Earl Howe did not live on the estate permanently; he used to come down at different times of the year. They always brought their own staff from their London residence, although a permanent skeleton staff was maintained at the hall. The family came to the estate mostly for the shooting season or for seasonal festivities such as Christmas. At this time of year, special Christmas boxes would arrive for the villagers and a game cart would go around, the villagers would get either venison or rabbits, and the farmers could have a choice of the feathered birds. Often Edith's uncle would get a piece of venison, or a pluck, which was the heart and other bits. The venison would be a reward for helping to cull the deer.

Woodmen at Gopsall

BY MESSRS- BLAKESLEY AND HOLLIER.

Gopsall Annual Timber Sale.

Messrs. BLAKESLEY & HOLLIER
Have been again honoured by instructions from the Right Hon. the Earl Howe,

TO OFFER BY PUBLIC AUCTION,
On Monday, March 2nd,

200 LOTS of very superior large Larch, Spruce, Ash, Elm, Oak, and Poplar Poles, and Six Lots of Poplar Timber. The above are now cut down and laying on Congerstone Hill, near to the Canal.

The Auctioneers respectfully request their friends to meet them at Mr. Dawkins at Congerstone, at Ten o'clock, to proceed to sale.

The pay day for last year's timber is fixed at the same place at Four o'clock.

Leicester Mercury, February 21st 1863.[1]

When the family came down to the estate, who usually came down?

It was mainly the immediate family and their guests, who were quite often famous, such as King Edward VII. One of the family, was quite well known for being a racing driver. Lady Howe was buried in the churchyard at Congerstone, and a monument was erected in her name. Her body and the monument were later moved down to Penn in Buckinghamshire. *(Francis Curzon, the 5th Earl Howe, was a racing driver between about 1928 and 1939, long after Gopsall was sold to Samuel Waring.)*

Jimmy Hodgkinson with his push mower in St Mary's churchyard. The memorial to Countess Howe is in the background.

A local story: A Mrs Fenton, who lived at the rectory, had a son who was a doctor when one day he said that there was always a funny smell in Congerstone church, and that the smell had gone down to Penn with Lady Howe.

The Earl had a special avenue of trees cut in order that he could see the monument to his wife from the hall itself. The churchyard was tended full time by Jimmy Hodgkinson from Bilstone. The whole family were very strict about going to church and Sunday school. The church was very well kept with crosses and stones, and even iron stakes with numbers so that a record could be easily kept. If anyone was ever seen messing about in the churchyard Mr Hodgkinson would be after their skins.

Can you remember any other people who worked on the estate?

The lodge-keeper was Mrs Tom Clarke who lived at Bilstone. Mr Smith was the gamekeeper for Twycross and Mr Spare the lodge-keeper at Shackerstone. The only lodge still standing is the one at Shackerstone, the others have all been pulled down. A lodge also existed at Snarestone but the keeper's name has slipped my mind. The Bilstone lodge was at what is now known as Bailey's turn, as you turn up the road to where the hall had used to be. There were gates at this entrance to the estate which the villagers were forbidden to enter unless told they could.

A local story which took place at a later date, when Lord Waring was the owner: Mrs Clarke had used to be on guard at the gates and Mrs Seekins' cousin once said to her, "*Excuse me Mrs Clarke but we have got to go to the Gopsall Hall.*" "*No you have not.*" she said. "*Yes we have, we're selling Alexander roses and I've got to see Major Miles.*" Major Miles was the man everyone had to see when you wanted to go fishing. *(Major Miles administered the estate from 1919 to about 1940.)*

The hall also owned a team of Suffolk Punch horses, a double team, which were obviously of great value. The wagoner was a man named Jimmy who lived at Snarestone.

Can you remember any social events which took place at the hall?

Most of the things we can remember are too late to be of use. Mrs Lampard had used to sing in the choir at the hall and in the Chapel. Her mother was a laundry maid, Mrs Seekins's great grandmother was a washer and ironer, as well as Mrs Hextall.

When the sale took place to Lord Waring can you remember any reasons that were suggested for Earl Howe selling the estate and hall?

Edith's dad was told by Earl Howe himself that he couldn't afford to keep the place and that he (Edith's dad) was first to go since he was on the golf links and not a necessity. This was around 1919. Edith's mother was not too upset because she did not approve of the Sunday golfing sessions.

Are there any more of the people who lived on the estate alive today?

Not really, they are mostly dead. Mr and Mrs Lee are dead. They had used to live in Nurse Watson's house at Bilstone *(now Ronaldsway House)*.

Mrs Edith Leek (nee Rock), Sheepy Magna, November 1981

What do you remember about Gopsall Hall?

It was a big stone, massive place about three miles around its circumference, going around one side and then the other, about three miles in all. *(Excluding Shackerstone drive, the perimeter of Gopsall Park is 6.2 miles or 9 miles by public roads.)*

Had you used to go to the hall?

Yes, I was in laundry there and had used to live in. Shooting parties had used to come down you see, from London, but we didn't go up there, we had to stay there and the laundry was sent by rail in big hampers. A man at the station had to bring it up and then take it back to Shackerstone station, to send it off again at the weekend. So, we were part of the permanent staff.

How many permanent staff were there?

Four in the laundry, four in another, two or three footmen and a butler, but some went up to London with the Earl. There was a night-watch, a house keeper and housemaids. Four in every department, and when there was a party, people came from the village, always extra 'helpmen' were needed.

Did they have parties regularly?

Well about three or four times a year, usually shooting parties. Gopsall Park was very big and they had three gamekeepers who reared birds for them to shoot and then there was a bit of deer stalking because they had red deer and roe deer. They regularly came and invited other people, around a hundred beds would be going when they all came down. *(Accommodation for the family and their guests at various functions is difficult to know as, from plans of the hall, there were only about 18 principal/guest bedrooms, excluding the large number of servants' bedrooms; Chapter 2.)*

Can you remember Lord Curzon's Coming of Age in 1905?

No, not him. He was married when I went. Curzon was the family name, and his son was married before my time there. She was supposed to be the most beautiful woman in society, she had a boy and a girl. They were little when I was there. *(The 'most beautiful woman' was Mary Curzon, the wife of Francis Viscount Curzon. Married in 1907, they had a son in 1908 and daughter in 1910. Mary Curzon, was feted for her loveliness in every fashion magazine and society periodical, right into her middle age.)*

They always had Lords and Ladies and Countesses visiting. King Manuel II of Portugal[2], who came over *(in 1911)* when he was twenty-one, didn't know how to shoot properly. King Edward VII came before that and before I was there. They had a silver bath and a private staircase put in for him, all with red carpets on them, very nice. The hall also had a beautiful picture gallery.

Pre-Christmas shooting party in 1911[2,3]

Top: 4th & 8th from the left standing are Viscount Curzon and his wife; 3rd, 4th & 5th from the left sitting are King Manuel, Dowager Countess Howe and Earl Howe. **Left:** The Earl and King Manuel II. **Above:** The beaters at work.

The large picture gallery (c.1890s), illuminated by two huge roof lights.[3] In the early 20th century it was also known as the salon and contained a grand piano and an Aeolian pipe organ (Chapter 3).

Were you allowed to wander around the hall?

Yes, you could go anywhere when they were not there, and we also went when there were parties to see the table set. The Earl had the best silver and gilt next to the Queen. When the dining room was laid out it was beautiful, genuine silver and pink carnations to set it off, a great big long table full of silver and then it was gilt, they had glasses with gilt edges all the other part was gold in the middle, all the flower vases on the table. It was lovely silver and gilt.

The picture gallery was magnificent with the Lady and Lord Howe; Lady Howe was really a Countess. They were just two paintings on one wall (about 12ft each), his uncle who was in the navy as well, all of them big pictures. The famous uncle was Admiral Howe. *(Admiral Richard Howe was the 1st Earl Howe by the first creation who died in 1799 and did not own Gopsall.)*

When did you start working there?

When I was twenty-one, just before that. I'm ninety-one now, so it was a long time ago! I've been married over sixty years. I was there eight years before that. *(Edith worked from about 1911 to 1919.)*

When did you leave?

I left after I'd been there eight years. The hall was still standing. It and the contents (furniture) had been sold to Lord Waring. From there I went to the 'Woodlands', his house near Oxford. After 12 months I got married. *(A lot of the furniture was sold by auction or taken away by the Earl; Chapter 12.)*

Did you go out on the estate itself?

Yes, you could go anywhere, they did not bother, as long as you did not interfere. There was all deer in the park and everything.

When they came down from London, who came? Did they come alone?

Oh no, they always had parties the same night they came down. They only really came down for the parties. It was not really their home. Earl Howe had to be in London because of the Queen, Queen Alexandra. He had to attend her regularly and he lived at Curzon House in London. Curzon Street belonged to him. He held small parties at the 'Woodlands' because he could slip down on the Metropolitan Railway from London to Oxford.

You said earlier that there were groups who worked at the hall. Who were they?

There were gardeners, eight young chaps in the glasshouses and odd ones in the kitchen garden. There was a large number of staff.

Did Earl Howe treat you well?

Yes, we were on board wages half the time and looked after ourselves when they were in London. Money was sent down regularly each month for our board wage. They used to be pretty free with us.

Were you able to be involved in the social events of the hall, such as parties?

Oh no, I never went to parties, I just did my work. We had our own place just across the yard, which was a big stone place that you entered by a big door. We had our own apartments but never had parties. They had the parties and the footmen looked after them. *(The 'big stone place' was probably the wing of the hall containing the servants' hall.)*

What sort of social events did they have for the servants?

The servants just did the work, waiting on all the guests and family. We enjoyed the fun of the people who came. We had some fun between ourselves because there wasn't much otherwise. They would bring all their maids and men to look after them. We only had to do our work and generally could go where we wanted. St Mary's, Congerstone was the church we went to and I went there every Sunday morning. We had nothing else to do.

I went round to the other girls when I wanted to but when there was a party on there was a lot to do and they didn't like knocking about with you much then, they liked to do their jobs.

So, were there any people who you used to go out with that didn't work at the hall?

Yes, we could go anywhere when there wasn't a party on and they weren't there.

Are there any memories that stick in your mind of when you worked there?

We had used to work with the boys and there were whist drives and dances that we could go to in the

Christmas 1903 - Fancy dress in the red drawing room at Gopsall[3]

Names of some present are: Earl Howe (dressed as Admiral Earl Howe), Mr A.D. Sassoon, Viscount Curzon (wearing a three-cornered hat), the Duchess of Manchester, Earl de Grey and the Marquis de Soveral are standing in the back row (*1st, 2nd, 8th, 12th, 15th & 16th from the left*). Countess Howe (wearing a diamond sunburst in her hair) is standing in front to the right of centre with Lady Sarah Wilson next to her (kneeling).

Lord and Lady Howe with their guests in Gopsall Park (1902)[3]

Those present include: Mr A.D. Sassoon, the Marquis de Soveral, the Duchess of Manchester, Lady Sarah Wilson and Earl de Grey are standing (*1st, 2nd, 4th, 7th, 9th from the left*). Lord and Lady Howe are kneeling (*1st & 2nd from the left*). Sitting in the front row are Winston Churchill and Count Albert von Mensdorff (*2nd & 4th from the left*).

villages - Congerstone, Appleby and Twycross. It was good because we were well placed to get to them because of the where the hall was.

Was the hall the centre of activity?

Oh Yes. It provided work for the people. There were electricians, carpenters, bricklayers, keepers, odd men and gardeners, everything like that. Practically all the villages around looked to Gopsall for work, especially when a party was on.

Electricity was available throughout the hall and provided by a generator. The electrician lived in one of the cottages near the gate and gardens. There were two cottages there, the odd-man lived in one and the electrician in the other. The electrician was always on hand when needed. He didn't seem to mind the work even though it was a big job with all those rooms. Most people enjoyed life and didn't bother about the work. *(It is probable that the two cottages mentioned were those built in 1901, at one time, used for the gardeners. They still stand today - Chapter 14.)*

Can you remember any of the other servants who might be alive?

No, I only remember that nearly all the boys got killed in WWI. All of them had to enlist and most got killed. I can't remember the girls. One had used to live in Nuneaton but she died when she was eighty. She was a housemaid. I don't remember anyone else.

Are there any other things that you can remember about the hall?

Nothing, only that King Edward VII came, it took a lot of money. Many Lords, Ladies, Counts and Countesses came for shooting parties, as well as King Manuel from Portugal. He left us all a tip, which is why we remembered him so well. All of us were given 10 shillings *(50p)*, a big tip in those days.

Do you remember Countess Howe and how she died?

No, that was before I got to the hall. They all used to wear knee breeches and wigs when she was alive. After she died, they all wore long black coats and striped waistcoats. They all went into mourning and they never came out and things never went back to how they used to be with plus fours and powdered heads.

Were you there when they moved Lady Howe's body and the Monument to Penn?

That was after they had sold Gopsall. Earl Howe had a gap cut in the hedge at Penn so that he could see the memorial from his bedroom window. *(A ride was cut in The Race Course wood at Gopsall so that the memorial in Congerstone churchyard could be seen from the hall [Chapter 9]; it is not possible to view the monument, now erected in Penn Street churchyard, from Penn House.)*

Mr and Mrs Charles Hayes, Congerstone, October 1981

What can you remember about the estate and hall ?

When I was a child, I had used to go beating with the shooting party from the hall. This was at weekends and the pay was a bird which was sometimes hung until the next shoot, perhaps a month away. At other times the beaters would get a piece of venison as their pay. Usually it was the gentry who went on the shoots, and on a number of occasions King Edward VII visited the estate but did not care to shoot *(This comment may refer to King Manuel rather than Edward VII)*. As a boy I remember all the forms at the school lining up in order to see the King, but we did in actual fact miss seeing him.

Both my wife and I remember when there was a party for the parents with food provided. Unfortunately, the weather was bad and as a consequence most people took umbrellas. When the party ended the parents were allowed to help themselves to the food. Since Mrs Hayes parents didn't take a bag they used their umbrella as a bag and took their share of the food that way. *(This 'party' may have been Viscount Curzon's Coming of Age celebrations in September 1905.)*

Earl Howe at one time had a parrot, which could say to him "*Good morning*". However, one morning the Earl went past it and the parrot said, "*Good morning you're bloody late*", naturally the bird was removed and never seen again.

Where did the employees live?

Some of the employees lived in the hall if they actually worked inside, this was mostly men, servants and handmaids. Others lived in lodges which were generally purpose built. People like the grooms lived above the stables, as did the rent man. The remaining staff were sometimes found accommodation. For example, Mr Lee lived at the Old Nurses House in the village of Bilstone *(now Ronaldsway House)*.

What land did the estate occupy?

A large amount of land belonged to the estate including Nailstone, Congerstone, Shackerstone, Bilstone, Osbaston, and the Tollgate, Barton-in-the-Beans, Odstone, Wellsborough, Twycross, and Norton-Juxta-Twycross. *(Only relatively small areas of land were part of the estate in some of these locations.)*

What did most of the employees of the estate do?

Most of the estate employees worked as farm labourers or in the saw mill. There were five keepers on the estate each living in a cottage just on the outskirts of the estate.

What sort of social events took place which you can remember?

Seasonal events such as the shoots were regular, when the gentry would come and visit the hall. There was once a regular annual dinner for the tenants who would pay their rents. Each rent payer would go to the bottom public house *(The Horse & Jockey, Congerstone)* and pay their 1s *(5p)* rent and then have something to eat.

Did the family stay at the hall a lot?

When the family first moved in, they had used to stay at the hall regularly but after the death of Lady Howe, the family visited less often and visited Penn in Buckinghamshire more often.

Can you remember anything about the estate and hall?

When we were both children, we had used to go acorn picking in the park. The deer were fed with these acorns and we used to get paid 1s *(5p)* for every bag that we collected. The park was really out of bounds for the village children but once a year the children were allowed to walk down it and look at the May flowers.

We were too young to remember a lot about the hall and most of our memories are of when the hall was taken over by the Warings. Many of the things we know about the hall were passed down from mouth to mouth. We do remember Mr McCullam, who used to go to the station to fetch the mail for the hall. It was said that people from Italy came to do beautiful carvings on the ceilings and that that may have been the reason why the money ran out. *(Probably a reference to the original 18th century plasterwork, rather than any work performed in the 20th century.)*

The whole hall was supplied with water from the water wheel in the park, where two big water holes were made into wells, but later the water came from Twycross (around 1,000 gallons per hour).

The whole family was very church orientated and the servants had to attend too, when they reached the lychgate they all had to change their shoes.

The lychgate at Castle Farm crossroads looking towards St Mary's Church

Mr and Mrs Ernest Brown, Congerstone, October 1981

What sort of labour was employed from the villages?

Most of the labour was from the village, around six or seven gardeners, and about seven or eight outside workers. Mr Challis was a head groom at the stable, which used to be at what is now the Curzon Arms Public House. There were six keepers and fourteen woodmen who had used to deal with the drainage of the land. *(As far as is known, the Curzon Arms was never a stable.)*

In the hall there were housemaids, kitchen maids and laundry girls, one of which was Mrs Hextall. The housekeeper at that time was Mrs Battey. Also, in the hall itself was a hallman and a coalman. Mr Spare was the hallman and Mr Godfrey was the coalman, who had to make sure that all the coal-buckets in the hall were kept full. Mr Prince was the butler in the hall. Four lodges existed at Twycross, Bilstone, Shackerstone and Snarestone.

1,000 deer in the park commanded attention and at Christmas venison was served at the table, as well as the fires using a whole ton of coal.

Rent was paid at the Horse & Jockey and a lunch prepared for the rent payers, who paid only one shilling *(5p)* a week.

In the estate grounds there were golf links and in the park four men were employed, one from Congerstone, two from Shackerstone, and one more from Norton-Juxta-Twycross; these included Jack Harris and lawn men, plus four or five more odd job men.

What can you remember of the events at the hall?

In 1905 the Viscount Curzon's Coming of Age took place when I was only four years old. I remember Mr and Mrs Hextall going to the hall for a drink of beer under the riding school *(the stables)*. The second Earl Howe was killed in a motor accident whilst racing. *(The 2nd Earl died in 1876.)*

When I was about twelve or thirteen, I remember Lady Howe's mourning after she had died, in 1913. Boats were at Gopsall wharf and a lot of people arrived by train. This all took place and was then followed by a two-week sale. A big flag pole was erected in the park with a flag flying from it, but after a while the monument and the flag were both moved from Congerstone to Penn, with the coffin of Lady Howe. Most of the permanent staff went to Penn too. *(This recollection combines the death of the 4th Earl's sister Evelyn in 1913, the death of Countess Howe in 1906 and the final sale of the estate to Waring and subsequent removal of Lady Howe's body and monument to Penn in 1919.)*

My father was a carpenter with three others - Jakes, Oliver, Willeby and a bricklayer. The carpenters made doors and fences for the estate. Dick Pear's father was a bricklayer. The farms on the estate supplied meat, eggs and milk for the hall. Mr Saunders was the bailiff at Snarestone and a Mr Burnett was the agent of the estate, which meant that he had to go to the hall in order to ask for improvements.

My father had used to live at a small holding which was pulled down in 1939. Most people had houses in the villages, or the staff that lived in, lived over the stables. When there were parties extra help in the kitchen was acquired from the villages. *(Most 'live in' staff had accommodation within the west service wing of the hall.)*

What sort of social events can you remember at the hall?

I can remember only one Hunt Ball; the rest were mainly shooting parties. In 1902, King Edward VII visited and a large number of extra beaters, who wore white smocks, were needed to beat the land. People used to come from miles around in order to shoot at Gopsall. Much of the game shot in the park was placed in cold storage ready to be taken to London when the family visited their town house.

At the Coming of Age of the Viscount Curzon in 1905 all the estate people were invited and took turns to sit and eat, since there was not enough room to seat them all in one sitting.

When King Edward and Queen Alexandra visited, a new road was built as well as a new avenue. Also, a new wing had been redecorated for the Kings arrival, and this caused a large financial strain on the Earl, but the thing which really strained his financial assets was the weather. During the King's visit the weather suddenly took a turn for the worst and forced the King and his entourage to remain for an extra six weeks. The cost of feeding the King in a manner to which he was used is said to have set Earl Howe on the path to bankruptcy. *(We are unaware of the building of a new road and avenue; the original plan was for the King to stay 3 days at Gopsall but the length of the stay was increased to 7 days some time before the actual visit; Chapter 8.)*

The Earl built a new billiard room in the hall and, in St Mary's Church, he put a new pulpit and boxes. A Mr Burns of Nuneaton also put in an organ which was later moved to Shackerstone. In the hall was an electric organ which, in those days, was a very modern thing and therefore very costly. *(This recollection probably combines a number of different actions by the 1st and 4th Earls spanning an 80-year period; the box pews installed in 1834 and the organ and pulpit installed in St Mary's in 1914 are still in place.)*

Only rarely were there events for the working people, but the whole family was very religious and as a consequence the Sunday School children would have a tea set for them in the park. The dray and horse would fetch them and after the tea there would be games.

What can you remember about the Howes themselves?

The Earl would not let anyone who did not work on the estate live in the villages, therefore everyone who lived in the villages worked for the Earl. Only farmers on the estate were allowed to have dogs and they were limited to one dog each.

The whole family went to church every Sunday, and the servants and grooms were made to go too. If everyone was not at church on Good Friday their wages were docked and their absence was counted as a day off. Only six-day licences were given to the public houses, so that Sunday could and would be for church. All the children were made to go to Sunday School and the Earl used to visit the Sunday School regularly. Bible classes were run by a Mrs John Dawkins, who lived at what is now Sutton's farm.

Georgiana, the Countess Howe at her writing desk in her sitting room (the blue boudoir).[3]

The Earl was generous in the fact that he allowed the village people to earn a few shillings by picking acorns in the park for the deer in the winter. We were paid one shilling a strike for all that were collected. Also, when we were children, we were allowed to go primrose picking on particular days. On Good Friday, palm crosses were made for the church by the villagers from the bits of wood in the park and on The Race Course. On special occasions the villagers were given permission to walk up the Avenue and earned 1d and 2d for the holiday horses and opening the gates for the gentry at Bilstone. The Howes were good people to work for because they looked after the villagers well.

Mr Brian McCullam, Twycross, February 1982

What was your family's connection with Gopsall Hall?

Well, my grandfather, John McCullam, was a coachman at Gopsall Hall and when Lord Waring took over he retired. When, he first came to Gopsall in 1880, or possibly 1888, he came from Scotland originally. Don't hold me to two years, because my father was born in 1895 and is still alive today at 87. As far as I can gather my grandfather was telling me the tale, that he met these people connected with Gopsall, the Howe family, that had gone to Scotland on a shoot as a guest of another wealthy person on an estate in Scotland. He came to Nuneaton station where he joined up with a party of people who were Irish people who were coming to work at Gopsall, and they had to walk from Shackerstone station up the Avenue to Gopsall, where he went into lodgings in what was the stables. After a period of time in the stables he was promoted to head coachman and his duties were to drive the Howe family to Shackerstone station and also to church in Congerstone where they had their own pew. The servants were encouraged to go to church in Congerstone but they had to walk, coming down an avenue of trees. I don't know if they are still there today. They came down by Castle Farm and it leads round and

Left: John and Elizabeth McCullam outside their cottage in Barton Lane, Congerstone.
Right: Beatrice McCullam, who worked at Gopsall Hall until she was married.

over a little foot bridge right up to a little door at the church which corresponds with where all the Howe family sat with their servants and their entourage, which were visiting. *(Part of the avenue of trees exists today and is the remnant of the 'New Walk' or 'Lady Georgiana Avenue', running between Castle Farm crossroads and St Mary's Church, created by the 4th Earl after his wife's death in 1906.)*

Anyway, he married my grandmother, who was a Jebbett, and I think her name was Phoebe *(it was Elizabeth)*, and she lived at Newton Burgoland. Great uncle Harry lived to a big age and he lived at Odstone until about 1850. He and his wife lived where Longwill's is now *(Ivy House Farm, Odstone)*, those cottages surrounded by trees; it's like in a little ground in Odstone, near the hall.

Going back to my grandfather, he lived to his eighties, he always smoked a pipe which he most of the time just held it in his mouth and never had it lit. My grandmother's family were in farming somewhere in Newton Burgoland or either had a smallholding and they moved when they got married to a house down Barton Lane in Congerstone which when they passed on, went to my Aunt Beatty who lives in it today. She's quite elderly and whether an interview with her would produce any results, I don't know. But she was left the family home and they kept chickens etc and she used cart the eggs to Shackerstone station and for other people in Congerstone at so much a dozen. She'd also take them to Nuneaton market using Bailiss' old charabanc *(Clarence coaches: WH Bailiss & Sons, Barton-in-the-Beans)*. From the proceeds she bought the house which is Clay's now and that was left to my uncle Harry in his will. The next house at the top of the drive was Brown's but I don't know whose it is now. It joins on the property, not where Bett Coleman lives but the next one. When they all passed on the town houses were sold.

He was quite proud of the fact that he'd got up to head coachman and was hobnobbing with nobility. It was quite a good job to get to go from groom to head coachman and they were able to get out and about. Most of the servants at the hall only did their particular job and it was a holiday if they went to Nuneaton or somewhere like that. That's why they were anxious to go to church for the mere fact that they got out of doing their duties and things.

He always used to wear these vivid waistcoats. In those days anyone to do with horses seemed to have loud clothes. He always used to wear a yellow waistcoat, which as children we had used to think quite frightful really. He also had one of those funny watches, a Hunter watch, which was posh. It had been given to him by a hall guest at a party at the time that the King came. My father and the other children were taken up to Gopsall and given a little bit of a party by all the people who lived on the estate to celebrate that he had come to the estate. This party was almost the highlight of their lives to a certain extent, and it stood out, and was a thing that was talked about, you know "*the day that the King came we had a Bun Party*", as they called them. *(This may be a reference to Viscount Curzon's Coming of Age celebrations in 1905 rather than the 1902 King's visit.)*

He was very friendly with someone he met at Gopsall, a Mr Wormington, who was head gamekeeper and lived on the Snarestone side of Gopsall. He had a house in the woods so he was among all his work and it backed up to the canal. It was there a few years ago but it's probably only a ruin now. It was at the back of Barker's farm *(Beanfields Farm)*. He was quite friendly with him almost until the time of his death. Mr Wormington lived to a great age and he was a very, very good shot. As a child I remember, when we used to have corn cutting, that he had used to be one of the top men who would come and space the men out with the guns to shoot the rabbits as they came out of the corn. When he was quite old he had used to live in a cottage in Shackerstone, as you go up Church Walk, he lived in the first one of those. As a young boy I remember him walking to Congerstone to see my grandfather when my grandfather was ill and they kept up their friendship until they passed on. *(The head keeper's cottage was on the southern edge of Shackerstone Fields Covert.)*

Head Keeper's cottage
The cottage no longer exists; some say that it was taken down brick by brick and transported to the USA but others tell the same story about Bilstone lodge!

The Wormington children used to have to walk from this cottage in the woods to Congerstone School across the park and, in those days, there were few footpaths. One of the Wormington daughters became Mrs Beauman who lived at Norton-Juxta post office until about twenty years ago. When I went to school, I was friendly with Cliff Beauman. We all had contact; my grandfather and his grandfather were friendly and we used to take various bits and pieces and eggs from Congerstone to Shackerstone to Wormingtons and Cliff was there. So, I knew him before I started school as a little boy and he was at Congerstone school at the same time as me.

Can you remember when your grandfather said anything about the estate whether it was self-sufficient or not and whether they grew all their own fodder for the horses?

I'm not absolutely certain about it. Certain parts of the park I know were woods. They were quite keen on the shoot and there were various keepers and under-keepers.

One of the Howe family was interested in motor racing and they had a race track somewhere there and so many of the estate workers had to maintain this part so it looked the part when the visitors came from London. They were always toing and froing from London. They mainly used the railway, more than I ever thought they did. It was the main means of transport. *(The 5th Earl was a racing driver years after the family sold Gopsall. Plans for a racing circuit in the park were made in the 1930s but never carried out [Chapter 10]. Speed trials were held along Shackerstone Drive from 1926-1934.)*

When my grandfather first came to the estate, the coal had to be fetched by cart from the wharf, and then taken into the kitchens etc for the heating of the hall. After two or three years as people passed on (died or moved to another estate), he got promotion. It was the Howes that were mostly in charge of the hall, and had the running of it when my grandfather was there. He was there for about one year with Lord Waring before he retired, as regards dates I couldn't really tell you. *(John McCullam probably retired in c.1920.)*

You've already mentioned the King coming. Can you remember any other events?

The significant part of the King coming was the party which all the children went to. *(There appears to be no evidence of a children's party at the hall; perhaps the children at school were given cakes to celebrate?)*

Do you remember being told about the Viscount Curzon's Coming of Age in 1905?

Nothing much really. It was a party again. *(A party for all the cottagers and their children over 10 years old was given at the hall on Tuesday 5th September 1905; this included John McCullam.)*

From what your grandfather has told you, would you say that the estate was a self-contained community?

Well, I would gather that it was but the estate deteriorated because of the death duties. Lord Waring took over but the place gradually went down and it was taken over by the Crown Lands Commission. But as regards dates I don't know. *(The Commissioners for Crown Lands purchased the estate, except the hall, park, Home [Shornhill] and Norton Barn Farms, in 1932.)*

So, your grandfather left the estate when he retired ?

Yes, in Waring's time. He was with the Howe family for whom he had a high respect. I don't think somehow too much feelings were lost on the Warings because he got the impression that they were trying to take too much out of the estate, and it changed. When you work for a boss and he is a great fellow and the other people come with new ideas, you don't seem to have the same affection for someone who comes and takes over. I get the impression from him of that. When he was a young man life was great when he first arrived with a group of Irish people. He was given the knickname 'Irish Johnny' even though he'd never been out of this country. *(Brian's grandfather, John McCullam, was baptised in Corcreaghy, Parish of Kilmore, County Monaghan, Ireland; Chapter 6.)*

From what people have said in other interviews your grandfather was considered a real joker, a proper character.

Oh, I think he was rather a character, even as an old man. They made their own entertainment.

It is said that one day he said to Mrs Battey, the housekeeper, that he hoped that he died on the same day as she did because the devil would be so busy with her he wouldn't have time for him.

You would have to have been in real contact with him to know of that incident. He was quite a character and lived to a great age. When I went to Congerstone School, he used to spend most of his time sitting in his rocking chair.

Is there anything else that you can remember?

Jones and Challis were some of his friends that lived at Twycross. Mrs Challis was the wife of Mr Jones who had used to keep the Curzon Arms. There was a June Jones about my age and then there was one or two younger children. Mrs Challis used to come down and see grandfather when he was old. Her father worked at Gopsall, something to do with the garden.

A group photo taken in the Curzon Arms in about 1940

Those present include Mrs Challis (*far left*), licensee of the Curzon Arms, Edward (Ted) Jones (*front centre*), Gopsall's last gardener and Margaret Jones (*second from the right*), Land Army girl who worked at Harris Bridge Farm during the Second World War.

A lot of staff were taken on and a lot settled locally, marrying local girls or other servants at the hall.

When my grandfather first moved to work at the estate he lived above the stables, and I should imagine most of the others did too. It wasn't until he got married and the fact that my grandmother had a little money, that they were able to purchase a house, even though it was a modest place in those days. He was quite happy with horses and his way of life. His wife was the business type, anxious to own property because property made her feel important in her own way. *(Some servants lived above the stables but others had rooms in the service wing of the hall. The cottage in Barton Lane was purchased in 1930.)*

I'm trying to think of people who had used to come visiting when I was a child. There was Mrs Jones, her father had passed on but she used to chat to him about the old days. He was between seventy and eighty when I used to know him and he passed on when I was fourteen or so. I'd just started to work and I remember his funeral being on a Saturday afternoon. I vividly remember hearing my parents say "*Well he's the last of the ....*". They used some funny name for him because he was at Gopsall.

Mrs Elsie Bennett (nee Hextall), Heather, February 1982

What was your family's connection with Gopsall?

My mother came to work at Gopsall Hall in the late 1890s - I don't know if she came twice but that's how she met father (Joseph Hextall) and she was there until 1901 - somewhere there because she was married on Christmas Day and she never went back to work at Gopsall Hall. Then of course the connection was that father was a wheelwright in the village and they were married and lived right up by the Horse and Jockey. I can't think who lives there now, but up that alley way, and that's where I was born *(now Kingfisher Cottage)*. We were there until I was about three and then we went to the Fox and Hounds and took so much ground with it. Dad carried on as a wheelwright at Shackerstone then, and mother managed the pub. That was when the fun was.

Elsie's mother, 'Granny Hextall', outside her cottage in Congerstone.

All sorts of things happened on the estate. In that day there would be five or six keepers. They wore a uniform like a policeman but in a khaki colour with buttons on and everything. Every entrance to the hall had a little cottage and a keeper lived there. There were two cottages down in the park where two keepers lived and there was another one towards Snarestone, and one up Barton Lane, it was a posh house and somebody named Paine (or Payne) lived there, he was keeper. Then there was a Mr. Wormington, a Peach, a Smith, and I knew all these personally. On top of that there were the woodmen, someone named Wilson was, I think, head woodman, but also there were others - Simon, Pegg and Twiggy; I knew them all as a child.

Things went on and the next period there was Viscount Curzon's Coming of Age and the death of Countess Howe. They had a big Coming of Age party and there is a photo of that. And then of course when Countess Howe died things began to deteriorate.

Mother remembers the King coming, he used to come regularly shooting, it was one of his outposts, I won't say why. Of course, everything was 'just so' inside the hall. There was a silver bath in the bathroom; some say it was gold but it was silver, I saw it. There was one room downstairs, they called it the cedar room. It was all panelled with cedar off the estate. *(The reason why, which Elsie was not willing to say, may have been a local 'story' that Edward VII used to meet with Lillie Langtry at Gopsall.)*

You've said how Mrs Hextall came to work there haven't you?

Well she was married, and she had been all over the place and all over England, Lord A............. and somewhere else quite a few places and her choice was to either go to Glamis Castle for the present Queen's mother, or go to Gopsall, and she came to Gopsall Hall. She was a laundress, there were two of them, the Head and the Second, and they never moved without one another. She was the Second but the elder one wouldn't go to another estate unless my mother went with her and she'd worked her way

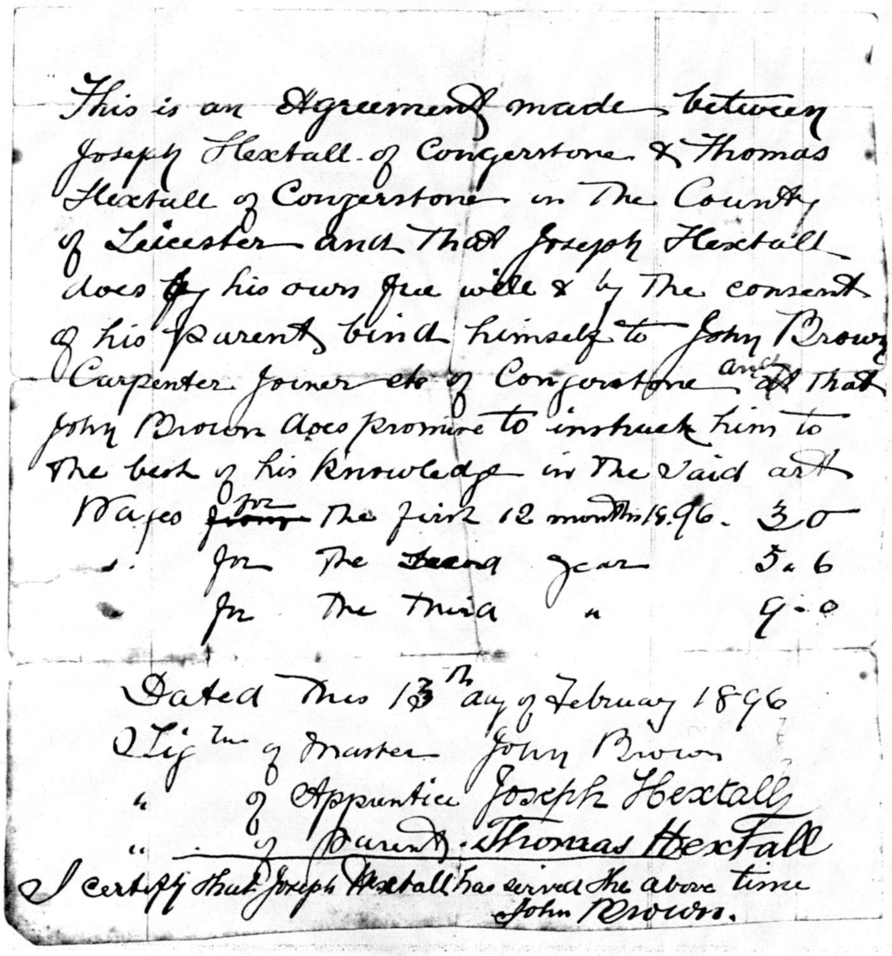

This is an Agreement made between Joseph Hextall of Congerstone & Thomas Hextall of Congerstone in The County of Leicester and That Joseph Hextall does by his own free will & by The consent of his Parents bind himself to John Brown Carpenter Joiner etc of Congerstone and That John Brown does promise to instruct him to The best of his knowledge in The said art

Wages for The first 12 months 1896. 3.0
for The second year 5.6
for The third " 9.0

Dated This 13th day of February 1896
Signature of Master John Brown
" of Apprentice Joseph Hextall
" of Parent Thomas Hextall
I certify that Joseph Hextall has served the above time
John Brown.

Apprenticeship agreement between Joseph Hextall and John Brown (13th February 1896).

up. That's how they moved along. I do remember the elder one, who was mother's friend, coming to see mother and they used to talk. When the family wasn't in residence at Gopsall, if they were down at Penn or in London, the washing all used to come to Gopsall Hall to Shackerstone station, a man used to fetch it. I can't remember if it was every day for washing but he definitely went every morning to the eight o'clock train to fetch the papers and all such things from the station, and be dispatched back again.

What sort of things had they used to wash, the linen, or personal clothing?

Now, the elder one did the gents clothing and my mother did the ladies, and they had to find their own special equipment, such things as sleeve boards. Mother's was like a board, with an arm up, and then it was like a sleeve, and you could pull a sleeve on either way. Like the ironing boards today they had a skirt board, well they had to lodge that. Ours used to lodge on the edge of the kitchen table and the back of a flat chair, and you could pull skirts on to that. Then there was a polishing board that was about eighteen inches by twelve and an iron that was used in that fashion, in grooves, and that was to polish the collars and cuffs, the lace and frillies all had to be goffered, the goffering irons were like curling irons, and you did this. I had used to be able to do it, and in fact I used to use the goffering irons sometimes to curl my hair. She never went back to Gopsall Hall.

Before the visit of the King and Queen, my dad cleaned every window in Gopsall Hall. He said that there were 365 windows and doors. *(A commonly held belief.)*

So, your father used to do odd jobs then?

Most people in the villages worked for the estate. My dad worked for a man named Brown who got contracts for various cleaning jobs in the hall, including the windows. Father was apprenticed to him.

The place began to deteriorate after the death of the Countess. She was buried in Congerstone churchyard, in the centre. Around the time of the First World War Earl Howe seemed to have lost his money. The visit of the King was one thing that led to his ruin. But he did a lot of entertaining with people coming from all over Europe. He was very interested in Russia. We often said that he had got a lot of money invested in Russia. When the Russian Revolution came just after the First World War things began to deteriorate. He never lived there much afterwards. *(Earl Howe sold the estate to Samuel Waring in 1918.)*

Once the Earl had sold the estate, the Countess's body and the monument were moved from the graveyard and taken down to Penn. I remember the body going ever so well. The undertaker and his mother came one Sunday evening and stayed with my gran. They had to have someone they trusted. The gentleman parked the hearse and hid it so that no one knew what was happening. The hearse left before eight o'clock in the morning. The undertaker had brought his mother because the body of the Countess was not allowed to travel without a lady in the hearse. I think the empty vault is still in the ground. *(Newspaper reports indicate that the body was exhumed on Thursday 10th July 1919.)*

The estate was sold to Lord Waring. However, some of the estate couldn't be sold - because nobody knew who owned parts of it. Elsie goes on at length to say that some thought that the Crown purchased the estate but that her dad always said it was in Chancery. Also, that the farm houses were not sold. *(This may be combining two unrelated events. The first, to do with the extended legal case in respect of inheritance of the Jennens' estates dating from after the deaths of Charles and William Jennens in the 18th century.[4] The second, may refer to the fact that when Waring attempted to sell the outer portions of the Gopsall estate in 1927, virtually none of the land or properties were sold.)*

For a long time, building in the village was not allowed. The first house in the village that was built, after the Howes had left, was on the left going from Congerstone School into Congerstone *(The Limes)*. When the Howes owned the estate, they wouldn't have anyone in the villages unless they were connected with agriculture or with running the hall etc - no miners. *(A common assertion is that miners did not live in the Gopsall villages until c.1920, however, cottagers who worked in the mining industry were invited to Viscount Curzon's Coming of Age celebrations in 1905.)*

At Christmas the older people, the poorer people all got either a piece of venison or a piece of beef. No-one ever went without. I don't mean they swamped them with food, but they made sure that they all had a Christmas dinner.

I remember well when the Howes sold up as I was about eighteen. That glass dish on there came from Gopsall. It was given to me by the head assessor who was doing the cataloguing. He lodged at my mother's and, because I was able to see him and give him his meal, he brought me that. In fact, he gave me two bowls. My daughter has got the other one.

The place was empty for quite a while before Lord Waring bought it. The hall was supposed to be a residence for his daughter, who married Able Smith *(married Captain A.C.B Critchley)*. They had a big wedding reception and I've got photographs taken of them standing in front of the hall with the late Reverend Rolleston and his family. I took the snap myself and it's a bit faded. We had quite a do. They lived there for quite a time off and on but times were nothing like they had been. The furnishings in the place were nothing to what they had been. They had a son and he died at Gopsall Hall. Afterwards they sold up and the estate then passed to the Crown. I know that for a long time it couldn't sell those four cottages where my mother lived; they were almshouses years back when the rent was 1s *(5p)* per year *(possibly should be 1s per month from what others have said about rents)*, which was a lot in those days when people hadn't got anything, only 5s a week pension. *(The outlying portions of the Gopsall estate were sold to the Commissioners for Crown Lands in 1932; the hall, park, Home [Shornhill] and Norton Barn Farms were retained in Waring's name; Chapters 1 and 12.)*

After the Warings took over they did quite a bit. Now who lives opposite Sutton's farm *(Old Ivy House farm, Congerstone)*? Churchills lived there at one time and someone named Hatton lived in the other end and he wanted them out. Miss Jennaway had what was the residence and then she allowed Hattons to build that house *(possibly The Limes in Congerstone)* and it was on a 99 year lease and that was the only stipulation. Everyone's eyes skinned because no one else was allowed to build one. Then Lord Waring owned it. It was a country club *(The Maltings or Malt House)* and when they had shoots and that sort of thing, they had a caretaker there named Mr Rose and his wife and they held the meals there when they had been shooting and hunting and the like. We used to have a dance there. We had the room free but we had to find the money for our own band. I think we paid 2s *(10p)* every Friday night or Saturday and we used to have these hops. Then, of course, that was closed and Waring lost all interest and gradually, as the farms emptied, he sold the houses and put the land to the other farms. *(Lord Waring sold over 3000 acres of land between 1920 and 1923; Chapter 5.)*

It seems that from what you've been saying that the Howes were quite strict on things, not letting people enter the village unless they worked for them, and as soon as Waring took over things began to slide and change .....

Oh, yes it did and then the next thing the army took over and they dilapidated it. I mean when I first remember it there were glasshouses and all sorts, I might have been the only child in the village who ever saw a peach or an apricot. They used to grow all those in the glasshouses and grapes. I don't know what happened to the vinery, but the grapes were beautiful. We used to go up there to the riding school *(stables)* for riding. It wasn't a school but it was where they exercised. It was all covered in. The man who looked after the place was virtually resident there even though his family lived in the village.

I can tell you who his daughter was, she still lives in Congerstone *(no name given)*.

Below and further up behind this riding place, there was what was called a cold room *(possibly the Deer Barn, see Chapter 14)*, no fridges in those days of course. It was a place where you needed a clothes peg on your nose to go in and see pheasant and venison and all sorts hanging there.

Do you remember there was a chapel that was part of the hall? Did you ever go near that?

Yes, I think that was the room lined with cedar. I went all through the hall but it was such a long time ago that I can't remember except that it was a marvellous place.

We were allowed into the grounds on Whit Sunday or Whit Monday, as a treat. We used to go into Twycross woods on Good Friday morning, to pick primroses to decorate the altar in Congerstone church and that was about all you were allowed to do. The temple was quite a little show piece. It was on the left as you went in from the Congerstone end. It was a circular one with pillars and a statue on the top. It's rumoured that Handel composed part of the Messiah there in Jennens' time, because he used to visit Gopsall. *(The statue of Religion that originally stood on top of the temple was removed in about 1835 and donated to Leicestershire Museums and Art Galleries in 1857.)*

In the laundry they had huge mangles with wooden rollers, and they had a man (one of the odd job men) to turn the handle for the rollers. Everything was washed by hand and used dolly pegs and punches. We can't miss that out because you lot, these days, you have automatic machines.

When the family were not in residence, the staff lived on what was called board wages, and they were better off then, because they got all their vegetables from the garden and there's no doubt that they often got meat. There was a resident housekeeper called Mrs Battey and she used to come into church and sit in the second big pew. All the housemaids who were still there used to follow her in and anyone would think that she was the Countess when she came in. She had a big hat on and you daren't bat your eyelids. Well, the laundry people sat in the next pew, they didn't mix. The top pew was the Howe's. Until the exhibition last year,[5] I'd never set my foot in that. You weren't even allowed to look over the door. It had a lovely carved oak table in the middle and a lovely red carpet on the floor. I think that their crest was on it: 'Let Curzon Hold what Curzon Held'. There were also hymn books in the pew and a fireplace. It is the truth, I was born, christened, married and all the rest of it in Congerstone and I'd never been allowed to set foot in the Howe's pew. No-one else did either except to keep it clean and tidy. The gardeners and the like used to sit it the little pew next to the door and near the altar. The Gopsall workers never mixed with anyone else in church and they used to come in as if they were in a procession.

So, going to church was the done thing by all?

Oh, yes. I remember mother telling me that she was in the Countess's funeral procession even though she had been left quite a few years. She is in one of the photographs taken at the time. After the burial, Earl Howe had the Countess' monument put up and had an avenue cut through all the woods to see Congerstone church. It was so planned that he could see all the churches on his estate because of avenues radiating in different directions. The estate went from Nailstone, Barton, Odstone, Shackerstone, then to Congerstone and then out to Twycross, Norton-Juxta-Twycross and to Harris Bridge. I don't remember whether the next village was in it but it went right out there. *(Sibson Manor was also part of the Gopsall Estate until sold by the 4th Earl in 1912; Chapter 1.)*

Can you remember any of the visitors who came to the hall?

They are all in that paper, although I do remember that they told me many times that I was only six weeks old when the King came and they took me to see him. That would have been in 1902.

Can you remember the Coming of Age at all?

I can't remember that, not clearly. There's a record of it in the paper and photos with the tenants sitting there. When my granddad was married, or perhaps when he was 21, Lady Howe gave him a bible which I have. Written inside it says 'To Thomas Hextall from the Lady Howe'. My mother had a photograph album with pictures of the Count, Countess, Queen Victoria and many other people connected with the estate.

When did your mother leave the hall?

She left when she got married. That was the reason for her leaving. I'm not quite sure when dad started collecting the rents for the hall, for the estate. I can remember as a child going in the pony and trap and a great gorgeous stick (?) under the seat while he went to all the houses in Twycross and so on, collecting the money. I'm not sure whether this was for Earl Howe or someone else. *(If she was a child at the time, this would have been for the 4th Earl Howe.)*

They began to allow miners in after the First World War. They had to pay their rent to my dad every Friday night and if they missed, they got notice. It wasn't very much that they paid, but they had to pay on time. That was a big concession. They went to live in that house opposite you *(Bates/Fox Covert Farm, Congerstone)* just around the corner. The first miner to move in was called Marshall. *(The house referred to was an 'eyebrow' cottage at the corner of Shadows Lane and Main Street, now demolished.)*

Are there any other things that you can remember about the hall?

They had an electrician and a head gardener Mr Lee was always the church warden and had always used to turn up to church in hat and tails. The electrician's wife a Mrs Garner played the organ and that was up in the gallery, above where the organ is now. I remember that organ being put in. We had a memorial service and it was put in for Lady Georgiana. Whether she was killed in an accident or what I'm not sure but her memorial book for her service is in there. *(The gallery organ was installed in 1834 by the 1st Earl Howe. It was replaced in 1914 by the current organ in remembrance of the 4th Earl's sister, Evelyn, who died in a pony and trap accident in 1913.)*

What about the school? You said that the school was built by the Howes?

That's right. I know he built it and there's a photograph of when a man named Bushby was the head master, but that was before my time. A Mr Bunting came to the school when dad was ready to leave. He had wanted dad to stay on but dad wouldn't and went on to apprentice to a wheelwright. Grandad didn't really work for the Howes. He worked at Wellsborough but he was really a drainage contractor. He was the man who was sent to put the (field) drains in. They were not put in like they are now but were put in a block, with a bit of straw in between. That would have been before 1900. In fact, I can remember farmers coming in to him when they had problems. They would say "*Tom can you remember where such and such drainage is because we've got a flood in the middle of a field*". I can remember tracing them out too. He never went to church but he'd read the bible at least seven times a week and you could ask him where to find a text. Granny would go to church but he wouldn't. He'd just sit there on a Sunday afternoon. *(Congerstone school was built by the 1st Earl Howe in 1825.)*

Congerstone School photo taken c1890

Mr Bunting (head) is on the left.

The two daughters of the Shackerstone stationmaster (Mr Cooke) at the time of the King's visit in 1902 are present.

Elizabeth Cooke is fourth from the left on the front row and her sister Violet is standing behind.

One of the boys may be Joseph Hextall, who would have been about 10 years old

Can you remember people like Mr McCullam?

Yes, I do. I wouldn't go down to Congerstone school unless he'd fetch me, when I was five. Sometimes he went to see the family but he always called at the Fox and Hounds. We opened at six and he'd always have a hot rum in the winter, well he always had rum in the mornings. We used to say

"*Chuberagin*" (his nickname) and he used to come in and pick me up. I got that I wouldn't go unless he took me. Our living conditions in the pub, then what was the bar in later years, was where we lived.

I knew Mr Lee very well, and I knew another gardener Mr Young, and he sang in the choir and all these other people. Jimmy Pegg, now he used to live where Mrs Lampard lived, and the man who lived in the house Mr Hayes lived in was Mr Hodgkinson. The Howes paid him and he did three or four days a week in Congerstone churchyard with a hand mower. It was like a tennis court from the front gates right through. There is a photo of him in Congerstone churchyard with a mower.

Did any social events take place for you and the village people?

I think we had a farmer's dinner once a year, when they paid the rent because they paid it at Twycross at the Curzon Arms. We had celebrations for the Coronation and that kind of thing and there was a big celebration when the Viscount Curzon came of Age. There was a party for something else but, as I say, we didn't see much of them.

If the Countess drove through the village in the open Landau and saw people in the village, she always expected them to acknowledge her and she did the same. She was a lovely looking lady.

Notes and References

1 Newspaper image © The British Library Board. With thanks to The British Newspaper Archive (www.britishnewspaperarchive.co.uk).

2 The December 1911 shooting party at Gopsall included King Manuel II and Paul Graf Wolff Metternich zur Gracht, the Prussian and German ambassador in London from 1901 to 1912. Manuel II was the King of Portugal and the Algarves from 1st February 1908 to the 4th October 1910. His reign ended with the dissolution of the monarchy in the 5th October 1910 revolution; he lived the rest of his life in exile in Twickenham, Middlesex. The identified members of the shooting party from left to right, in the back row: 1, Lord Alastair Innes-Ker; 3, Countess Metternich; 4, Viscount Curzon; 5, Sir Charles Frederick (Master of the King's Household and an Extra Equerry to King Edward VII and to Queen Alexandra); 6, The Hon. Harry Stonor (British courtier); 8, Viscountess Curzon; 9, Count Metternich; 11, Lady Alastair Innes-Ker; 12, Mr Arthur Sassoon (personal friend of King Edward VII); 13, Mr Murietta; 15, Lady Cynthia Graham. In the front row (left to right): Lady Evelyn Eyre (Earl Howe's sister), the Marchioness Dufferin, King Manuel, the Dowager Countess Howe, Earl Howe and the Countess of Craven.

3 Image courtesy of The Rt Hon Frederick Richard Penn Curzon, 7th Earl Howe, GBE, PC.

4 William Jennens ('the Rich') was Charles Jennens juniors' cousin. When he died intestate in 1798, it was claimed that he was worth £2m (~£259m today). Three aristocratic families hoped to benefit from William's estate: the Howards, the Curzons (who had inherited Charles Jennens' estate after his death in 1773) and the Lygons. It appears that the Curzons (later the Earls Howe) and Lygons (later the Earls Beauchamp) aquired the majority of the inheritance. Thereafter, a large number of claims on the Jennens estate were made by would be beneficiaries, the last being made by an American lady (Mrs Elizabeth Barnett) against Earl Beauchamp in 1933, 134 years after the death of William the Rich. This case was almost immediately struck out by the court, but in 1943 Mrs Barnett changed her target and stated that she intended "*to go to England after the war and have it out with Lord Curzon*" who, she insisted, "*had nine castles which belonged to her*". For more detailed information about this, see:

The Great Jennens Case being an epitome of the history of the Jennens Family. Messrs. Harris & Willis, Sheffield 1879.

Stranger Than Fiction? The Jennens Inheritance in Fact and Fiction Part 1: The Jennens Fortune in the Courts. Patrick Polden. Common Law World Review (2003) 32 (3), 211-247.

Stranger Than Fiction? The Jennens Inheritance in Fact and Fiction Part 2: The Business of Fortune Hunting. Patrick Polden. Common Law World Review (2003) 32 (4), 338-367.

5 *Portrait of a Village in Flowers and Bygones*. This exhibition, organised by Madge Rowbotham and Philip Kendall (churchwardens), was held in St Mary's Church on 28th and 29th June 1981.

A Royal Visit

"Visits of Kings to Leicestershire have not always been of such a peaceful nature as the one King Edward is about to undertake............................ In the neighbourhood is Radmore Plain, where, in 1485, was fought the last battle of the Wars of the Roses, which ended the line of the Plantagenet Kings of England."

The Birmingham Post, 15th November 1902[1]

On Tuesday 9th December 1902 King Edward VII and Queen Alexandra, together with Princess Victoria, arrived at Gopsall for a 7-day visit that had originally been planned to last just 3 days. This was his Royal Highness' first trip to Gopsall since becoming King in January 1901 and his delayed coronation on the 9th August 1902, although he had visited several times as Prince of Wales. Social visits from the Royals were not anything new for the Howes and previous Earls had played host at Gopsall Hall and at Curzon House in London. The King had visited the 4th Earl at Penn House (Penn Street, near Amersham) several times, including in January 1902,[2] where the pheasant shooting was *"the best in Buckinghamshire"*. Penn House is the current residence of Frederick Curzon, 7th Earl Howe who, according to the Daily Mail in 2013, ended the shoot which had been in place since 1875. However this newspaper report was media hype and incorrect.[3]

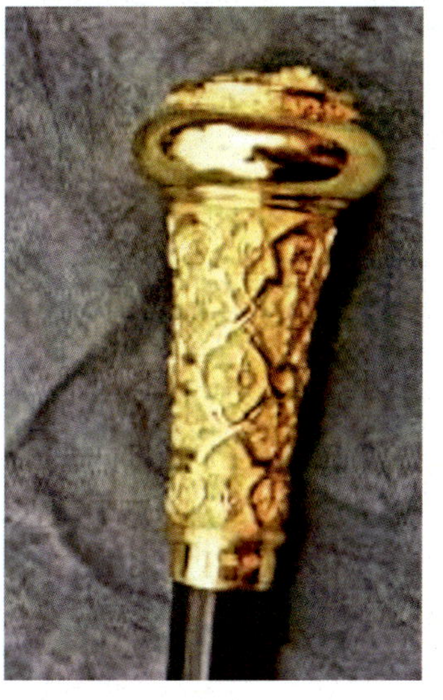

The head of the Gold Stick.

The Howes' connection to the Royal Household was long standing and well established. For five of the seven years of King William IV's reign (1830-1837), the 1st Earl was Lord Chamberlain to Queen Adelaide. After King William's death, Adelaide, as dowager queen, visited Gopsall every autumn from 1839-1844. Subsequently, the 2nd Earl was also host to the Royals at Gopsall. The 3rd Earl was Gold Stick[4] to Queen Victoria and the 4th Earl, when still Viscount Curzon, served as Treasurer of the Queen's Household, as well as being a friend of the Prince of Wales and future King. From 1903 to 1925 the 4th Earl was Lord Chamberlain to Queen Alexandra.[5]

The office of Gold Stick goes with the colonelcies of the Household Cavalry regiments (the Life Guards and the Royal Horse Guards, from 1820-1969; the Life Guards and the Blues & Royals today). For the last 180 years, the Sovereign's bodyguard positions of Gold Stick and his deputy, Silver Stick, have been ceremonial, but they were originally created in 1678 as a response to a supposed Catholic conspiracy to kill King Charles II.[6] The titles given to these bodyguards conjure up the vision that, if a Popish Plot had emerged, the Gold Stick-in-Waiting (i.e. on duty) would step into the fray wielding his gold-headed stick and, if overcome, the Silver Stick-in-Waiting would wade in as the backup! However, even the ceremonial duties could be too much at times, as Queen Victoria wrote in her diary about her diamond jubilee procession as it passed down the Mall on 22nd June 1897: *"The heat during the last hour was very great, and poor Lord Howe, who was riding as Gold Stick, fainted and had a bad fall, but was not seriously hurt"*.[7]

Preparing for the royal visit to Gopsall had taken approximately one year, with the King loath to commit to definite dates until near the time. This was apparently because he had health concerns; his coronation had been delayed 6 weeks because of illness earlier in the year, hence the change from a 3-day to a 7-day affair. The hall was repainted, new curtains hung, furniture revived, an organ installed in the cedar chapel and a power house built, complete with a generator to supply electricity to the hall. In addition, a new larder was constructed but, unlike today's larders, this was big enough to dress and hang game, including complete deer carcasses (Chapter 14). While many of these activities will have been prompted by the impending Royal visit, some were probably changes made by Viscount Curzon on becoming the 4th Earl in September 1900. Immediately before the visit, extra telephone lines were installed for the King's use, and no doubt the staff had been hard at work with brooms and on grass cutting and weeding duty in the gardens.

200-year-old mansion is stripped

LEGEND OF A BATH IS SHATTERED

A 50-YEAR-OLD legend was shattered yesterday when the auctioneer's hammer fell on lot 155 at the auction at Gopsall Hall—a 200-year-old mansion near Nuneaton.

Legend had it that Lord Howe—the mansion's former owner—had a silver bath specially fitted for the visits of his home of King Edward VII.

But a murmur went up from the prospective buyers, who believed the story, when the auctioneer announced: "I have been told it is silver, but I am selling it as tin.

"I have no objection, however, to you giving me the silver price," he added, and the lot was sold for £20.

A few minutes later a telegram was handed to the auctioneer. It was from the owners of the Hall, instructing: "Withdraw all baths and washbasins from sale."

No explanation was given and the names of the Hall's present owners are being kept secret. If the telegram had arrived 10 minutes earlier the secret of the bath would have been kept, too.

Gopsall Hall has been scheduled for demolition by a Ministry order.

The Birmingham Daily Gazette 1st June 1951
Jim Garvey, a demolition worker, and the 'silver' bath.

Widely reported after the event, although interestingly not once in the scores of 'Royal Visit' newspaper articles printed that week, was the introduction of a silver bath for the King's use. This 'mythical' bath did exist and pictures and local stories appear to prove it. One local farmer recalls how, as a child, he was put in the bath on a visit during the 1940s while the army still occupied the park. Lot number 316, an 'oxidised silver bath', was auctioned by Perry & Phillips Ltd on 31st May 1951. The lot was sold to Chris Lloyd, a scrap metal dealer in Ashby-de-la-Zouche for £20, just before a telegram was received withdrawing it from sale! We will never know whether it was really solid silver.

Entertainments for the week included shooting around the estate (see Appendix for more information about shooting at Gopsall) and golf on the nine-hole course. For the latter, two golf professionals were on hand to give demonstrations and coaching. There was to be no special meet of the Atherstone hunt during the visit and, more importantly, no meet during the week before, lest it disturbed the pheasants. If the lake remained frozen over, skating was a possibility for the guests and *"a motor car excursion"* was planned.

A selection of musical entertainments was also programmed for the duration of the visit. A performance by the choristers of Lichfield cathedral was to be heard and M.F. Casano's orchestra would be in attendance to play each day at tea and in the evenings. Mr Charles Perkins (organist at Birmingham Town Hall) would oversee the musical interludes and play the new chapel organ during Sunday service. The Royal Caledonian Boys (all 14 of them, who were appearing at the Leicester Palace) were also commanded to appear on the Saturday afternoon.

In addition to the King, Queen and Princess Victoria, other guests at various points during the week-long visit included: The Duke & Duchess of Marlborough; The Duke and Duchess of Devonshire; The Duke and Duchess of Portland; Mr Winston Churchill; Lord and Lady Gosford; Lord and Lady Cadogan; Lord and Lady De Grey; Mr and Mrs Arthur Sassoon; Lord Herbert Vane-Tempest; Marquis de Soveral (the Portuguese minister); Major and Lady Sarah Wilson (Countess Howe's sister); The Duke of Roxburghe; Sir F. Lascelles; Lady M. Warrender; Sir G. Warrender; Lady Juliette Lowther; Lady Norreys; The Duchess of Manchester; The Earl of Rosebery; Colonel the Hon. H. Legge; Count Albert von Mensdorff; Mr Arthur Balfour (the Prime Minister); Admiral Lambton; Captain Ponsonby; Mrs Sneyd and Viscount Curzon.

Countess Howe had returned on the 6th December from a trip to South Africa for her health, with her sister Lady Sarah Wilson aboard the 'Briton'.[8] The Daily Express reported *"She has very much benefitted by her trip, and will be hunting and riding again this season as vigorously as ever"*.[9] The Countess had not enjoyed good health for some time but the details were not disclosed.

Arthur James Balfour, 1st Earl of Balfour and Prime Minister (1902) NPG x 8451

The King travelled from Sandringham on Monday 8th December from a shooting party with other guests to London. That evening, he attended a special performance by Lillie Langtry of her play, 'The Crossways', before travelling to Gopsall by train on Tuesday, with low profile security provided by plain clothes detectives. The London and North Western Railway (L&NWR) was in charge of arrangements to get the King from Euston (3:45pm departure), via Nuneaton, to Shackerstone (6:00pm arrival). The Royal train was preceded by a pilot engine which ran 15 minutes ahead to ensure that the route was clear. The special train was hauled by locomotive 'Warrior' (L&NWR No. 1925, a 4-4-0 Webb Jubilee Class 4-cylinder compound locomotive built in 1900) and, as it travelled along the Ashby branch line to Shackerstone, it passed stations that were "*gaily decorated*" on an "*elaborate scale*", despite the visit being private in nature.

The King and Queen travelled in two newly built Royal saloons provided by the L&NWR company,[10] at a cost of £60,000, and were able to enjoy "*electric heaters so that any temperature desired can be laid on, while for warm weather, electric waving fans have been provided*". Electric cigar-lighters were also specially provided for the King! Prior to leaving Euston, the Royal couple were shown around the new saloons, delaying the departure by five minutes. Their Majesties declared themselves very pleased with the new saloon cars. Indeed, the sumptuous detail of the new coaches gathered many column inches in the newspapers, including the French press, which seemed as enthusiastic as the British press.

Just before departure from Euston, railway attendants removed the red baize-covered ramps attached to the floor of the carriages at the doors. They then proceeded to shut the double doors of the saloons but the operation seemed particularly difficult at the doors of the King's saloon. According to the Yorkshire Post, *"By an extraordinary effort on the part of the attendants the doors, which should have swung together almost automatically, were forced together and securely closed, and the train steamed out of the station"*.[11]

Especially for the Royal visit, a new platform surface of Victoria slabs had been laid at *"the rough and ready"* Shackerstone station. In addition, a canopy, picked out in red and white, had been fixed from the station door to the edge of the platform and a similar porch was erected at the station entrance, in order that the Royal guests could be under cover from the train to the carriage which would take them to the hall. The stationmaster, Mr George Cooke, had been working with Earl Howe's head gardener, Mr Lee, to decorate the platform with evergreen foliage and shrubs, the heavy frost not permitting flowering plants to be used outside. Electricity had been laid on for the first time at the station to illuminate the Royal visitors' way off the train across the platform and through the porch to their waiting carriage by way of a red carpet.

Shackerstone Station in 1902. Note the slight 'hump' in the platform where the Victoria slabs were laid (Chris Simmons).

In addition to the Earl, the reception committee on the platform included the chief

The new Royal saloons used for the visit to Gopsall. They were well built, elegant and modern by the standards of the day and served through three reigns and into a fourth. Two new, armour plated Royal saloons were completed in 1941, as the 1902, wooden bodied saloons were considered too vulnerable (Chris Simmons).

Top (L-R): The 'problem' doors and the King's day saloon; the smoking room is through the end door.[12]
Bottom (L-R): The control compartment with switches for lights, fans etc and the King's bedroom.[12]

Mr George Cooke (stationmaster; *3rd from the left*) with other railway officials awaiting the arrival of the Royal Train.

constable of Leicestershire, the stationmaster and various L&NWR officials. A man stood at the far end of the platform with a red light in readiness to bring the train to a standstill at the required point. Thirteen minutes after the pilot engine passed through the station, the royal train arrived on time and pulled up so that the doors of the King's saloon were opposite the waiting room.[13] A red carpeted ramp was quickly put in place at the doors of the King's saloon, ready for him to easily step onto the platform. Unfortunately, attempts to open the King's double doors failed and it was initially thought that it was because the bottom of the doors were lower than the ramp. However, it was then discovered that the doors opened inwards and were stuck.[14] By that time the King had already answered the Queen's call for him to leave through her saloon. Earl Howe offered the use of the ramp again, but all three Royals chose to step down onto the platform. His Majesty seemed to consider it amusing, but one might assume that the Earl was a little red faced, even if it was the fault of the L&NWR!

As the Royal party left the station some villagers, who had assembled at the station gates in spite of the biting cold, gave hearty cheers. Along the short drive through Shackerstone village to Gopsall Hall the local villagers had painted and tidied the fronts of their cottages and hung them with flags. Arches had been erected over the road and the bellringers at St Peter's Church rang a "*merry peal of welcome*". On arrival at the hall, the Howe flag was furled and replaced by the Royal Standard for the duration of the stay. Soon after their arrival at the hall, their Majesties dined with the rest of the house party and after dinner, Casano's band played a selection of music in the picture gallery. *"Dinner was served on the Howe gold plate, a magnificent service. The table was decorated with red geraniums* (well done Mr Lee, this was December) *and the rest of the decorations, candle shades etc were of the same deep colour. The old original candelabra have been converted into electroliers and additional softened light is admitted from behind the cornice which runs around the ceiling. The ceiling itself has a large centre piece representing Neptune riding in a Nautilus Shell drawn by horses. The furniture is upholstered in green leather"*.[15]

State dining room table laid with Gopsall's finest tableware.[16] A portrait of Richard William Penn, 1st Earl Howe, in his 1821 coronation robes is on the far wall.

The Morning Leader reported "*The king will occupy the famous blue and white suite of*

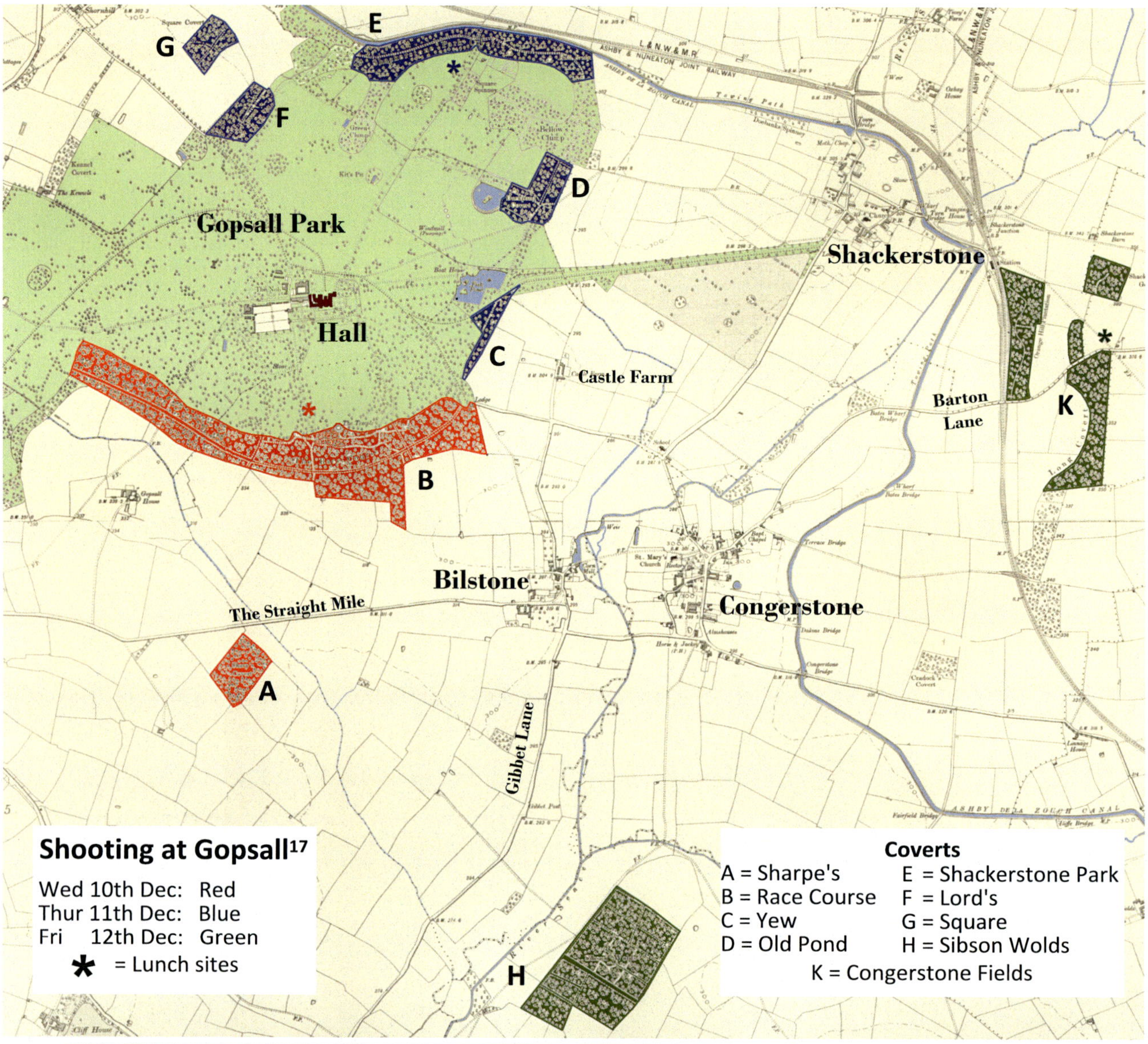

The King's beaters assembled at Shackerstone, December 1902

apartments, while the Queen will have Lady Howe's and the Princess Victoria, Lord Howe's suite." These rooms were also referred to as the Chapel rooms as they were next to, and above, the cedar chapel in the west wing of the hall and only accessible via private staircases (see Chapter 2 for floor plans of the hall).

Wednesday saw the start of three days of shooting for the King. A shooting party, including the King and Earl Howe, drove through Bilstone and shot over Sharpe's Covert (a wood just south of the Straight Mile) before shooting over the Race Course Covert, while some of the other house guests played golf. The shooting party was joined by the Queen and Princess Victoria and others for a hot lunch at 1pm in a very large marquee, erected near the covert. The marquee was made of stout canvas and featured glazed timber window frames. Coconut mat flooring was laid over the entire floor area and carpeted throughout. After lunch shooting resumed over the Race Course until 3:30pm. About 60 beaters were employed, dressed in Holland (plain woven unbleached or dull-finish linen, Khaki coloured) and trimmed in red. They also wore caps of Holland with red peaks. The press reported that the total bag for the day was 729, consisting of mostly pheasants but also many hares.

The House Party during the King's visit

Countess Howe, Earl Howe, Queen Alexandra and King Edward VII are standing centrally in the back row [4th - 7th from the left respectively]. Other guests include Capt Fritz Ponsonby (Assistant Private Secretary to the King), Rear-Admiral the Hon Hedworth Lambton* and Prime Minister Arthur Balfour [standing 1st, 3rd & 10th from the left]; Princess Victoria, Lady Sarah Wilson, the Marquis de Soveral, the Duchess of Manchester and Lady Juliette Lowther* [sitting 2nd, 4th, 5th 7th & 8th from the left] and, in the front row [*left to right*] Lord Herbert Vane Tempest, Frederick Robinson, Earl de Grey (later Marquess of Ripon), Mr A.D. Sassoon and Sir George Warrender* (7th Baronet of Lochend, Captain and Extra Equerry to the King; Vice-Admiral in 1913).[16]

* probable identity

On Thursday morning, the King and Earl Howe drove to the top of Shackerstone Avenue, while other members of the shooting party, now including Viscount Curzon who had arrived the previous evening, made their way on foot. The King took position between the main drive and the Fish Ponds while the beaters entered Yew Covert from near the Congerstone gates (by Bilstone Lodge). After some *"fair sport"* the party moved on to Old Pond Covert (Duckpond Covert) where an enormous number of pheasants were flushed and shot. From the Old Pond Covert, the shooters walked on to Shackerstone Park Wood for the last drive before lunch. The luncheon marquee was erected close to the keeper's cottage in Shackerstone Park Paddocks. The ladies joined the party for the 1pm lunch: all of them walking from the hall except Lady Howe, who rode out in an American spider carriage. After lunch the whole group was photographed[18] before the guns proceeded to Lord's Covert, where several foxes were *"disturbed"*; it is not recorded if they came to a similar end to the pheasants. The shooting finished at 3:30pm over

Square Covert and the King rode back to the hall on a cob, *"smoking a cigar, and evidently well pleased with his day in the woodlands."*

According to the Leicester Advertiser, dinner was again an impressive affair: *"the dinner table was again charmingly decorated, the flowers used being of that beautiful variety of begonia known as Glorie de Lorraine. A silver dinner service, bearing the initials 'A.R.' was used, this being the service which was bequeathed to the family by Queen Adelaide".*[15] Interestingly, the flowers for the dinner table were changed daily, Tuesday to Sunday: scarlet geraniums; lilies of the valley with smilax; pink begonias; bronze chrysanthemums; lilies of the valley with asparagus fern; *Plumbago rosea*. All the flowers were produced on site and tastefully arranged by the head gardener, Mr Lee.

Friday dawned a calm and bright winter's morning, favourable for the day's shooting planned at Sibson Wolds (Gibbet Lane) and 'Congerstone Fields' (Barton Lane). The King and Earl Howe drove from the hall down the main drive to Congerstone in an open Victoria drawn by a pair of black horses. When they arrived at 'Bilstone Turn' (Castle Farm crossroads) they found that the Rev. Ottley Warner and Mr Bunting (headmaster) had gathered together the children from Congerstone school to sing the National Anthem as the carriage passed by. After shooting over Sibson Wolds the party made their way through Congerstone village, where they were *"heartily cheered"*. When they arrived at the luncheon tent, erected near the keeper's cottage on Barton Lane, the ladies from the hall were already there. A hot lunch was again provided despite an accident witnessed earlier in the day by Princess Victoria and the other ladies while walking in the park. A pair-horse wagonette, with the servants being driven to Congerstone Fields to set up the lunch, bolted and collided with a gateway. The coachman, named Jacobs, sprained his ankle whilst wrestling with the horses who also sustained some injury, but luckily the lunch survived intact! After lunch, shooting continued over Congerstone Fields until sunset (see Appendix for more information about shooting on the Gopsall Estate, including the shoots during the visit of King Edward VII).

Mr Balfour (the Prime Minister) arrived in the evening in time to dine with the other house guests and be entertained afterwards by Casano's band. It is likely that a significant reason for his presence was the fact that he was a keen golfer and wanting to play the Gopsall course.

Throughout the King's stay everyone was much exercised as to who the handsome Turkish gentleman, in full national costume might be. This was Amin Ibraham, and his duty was to make coffee for the King, obviously.

The weekend was to be a more relaxing couple of days, with the only sport on offer being golf.[19] On Saturday morning, the King viewed the gardens and planted a cedar tree (*Cedrus atlantica*) on the east lawn before lunch. After lunch, the Queen and Princess Victoria also each planted an ornamental tree (*Picea nobilis*) on the east front. The King, who wished to view the Earl's fat stock which had won prizes on Monday at the Ashby Christmas Show, was taken to inspect Home Farm by Countess Howe, who drove them using an American spider carriage drawn by one horse. In addition, the King toured the dairy and newly installed larder facility, the latter containing all the game shot in the previous three days. After tea, the house party assembled in the red drawing room where a performance was given by the Royal Caledonian Boys. Dressed in Highland costume they performed nine or ten items and, of course, the programme was bound in blue satin. Macfarlane, a member of the troupe, performed the Highland Fling, followed by a sword dance. The latter took the *"best part of an hour"*; the Royal visitors must have had great powers of concentration!

Reverend Leonard Ottley Warner.

Sunday was spent quietly at the hall. Services (morning, afternoon and evening) in the cedar chapel were to be officiated by the Congerstone Rector, the Rev. L. Ottley Warner. There was no sermon, but a recital from a small choir from Lichfield Cathedral accompanied by Mr Perkins on the organ. The Rev. C. J. Taylor from Twycross was also to assist, but due to an outbreak of scarlet fever in his parish, his attendance was in doubt. It is not certain whether he managed to attend the service as only the Rev. Ottley

Warner took lunch at Gopsall with the King's party, with no mention of Rev. Taylor. After lunch and the afternoon service, the Lichfield Choristers were presented with leather bound writing cases by the Queen, each with their names and *"Gopsall Hall, December 14th 1902"* inscribed on them. Mr Perkins was given a diamond pin monogramed *"E. R."*; lucky Mr Perkins.

The Royal guests returned to London by train on Monday morning. Although this had been a private visit, the King requested that Shackerstone Avenue should be opened up for the public to view his departure. The Royal party left Gopsall Hall escorted by 34 members of the Leicestershire Imperial Yeomanry. The men, on horseback, came down the avenue at a slow trot with swords drawn. As they entered the avenue, which was lined with well-wishers down its entire length, children from Congerstone and Shackerstone Joint School sang the National Anthem. Further on, when the party passed through the village, the church bells rang and cheers continued all the way to the station where the Hugglescote and Ellistown Brass Band played the National Anthem as the King and Queen appeared on the platform. The Royal train was waiting and, after the farewells, the Prime Minister and the other members of the house party who were travelling with the Royal party entered their saloons before the Queen, Princess Victoria and the King boarded. The doors were then closed, without incident!

Alfred the Great Class locomotive 'King Edward VII' (L&NWR No. 1942; built May 1901), photographed in grey livery at the Crewe works in 1901 (Public Domain). The Alfred the Great Class L&NWR locomotive number 1943, built June 1901, was named 'Queen Alexandra'. It seems strange that neither of these locomotives was used for the visit, especially as this was the first time the new Royal saloons had been used. However, compound engines of this type were notoriously unreliable and it is possible that both 'King Edward VII' and 'Queen Alexandra' were not serviceable at the time.

The Royal train was hauled on the return to London by a 4-4-0 4-cylinder compound engine 'Francis Stevenson' (L&NWR No. 1960; built March 1902), a locomotive of the Alfred the Great class. It pulled out on time, having severely disrupted the normal rail traffic.

The newspapers at the time reported that there were *"well over 10,000"* people cheering and waving on the mile and a half drive down Shackerstone Avenue to the station and that no police were needed to control the well-wishers and there was no crowding. The large numbers present had travelled to Shackerstone by train from Leicester and intermediate stations much earlier in the morning, as well by special coaches laid on from the surrounding towns.

As a memento, The Leicester Advertiser produced five special copies of its coverage of the Royal visit, printed in gold, which were given to King Edward VII, Queen Alexandra, Princess Victoria and Lord and Lady Howe.[20]

APPENDIX

Shooting on the Gopsall Estate

Examination of census records, game certificate lists and newspaper reports, demonstrates that shooting game was an important activity on the Gopsall Estate throughout the Curzon-Howe ownership. Even in the 21st century, shoots exist within what used to be Gopsall Park and the outlying areas of the estate. Throughout the 19th century game licences were held by the Earls Howe, and gamekeepers had been on the estate staff since 1810 (at least), when Joseph Hodson[21] was keeper to Baroness Howe. While the shooting today is strictly for game birds (pheasant and partridge), 19th and early 20th century shoots included deer, not to mention almost anything that was flushed by the beaters. Shooting record books contained columns for hares, rabbits, woodcock, snipe, wild duck and 'various', presumably anything not listed that moved.

Deer shooting in the 500 or so acres of Gopsall Park occurred through the 19th and early 20th centuries but, in such a confined area, could not really be considered sport. The small size of the park and large number of deer present would also not give staghounds much of a run, but there is at least one report of Lord Brudenell's staghounds being let loose at Gopsall in 1821.[22] Most of the deer shooting at Gopsall was performed to maintain the size and health of the herd and to provide meat.

1894 - The billiard room at Glen Quoich showing two 11-pointers (one overlooking the glass, & the other to the right of same, & over billiard marker), which I shot on Kingie and on the East Beat in 1891!! (Caption as written by Lord Curzon).[16]

Detailed records of the shoots at Gopsall are in the archive of Lord Howe who has kindly provided us with information covering the period from 1894 to the final shoot under the Howe stewardship on February 1st 1918. Lord Howe comments: *"The 3rd Earl Howe does not appear to have had a particular passion for shooting, at least towards the end of his life, although latterly he clearly did take part in the shoot at Gopsall in a very informal way. Rather, it was his son, Viscount*

Lord Curzon standing between Prince Philipp and Princess Louise of Saxe Coburg with the day's trophies.[16]

Curzon, later 4th Earl Howe, who was absolutely mad keen on the sport and kept meticulous records to prove it. 1897 and 1899 were especially busy years, though in 1895 there appears to have been no shooting at Gopsall at all: instead, Lord Curzon went deer-stalking in Scotland and later, stag hunting in the Carpathians as a guest of HRH Prince Philipp of Saxe Coburg. There was a successful pheasant shoot at Penn at the tail end of that year".

Earl de Grey at Gopsall (1903)[16]

The shooting season at Gopsall usually included the months of October through to the end of January and, in the early 1900s, Christmas and New Year shoots were a particular highlight and associated with house parties with distinguished guests. Lord Howe hosted large Christmas gatherings at Gopsall in 1902, after the King's visit, and in the following year. Both involved fancy dress parties in addition to shooting, and included many of the same guests present during the King's visit.

The Marquess of Ripon's son, Earl de Grey (1852-1923), known as the Marquess of Ripon after his father's death in 1909, was a top-notch shot and a regular guest of Lord Howe at Gopsall and Penn and of other nobility at weekend shooting parties. He was a long time friend of King Edward VII and was appointed Treasurer to Queen Alexandra in 1901. Wikipedia states: "*Lord Ripon was a fast, accurate game shooter, who was noted to down 28 pheasants in sixty seconds as a shooting party guest on the Sandringham House estate. He also holds the record of the greatest recorded lifetime bag of birds shot: 556,000, including 241,000 pheasants*".[23] It seems that his passion for shooting was inherited. His father, while Viceroy of India (1880-1884), joined a shooting party organised by the Maharaja of Darbhanga which had a total bag of 1,683, including 4 tigers, 47 buffaloes, 280 pigs and 467 deer. The remainder being 'small game'. There was some criticism at "*such wholesale destruction, particularly as it happens to be the breeding season*".[24]

Christmas 1902 - Fancy dress in the entrance hall at Gopsall

Names of some present are: Viscount Curzon (*5th from the left, back row*), the Duchess of Manchester, Countess Howe (as Joan of Arc), Lady Sarah Wilson (as Bonnie Prince Charlie), Mr AD Sassoon and Earl Howe (*1st, 3rd, 4th, 6th & 7th from the left front row*). The Marquis de Soveral is standing behind the Duchess of Manchester, to her left.[16]

Details of Gopsall shoots between January 1894 and 1st February 1918

Season	Days shooting	Birds etc shot		Remarks	
		Total[a]	Per day		
1893/4	4	699	175	No details for 1893 part of the season. Guns: Lord Curzon, WE & E de C Oakeley of Cliff House, Twycross.	
1894/5	5	1,900	380	Guns: Lord Curzon, Lord Clifden, Lord Hindlip, Sir Archibald Edmonstone, Mr E Hulse MP, Mr C Wilson MP and WE & E de C Oakeley. No shooting in 1895.	
1895/6	3	1,734	578	In 1895, Lord Curzon went deer-stalking in Scotland and later, stag hunting in the Carpathians as a guest of HRH Prince Philipp of Saxe Coburg. January 1896 guns: Hon H Stonor, Hon A Walsh, Rt Hon A Morley, Hon A Walsh, A von Andre Esq, WE & E de C Oakeley .	
1896/7	10	5,485	549	Guns: Lord Curzon, The Earl of Clarendon, Lord Herbert Vane-Tempest, Hon H Stonor, Hon Cyril Ward, Hon J Ward, Sir James Miller, Mr A von Andre, Mr Hwfa Williams, Mr A Sassoon, Hon FG Curzon.	
1897/8	9[b]	3,930	437	Guns: Lord Curzon, Sir E Sassoon, Hon H Stonor, Hon D Marjoribanks, Colonel Swayne, Hon FG Curzon, self, Rt Hon A Morley, Mr A von Andre and Mr Charles Wilson.	
1898/9	9	3,276	364	Guns: Lord Curzon, The Hon Frederick Curzon, Earl of Chesterfield, Lord Herbert Vane-Tempest, Sir E Colebrooke, Sir E Sassoon, Mr A von Andre, Mr E Cassel, Capt WF Ricards, Hon H Stonor, Hon J Ward, Hon A Walsh, Mr H Milner	
1899/1900	11[c]	3,883	353	Guns: Lord Curzon, Lord Tweedmouth, Col Hon Montagu Curzon, Mr JM Paulton MP, Mr Henry Foley, Hon Francis Curzon, Hon FG Curzon, Capt Hon S Fortescue, Hon J Ward, Sir E Cassel, Capt WF Ricards, Capt Stewart, Mr A Sassoon & Mr H Harris.	
1900/1	11	4,639	422	Guns: Lord Howe [4th Earl], Hon FG Curzon, Viscount Curzon [Francis, later 5th Earl], Mr JM Paulton MP, Lord Lurgan, Lord Herbert Vane-Tempest, Hon Dudley Marjoribanks, Mr Ludwig Neumann & Woods.	
1901/2	17	5,423	319	Guns: Lord Howe, Lord Curzon, Lord H Vane-Tempest, Gen Sir Ian Hamilton, Capt G Holford, Earl de Grey, Lord Tweedmouth, Sir John Willoughby, Col F Rhodes, Capt G Wilson, Mr A Sassoon, Winston Churchill, Duke of Marlborough, Mr G Cornwallis-West & Woods.	
1902/3	12	4,484	374	Guns in the King's shoots in Dec 1901: Lord Howe, HM The King, Earl de Grey, Adm the Hon Hedworth Lambton, Sir George Warrender, Col the Hon H Legge, Captain Fritz Ponsonby, Mr AD Sassoon, Lord Herbert Vane-Tempest and Woods (3-day shoot total = 3,493).	
1903/4	9	4,956	551	Guns inc.: Lord Lovat, Winston Churchill, Earl de Grey, Lord Vane-Tempest, Hon H Stonor, HRH Prince Francis of Teck, Mr E de C Oakeley.	
1904/5	25	1,767	71	Note in album: *"We went to Egypt and I asked Mr Oakeley to do the shooting"*. Second busiest season with lowest average daily kills..	
1905/6	17	4,245	250	There were three days when over 1,000 birds were shot.	
1906/7	13	4,001	308		
1907/8	9	3,035	337	Guns inc.: HRH The Grand Duke Michael of Russia, the Marquis of Dufferin and Ava*, the Earl of Craven	
1908/9	12	4,254	355		
1909/10	19	4,895	258	Guns inc.: the Marquis of Dufferin & Ava, Earl of Craven, HRH Prince Francis of Teck, Earl of Chesterfield, Earl of Clarendon, Lord Vivian	
1910/11	12	3,727	311	Guns inc.: HRH Prince Nicholas of Greece, the Marquess of Dufferin and Ava, Earl of Craven, HRH the Grand Duke Michael of Russia	
1911/12	11	4,691	426	Guns inc.: HM King Manuel, H.E. The German Ambassador, Lord Herschell; 1,113 birds etc shot on one particular day.	
1912/13	9	3,791	421	Guns inc.: the Marquess of Ripon	
1913/14	7	1,735	248	Guns inc.: HH Prince Albert of Schleswig-Holstein. The last Gopsall shoot in which Lord Howe took a part was on January 30th 1914.	
1914/15	7	2,883	412		
1915/16	12	2,633	219	The total does not include 949 killed by keepers and tenants.	a = Total shoot tally for the period shown = 89,074 kills
1916/17	42	3,251	77	The busiest shooting season but with low daily kills.	b = Does not include 14 keeper days with few birds shot
1917/18	18	2,808	156	Guns inc.: Sir Oswald Mosley, but see Notes on next page.	c = Does not include 18 keeper days with few birds shot

* Died in February 1918. His widow married Lord Howe in December 1919.

Details of the drives used for the Gopsall shoots between 1888 and 1902

Part of the Gopsall Estate	Drive	No. of Drives	Period Used
Gopsall Park & Home Farm	Shackerstone Park & Farm Coverts	19	1894-1902
	The Race Course	18	1894-1902
	Gopsall Woods	17	1894-1902
	The (Shackerstone) Avenue	6	1894-1902
	Moore's Covert/8 Acre Covert (Shornhill Farm)	6	1894-1901
Congerstone	Sibson Wolds & Fields (south of Congerstone, east of Gibbet Lane)	21	1894-1902
	Congerstone Fields (Barton Road, fields near Keeper's Cottage)	13	1894-1902
	Osier beds/Harris Bridge Farm/Gibbet Lane	9	1896-1901
	Roby's/Robies Gorse (Robies Gorse Farm)	4	1896-1901
	Cradock's Covert (Fox Covert Farm)	2	1888-1901
Twycross	Twycross Fields	10	1894-1901
	Clare's (Barn) Farm (Sheepy Wood)	6	1888-1899
	Lea Grange Farm (Orton Wood)	5	1897-1902
Norton-Juxta-Twycross	Norton Fields & Coverts (Cottage Farm & Norton Barn Farm)	13	1888-1900
	Culloden/Appleby side (Culloden Farm)	3	1897-1899
Bilstone/Twycross	Sharpe's Covert	13	1894-1902
Nailstone	Nailstone (inc. Nailstone colliery; Knowles Farm & Nailstone Moor)	11	1888-1901
	Belcher's Bar	2	1897-1899
Carlton	Poplar Spinney	7	1897-1901
Barton in the Beans & Odstone	Drive not specified	4	1897-1899
Not known	Harry's Grove	3	1888-1901
	Lady Byron's Spinney	2	1888
	Shipston Farm	2	1888-1897

Notes about Gopsall shoot records

1. All guns are listed for shoots from 1894 up to and including the shoots with King Edward VII in December 1902. After 1902, only the names of notable guns are shown.
2. Names of gamekeepers noted in the Gopsall shooting album: Woods is named repeatedly as keeper in 1903/04; Woods and Peach in 1904/05, 1905/06, 1906/07, 1907/08, 1908/09, 1909/10; Peach only in 1910/11; Peach and Wormington in 1914/15 and 1917/18.
3. Notable absence of royalty and aristocracy during the years of the First World War.
4. The final shoot at Gopsall during Lord Howe's ownership took place on 1st February 1918. The guns were: Mr Turner, Mr Thompson, Mr Green, Mr Emery, Mr Emery Jnr and Mr Howe. In that final season, this group of men shot on a majority of days: other, more occasional, guns were Col Radcliffe, Mr Radcliffe, Mr Ford, Mr Evershed, Mr Moore, Mr Cox, Mr Yeomans, Mr Blackwell, Mr Hanmer, Mr Elsom, Mr Hardy, Mr Beresford, Mr Mammoth (?) and Sir Oswald Mosley.
5. Total shoot tally for the period 1894-1918 = 88,125 (89,074 including the kills by keepers and tenants during the 1915/16 season).

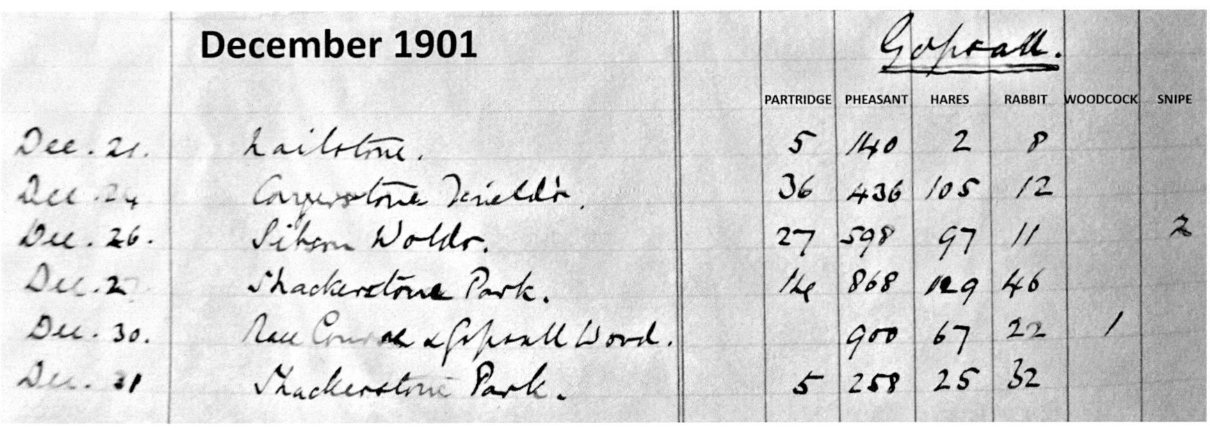
December 1901 — Gopsall.

		PARTRIDGE	PHEASANT	HARES	RABBIT	WOODCOCK	SNIPE
Dec. 21.	Nailstone.	5	140	2	8		
Dec. 24	Congerstone Fields.	36	436	105	12		
Dec. 26.	Sibson Wolds.	27	598	97	11		2
Dec. 27	Shackerstone Park.	14	868	129	46		
Dec. 30.	Race Course & Gopsall Wood.		900	67	22	1	
Dec. 31	Shackerstone Park.	5	258	25	32		

Over the 24 seasons from 1894 to 1918, there were 313 days of shooting (excluding keeper days), averaging 13 days per season and 334 kills per day. Although the shoots were ostensibly for pheasant and partridge, more hares and rabbits were shot than partridge, especially during December and January. For example, in the 9 days of shooting over Christmas and New Year 1903-1904, the total bag was 4,962, consisting of 3,340 pheasants, 928 hares, 323 rabbits, 280 partridge, 14 woodcock, 6 snipe and 71 'various'.

The House Party in December 1903

Earl Howe, Mr A.D. Sassoon, the Marquis de Soveral, Countess Howe, Viscount Curzon and Lord Gosforth* are standing (3rd, 5th, 8th, 9th, 17th & 18th from the left). Earl de Grey, Winston Churchill, Lord Herbert Vane-Tempest, Lady Sarah Wilson and the Duchess of Manchester are sitting (1st, 2nd, 4th, 5th & 6th from the left).[16]

* probable identity

A carriage with six 'guns' leaving the hall for a shoot (Christmas 1902). It is about to pass through the main north entrance gates of the hall.[16]

A third of all shoots took place within the confines of Gopsall Park and Gopsall (Shornhill) farm but drives in the Congerstone and Twycross areas were also popular and accounted for half of the shooting recorded between 1894 and 1918. Shooting in other areas was relatively uncommon, possibly due to the extra travelling distance required and the lower density of woodland in the Nailstone, Carlton and Barton in the Beans parts of the Gopsall Estate. A surprising feature is the complete lack of shooting on the Sibson part of the estate. The 'Sibson Estate' was sold by Earl Howe in 1912[25] with "*The Shooting is Excellent*" being an important selling point (Chapter 1). However, it may be that the shooting was let to a tenant in the late 19th and early 20th centuries, as it was when the estate was sold in 1912.

The final shoot at Gopsall during Lord Howe's ownership took place on 1st February 1918. This coincided with at least one of Gopsall's long-standing keepers moving to the Bosworth Estate (Herbert Peach). Shooting continued at Gopsall under Samuel Waring's ownership up to the outbreak of the Second World War, overseen by Major Miles. They were not family affairs.

Notes and References

1 The 'private' visit of King Edward VII and Queen Alexandra to Gopsall was covered extensively in both the local and national press at the time. For example, The Leicester Advertiser covered the whole visit in two editions dated 13th and 16th December 1902. The daily press reports of the visit form the basis for the contents of this chapter and specific references are not generally given. Precise details of some aspects of the visit are uncertain because of apparently contradictory accounts.

2 *The King at Penn*. Buckinghamshire Examiner 17th January 1902. At this time Penn House was the home of the dowager Lady Howe (Isabella Maria Katherine [née Anson], Countess Howe; died 1922; Wife of 3rd Earl Howe).

3 *You're fired! Earl kills off historic shoot*. Richard Kay. Daily Mail Online 12th February 2013.

In fact, the lease of the large syndicate renting the shooting rights came to its natural end. Because such a large shoot was causing major damage to crops on the farm, the lease was not renewed. Shooting rights were leased to a smaller syndicate three years later.

4 Gold and Silver Stick (created 1678): The Colonels of the regiments of the Household Cavalry hold the Court appointment of Gold Stick in rotation. The Lieutenant Colonel Commanding the Household Cavalry normally holds the post of Silver Stick. The emblem of office - an ebony stick or truncheon with gold head engraved with the Royal crown and cipher – gives the name to the holder. The Silver Stick assists the Gold Stick, who is also aided by brigadiers who carry ebony and ivory staves. Gold Stick's main duty on ceremonial occasions is to convey the Sovereign's orders to the Household Cavalry.

5 *Richard George Penn Curzon, 4th Earl Howe*. The Peerage compiled by Daryl Lundy, accessed 4th August 2021: https://www.thepeerage.com/p10633.htm#c106325.2

6 The Popish Plot was a fictitious conspiracy invented by Titus Oates, an English priest. It resulted in the executions of at least 22 men between 1678 and 1681. Oates alleged that there was an extensive Catholic conspiracy to assassinate Charles II, In 1786, Oates was eventually tried for perjury and jailed for life, but was pardoned after 3 years in prison when William of Orange (King William III) came to the throne in 1689.

7 Queen Victoria's diaries can be read at: http://www.queenvictoriasjournals.org/

8 *The Royal Visit to Gopsall.* Birmingham Post 3rd December 1902.; *The Royal Visit to Gopsall - The House Party.* Leicester Daily Post 4th December 1902.

9 *The King's Hostess*. Daily Express 2nd December 1902.

10 Following King Edward VII's accession to the throne in 1901, the L&NWR asked if His Majesty would approve the building of a new Royal Train. At the King's request, twin vehicles (Nos. 800 and 801) were constructed in 1902 with the interior decoration as close as possible in style to that of the Royal Yacht. This would appear to have been achieved to his satisfaction, complemented by loose furniture from Messrs Waring of London, forerunners of Waring and Gillow, who also supplied furniture for the Royal Yacht. The L&NWR had been particularly frustrated by Queen Victoria's reluctance to change; she had insisted on keeping oil and candle light (despite the presence of electric lighting) in her favourite L&NWR royal saloon. The new L&NWR Royal Train was magnificent. The two principal saloons for the King and the Queen were so well built, elegant and modern by the standards of their day that they served through three reigns and into a fourth. (John Arthur, National Railway Museum, 2020). The Royal saloons can be viewed in the National Railway Museum in York.

Description of the Royal Saloons: The Standard, 10th December, 1902: For the first time, his Majesty and the Queen saw and used the new Royal saloons built for them at the Company's works at Wolverton, from the designs of Mr. Park. The saloons are models of all that could be wished in the way of comfort and elegance. They are intended for use both on long and short journeys, and for day or night travel. Each saloon is of the standing pattern as regards length, equipment of bogey, and so forth, of the North-Western Railway, and is finished externally in the familiar white and chocolate, picked out with gold, which distinguishes the Company's carriages. One saloon is fitted up for the King, the other for the Queen and her constant companion, Princess Victoria. His Majesty's saloon (No. 800) is divided into smoking-room, day compartment, bed and dressing room, and at the, end is an observation compartment. The Queen's is similar in general arrangement, and the saloons are so arranged that the living apartments, so to speak, in each car are next each other, and are connected by a corridor. The King's smoking-room is in mahogany, with fine inlays of rosewood and satinwood. The chairs are in green leather, and the curtains, carpets, and hangings are in similar tones of colour. The King's day compartment is decorated in the 'Colonial' style, and is in white enamel. The furniture is in satinwood, inlaid with ivory. This room is also in green, though of a lighter tone of colour. Electric heaters have been introduced, and each room can be warmed to any temperature desired. In hot weather, electric waving fans will help to keep down the temperature, and, if desired, the windows can be lowered and fine dustproof ventilators inserted. His Majesty's bed and dressing rooms are in white enamel with silver-plated fittings, the upholstery generally being of a soft green shade. His Majesty's saloon is also fitted with electric cigar lighters.

The Queen's saloon (No. 801) is similar in general arrangement to the King's, and accommodation is also provided for Princess Victoria. The two beds have pink hangings, and at the head of the Queen's is a set of switches giving absolute control of the lights. All the rooms are in white enamel, but the predominating colour is blue, with light brocades and a very soft shade of pink to tone the electric lights. Her Majesty's bedroom has been draped in soft pink, and with the silver-plated bed and the fittings in the room, has a very beautiful effect. Adjoining this are her Majesty's dressing rooms. There are balconies to each saloon which are so fitted with windows that they can be used as observation cars.

11 Yorkshire Post 11th December 1902.

12 Images of the saloon doors and control compartment are by Hugh Llewelyn used under the CC BY-SA 2.0 Creative

Commons licence. Both images have been cropped. Photograph of the King's bedroom taken by Mick Higgins.

13 The granddaughter of the Shackerstone Stationmaster (George Cooke) has told us that the family legend was that the train actually overshot the place prepared for the Royal party to alight from the train and had to shunt back, much to the embarrassment of the station staff! There are various 'stories' about the failure of the doors of the King's saloon to open, both from the press and local oral history.

14 *The King and Queen - Departure to Gopsall - A New Royal Train*. Morning Advertiser 10th December 1902.

15 *The King and Queen at Gopsall*. Leicester Advertiser 13th and 16th December 1902.

16 Image courtesy of The Rt Hon Frederick Richard Penn Curzon, 7th Earl Howe, GBE, PC. Digital copies of the original photographs have been processed using Corel PaintShop Pro 2019.

17 Composite map produced from scans of 6 inch OS maps of Gopsall Hall and Park (1903; sheets XXVIII NE & XXIX NW) and online images of the 6 inch OS map dated 1955 for the remaining areas (Reproduced with permission of the National Library of Scotland under licence CC BY 4.0).

18 Russel & Sons photographers from London were employed to record the visit along with two local (and unnamed) photographers. The whereabouts of these photographs is unknown.

19 The 4th Earl enjoyed golf and Gopsall boasted a fine, 9-hole course that provided an important entertainment for guests staying at the hall. Golf was popular with many of the house guests in December 1902 during the visit of King Edward VII and Queen Alexandra. The ninth hole provided a considerable challenge to players, as it was positioned on the lawn immediately in front of the main hall entrance. The approach shot must negotiate "*a dip and the tall iron pallisadings and massive entrance gates which enclose the grounds in front of the hall*" (Birmingham Post, 12th December, 1902).

20 *The King and Queen at Gopsall. Planting of Commemorative trees*. The Departure: enthusiastic scenes. Leicester Advertiser, 20th December 1902.

21 It is possible that Joseph's wife was the Mrs Anne Hodson who was burnt to death in December 1824 aged 60, having served the Curzon family for 30 years (Chapter 6).

22 Morning Herald (London), Monday 19th November 1821.

23 *The Guinness Book of Records*. McWhirter, Norris and Ross (editors) (1972).

24 Derby Daily Telegraph, Friday 27th April 1883.

25 *Auction announcements of Messrs. KNIGHT, FRANK and RUTLEY, landed estates extending to 208,525 acres*. The Times, Tuesday 23rd April, 1912.

"*Now gentlemen, thro' there if you please*"

Original cartoon drawing in the Gopsall shooting album depicting a shoot.[16]

Celebrations and Sadness at Gopsall

After the well-publicised visit of King Edward VII and Queen Alexandra in 1902 (Chapter 8), there were two other notable events at Gopsall prior to the sale of the estate to Samuel Waring in 1918. In 1905, lavish celebrations were held at Gopsall marking the coming of age of the 4th Earl Howe's son, Francis Richard Henry Penn Curzon, Viscount Curzon (later 5th Earl Howe; Chapter 10). By contrast, the following year witnessed the death and funeral of the 4th Earl's wife, Georgiana Elizabeth Spencer-Churchill, the Countess Howe. Both of these family events affected and involved the workers, the tenantry and the villagers in the Gopsall Estate and other estates and properties owned by Lord Howe.

Francis Richard Henry Penn Curzon was born in Mayfair, London on the 1st May 1884. Francis was educated at Eton and Oxford and joined the Royal Navy Reserve after leaving school. In 1900, on the death of his grandfather, he assumed the title Viscount Curzon and his father became the 4th Earl Howe. In 1905, Viscount Curzon was a sub-lieutenant in the Royal Navy Volunteer Reserve (RNVR) and, owing to service commitments, his 21st birthday celebrations could not take place on the 1st May, but had to be delayed until the first week of September. He was serving with H.M.S. Barfleur in Portsmouth at the time of the Gopsall celebrations, but on 9th September the navy issued an undated appointment for him to join H.M.S. Terrible.[1] H.M.S. Terrible acted as escort to the Royal Yacht (the pre-dreadnought battleship 'Renown' reconfigured as a Royal Yacht) carrying the Prince and Princess of Wales on their tour of India in November 1905-March 1906.[2]

Above: H.M.S. Barfleur in 1896, a Centurion-class, pre-dreadnought battleship when part of the Mediterranean Squadron (launched 1892, scrapped 1910).[3]
Right: Viscount Curzon at Gopsall on 5th September 1905 (*top*) and in early 1919 when he was a RNVR Commander (*bottom*; photo by Walter Stoneman, NPG x65498). He was promoted to Captain on 5th April 1919.

The coming of age celebrations for Viscount Curzon at Gopsall extended over 2 days; the 4th and 5th of September 1905. On the Monday, the tenant farmers on the Earl's estates in Suffolk and Essex, Nottinghamshire (Gotham) and Gopsall, with their wives and families were, in the words of the Hinckley Times, *"entertained in a manner characteristic of the hospitable traditions of the family"*.[4] Gopsall tenants and families, together with some specially invited local people (eg. the rectors of Congerstone, Market Bosworth and Nailstone), began to arrive at about ten o'clock and were met at the front of the hall by Lord and Lady Howe and introduced to Viscount Curzon. The guests

The tenants and their families at Gopsall on Monday 4th September.

travelling from both the Nottinghamshire and the Suffolk estates came by special trains and started arriving around midday. Newspaper reports at the time said that the total number of guests arriving for Monday's celebrations was between 450 and 550. After being greeted and introduced to Viscount Curzon, all the guests were allowed to go through the hall to view its rooms and treasures, and to wander around the gardens and greenhouses; all the while listening to music being played by the band of the Royal Horse Guards, who had come down to Gopsall by special permission of the King.

In addition to the tenantry and local guests, there was a distinguished house party consisting mainly of members of the Howe and Marlborough families.

Lunch was served shortly after two o'clock in the 'covered gallery' (ie. the stable court, also known as the riding school), which had been specially decorated for the event. Lord Howe presided over the meal and members of the house party were seated at his table, with Viscount Curzon sitting between his father and mother. The band of the Royal Horse Guards played selections of 'national airs' throughout lunch.

The lunch menu was extensive, including roast meats (beef and mutton), pies (venison, veal and ham, chicken), cold ham and tongue, vegetables and salads, finishing with a variety of fruit tarts, jellies, tipsy cake and cheese. The tipsy cake (sponge cakes soaked in sherry and brandy and topped with almonds) might well have cheered the guests prior to the toasts and speeches that followed.

Lord Howe, after extolling the virtues of Edward VII, *"the great monarch who now sat upon the throne of their empire"*, proposed the toast of *"The King"* and the band played 'God save the King'. Ralph Arnold, of Shackerstone, the oldest tenant on the Gopsall Estate, then rose and proposed a toast to Viscount Curzon; he was supported by the senior tenants from Ratcliffe-on-Soar and from Suffolk. In response, Viscount Curzon thanked the tenants for their good wishes and said that he hoped to be able to emulate his forbears in running the estates (when the time came) and in his duties as an officer in the Navy.

The House Party at the north entrance to the hall: The Earl Howe, Viscount Curzon and Countess Georgiana Howe are in the front row (2nd, 3rd & 4th from the left respectively; *above*). Mr and Lady Evelyn Eyre and Lord Tweedmouth (*below*).

The Duke of Marlborough then rose and praised our farmers who *"during the last half-century had produced by their ability, energy and knowledge, the finest horses, the best cattle, and the finest sheep the world had ever known - and that the rest of the world today that possessed fine flocks and herds owed it entirely to the fact that they had been able to buy the best blood from the United Kingdom"*. After suggesting that the tenant farmers should combine when purchasing labour, machinery, feed, etc to help increase profit margins, he congratulated Lord Howe, and especially his long serving Gopsall agent Mr Burnett, for the successful running of the Gopsall Estate and proposed a toast to *"Agriculture and Mr Burnett"*. Mr Burnett gave a short reply before Lord Tweedmouth proposed the final toast to *"Lord and Lady Howe"*. They, in turn, replied and drank to the health of the tenants.

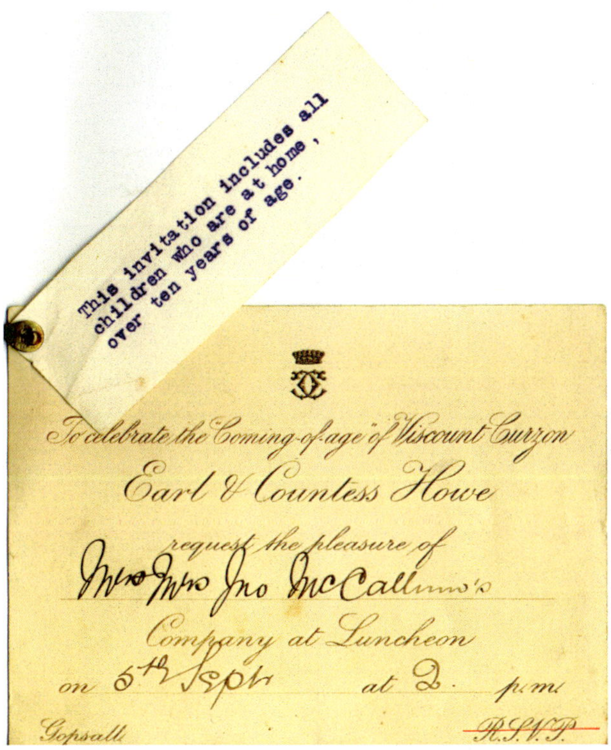

This invitation includes all children who are at home, over ten years of age.

To celebrate the Coming-of-age of Viscount Curzon

Earl & Countess Howe

request the pleasure of

Mr & Mrs Jno McCallum's

Company at Luncheon

on 5th Sept at 2. p.m.

Gopsall

R.S.V.P.

After the toasts, guests filed up to a table on which the gifts to Viscount Curzon were exhibited. These included a huge bronze urn from the tenants of Ratcliffe-on-Soar; a handsome clock from the tenants of Gotham; a silver urn from the tenants of Suffolk and Essex; a silver candlestick and inkstand from the outdoor and indoor staffs of Gopsall, Woodlands and Curzon House; a silver tray from the Gopsall tenantry and several private gifts. Shortly afterwards, tea was served in the riding school before the guests left.

The second day of celebrations was held for the Gopsall cottagers, their wives and children over ten years old, who were invited for lunch. All those living in estate property were invited, including both those working on or for the estate as well as many tenants engaged in coal mining. According to the newspapers at the time, some ten or eleven hundred guests attended the hall;

Tuesday 5th September's guests viewing the house (*top*) and in the formal photographs taken at the north front of the hall (*bottom*).

The guests having tea in the riding school (stable yard) on Tuesday 5th September.

almost certainly a gross exaggeration!

Lunch was again in the riding school, with the family and house guests in attendance. Today's music was provided by the Hugglescote and Ellistown Brass Band during lunch and at various times throughout the afternoon. At the end of the meal, cigars and tobacco were handed round, while champagne[5] and wines were placed on the tables for the guests to drink to Viscount Curzon's health. After the loyal toast, Mr Sentance, bailiff at Gopsall Lodge Farm (Shornhill farm), who had worked on the estate for 45 years, proposed the health of Viscount Curzon.

In reply, Viscount Curzon thanked all those present and then reiterated his sentiments of the day before saying that he would try to follow in the footsteps of his parents and live up to the example of one of the greatest admirals that England had ever seen (ie. his great-great-great grandfather, Admiral Earl Howe, 1726-1799). He concluded by saying that for the wellbeing of the country, Britain should have a strong navy. Thereafter, Mr Sheppard of Congerstone, with 50 years of service as carpenter on the estate, said he was pleased that both Admiral Sir Assheton Curzon Howe and Colonel the Hon. Montagu Curzon were present and gave the toast to "*the Army and Navy*". Both the Admiral and Colonel responded by thanking those present for proposing a toast to their armed services.

Mr Burnett submitted the toast of *"Lord and Lady Howe"*, saying that all would agree that it would be difficult to find a better landlord than Earl Howe or a more considerate employer. Lord Howe replied saying that, when his son took over the estate he knew that all those present would support him, as they had invariably done to the house of Curzon.

After the toasts and short speeches, the guests dispersed, some going through the house to view the state rooms and others strolling round the grounds and greenhouses. Later, tea was served in the riding stables and the band played for dancing until the festivities ended in the evening.

Today, it is interesting to note that the celebrations at Gopsall were held during the week. However, in the early 20th century, most people would have worked for part or the whole of Saturday, as the 48-hour weekend was only established in the 1930s. Furthermore, having a party on a Sunday would have been unacceptable. As most of the 'ordinary' guests worked for the Earl, a weekday would not have been a bar to attendance, and it is likely that most guests were delighted to have a day off, a good meal and a view of the house! Whether those Gopsall staff

Top: Lady Georgiana, the Countess Howe wearing her coronation robes.[7]

Bottom: The Countess on horseback. She was better known as Lady Georgiana Curzon in the sporting world.[8]

preparing and serving lunch and tea during the celebrations were given time off *in lieu* is unknown.

During the coming of age celebrations, Lady Georgiana, the Countess Howe, attended the lunches and, with the Earl, greeted guests as they arrived at Gopsall. At the time, the newspapers recorded that she appeared to be in better health than for some time and could walk a few steps with the aid of a stick but still had to rely on a bath chair to move any distance[3].

Lady Georgiana Elizabeth Spencer-Churchill was born on May 14th 1860 and was the 5th daughter of John Spencer-Churchill, the 7th Duke of Marlborough. In 1883 she married Richard George Penn Curzon (Viscount Curzon), who became the 4th Earl Howe on the death of his father in 1900. Lord and Lady Howe were close friends of royalty, especially King Edward VII and Queen Alexandra, both before and after Edward ascended to the throne on January 22nd 1901, and entertained them on many occasions at Gopsall Hall, Penn House and at Curzon House in London (Chapter 8).

During her early married life, Georgiana devoted her efforts to supporting her husband's political career and campaigned tirelessly until he successfully won the parliamentary seat of Wycombe and took his place in the House of Commons in 1885. The Countess was one of the most popular ladies in society and was known as an accomplished sportswoman. She was a fine shot and a fearless rider to hounds, following the Quorn and Cottesmore hunts and occasionally having a day with Lord Rothschild's staghounds. However, her skills as a horsewoman were probably most publicly recognised as a whip.[6] She was often seen in Mayfair and Hyde Park driving her four-in-hand, clad in a bright scarlet coat adorned with large buttons.[8,9]

Georgiana, used her position in society to support and promote a variety of religious and philanthropic movements. She is probably most remembered for her work to help British troops during the Second Boer War (11th October 1899 - 31st May 1902).[10] In a disastrous week in December 1899 ('Black Week') the British army suffered crushing defeats at Colenso, Stormberg,

Georgiana, the Countess Howe in her bath chair
Gopsall Park, October 1904.

and Magersfontein, with a total of 2,776 men killed, wounded or captured. Together with Lady Chesham, Georgiana wrote a letter[11] to a number of newspapers in favour of provision of special hospitals for the Imperial Yeomanry; a volunteer mounted force, members of which were being recruited to fight in South Africa. At this time her husband was a captain in the Prince Albert's Own Leicestershire Yeomanry, as well as being a Member of Parliament. The appeal resulted in donations of over £100k and the establishment of the Imperial Yeomanry Hospital in South Africa, which was reputed to surpass the Government's own medical provisions (Army Medical Service) in both quality of the staff and efficiency. The Graphic wrote: "*Never, in the history of warfare, has so completely equipped a hospital as that which now finds its home on the veldt at Deelfontein been sent out to administer to the wants of the wounded. When it was decided to send out a force of Imperial Yeomanry to South Africa several ladies, whose good works have rendered their names household words, banded themselves together with the intention of raising money, by voluntary subscription, for the purpose of providing a special hospital for the Yeomanry. Among these we may mention the names of Lady Georgiana Curzon and Lady Chesham*".[12]

Star of the Dame of Grace of the Order of St John of Jerusalem.
(David Bowen; Public Domain)

According to the Sphere the "*food and liquids*" provided at the hospital in Deelfontein were better than one would expect; the July 1901 supplies included 4,500 bottles of stout, 400 bottles of port, 150 bottles of brandy, 140 bottles of whisky, 230 bottles of champagne and 14 gallons of rum. The article added that "*not a single drop of the above intoxicants could be administered to a patient without the exact dose being tabulated on the diet sheet signed by the doctor in charge of the case*"![13]

Georgiana was chairman of the hospital organising committee for 2 years and both Lady Chesham and Lady Georgiana were appointed Dames of Grace of the Order of St John of Jerusalem for their work.[14]

While Lady Georgiana also supported another high-profile Boer War appeal, for the relief of those besieged in Mafeking, she also played a part in a variety of less well known charitable and

Members of the Sparkenhoe branch of the Girls Friendly Society at Gopsall Hall photographed on the south terrace.

Detail from one of several postcards printed to mark the death of Countess Howe. This card was sent from Twycross to a Mr Battersby of Wilson St, Timaru, New Zealand in July 1906.

humanitarian organisations, including the Girls Friendly Society.[15] This society was established in 1875 with the support of the Anglican Church as a pioneer youth organisation to protect working-class country girls who left home to take up urban employment. Georgiana's friend, Queen Alexandra, succeeded Queen Victoria in being the Society's patron.

In early 1902, Georgiana became ill with what was variously described as neuritis, blocked vein and paralytic seizure. Later in the year she spent several months taking a sea voyage to the Cape and back for her health, but only partially recovered, and from that time on, frequently required an invalid chair to move about. Georgiana's chronic ill-health ended her sporting activities, but she still tried to maintain her duties as a hostess when entertaining guests. In the August of 1904, the King placed one of the Royal Yachts (H.M.Y. Osborne, a paddle steamer) at the disposal of Earl Howe in order that Georgiana might have sea air.[16] While her time aboard and the short cruise was reported to have had a positive effect on Georgiana's health, her condition waxed and waned, and her last appearance at a large gathering appears to have been at her son's coming of age celebrations in September 1905. Georgiana Elizabeth Spencer-Churchill, the Countess Howe died at Curzon House, London in the evening of the 9th February 1906.

It is said that, because Georgiana was fond of Gopsall and St Mary's Church, Earl Howe arranged for her funeral and burial to take place in Congerstone. The funeral was scheduled for the afternoon of Thursday 15th February, giving only five days, including a Sunday, to make all the preparations.[17] This must have meant that the building of the brick vault (with room for several bodies) in St Mary's churchyard by the estate bricklayers would have started almost immediately.

The coffin being carried to the hearse at Shackerstone station.

On Wednesday 14th February, three special saloons, containing Georgiana's coffin, Earl Howe and some other members of the family and the floral tributes, which had been delivered to Curzon House up to that time, were brought down by the eleven o'clock express from Euston to Nuneaton. These saloons were then hitched to a special engine to cover the remaining few miles to Shackerstone station. The carriage carrying the body was draped in violet and white, with a low catafalque (a decorated wood frame) supporting the coffin. The lead-lined coffin was made from English oak with brass furniture and a brass inscription plate that read - "*Georgiana, Countess Howe Born 14th May, 1860 - Died 9th February, 1906*".

As the coffin was removed from the train, it was covered by a white corded silk cloth with a central golden cross reaching nearly the length of the coffin. Earl Howe then placed a large chaplet of Parma violets and lilies of the valley on the coffin before eight bearers carried the coffin to the waiting hearse. The hearse, followed by two coaches carrying the mourners, drove slowly to Gopsall Hall via Shackerstone Drive. Some villagers stood along the route to the hall, house blinds were drawn and the church bell rang half muffled. Servants from Gopsall, who had been at Shackerstone station awaiting the arrival of Georgiana's remains, also made their way back to the hall. On arrival at the hall, the coffin was placed in the chapel and a brief service was held by the Rev. Ottley Warner, Lord Howe's domestic chaplain and rector of St Mary's Church, Congerstone. Thereafter, the body was watched over by relatives during the night.

In the early afternoon of the following day, mourners coming down from London arrived at Shackerstone station by special train and were taken to Gopsall Hall in carriages. At this time, tenants on the Gopsall Estate also made their way to the hall on foot, while many other villagers

The floral tributes.

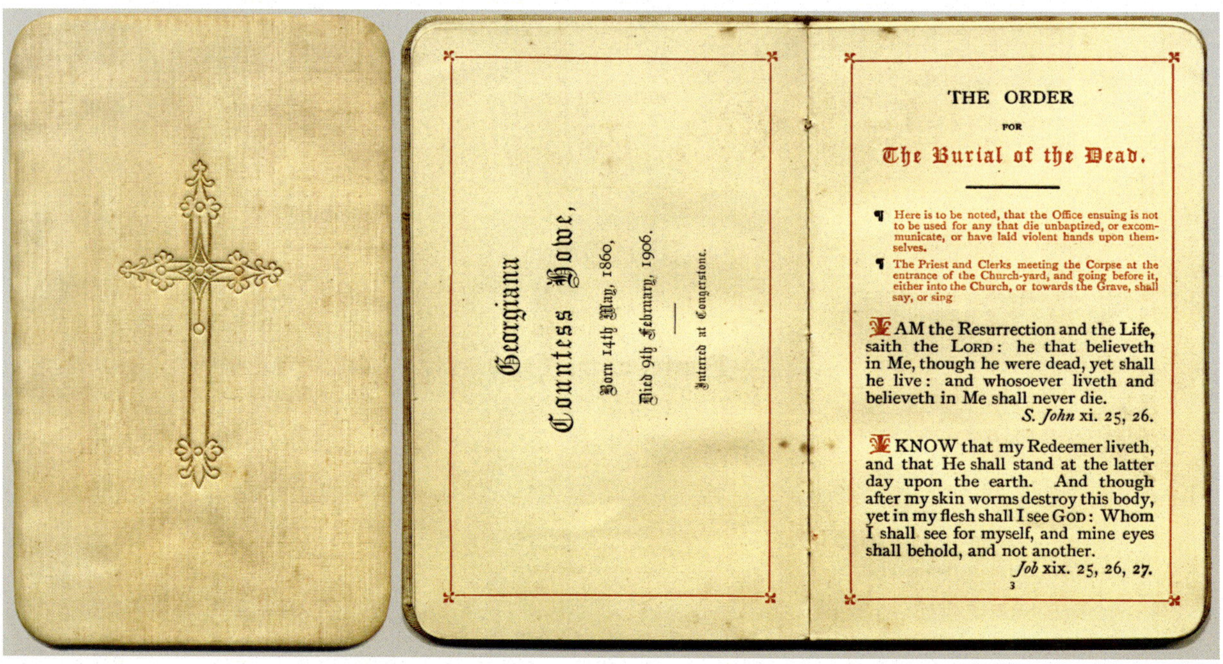

The silk bound Order of Service.[18]

started to congregate near St Mary's Church in Congerstone. The wreaths and flowers from the hall and those sent directly to the church were unpacked in the churchyard and placed in the chancel or outside; laid along the south chancel wall in preparation for the arrival of the funeral procession. At this time the public were not allowed into the churchyard and the police kept the road clear.

At about two o'clock, the satin cloth was removed from the coffin and the wreaths and floral tributes from Queen Alexandra and close relatives were placed on top. Eight bearers then carried the coffin to the waiting hearse at the north entrance. The mourners, with the tenantry and servants behind, formed into one long procession and followed the hearse and pair, walking to the gates of St Mary's churchyard, which were then at the roadside and immediately opposite the village post office. The hearse was met by the Rev. Leonard Ottley Warner, rector of Congerstone, and chaplain to Earl Howe, with whom were the Rev. W.H. Neep (rector of Shackerstone) and the Rev. C.J. Taylor (rector of Twycross), a cross-bearer and the church choir of St Christopher's, Ellistown. The coffin, carried shoulder high by eight estate workmen, was taken into the church by the south door of the chancel and placed on a purple cloth-covered bier. The coffin was followed by the mourners, local gentry, the tenantry, steward, head gardener, stud groom, the nurses who had attended the Countess during her illness and the servants, who all entered the church by the nave door. As they entered the church, Chopin's funeral march was played on the organ by Mr C.W. Perkins, the renowned

The procession arriving in Congerstone and the coffin being taken through the churchyard gates.

The coffin being carried from the church via the rectory walk to the vault surrounded by matting.

Placing the coffin at the vault entrance and the committal - "In Sure & Certain Hope".

organist from Birmingham Town Hall. All 3 clergy were involved in the service, but the opening and committal portions were read by the Rev. Ottley Warner.

Siegfried's funeral march by Wagner (Trauermarsch) was played when the coffin was carried out of the church and around the walk by the rectory before being placed by the side of the vault. A large part of the ground surrounding the newly made brick vault was covered with matting and sides of the opening to the vault were decorated with ivy, snowdrops and lilies (under the direction of the head gardener, Mr Lee). For the committal, the three clergy stood at the foot of the coffin, with Earl Howe at the head, and the chief mourners behind. After the service, the public were allowed into the church and churchyard to view the floral tributes and the coffin resting in the opening to the vault.

On the coffin was a chaplet of Parma violets and lilies of the valley - "*So, sleep, forever sleep. To our loved one, from Her grateful and devoted husband and child*"; a cross of lilies, tulips and white lilac from Queen Alexandra - "*In sorrowful remembrance dear Lady Howe, from Alexandra. Peace, perfect peace, now comes rest*"; four other floral tributes. The one significant person missing at the funeral was her son, Viscount Curzon, who was aboard H.M.S. Terrible escorting the Royal Yacht 'Renown' carrying the Prince and Princess of Wales on their tour of India.

Simultaneously with the funeral in Congerstone, a memorial service was held in St Margaret's, Westminster conducted by Rev. Canon Hensley Henson, assisted by the Dean of Westminster. Such was the standing of Georgiana in society, there were many notable attendees, foremost of whom were representatives of the King, the Queen and the Prince and Princess of Wales.

In remembrance of Georgiana, a twelve foot monument mounted on a three-step pedestal was erected over the vault in St Mary's churchyard during early 1907. In addition to the family motto, "*Let Curzon hold what Curzon held*," the monument was inscribed, "*The bitterness of death only touches the living*" (photos of the monument at Penn Street are in Chapter 13).

The death of Georgiana greatly affected the Earl who, in order to be able to see St Mary's

Lychgate at the start of New Walk or Lady Georgie's Avenue, as it would have been seen when returning to Gopsall Hall after a service at the church.

View from the south terrace of Gopsall Hall. St Mary's Church can be seen through the ride cut in The Race Course wood.

Historic England Archive

churchyard from the south front of Gopsall Hall, had a ride cut through the eastern end of The Race Course. He also built a direct, tree-lined path from the bottom of Gopsall's Congerstone drive across the fields and river Sence to St Mary's Church. At the start of this path, variously called New Walk and Lady Georgiana's Avenue on postcards, was erected a large, ornate wooden lychgate. According to the carved top of the gate, its true name was "*Lady Georgie's Avenue*".

Lady Georgiana's lychgate in Penn Street churchyard. Lord Howe (7th Earl Howe) is leaning on the gate.

At this time, it is obvious that the 4th Earl intended to live out his life at Gopsall and be buried with his wife in the vault built to accommodate a number of bodies. Indeed, from the speeches made by both the Earl and his son at the coming of age celebrations in 1905, the expectation was that when Viscount Curzon succeeded his father and became the 5th Earl Howe, the Gopsall Estate would be a part of his inheritance and responsibility. However, times were changing quickly in the early 20th century, Earl Howe's sister sadly died after a driving (horse and trap) accident in 1913[18] and the First World War started the next year. Whatever the reason, in 1918, Lord Howe decided to sell the Gopsall Estate and move to his other estate at Penn, Buckinghamshire.

Once the Earl had moved to Penn, he obtained a special Home Office Licence to allow the exhumation, transfer and reburial of Countess Howe's remains in the churchyard of Holy Trinity, Penn Street.[19] The exhumation took place early on the morning of Thursday 10th July 1919. In addition both the monument and lychgate were transferred to Penn Street churchyard, where they can be seen today.

Left: The Hon Francis Curzon and his mother, Viscountess Curzon (nee Spencer-Churchill) c.1887.[7]

Right: The "handsome clock" given to Viscount Curzon on his coming of age in 1905.[7]

The engraved presentation plaque on the base reads:

FROM THE TENANTS, RECTOR AND FRIENDS AT GOTHAM TO

VISCOUNT CURZON

ON THE OCCASION OF HIS COMING OF AGE 1905

On October 28th 1907, twenty months after his mother's death, Francis, Viscount Curzon married his cousin Mary Curzon in the little church of St Mary-in-the-Elms, Woodhouse.[20] The church was immediately opposite Mary's family home of Garat's Hay House, but the wedding was a subdued affair because the bride's father, The Hon. Montagu Curzon had died at the beginning of September. There were no bridesmaids and the small party of wedding guests, including Earl Howe and Isabella, dowager Countess Howe, shared the church with the resident villagers. The officiating clergy were the Rev. W.A. King (vicar) and the Rev. L.O. Warner of Congerstone, chaplain to Earl Howe. The organ was played by the Birmingham city organist who was accompanied by the choir of St Martin in the Bull Ring, Birmingham.

Immediately after the ceremony Viscount and Viscountess Curzon were "*greeted with cheers and waving of handkerchiefs by the villagers*". The couple had lunch with their wedding guests and then honeymooned at Woodlands, Earl Howe's house in Uxbridge.

Earl Howe and Isabella, the dowager Countess Howe leave the church after the service, their way cleared by the police.

The happy couple leave the church. Whether they walked across the road to Garat's Hay House or took a carriage is unknown!

Notes and References

1 *Naval Appointments.* The Globe Saturday 9th September 1905.

2 *The royal tour in India : a record of the tour of TRH the Prince and Princess of Wales in India and Burma, from November 1905 to March 1906.* Sir Stanley Reed, Bennett & Coleman, Bombay 1906.

3 *H.M.S. Barfleur of the Mediterranean Squadron.* Army & Navy Illustrated. 1st January 1896, p. 163. Photo by Symonds & Co, Portsmouth. H.M.S. Barfleur was described as follows:

The 'Barfleur' is a steel copper-sheathed first-class battleship, completed for sea in 1894. She was built at Chatham Dockyard, and engined at Greenock Foundary. Her displacement is 10,500 tons; I.H.P. 13,163. Length, 360 ft. Beam, 70ft. Maximum draught 25 ft. 6 ins. She carries, as her principal armament, four 29-ton guns; with ten 7-in., eight 6-pounder and twelve 3-pounder quick firers. She has a partial belt of 12 ins. Her speed is 18.5 knots, and her complement, 606 officers and men. She is commanded by Captain Reginald N. Custance, and her sister ship the 'Centurion' is the flagship on the China station. These are the two fastest battleships in any Navy.

4 *Festivities at Gopsall Hall. The Coming of Age of Viscount Curzon.* Hinckley Times Saturday 9th September 1905.

5 Provision of Champagne seems unlikely, perhaps an embellishment of the truth by the press of the time.

6 The 'whip' is a hunting term; more fully the 'whipper in'. The whip is the person responsible for guiding the hounds to follow the huntsman's horn and to ensure that strays returned to the pack. However, the term whip also applies to someone who is expert/experienced in driving a horse and carriage.

7 Image courtesy of The Rt Hon Frederick Richard Penn Curzon, 7th Earl Howe, GBE, PC.

8 *British Hunts and Huntsmen. The South-East, East, and Eastern Midlands of England.* Compiled in conjunction with The Sporting Life. The Biographical Press, London 1909.

9 *Obituary. The Countess Howe and sister of Randolf Churchill.* The Yorkshire Post Saturday 10th February 1906; *The death of Countess Howe. A patriotic and popular English woman.* The Birmingham Daily Mail Saturday 10th February 1906; *The death of Countess Howe.* South Bucks Standard Friday 16th February 1906.

10 In the second half of the 19th century several European countries (Germany, Belgium, France, Britain) sought to establish their hold on much of southern Africa. Britain 'officially' aquired the Cape of Good Hope from the Dutch in 1815 and annexed Basutoland in 1868 (now Lesotho) and the Transvaal in 1877. However, Britain had recognised the Transvaal as an independent Boer (Dutch-speaking inhabitants of the Cape) republic in 1852; the Orange Free State was similarly recognised in 1854. After several years of unrest, the Transvaal declared independence and the 1st Boer War began on 16th December 1880. The war went badly and the British government ordered a truce; a peace treaty was signed on 23rd March 1881 giving the Transvaal complete Boer self-government.

After losing the 1st Boer War, the British government had not given up its aim of unifying South Africa under Imperial British rule, especially with the discovery of diamonds, in 1866, on the borders of the Orange Free State and gold, in 1886, in the Witwatersrand basin, southern Transvaal. The origins of the 2nd Boer War were complex and stemmed from more than a century of conflict between the Boers and Britain. Of particular immediate importance, however, was the question as to who would control and benefit most from the very lucrative Witwatersrand gold mines. On 11th October 1899 the South African Republic (the Transvaal), together with the Orange Free State, declared war on the British Empire. It started after Britain rejected the Transvaal ultimatum, which demanded that all British troops on the borders withdrew and troops bound for the South African Republic by ship not disembark. After nearly 30 months the last Boers surrendered to the British in May 1902 and the war officially ended on 31st May 1902. The conflict was costly economically and in lives, with the death of about 25,000 Boers, 22,000 Britsh soldiers (including men from Australia, Canada and New Zealand) and 12,000 Africans. The peace treaty ended the existence of the South African Republic and the Orange Free State as independent Boer republics and placed them within the British Empire. The Union of South Africa was established as a dominion of the British Empire in 1910.

11 *Hospital arrangements for the Yeomanry. Beatrice Chesham & Georgiana Curzon.* Daily Telegraph & Courier (London) Friday 29th December 1899; Copy of the appeal published by the Countess Howe in all the leading newspapers on the 9th February, 1901. *Appeal for the Imperial Yeomanry Hospitals Funds. Georgiana Howe (Chairman of the Imperial Hospital Fund Committee).* Cambridge Independent Press Friday 29th March 1901.

12 *The Imperial Yeomanry Hospital (from a medical correspondent).* The Graphic Saturday 28th April 1900.

13 *What a big South African war hospital is like.* The Sphere Saturday 29th March 1902.

14 The Order of St John (The Most Venerable Order of the Hospital of St. John of Jerusalem) is a British Royal Order of Chivalry constituted in 1888 by Queen Victoria. Appointments to the Order are recommended "for service to humanity" and are confirmed by the sovereign.

15 The Girls Friendly Society (est. 1875) continues to support girls and young women today.

16 *The Royal Yacht Osborne.* Jersey Evening Post Tuesday 16th August 1904; *Local news and jottings.* Birmingham Mail Friday 19th August 1904.

17 *Death of the Countess Howe. Touching signs of regard and love. End of a brilliant life. The funeral at Congerstone.* The Hinckley Times. Friday 16th February 1906. Many local and national newspapers covered the death and funeral of Georgiana, the Countess Howe. The Hinckley Times article is particularly detailed.

18 A very similar, silk bound Order of Service was used for the burial of the 4th Earl's sister, Evelyn Alice Eyre, interred in Penn Street churchyard in 1913. *Lady E. Eyre's Death. Fatal injuries received through kind act to pony.* Cheltenham Chronicle & Gloucester Graphic, Saturday 11th October 1913.

19 *Famous Countess' Remains Removed from Gopsall Estate.* Shields Daily News. Saturday 12th July 1918.

20 *Fashionable weddings - Viscount Curzon & Miss M. Curzon.* Daily Telegraph & Courier, Tuesday 29th October 1907.

The 5th Earl Howe and the Gopsall Park Motor Racing Circuit

The Race Course at Gopsall is just a third of a mile south of the hall site and has been recorded on all Ordnance Survey maps of Gopsall Park since they were first published in 1885. Surprisingly, although visitors to the area have been known to ask villagers where Gopsall Park is, thinking that it was a recreational park, none have been known to ask the whereabouts of Gopsall race course. The Race Course is actually a wood which was almost exactly 1 mile long up until the early 1960s, but felling of the eastern part to provide more arable farm land has made it a little shorter today (1,500 yards). However, a wide avenue, the full length of the wood, is shown on all maps perhaps suggesting that it formed part of a hunt race course (called point-to-point in the latter half of the 19th century). Lord Vernon of Sudbury hunted the Gopsall country and kennelled his hounds at Gopsall prior to the coming of age of Richard William Penn Curzon (later 1st Earl Howe) in 1817.[1] Both the 1st and 2nd Earls Howe were keen huntsmen and Gopsall was known as one of the best 'countries' for fox hunting in the region. The 1st Earl rode with the Atherstone Hunt and chaired many of its meetings, and George Curzon-Howe, as Viscount Curzon, was master of the Atherstone for 11 years until he became 2nd Earl Howe in 1870.[2]

George Curzon-Howe, Viscount Curzon and Master of the Atherstone Hunt 1859-1870[2].

Although there is no direct evidence, it is quite likely that the Meynell Hunt and subsequently the Atherstone Hunt organised race meetings at Gopsall with the Earl's agreement or at his instigation. Certainly, the Earls in the late 19th and early 20th centuries had more than a passing interest in horse racing judging by the various races at Leicester bearing the Gopsall name. The Gopsall Park Plate was the first race on the card of the inaugural race meeting held at Leicester's new course at Oadby in 1883.[3]

Derby and District Motor Club
(Affiliated to A.C.U and R.A.C.)

CLOSED
SPEED TRIALS
(Held under the General Competition Rules of the A.C.U., and R.A.C. General Competition Rules)
ON THE
Shakerstone Drive, Gopsall Park,
SHAKERSTONE.
(PRIVATE ROAD)
by kind permission of Lord Waring
EASTER MONDAY, April 5th, 1926,
at 1-30 p.m. sharp.
Half-mile flying start.

OFFICIALS-
Judges—Capt. BEMROSE. Messrs. F. WALSH and CYRIL R. TOPPING.
Timekeeper—Mr. J. SIMMONDS.
Chief Marshal—Mr. L. WOZENCROFT.
Starter—Mr. F. J. MOORE.
Competitors' Stewards.—Mr. F. PEPPER and H. HANSON.
Hon. Sec.—Mr. F. CRANER.

Admission by Programme—SIXPENCE.

Remember the Amateur Trial on May 2nd, 1926, and the Races on Skegness Foreshore on Saturday, May 29th, 1926. . . . Particulars later.

In contrast to the above, there is a great deal of evidence that Gopsall was used for speed trials and that the park very nearly became a motor racing circuit, complete with its own aerodrome and country club. Records exist of speed trials held at Gopsall between 1923 and 1934.[4-7] The 4th Earl Howe sold the Gopsall Estate to Samuel Waring (later Lord Waring) in 1918. Waring, who never lived at Gopsall and rarely visited, gave permission for speed trials, for both cars and motorcycles, to be held on the relatively straight Shackerstone Drive. One of the last speed trials at Gopsall appears to have been organised by the Cambridge Automobile Club in 1933. The course was described as being half a mile in length, with a poor surface of sandy gravel, slightly uphill, with two gradual turns.[7] Various classes of car were raced from *"Up to 850cc sports and racing cars"* to the *"Over 3,000cc"* and *"Any capacity"* classes. The latter classes were dominated by the 10,688cc Delage of Oliver Bertram (26.8 secs; average speed of 67.2

mph) and the 7,912cc Bentley of Whitney Straight (30.6 secs; 58.8 mph). Interestingly, the next fastest car of the day was a 746cc single-seat MG Midget driven by K.D. Evans which completed the course in 31.1 seconds (57.7 mph), beating many Bentleys, Bugattis and Lagondas with considerably larger engine capacities. At about the same time that this meeting at Gopsall took place, 13 miles to the northeast, the Derby and District Motor Club held the first ever car road-racing event at Donington Park.[8] The circuit at Donington then was 21 miles in circumference and the roads tarmacked and at least 20ft wide!

As far as is known, Francis Richard Henry Penn Curzon, 5th Earl Howe, a motor racing enthusiast and accomplished racing driver, never took part in the speed trials held at Gopsall. The 5th Earl was a car enthusiast from childhood and drove a car for the first time in 1898, when he was only 14 while working as a mechanic in a French garage during his holidays from Eton![9,10] Francis Curzon's race debut was at the Irish TT driving a Bentley Type 43 in 1928 at the age of 44, before he became Earl Howe the following year. In motor racing circles he was affectionately known as *"The Grand Old Man of Racing"*[11] and today it is inconceivable that someone in his forties could embark on a motor racing career. However, the 5th Earl was not just an aristocrat with lots of money to fuel his dreams but a truly successful racing driver.

An Alfa Romeo Tipo B Monoposto (single-seat) - the fast but unstable car that Alfa Romeo refused to sell to the Earl.

Motor racing in the 1920s and early 1930s was dangerous for drivers, mechanics and spectators. The original large racing cars were two-seaters for the driver and, pre-1925, his mechanic, as breakdowns during a race were common and repairs would be attempted at the side of the track – no safety cars or 'red flags' in those days! The first lightweight single-seater car, the Alfa Romeo Tipo A Monoposto, was introduced in 1931. It had a top speed of 149 mph but was so unstable that lead weights had to be added over the rear axle to make it easier to handle.[12] Earl Howe's comments about the upcoming 1934 Grand Prix season emphasised the dangers: "*My own idea is that Grand Prix racing in 1934 will be nearly as dangerous for the spectators as for the drivers; and marshals, photographers, and other folk who have to stand on the edge of the course would be wise to station themselves near a 'funk-hole', where they can take refuge in the event of an uncorrected skid.*" [12]

Politics in the early 1930s had a big influence on motor racing such that Hitler banned the sale of Mercedes cars to any non-German driver[13] and Alfa Romeo refused to sell their Monopostos to non-Italian drivers. Indeed, when Earl Howe tried to purchase a Tipo B Monoposto for the 1934 race season, his deposit was quickly returned with an explanatory note from the manufacturers.[12] This, despite the Earl and Tim Birkin having been personally congratulated by Benito Mussolini for their *"victory for Italy"* after winning the 1931 Le Mans 24h race in an Alfa Romeo 8C. Sir Henry 'Tim' Birkin was, like the Earl, a very successful British gentleman racer.

Celebrations at Le Mans in 1931 after Sir Henry 'Tim' Birkin (with goggles) and Earl Howe won the 24h race (Agence de Presse Meurisse / Public Domain).

Left: Tim Birkin driving the Alfa Romeo 8C 2300 during the Le Mans race in 1931 (Motorsport Images).
Right: Tim Birkin at Le Mans in 1929 when he won the race with Woolf Barnato (Public Domain).

Francis Penn Curzon was educated at Eton and Oxford. He joined the Royal Navy Volunteer Reserve (RNVR) after leaving school and, during the First World War, was Battalion Commander, Howe Battalion of the 2nd Royal Naval Division. This was an infantry unit and Francis Viscount Curzon saw action in Gallipoli, Greece, France and Belgium. In 1918 he became the Member of Parliament for Battersea South, and in 1921 he was also appointed Commanding Officer and Captain of the Sussex Division of the RNVR. He became interested in motor racing in the late 1920s and was instrumental in the formation of the British Racing Drivers' Club (BRDC) in 1928, his debut year as a driver. He was president of the BRDC from 1929 until his death in 1964.[14] He stood down as an MP on becoming 5th Earl Howe on the death of his father in 1929.

The 5th Earl was involved in many racing formulae: Grand Prix (GP) and circuit racing, hill starts, short sprint and continental road racing. He even lobbied government to make road racing legal in the UK, happily without success! He travelled across Europe racing, and was often seen in the paddock with a blue golf umbrella, wearing his red cap and a red buttonhole carnation. Several years passed after his first race before he scored his first great and well-deserved victory - Le Mans in 1931, partnered by Tim Birkin at the wheel of an Alfa Romeo. In that year he acquired the famous 11-litre Delage, with which he set up a Brooklands Outer Circuit class record of 127.05 mph which still stood in 1939. He piloted a variety of marques including Bugatti, Lea Francis, Mercedes, Talbot, Alfa Romeo, Delage, M.G., Maserati and English Racing Automobiles (ERA) and raced on almost every circuit in Europe, on the Roosevelt Raceway in New York and on several circuits in South Africa.[11]

The Earl finished on the podium many times during his racing career between 1931 and 1939 and races won included the Junior Car Club Brooklands 12h race (1931); Le Mans 24h race (1931); Dieppe GP (1931); Empire Trophy at Donington Park (1932); AVUS Voiturette[15] in Germany (1932); Eifel Voiturette (1933); Nurburg GP (1933); Donington Park Trophy (1933); Grosvenor GP, South Africa (1938).[14] His last race was at Brooklands where he missed a corner and crashed, without injury to himself and relatively minor damage to his car, an ERA R8B.[16] Earl Howe had several racing accidents, the worst being in May 1937 during the inaugural race on the Campbell road racing course at Brooklands where he overturned his ERA and suffered a bad head wound and several internal injuries that stopped him racing for the rest of the season.[17] From his early years of racing, the Earl had a 'down to earth' approach to accidents; when he crashed his Delage into a tree during the 1932 Monza GP his immediate response was to say "*I'm afraid I have one car less*".[14] However, this did not mean that he was reckless. The fact that the Earl survived his racing career was probably due to the fact that he was one of the first racing drivers to wear a crash helmet;[14,18,19] blue to match the blue and silver livery of his cars.[11]

Left: Earl Howe in his 2.3 Alfa Romeo at the Dundonald Hairpin (1932 Ulster TT).
Right: The Earl fixes his Type 41 Bugatti's hub in the 1930 Brooklands Double-12, having run to the pits for parts.
Motorsport Images

Above: Earl Howe and Tommy Thomas in an SS Mercedes being chased by Caracciola in the 1930 Irish GP.
Below: Earl Howe (16) and Bira (17) in ERAs ahead of Seaman's Delage (9) in the Isle of Man 200 mile race.
Motorsport Images

Lord Howe (finished 3rd) with the other two Mercedes Benz SSK drivers at the Dublin Grand Prix in 1930. The photograph is signed by Malcolm Campbell (finished 5th) and Rudolf Caracciola, who won the 300-mile race at an average speed of 86.37 mph.

Image courtesy of Lord Howe

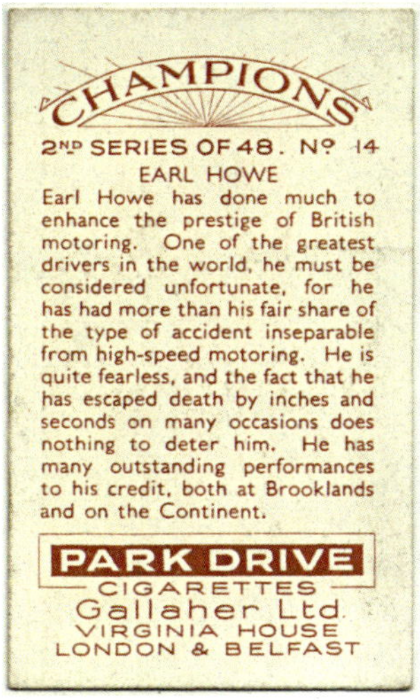

Cigarette card featuring Earl Howe.

The Talbot 105, registration number GO54 was one of four Talbot Team cars until 1932. It was driven by Lord Howe in the 1934 RAC International Tourist Trophy Race at the Ards circuit, Belfast when he finished 13th. In the same fixture held in 1932 and 1933, the Earl finished 3rd and 5th driving an Alfa Romeo.

Motorsport Images

Tommy Thomas, with Earl Howe in his Delage (1932 Dieppe GP).
Motorsport Images

Francis had a mechanic who travelled the world with him, Percy E Thomas, known as 'Tommy' Thomas in racing circles who looked after all the Earl's cars.[20] He was always referred to by the Earl as Thomas and he, in return, referred to the Earl as your lordship. However, such was the relationship between them that Tommy always stayed in the same hotel as the Earl. Tommy had been working for Malcolm Campbell, of Bluebird fame, when the Earl asked if he could take Tommy on. As Tommy was not involved in the speed tests of Bluebird, he was happy to work in Earl Howe's team. At this time racing cars were transported on trailers from race to race and Tommy suggested a van might be a better facility and, taking Tommy's advice, the Earl bought a Comma van, fitted out as a mobile service centre complete with sleeping accommodation. Neither Tommy nor the Earl ever used the sleeping accommodation, but this probably represented the first example of a racing team motor home, which today have price tags in the millions of pounds. When not racing the Earl kept Tommy busy with his collection of road cars, from an Isotta Fraschini to A7's and Fiat 500s!

Commodore the Earl Howe, PC, CBE, VD, RNVR with his tiny Fiat car, October 1943, Leith (© IWM A 19997).

The Earl's racing career was essentially ended by the outbreak of war in 1939. During the Second World War (WWII) he was a Commodore in the RNVR and his headquarters were in Leith, Scotland. When on official duties in his area he would drive around in a tiny Fiat car, presumably purchased prior to the outbreak of the war with Italy.

After WWII, the Earl maintained a keen interest in motor racing and was a passionate advocate for the sport. Although not racing himself, he continued to prepare and enter cars in races for other drivers and was involved in organising the first British Grand Prix at Silverstone in 1948. As President of the BRDC, he secured Silverstone, as the country's premier motor racing circuit, with full Formula One World Championship status in 1950, and represented the country's interests at the Federation Internationale de l'Automobile (FIA). Gerald Lascelles replaced the Earl as President of the BRDC in 1964; today's President is David Coulthard (2021).

Although Francis, 5th Earl Howe was never the owner of Gopsall, as his father had sold the estate to Samuel Waring in 1918, he knew it well. In 1932, he would have also known that Lord Waring still had a mortgage outstanding to his family trustees, meaning that the hall and park could potentially be repossessed and made available for his use (Chapter 1). Thus, it would have been in Lord Waring's interest to support a motor racing circuit at Gopsall, which had the potential to generate income from 'his' property. It is this background and the increased interest in motor racing, demonstrated by plans to develop race tracks at nearby Donington and Drakelow Parks, that probably caused the germination of the idea to transform Gopsall Park into a racing circuit and country club.[21-23] At that time Donington[24] was used for motorcycle racing and the

Automobile Racing Association (ARA) had already staged their inaugural meeting at Drakelow in May 1932 and were actively advertising for members.[25-26] However, the Drakelow Country Club meet was a failure, probably due to the weather, and the ARA was evicted from the property in the July.

Thus in 1932, the Earl was ideally placed to turn the Gopsall Park Club idea into reality. He mixed in the right circles, had intimate knowledge of Gopsall Park and a practical understanding of the needs of motor racing, not to mention access to people with money to fund the project and his own impeccable racing credentials. The idea was to use Gopsall Hall as a Country Club and Gopsall Park primarily as a motor racing circuit, but also incorporating an aerodrome; some newspapers called it the Midland Motordrome project.[27] As the hall and park still retained many original features intact, it was also proposed to provide facilities for members of the club, including tennis, cricket, croquet, squash, badminton, horse riding, boating and fishing, as well as the pleasure grounds surrounding the hall. The founder and general organiser of the Gopsall Park Club, was William Haines Hutchison, who had extensive experience in railway, canal and road building. In addition, Sir Malcolm Campbell[28] and Sir Henry 'Tim' Birkin[29] were members of the

Map showing the proposed Gopsall Park motor racing track. The full track is 6.2 miles long with a 1 mile straight. Provision is also made for two different ~2-mile short tracks, 6 stands, 5 car parks and an aerodrome. The hall and gardens were for the exclusive use of members and their guests. Provision of garage facilities was not included on the map. One comment in the motoring press at the time suggested that the hall stables were to be used as the garages, but the prospectus talks of "*loose box accommodation for 30 horses*", presumably referring to the stable block.

advisory committee for track and racing ensuring the credibility of the project.

The Gopsall Park Club prospectus (see Appendix) boasts a circuit 8 miles long (around twice the length of a modern day F1 circuit) with a 1.5 mile straight, all to be finished in a non-skid surface. The map detailing the circuit, car parks, stands etc contradicts these dimensions and shows a 6.2-mile main circuit, with the members' enclosure being a third of the way along the 1 mile straight. Although the racing circuit and park would be open to paying members of the public, the 34-acre pleasure grounds would only be available to members and their guests.

Lord and Lady Howe at the Donington Park JCC 200 mile race in August 1937.[30]

Motorsport Images

The proposal was before its time in terms of the participation of women in motor racing:

"At Gopsall Park women as well as men can indulge in their love for speed. We hope that women-only races will be popular, as well as the 'mixed' event, and we are anxious to introduce the sport to women who have never tasted a greater thrill than doing 60 miles an hour on the road."

As for the hall, this would be converted to a residential Country Club, with bedrooms for 100 members, several dining rooms and reception rooms, a ballroom accommodating 200 dancers and function rooms for all sorts of social occasions. The body of the hall only contained 20 bedrooms, so conversion would have been expensive, requiring refurbishment of the servants' quarters for use by members.

Earl Howe driving his ERA R8B at Donington Park, 2nd October 1937 where he finished 7th in the Donington Grand Prix.

Photo by TW Green (© MONZA Ltd on behalf of the Green Estate)

The relative remoteness of Gopsall Park to London was cited as a problem with the scheme from it first being announced. However, the Earl and Tim Birkin promoted this as an advantage because it would allow the running of 24-hour, Le Mans-style, road races as it would cause disturbance to very few people. This was considered significant as Brooklands, the only motor racing circuit in Britain at that time, was limited to running races with a maximum duration of 12 hours.[31]

Some information about the facilities at, and types of membership of, the Gopsall Park Club were being publicised in the press in April 1932[32] and Lord Howe visited Gopsall in May to drive the course (in an all-terrain vehicle built for the army) and finalise the layout of the track.[33] By July 1932, the prospectus had been distributed to interested parties,[22] the advisory committee confirmed and the Gopsall Park Syndicate Ltd registered as a private company.[23] Unfortunately, a Government embargo on the issuing of all company stock held up the project.[34] Despite this, in November 1932, the Royal Automobile Club list of international motoring fixtures for 1933 included a Gopsall Park Race Meeting in September.[35]

Surprisingly, in January 1933 the Gopsall project appeared to be progressing well.[36] Newspapers reported that contracts for £250k had been signed, the track layout had been approved and two firms had contracts for laying the track. In addition, stands had been designed for 50,000 spectators, arrangements made for laying out car parks and the work was due to start in a few weeks, once the company had been registered. Such was the expectation that all would go to plan, it was confirmed that Gopsall Park had been allotted a date in the International Motor Racing Calendar for the 30th September 1933, the opening date for the circuit!

No building work at Gopsall was undertaken during 1933 or the first 6 months of 1934, and meetings were still being held explaining the Gopsall Park project to possible investors in June 1934.[37,38] It appears that there were changes in both the company directors and racing advisory committee and a re-launch of Gopsall Park Ltd with the aim of issuing 1,200,000 ordinary shares of 5/- (25p).[39,40] However, the share issue was not a success and the scheme was abandoned in August 1934.[41] In the October of that year a proposal was put forward for a pony racing track at Gopsall;[42,43] presumably an attempt by Lord Waring to create income from the park rather than the continued participation of Earl Howe and his motor racing circle.

Derby Daily Telegraph, 26th May 1950.
Reach Licensing

The principal reason that the motor racing track never came to fruition was lack of funds and there were probably two main reasons why financial backing for the project was not forthcoming. The financial crisis due to the 'Great Depression' had begun to overwhelm Britain in 1931, amplifying the risks involved in investing in an entertainment project, principally aimed at the wealthy members of society. This, together with the failure of several similar country club and motor racing schemes during the two years leading up to the summer of 1934,[44] would also have weighed heavily with potential investors. Additionally, the opening up of Donington Park for official car race meetings in 1933,[8] when Gopsall was still in its planning stages was probably also a major factor. That the opening of Donington Park was significant in the demise of the Gopsall circuit is supported by the fact that in the summer of 1934 Earl Howe, together with a number of the proposed Gopsall racing committee, joined the racing committee of the Derby and District Motor Club who ran the events at Donington Park.[41]

Coventry Evening Telegraph, 23rd August 1950.
Reach Licensing

Surprisingly, motor racing of a sort returned briefly to Gopsall Park in 1950. The Hinckley and Donisthorpe Districts Motorcycle and Light Car Clubs jointly organised three motorcycle grass track events in the park during the May and August Bank holiday weekends and on the 9th July. Entry was 2/- (*10p*) for adults and 1/- (*5p*) for children and special buses ran from Ashby, Hinckley and Atherstone.[45] However, the last recorded motoring event involving Gopsall appears to have been in 1972 during the 432 Solihull Motor Club's Rally of the Tests.[46] The rally had an entry of over 150 cars and a 200-mile route including 10 special stages; a very muddy Gopsall Park being one. The winner, driving a Ford Escort TC, was Barrie Malkin who had won the Tour of Epynt in 1968. The Welsh Epynt rally in Breconshire still runs and is part of the Protyre Motorsport UK National Asphalt Rally Series.

The failed attempt to transform Gopsall Park into a Country Club and Racing Circuit was probably its death knell: with the hall being demolished and the park reverting to farm land in 1951, after the financial problems encountered by Lord Waring and Panton Investments (Chapter 1). It is almost certainly true that many of the current residents of the estate villages of Twycross, Norton-Juxta-Twycross, Bilstone, Shackerstone and Congerstone would be living elsewhere today if the racing circuit had come to fruition, even if they do regret the fact that Gopsall Hall is no more!

APPENDIX

GOPSALL PARK

MOTOR RACING CIRCUIT, AERODROME AND COUNTRY CLUB

★

PATRONS

The Rt. Hon. The Earl Howe, P.C., C.B.E., V.D.
The Right. Hon. The Countess of Harrington, M.F.H.
The Lady Iris Capell
W. Lindsay Everard, Esq., M.P., D.L., J.P.
Major Algernon Burnaby, D.L., J.P.
Horace Crossley, Esq., J.P.

ADVISORY COMMITTEE (TRACK AND RACING)

The Rt. Hon. The Earl Howe, P.C., C.B.E., V.D.
Sir Henry Birkin, Bart. Sir Malcolm Campbell
S. C. H. Davis, Esq.
Hugh P. McConnell, Esq., M.S.A.E., A.M.I.A.E.
C. S. Staniland, Esq. Brian Lewis, Esq.

FOUNDER

W. H. Hutchinson, A.M.INST.C.E.

HEADQUARTERS

Gopsall Park, Atherstone, Warwickshire.

ORGANISING SECRETARY, LONDON OFFICE

Col. J. B. Cameron, D.S.O.
1a Grosvenor Gardens, London, SW 1

1

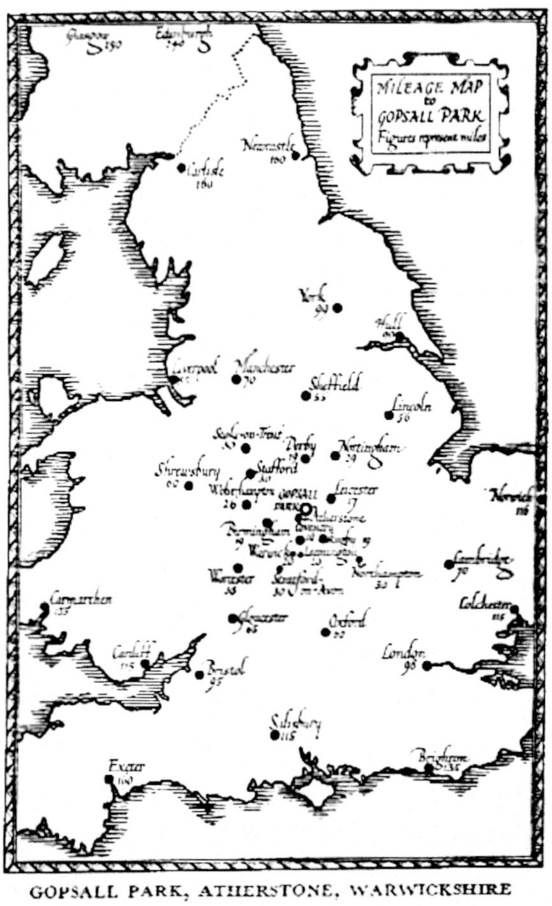

GOPSALL PARK, ATHERSTONE, WARWICKSHIRE

THE KINGS OF SPEED

★ ★

OUR ADVISORY COMMITTEE

EARL HOWE was a pioneer of speed. In his more mature years he has contributed greatly to the domesday book of fast sport. Last year, at Brooklands, he won The Gold Star, and by his infinite daring he has become associated with the first flight of heroes whose hobby is that of "crowding miles into minutes." He has recently added to his laurels by his success in the 1932 Monaco Grand Prix.

★ ★

SIR MALCOLM CAMPBELL. His name is a synonym for record speed. More than any other man he has, to use a phrase of the popular press, "diced with death." Holder of the World's land speed record, he has explored the World for suitable venues, and the fact that he has decided to join the Advisory Committee adds a plume to our cap.

★ ★

SIR HENRY BIRKIN is the holder of the Brooklands lap record. More than any other of our speed heroes, he is a master of racing on track and road. His experience makes him a very valuable member of the select committee. If you have seen SIR HENRY BIRKIN handling a car on the Ards Circuit or in Phœnix Park, you will know what we

3

mean by the spectacle of speed. He epitomises the sport which we have to offer.

* *

SAMMY DAVIS is the man who, when a boy, pressed his face against the window at Westminster School and visualised a future which came to him. His book on motor racing is likely to become a best seller among adventure books for boys. He is a journalist and therefore a man of keen observation. Because he is a press man he is necessarily discriminating, and SAMMY DAVIS is on the Advisory Committee for Motor Racing. His wide experience as a racing driver has placed him in the forefront of motor sport to-day.

* *

HUGH MCCONNELL represents the official side of the movement. He was a racing man, but is primarily concerned with the technical side. Whenever the Royal Automobile Club or other well-known Motor Club desire to be satisfied as to the eligibility of a competing car in a race, a rally or a trial, HUGH MCCONNELL is the man on whom the Clubs rely. He joins the racing men on the Advisory Committee.

* *

BRIAN LEWIS has had a wide experience of road and track racing. He has the reputation of being the most consistent of all racing motorists. Recently he competed in the famous Mille Miglia or Italian 1,000 miles race, and finished the course

4

after an exciting adventure during the night. His car had to be dragged from a ditch on to the road again by enthusiastic Italian villagers. Brian Lewis is a keen airman and an expert pilot of a Moth aeroplane. His experience and practical suggestions will be of great value.

* *

C. S. STANILAND.—Flight-Lieut. C. S. Staniland is a young man whose sense of speed is very highly developed. He holds the Gold Star for lapping Brooklands on a motor cycle at over 100 miles an hour, and has driven a car round the track at over 120 miles an hour. He is chief tester to a famous aeroplane construction firm, and is an airman of great distinction. As a member of the Royal Air Force High Speed Squadron, he acquired an appetite for speed which he now satiates with "the power dive," in which, under full power, he dives an aeroplane from high altitude at a speed exceeding 400 miles an hour.

* *

We are proud of the achievements and the prowess of our Advisory Committee, and we are happy in the knowledge that their experience will be practically applied to the pioneer work in connection with Gopsall. They are of the opinion that Gopsall Park is ideal for the purpose intended, and lends itself to the laying out of a road-racing circuit second to none.

5

GOPSALL

GOPSALL PARK, whose exact location is shown in the accompanying map, is within easy access of many large towns and cities. For example, Birmingham, with its population of a million, is only thirty miles away; Coventry (167,000) is nineteen miles; Leicester (239,000), seventeen miles; Derby (142,000), nineteen miles. Nottingham (269,000), 29 miles. The combined population of large towns within thirty miles is more than two millions. It is from these populous centres that Gopsall Park, with its many attractions, will draw its chief support.

The property itself consists of a Mansion House (originally built in 1758) standing about 400 feet above sea level in beautiful parklands. The mansion, with its large and handsome reception rooms, its bed and dressing-room accommodation, is eminently suitable for a magnificent Country Club, and though the primary purpose of the Gopsall Park enterprise is the provision of a road for motor racing, there will be other amenities. Assurances of enthusiastic support for the venture have been received from important citizens throughout the Midlands, from the motor industry, and from the prominent motor-racing drivers of the country.

On all hands the scheme is hailed with delighted enthusiasm because the need of such a motordrome is so great.

6

It is expected that private racing men will use the road extensively. There will be periodical race meetings which are calculated to draw many thousands of spectators.

It is certain that many important organisations will seek association with the Gopsall Park Club, with a view to the adoption of the estate as Country Headquarters.

National bodies will discover in it facilities for the futherance of their interests such as are not now available. Motoring clubs will want to meet there. Indeed, there are limitless possibilities in connection with this great home of sport. Attractive affiliation schemes will be arranged to the benefit of such organisations and the Club.

AN INTERIOR VIEW OF THE CLUBHOUSE

SOME PROPOSALS

The Hall. This will be transformed into a residential Country Club to be run on first-class and up-to-date lines.

There will be plenty of accommodation for members and guests, and every form of recreation and amusement will be available.

Reception Rooms. The suite of reception rooms is superb. There is an oak-floored ballroom of majestic proportions capable of accommodating 200 dancers. There are also many private dining rooms.

Bedrooms. There is Bedroom and Dressing-room accommodation for 100 members in the mansion.

Hunting. The estate is in the centre of magnificent hunting country, and there is loose box accommodation for thirty horses. Undoubtedly, there will be many people to whom such excellent facilities will appeal.

Cricket. The Leicestershire County Gentlemen play on the beautifully situated cricket ground, which is at present laid out in the Park.

Social Functions. The premises will be available for private social functions such as banquets, dances, receptions, etc., given by members.

8

Lawn Tennis, etc. It is proposed to lay down at least twelve lawn tennis courts within the grounds as supplementary to those already in existence. There will be squash racket courts, croquet lawns and badminton. Tournament competitions will be organised.

Two lakes, each of about six acres, make provision for fishing and boating.

The Members' Park. The glorious park will be reserved for members of the Club, the public being admitted only on payment of admission money. The Pleasure Grounds, which extend to approximately thirty-four acres, will be for the use of members and their guests only.

The Park is well suited to motor rallies and gymkhanas.

GOPSALL PARK

by LAURENCE H. CADE

THERE are approximately 1,100 acres in Leicestershire known as Gopsall Park, surrounding a magnificent mansion, which have been acquired from Lord Waring so that they may be adapted to modernity and transformed into a Country Club. The prime object of the sponsors is to achieve that which the law forbids, but in doing so they are not in any way transgressing the law.

Motor racing on public roads is prohibited. It is not our purpose to criticise the paradox of the fact that the second greatest car producing nation in the World is precluded from enjoying the facilities which go to make a great motoring nation, but it is our intention to remedy a monstrous defect.

Nor is this all. We are concerned with the thrill of speed—so will be many thousands of visitors to Gopsall Park. There are few spectacles to compare with that of racing cars competing against each other, and at Gopsall Park motor racing at its most exciting best will be seen. Imagine the mile-and-half-straight along which the competitors will dash at their utmost speed! Imagine the tens of thousands of spectators flanking the course!

It is twenty-five years since a motor track was built in England, and during that period cars have become incomparably faster. Try to visualise the cars of twenty-five years ago and those of to-day, and then realise how great is the need for a modern arena of speed—an arena which will provide for the public unprecedented spectacles.

10

The speed enthusiasts of the country are not well catered for. They search the shores of the country for suitable places on which to test their cars. They are like accidents looking for somewhere to happen. At Gopsall Park they will find all that they need, for the road-circuit will be adapted specially to the requirements of modern speed and speedmen.

Further Application Forms may be obtained from

GOPSALL PARK, ATHERSTONE, WARWICKSHIRE

and from the

Organising Secretary, London Office

COL. J. B. CAMERON, D.S.O.

1A GROSVENOR GARDENS

LONDON, S.W.1

THE ROAD RACING CIRCUIT

The public, the hundreds of thousands of sport-loving men and women who have been denied the thrill of road racing because it is not legal in this country, will throng the course at Gopsall Park. There they will see speed at its most thrilling. There the racing aces will compete against each other, manœuvring with infinite daring on the corners and the hazards of the circuit, swooping in glorious sprints along that magnificent straight of a mile and a half. Racing at Gopsall Park will come to be one of the most exciting and attractive sports in the country, and there is no doubt about the manner in which the public will respond to the provision of such hectic entertainment.

The *pièce de résistance* is, of course, the Road Racing Circuit. It is intended to build an eight miles course with a non-skid surface which will be designed, on the recommendation of the Advisory Committee, so that racing along the lines of that held on the Ards Circuit and le Mans can be held.

The course will include a straightway of 1½ miles—a magnificent stretch which will permit of superb racing spectacles during the periodical meetings.

The course will also be available for motor-cycle racing.

THE AERODROME

The promoters are mindful of the great future which exists in connection with private flying, and adequate arrangements are being made for the construction of an aerodrome. It will be equipped with repair shops, hangars, storage depots and landing grounds.

The development of civil aviation will be encouraged in every way. Airmen will be able to fly to Gopsall Park and enjoy the amenities of the Country Club.

Week-end air visits to the Park for the various tournaments or motor racing should be a popular feature.

The ground is well suited to the creation of excellent landing grounds and the best technical advice will be obtained in connection therewith.

The Gopsall Park aerodrome will become a " Sports Station " for air travellers.

It is the intention of the promoters to make Gopsall a comprehensive sports and pastimes Centre.

A WOMAN'S THOUGHT

By FAY TAYLOUR

Winner of 1931 Women's Race at Brooklands

Gopsall park motor road track—the realisation of a dream. Somewhere to race without restrictions, somewhere to pit our pluck and our prowess against man's.

Only to think of it. In the past we have been tolerated very infrequently on tracks ; never have we been allowed to race on a real road circuit.

At Gopsall Park women as well as men can indulge in their love for speed. We hope that women-only races will be popular, as well as the " mixed " event, and we are anxious to introduce the sport to women who have never tasted a greater thrill than doing 60 miles an hour on the road.

Under the stately elms and ancient yews of Gopsall, modern women will make road-racing history, and we hope to prove that woman's place on the circuit is as great as man's.

THE PRIME MOVER

* *

Mr. William Haines Hutchinson is the Founder and General Organiser of the Gopsall Park scheme. All his life has been devoted to transport and progress. It was Mr. Hutchinson who constructed the principal railways which opened up the great coalfields of Nottinghamshire and Derbyshire, and he has been associated with innumerable railway developments.

Mr. Hutchinson was Director-in-Charge of construction on three sections of the Welland Ship Canal, the great Canadian enterprise, the locks of which are comparable, in magnitude, to the locks of the Panama Canal.

As Director of General Contracting for Sir William Arrol and Co., Ltd., he supervised the construction of the Bexleyheath, Sidcup and Dartford by-pass roads.

His experience should prove most valuable in laying out the road circuit and other Engineering features entering into the general scheme at Gopsall.

Printed by Spottiswoode, Ballantyne & Co. Ltd. London, EC4

5/39

Application Form

To The Secretary
GOPSALL PARK CLUB
(Motor Racing Circuit, Aerodrome and Country Club)
Atherstone, Warwickshire

DEAR SIR :

I beg to apply for ★ .... Class Membership of the Club, on its being constituted in accordance with the descriptive Brochure dated May, 1932, which has been submitted to me.

I am, Yours faithfully,

(*Signature*) ....

FULL NAME ....

ADDRESS ....

....

OCCUPATION ....

DATE ....

★ Insert Class of Membership desired, A, B, or C.

NOTE. No application for membership incurs any liability whatsoever beyond the amount of the annual subscription, and that only from the date of the actual opening of the Club premises.

50 (*please note overleaf*)

MEMBERSHIP

The Classes of Membership to be offered by the Club are as follows :

A...FULL MEMBERSHIP, which entitles members to the use of the Club House, grounds and park, and to free admission to the Members' Enclosure for all Sporting events within the grounds with two lady friends, and to free parking for one motor car within the areas reserved for the parking of members' cars. The subscription for Full Membership is £5 5*s.* 0*d.* per annum.

B...MOTOR-CAR ASSOCIATE MEMBERSHIP, which entitles Members to free admission and car parking with one guest to view all sporting events within the Park to which the public have access, but does not include use of the Club House and Full Members' private enclosures. Associate Members also have the right to enter for events which are declared to be limited to members of the Club. The subscription for Associate Membership is £2 12*s.* 6*d.* per annum.

C...MOTOR CYCLE ASSOCIATE MEMBERSHIP, which entitles Members to free admission to view all motor cycling events within the portion of the Park to which the public have access, but does not include the use of the Club House or Full Members' or Associate Members' private enclosures. Motor Cycle Associate Members have also the right to enter for any motor cycle events which are declared to be limited to Members of the Club. The subscription for Motor Cycle Associate Membership is £1 11*s.* 6*d.* per annum.

NOTE.—A limited number of Members will be admitted to the above classes of Membership without the payment of any entrance fee, but after this limited number has been admitted an entrance fee will be charged for all classes of Membership of the Club.

Gopsall Club prospectus courtesy of The Rt Hon Frederick Richard Penn Curzon, 7th Earl Howe, GBE, PC.

Notes and References

1 *History of the Meynell Hounds and Country: 1780-1901* (Vol. I). J.L. Randall. Sampson Low, Marston & Co. Ltd,: London, 1901, p. 9.

2 *British Hunts and Huntsmen (The south-east, east, and eastern midlands of England).* Compiled in conjunction with The Sporting Life. The Biographical Press: London, 1909, p. 199.

3 *The Leicester and Leicestershire Club and County Races.* Leicester Journal, Friday 27th July 1883.

4 *Gopsall Park Trials.* Birmingham Daily Gazette, Tuesday 11th September, 1923.

5 *Motorists Rally. 5,000 spectators at Derby Club's Speed Trials. Records at Gopsall.* The Nottingham Journal, Tuesday 6th April 1926.

6 *Ace Motor Club. The forthcoming speed trials at Gopsall Park.* Coventry Herald, Friday 6th May 1927.

7 *..... and at Gopsall Park.* Motor Sport IX (6) April 1933, p. 49.

8 *Motor racing at Donington Park. Successful Experiment by Derby and District Motor Club.* Motor Sport IX (7) May 1933, pp. 314-317.

9 *Britain's sadly forgotten gentleman racer.* The Irish Times, Wednesday 27th August 2008.

10 *Personality Parade - No. 1 - Earl Howe.* Motor Sport XXII (1) January 1946, p. 3.

11 *Earl Howe. The Grand Old Man of Motor Racing.* MotorSport June 1998, pp. 772-775.

12 *Lord Howe gives his Impressions of the Coming Racing Season (in an interview).* Motor Sport X (3) January 1934, p. 114.

13 *Hitler's Motor Racing Battles: The Silver Arrows under the Swastika.* Eberhard Reuss. J.H. Hayes & Co Ltd, 2008.

14 *Earl Howe Biography. MotorSport Database*: https://database.motorsportmagazine.com/database/drivers/earl-howe - Accessed January 2021.

15 Voiturette racing took place between 1931 and 1940 and was the training ground for Grand Prix racing, equivalent to Formula 2 today. These races were considered so good that the formula became the official Grand Prix class in 1945, which lasted until 1952.

16 *Another Big Victory for "BIRA"*. Motor Sport XV (6) June 1939, pp. 165-166.

17 *Maserati wins the BARC Campbell Trophy Race*. Motor Sport XIII (6) May 1937, pp. 196-198.

18 *Earl who thrilled TT fans on Ards circuit dies*. Belfast Telegraph, Monday 27th July 1964.

19 *Motor-cyclists' Crash Helmets*. House of Lords Debate. Hansard Vol. 180 (cc49-66) 28th January 1953. Although Lord Howe was in favour of crash helmets, he was unsure of the proposal to make wearing them compulsory. In another debate on the subject in March 1953, the Earl appeared to be wanting the Government to encourage the wearing of crash helmets by abolishing purchase tax on them. Crash helmets only became compulsory for motorcylists on June 1st 1973.

20 *'Tommy' Thomas - Earl Howe's Mechanic*. Motor Sport November 1994, pp. 1204-1206.

21 *Future of Gopsall Park. Massive Racing Track Proposals.* The Atherstone News, Friday 18th March 1932.

22 *Gopsall Park Scheme. Progress of the Leicestershire Project*. Sheffield Daily Telegraph, Friday 24th June 1932.

23 *Gopsall Park LTD. Syndicate formed for road races*. Tamworth Herald, Saturday 2nd July 1932.

24 Donington Park motor racing circuit was the first permanent park circuit in England. The original track was 2 mile 327yd in length, and based on normal width unsealed estate roads. The first motor cycle race took place on Whit Monday, 1931. In 1933 a permanent track was built, with the original layout widened and sealed at a cost of £12,000. The first car race was held on 25 March, followed by three car meetings later that year. The first Donington Park Trophy race was held on 7 October 1933, and the 20-lap invitation event was won by the Earl Howe in a Bugatti Type 51.

25 *Associate membership application to the Automobile Racing Association*. Derby Daily Telegraph, 11th April 1932.

26 *Rain spoils Drakelow Hall Sports*. Derby Daily Telegraph, 17th May 1932.

27 *Midland Motordrome Progress. The Gopsall Project*. The Nottingham Journal, Friday 20th May 1932.

28 Sir Malcolm Campbell (1885-1949) was a British racing driver and journalist. He won the Grand Prix de Boulogne twice (1927 & 1928) and broke the land speed record 9 times between 1924 and 1935. During his final land speed record on 3rd September 1935 he became the first person to drive an automobile over 300mph (av. speed 301.337mph). He also set the water speed record 4 times attaining 141.74mph in Blue Bird K4 on 19th August 1939.

29 Sir Henry Ralph Stanley 'Tim' Birkin (1896-1933) was a British racing driver and won the Le Mans 24 hour race in 1929 (with Woolf Barnato) and 1931 (with Earl Howe).

30 This was the Earl's first race after his big accident in May 1937 during the inaugural race on the Campbell road racing course at Brooklands.

31 *Gopsall Hall.* Tamworth Herald, Saturday 26th March 1932.

32 *Famous Speed 'Stars' to Visit Gopsall Park*. Leicester Evening Mail, Saturday 9th April 1932.

33 *Earl Howe visits Gopsall Park. Motor track lay-out inspected. Improvements suggested*. Leicester Evening Mail, Saturday 7th May 1932.

34 *Gopsall Park Racing Scheme Held Up*. Leicester Evening Mail, Saturday 23rd September 1932.

35 *Motor Dicta*. The Sketch, Wednesday 2nd November 1932.

36 *Gopsall Track. £250,000 contracts signed*. The Atherstone News, Friday 27th January 1933.

37 *Gopsall Park Track Scheme*. Tamworth Herald, Saturday 27th May 1933.

38 *Road Racing at Gopsall Park. An International Centre Planned*. Leicester Evening Mail, Monday 11th June 1934.

39 *New £300,000 speed track*. Daily Mirror, Thursday 21st June 1934.

40 *Race Track Plan Development*. Leicester Evening Mail, Wednesday 4th July 1934.

41 *Rumblings - Gopsall Scheme Abandoned*. Motor Sport X (10) August 1934, pp. 474-476.

42 *Pony Racing Plan.* Nottingham Journal, Saturday 20th October 1934.

43 Pony racing became popular in the 1920s and 1930s, particularly in the south of England where a number of dedicated racetracks were opened, the first being at Northolt, Middlesex in 1929.

44 These included the ARA country club at Drakelow and their 15 mile speedway on Skegness sea wall, the Ivinghoe course near Tring and tracks near Bexhill and Brighton.

45 Newspaper adverts downloaded from www.britishnewspaperarchive.co.uk and reproduced courtesy of Reach Licensing / Mirrorpix.com.

46 *Malkin leads through mud and ice*. Birmingham Daily Post, Monday 31st January 1972.

Military Occupation of Gopsall during the Second World War

Much of the information about the army occupation of Gopsall that follows is based upon the memories of military personnel who were posted there during the war and the memories of local villagers and members of the Women's Land Army (WLA) working on local farms during the Second World War (WWII). These memories were collected between 1997 and 2005 and have been published in unedited form elsewhere.[1]

Gopsall Park was initially occupied by a Royal Army Service Corps Vehicle Reserve Depot but, in 1942, this was transferred to the Royal Army Ordnance Corps. Prior to August 1942, the hall appears to have been used as the headquarters for a Royal Artillery training and transit camp. Thereafter, the hall and gardens were taken over by the Royal Electrical & Mechanical Engineers as the No. 2 Radio Mechanics School (RMS). The RASC, RAOC and REME units at Gopsall all included a significant number of women from the Auxiliary Territorial Service.

Brief history of the RAOC, REME and the ATS[2-6]

It was only with the development of explosives and more complex weapons that it became necessary for the British government to establish arsenals (places were arms and ammunition are made, repaired and stored) in which civilian tradesmen were employed. However, in 1896, these civilians became military tradesmen and, together with the providers of military stores, formed the Army Ordnance Corps (AOC).

After the First World War (WWI; 1914-1918) many of the army Corps gained their 'Royal' prefix including the AOC and, at this time, the Royal Army Ordnance Corps (RAOC) was both a supply and repair Corps. It had responsibility for the supply of weapons, armoured vehicles and other military equipment, ammunition and clothing and some minor functions (laundry, mobile baths and photography). The RAOC was also responsible for a large part of the repair and maintenance of army equipment including small arms, guns and instruments. However, other branches of the army (e.g. Royal Tank Corps, Royal Engineers, Royal Corps of Signals) maintained and repaired their own specialist equipment, with the Royal Army Service Corps (RASC) being generally responsible for the supply, storage and repair of mechanical transport.

Thus, the army had a variety of different repair organisations functioning simultaneously; with many other regiments and Corps having their own tradesmen to carry out minor repairs. Although it had been acknowledged for years that this system for the repair and maintenance of military equipment was inefficient and fragmented, it lasted well into WWII.

Rearmament in the late 1930s and the outbreak of WWII (1939-1945) resulted in a huge increase in the quantity and complexity of military equipment and an accompanying shortage of qualified tradesmen. In response, the Corps of Royal Electrical and Mechanical Engineers (REME) was formally established in October 1942 to rationalise repair services within the army and to meet the technological challenges posed by advances in weaponry and associated fields such as radio location (Radar). Thus technicians,

RAOC, RASC & REME cap badges

mechanics and electricians were drawn from the RAOC, RASC, the Royal Engineers and the Royal Signals to form REME. At this time, the repair function of the RAOC was also transferred to REME and the vehicle storage and spares responsibilities of the RASC were passed to the RAOC. Thus, in 1942, REME became responsible for the maintenance, repair and modification of a vast array of military equipment including radar (RAdio Detection And Ranging), a role still played today by the electronic technicians serving in REME.

ATS recruitment poster (Public Domain) and cap badge

The Auxiliary Territorial Service (ATS) was formerly the Women's Auxiliary Army Corps (WAAC), established in 1917 as a voluntary service. The ATS, formed in September 1938, was also a volunteer service for women between the ages of 17 and 43 providing support roles as waitresses, telephonists, orderlies, clerks and cooks. However, in the December of 1941, unmarried women between the ages of 20-30 were required to work in industry or join one of the auxiliary services including the ATS, the Women's Auxiliary Air Force (WAAF), the Women's Royal Naval Service (WRNS), the Women's Land Army (WLA) and the Women's Voluntary Service (WVS).

Although the ATS women were only allowed to participate in non-combat roles, many of the tasks they did perform were not without risk. In 1941, with numbers reaching 65,000, the ATS rank structure was reorganised and the ATS was given full military status. This change reflected the reality that members were no longer volunteers and that they had become a significant presence within a variety of active army units within Britain. Members of the ATS were involved in the defence of the country taking on tasks such as supply drivers, mechanics and radar operators, and were members of the military police as well as forming part of the crews of the Royal Artillery's Heavy Anti-Aircraft (HAA) batteries. By 1943 three-quarters of Anti-Aircraft Command's HAA batteries included members of the ATS.[7]

The Army at Gopsall

The Crown Commissioners purchased the "outlying" parts of the Gopsall Estate in 1932, while the hall, gardens and park were retained by the Waring Family but not lived in (Lord Waring purchased the Gopsall Estate from the 4th Earl Howe in 1918). Subsequently, the hall, gardens and parkland were purchased by an investment company in 1941 after the death of Lord and Lady Waring (Chapter 1).

Gopsall was only one of the thousands of country houses (large and small) and estates requisitioned by the Government during WWII for use as hospitals, maternity units, schools and command centres and for military use. Unlike Gopsall Hall, most of the houses requisitioned were inhabited. The Rothschilds were given four days' notice that Waddesdon Manor was to be used to accommodate 100 very young children evacuated from London. Blenheim Palace was taken over by MI5 (an open secret at the time) and Bletchley Park became the centre of Allied code-breaking, but other places were not so lucky and were occupied by the army. After army occupation many owners returned to damaged buildings and property; with a number being partially or completely burned down. The north wing of Melford Hall in Suffolk was burned down in February 1942 after an 'out of bounds' party by junior officers of the Berkshire Regiment. On returning to the hall in 1944, the owners also discovered that the soldiers had drunk all the wine in their cellar and refilled the bottles with water, replacing the corks and foil as if they were untouched.[8]

The date when Gopsall Hall and park were requisitioned for use by the army is difficult to know and specific details about the use of the hall by the army before it became the REME No. 2 RMS are sparse. However, there is evidence that the park had been used for army manoeuvres prior to August 1939 as the grounds then were criss-crossed with the tracks of Bren gun carriers and there were signs of slit trenches being dug and re-filled. There is however, no evidence that the hall had been used by the army and, according to an Ibstock Boy Scout on Summer Camp at Gopsall in 1939, *"the magnificent ceilings, depicting angels, floating on high and tapestries hung on wood panelled walls"* were still on view.[1]

This changed in early 1940 when the Sappers (the Royal Engineers) moved in. They covered the wall hangings and wood panels, re-plumbed the building, connected water and electricity supplies, fitted new toilets, upgraded the kitchens and started to build Nissen huts in the park ready for army occupation. From early on, while the renovations of the hall were ongoing, Royal Artillery (RA) trainees were at Gopsall undergoing general military training. Similarly, the Sappers were still working at Gopsall at the end of May/early June 1940 when the camp saw the arrival of some of the survivors of Dunkirk (26th May - 4th June). It is probable that the Dunkirk veterans underwent some general training prior to being allocated to new army units. Large numbers of troops were camped in the parkland and in fields close to Norton-Juxta-Twycross at this time.

Gopsall Park was being used as an RASC Vehicle Reserve Depot (No. 28 VRD) at least from January 1940, as the first Royal Artillery trainees reporting to the hall remember large numbers of army vehicles parked under the trees. Initially the trainees were billeted in dormitories in the hall and meals were taken in mess tents. It was only later in 1940 that Nissen huts were erected in the park for the trainees/lesser ranks, with the officers having quarters in the hall. Gopsall Hall and Camp, not the RASC vehicle depot, appear to have been used for general military training and as a transit facility for military personnel until the end of 1941 or summer 1942. On leaving Gopsall, soldiers were deployed to their army units or sent for specialist training at colleges or universities around Britain. It was in August 1942 that the Radio Mechanics School (RMS) was moved from Cheltenham to Gopsall where it occupied the hall and gardens. The following October, after the reorganisation to rationalise repair and maintenance services within the army, the RMS became part of REME as the No. 2 RMS and the RASC vehicle depot was transferred to the RAOC.

From 1941 onward, Gopsall Camp and the vehicle depot were guarded by the Vulnerable Points Wing of the Military Police (MP).[9] This branch of the Corps was formed after the start of WWII to provide security for static locations and establishments such as ammunition and fuel dumps, docks, bridges and power stations. They were commonly known as 'blue caps' from the Oxford blue cloth covers worn on their service dress caps. At Gopsall they had guard posts at the lodges (Snarestone, Shackerstone, Bilstone and Twycross) at the four entrances to the park and a guard room in the hall gardens. Although they were armed with submachine guns and at night they patrolled the park with guard dogs, their effectiveness in securing the site was questionable, as soldiers based at Gopsall frequently exited and entered the camp unnoticed via Gopsall Wood to get to the B4116 and Measham. From all accounts, the blue caps' only success was the detention of the 8-year-old

Bilstone Lodge (now demolished) stood next to the entrance gates guarded by the Military Police.

paper boy from Congerstone who happened to be at the camp when some equipment went missing. He was finally returned home in an MP jeep after midnight.

The blue caps did provide a useful social function. Many of the REME students and permanent staff billeted at Gopsall owned bicycles, so that they could access the local pubs and villages. When the students left Gopsall they often sold their bicycles on to new students, so a bicycle numbering scheme was operated by the blue caps, as the new owners were apt to ride the wrong bicycle in error.

The first impressions of those who found themselves sent to Gopsall, whatever their function or rank, were generally not good. Until late 1942, most of those posted to Gopsall arrived by train at Ashby-de-la-Zouch or Atherstone stations and were then transferred to the camp by army lorry. This changed after some of the first trainees at the RMS were detailed to prepare Shackerstone station for military use, prior to finishing their radio course in December 1942. Thereafter, most REME staff and trainees arrived at Gopsall on the 'Shacky Flier', a single carriage train running from Nuneaton to Shackerstone. This journey, bypassing Market Bosworth and the few other villages en route, reinforced the feeling of new arrivals that Gopsall was a long way from civilisation.

The gates to Shackerstone Drive and the first glimpse of Gopsall Hall seen over the ornamental lake by new arrivals.

From Shackerstone station new trainees would be marched or taken by lorry, via the Shackerstone entrance and three-quarter mile straight drive, past the ornamental lake to Gopsall Hall. During this journey, resident students would often greet the new intake by swinging from the trees and making simian noises, to demonstrate to them that Gopsall was the 'back of beyond'. When they did get to the hall they were dumped in the stable yard and left until one or other of them went to find out what they were supposed to do!

Most of those actually billeted at Gopsall, in the hall or in huts in the gardens and park managed to find some solace in the local pubs and entertainment in the cinema at Measham (The Empire). Indeed, the REME and RAOC officers had a room especially reserved for them in the Curzon Arms in Twycross; they used to signal for a refill by throwing an empty tea tray into the corridor!

In the early days of Gopsall Camp and the RASC vehicle depot, recreational visits to Nuneaton or Leicester were rare and involved transport in army trucks. However, from about 1942 onward, weekend coach outings to these destinations were one of the highlights of a Gopsall posting.

The bar in the Curzon Arms run by the Jones family during WWII (*L to R*: Margaret Jones, Tommy Tunks and Mrs Challis, licensee) and one of the coaches used to take soldiers to Nuneaton and Leicester.

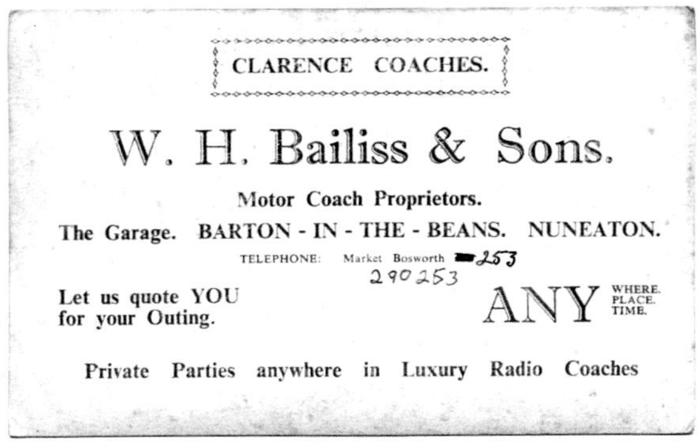
CLARENCE COACHES.

W. H. Bailiss & Sons,

Motor Coach Proprietors.

The Garage. BARTON - IN - THE - BEANS. NUNEATON.

TELEPHONE: Market Bosworth ~~253~~ 290253

Let us quote YOU for your Outing. ANY WHERE. PLACE. TIME.

Private Parties anywhere in Luxury Radio Coaches

These coaches were run by W.H. Bailiss & Sons (Clarence Coaches) of Barton and were usually so overloaded that the tyres would rub on the wheel arches and fares had to be paid to the conductor before passengers were allowed onboard. Inevitably, some missed the return bus and had a long walk back.

A consistent complaint voiced by all those at Gopsall was the intense cold during winter. Much of the time was spent outside or, at best in the barely heated hall and Nissen huts. Coal was delivered from the local mines, but most appears to have been used in the hall and offices with little, if any, being allowed to be used in the accommodation huts. The cold was a significant memory for those who were billeted in Nissen huts in the park and gardens as heating was limited to a single stove and fuel was whatever they could find in the woods. In addition, they had to suffer the problems of having no mains water, barely adequate latrines and water that was undrinkable unless obtained from the Navy, Army and Air Force Institutes (NAAFI) canteen when it was open. However, drinking water was only available after the daily water wagon from Leicester had brought its load!

From the time that the Sappers arrived in early 1940, the hall contained none of its original furniture. The only contents of note were the two organs still present in the chapel and library/music room. Although it is often asserted that one of these instruments was designed and possibly played by Handel, this was not the case (Chapter 12). A number of the hall walls, inside and out, were shored up by large timber beams, as was the chapel ceiling. The wall coverings and tapestries were covered with hardboard and hessian, leaving only the ornate ceiling plasterwork to give a glimpse of what the hall had been like in times gone by. The picture gallery's large skylights were 'blacked-out', making it a rather dark place, but it was easy to see where pictures had hung, preventing dust and dirt reaching the wall coverings.

The ornate library ceiling

After the RMS moved from Cheltenham to Gopsall in 1942, there was a distinct divide between the RAOC administered vehicle depot in the parkland and the radar training school, based in the hall and gardens. A one-way traffic flow system was set up with all traffic entering via the Snarestone lodge entrance and leaving via the Twycross lodge 'exit'. The Shackerstone entrance was mainly used to ferry REME staff and students to and from Shackerstone station, although the drive also provided access to the fields for farmers and the woods around the ornamental pool, which for a short time, still had a working, steam powered sawmill. From all accounts, the Bilstone lodge entrance was only used by the paperboy!

The Twycross 'OUT' gate (c. 1950)

Madeline Wardle and her grave in the churchyard of Holy Trinity Church, Norton-Juxta-Twycross.

Italian prisoners of war (PoW) worked on many farms and performed forestry work throughout the latter part of the war (late 1943 onward), including at Home Farm (Shornhill Farm) and in the woods at Gopsall. It was an army lorry taking Italian PoWs to Home Farm that sadly knocked down and killed Madeline, a little girl who lived at Snarestone lodge next to the 'IN' gate to the Gopsall Camp. Her funeral was attended by many of the soldiers and ATS from Gopsall.[10]

Records of the bombs dropped in Leicestershire during WWII indicate that Gopsall was not deliberately targeted by the German Luftwaffe.[11] Apart from two high explosive bombs landing in the park to the north of the hall, no other devices were reported within a 1.5 mile radius. Quite a few bombs were dropped in this area of Leicestershire, particularly to the south and southeast of Gopsall in the Hinckley and District area. However, this area was at the 'cross-roads' of the Luftwaffe activity around Birmingham, Coventry, Nottingham and Derby, making it at considerable risk from aborting or damaged aircraft looking to unload bombs. There were a considerable number of aircraft crashes within a radius of about 7 miles of Gopsall Hall between 1939 and 1945, but all except a German Heinkel were flight training accidents.[11] Crashes at airfields were not recorded, nor was the crash of a Tiger Moth in Gopsall Park. This was believed to be the RMS's 'target' plane that used to fly around the Gopsall area, which was based at the RAF Desford (Tiger Moth) Flight Training School.

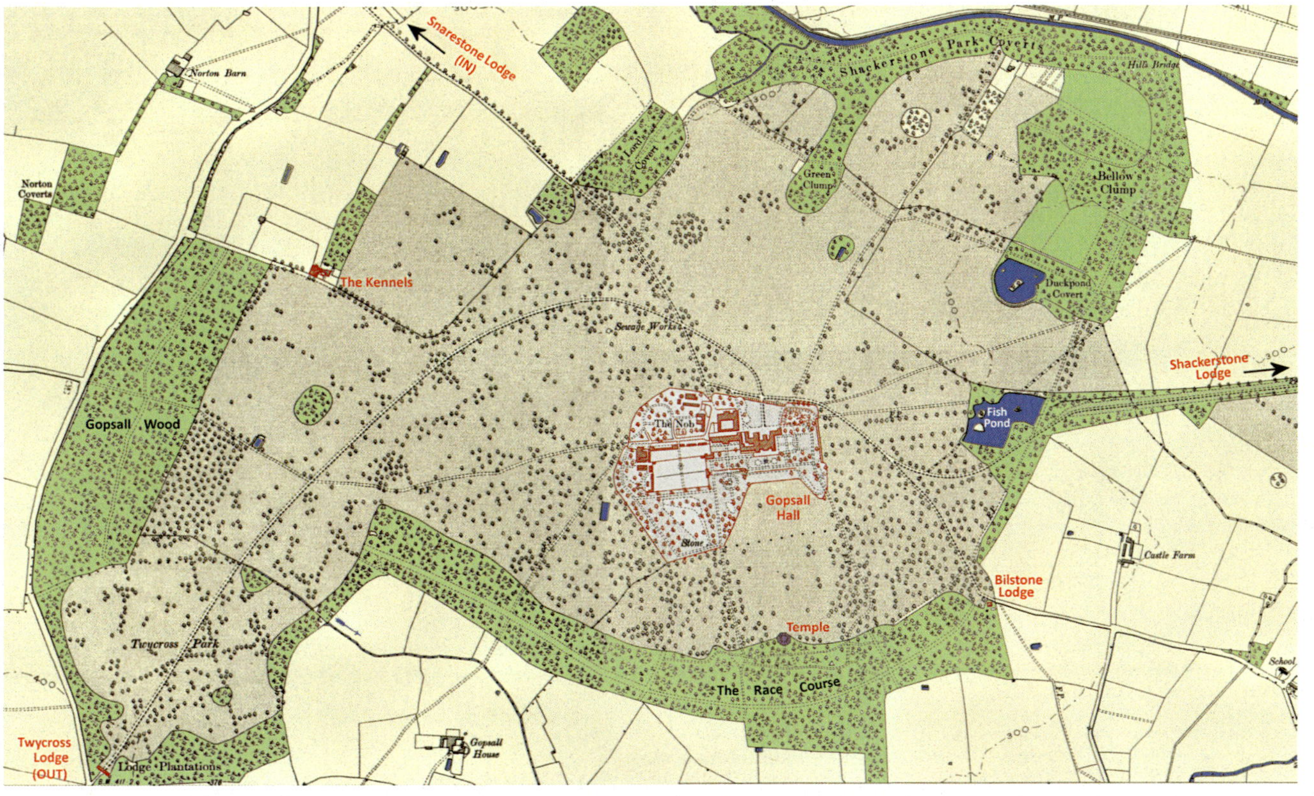

Map of Gopsall Park showing the hall, temple, The Kennels and the entrance lodges

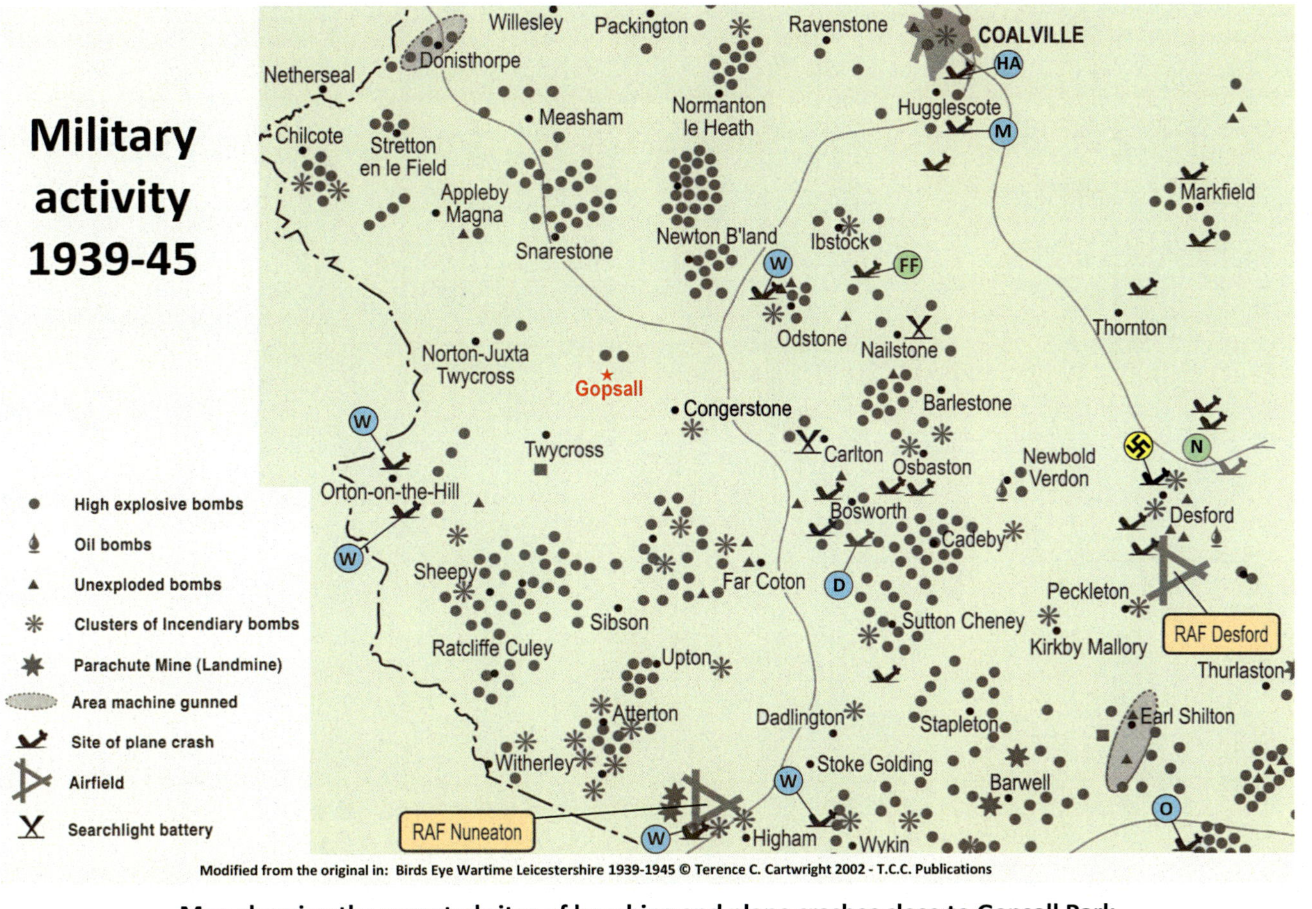

Map showing the reported sites of bombing and plane crashes close to Gopsall Park

Only 2 bombs were dropped within Gopsall Park, to the north of the hall. The closest, apparently deliberate bombing of a military installation was directed at a searchlight battery at Carlton.

Plane crashes: *British*: W = Wellington bomber; O = Oxford; M = Mosquito; D = Defiant; HA = Hawker Audax; Unlabelled = Tiger Moth (trainer). *American*: FF = Flying Fortress; N = Norseman. *German* = Heinkel HE 111 (originally damaged over Coventry). All allied crashes were of aircraft on training flights.

The No. 28 Vehicle Reserve Depot at Gopsall

Gopsall Park provided a perfect location for a military vehicle depot. It was surrounded by woods and provided ample, secluded space and tree cover for the storage of a large number of vehicles without the need for any major preparatory work. In addition, it was in a geographically good location, being centrally located within the country and close to major highways and the Midlands motor manufacturing industry. Thus, the site was ideal for the collection of new vehicles from factories and their distribution to military units across the country.

Top: Lindley lodge, used by the army's Scottish Regiments, the Royal Marines and finally, the ATS of No. 28 VRD, Gopsall.
Bottom: ATS drivers about to drive to Scotland (winter 1942).

During WWII there were two Vehicle Reserve Depots (for light vehicles; VRD) and two Armoured Fighting Vehicle Depots (for tanks; AFVD) in Leicestershire.[12] Although they were run by the RAOC, each had a small detachment of REME mechanics to carry out maintenance of stored vehicles, as well as a significant contingent of ATS women serving various functions. The VRDs were at Gopsall and Syston and one of the AFVDs was at New Parks Estate in Leicester (No. 8 AFVD), where the newly built roads for a proposed housing estate provided ideal hardstanding for tanks! The precise site of the other AFVD in Leicestershire is unknown.

The No. 28 VRD at Gopsall appears to have been predominantly 'manned' by members of the ATS, many of whom were drivers and/or mechanics. The RAOC and REME officers of the depot were billeted in The Kennels, about threequarters of a mile northwest of the hall, and other ranks in Nissen huts erected in the park. None of the ATS working at the vehicle depot was billeted at Gopsall. ATS headquarters was at Cliff House in Twycross, which also provided accommodation for about 20 members of the ATS. Other ATS members were billeted with families in Atherstone, at Copton Ash Farm and at Lindley lodge, next to RAF Lindley (RAF Nuneaton) on the A5.[11,13] A number of the ATS became friends with members of the aircrew from RAF Lindley, which served as a base for British and Polish air training units that flew Vickers Wellingtons, Avro Ansons

Molly Page (ATS) servicing one of the army vehicles

Vehicle ramp close to Twycross Lodge (∗)

The 1948 aerial photo (*top left*) shows that the ramp was covered to allow vehicle repairs in all weather. There were about 7 VRD service areas in the park; some are marked on modern OS maps and can be seen on Google Earth.

and twin-engine Airspeed Oxfords.[11,14] Transport for the ATS was provided by army lorries which ran daily between Lindley lodge and the Gopsall vehicle depot via Atherstone and Cliff House.

The drivers were responsible for the collection of military vehicles from factories or the docks as well as the delivery of vehicles from the Gopsall depot to units all around the UK. The ATS also ensured that vehicles in the depot were kept in full operational condition, which required regular maintenance checks, greasing and movement of vehicles to prevent deterioration of the tyres. Greasing was the most hated job as it was incredibly boring and meant that you were generally outside, no matter what the weather.

Corrugated iron Nissen huts serving as the Vehicle Reserve Depot's offices by the cross-roads just to the northwest of the hall. The WVS tea wagon used to park close to the cross-roads. Two of the volunteers from Twycross who used to run it were Mrs Manley and Mr Foster. They were considered 'angels' by the vehicle depot personnel for providing hot, drinkable tea, especially in winter. Note the 'soft top' fire car parked out front.

Throughout the war thousands of vehicles were stored in the park at Gopsall; most were carefully parked beneath trees (4 per tree) to make observation from the air difficult. British-, American- and Canadian-made vehicles were stored at Gopsall; these included lorries, jeeps, amphibious vehicles and light armoured vehicles such as Bren gun carriers. It is often rumoured that the Gopsall depot was specifically created for the storage and supply of vehicles for the D-Day landings. While this is not correct, it is probable that a significant number of vehicles stored at Gopsall were part of the follow-up landings after D-Day itself. In late 1943 there were already thousands of American, left-hand drive, Dodge and Ford army lorries (3- and 5-ton) stockpiled at Gopsall; the numbers decreased significantly immediately after 4th June 1944.

In late 1943 and the first half of 1944, members of the local defence forces were drafted in to help vehicle depots all over the country to prepare vehicles prior to the D-Day landings.[15] Thus, the Ibstock Home Guard spent every Sunday working in the depot removing protective grease,

Aerial photos of Gopsall Park in 1948[16]

Above: Vehicle tracks in the snow to the north of the hall.
Right: Large numbers of parked vehicles covered in snow.
Below: Vehicles parked in rows; lines on the grass show that many more were present before the photo was taken (March 1948).

Black arrows = vehicle service areas.

Without Reserve.
By Order of The Minister of Supply.
GR
No. 28 V.R.D.
GOPSALL PARK,
LEICESTERSHIRE.
(6 miles Ashby-de-la-Zouch and Atherstone, 10 miles Nuneaton and Hinckley).
Sale of Approximately
1,000 MOTOR VEHICLES AND TRAILERS
comprising:
Light and Heavy Lorries and Trucks (including Diesel), Breakdown Lorries, fitted with cranes and/or winches, Tippers, Wireless and other Vans, Crew Carriers, Tank Transporters, Tractors and Trailers of various types, Foden Diesel Lorries, White Scout Cars, Morris Recce Cars, etc., by the following makers:—Albion, Austin, Cressley, Chevrolet, Dodge, Ford, Fordson, Foden F.W.D., Guy, Humber, Karrier, Leyland, Morris, Mack, Studebaker, Thorneycroft, and Ward La France, etc., together with
TWO, FOUR, EIGHT AND TWELVE-WHEEL TRAILERS
including: Articulated, Platform Low Leading, Smoke Generators (with Lister Engines), and Tank Transporters, which Messrs.
NIXON, TOONE & HARRISON
Will Sell by Auction on the Site, on
TUESDAY, WEDNESDAY, AND THURSDAY,
SEPTEMBER 9th, 10th & 11th, 1947
Commencing each day at eleven o'clock prompt.
View Days: Monday to Friday, September 1st to 5th inclusive; Monday, September 8th, from 9 a.m. to 4 p.m.; and on Saledays from 9 a.m. to 10.30 a.m.
Catalogues: Sixpence each (postal order only) which admits two persons to view and one person to the sale, obtainable from the Auctioneers.
Offices: 12 and 14, Newdegate Street, Nuneaton; also at Hinckley and Lutterworth.

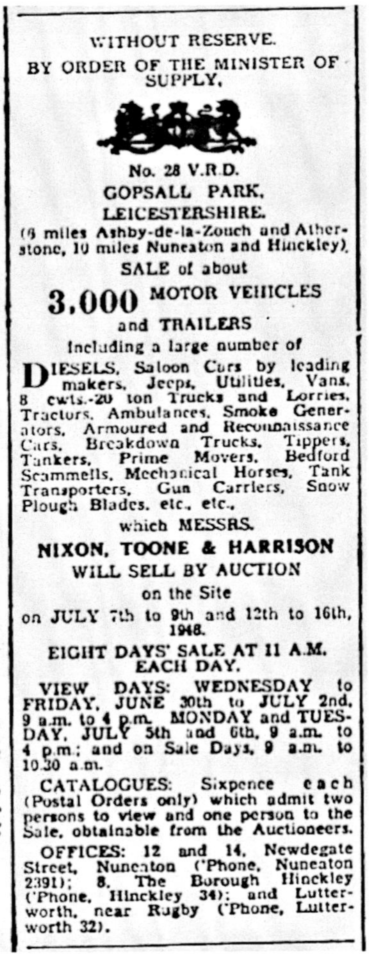

WITHOUT RESERVE.
BY ORDER OF THE MINISTER OF SUPPLY.
No. 28 V.R.D.
GOPSALL PARK,
LEICESTERSHIRE.
(6 miles Ashby-de-la-Zouch and Atherstone, 10 miles Nuneaton and Hinckley).
SALE of about
3,000 MOTOR VEHICLES and TRAILERS
Including a large number of
DIESELS, Saloon Cars by leading makers, Jeeps, Utilities, Vans, 8 cwts.-20 ton Trucks and Lorries, Tractors, Ambulances, Smoke Generators, Armoured and Reconnaissance Cars, Breakdown Trucks, Tippers, Tankers, Prime Movers, Bedford Scammells, Mechanical Horses, Tank Transporters, Gun Carriers, Snow Plough Blades, etc., etc.,
which MESSRS.
NIXON, TOONE & HARRISON
WILL SELL BY AUCTION
on the Site
on JULY 7th to 9th and 12th to 16th, 1948.
EIGHT DAYS' SALE AT 11 A.M. EACH DAY.
VIEW DAYS: WEDNESDAY to FRIDAY, JUNE 30th to JULY 2nd, 9 a.m. to 4 p.m. MONDAY and TUESDAY, JULY 5th and 6th, 9 a.m. to 4 p.m.; and on Sale Days, 9 a.m. to 10.30 a.m.
CATALOGUES: Sixpence each (Postal Orders only) which admit two persons to view and one person to the Sale, obtainable from the Auctioneers.
OFFICES: 12 and 14, Newdegate Street, Nuneaton ('Phone, Nuneaton 2391); 8, The Borough Hinckley ('Phone, Hinckley 34); and Lutterworth, near Rugby ('Phone, Lutterworth 32).

Postwar vehicle sales at Gopsall

Rugby Advertiser, 29th August 1947 — Warwick & Warwickshire Advertiser, 2nd July 1948

Reach Licensing

waterproofing and fitting out vehicles. This work was done in large open-ended canvas shelters that housed compressors and air-driven spray guns. The latter were used, with a template, to spray the Allied white, 5-pointed star aircraft recognition logo onto vehicles.

The vehicle depot at Gopsall remained active until at least the early part of 1949, well after the end of the war, and aerial photographs of the area in 1948 show thousands of vehicles in the park[16]. It was around this time that vehicle sales were held and many local farmers purchased, 'as seen', vehicles for use on their farms at very good prices. Lorries could be had for £20. One 'lucky' purchaser of a six-wheeled Austin, previously used as a mobile workshop, found out after the auction that he was also the surprised owner of seven motor cycles that he had subsequently discovered inside!

The Ministry of Supply held multi-day vehicle sales at No. 28 VRD Gopsall Park in September 1947 and July 1948. As can be seen from the newspaper adverts at the time, anything from saloon cars to tank transporters, armoured cars and gun carriers could be purchased. Such was the number of vehicles involved, prices were low, as there were no reserve prices. Essentially, the Government wanted to get rid of its vast number of now redundant vehicles and get money flowing into the Treasury.

Similar vehicle auctions were held at a number of other VRDs across the country in 1947 and 1948.[17] The last vehicle sale at Gopsall seems to have been in July 1948, and public auctions of surplus vehicles across the country do not appear to have continued after 1948.

The No. 2 REME Radio Mechanics School

Research in Britain leading to radar technology, then called RDF (Range and Detection Finding) began in 1935, led by the RAF. The research was pioneered by Robert Watson-Watt and Arnold Wilkins who, after discounting the feasibility of using strong radio waves as a 'death ray', demonstrated that reflected radio waves might be used to detect aircraft (the 'Daventry Experiment', 26th February 1935).[18-20] In March 1936 RDF research and development was moved to Bawdsey Research Station (Suffolk) and included input from the RAF, army and navy. The army programmes were for gun-laying, searchlight control and coastal defence artillery systems. However, at the outbreak of WWII, the RAF research unit (called the Telecommunications Research Establishment; TRE) was temporarily moved to Dundee and then to Worth Matravers, near Swanage, Dorset. It was finally moved to Malvern College in April 1942. Similarly, the army RDF research unit (called the Air Defence Research and Development Establishment; ADRDE) moved to Great Malvern in 1942 after previously being based at Christchurch in Dorset for some 2.5 years. By contrast, the Navy RDF research unit, initially based in Portsmouth, was relocated to a safer base in Witley and Haslemere in Surrey in 1942.[19,20] These moves inland were ordered by Churchill based upon intelligence reports indicating that the Germans were going to target the coastal research sites in May 1942[21]. Thus, from May 1942 onwards, all the secret British military research and development activity on RDF/radar was based at two sites in England.

By mid-1940 the RAF had incorporated radar into the national air defence and the army was beginning to use it to increase the efficiency of searchlights and artillery to find targets. The requirement for qualified technicians to maintain and repair radar equipment increased rapidly and training courses were developed and run by many colleges and specialist military schools; the REME No. 2 Radio Mechanics School (RMS) at Gopsall Hall was one such school. Although it was not a secret radar research unit, the radar equipment, training manuals and detailed technical documentation present at Gopsall Hall were secret and all the work was covered by the Official Secrets Act.

It is often said that the No. 2 RMS was located at Gopsall because it was an isolated site. While Gopsall can be said to be 'in the sticks', it is unlikely that this was of paramount importance as the No. 1 RMS was based at Lower Croft Camp, only 1.7 miles from the centre of Bury and less than 10 miles from the centre of Manchester.[22] Gopsall, which was already set up as an army camp with a hall and gardens containing many mature trees surrounded by parkland, would seem to offer an ideal, ready-made secluded site.

Top: GL Mk II receiver cabin. The cabin swings around on a pivot to keep it pointing at the target. The 3 sets of aerials are used for range, bearing and angle of sight.

Bottom: Centrimetric GL radar Mk III(b) - the British version of the Mk III, 'manned' by the WRAF (Gilkicker Training Camp).

(www.fortgilkicker.co.uk; CC BY-NC-ND)

The No. 1 RMS, sometimes quaintly called the 'School of Electric Lighting', specialised in training for the servicing and repair of Searchlight Control Radar (SCR); radar that was designed to locate an aircraft and direct a searchlight to immediately light up the target. By contrast, No. 2 RMS specialised in the development of service protocols and the training in the setup, use and repair of Gun-Laying Radar (GLR). While the radar was essentially similar in both cases, the processing of the information after the radar had located an aircraft was more complicated because the gun had to be directed to a point where the target would be by the time a (slow) anti-aircraft shell reached it.

Up until 1943, the only GLR models in use were the British GL Mk I, I* and II. The GL Mk I radars were very inefficient and could only determine the slant distance to an aircraft and, on average, required 18,500 rounds to hit the target. However, this was a great improvement over the 41,000 rounds required by anti-aircraft guns without radar. The upgraded Mk I* and Mk II models, used throughout the war, had the ability to accurately determine bearing and elevation and reduced the rounds per hit to 4,100 and 2,750 respectively.[19,23] The GL Mk II radar consisted of two trailer-mounted timber cabins for the transmitter and receiver, and a generator, with the three units making up a mobile convoy which, in theory, could be brought in and out of action quickly. Virtually all the mobile radar units at Anti-Aircraft sites in Britain were static and were rarely moved.[24] In 1943, the British and Canadian versions of the more compact, microwave-based, GL Mk III were introduced, followed in 1944 by the American SCR-584 units, both having improved hit rates. These new gun-laying radars were able to detect smaller objects than the previous lower frequency radars (GL Mk I & II), and the American equipment played a big role in the defence of London and other cities against the V-1 flying bomb ('doodlebug').[20,25,26]

An SCR-584 radar unit deployed on Peleliu (Micronesia) during WWII. The antenna on the left is for the 'Identification Friend or Foe' system. This American radar was advanced for its time and was used extensively from February 1944 onwards in Europe and the Pacific. After deployment on the south coast, the SCR-584 resulted in the shells required to destroy a V-1 rocket being reduced from 2,500 to 100.
(US Dept of Defence; Public Domain)

Throughout the time that the No. 2 RMS was at Gopsall, training was given in the maintenance and use of all the types of gun-laying radar in use, meaning that near the end of the war this included the old Mk I, Mk II and Mk III GL radars plus the new American SCR-584 units introduced in 1944. However, the training staff were not always on top of their subject. In late 1943 a contingent of mechanics, who had been assembling Naval 271 microwave radar sets at the REME workshops at Old Dolby were sent to be trained on the new microwave-based radar systems. When they arrived, the teaching staff had to admit that they had no experience in such equipment, having assembled, but not turned on, their only such radar set. This intake of 'students' taught the staff and then set their own exit exam, which they all passed and subsequently increased their army pay by 50%!

Although the Royal Engineers had made the hall useable as the headquarters of the Gopsall Camp for the general military training and forward deployment of troops in 1940, further work was undertaken when the RMS was moved from Cheltenham in August 1942. All the greenhouses in the walled and formal gardens were taken down and the glass removed from the large show house to prevent sunlight reflections and the possibility of being seen from the air. Nissen huts were erected in the walled gardens, in the Cedar Walk area to the south and on the south terrace, complementing those already in and around the area known as 'the Nob', to the northwest of the hall. Those on the south terrace were used as technical administration offices and some training accommodation. The large numbers of huts amongst the trees in the Cedar Walk area of the gardens to the southwest and west of the hall, were used as accommodation for the trainees and lower ranks, lecture rooms, equipment demonstration rooms, a gymnasium, and shower and latrine blocks. Nissen huts were also present within the walled garden, which provided more

Aerial photo (1948): Nissen huts are in Cedar Walk, in/around the Nob and on the hall terrace; mess huts and the NAAFI are in the north part of the walled gardens.[16]

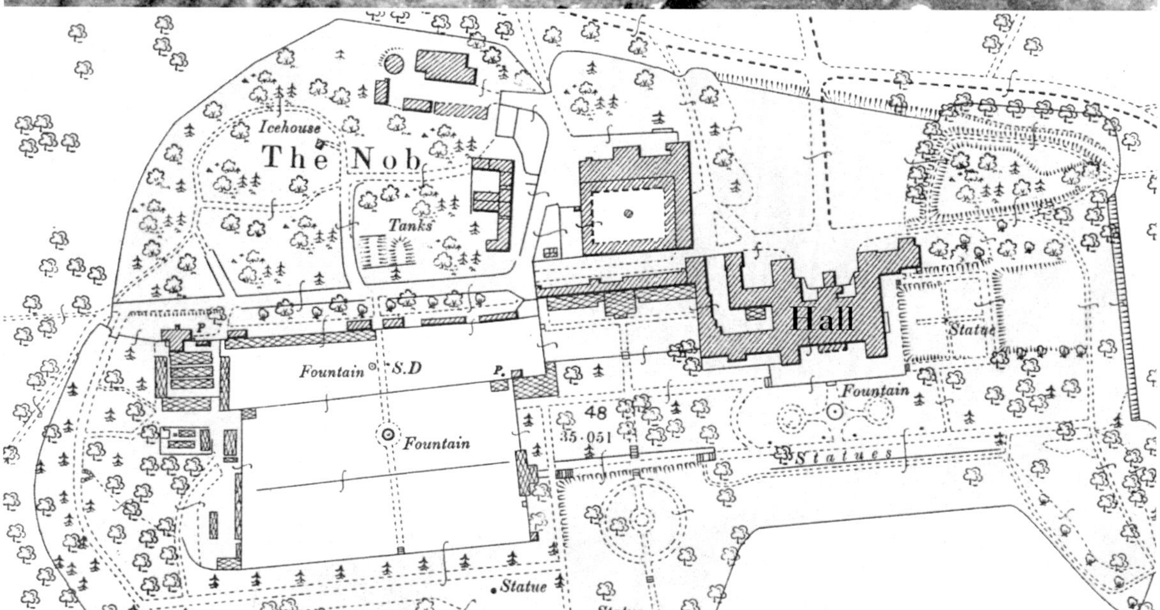

teaching accommodation and, more importantly, the other ranks' dining halls, cookhouses and NAAFI-run canteen, which actually served beer! The officers dined in the hall.

The stable yard housed the generators for powering the radar equipment in the hall and stables that was used for practical teaching sessions. In addition, there were a number of camouflaged mobile radar cabins in the grounds, linked to their own mobile generators, which provided trainees with practical training under conditions they would meet in active service.

Aerial photo of Gopsall Hall after it was vacated by the army. Huts are on the south terrace, 2 each side of the fountain, and one is close to the library wall on the east terrace. Holdsworth's cenotaph, commissioned by Charles Jennens (Chapter 4), stands at the centre of the east garden, in which is another hut. Note that the roof lights in the picture gallery and smoking/billiard room (arrows; Chapter 2) are blacked out.

The staff at the RMS consisted of about 20 REME instructors/technicians plus other male support staff and about 50 ATS clerks, orderlies, cooks, drivers and cleaners, and one female radio technician. The REME officers were accommodated within the hall, but other ranks were billeted in the Nissen huts erected in the Cedar Walk area of the gardens. However, some of the non-officer staff managed to get permission to be quartered in 'basement rooms' which were considered to be far better than the Nissen huts. These rooms were probably ground floor rooms within the west service wings (Chapter 2). Unsurprisingly, the Commanding Officer's quarters were the suite of rooms, including the silver bath, said to have been used by King Edward VII when he and Queen Alexandra visited the Earl and Countess Howe at Gopsall in 1902. Unlike the ATS attached to the RAOC vehicle depot who were billeted outside Gopsall, those attached to the RMS were accommodated in the attic rooms of the hall, which used to be the servants' quarters.

In addition to staff quarters, the hall contained administration offices, some teaching rooms on the first floor and, in 'the basement', a number of small workshops for the maintenance of equipment and the production of training aids. These workshops were almost certainly in the 'ground floor' of the kitchen wing, half a floor below the main ground floor of the hall (Chapter 2). Many of the permanent staff and some trainees had bicycles, which they also stored in the basement. The library, used as the examination room at the end of each radio course, was widely known as the music room at the time. It contained no books but did have an Aeolian pipe organ and a small stage complete with curtains and lighting rig erected at the south end of the room. Some of the trainees managed to resurrect the 110-volt electric organ by using a searchlight generator, a 12-volt lorry battery and two heavy sandbags to replace the missing windchest weights! This room served as a cinema, concert hall and theatre. Regular dances were held in the hall which were attended by both RMS and vehicle depot staff. As well as members of the ATS, girls in the Women's Land Army working on farms in the area were invited to events in the music room and, especially the dances. Attendance by the Land Army girls was strictly by invitation and security pass only.

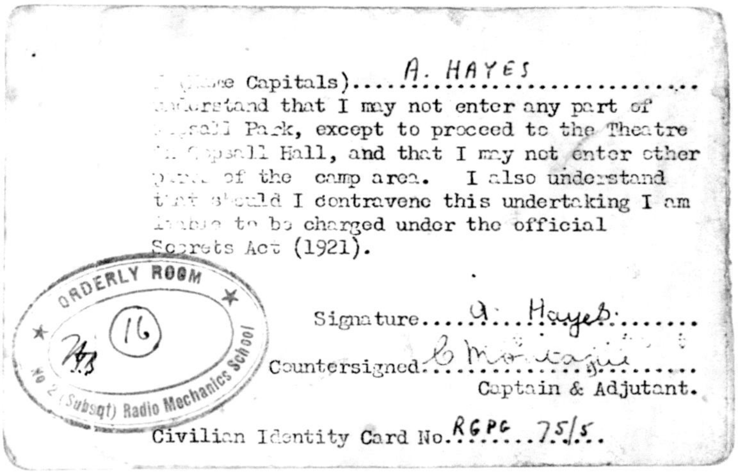
...e Capitals)........A. HAYES..........
...understand that I may not enter any part of ...sall Park, except to proceed to the Theatre ... Gopsall Hall, and that I may not enter other ... of the camp area. I also understand that should I contravene this undertaking I am ... to be charged under the official Secrets Act (1921).

ORDERLY ROOM
No 2 (Subsqt) Radio Mechanics School

Signature....A. Hayes.......

Countersigned:..................
Captain & Adjutant.

Civilian Identity Card No. RGPG. 75/5.

Pass issued to Audrey Hayes of the Women's Land Army for admission to the theatre at Gopsall and nowhere else in the camp!

The RMS staff and trainees at Gopsall largely made their own entertainment, as there were usually a number of individuals with amateur or sometimes professional experience in music and entertainment. Not surprisingly, the school had a virtually permanent 'Entertainments Party' who put on a variety of shows and plays. Sometimes shows were taken 'on tour' to other service units and, on at least two occasions, were presented at a theatre in Leicester and the playhouse in Nuneaton.

Peter Casson (1921-1995) ran hypnotherapy clinics in London and Yorkshire, spending only a quarter of his time performing. The poster is dated December 1958.

A memorable one-man show at Christmas 1942 was put on by Peter Casson, a Gopsall trainee from the Royal Marines; he hypnotized his subject on the stage and half the audience! His skill at hypnotising fellow recruits soon spread and, after leaving Gopsall, his first 'official' stage show was in the Sergeants' Mess at his Portsmouth Barracks at the request of the Colour Sergeant. He became a well-known hypnotherapist and entertainer and was performing at the London Palladium in 1946; his last performance was in 1991, at the same venue.

In addition, an enterprising group of musicians formed the nucleus of a dance band which would be augmented by any other likely volunteer passing through the camp. The 'Gopsall Dance Band' was made available for outside dances at the request of various organisations and was very popular; playing in many village halls and small dance halls over a wide area, from Shepshed in the north to Hinckley in the south.

One of the first intake of trainees to the RMS had a number of members who, before the war, had been teachers of Latin. During their spare time, they took to inspecting the Latin inscriptions on the many statues, monuments and obelisks that were present in the grounds. This sparked interest amongst the other courses, so a conducted tour was organised. As the procession arrived at a monument, one of the teachers, with an army blanket thrown over his shoulder to simulate the appropriate dress, read the inscription in the style of Roman orator, after which a few of the others would give an *ad hoc* translation. When these trainees finished their course, they made a shield with drawings relating to various facets of their stay at Gopsall, and added an appropriate Latin motto. When they left, it was hung in one of the trees near to the house, and this practice became a tradition and was repeated by later courses. However, rather than being hung on the trees, the colonel decreed that the shields should be hung in the library so they would not be exposed to the elements. The passing out shields that hung in the library eventually made their way to the REME museum in Arborfield after the No. 2 RMS left Gopsall. Hopefully, these relics of the No. 2 RMS are still held by the museum after its relocation to Lyneham, Wiltshire in 2015.

Sunday was usually free for the trainees and, depending upon when they were at Gopsall, they would attend a service in the library or be marched to St James' Church, Twycross. For a short period, Gopsall Hall chapel also seems to have been used for services, the organ having been temporarily repaired by some trainees. However, the bass notes had to be blanked off because it was feared that if low notes were played it would bring down the chapel ceiling which was held up by huge timber braces!

Morning and afternoon parades were held on the large forecourt in front of the north entrance before the trainees were marched off to their classes. The trainees, normally about 20 per intake, worked long hours and had little free time during their course, which normally lasted 8 weeks. Initially only members of the British army with school certificates in maths and physics who passed a basic 16-week course in electronics and wireless technology could enrol as trainees at the RMS. Later, enrolment was extended to military men with similar basic training from Norway, the Netherlands, Canada, France, the USA and Poland. In late 1943/early 1944 women from the ATS and a few RAF meteorologists were also admitted for training. Most of the trainees' enjoyable memories of Gopsall focussed on playing jokes on each other, dances and shows held in the hall, vying with each other to dance with ATS and Women's Land Army girls, sneaking in and out of the base via the woods, walking /hitching to Measham to go to the Empire Cinema and the bus outings to Nuneaton and Leicester.

Successful completion of the course entitled you to a significant increase in pay as well as the right to wear the radio mechanics badge on your arm. As all diagrams and notebooks were classified as 'secret', and bore a label quoting the Official Secrets Act, they were collected by the school and forwarded to those who qualified after they had joined their unit. As radar developed during the war, many of the students returned, some more than once, to be trained on new equipment.

Unlike the RAOC vehicle depot at Gopsall, the No. 2 RMS was closed soon after the war ended in a general consolidation of training establishments. Gopsall classes and instructors were moved, mid-course, along with the Officer Training School at Petersham, to the Electrical Wing in Arborfield.

Activity at Gopsall immediately after the war

Apart from knowing that the park was used as a vehicle depot up to at least early 1949, little is remembered about Gopsall by local residents until the hall was demolished in 1951. However, it would appear that British troops returning from abroad were billeted at Gopsall in 1947, prior to being demobbed or re-deployed; a function it served after the Dunkirk evacuation in 1940. Members of the vehicle depot ATS remember the Green Howards staying at Gopsall after returning from Germany: "*They were a fighting unit and couldn't seem to forget it. Several unpleasant incidents occurred which did nothing for their reputation.*"

One inscription on the temple ruins (21 Army Group) may also support this final military role of Gopsall. The 21st Army Group (21st AG) was established in July 1943 and controlled all ground forces in Operation Overlord (the D-Day landings and Battle of Normandy) and operated in Northern France, Belgium, the Netherlands and Germany from June 1944 to August 1945, when it was renamed the British Army of the Rhine.[27] The majority of the British contingent of the 21st AG, consisting of the British Second Army, would have been involved in the immediate post-war reorganisation of Germany and did not return home until sometime after war ended.

A resident in Measham recalls German prisoners of war (PoW) being held at Gopsall in the winter of 1946-47.[1,28] Overall, there were about 402,000 German prisoners in Britain in September 1946, a number that fell to 220,000 by the following September. That German prisoners were in the area at this time is supported by another memory of a resident of Congerstone who, as a young boy, remembers two German officers working on his parents' Farm in Austrey and eating lunch with the family. However, Gopsall is not mentioned in any list of WWII PoW camps.[29] The PoW camps that are listed in the area were at Stretton Hall (Stretton en le Field), Merevale Hall (Atherstone) and Arbury Hall (Nuneaton). Stretton Hall was only 3 miles by road from Measham and 3.5 miles from Austrey, perhaps suggesting that these PoWs were from there rather than Gopsall. However, there are several inscriptions left on the temple ruins at Gopsall that provide evidence that some German PoWs were at Gopsall in 1948, either as visitors or prisoners.

Interestingly, there is anecdotal evidence that Lowercroft Camp near Bury, the site of the No. 1 RMS became a PoW camp at the end of the war. As with Gopsall, the site does not appear in any list of British PoW camps.[22]

The temple at the edge of the Race Course wood was often visited by both the soldiers based at Gopsall and local villagers. Signs of the wartime occupation of Gopsall are carved into some of the stones and 'Chad', the wartime equivalent of a 21st century emoji, representing complaints about rationing and the like, is featured on several stones. A number of the trainees at Gopsall claimed that 'Chad' originated there, and one even wrote to the Daily Mirror making the claim![30]

Many of the temple inscriptions made during WWII are a lasting testament to the military personnel who passed through Gopsall.

German prisoners of war at Merevale Camp

(The Wright Family Rural North Warwickshire Archive)

The temple ruins ('Chad's Chapel') in 1942

21 ARMY GROUP

J EASTON REME

WEGAR
Zachert German P.o.W. 48

HERBERT LANGE GERMAN

MARY COLMAN
MARY LEADBETTER
ATS
Age 19 of Cheshire
1945

Notes and References

1 *Gopsall & Congerstone at War.* J. Matthews & L. Stoney. Independent Publishing Network. Congerstone, 2020.

2 *History of REME.* REME Connect webpage: https://remeconnect.org/corps/history/ accessed 17th February 2021.

3 *History of the Royal Army Ordnance Corps, 1920-1945.* Brigadier A. H. Fernyhough. Published by Royal Army Ordnance Corps, 1967.

4 *History of the Army Ordnance Services: The Three Volume Compilation.* Major General A. Forbes. Published by Naval and Military Press, 2020.

5 *The history of the Auxiliary Territorial Service.* https://www.thehistorypress.co.uk/articles/the-history-of-the-auxiliary-territorial-service/ The History Press, accessed on 17th February 2021

6 *Girls in Khaki. A history of the ATS in the second world war.* Barbara Green. Spellmount; Illustrated edition, 2012.

7 *Anti-aircraft Artillery, 1914-55.* N. W. Routledge. Brassey's: London, 1994.

8 *Our uninvited Guests. The secret lives of Britain's country houses 1939-45.* Julie Summers. Simon & Schuster, 2018.

9 *History of the CMP.* 245 Provost Company Corps of the Royal Military Police website, accessed 17th February 2021 https://245provostcompany.co.uk/index.php/history-of-the-cmp/.

10 *Twycross Girl Killed. Dashed into Army Lorry. Just received book from Italian Prisoner.* Atherstone News, Friday 29th October, 1943.

11 *Birds Eye Wartime Leicestershire 1939-1945.* T. C. Cartwright. TCC Publications: Wigston. 2002.

12 *But for these things. Leicester and its people in WWII.* Vincent Holyoak. Matador: Leicester, 2014, pp. 161-162.

13 Cliff House, Twycross was demolished to make way for the building of the headquarters of Rare Computing Ltd, a video game development company founded by Tim and Chris Stamper (Chris Stamper now owns the 'Shackerstone Estate'). Lindley Lodge, on the A5, is now called 'The King's Lodge' and is the home of the Christian organisation, Youth With A Mission (YWAM). RAF Lindley is now Horiba MIRA Ltd, formerly the Motor Industry Research Association.

14 *RAF Nuneaton (Lindley).* Airfield Research Group website: http://www.controltowers.co.uk/N/Nuneaton.htm accessed 17th February 2021.

15 *Army cadets prepare for D-Day.* BBC WW2 People's War Article ID A6143609, accessed on 17th February 2021 (https://www.bbc.co.uk/history/ww2peopleswar/stories/09/a6143609.shtml). A variety of volunteer groups were involved in preparing vehicles for D-Day and the subsequent invasion of Europe.

16 *Aerial photographs of Gopsall.* The Record Office for Leicestershire, Leicester and Rutland. File Ref: DE9293/21/2/1.

17 Vehicle sales were held at many sites across the country during 1947 and 1948, including: No. 22 VRD, Cornbury Park, Charlbury Oxon; No. 246 RAF Maintenance Unit, Bicester, Oxon.; No. 31 VRD, Douglas, Lanark, Scotland; No. 52 VRD, Knole Park, Sevenoaks, Kent.

18 *Robert Alexander Watson-Watt 13 April 1892-5 December 1973.* J. A. Ratcliffe. Biographical Memoirs of Fellows of the Royal Society 21: 1975, pp. 548–568.

19 The development and use of radar by Britain in WWII is a large subject and there are no sources that present a broad, readable overview relevant to this chapter other than Wikipedia (https://en.wikipedia.org/). Search for: *Radar in WWII, Gun Laying Radar and Telecommunications Research Establishment.*

20 *Army Radar: The story of its Development and Employment in World War II.* David Wilcox. Menin House, 2004. This is a relatively readable account of radar for gun laying, searchlight control and coastal defence and its role in combating the V-1 flying bombs.

21 *Purbeck - Worth Matravers.* Purbeck Radar Museum Trust website (http://www.purbeckradar.org.uk/). Accessed on 18th February 2021. *Dorset's Radar Days.* Bill Penley & Reg Batt. Purbeck Radar Museum Trust: 6th ed., 2006.

22 *Lowercroft Camp, Bury.* Lancashire at War website, accessed 19th February, 2021: http://www.lancashireatwar.co.uk/lowercroft-camp/4583041255. Also see: Cecil Ramsbottom in reference 1.

23 *Schonland: Scientist and Soldier: From lightning on the veld to nuclear power at Harwell: the life of Field Marshal Montgomery's scientific adviser.* Brian Austin. CRC Press, 2016, p. 211.

24 *World War Two GL Radar Mark II.* Fort Gilkicker website: https://www.fortgilkicker.co.uk/radar.htm, accessed 18th February 2021.

25 *Radar Screening for Low Flying Objects.* Lieutenant Colonel Albert J. Weinnig. Coastal Artillery Journal 89 (2) March/April, 1946, pp. 9-12.

26 *Citations and Commendations. Distinguished Service Medal to Brigadier General Clare Armstrong.* Coastal Artillery Journal 89 (1) January/February, 1946, p. 75. 97% of V-1 all flying bombs aimed at Antwerp docks were destroyed between November 1944 and April 1945.

27 *A concise history of 21 Army Group (History & Personnel).* See: https://www.britishmilitaryhistory.co.uk/wp-content/uploads/sites/124/2020/06/21-Army-Group-History-Personnel.pdf - Downloaded 17th February 2021.

28 *Anglo-German friendship. Dortmund woman visits Measham.* Leicester Evening Mail, Friday 29th June 1962.

29 Prisoner of War Camps (1939-1948). Twentieth Century Military Recording Project Report by R.J.C. Thomas. English Heritage, 2003. The report was accessed on 19th February 2021 and is downloadable from: https://historicengland.org.uk/images-books/publications/prisoner-of-war-camps/prisoner-of-war-camps/.

30 We've had Chad! The Daily Mirror, Monday 24th September 1945.

The Last Days of Gopsall Hall

On Thursday 31st May 1951 at half past ten prompt, auctioneers Perry and Phillips Ltd of Bridgnorth began to sell off Gopsall Hall piece by piece. During the previous week, after purchasing the sale catalogue for one-shilling, prospective buyers were allowed to view the *in situ* 'fixtures and fittings' within the hall. These were some of the very last people to enter the hall before the demolition men started their work in June.

Historic England Archive

The south front of Gopsall Hall awaiting demolition. Most of the windows have been removed and the gardens are overgrown.

GOPSALL HALL

Twycross, Near Nuneaton.

Atherstone 9 miles, Nuneaton 10, Hinckley 11, Coventry 20, Birmingham 30.

CATALOGUE OF THE

INTERIOR & EXTERIOR

FIXTURES and FITTINGS

to be offered for SALE by AUCTION on the Site on

THURSDAY, 31st MAY, 1951

Commencing at 10-30 a.m. prompt.

ON VIEW WEEK PRIOR TO SALE.

AUCTIONEERS:

PERRY & PHILLIPS LTD.

59, HIGH STREET, BRIDGNORTH. TEL. 2248.

Catalogues: Price 1/- each.

Bridgnorth Journal Co

Historic England Archive

Ironically, the fixtures and fittings catalogue gives some of the best descriptions of the hall rooms. The "*Extremely fine statuary marble mantelpiece (8ft x 5ft 9in)*" with large size figures of angels secured a top price of £25. Other marble mantelpieces sold for much less, some for only £1.

LOT **BOUDOIR**

51 A PAIR OF HANDSOME MAHOGANY PANELLED DOORS, each 3ft. × 11ft., with carved panels, also the carved wood framing on each side of the lining

52 THE OAK FLOOR AS LAID, 42ft. × 23ft. 6in., and the carved wood skirting

53 Oak frame sash window, 4ft. × 8ft., with carved wood framing. folding shutters and panelling below

54 Ditto

55 Ditto

56 A 4ft. 6in. carved gilt consul table with marble top and mirror at back

57 A gilt frame mirror, 10ft. × 5ft.

58 Ditto

59 A 7ft. 9in. HANDSOME CARVED WHITE MARBLE MANTELPIECE. The fluted pilasters have carved swags of fruit beneath a carved mask. The frieze has three carved panels of musical instruments with carved vases at either side. Also the iron grate and hearthstone

60 The whole of the silk damask as fitted to the room

ANTE-ROOM

61 A MAHOGANY PANELLED DOOR WITH CARVED WOOD PANELS, 4ft. × 7ft. 8in., together with the carved wood framing on either side of the deep lining

62 THE OAK FLOOR AS LAID, 20ft. × 24ft., and the carved wood skirting

63 The oak frame sash window, 4ft. × 8ft., with carved wood folding shutters, framing and panelling below

64 A pair of deal ledge doors. each 2ft. × 7ft. 4in., together with the carved wood framing and deep lining to same

65 Gilt frame wall mirror, 13ft. 6in. × 5ft. 6in.

66 The green hessian as fitted to the walls

67 The green silk brocade as fitted to the walls

68 THE EXTREMELY FINE CARVED WHITE MARBLE MANTELPIECE, having carved scroll pilasters decorated with swags of grapes. The frieze, which is richly carved with festoons and garlands of flowers, has a centre panel with carved dove in shell scroll with bunches of fruit. Also the iron grate and hearthstone

LIBRARY

69 A PAIR OF HANDSOME MAHOGANY PANELLED DOORS, each 3ft. 1in. × 11ft. 6in., with carved panels, also carved wood framing on both sides and the carved lining

70 THE OAK FLOOR AS LAID, 54ft. × 22ft.

71 Six sheets of asbestos

72 Painted deal counter, 9ft. 6in. wide. with flap

73 A HANDSOME CARVED WHITE MARBLE MANTELPIECE, 7ft. 6in. × 6ft., having plain panelled pilasters surmounted by carved scrolls. The centre panel is of plain marble with panels of carved festoons of flowers and ribbons at either side. Also iron grate and hearthstone

74 A SIMILAR MANTELPIECE, with carved festoons of acorn and leaf decoration, also iron grate

75 THE HANDSOME ANGLE FITMENT OF MAHOGANY BOOKSHELVES, fitted with six glazed doors, extreme size 8ft. 6in. × 12ft. 6in., together with two fluted pilasters having carved capitals

LOT **OUTSIDE**

359 A PAIR OF HANDSOME WROUGHT IRON GATES, each 6ft × 6ft. 6in. high, with wrought iron pillars, also the two side gates, the stone pillars surmounted with ball ornaments and the length of pallisading at each side

360 A brass call bell

361 THE ERECTION OF GLAZED SPAN-ROOF CAR WASH

362 A VALUABLE OLD TWO-DIAL TOWER CLOCK, by Thomas Mudge, of London

363 A COMPOSITION PEDESTAL, 3ft. HIGH, decorated with carved rams heads

364 DITTO

365 DITTO

366 DITTO

367 A HANDSOME SQUARE MARBLE PEDESTAL ON SQUARE BASE, 9ft. HIGH, the base having carved figure decoration and inscription, surmounted by carved marble vase with scroll decoration on base

368 A SET OF FIVE STONE STEPS, 10ft. wide, and stone stringing

369 AN ORNAMENTAL FOUNTAIN WITH DOLPHIN SUPPORT, also the stone surround, 13ft. 6in. × 8ft.

370 A PAIR OF HANDSOME WROUGHT IRON GATES, each 2ft. × 6ft., with wrought iron scroll work, four pillars and side pieces. Extreme width 11ft. 6in.

371 A SET OF FIVE STONE STEPS, 11ft. wide

372 A LENGTH OF STONE BALUSTRADING WITH MOULDED COPING, 50ft. long × 3ft. high

373 A SIMILAR LOT, 75ft. × 3ft. high

374 A SIMILAR LOT, 35ft. × 3ft. high

375 The handsome carved marble linings to the archway, with carved coat of arms panel surmounted with cupids and other figures

376 STONE BALUSTRADING WITH TURNED BALUSTRADES and moulded stone coping, about 30ft. long

377 DITTO

378 A PAIR OF FINE IRON ENTRANCE GATES, 12ft. 4in. × 7ft. 6in., with side gates each 4ft. wide, together with the wrought iron piers, 9ft. high

379 A PAIR OF FINE WROUGHT IRON GATES to the Twycross Entrance, 11ft. 10in. × 10ft. 6in.

END OF SALE

Pages from the May 1951 sale catalogue listing some of the lots: sheets of asbestos, hessian and silk brocade on the walls, oak floors, doors, mantelpieces, the tower clock, the entrance gates to the hall (Lot 359) and those at Bilstone and Twycross lodges (Lots 378 & 379) and the Holdsworth cenotaph (Lot 367).

Prices achieved included: The entire mahogany library fittings, £230; gilded carved wood overmantel from the library, 100gns; pitch-pine door, £60; main hall gates, £30; 2-dial tower clock, £20; the 'silver' bath, £20; complete glazed windows, £3; 3ftx6ft oak sash windows with framing, shutters and panelling below, £1.50; marble mantelpieces from £1; oak flooring £1/sq ft; pine flooring, 3s (15p)/sq ft.

The cedar tea room mantelpiece (Lot 97; Historic England Archive) is described as "*An extremely fine carved white marble mantelpiece, the pilasters having carved trusses with carved doves in a shell background pecking fruit. The frieze of Sienna marble has a carved centre panel of man with angel and lions.*"

Some items (eg. the chapel organ, pews and pulpit) do not appear in the sale catalogue and had presumably already been sold privately, or had been reserved for private sale by the liquidators of Panton Investments Ltd or the demolition company (Thomas Oakley Ltd) (see later).

The 1951 Fixture & Fittings Sale

The auctioneers went around the hall and gardens bringing the hammer down on almost anything the crowd would buy - except the chapel organ and pulpit, which were not included in the sale.

The day before the fixture and fittings sale, the Leicester Evening Mail told its readers a little about one of Gopsall's last retainers:

> *"Today Miss Annie Clarke, one of the last retainers, was opening the wrought iron gates of the Bilstone entrance to admit prospective buyers. Her mother, 88-year-old Mrs Francis Clarke, widow of Thomas, one of the staff, is bedridden in the nearby lodge where they have lived rent free since the estate decayed. They remember the time 50 years ago when Gopsall, then the seat of the Howes, was in its heyday".*[1]

The Clarkes, in service at Gopsall for all those years, witnessed royalty, the aristocracy, government officials and thousands of members of the armed forces pass through the gates and, on the last day, the final visitors arrived to pick through the carcass of the hall. Bilstone gates were the penultimate lot sold in the auction and they still survive in Market Harborough (see later).

It is estimated that during the 20th century, between 1,200 and 1,600 country houses were demolished in England alone; an average of 12 to 16 per year.[2,3] The number of houses lost during the 1920s and 1930s was triple that seen in the first two decades of the century, no doubt due to the after effects of WWI and the great economic depression that lasted throughout the 1930s. This increase was slowed by WWII, which diverted men and machines to fighting and civil defence duties, and resulted in many country houses being requisitioned by the government for military and other uses.[4] However, the loss of country houses peaked in the 1950s, with an average of 42 houses being demolished each year. Since then, the number of houses demolished has fallen rapidly, with less than one each year being the average over the first two decades of the 21st century. Although this decline may be the result of interventions by Historic England and The National Trust, the major reason is undoubtably the smaller pool of country houses existing after the preceding decades of destruction.

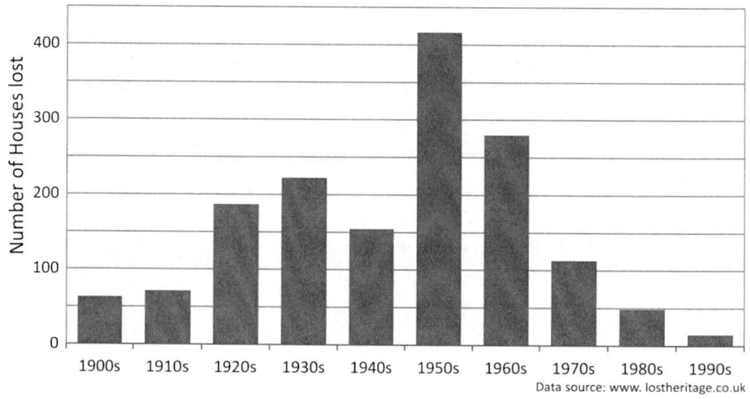

It is easy to overlook the social effect this loss had on local communities. In the 19th and early 20th centuries, it was common for the local gentry in 'the big house' to provide employment and housing for the local population, and for the village school and church to benefit from their patronage. The Gopsall villages were big beneficiaries of the Earls Howe (Chapter 13), and the hall and estate were the bedrock of local society, as was the case in the majority of rural England at the time. Demolition of the 'big houses' and the selling off of the estates before WWII meant significant unemployment for the local community. The Gopsall villages had, however, lost their main local employer some 30 years before the demolition of the hall, which had essentially not been lived in since the estate had

The windowless, ivy-clad east front of the hall with the salon and billiard room additions on the left. Holdsworth's cenotaph stands in the middle of the overgrown east flower garden.

been sold to Samuel Waring in 1918 (Chapter 1). Large English country houses were being abandoned as homes mainly because they became economically impossible to support in a changing society after WWI, the great depression, WWII and the subsequent expansion of the welfare state. In 1951, Gopsall Hall, once considered the finest mansion in Leicestershire, lay stranded in its park, waiting to be picked over for the sum of its parts, with no value given to it as whole. The elaborate and exquisitely fashioned plasterwork ceilings, still remembered in 1982 (Chapter 7) were too difficult to remove, so fell to the wrecking ball.

The north front of the hall

Historic England Archive

The road to that wrecking ball and sale of Gopsall Hall as 'building materials' was not straight forward. We do not know why the 4th Earl Howe sold the Gopsall Estate in 1918. However, several events may have contributed to the Earl spending less time at Gopsall than previously: the death of Georgiana, the Countess Howe, in 1906 (Chapter 9); the subsequent death of the Earl's beloved sister Evelyn in 1913 and the outbreak of WWI in 1914. Gopsall was very much used by the Howes for entertaining, but in light of these events, it is easy to see why the fashionable parties and balls, the shooting parties and visitor weekends declined. The Earl's relationship with, and subsequent marriage to Florence Hamilton Davis (the Marchioness of Dufferin and Ava) in December 1919 is unlikely to have played a role, as Florence's first husband (Lord Dufferin) died in February 1918 and the sale of Gopsall to Samuel Waring was reported at the beginning of August that year (along with the auction sale of the Earl's Gotham Estate in Nottinghamshire).[5-7]

The south front of the derelict hall viewed from an area just to the south of the sunken garden. The iron park fence is in the foreground.

After the August reports of Gopsall's sale to Samuel Waring, the extensive and valuable collections of books, furniture and paintings were catalogued. Some items were removed from Gopsall but the majority of the hall contents were lotted and listed by Messrs. Trollope to be auctioned at the hall on Monday 14th October 1918 and following days.[8] This auction was preceded by a sale of the agricultural implements and effects held on the 9th and 10th October 1918 at Home Farm and gardens.

BY MESSRS. TROLLOPE.

By Direction of the Right Hon. Earl of Howe G.C.V.O., First Portion.

THE HOME FARM AND GARDENS, GOPSALL PARK, LEICESTERSHIRE.

Nearest Stations, Shackerstone and Snarestone.

MESSRS. TROLLOPE having sold the Estate, will SELL BY AUCTION, at the above, on WEDNESDAY and THURSDAY, 9th and 10th OCTOBER, 1918, at 12 o'clock precisely each day,

THE AGRICULTURAL IMPLEMENTS AND EFFECTS, including—

Two Bamblett's Mowing Machines, Tip Carts, Drills, Waggons, Floats, Timber, Wheels, Dring Winnower, Chaff Machines, Crushers, Barrows, Blacksmith Tools, Old Timber and Iron, Lead Lined Troughs, etc., etc. The Keeper's Effects, comprising Coops, Setting Boxes, Deer Nets, 3 Huts, 2 Fowl Houses, an Aged Mare and Cart, Wire Netting, etc. The Contents of Power House, Blacksmith's and Painter's Shops, the Garden Tools, and Plants.

On View day preceding sale. Catalogues may be obtained at the Royal Hotel, Ashby-de-la-Zouch, and at the Auctioneers' Offices, 25 Mount street, London, W. 1.

Tamworth Herald, Saturday 5th October 1918.
Reach Licensing

MAIN PORTION.

By Direction of the Right Hon. EARL HOWE, G.C.V.O.

GOPSALL, LEICESTERSHIRE.

Shackerstone two miles. Ashby-de-la-Zouch eight miles.

CATALOGUE

OF THE

Fine Antique and Modern

Furniture in the Mansion

WHICH INCLUDES

FENDERS, IMPLEMENTS, CURTAINS,
PERSIAN, INDIAN, TURKEY AND PILE CARPETS AND RUGS,
BEDSTEADS AND BEDDING, including

A PRINCE CHARLES STATE BEDSTEAD

with the Stuart Tartan Silk Drapery,

SETS OF COUCHES, SETTEES, EASY, LOUNGE, AND STANDARD CHAIRS,

Writing Tables, Side Tables, Commodes, Court Cupboards, Screens, Cabinets, Sideboards, Buffet, Torchieres, Secretaires, Wardrobes, Armoires, and Mirrors in Very Choice Carved Frames.

COLLECTION OF PICTURES,

English, Dutch, etc., Schools by Eminent Old Masters, including a Series relating to the Pretender Period,

Engravings, Prints, and Drawings,

GRANDFATHER, MANTEL & BRACKET CLOCKS IN CHOICE CASES,

A FEW ORNAMENTS,

THE EXTENSIVE LIBRARY OF BOOKS,

BILLIARD TABLE & ACCESSORIES by COX & YEMAN,

The Usual Furnishings of the Bedchambers & Domestic Apartments, Garden Vases, Summer House, a Station 'Bus, a Wagonette and a Brougham, Harness, a Manual Fire Engine and Appliances.

Messrs. TROLLOPE

Having Sold the Estate, will Sell the above by Auction, on the Premises,

On MONDAY, 14th OCTOBER, 1918, and Following Days,

At Twelve o'clock precisely.

ON VIEW: PRIVATELY, by Catalogue and Card only, on THURSDAY; and PUBLICLY, by Catalogue, on the FRIDAY and SATURDAY preceding the Sale. Catalogues to admit to View (1/- each) and Card for Private View may be had at the Auctioneers' Offices—

*25, MOUNT STREET, GROSVENOR SQUARE, W. 1;
Hobart Place, Eaton Square, S.W. 1;
West Halkin Street, Belgrave Square, S.W. 1; and
5, Victoria Street, Westminster, S.W. 1.
LONDON.

In addition to agricultural implements, the sale at Home Farm included gamekeeper's effects, timber, the contents of the power house, blacksmith's and painter's shops, and garden tools and plants. The sale of the 'Furniture in the Mansion' starting on the 14th October 1918 was, in reality, a sale of the furnishings and included virtually all movable items: furniture, curtains, carpets, paintings (see Appendix), clocks and books[8]. The sale was a prolonged process and two days, 28th and 29th October 1918, were devoted to selling the vast collection of books in the library.[8,9] High priced purchases included 'Tobit Curing his Father's Eye', attributed to Rembrandt (1,000gns); 'River Scene' by Van Goyen (425gns); a Chippendale carved mahogany State bedstead, with Stuart Tartan hangings (£1,000); a pair of mid-18th century tables (£1,000) and a set of seven Chippendale chairs (£800).[10,11] Two years later, Messrs. George Trollope and Sons auctioned the *"Second Portion of the well-known Collection formed at Gopsall, Leicestershire"* which consisted of *"rare examples of furnishings of the 17th and 18th centuries"* including furniture of Carolean (the reign of Charles II), William & Mary, Queen Anne, Chippendale, Sheraton and Georgian periods, a few pictures and a selection of more mundane things (eg. an iron safe, silk curtains, oxidised metal electric standards). The three-day auction in London began on 21st July 1920, and Messrs. Trollope and Sons targeted a specific group of bidders: *"Of particular Interest to American Visitors on Account of The Family's Connection with William Penn"*.[12]

"*Stream in a wooded mountain landscape*" by Jacob Van Ruisdael (early 1650s). The painting is thought to have been passed down from Charles Jennens via Penn Assheton Curzon, and was sold for 245gns in 1918.

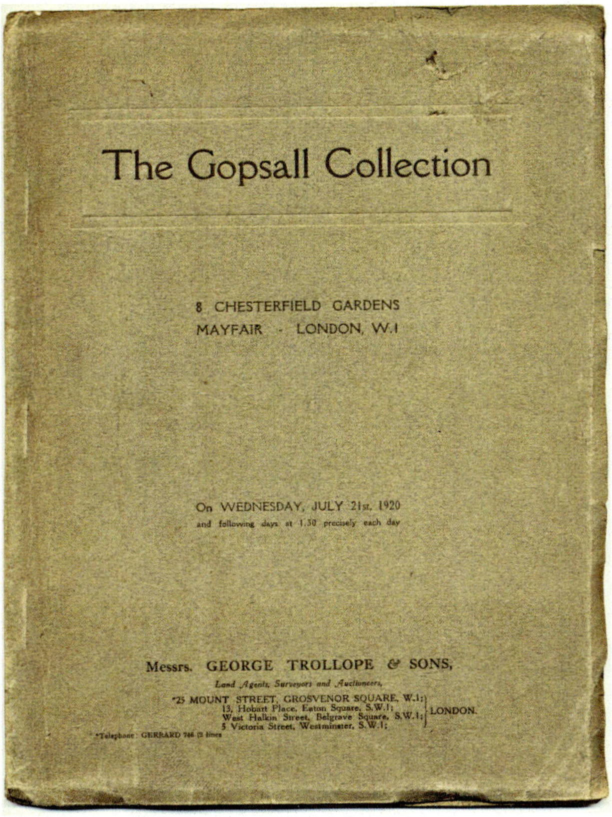

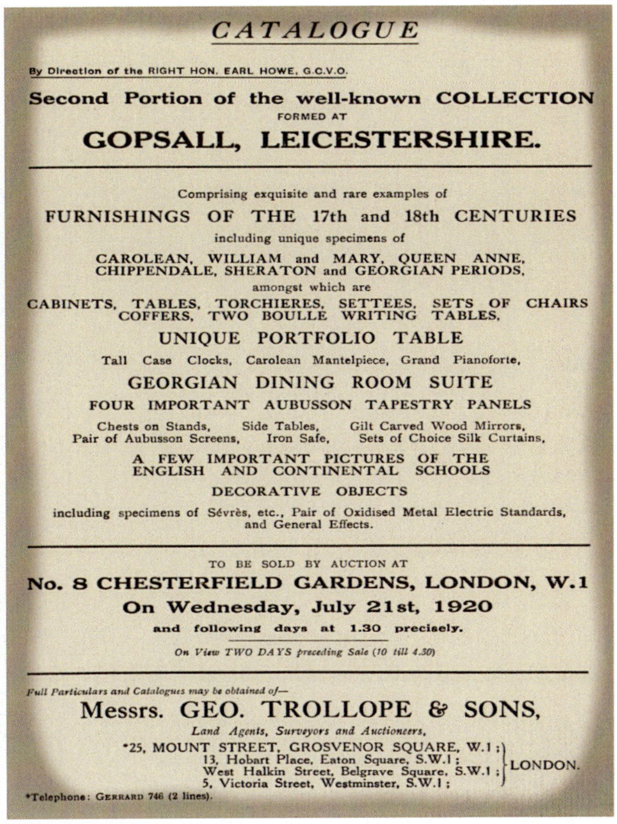

CATALOGUE

By Direction of the RIGHT HON. EARL HOWE, G.C.V.O.

Second Portion of the well-known COLLECTION
FORMED AT
GOPSALL, LEICESTERSHIRE.

Comprising exquisite and rare examples of
FURNISHINGS OF THE 17th and 18th CENTURIES
including unique specimens of
CAROLEAN, WILLIAM and MARY, QUEEN ANNE, CHIPPENDALE, SHERATON and GEORGIAN PERIODS,
amongst which are
CABINETS, TABLES, TORCHIERES, SETTEES, SETS OF CHAIRS COFFERS, TWO BOULLE WRITING TABLES,
UNIQUE PORTFOLIO TABLE
Tall Case Clocks, Carolean Mantelpiece, Grand Pianoforte,
GEORGIAN DINING ROOM SUITE
FOUR IMPORTANT AUBUSSON TAPESTRY PANELS
Chests on Stands, Side Tables, Gilt Carved Wood Mirrors, Pair of Aubusson Screens, Iron Safe, Sets of Choice Silk Curtains,
A FEW IMPORTANT PICTURES OF THE ENGLISH AND CONTINENTAL SCHOOLS
DECORATIVE OBJECTS
including specimens of Sèvres, etc., Pair of Oxidised Metal Electric Standards, and General Effects.

TO BE SOLD BY AUCTION AT
No. 8 CHESTERFIELD GARDENS, LONDON, W.1
On Wednesday, July 21st, 1920
and following days at 1.30 precisely.
On View TWO DAYS preceding Sale (10 till 4.30)

Full Particulars and Catalogues may be obtained of—
Messrs. GEO. TROLLOPE & SONS,
Land Agents, Surveyors and Auctioneers,
*25, MOUNT STREET, GROSVENOR SQUARE, W.1;
13, Hobart Place, Eaton Square, S.W.1;
West Halkin Street, Belgrave Square, S.W.1;
5, Victoria Street, Westminster, S.W.1;
LONDON.
*Telephone: GERRARD 746 (2 lines).

Front cover and title page of the 1920 sale catalogue.[13]

The 1918 eleven-day 'furniture' auction also included the sale of 622 lots of books, 273 paintings, 49 prints and 7 water colour/pastel drawings, taking four complete days. The Midlands County Tribune reported that the books were "*mostly bought by Mr Sam Waring*".[9] Although the sale included some significant pieces of furniture, much was utilitarian and many other lots consisted of a multitude of articles such as bedding, chopping boards, linoleum, carpets, fenders and fire implements, not to mention a pair of stuffed wild ducks in a glazed case (Lot 508)! However, significant amounts of furniture, ornaments and paintings were removed from the hall prior to the sale and were either kept by the family or sold in the London sale two years later.

In December 1918, Messrs Trollope produced a schedule of the pictures, drawings, prints etc (252 in total) removed from Gopsall and hung or stored in various rooms in Assheton House, Twycross.[13] This use of Assheton House was possible because, although the sale of the Gopsall Estate to Samuel Waring had been agreed earlier in 1918, the formal purchase did not occur until August 1919. The date when the paintings etc were finally removed from Assheton House is not known. Comparison of the December 1918 schedule with the 1920 sale catalogue indicates that only 5 of the Assheton House pictures were sold, with the rest being retained by the family.

The 1920 sale in London, billed as "*The Gopsall Collection*", lasted three days and, together with a significant quantity of 17th and 18th century furniture, included high quality 'ornamental items' (e.g. Wedgwood, Coalport and Dresden china, oriental porcelain, clocks and barometers), cushions, curtains and tapestry panels, as well as a further 61 paintings and 6 engravings. The Appendix to this chapter gives a full list of the 334 paintings and various lots of prints, engravings and drawings sold in the two sales, as well as the list of items in the Assheton House schedule.

Several reasons have already been put forward suggesting that the purchase of the Gopsall Estate by Samuel Waring was a speculative investment (Chapter 1). The most compelling evidence for this is the fact that he purchased the bulk of the Duke of Buccluech's Dunchurch Estate in Warwickshire in December 1917, only to sell off most of his holding in two auctions held in June 1918 (4,550 acres) and June 1919 (3,200 acres).[14] Indeed, Messrs. May and Rowden (auctioneers) placed newspaper adverts for the 2nd June 1919 Dunchurch Estate sale alongside one for the auction of 5,600 acres of the outlying portions of the Gopsall Estate, to be held on the 24th and 25th June. This latter auction was withdrawn (Chapters 1 & 5).

The sale of the Gopsall Estate to Samuel Waring was done on the basis of a very large private mortgage (£340,000) secured on the freehold.[15-17] It is probable that both his aborted and successful sales of parts of the Gopsall Estate between 1919 and 1923 (Chapters 1 & 5) were to generate funds to reduce his mortgage debt, which in March 1924 was £214,873. However, a subsequent attempt to sell the outlying portions of the estate in 1927 failed, and by 1931 Lord Waring was in financial difficulty, with £170,310 still outstanding on his mortgage.[16] At this point, the mortgagees (Howe Family Trustees) agreed to sell 6,107 acres of the estate to the Commissioners for Crown Lands for £128,000, effectively calling in part of Waring's mortgage (Chapter 1).

Lord Waring never lived at Gopsall and, between 1932 and 1934, attempts were made by Francis Richard Henry Penn Curzon, 5th Earl Howe and associates to transform the hall and park into a motor racing track and country club (Chapter 10). This scheme failed due to lack of investors, and the empty hall and park remained with Lord Waring who still had about £42,000 owing on his mortgage.

In 1935, there was a glimmer of hope that Gopsall Hall might again be a family home, but not for the Waring family. When Edward Richard Assheton Penn Curzon, Viscount Curzon (later 6th Earl Howe), married Priscilla Weigall in July 1935, the couple had been given a choice of living at Penn House or at Gopsall Hall by the Howe Family Trustees.[17] They chose Penn, but not before they had travelled to view Gopsall and arranged for various garden ornaments to be removed to the Penn House gardens, where they remain today.

LEICESTERSHIRE.

In the Parishes of ODSTONE, NAILSTONE, BARTON-IN-THE-BEANS, TWYCROSS, SIBSON, ORTON-ON-THE-HILL, and NORTON-JUXTA-TWYCROSS

The Outlying Portions of the

GOPSALL HALL ESTATE,

Comprising:—

30 Excellent DAIRY, CORN, and REARING FARMS,

NUMEROUS SMALL HOLDINGS,

ACCOMMODATION LANDS,

134 COTTAGES,

ALLOTMENTS, LICENSED PREMISES,

VILLAGE STORES,

The Whole Extending to an area of about

5,600 ACRES,

Producing an Inadequate Rent Roll of Upwards of

£7,900 PER ANNUM,

Which

MESSRS MAY AND ROWDEN, have received instructions to SELL by AUCTION, in Lots, at the CORN EXCHANGE, LEICESTER on TUESDAY and WEDNESDAY, June 24 and 25, 1919, at Three o'clock.

Illustrated Particulars, Plans, and Conditions of Sale, may be obtained of Messrs JOHN B. and F. PURCHASE, Solicitors, 14 Regent Street, London, S.W.1.; or of the Auctioneers, 27, Maddox Street, W.1.

WARWICKSHIRE.

Adjoining Dunchurch Station (L. & N.W.R.), 3 Miles from Rugby, 12 from Leamington Spa, 14 from Warwick, 12 from Coventry.

IMPORTANT SALE OF THE OUTLYING PORTIONS OF THE

"DUNCHURCH ESTATE,"

Situate in the Parishes of Dunchurch, Thurlaston and Church Lawford (3 Miles from Rugby), extending to about

3,200 ACRES,

And Including:—

15 FIRST-CLASS FARMS,

3 GENTLEMEN'S FARMS & HUNTING BOXES,

SEVERAL SMALL HOLDINGS,

ACCOMMODATION LANDS, GARDENS,

ALLOTMENTS, BUILDING SITES, VILLAGE RESIDENCES, BUSINESS PREMISES, and the VILLAGE OF THURLASTON.

To be SOLD by AUCTION in NUMEROUS LOTS by

MESSRS MAY AND ROWDEN,

In conjunction with Messrs

JAMES STYLES AND WHITLOCK.

Under instructions from Sir Samuel J. Waring, Bart., at the CO-OPERATIVE HALL, RUGBY on MONDAY, June 2, 1919, at Two o'clock precisely.

For Illustrated Particulars, Plans, and Conditions of Sale, apply to Messrs JOHN B. and F. PURCHASE, Solicitors, 14, Regent Street, London, S.W.1; Messrs MAY & ROWDEN, Auctioneers, 27, Maddox Street, Regent Street, London, W.1; or Messrs JAMES STYLES & WHITLOCK, Estate Agents, Rugby.

Western Daily Press, Thurs 15th May 1919. The Dunchurch advert names Samuel Waring whereas the Gopsall sale is anonymous.
Reach Licensing

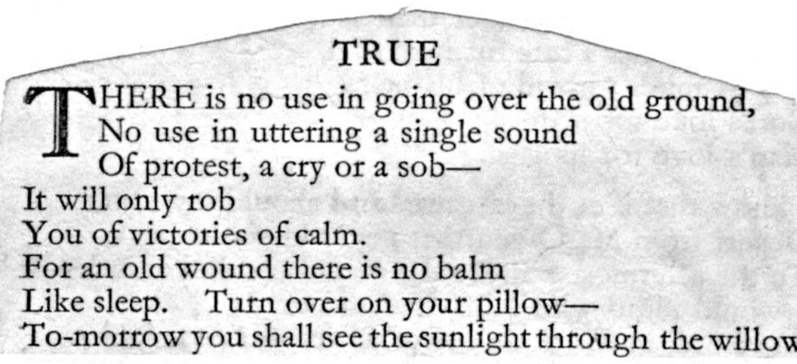
TRUE

THERE is no use in going over the old ground,
No use in uttering a single sound
Of protest, a cry or a sob—
It will only rob
You of victories of calm.
For an old wound there is no balm
Like sleep. Turn over on your pillow—
To-morrow you shall see the sunlight through the willow.

A cutting in the Howe family album surrounded by photos of Gopsall taken in October 1934, perhaps lamenting the decline of the hall and gardens.[13]

Thus, when Lord Waring died in January 1940, he was still in possession of Gopsall, with a mortgage debt. He left a gross estate of £138,943 18s 4d, with net personalty nil.[18-20] His property, which included Foots Cray Place in Kent and Gopsall (hall, park, Shornhill Farm and Norton Barn Farm), passed to his wife Eleanor, who died just over a year later in April 1941. The executors of Lady Waring's will sold the contents of Gopsall Hall by auction in London on 12th and 19th December 1941.[21] This auction included a billiard table and accessories by Cox and Yeman who were taken over by another billiard table manufacturer (Burroughes & Watts Ltd) in 1911,[22] suggesting that this table was the one originally sold in the 1918 sale of Gopsall furnishings by Earl Howe. The hall, park and the two associated farms were subsequently sold to Panton Investments Ltd in October 1942;[23] the hall and park were occupied by the army at this time (Chapter 11). The two Gopsall farms, Shornhill and Norton Barn, were purchased from Panton Investments Ltd by the Crown Estate Commissioners in December 1943 for £18,000.[24]

In October 1949, when there was still a small Royal Engineers' depot at Gopsall, 4cwt of lead was stolen from the disused NAAFI and cookhouse that stood within the walled kitchen gardens, but the hall was not affected.[25] The army vacated Gopsall by the end of 1949 and the hall was left empty and was said by many to be in a poor state of repair. In May 1950 a small amount of lead

Gopsall garden ornaments now at Penn House

The obelisk, together with the adjacent urns, believed to be by William Kent, was originally situated at Pope's Villa, in Twickenham and was erected by Alexander Pope in memory of his mother. The stone seat was where he used to sit and meditate. Lord Howe says: "*The reason why these items found their way to Gopsall is that in 1807, my predecessor, Baroness (Sophia) Howe (1762-1835), eldest daughter of Admiral of the Fleet, Earl Howe, purchased Pope's Villa, which she proceeded to demolish, replacing it with an amalgam of buildings, including some in Strawberry Hill Gothic style. This act of vandalism caused a public outcry, but there was little to be done once the destruction had occurred. Exactly when the obelisk was removed to Gopsall is uncertain, but I have always assumed that it would have been in the mid-1830s, immediately after Baroness Howe's death, when the sale of the Villa took place*". Images courtesy of Lord Howe.

At one time the recumbent lions were positioned either side of the east front garden entrance. The two lead putto (*top, middle and right*) and four sculptured putti were displayed in the gardens.

was stolen from the hall by an ex-soldier who had been billeted at Gopsall during the war and later, in November, the flat roof of the carriage porch was completely stripped of lead.[26,27] This latter lead theft occurred the night after the hall had been surveyed by the Society for the Protection of Ancient Buildings, with a view to considering the preservation of the building; the survey report concluded that the structure of the building was sound and that a few relatively minor repairs would render it weatherproof for many years.[28] While the theft of the carriage porch lead may not have meant the end for Gopsall Hall, its coup de grâce was surely the theft of a large area of lead from the main hall roofs over the weekend of the 16th and 17th December 1950.[29]

At this time, Panton Investments Ltd was going bankrupt and it was their liquidators who officially sealed the fate of Gopsall Hall by selling the building to a demolition company; Thomas Oakley (Luton) Ltd. Oakley's demolition team started demolishing the hall as soon as the 3-week period allowed to purchasers of fixtures and fittings in the 31st May 1951 auction to remove their items from the hall had ended.

On 11th July 1951, six weeks after the hall fixtures and fittings sale in May, the Crown Commissioners purchased Gopsall Park (including the gardens and hall site) from the liquidators of Panton Investments Ltd.[30] This was just eight days before the first sale of building materials recovered from the first weeks of demolition.

South front of Gopsall Hall in early 1951. The windows are intact but ivy is climbing the library walls and the terrace and gardens are overgrown.

If you had taken an illicit walk through Gopsall Park in early July 1951, you would have found the hall near to dereliction; great baulks of wood holding up sections of the walls, gaping holes in the roof, ceilings inside propped up against collapse. Closer inspection would have shown the scarring from a series of small fires that had taken place. Around the hall, the once manicured lawns and borders were overgrown with weeds, and the gardens, effectively destroyed by the army occupation in WWII, now only had the ancient *Wellingtonia* and cedar trees left intact. Nissen hut foundations littered the area, including within the once productive walled gardens where skeletal outlines on the lime-washed brick walls provided the only indication of where glasshouses used to stand. However, there was some order in this chaos. Neat piles and stacks of components of the

Ladders in place on the clock tower to allow the 'official' removal of the lead roof and gutters; the clockface has already been removed.

The carriage porch with damaged ceiling after the theft of the roof lead. One of the 3 upper windows in the double storey entrance hall can be seen (*arrow*), its top half being false.

hall fixtures and structure were placed around the hall, especially on the north front: 100 pine-panelled doors; 100 glazed sashes; 25 wash basins; 10,000ft each of rafters, oak joists, cast iron pipe, heavy oak and pine beams, and floorboards; 9,000 blue Welsh slates and many other lots of useful building materials. These were all stacked and ready for the first building materials sale by Perry & Phillips Ltd on Thursday, 19th July.[31]

Such was the size and toughness of the hall's structure that in the 2nd or 3rd week of August the demolition contractors turned to explosives to hasten their task. Some reports suggested that the gelignite had destroyed the hall, saying that *"Gopsall had been stripped of every saleable treasure before it was blasted off the sky-line"*.[32] However, the reality was not quite so final: *"When the rumble of destruction died down the old house, if not unscathed, was only scarred"*.[33] It was power rams and clawed grabs that finally flattened the hall and amongst the rubble, the 2nd and final building materials sale was held on

Demolition of the northwest parts of the two west service wings. The clock tower still stands but the rest of the wing, including the steward's room has been flattened. The far west service wing containing the laundry, ironing room, bakery and servants' bedrooms still stands, without a roof or windows. 'Building materials' are laid out in piles on what used to be the north lawns.

Top: The north front of the hall with two contractors' vehicles parked by the carriage porch. Most of the windows and doors have been removed, as has the roof of the northeast (red drawing room) wing. Note the white, false top halves of the two upper entrance hall windows that are to the left of the carriage porch.

Middle: The south front of the hall showing the fountain and portico. Many windows and doors have been removed and wood beams and floorboards are stacked on the terrace.

Bottom: The view southeast towards Congerstone showing the fountain in the overgrown south gardens.

Kennel Cottages, Gopsall, Atherstone (July 2020). These cottages stand on the site shown as The Kennels on old OS maps. Whether they retain any of the original 19th century structures is unknown. Both cottages were refurbished by the Crown in 1999.

Thursday 6th September 1951.[34] Once again, staggering amounts of materials were up for auction including 10,000ft each of heavy oak and pine beams, oak joists, rafters, matching, and floor boards; 7,000 blue Welsh slates; washbasins; cisterns; glazed sash windows and other lots. The contractors filled *"a cavity in the grounds"* and the cellars with rubble and invited anyone wanting rubble to come to the site site with their lorry.[33,34] The rubble was free and the demolition company was pleased to use its own equipment and men to load all comers.

Because debris from the final destruction of the hall was freely available, it is likely that rubble from Gopsall now forms the base for many farm tracks, buildings and houses in the area. Incredibly, even as recently as last year (2020), reclaimed 'Gopsall bricks' were used to renovate number 2 Kennel Cottages, Gopsall, Atherstone. Unfortunately, where most of the fixtures, fittings and building materials from the demolition sales went is unknown, but a few items have been located and some stories as to other locations have been passed down by word of mouth or, in the case of Mr Cudmore of Fleckney, by letter.

Mr J.E. Cudmore wrote to Lynn Stoney in 1997 about his recollections of the demolition of Gopsall Hall and the small part he played in it.[35] He also enclosed 4 large photos of the hall during demolition, which are reproduced on the previous 2 pages. Mr Cudmore wrote:

> *"In 1951 I worked for W.E. Sturgess and Sons the well known Leicester garage firm, who at that time had a garage in Braunstone Gate Leicester.*
>
> *One morning I was told by my boss the late Frank Sturgess, to go with a mechanic George Pollard, in the firm's old Commer lorry, to Gopsall Hall, to lift and transport to his house at Hoby, the entrance hall floor which he had purchased from the demolition contractors.*

> *We arrived at Gopsall Hall and were shown the floor we were to remove, and told not to wander about, as they were blowing up the stable block, that day. The floor consisted of stone slabs about 2 feet square, with the corner cut off and a small piece of slate about 4 inches square set in where the corners of the slabs met. I think the slabs were Portland stone but I am not sure about this. The corner pieces were polished slate about 4 inches square.*[35]
>
> *They weighed about 1 cwt each and we found we could get 50 slabs on the lorry. On the first day we managed two loads from Gopsall to Hoby, the next day we took one load from Gopsall but on our way with the second load the lorry broke down, and we only just managed to get it going and limp back to the garage in Leicester. Next morning we got the lorry going again and delivered another load to Hoby. After returning to Gopsall and loading for a second time, the lorry decided that it had had enough and refused to start."*

Mr Cudmore goes on to say that when they looked round the lorry after it was towed back to the garage they discovered that the maximum load was 30 cwt and he had been carrying 50 cwt, nearly twice the suggested load. His boss had to employ a removal firm to transport the rest of the entrance hall floor to his home, where he eventually had it installed.

Local stories claim lots of crockery from Gopsall Hall were unceremoniously dumped into the Lake (the Fish Pond) at the end of Shackerstone Drive, presumably because it had not sold. Several villagers remember, as chidren, finding and smashing crockery in the lake, supporting the stories.

Two of the most accessible remnants of Gopsall that can be seen today are the cenotaph, commissioned by Charles Jennens and dedicated to his friend Edward Holdsworth, and the Bilstone lodge gates. The listed grade II* cenotaph by Richard Haywood, Lot 367 in the fixtures and fittings sale, was purchased for £18 and can now be viewed in the gardens of Belgrave Hall, Leicester. Close by in the east gardens stands the statue of Religion carved by Roubilliac (grade II*), which once stood on top of the temple containing the cenotaph at the edge of Race Course wood at Gopsall (Chapter 4). The set of 4 gates and 4 piers forming the Bilstone entrance to Gopsall Park can be seen in the centre of Market Harborough, where they make an imposing approach to the garden of remembrance.

Left: Holdsworth cenotaph (Haywood, 1764) with a relief of a ruined pyramid thought to represent Virgil's tomb.
Centre: Bust of Virgil (left side panel; *top*) and a mourning winged Genius leaning on a reversed torch (rear panel).
Right: Statue of Religion by Roubilliac (c.1760), a gift from Richard William Penn Curzon, 1st Earl Howe to Leicestershire Museums and Art Galleries in 1857.

Left: Blue-painted wrought iron gates to the garden of remembrance in Market Harborough, opened in 1954. The two central cast iron piers bear bronze plaques commemorating the fallen of WWII. Market Harborough Council decided to buy the gates in November 1951,[36] suggesting that they were originally purchased by an unknown dealer.

Right: The gates in their original position at the Bilstone entrance to Gopsall Park (Lot 378 in the fixtures and fittings sale in May 1951).

Perhaps the most surprising thing about the sale of fixtures and fittings is the absence of any items from the cedar chapel, notably the organ, eagle pulpit and the pews (Chapter 3). However, on the 20th July 1951 several newspapers reported that the chapel organ was to be rebuilt by F.W. Burns & Son of Lutterworth Road, Attleborough before being installed in Attleborough Baptist Church (The Green, Attleborough) at a cost of between £1,200 and £1,300.[37-39] John Burns, 'the Son', still has the workshop in Attleborough Road where he repairs and rebuilds pipe organs. In October 2020, aged 88, John was busy 'electrifying' an organ from a Roman Catholic church while talking about the Gopsall chapel organ.

John Burns in his workshop in Lutterworth Road, Attleborough.

"The organ was built by William Hill & Sons who merged with Norman & Beard in 1916. When the organ was removed from the chapel in 1951, the cedar case was riddled with woodworm but the inside of the instrument was in reasonable working order. It was elecrically pumped, a WWII conversion, but was originally hand pumped. The organ was installed up against the chapel wall meaning that it was impossible to get to the swell soundboard, which would normally be accesssed from the rear. Tuning of the swell was difficult because it had to be done via the grate."

In Attleborough Baptist Church, the organ was installed free-standing with a new wooden case, new manuals (keyboards), a new 4ft stop to the great organ and easy access for maintenance and tuning via rear doors. As first installed the pedal board was concave and straight, but it was changed to a radiating concave configuration in the 1960s by F.W. Burns & Son. The arrangement of the pipes at Attleborough is very different from that of the organ as installed in Gopsall chapel, and today it is unrecognisable as the instrument originally at Gopsall Hall (see Chapter 3). This difference in appearance is more pronounced because the pipes have been painted matt grey.

The 5 rows of pews that were present on the east side of Gopsall chapel were installed in St Mary's Church, Sandwich in 1956;[40] the year proposals for its demolition were put forward. However, for architectural and historic reasons the church was restored and is now run by the Churches Conservation Trust.

The whereabouts of the other pews and the ornate 'eagle pulpit' designed by the Hiorns brothers for Charles Jennens are unknown (Chapter 2).

Above: Gopsall chapel organ in Attleborough Baptist Church with matt grey pipes and F.W. Burns & Son name plate. The original ornate organ pipes are shown for comparison.
Right: The chapel pews in St Mary's Church, Sandwich.

The organ designed by Handel for Jennens in St James' Church, Great Packington.

For many years there has been confusion about the Gopsall chapel organ, installed in 1901, and the organ, designed by Handel and built in 1749-1750 by Thomas Parker.[41] Parker was trained by Richard Bridge and graffiti on the rear of the great key slip confirms Parker as builder.[42] The 'Handel organ' was installed in the music room at Gopsall;[43] a room known as the red drawing room in the late 19th and early 20th century. Following the death of Charles Jennens in 1773 the organ was moved to Packington Hall by his cousin (the Earl of Aylesford), to whom he had bequeathed his music books and instruments. It was originally installed in a new music room, but in 1792 the organ was transferred to St James' Church in the grounds of Packington Hall, where it can be found today.

At the same time that the chapel organ was removed in 1951, an Aeolian organ, used for entertainment by the soldiers stationed at Gopsall during WWII (Chapter 11), was also removed from the 'ballroom' (the library) and sold to the UK agents for Aeolian (Davies & Sons of Northampton). This organ had originally been installed in the salon in 1901 but was moved into the library sometime before 1941. The organ was put into a beautiful, old wooden case and the manual replaced before it was sold to Mancetter church by Davies & Son. The instrument was eventually scrapped after about 15 years at Mancetter.[44,45]

Nothing existed of Gopsall Hall above ground since its demolition in 1951 until recently, when the current owner of Gopsall Hall Farm excavated the cellars in 2020. Now the seven wine cellars and the underground passageways are above ground revealing the excellent workmanship of the builders (Chapter 2).

Notes and References

1 *A hammer will rap the knell of fantastic Gopsall Hall*. Leicester Evening Mail, Wednesday 30th May 1951.

2 *England's Lost Houses: From the Archives of the Country Life*. Giles Worsley. London: Aurum Press, 2002.

3 *Complete list of lost English country houses*. Information compiled by Matthew Beckett. Accessed 8th March 2021: http://www.lostheritage.org.uk/lh_complete_list.html.

4 *Our Uninvited Guests*. Julie Summers. London: Simon & Schuster, 2018.

5 *The Gopsall Estate*. Coventry Herald, Saturday 3rd August 1918.

6 *Earl Howe's Estate. Reported sale of Gopsall and Gotham Estates*. Leicester Journal, Friday 9th August 1918.

7 *Gotham Estate Sold for £41,860*. Nottingham Evening Post, Thursday 1st August 1918.

8 *Gopsall Leicestershire. Catalogue of the Fine Antique and Modern Furniture in the Mansion*. Messrs. Trollope. The Record Office for Leicestershire, Leicester and Rutland. File Ref: L333 (LSP 7 - G).

List of items auctioned in October 1918: Fenders, implements, curtains, Persian, Indian, Turkey and pile carpets and rugs, bedsteads and bedding, including a Prince Charles State bedstead with the Stuart Tartan silk drapery, sets of couches, settees, easy lounge and standard chairs, writing tables, screens, torchieres, side tables, cabinets, secretaires, commodes, sideboards, wardrobes, court cupboards, buffet, armoires and mirrors in very choice carved frames, collection of pictures, English, Dutch, etc. schools by eminent old masters, including a series relating to the Pretender Period, engravings, prints and drawings, grandfather, mantel and bracket clocks in choice cases, a few ornaments, the extensive library of books, billiard table & accessories by Cox & Yeman, the usual furnishings of the bedchambers and domestic apartments, garden vases, summer house, a station bus, a wagonette and a Brougham, harness, a manual fire engine and appliances.

9 *Gopsall Hall Sale*. Coventry Herald, Saturday 26th October 1918.

According to the Midland Counties Tribune (Friday 10th November 1918) "*The sale at Gopsall Hall last week brought down from London a crowd of dealers in antique furniture, china and old books. The hall has now been stripped of the rare articles which made it famous, and which used to excite the admiration of King Edward and other famous visitors. The old books, however, were mostly bought by Mr Sam Waring, the new owner of the place, and the dealers in ancient pages did not get much for their trouble*."

10 *Gopsall Hall Sale*. Leicester Journal, Friday 25th October 1918.

11 *Gopsall sale*. Uxbridge & W. Drayton Gazette, Friday 1st November 1918.

12 *Messrs. Trollope & Sons advert*. Yorkshire Post and Leeds Intelligence, Tuesday 29th June 1920.

13 Courtesy of The Rt Hon Frederick Richard Penn Curzon, 7th Earl Howe, GBE, PC.

14 *£126,500 Property Sale. Dunchurch Farms*. Coventry Evening Telegraph, Friday 7th June 1918.

15 *Abstract of Title detailing Indenture dated 13th August 1919 between the Earl and Countess Howe Trustees and Samuel Waring*. The National Archives. Doc. Ref: CRES38/1002.

16 *Gopsall Estate to be Sold. No Injunction for Lord Waring*. Leicester Mercury, Friday 11th December 1931.

17 Personal communication - The Rt Hon Frederick Richard Penn Curzon, 7th Earl Howe, GBE, PC.

18 In England, personalty (personal estate, chattels or choses) includes all the investments and belongings of a person except for freehold land and buildings.

https://www.gov.uk/hmrc-internal-manuals/trusts-settlements-and-estates-manual/tsem6015 & 6016 accessed 10th March 2021.

https://cilexlawschool.ac.uk/wp-content/uploads/2018/10/HQ09-Land-Law-Sample-2018.pdf accessed 10th March 2021.

19 *Index of wills and administrations*. https://probatesearch.service.gov.uk/#calendar accessed 12th March 2021. Probates do not show joint property passing by survivorship or settled property. It is likely that Gopsall and Foots Cray Place were either in joint ownership, with the properties passing to Lady Waring by survivorship, or held in a trust with Lady Waring as beneficiary.

20 *Latest Wills*. Lord Waring's Estate: Net Personalty Nil. Birmingham Daily Post, Saturday 22nd June 1940.

21 *Removed from Gopsall Hall*. Birmingham Daily Post, Saturday 6th December 1941.

22 The Billiard Monthly, January 1912, p. 8.

23 *Conveyance dated 2nd October 1942*. National Archives. File Ref: CRES38/1002.

24 *Panton Investments Ltd. Crown 1943, Dec. 1 Gopsall: conveyance of Shornhill and Norton Barn Farms*. The National Archives. Doc. Ref: CRES 38/998.

25 *Stole lead at Gopsall Park: Four men fined*. Leicester Evening Mail, Friday 4th November 1949.

26 *Stole lead from his old billet*. Leicester Evening Mail, Thursday 25th May 1950.

27 *Gopsall Hall Stripped of £500 Lead*. Leicester Daily Mercury, Friday 24th November 1950.

28 *News & Notes: Departed Glory and Now Vulnerable*. Leicester Daily Mercury, Saturday 2nd December 1950.

29 *Gopsall Hall again raided for lead*. Leicester Evening Mail, Monday 18th December 1950.

30 *Panton Investments Ltd. Crown 1951, July 11 Gopsall: conveyance of Gopsall Park*. The National Archives. Doc. Ref: CRES 38/1002.

31 *Gopsall Hall building materials sale*. Coventry Evening Telegraph, Saturday 14th July 1951.

32 *No gelignite charge for Shenton Manor*. Leicester Evening Mail, Thursday 30th August 1951.

33 *Wreckers attack on Gopsall Hall nears end*. Leicester Evening Mail, Friday 7th September 1951.

34 *Second building materials sale*. Coventry Evening Telegraph, Thursday 23rd August 1951.

35 *Reminiscences in letters of Mr. J.E. Cudmore of the demolition of Gopsall Hall - including photo. negatives - see DE8131 - in 1951*. The Record Office for Leicestershire, Leicester and Rutland. File Ref: DE10125/5). According to John Grundy (1750), the floor slabs were Ketton stone (limestone) with black marble inserts. See Appendix I, Chapter 2. The freehand drawing of the slabs was included in Mr Cudmore's letter.

36 *Gopsall Hall gates for Harborough*. Leicester Evening Mail, Wednesday 28th November 1951.

37 *Gopsall Hall organ for Attleborough Baptists Church*. Midlands Counties Tribune, Friday 20th July 1951.

38 *'Messiah' organ for Baptists*. Coventry Evening Telegraph, Friday 20th July 1951.

39 *An original idea in money collecting*. Midlands Counties Tribune, Friday 7th December 1951.

40 *Historic England listing of St Mary's Church, Sandwich, Kent*. https://historicengland.org.uk/listing/the-list/list-entry/1069541 accessed 20th March 2021.

41 *The Chamber Organ in Britain, 1600–1830*. Michael Wilson. 2nd Ed. Routledge, 2016.

42 *History of 1749 Thomas Parker, Gopsall Hall*. The National Pipe Organ Register (NPOR) V2.19.1. Accessed 20th March 2021: https://www.npor.org.uk/NPORView.html?RI=E00968

43 1750 description of Gopsall Hall by John Grundy. See Appendix I, Chapter 2.

44 Personal Communication. John Burns, October 2020.

45 *Gopsall Hall - House Organ*. The National Pipe Organ Register (NPOR) V2.19.1. Accessed 20th March 2021: https://www.npor.org.uk/NPORView.html?RI=E00970.

Newspaper adverts were downloaded from www.britishnewspaperarchive.co.uk and reproduced courtesy of Reach Licensing / Mirrorpix.com.

APPENDIX
Prints, engravings and pictures at Gopsall Hall

The lots are listed as in the original catalogues (without lot numbers) and in the December 1918 Assheton House schedule. The list clearly indicates the quantity and quality of the artwork on display in the hall during the early 20th century.

1918 SALE

THE PRINTS, ENGRAVINGS, etc.

Two antique Prints, "Italian Ruins," etc.

Twenty-two similar lots

Four prints, "Allegorical Subjects"

Three ditto

A series of 5 old coloured prints, "Views in the County of Leicestershire"

Two similar lots

A pair of aquatint drawings, "Landscapes & Buildings"

A similar lot

A pair, by W. Geller, after W.P. Parker," Looking Out "and "Looking In"

"Deed Hounds" by Alfred Lucas, after J. Bateman

A pair, "Picking out the Lambs" and "Going to Market," by C.G. Lewis, after R. Ansdell

"A Distinguished Member of the Royal Humane Society," by Thomas Landseer, after Sir E. Landseer, R.A., in a carved frame

Three, portraits, "Lord Radstock," "Marquis of Downshire" and "A French Prince

"Four portraits

A similar lot

"Sir Isaac Newton," a mezzotint, by James Macardel, after Enoch Sieman, 1760

"The Right Hon. William Pitt," by F. Bartolozzi, R.A., after T. Gainsborough, R.A.

Two, "Lord Raglan" and "Henry Liddell, Esq"

"The Chase" - an eventide landscape

A Set of 4, Modern Love - "Courtship," "The Elopement," "The Honeymoon" and "Discordant Matrimony," by J. Goldar, after J. Collett, 1766

"A Gipsy Encampment," a mezzotint, in colours

"Grouse Shooting," an artist proof etching, by T.G. Appleton, after A. Stuart Wortly

A set of 4, "Rent Day," "Blind Man's Buff," "Village Politicians" and "The Blind Fiddler" by A. Raimbach, after Sir David Wilkie, R.A.

"Mrs. Flora Macdonald, 1747," a mezzotint, by J. Faber, after T.Hudson

"Charles I and Attendant," in colours, by J. Sympson, after Sir A. Vandyke

"Blenheim Palace," a large engraving

"Dr. Kirkland," a mezzotint, in colours, by J.R. Smith

"H.R.H. George, Prince of Wales," a mezzotint, by J.R. Smith, after T. Gainsborough

THE WATER COLOUR DRAWINGS & PASTELS

"Hunting Scene"

"A Cascade, Fisher Folk in the centre"

"A Landscape with Cattle at a Ferry"

A half-length portrait of a gentleman, wearing wig, a pastel, by Saxton

A port scene, "Building, Ship & Boat"

A bust of a gentleman, black coat, lace collar, Stuart period, in pastel, (19-in. by 13 1/2-in)

"Mountain, Stream, Bridge & Figures," by Paul Sandby

THE PICTURES

W. Aikman, l682-l73l.
A 3/4 length portrait of "The Honorable Mrs Page" in fancy costume
(Canvas 49 1/2 by 39 1/2-in.)

Francis Barlow.
"A Hawk with Prey, on Tree Stump"
(Canvas 30 by 22-in.)

Sir Geo. Beaumont.
A sketch, "A Landscape at Coleorton"
(Panel 6 3/4 by 5 1/2-in.)

Both & Bergheim.
A large " 'Woody Landscape," muleteers, 3 mules & a dog to the left, a stream to the right
(Canvas 36 by 36-in.)

Bogdané.
Swans, heron, pheasants & water fowls, lake & temple background (Canvas 79 by 49-in.)

Bogdané.
Peacock, turkeys, & ruins (Canvas 79 by 49-in.)

A. Canaletti. l697-l768.
"A Canal Scene," numerous boats & buildings
(Canvas 39 by 25-in.)

A. Canaletti.
"A Venetian Scene" (Canvas 64 by 36-in.)

A. Canaletti.
" A Venetian Scene" (Canvas 64 by 36-in.)

Coéssin (Signed and dated 1863).
"A Group of Arabs attack upon a Lion"
(Canvas 100 by 60-in.)

D. Costa (signed and dated 1888)
Dead Game a hunting horn and gun hanging to the top of trophy (Canvas 80 by 50-in.)

R. Croos (signed and dated 1635.)
A Dutch Landscape, two figures seated to the left (Panel 23 1/2 by 13 1/2 in.)

A. Cuyp, l606-1672.
Interior of a Stable, two horses, a man, a boy and three fowls (Panel 15 by 10 1/2 -in.)

John De Heem, l693.
"Still Life", (Panel 33 by 25-in.)

De Vuigers.
A Sea piece, a quay on the right, ships & boat to the centre (Canvas 21 by 14-in.)

A. Diegt.
A Coast Scene, mountain and tall buildings to the right figures and boats in foreground
(Canvas 40 1/2 by l5-in.)

A. Diegt.
River & Hilly Landscape, ruins to the centre
(Canvas 40 1/2 by 15-in)

Domenichino, 1581-1641.
A bust portrait of an aged man wearing grey hair and long beard (Canvas 24 by l9 1/2 -in)

Jean Faust.
"A Japanese Beauty" (Canvas 35 1/2 by 23-in)

Alfred Grey, R.H.A., 1879.
"Highland Cattle" (Canvas 86 by 60-in.)

Alfred Grey, R.H.A., 1879.
"Highland Cattle" (Canvas 86 by 60-in.)

J. Griffier, 1645-1718.
A small Landscape, trees, cart & figures in foreground (Canvas 7 by 5-in.)

J. Griffier.
A Landscape, equestrian figures and trees in foreground (Panel 7 1/2 by 5-in.)

J. Griffier.
A distant open Landscape, river to centre, figures in foreground (Panel 12 by 9 1/2-in.)

F. Haymen.
"David Garrick as Richard III."
(Canvas 35 by 27 1/2-in.)

M. Hondecoeter 1636-1695.
Geese, ducks, doves, water fowl, lilies, etc.
(Canvas 72 by 92-in.)

M. Hondecoeter 1636-1695.
Duck, water fowl, etc in a landscape
(Canvas 30 by 24-in.)

M. Hondecoeter 1636-1695.
A white fox and a dead cockerel in a landscape
(Canvas 32 1/2 by 38-in.)

M. Hondecoeter 1636-1695.
Chickens & pigeons (Canvas 47 1/2 by 27-in.)

M. Hondecoeter 1636-1695.
Six chicks (Panel 12 3/4 by 10 1/4-in.)

C. Huysman, 1648-1727.
A Rocky Landscape, with cattle and figures
(Canvas 14 3/4 by 12 3/4-in.)

J. Van Kessel, l626-l670.
A Woody Landscape, figures, trees and river in foreground (Canvas 36 by 28-in.)

Sir Godfrey Kneller l648-l723.
A life-size whole-length portrait of a Queen, seated, wearing blue dress, ermine trimmed cloak, crown and sceptre on a table to her left
(Canvas 90 by 56-in.)

Sir Godfrey Kneller 1648-1723.
"H.M. King Charles II," life-size, seated portrait, a crown, orb and sceptre resting on table to his right (Canvas 87 by 55-in.)

Sir Godfrey Kneller, 1648-1723.
"H.M. King]ames II" life-size standing portrait
(Canvas 90 by 56-in.)

Sir Godfrey Kneller, 1648-1723.
A life-size whole-length portrait of a Queen in blue dress, ermine trimmed blue cloak, a crown, orb and sceptre resting on a table to her left
(Canvas 90 by 56-in.)

Sir Godfrey Kneller, 1648-1723.
A King in full dress, whole length standing portrait, sceptre in left hand, resting on a table on which is the crown (Canvas 91 by 57-in.)

Sir Godfrey Kneller, 1648-1723.
A Queen, whole-length, standing portrait her righthand extended resting upon her crown .
(Canvas 91 by 57-in.)

Sir Godfrey Kneller, 1648-1723.
A half-length portrait of a gentleman wearing wig, brown dress and lace cravat
(Oval canvas 36 by 30-in.)

Sir Godfrey Kneller, l648-l723.
A life-size portrait of a young Nobleman, to the knees, to the right, facing spectator, wearing wig, brown coat, blue cloth, his right hand in vest (Canvas 47 by 53-in.)

Sir Godfrey Kneller, 1648-1723.
A life-size 3/4-length portrait of a young lady, seated, facing spectator, a pet: lamb by her side
(Canvas 47 by 53-in.)

Sir Godfrey Knéller, l648-l723.
A 3/4-length portrait of a gentleman, seated, wearing green coat, wig, linen vest, drapery and landscape background (Canvas 63 by 49-in.)

Sir Godfrey Kneller, l648-1723.
A 3/4-length portrait of a lady, slightly to the

left, facing spectator, wearing light dress, open low and blue sash, her left hand raised to her breast (Canvas 49 by 37-in.)

Sir Godfrey Kneller, 1648-1723.

A 3/4-length portrait of a gentleman, to the right wearing wig and red coat (Canvas 49 by 37-in.)

Sir Godfrey Kneller, (signed and dated 1683).

A life-size 3/4-length portrait of a lady, seated, nursing her pet dog (Canvas 49 by 40-in.)

Sir Godfrey Kneller (signed 1722).

A 1/2-length portrait of a young man, wearing powdered wig

Sir Godfrey Kneller, 1648-l723.

A 3/4-length portrait of a Queen, wearing ermine cloak, a crown resting upon a table to her right (Canvas 48 by 38-in.)

Sir Godfrey Kneller, l648-l723.

A 1/2-length portrait of a gentleman, wearing velvet coat and vest (Canvas 29 1/2 by 24-in.)

Sir Godfrey Kneller, 1648-1723.

A 1/2-length portrait of a gentleman wearing wig and light coat and vest, within an oval (Canvas 29 1/2 by 24-in.)

Sir Godfrey Kneller, l648-l723.

A family group, lady, gentleman and 6 children- A Gallery picture (Canvas 132 by 90-in.)

Sir Godfrey Kneller School.

A 1/2-length portrait of a gentleman wearing olive green coat, embroidered waistcoat and wig (Canvas 28 1/2 by 23 1/2-in.)

Claude Lorraine, l600-l682.

A wide Landscape, figures dancing in the foreground (Canvas 44 by 36-in.)

Claude Lorraine, l600-l682.

A Landscape, with two figures and cattle, in the foreground A Bull (Canvas 52 by 37-in.)

J. Loweck, 1656.

A Bull (Panel 29 by 19-in.)

Le Duc.

An Interior, Corps du Garde groups playing cards on drumhead and smoking (Panel 16 by 12-in.)

Sir P. Lely, l6l7-l680.

A 1/2-length portrait of a nobleman wearing wig and Order of the Bath (Canvas 30 by 24-in)

Sir P. Lely, l617-l680.

A 1/2-length portrait of a nobleman wearing wig, armour and lace cravat (Canvas 30 by 24-in.)

Sir P. Lely, l6l7-l680.

A 3/4-length portrait of a nobleman wearing long curling wig, lace cravat, armour, hilt of sword to the left hand; sea and ships to the left (Canvas 50 by 42-in.)

Sir P. Lely, l617-l680.

A life-size 3/4-length portrait of a nobleman wearing long curling wig, brown coat, armour, sword in left hand, staff in right hand, a battle in background (Canvas 50 by 42-in.)

Sir P. Lely, 1617-1680.

A 3/4-length portrait of a lady, seated, wearing green dress, crimson shawl, pearl necklet and earrings, holding flowers in her right hand, landscape and drapery background (Canvas 53 by 49-in.)

Sir P. Lely, l6l7-l680.

A life-size 3/4-length portrait of a gentleman, wearing long curling wig, brown cloak, lawn sleeves, landscape background (Canvas 53 by 49-in.)

Sir P. Lely, l6l7-l680.

A life-size 3/4-length portrait of a gentleman, seated, wearing wig, brown cloak, lawn sleeves, lace cravat (Canvas 49 by 40 1/2-in.)

Sir P. Lely, 1617-1680.

A small 3/4-length portrait of a Butler, wearing a loose gown and wig . (Panel 13 1/2 by 10-in.)

Sir Peter Lely (signed), l617-l680.

A life size 3/4-length portrait of a gentleman, seated, wearing brown dress, white cravat and light curling hair, landscape to the left . (Canvas 46 by 38-in.)

Sir P Lely School.

A 1/2-length portrait of a young lady wearing grey and blue evening dress (within an oval) (Canvas 29 1/2 by 23 1/2-in.)

Sir P. Lely School.

A 1/2-length portrait of a lady wearing evening dress and pink shawl (within an oval) (Canvas 29 1/2 by 23 1/2-in.)

Sir P. Lely School.

A1/2-length portrait of a lady, wearing blue dress, open very low (within an oval) (Canvas 29 1/2 by 24-in.)

Sir P. Lely School.

A -1/2-length portrait of a lady, wearing white low dress, red and blue shawl and jewelled ornaments (Oval canvas 29 by 24-in.)

Sir P. Lely School.

A 1/2-length portrait of a lady, facing spectator, wearing white low-neck dress, embroidered blue shawl and pearl ornaments (Oval canvas 29 by 23 1/2- in.)

Sir P. Lely School.

A 1/2-length portrait of a gentleman, wearing olive green satin coat, linen collar and cuffs, shawl over left shoulder (Canvas 30 by 24-in. in a carved, frame.)

Sir Peter Lely School.

A 1/2-length portrait of a lady wearing evening dress, pearl necklet and earrings (Canvas 29 1/2 by 24-in.)

Ester Van Marc.

A Battle Scene, castle on a hill, to the right (Canvas 32 by 22 1/2-in.)

Este Van Marc.

Battle Scene, numerous equestrians in foreground, castle to the left (Canvas 48 1/2 by 26 1/2-in.)

Este Van Marc.

A Battle Scene, a city and lake in background (Canvas 52 by 24-in.)

Este Van Marc.

Battle Subject, combatants and tower to centre (Canvas 40 by 29-in.)

Jan Meol.

Two figures seated on a terrace (Canvas 13 3/4 by 10 3/4-in.)

A. Frans Vander Meulen, 1667.

A Battle Subject, equestrian and foot soldiers at close quarters (Canvas 22 1/2 by 32-in.)

P. Neefs & D. Teniers.

An Interior of a Cathedral, with Procession in foreground (Panel 24 1/2 by 19 1/2-in.)

P. Pannini, 1691-1758.

"The Coliseum" (Canvas 28 by 17-in.)

Patel, 1648-1703.

A Landscape, building, trees and figures to the right, mountain background (Canvas 16 by 11 1/2-in.)

G. Peters.

"A Dutch Winter Scene," an old mill, boats, and numerous figures (Panel 22 by 13-in.)

C. Poelemberg.

"The Salutation of The Virgin," Angels all around (Panel 19 1/2 by 17-in.)

Rembrandt School.

"Jobit Curing his Father's Eye" (Canvas 47 1/2 by 42-in.)

[Sold for 1000gns; Jobit, misprint for Tobit]

S. Riccl.

Ruins and figures (Canvas 14 3/4 by 11 3/4-in.)

Ribera, G.

A 1/2-length portrait of an aged man with grey hair and beard holding a statuette (Canvas 30 by 24-in.)

Rombus.

A bust portrait of aman, to the right wearing lace ruffle (Canvas 18 by 14-in.)

P.P.Rubens.

A view in an old Dutch town. a stream and bridge to the centre. (Canvas 14 by 10-in.)

J.Ruysdael, 1630-1681.

Hilly and wooded landscape, wagon, figures and sheep in foreground (Canvas 24 1/2 by 20 3/4-in.)

J Ruysdael 1630-1681.

Landscape with stream, cattle, shepherd and dog. (Canvas 24 3/4 by 19 1/4-in.)

["Stream in a wooded mountain landscape" - see image earlier in this chapter]

"*Tobias curing his father Tobit's blindness*" (c.1650) sold in 1918 for 1000gns with the 'Rembrandt School' attribution. The painting is now in the Museum Catharijneconvent, Utrecht and currently attributed to Gerrit Willemsz Horst (1612-1652), a student of Rembrandt during the years 1635-1640.

J. Ruysdael 1660-1681.

A rocky landscape, a man fishing from a burn (Canvas 30 by 20 3/4-in.)

School of Ruysdael.

"Ships in Storm" (Panel 19 by 16-in.)

Salvator Rosa

A woody landscape, figure in foreground. (Canvas 54 by 40-in.)

F.Sartorius.

A Horse in a landscape buildings and river to the right (Canvas 46 by 40-in.)

F.Sartorius.

A lady and gentleman on horseback, a groom standing holding a hare, two dogs and a horse at side. (Canvas 48 by 38-in.)

F. Sartorius (signed).

A Landscape with a pointer, a groom, 2 horses and a gentleman with gun and dog (Canvas 44 by 35-in.)

F. Sartorius.

"Hyale Beating Aniseed, at York, 1801" (Canvas 23 by 17-in.)

F. Sartorius.

"Two Racehorses Exercising" (Canvas 31 by 22-in.)

P. G. Syamaar.

An Interior with numerous figures seated around a table, on which rests a lighted candle (Panel 19 1/2 by 14.1/2-in.)

Stuart Period.

A 1/2-length portrait of a gentleman wearing wig, blue coat (Canvas 29 1/2 by 24-in.)

Stuart Period.

A 1/2-length portrait of an aged gentleman, grey hair, claret coloured coat, (within an oval) (Canvas 29 1/2 by 24-in.)

Stuart Period.

A 1/2-length portrait of a gentleman, curling wig, lace cravat, light coloured coat, (within an oval) (Canvas 29 1/2 by 24-in.)

Sir Godfrey Kneller.

A life-size 3/4-length portrait of a nobleman (Stuart Period) in armour, facing spectator, lace cravat, Blue Ribbon Order, soldiers in combat to the left (Canvas 47 by 37-in.)

Stuart Period.

A 1/2-length portrait of a Nobleman, wearing wig, armour, blue shawl (within an oval) (Canvas 29 1/2 by .24-in.)

Stuart Period.

A 1/2-length portrait of a gentleman, with long dark hair black coat light sleeves and linen collar (within an oval) (Canvas 29 1/2 by 24-in.)

Early English School (Stuart Period).

A 1/2-length portrait of a gentleman, wearing curling wig, armour, (within an oval) (Canvas 29 1/2 by 24-in.)

Stuart Period.

A small bust portrait of a gentleman, dark curling hair, lace collar (Canvas 18 by 13 1/2-in.)

Stuart Period.

A Set of 7 Miniatures, 3 ladies and 4 gentlemen (in 1 frame) Stuart Period. A 3/4-length portrait of a nobleman, wearing wig, armour, blue ribbon Order, lace cravat, brown shawl, baton in his left hand (Canvas 49 by 39-in.)

Stuart Period.

A bust portrait of H.M. King James I, lace cravat, crimson cloak (Canvas 29 by 24-in)

Stuart Period.

A life-size bust portrait of The Marquis of Montrose wearing linen cravat and armour, facing spectator (Oval canvas 29 by 23 1/2-in)

Stuart Period.

A small portrait of a gentleman wearing longhair and armour, (within an oval) (Panel 12 by 10-in)

Stuart Period.

"H. M. King Charles I" a bust portrait (Canvas 29 by 24 1/2-in)

Stuart Period.

A 1/2-length portrait of Charles Edward Stuart, crimson embroidered coat, lace cravat, Blue Ribbon Order (within an oval) (Canvas 29 by 24-in.)

Stuart Period.

A 1/2-length portrait of the Consort of Charles Edward Stuart, wearing blue embroidered dress, open low, (within an oval) (Canvas 29 1/2 by 24-in.)

Stuart Period.

A 1/2-length portrait of a Nobleman, wearing powdered wig, green coat, armour and Blue Ribbon Order (Canvas 23 by 19-in.)

Stuart Period.

A 1/2-length portrait of a young Court lady, to the right, facing spectator, wearing white satin dress, open low, ermine-trimmed cloak and jewels (Canvas 23 by 19-in.)

D. Teniers (signed), I582-I649.

"Boors Playing Skittles" (Panel 14 by 9 1/2-in.)

David Teniers, I582-I649.

Exterior of a Hostel, figures carousing (Canvas 37 by 23 1/2-in.)

R. E. Tork.

A Landscape, a pedlar in the foreground, an equestrian, on a white horse, to the right, distant landscape (Panel 22 1/2 by 12 1/2-in.)

Louis De Vadder, I560-I623.

River Scene, buildings and trees to the right, boat and fowl on the stream (Panel 23 by 16 1/2-in.)

Van Goyen.

A River Scene, with numerous boats (Panel 24 1/2 by I5 1/2-in.) *Sold for 425gns*

Valesquez School.

A half-length portrait of a gentleman, to the right, facing spectator, wearing moustache, and fur coat. (Canvas 25 by 20-in.)

Valesquez School.

A 1/2-length portrait of a gentleman wearing dark coat, red order nad deep lace collar, to the right facing spectator. (Canvas 30 by 24-in.)

F. Vandebonke.

A pair "Lions" and "Tigers" (Panels 30 by 24-in.)

W. Vande Velde, 1610-1693.

[Willem van de Velde, the elder]

A stormy Seascape with fishing boats (Canvas 21 by 15 1/2-in.)

W. Vande Velde 1610-1693.

A coast scene with fishermen and boats on the foreshore (Canvas 19 1/2 by 14 1/2-in.)

W. Vande Velde. 1610-1693.

A cost scene with boat and two fishermen. (Panel 12 1/2 by 9 1/2-in.)

END OF FIFTH DAY'S SALE

THE PICTURES — (Continued.)

Sir A. Van Dyke School.

"H.M. King James I" life-size, to the knees, in armour, holding baton, crown on table to his left (Canvas 63 by 49-in.)

Sir A. Van Dyke School.

A life-size 3/4-length portrait of a Nobleman, wearing the cloak and Order of the Knight of the Bath (Canvas 49 by 40-in.)

Sir A. Van Dyke School.

A 3/4-length portrait of a Nobleman, wearing armour and lace cravat, ship to the right (Canvas 48 by 38-in.)

Sir A. Van Dyke School.

A 1/2-length portrait of a Young Nobleman, wearing wig and lace cravat, (within an oval) (Canvas 29 by 24-in.)

J. W. Waller.

A bust portrait of a Lady, wearing black dress & tall linen & lace collar (Canvas 17 by 14-in.)

Wm. Webb (signed and dated I826).

A Groom and 4 Horses, 2 Dogs and Deer, in a Landscape (Canvas 65 by 52-in.)

Jaques de Wet.

"Moses Dividing the Red Sea" (Panel 25 1/2 by 19 1/2-in.)

G. Wilson (signed and dated 1706).

A Landscape, with Girl and Youth Seated, Dog, Cat and Dead Game (Canvas 102 by 78-in.)

J. B. Weenix, I62I-I660.

Figures & Dead Game (Canvas 81 by 57-in.)

P. Wowermans, I620-1668.

A Rocky Scene, with 2 Figures, a Horse and 2 Cows (Panel 15 by 12-in.)

P. Wowermans' School.

A Battle Subject, tall tree to the left (On copper, 12 by 10-in.)

P. Wowermans.

A Battle Subject, numerous combatants in the foreground (Canvas 11 3/4 by 9 1/2-in.)

Zuicarelli.

A Group of many Classical figures (Canvas 20 by 16 1/2-in.)

School of Zucchero.

A bust portrait of a Gentleman with dark hair, moustache and beard and frilled ruffle (Canvas 24 by 20-in.)

Hendrik Van Zuylen

(signed and dated I888).

"The Lion & Lioness in Cave" (Canvas 80 by 59-in.)

H. B. Ziegle.

An Old Oak Tree in Bushy Park (Canvas 12 by I0-in.)

Dutch' School.

A Youth with a dog, a hare and other dead game (Canvas 48 by 30-in.)

Dutch School.

Coast Scene, Ships, Boats, Figures (Panel 32 by 26-in.)

Dutch School.

Quay Scene, Church, Figures, ships and Boats (Panel 32 by 23-in.)

Dutch School.

A Landscape, with House and Figures in foreground, Hills in distance (Panel 23 by 16-in.)

Dutch School.

Buildings, River, Bridge, Figures and Cattle (Panel 24 in by 20-in.)

Dutch School.

Landscape, Figures to the left, Ruins on an eminence, to the centre (Panel 12 1/2 by 19 1/2-in.)

Dutch School.

Landscape with figures, cattle and sheep in foreground (Panel 30 1/2 by 23 in.)

Dutch School.

A rocky distant landscape, tall trees and figures to the left. (Panel 11 by 9-in.)

Early Dutch School.

An interior, figures seated at a repast at a table, a faun by an open door to the left, a dog and spinning wheel near (Panel 20 by 15-in.)

Dutch School.

An Encampment Figures to the right, River to the left (Canvas 26 1/2 by 19 1/2-in.)

Dutch School.

Ruins, Soldiers Halting by the Way (Canvas 25 1/2 by 20-in.)

Dutch School.

A Homestead, Figures to centre, Boat on River to the right (Panel 24 by 11-in.)

Dutch School.
The companion, A Homestead; Boat on River to the left (Panel 24 by 11-in.)
Dutch School.
A Distant Landscape, Figures beneath Trees to the right, Sheep and Buildings in mid-distance (Canvas 48 1/2 by 29-in.)
Dutch School.
A Battle Subject, numerous Equestrians (Panel 17 by 7 1/2-in.)
Dutch School.
A Battle subject, Buildings on high ground, to the right (Canvas 60-in. by 29-in.)
Dutch School.
A Distance Mountainous Seascape-A Dutch Allegory (Panel 35-in. by 24-in.)
Dutch School.
Donkey, Goat, Sheep, etc.-a Gallery picture (Canvas 58 by 49-in.)
Dutch School.
A Pastoral and River Scene, Buildings, Figures and Boat to the centre (Canvas 90 by 52-in.)
Dutch School.
A bust portrait of a Gentleman, to the left, facing spectator, Wearing dark coat and ruffle (Panel 29 1/2 by 24 1/2-in.)
Dutch School.
A wood bridge spanning a Stream, Sailing Boats, to the right (Panel 13 1/2 by 12 1/2-in.)
Dutch School.
A Rocky Landscape, with Stream, trees and Figures (Canvas 38 by 31 1/4-in.)
Dutch School.
A 1/2-length portrait of a woman with Vegetables at a Table (Canvas 32 by 24 1/2-in.)
Dutch School.
A 1/2-length portrait of an aged Lady, wearing open blue dress and black head shawl (Canvas 29 by 24 1/2-in.)
Dutch School.
A Small Rocky Landscape, Figures and Tree Stumps to the right (Panel (10 3/4 by 8-in.)
Dutch School.
An allegorical landscape, a Castle in mid-distance, to the centre (Panel 25 1/2 by 19 1/2-in.)
Dutch School.
A Landscape, an old Mill House to the left (Canvas 29 3/4 by 22-in.)
Dutch School.
Ruins with Cattle (Canvas 24 1/2 by 20 1/2-in.)
Early English School.
A 1/2-length portrait of a Gentleman, wearing wig and red waistcoat (Canvas 29 1/2 by 24-in.)
Early English School.
A 1/2-length portarit of a gentleman wearing blue coat. white cravat, powdered hair (Canvas 23 1/2 by I9 1/2-in.)
English School.
A bust portrait of Aged Lady, to the right, wearing lace collar and tall cap, chain and locket (Panel 16 by I4-in.)
English School.
A 3/4-length portrait of a Young Lady wearing ringlets, tall lace collar, red evening cloak, trimmed ermine, holding a fan, feathered hat (Canvas 44 by 32 1/2-in.)
English School.
A bust portrait of a Lady, wearing feathered black hat, pearl necklet, lace collar, black dress and a gold chain (Canvas 16 by I4-in.)
English School.
A 1/2-length portrait of a Gentleman wearing wig and violet coat (Canvas 28 1/2 by 23 1/2-in, in carved frame.)
English School.
A 1/2-length portrait of a Military Officer, to the right, facing spectator, right hand outstretched. left resting on his feathered helmet (Canvas 35 by 29-in.)
English School.
A 3/4-length portrait of a Gentleman wearing brown embroidered vest, blue coat, wig, stick in his right hand (Canvas 38 by 28-in.)
English School.
A 1/2-length portrait of a Gentleman wearing wig, blue coat and silk scarf, (within an oval) (Canvas 29 1/2 by 24-in.)
French School.
A 3/4-length portrait of a Nobleman, wearing embroidered brown coat, powdered wig, holding a pencil and a book in his hand (Canvas 31 by 25-in.)
Flemish School.
A 1/2-length portrait of a Lady, wearing dark low-neck dress, her left hand raised, pearl necklet and earrings (Canvas 28 1/2 by 24-in.)
Flemish School.
Landscape, with Castle and Ruins (Panel 9 by 6 1/4-in.)
Italian School.
"Near Rome - St. Peter and Our Saviour" (Canvas 29 by 23-in.)
Italian School.
Ruins, Figures and Hercules Statue to the right (Canvas 25 by 19-in.)
Spanish School.
A 1/2-length portrait of an Aged Man, pointing with his right hand (Canvas 20 by 15 3/4in.)
Spanish School.
A 1/2-length portrait of an Aged Man (Canvas 29 by 22-in.)
Spanish School.
"Madonna & Child, with St. John" (Panel 41 by 34-in.)
Spanish School.
Head of an Aged Man, with grey hair (Panel I9 by 14 11/2-in.)
Unknown.
"A Youthful Artist," a Scene in a Studio, a palette resting on a chair, 2 portraits by an easel (Canvas 29 1/2 by 24-in.)
Roman Soldiers & Figures A (Panel 25 by 20-in.)
A 1/2-length portrait of a Bishop wearing a Cap, (within an oval) (Canvas 29 1/4 by 25-in.)
A bust or an Aged Man. wearing scarlet coat, a staff in his right hand, (within an oval) (Panel I9 by I5-in)
An Interior - Two whole-length portraits of gentlemen with a Horse (Canvas 29 by 24-in.)
Continental School.
A bust portrait of an Aged Gentleman wearing black coat and lace collar (Canvas 22 1/2 by 18 1/2-in.)
Continental School.
A Head of a Man, wearing dark coat, deep collar and a medal (Canvas 19 by I6-in.)
"The Eagle's Nest, with Prey," mountain and burn in back- ground (Canvas 46 by 59-in.)
A Stag's Head (Canvas 24 by 28-in.)
Two Spaniels (Canvas 20 1/2 by I6 1/2-in.)
"Still Life" (Canvas 28 by 22 1/2-in.)
"Still Life" (Canvas 32 1/2 by 25-in.)
Huntsmen and Hounds, kennels in background (Canvas about 42 by 37-in.)
Three Boys and a Dog, a group seated on a terrace (Canvas 72 by 45-in.)
A Pastoral Landscape, Figures by a Lake (Canvas 79 by 35-in.)
The companion picture, River Scene, Buildings and Trees
A Landscape, with a Cleft Rock and Figure (Canvas 21 by 18-in.)
A Seapiece with wrecked Ship on the Rocks (Canvas 29 by 23 1/2-in.)
A Landscape, with Lake and Mountain (Panel 19 by I0 1/2-in.)
A Landscape, with Monument, Buildings and Figures (Canvas 39 by 33-in.)
A wide open Landscape, a River and Buildings to the centre, Figures on the Bank, to the right (Canvas 39 by 21-in.)
A Rural Landscape, a Figure Seated beneath a Tree, to the centre (Panel 9 1/2 by 11 3/4-in.)
A River Scene, with Buildings and Figures, on high ground, to the left (Canvas 18 by 13-in.)
A Landscape, with Church in centre, Figures and Sheep to the right (Canvas 28 by 23-in.)
An open Landscape, Buildings, Horsemen and Caravan to the right, a River to the centre (Canvas 29 1/2 by 38-in.)
Ruins and Figures, Seascape and Boats to the right (Canvas 12 1/2 by 17-in.)
A Classical View of Rome, numerous Figures, Boats and Buildings (Canvas 40 by 35-in.)
Ruins with Cattle and Figures (Canvas 18 by 13 1/2-in.)

"*Landscape with Saint Jerome and the Lion*" painted by Gaspard Dughet (called Gaspar Poussin) c1638. It was originally owned by Charles Jennens, inherited by the Curzon-Howe family and sold in 1920 when it was attributed to Poussin and titled "A Large Rocky Landscape." It is now housed in the Museum of Fine Arts, Boston, USA (https://www.mfa.org/).

A Naval Battle, numerous Frigates in action, heavily laden boats in foreground (Canvas 32 by 24-in.)

A Mansion standing in a Park, Waterfall in foreground (Canvas 16 by 11-in.)

"The Meditating Magdalen" (Canvas 28 by 23-in.)

"Jephtha's Vow" - a Gallery picture (Canvas 85 by 65-in.)

"The Transfiguration " (Canvas 50 by 34 1/2-in.)

"The Magdalene at Prayer" (Canvas 18 1/2by l4-in.)

"The Assumption of The Virgin " (Canvas 28-in. by 18-in.)

The Magdalen with White Headdress and Nimbus (Canvas 19 by l5-in.)

"The Holy Family and Cherubs" (On panel 6 1/2 by 6 1/2-in.)

"The Holy Family with St. John" (Panel 11 by 8 1/2-in.)

"An Angel Appearing to Hagar" (Canvas 31 1/2 by 21 1/2-in.)

"Christ and a Woman at the Well" (Canvas 30 1/2 by 25-in.)

"The Baptism of Our Lord, in the River Jordan" (Canvas 36 by 27 1/2-in.)

"The Holy Family" (Canvas 28 1/2 by 24-in.)

"The Descent from the Cross, with the Two Marys" (Canvas 29 by 24-in.)

"The Agony in the Garden" (Canvas 19 by 15 1/2-in.)

"The Madonna at Prayer" (Canvas 16 1/2 by 21-in.)

"Our Lord Healing the Sick" (Canvas 25 by 12-in.)

P. P. Rubens (after).

"Ecce Homo" (Canvas 19 1/2 by 15-in.)

"Christ Walking on the Sea" (On copper, 12 1/2 by l0-in.)

"Salome with Head on a Charger" (on canvas.)

An Allegory - An Angel seated holding a Wreath and Pointing to an open Book (Canvas 46 by 31 1/2-in.)

An Allegory - Four Figures in a Landscape (Canvas 19 by l4-in.)

"Our Saviour with His Disciples Preaching on the Mount" (Canvas 58 by 77-in.)

" The Holy Family" (Canvas 19 by 13 1/2-in.)

An Allegory - Figures at a Well (Canvas 27 1/2 by 22-in.)

"The Last Supper"- a Gallery picture (Canvas 56 by 43-in.)

An Allegory - "The Flight into Egypt" (Canvas 23 by 28 1/2-in.)

"Our Lord in the Temple" (Panel 31 1/2 by 25-in.)

"The Madonna & Child" (Oval canvas 35 by 28-in.)

An Allegory - Numerous Figures in foreground (Canvas 56 by 54-in.)

"Christ Visited by Two Angels" (Canvas 36 by 28 1/2-in.)

"Our Saviour and a Woman at the Well" (within a floral chaplet.)

Dutch School.

(Canvas 46 by 54-in.)

"Our Saviour Working a Miracle"

Italian School.

(Canvas 68 by 48-in.)

"The Last Supper " (Panel 16 1/2 by 12-in.)

"The Holy Family and attendant Figures" (Canvas 34 by 24-in.)

"The Magdalen Meditating" (Canvas 42 1/2by 28-in.)

Head of a Saint

Spanish School.

(Panel 18 by 13 1/2-in.)

"The Ascension" (Canvas 60 by 47-in.)

"St. Mary Anointing Our Lord's Feet" (Canvas 60 by 43-in.)

"The Temptation of St. Anthony" (Canvas 54 by 42-in.)

"Saint & Infant Christ" (Canvas 38 by 28-in.)

"Our Saviour Appearing to Mary Magdalene" (Canvas 28 by 23-in.)

"Infant Christ - Recumbent" (Canvas l8 by 15 1/2-in.)

Classical figures (Canvas 4 1/2 by 15 1/2-in.)

A Scriptural Subject (Canvas 2 1/2 by 15-in.)

Two oil paintings

Lion and Cubs

Two - Allegorical subjects

Two - Allegorical subjects

Landscape and Figures

Cow in Landscape (Panel 12 1/2 by 9-in.)

A Classical Hilly Landscape, numerous Buildings and Figures (On copper 13 1/2 by 10 1/2-in.)

"The Holy Family" (On copper, 12 1/2 by 9 1/2-in.)

"A Carriage Hound," in a Landscape (Canvas 45 by 33-in.)

"A Horse," in a Landscape (Canvas 41 by 27-in.)

END OF SIXTH DAY'S SALE

1920 SALE

THE PICTURES

** indicates that the picture was listed in the December 1918 Assheton House schedule*

Henry van Balem.*

"The Baptism of Christ" (on copper, 8 3/4 x 7 1/4-in.)

H. van Balem.*

"Cupids and Lamb" (on copper, 9 1/4 x 7 1/2-in.)

Bassano.

"Christ Before Pilate" (canvas, 36 x 18-in.), in a carved wood frame

Bassano.

The companion picture, "Christ Being Led to the Crucifixion"

D. De Bast.

"A Harbour Scene," ships in full rig in the foreground (panel 22 1/2 x 17-in.)

Nicholas Berghem.

"A Landscape": Equestrians to the right (panel 19 1/2 x 14 1/2-in.)

N Berghem.

"A Landscape": Two Badgers to the left (panel 16 1/2 x 12 3/4-in.)

N Berghem.

"A Landscape," with herd of Goats and Figures (panel 18 1/4 x 13 3/4-in.)

N Berghem.

"A Rocky Landscape," Cattle and Equestrian, to the left (panel 19 1/2 x 14 1/2-in.)

Brill.

"St. Sebastian" (on copper, 13 x 7 1/4-in.)

Brooking.

"A Stormy Seascape," with two Vessels in distress (canvas 24 x 27 1/2-in.)

Thos. Cole.

"The Coliseum" (panel 12 1/4 x 9-in.)

Old Chrome.

"A Woody Landscape" (panel 22 x 18%-in.)

Cornelius Decker.

"A River Scene" : Old Building and Boat with Figures to the right (panel 21 3/4 x 17 1/2-in.)

"Still Life and Dog" (Canvas 45 1/2 x 34 3/4-in.) In a carved wood frame

Francis Desportes.

The companion Picture

Dominico.

"A Classical Subject," with buildings and numerous figures (panel 5 x 4 1/4-in.)

Van Falens.

"Exterior of a Stable": Figures and Horses in the foreground (panel 15 3/4 x 11 1/4-in.)

Dom. Fatti.

"Our Saviour at Emmaus" (panels 15 1/4 x 12 3/4-in.)

Griffier.

"A Moonlight River Scene," numerous Boats, Figures and Buildings (canvas 19 1/4 x 15 3/4-in.)

L. de la Hyre, Signed and Dated.

"A Landscape": Ruins and a Temple to the left; Equestrians, Figures, and Cattle in foreground (canvas 33 3/4 x 25-in.)

G. Lambert.

"An English Landscape," River to the centre (canvas 28 x 22-in. in a carved wood frame)

G. Lambert.*

"A Landscape," Satyrs disporting, to the centre (canvas 25 x 19-in.)

Peter Neefs.

.Interior of a Church (panel 24 1/4 x 16 1/2-in.)

Orizonti.

"A Rocky Open Landscape," Figures and tall Trees in the foreground, Buildings on an eminence, in mid-distance (canvas 54 1/2 x 49-in.)

Orizonti.

"An Open Landscape," Figures, Trees and Stream, in the foreground, high ground in mid-distance (canvas 54 1/2 x 49-in.)

G. Poussin.

"An Allegorical Landscape": two Figures and a Dog, on the road, to the centre (canvas 25 1/2 x 19-in.)

N. Poussin.

A large Allegorical Landscape: Three Figures seated, in the foreground (canvas 68 x 45-in.) in a very fine carved frame

(N.B. - Exhibited in the Royal Academy Exhibition of the Works of Old Masters, 1885)

N. Poussin.

"A Large Rocky Landscape," a crouching Lion and Figure, to the right (canvas 69 x 48-in.) In a very massive carved wood frame

(N.B.--Exhibited in the Royal Academy Exhibition of the Works of Old Masters, 1885)

[Image on previous page]

A. Pynake.

"Buildings, Figures and Cattle" (panel 14 1/2. x 12 1/2-in.)

Salv. Rosa.

"A Woody Landscape," Cattle and Figures at a stream, in the foreground, to the right (canvas 26 x 19 1/4-in.)

Salv. Rosa.

"A Landscape," storm raging, with Equestrian to the right (canvas 34 1/4 x 22 1/2-in.)

J. Ruysdael.

"A Dutch Coast Scene," numerous Fishing Boats and Folk, on the foreshore (panel 21-in. x 15 1/2-in.)

P. P. Rubens.

"The Death of a Saint" (panel 22 x 13 3/4-in.)

I. P. Scarsella.

"An Allegory" (panel 121/2 x 9 1/4-in.)

Snyders.

"Still Life," with Hound and Cat (canvas 37 x 27 1/4-in.)

Swanevelt.*

"The Flight Into Egypt"

Figures to the left, River and Landscape to the right (panel 20 1/2 x 13 1/2-in.)

Swanevelt.

"A Rocky Landscape," numerous Figures in the foreground (Canvas 20 3/4 x 15-in.)

Swanevelt.

"A Hilly Landscape," with Building on an eminence to left, Figures and Equestrians on bridge and in the foreground (canvas 50 1/2 x 37 1/2-in.)

D. Teniers.

"A Stump Orator addressing Peasants" (panel 5 3/4 x 3 1/4-in.)

D. Teniers.

"A group of Figures outside a Hostel" (panel 5 3/4 x 3 1/4-in.)

Van Der Velde. ***[also van de Velde]***

"A Seascape": British Vessels bringing up, and numerous Dutch boats (canvas 28 3/4 x 20 1/4-in.)

Weenix.

"Still Life," with Deer, etc. (canvas 37 x 78 1/4-in.)

Weenix.

The companion picture, " Still Life," with Hare and Hounds (canvas 38 1/4 x 78 1/4-in.)

Wynants.

"A Hilly Landscape ": A Temple on an eminence, with waterfall, to the left; Figures and Equestrians, on a road, to the right (panel 27 x 19 3/4-in.)

English School after
Sir Joshua Reynolds, P.R.A.

"The Snake in the Grass " (canvas 50 x 40-in.)

School of G. Romney.*

A life-size three-quarter-length portrait of a Lady, in white dress (canvas 43} 14/ x 54 3/4-in.)

Early English School.

A life-size three-quarter-length portrait of a Lady, seated, wearing satin dress cut low, and a loose blue shawl (canvas 52 1/2 x 42-in.)

Continental School.

"Classical Figures and Landscape" (canvas 63 x 48-in.) in a carved wood frame

Dutch School.

"A Stormy Coast Scene," with Wreckage and a Vessel in distress, in the foreground (canvas 30 1/2 x 24 1/2-in.)

Early Dutch School.

"A Wide Open Landscape," River to the centre, a Temple on high ground, to the left (panel 23 x 18 1/2-in.)

French School.

"Nymphs at Play," four sheep to the right (canvas 66 x 39-in.)

French School.

The companion picture, "A Group of Three Nymphs with a Chaplet of Flowers " to the centre and a Chanteclere to the left

Flemish School.

"A Rocky Landscape," Mules and Figures, and Lake to the centre (canvas 62 x 47-in.)

Flemish School.

"An Open Landscape," Cattle and Herdsman to the left, stream to the right, a Monastry to the centre (canvas 40 1/2 x 36-in.)

Flemish School.

"Head of a man," working by candle-light (panel 6 1/2 x 5 1/4-in.) in a carved wood frame

Italian School.

"A Feast": Numerous Figures seated at Table, the head of]ohn the Baptist being borne on a Charger, to the centre (panel 29 x 18 1/4-in.)

Italian School.

A Landscape, with Buildings, Figures and Equestrians; an old Roman bridge to the centre (on copper 11 1/2 x 9 1/4-in.)

Italian School.

"The Madonna and Child" (on copper 8 x 6-in.)

Italian School.

"The Crucifixion"

(panel 13 x 10-in.) in an ornate frame

Italian School.

" A Woody Landscape " (panel 14 x 10 1/2-in.)

A Drawing in Pastel, A Lady wearing evening attire, playing a harp

THE ENGRAVINGS

An artist proof by **W. Davies**, "Oxen Team"

An artist proof by T.L. Atkinson, after Heywood Hardy, "Watering the Brood Mare"

"Forgotten," by **C. Mottram**, after J.S. Noble

"A Picnic," a proof by ***C.G. Lewis***, after W.H.B. Davis

"Driving in Highland Cattle," proof before letters

" Going to the Horse Fair," proof before letters, **after Rosa Bonheur**

ASSHETON HOUSE SCHEDULE

*** indicates that "London" was written next to the picture in the typed list. These are generally either by a more valuable artist or family related.*

A stormy subject. Ship in foreground a wreck to the right. (canvas 27 x 24")

A life-size bust portrait of Marchioness of Sligo wearing dark dress, lace collar, Jewelled necklet and head ornaments. (Canvas 29 x 24") By **Sir Wm Beechey****

A replica of same.

A life-size ¾-length portrait of Lady Curzon, daughter of Ralph Assheton wearing yellow dress blue shawl over left arm, dog to right. (Canvas 48 x 40") By **Jervaise**

A Marine Battle Subject. (Canvas 73 x 42") By **Booking**

A life size ¾-length portrait of Esther Hanmer (when young) wearing embroidered dress - her left hand resting upon a basket of flowers on a table. (Canvas 49 x 39½") in a carved wood frame.

A whole length portrait of a young girl dressed in red embroidered dress holding feathered hat in her left hand. (canvas 48 x 36") in a carved gilt wood frame.

A river scene by a **Cuyp**. Boating to centre, on the bank in foreground are a man standing and a woman milking a cow, other cows to the right and on an eminence. (panel 28½ x 18")

A life size recumbent Child (George A. Viscount Howe) holding a bow, right arm on a quiver of arrows. (Canvas 42½ x 26½")**

A stormy landscape (**Dutch School**) Horses Caravans and figures in foreground. (Panel 27 x 15")

A shepherdess, with sheep in foreground. By **Karolder Jardin** (Panel 9 x 8")

Youth with donkey equipment, dog to centre. By **Karelder Jardin** (Panel 8¾ x 7¾)

A Dutch Interior, a Female seated, a man to her right, lighted lamp on a tall stand to her left. By **Schaken** (Panel 12 x 8")

An Aged philosopher, seated, sharpening his quill, a globe to the right.

By Adrian de Pape (Panel 15¾ x 11 ½")

A pair of miniatures in oil on ivory. H.M. George II and His Consort.

A marine subject numerous ancient sailing Vessels on a strong sea. (Canvas 29 x 19¼")

Dutch children carousing outside a Hostel.

By **Phillip Wouvermanns** (Panel 11 x 9")

Interior of a Dutch Stable, Three horses and numerous figures. (Panel 15½ x 11¼")

A bust of a Cavalier, facing spectator wearing dark coat lace cuffs and deep collar and broad hat and holding a watch in his right hand. By **Fran Hals** (Panel 24½ x 18½")**

A Dutch Woody Lane. Buildings to the left. Equestrian, Horses, Dogs - Figures to the centre. By **Hertz?** (Panel 17 ½ x 15")

A Miniature, in oils on ivory - a half length Portrait of a Lady wearing a rope of pearls, white evening dress and gold embroidered blue shawl.

A Miniature in oils on ivory. A lady seated at a pianoforte wearing black dress lace trimmed. Royal Blue embroidered shawl. By **J. C. Engleheart**

A pair Vases of Flowers. (Canvas 21¾ x l7½ & 22 x 18½")

A half length portrait of Richard Lord Howe wearing Admirals dress and Ribbon of the Garter. (Canvas 28½" Diameter)**

A Dutch landscape Cattle & Herdsmen to the left, tall trees to the right. (Panel 19 x 16½")

A Dutch shipping subject. A Port Scene. (Panel 22½ x 17½")

Head of aged man. By **Denner** (Canvas 19½ x 16½") in carved gilt wood frame.

A Dutch Coast Scene. Sail vessel nearing the foreshore, a boat and figures nearby. (Panel 12½ x 9½")

A Saint Visiting by **Angels**. (on copper 17½ 12¾") In a carved Giltwood frame.

The Nativity - Numerous figures around Our Saviour who lays upon a cushion to the centre. (Panel 19 x 14¼")

A mezzotint by **Wm. Say** after Devis, Viscount Curzon.

A stormy Marine Subject. A ship in distress to the centre. By **Ruysdael** (Canvas 30½ x 24½")

An Interior of a church. By **Peter Neefs** (Panel 16½ x 24¼")

A Life-size whole-length portrait of two young ladies in a garden. (Canvas 48½ x 39")

The Madonna & Child. (Panel 22¾ x 15¾) in a carved gilt wood massive frame.

A Life-size three-quarter-length portrait of Lady Arabella Howe. By **Sir Peter Lely** - Seated wearing a brown dress blue shawl pearl ornaments holding flower in her right hand on her lap. (Canvas 46 x 30½")

A life-size three-quarter-length portrait of a gentleman, wearing long hair, linen cravat, yellow vest, red cloak. (Canvas 46 x 30½")

A life-size whole-length portrait of a Lady standing on a terrace in blue dress, brown shawl, and holding her pet dog on her right arm By **Thomas Murray** (A Gallery picture)

A life-size whole-length standing portrait of Richard Admiral First Earl Howe, by **Thomas Gainsborough**. as a young man wearing uniform & hat. (A Gallery picture)**

[see the painting hanging in the red drawing room in Chapter 3]

A water coloured drawing signed **Edith 1851**. Eastern Ruins, Mountains and Lakes Scene

A presentation address to The Right Hon: Richard William Penn Earl Howe, from Tennants in Leicestershire, Nottinghamshire, Suffolk, Essex Warwickshire and Buckinghamshire.

An engraving by **Wm. Bromley** after Sir Thomas Lawrence, "The Duke of wellington".

A mezzotint by **S.W. Reynolds** after J Northcote R.A. "H.M. King George the Fourth on his charger"

Antique Print A General view of Mount Edgecumbe" from St Nicholas Island.

A whole-length life-size portrait of a young lady as Diana. By **Sir Goefrey Lneller** ***[misprint - Sir Godfey Kneller]*** (A Gallery Picture)

A whole-length life-size portrait of a Nobleman in court attire, his right hand raised to a table on which his coronet rests. (A Gallery Picture)

A life-size to the knees portrait of Handel (when young) holding an open book (canvas 48 x 36½") in a carved gilt wood frame.

A proof engraving. The Duke and Duchess of Beaufort on Hunters, 2 hounds by the side.

A half-length portrait of The Rt. Hon: Richard William Penn Earl Howe, wearing dark coat. (canvas 29 x 24")

A life-size whole-length presentation portrait of The Rt. Hon: Richard William Penn Earl Howe. By **Sir Francis Grant** (A Gallery Picture)** ***[The painting is now in the library at Penn House]***

A pair of life-size whole length portraits of The Rt. Hon: Georgiana Countess Howe and Richard George Penn Fourth Earl Howe in court attire (A Gallery Picture)

A bust portrait of a Cavalier playing a Mandolin **after Franc Hals.****

A life-size whole length portrait of H.M. Queen Alexandra **by Hughes** (A Gallery picture)**

A Port scene at Malta British State, shipping and Figures. (canvas 33½ x 23½")

A Dutch River scene - Craft in heavy water a storm approaching. By **Jacob Rayshasl** ***[misprint - Ruysdael]***. (Canvas 23½ x 16¼")

A bust portrait of an aged Lady by **Denner**, wearing white linen head shawl and fur collar. (On copper 16¼ x 12½")

A mezzotint. H. M. King George the Fourth in State attire.

A life-size whole-length portrait of Handel seated at a table on which is an open book. By **Thomas Hudson.**** (Gallery portrait) in a massive carved gilt frame.

A Life size ¾-length portrait of a nobleman (? Duke of York) wearing Blue coat, white facings gold braid embroidery and Ribbon of the Garter, left arm outstretched. (A Gallery picture) in a massive carved gilt frame.** ***[This is the Duke of York by Pompeo Batoni]***

A bust portrait of a young Nobleman (Stuart Period) wearing long curling wig, brown dress, within an oval. (Canvas 29 x 24")

A Dutch moonlit scene. (panel 20¼ x 16") By **Arnold Van der Neer**.

A life-size seated portrait of Queen wearing mantilla. (Canvas 35½ x 27½")

A life-size seated portrait of Mrs. Eliz. Hanmer Mother to Mrs Esther Curzon wearing cap, lace necklet brown dress trimmed lace - Book on lap. (Canvas 50 x 39½")

Full-length portrait of the Earl Howe, presented to the family by the tenants of the estate in 1858, hanging in the libary at Penn House.

The Duke of York (Edward Augustus, 1739-1767) by Pompeo Batoni painted in Rome in 1764 (*on far wall*). It was in the picture gallery at Gopsall, moved to Assheton House at the end of 1918 prior to being hung in the entrance hall of Curzon House in London (as shown). The painting was originally gifted to the Admiral Earl Howe by the sitter.

The Batoni portrait was removed from the frame at some point in the 20th century and sold in 1990. The large George III carved giltwood frame in the manner of Chippendale was sold in 2012 for £34,850 inc. premium.

Images courtesy of Lord Howe.

Seated portrait of Charles Jennens wearing a wig and blue coat[13]

A life-size seated portrait of Chas. Jennens Esq., of Gopsal uncle to Mrs Ester Curzon, wearing wig, blue coat, facing spectator. ***[above]*** (Canvas 49½ x 39")

A life-size seated portrait of Countess Howe, wearing ringlets and dark brown evening dress, her hands crossed resting on the lap. (**After Sir T. Lawrence**) (Canvas 50 x 40")

A life-size seated portrait of Viscount Curzon aged 89. By **Wm. Devis**, wearing robes, red drapery back ground. (A Gallery picture)

An Allegory. Adam and Eve - Numerous Birds, Beasts and animals. (Canvas 41 x 30")

A young girl holding dove. Blue dress, lace & black hat. (Canvas 20½ x 16½")

A Dutch Interior of a Cathedral. (On copper 14½ x 9½")

An Old print view of "Blenheim Palace".

18 Lithographs. Views in Leicestershire.

An Artist proof Mezzotint by **J.C. Webb after The Hon: John Collier**. A portrait of a Gentleman.

A series of 7 Miniatures in oils on ivory Portraits of Ladies and Gentlemen.

A small landscape; nr Coleorton. (Panel 6¾ x 5½")

Photographs etc. all framed and glazed.

The Judgement of Our Saviour. (Canvas 36 x 18")

An Allegorical Landscape Fauns etc dancing in foreground. (Canvas 25¼ x 19")

The Procession to Calvary. (Canvas 36 x 18½")

A Port scene at Malta, British Ships Boats and Figures. (Canvas 32½ x 23¾")

A Dutch Stormy landscape. An equestrian and another folk on the road to the centre. (Canvas 34¼ x 22½")

Two Dogs and a Cat. By **A. Cooper**.

A Hack, Gopsall & hounds. By **H. Barraud**.

A view of a Mansion with lake in foreground.

A Dutch Woody landscape with stream to centre across which is a bridge & numerous figures (Canvas 28 x 22½") in a carved frame.

The Flight into Egypt, a fine open landscape (Panel 21½ x 13½") in a carved frame.

A Castle view, cattle and figure in foreground.

A landscape figures to the left. Buildings on a cliff to the right. By **Swanevelt** (Canvas 20½ x 15")

Our Saviour on the Cross. (Canvas 52 x 47")

A Landscape with cattle a boy and dairymaid to the left. A stump of a tree & Buildings also to the left. To the right beneath an eminence are gypsies kindling a fire. By **T. Gainsborough** (Canvas 54 x 28¼")

A Dutch Landscape. Tall buildings & figures at a well to the left. Equestrians to centre. Cattle and tall trees to the right. (Canvas 33¾ x 24¾")

A Grey pony and a dog. A gallery picture.

Two cobs outside a stable. By **A. Cooper**.

A life-size bust portrait of a Lady by **F.K. Wm. Terhalter** wearing evening dress and pearl necklet. (Canvas 23½ x 19½") ***[This is almost certainly the portrait of Anne, Countess Howe, by FX Winterhalter, now in the library at Penn House]***

A Dutch river scene. Boat Buildings Windmill to the left, numerous figures on the right bank. By **Molenaen** (Panel 24¾ x 18")

A horse and a terrier in a landscape.

Two enlarged photographs. "Group of Royalty".

A bust portrait of Adml (Earl) Howe.

Head of an aged Lady, lace collar. Feathered hat. (Canvas 16¾ x 13½")

A Drawing. North view of Gopsall.

Two Prints Kedleston House in Derbyshire.

A pair "Horse and Jockey". By **H. Hall** of Newmarket

Three Dogs in a stable Signed **J. C. 1874**.

Two engravings **after Geo. Richmond Richard**. Wm. Penn Earl Howe.

Two coloured crayon drawings. A bust portrait of young ladies.

A water colour drawing by **Geo. Richmond** 1845. A small ¾-length portrait of a lady in evening black dress seated.

A Black & White drawing. A bust portrait of a gentleman.

Two enlarged photographs. Groups Gopsall December 1902.

An engraving Viscount Curzon. Feb 13 1813 aged 84. ***[Reproduced in Chapter 1]***

A Photograph of Chas. Jennens Picture.

A proof print in colours **after C. Cutler**. H.M. King Edward VII.

A Mezzotint. An Admiral.

A large engraving in colours Huntsmen and Hounds.

An artist proof etching **after Sir Luke Fildes**. H.M. Queen Alexandra.

A print **after Sir F. Leighton**. "Solitude".

An engraving by **B.I. Pouney after Robert Cleveley**. Morning (of the) Glorious 1st June 1794. ***[This is probably the Benjamin Thomas Pouncy engraving of the painting by R. Cleverley of the Royal Navy; reproduced in Chapter 3]***.

Fourteen photographs, prints etc.

A series of eighteen antique coloured prints **after T. S. Boys**. Views of old London early 19th century.

A set of four Old British Ships.

A Dutch coast scene - A cottage and equestrian figures to the right. Cows and goats to the centre. Shipping and boats beyond. By **Backhuysen**. (Panel 20¾ x14¾")

A bust portrait of a Lady, **Kneller School**, wearing red dress blue shawl. (Canvas 28½ x 24")

An enlarged photograph H. M. King Edward VII and Queen Alexandra in coronation robes.

A view of a coast town - A cart & equestrians fording a stream to the centre. Two pedlars to the right nearby. **signed S.R.** (Panel 25½ x 18")

A Swiss mountain scene with church to centre fitted a time piece.

A Venetian scene. By **Canaletto** (canvas 37 x 23½")**

Two Hounds coupled by **R. Drury Lowe**.

A Rocky & wooded Landscape cascade to left. Lion & recumbent figure to the right. By **N. Poussin**. (Canvas 58 x 47") in a massive carved frame.

A wide open landscape Buildings to left and centre. Trees & numerous figures. By **N. Poussin**. (Canvas 67 x 45") in a massive carved frame.

A life-size half-length portrait of a seated lady holding a rose. (Canvas 38½ x 23½")

A Cob and 2 dogs in stable signed **J. C. 1874**.

A landscape. Equestrian & cattle in foreground. By **Berghem** (Panel 19½ x 14¾")

A life-size ¾-length portrait of Georgiana Countess Howe 1900. (Canvas 48 x 35")**

A life-size to the knee portrait of a young lady **School of Romey**. (Canvas 55 x 43")

A Dutch winter scene. Numerous Figures skating, a tall building and a tent right. By **Cuyp**. (Panel 35 x 27½")**

A female playing musical instrument. Cupid in front, cherubs above, within an oval of flowers (17½ x 13") in a carved frame.

A marine subject Ships Boats and Figures. By **W. Van der Velde** (Panel 7½ x 7")

A life-size seated portrait of Charlotte De Kielmansegg, **M. Scrope**. Lord Viscount Howe 1719. Spaniel by her left side. (Canvas 49 x 36") ***[This is the painting of Charlotte, Viscountess Howe by Michael Dahl, which used to hang in the entrance hall of Gopsall Hall - see images in Chapter 3]***

A life size ¾-length portrait of a young nobleman to the right, facing spectator wearing embroidered vest, brown coat his left hand tucked in his vest. (Canvas 49 x 36")

A bust portrait of a Lady wearing blue dress, brooch & veil (within an oval 29½ x 24½") in a carved wood frame.

A marine subject - Sailing boat in foreground. By **Van der Velde**. (Panel 12¼ x 7½")

Cattle and figure in Landscape. By **Bergham**. (Canvas 17 x 15")

A Woody Landscape. By **Jacob Ruysdael**. (canvas 20 x 14¼ ") in a carved frame.

An Interior with figures by **David Teniers Jnr**. (On copper 19 x 13½") in a carved frame.

A Dutch River scene with numerous ships a boat with two figures to the right. (Panel 14 x 11¼")

A Landscape. Sheep Goats & Shepherdess on a sloping road to the left. (Panel 18¼ x 13¾")

The Lime Kiln by **Ruysdael** (Panel 17¼ x 14½")

A life-size half-length portrait of Prince Charles wearing curling long hair white shirt, blue cloak. (Canvas 29 x 24") in a carved frame.

An Allegory. Figure lashed to tree - Angel above. (On Copper 13 x 7¼")

An Allegory Our Saviour Baptising saints. By **H. van Balem**. (On copper 8¾ x 7") in a carved wood frame.

An Interior. Boars drinking seated around a tub to the centre. By **A. Ostade**. (Panel 12¼ x 10½") in a carved frame.

A Head of an aged man wearing red cap. By **Rembrandt**. (Panel 7¾ x 6½")**

A Dutch landscape. Trees and stream & figures to centre. By **Hobbema** (Panel 13 x 10¾")**

A water colour drawing. Dog sketched at Gopsall 1848.

A Head of an aged man with grey hair. By **Rembrandt**. (Panel 10 x 8")**

A Woody landscape. Hill in distance to centre, Figures in foreground. (Panel 14 x 10½") in a carved frame.

An Allegory. Three Angels one on a lamb. By **H. van Balem** (9¼ x 7½") in a carved frame.

A Dutch seapiece. By **Van der Velde**. (on Copper 9 x 6¾")

A Venetian scene. By **Caneletto**. (Canvas 39 x 24")**

A Dutch coast scene. By **Van der Velde**. (on copper 9 X 6¾")

The Magdelen in the Desert. Angels on clouds to the left (Panel 16 x 12") in a carved frame.

A fox hunt. By **Wootton**. A gallery picture.

A half-length portrait of an Aged Man, seated reading, wearing long beard, velvet cap & fur coat. **School of Rembrandt**. (Canvas 29 x 24")

A Naval Battle Scene. A gallery picture.

A bust portrait profile of a Queen wearing crown and robe. (Canvas 29 x 24")

A portrait of a Youth wearing deep lace collar, yellow dress and blue ribbon of an order. By **Cornelius Jansen**. (Canvas 29½ x 24½")

A Moonlit River scene. By **Griffier**. (Canvas 19 x 16")

Ruins & Cattle. By **Bergen**. (Canvas 25½ x 22")

A Hilly Landscape with figures to the right. By **Swanevelt**. (Canvas 51 x 37")

A three-quarter life-size portrait of a Nobleman to the right wearing lace collar, armour and sword, his plumed helmet and gauntlet on table to his left (A gallery picture)

A stormy coast scene. A Tower and boats on beach. Boats & shipping afloat. By **Ruysdael** (Canvas 56 x 41")**

A life-size portrait of Thomas, Earl of Pembroke & Montgomery etc wearing curling wig lace tie, armour, batten in right hand. Ship in background. (A gallery picture)

A Young Gentleman, a cob & a terrier in a Park. (A gallery picture)

Ruins, cattle buildings and Trees. Signed **W. Marlow** (Canvas 20¼ x 16¾")

Cattle and Sheep in Landscape. By **A. Van der Velde** (Canvas 22 x 19¾")

A Woody landscape. Cattle and figures to the right. By **Swanvelt**. (Canvas 26 x 19¼") in a carved frame.

Two photographs (Group of Scotch Terriers and photograph screen)

Building, dogs dead game and figures. By **Weenix**. (A gallery picture)

A whole-length life-size portrait of a Queen. Wearing robes, holding crown and left hand. (A gallery picture)

A life-size seated portrait of Handel wearing wig, red coat & vest, & holding book in right hand. (Canvas 36 x 27") no frame.

Fowls, Geese & Ducks. Seascape to right. By **Hondecoeter** 1651. (Canvas 65 x 51") ***[Name misspelled throughout]***

A life-size to the knee portrait of The Hon; Curzon his right elbow resting on a column, riding whip in right hand. (A gallery picture)

A Dutch coast scene. Fishing boat to right other vessels to the left. (Panel 21 x 15½")

A whole-length portrait of lady seated. Pug dog to her left. (A gallery picture)

Two whole-length portraits of the Ladies Curzon in landscapes. (Gallery pictures)

Three aquatint engravings "Sea Battle Subjects"

A stepple Engraving by **I. Gangain, after Sir Joshua Reynold**. Lady Catherine Manners".

An Engraving. Grand Fleet Under Admrl. Earl Howe 1790.

An oil painting a Young Girl (Canvas on panel) no frame.

A ditto. Horses exercising.

A Mezzotint. **By W. Say after A. W. Devis** "Viscount Curzon."

An engraving "Shipping" 1st June 1794.

An oil painting by **Sartorius**. Horseman & Hound leading, high wall. (Canvas 13¼ x 11½")

A private mezzotint **after Perignon by W. Walker**. A Lady with a hound.

Seventeen photographs etc. framed & glazed.

A Marine subject. "A Man o' war firing her guns on the right". (Canvas 21 x 14¼")

A Dutch River Scene. Buildings to centre church and other buildings to the right. By **Jacob Ruysdael** (Panel 19 x 15¼")

An Allegory. Herod's feast. (Panel 29 x 17")

A Wide Open Landscape, equestrians to right. By **N. Porrghem** (Panel 19½ x 14½")

A Woody Landscape. 2 animals to the left. (Panel 16½ x l2½")

An Allegory. Nude figures & other figures around. (Panel 22 x 13½")

A water colour drawing by **Cordon**. "Head of a Terrier".

A Woody Landscape, sheep and shepherdess to the right a Homestead to the left, a pond in foreground. (Panel 22 x 18½")

A Grey Hack with groom, Huntsmen & Landscape. (Canvas 50 x 43½")

A Huntsman in Landscape. Hunters & Hounds in distance. (Canvas 50 x 43½ ")

A Print. "Lady and Dog".

Dead Game - A pair by **Jan Fyt** (Gallery picture)

Dead Game - Dog and Cat. By **Jan Fyt** (Canvas 37 x 27")

A Landscape. Cascade to left Equestrian and other figures to centre, a Town in mid distance. (**Dutch School**) (Panel 27 x 19¾")

A Dutch seashore scene. figures and boat. By **Van der Velde**. (Panel 11½ x 9¼")

A Landscape, A ruined archway across a road under which a flock of sheep has just passed. By **W. Marlow** (Canvas 27¾ x 20½")

Fowls and other Birds. By **Hondecoeter**. (Canvas 50 x 39")

Fowls, Hawk, Pheasant etc. By **Hondecoeter**. (Canvas 49 x 39½")

The Infant Saviour sleeping, Cherubs above. By **Murillo**. (Canvas 56 x 42") In a massive carved gilt wood frame.**

Four oil paintings Horses. By **G. Morey**.

22 Prints photographs etc. (Family groups etc)

A Dutch stormy seascape. By **Van der Velde**. (Panel 10 x 7½")

Recumbent sleeping Infant. Saviour, Cherubs above. (Canvas 9¼ x 6½")

A Rocky Roadside scene. Two figures in discussion to the right. By **D. Feniers**. (Panel 12 x 7½") ***[possibly Teniers]***

Hound & Whelps. (Panel 8¾ x 6½")

A Gentleman in cricket attire, Cambridge cap.

Figures at a bridge, and a well. Buildings to right. **Dutch school**. (On copper 11½ x 9¼")

Dutch Boers seated at a table. **D. Feniers or Bronwer**. (Panel 11¾ x 8½") ***[Possibly Teniers; Bronwer unknown]***

A small head of a youth (**Bourdon**) (Stuart period) (Panel 6 x 4½")

A Black & White drawing. By **E. Anderson** "Viscountess Curzon".

A Pastel drawing - "George" A. W. & Marianne Curzon. By **A. Torretti** 1794.

Herculean Wrestlers (**Murello School**) (Panel 11¾ x 8")

A Dutch stormy seascape, Three ships in a rough sea. (Panel 6½ x 5")

Fox & Hounds crossing river. (Panel 8¾ x 6½")

A Dutch girl at needlework. (Panel 8½ x 6½")

A Marine subject. A Haulk on foreshore - sailing ship & boats to the right. By **W. Van der Velde** (Panel 7¾ x 7")

A Marine subject - A fleet of fishing smacks. By **Van der Velde**. (Panel 10 x 7½")

A Dutch woody Landscape. Figures & cattle to the left. (Panel 12½ x 9")

The Holy Family. **School of Van Dyck** (Panel 4¼ x 3½")

Our Saviour and 2 attendants. By **Dom. Fetti**. (15 x 13")

An Allegory, numerous figures at a bed and above. (Panel 12½ x 9½")

A Dutch Interior. Four figures seated carousing. Cabbage, Fish & utensils. (Panel 12¾ x 9½")

A Dutch Moonlight seashore scene. (Panel 12¼ x 11")

A Landscape. Two figures on the Road. By **D. Teniers**. (Panel 12 x 7½")

A Landscape with figures. (Flight into Egypt) By **Polemburg**. (Panel 9 x 7") ***[probably Poelenburgh]***

A Marine Subject - numerous craft near foreshore. Signed **W. V. Drost** [?] 1637 (Panel 13¾ x 7")

Buildings figures and cattle, by **A. Pynackery** (Panel 14¼ x ½") ***[probably Adam Pynacker]***

The Coliseum (Panel 12 x 9")

Fowls, Peacock, Turkey etc. (A Pair by **Hondecoeter**) (Canvas 19½ x 15¾")

A Dutch Stump Orator a line of figures in front. (Panel 5½ x 5")

The Crucifixion with the Three Marys. (Panel 18 x 10")

Madonna & Child. (on copper 8 x 6¼")

A small coloured drawing. A Riverscape - animal on tree stump.

The Country Mansion & a Church at Penn.

A Classical Landscape. By **Poussin**. (Canvas 25½ x 18½ ")

A whole-length small portrait of a Gentleman standing in a landscape.

An engraving H. M. George III on charger.

A water colour drawing signed **G. H.** "Ruins"

An engraving H. M. George IV.

An engraving Louis XVI.

A Dutch Homestead, a cow, Man, Boy, & Dog fording a stream. Landscape in distance. (Panel 25¾ x 18½")

A Dutch Hilly Landscape, cattle, horses and figures. (Panel 23¾ x 18¼")

An engraving "A Naval Battle after action".

The Gopsall Villages

Through the years there have been a number of villages that fell within, or on the border of, the Gopsall Estate and during the 19th century the Earls Howe were Lords of the manors of Barton in the Beans, Bilstone, Congerstone, Nailstone, Norton-Juxta-Twycross, Odstone, Shackerstone, Twycross and Wellsborough, in addition to Gopsall. They also held significant areas of land within the manors of Orton-on-the-Hill and Sibson, including virtually the whole of the village in the latter, without having manorial rights.[1]

Today most people would probably name just six villages that could be called 'Gopsall Villages': Bilstone, Congerstone, Norton-Juxta-Twycross, Odstone, Shackerstone and Twycross (including Little Twycross). These six villages were within the Gopsall Estate when Samuel Waring attempted to sell the outlying parts in 1927 and featured prominently in the sale catalogue, which represents the last detailed inventory of properties within the estate. However, even at that time, the estate included some land and properties in and around Barton in the Beans, Orton-on-the-Hill and Nailstone; the 4th Earl Howe having sold the 'Manor of Sibson' in its entirety in 1912 (Chapter 1).

The Lords of Gopsall have always influenced the lives of those living within their estate lands and certainly throughout the 18th, 19th and early 20th centuries they were the major employers and benefactors of the inhabitants of their villages. While their role as the major employers and village property owners of the area decreased significantly after the purchase of the majority of the Gopsall Estate by the Crown in 1932, some 7,000 acres of land were farmed by tenants until its final sale and breakup in 2017-2018. Today, the legacy of the Lords of Gopsall, which dates from the early 18th century when Gopsall was owned by Charles Jennens Snr, is most clearly seen in the churches, schools and houses of the estate villages.

The oldest surviving link between Gopsall and its villages is marked by gifts of communion silver to the churches in Twycross and Congerstone. St James' Church in Twycross has two silver cups and two silver patens thought to have been a gift from Charles Jennens Snr. The silver is dated 1717 and bears the hallmark of Richard Greene but no other inscription or decoration.[2] By contrast, the church plate of St Mary's Congerstone includes a silver paten made by William Spackman and inscribed *"The gift of Mrs. Felicea Iennens to the Church of Congeston. 1718"*.[3] Felicea Jennens (c.1668-1744) was an unmarried sister of Charles Jennens Snr who may have lived with her brother at Gopsall after the death of his second wife in 1708.

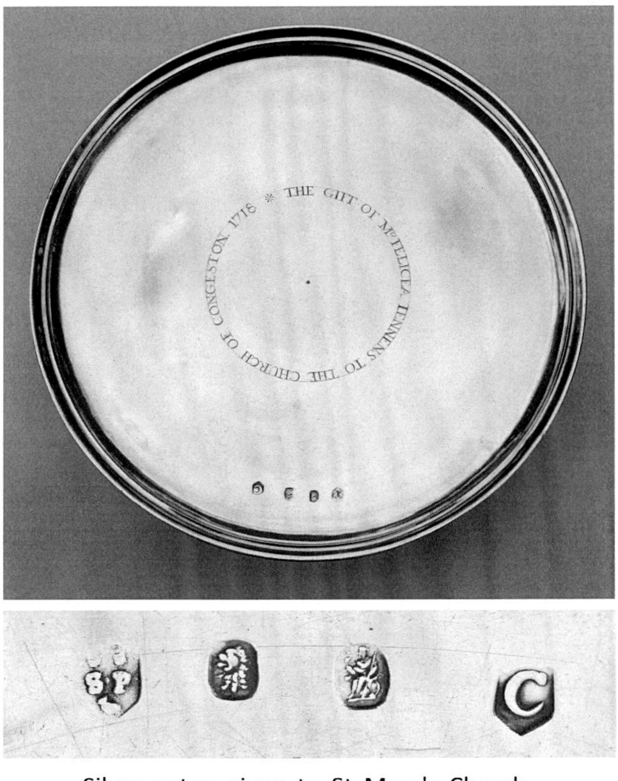

Silver paten given to St Mary's Church, Congerstone by Felicea Jennens in 1718.

In addition to the 1718 paten, the Congerstone Church silver includes a flagon, a paten, two cups and two large plates donated by the dowager Queen Adelaide while on one of her regular visits to Gopsall Hall. All the pieces are engraved with the sacred monogram (IHS)[4] with a cross above and three nails below, within a circle of glory, and all bear the inscription *"To Congerstone Church, August 1840"*, which appears beneath the monogram *"A.R."* surmounted by a crown.

The churches in Congerstone, Twycross, Norton, Nailstone and Shackerstone bear witness to their association with the Lords of Gopsall. Charles Jennens Jnr is known to have installed a clock in Holy Trinity Church, Norton-Juxta-Twycross in 1756[5,6] and erected a *"handsome singing gallery"*

Date **Church restorations funded by, and other historic links to, the Earls Howe**[7]

St Mary's, Congerstone

1824 Marble plaque in memory of Mrs Anne Hodson, a faithful servant with 30 years' service
1834 Replacement of the original chancel with an 'oversized' chancel the full width of the nave and north aisle
Building a gallery in the tower arch
Installation of:
a west window in the north aisle
box pews for the family and servants to the north side of the chancel
two small servants' box pews to the south of the altar
seats to nave and north aisle, central seats with 'poppy-heads'
1841 Installation of five new bells in wood frame
1845 Installation of a Bishop organ in the gallery
c.1880 Installation of the stained-glass altar window in memory of the 2nd Earl Howe
1897 Re-roofing the nave
Erection of a new porch of Hollington stone (actually rendered brick)
Repair to cracks in the tower and south wall of the nave
Commemorative brass plaque about the restoration work erected in the church
c.1903 Installation of the south chancel stained-glass window in memory of the 3rd Earl Howe
1906 Burial of Georgiana, Countess Howe; monuments erected in the churchyard and the chancel sometime later
1914 Removal of the tower arch gallery and Bishop organ (organ relocated to Holy Trinity, Norton-Juxta-Twycross)
Installation of the current Willis-built organ in memory of Lady Evelyn Eyre (Sister of 4th Earl)
1914 Marble plaque in memory of Emily Hales Chapple, "devoted nurse" to the Curzon-Howe family
1915 Marble plaque in memory of Susan Dolby, "devoted nurse" to the Curzon-Howe family
1919 Countess Howe's remains and monument transferred to Penn Street churchyard

St James', Twycross

1840 Repairs and additions to the church including[8]:
New roof over nave and chancel
Extension of the north aisle and installation of box pews for the family and servants
Addition of a vestry adjoining the tower at the NW end of the north aisle
Relocation of the pulpit from the centre of the church to the south wall of the chancel
Installation of 'free sittings' in the body of the church
Installation of a Bishop organ
1841 Stained glass window of Queen Adelaide's Coat of Arms in a new window within the north aisle
Presentation of an altar chair
1870 Richard William Penn Curzon-Howe, 1st Earl Howe buried in a new vault in Twycross churchyard
Memorial plaque in memory of the 1st Earl erected in the church
Memorial stained-glass window to the late Earl Howe; east end of the north aisle – by Holland of Warwick
1877 Anne Frances, Countess Howe buried (2nd wife of 1st Earl); memorial plaque in the church
1882 Capt. the Hon. Frederick Curzon RN buried (3rd son of 1st Earl); memorial plaque in the church
1885 Col. the Hon. Ernest George Curzon buried (6th son of 1st Earl); memorial plaque in the church
1893 Restoration of the church including:
Repointing and renovation of the east chancel window
Interior cleaning and recolouring
Restoration of a piscina and a staircase in south wall opened
Installation of a new stove in the north aisle and remodelling of the pulpit
1899 Robert Lothian Curzon buried (2nd son of Hon. Col. Earnest George Curzon); memorial plaque in the church
1901 A brass eagle lectern presented by The Hon. Mrs Ernest Curzon in memory of her husband and son

Holy Trinity, Norton-Juxta-Twycross

1841 Contribution to the stained-glass altar window bearing the Curzon, Moores, Gresley & Peveral Coats of Arms
1843 Donation of a new altar made from wood from Gopsall Park and contribution to:
New pews decorated with 'poppy-heads' and new hexagonal pulpit
Relaying the floor with Minton's encaustic tiles
Purchase of new harmonium
c.1890 Part contribution to:
Removal of the unsafe spire
Rebuilding the top of the tower, repointing and covering with a lead roof
Repair of the internal plaster walls and revarnishing the internal wood work (pews, pulpit etc)
1914 Installation of the Bishop organ removed from Congerstone Church

All Saints', Nailstone

1844 Presentation of a new organ
1853 Church restored by the architect Ewan Christian; £1,250 of total £1,650 cost paid by Earl Howe.
Work included: Repair of the nave walls, re-roofing and new pews, porch and pulpit

St Peter's, Shackerstone

1845 Complete restoration of the church including:
Rebuilding and shortening the chancel
Rebuilding the south aisle and part of the nave
Installation of a gallery organ,[9] new pews and pulpit

St Mary's Church: 1840 silver presented by Queen Adelaide *(top left)* and memorial window for the 3rd Earl (*top right*). **St James' Church:** Box pews in the north aisle (*middle*), Queen Adelaide's stained-glass window (*bottom left*) and the Curzon hatchment (*bottom right*).

Holy Trinity Church

Looking east from the gallery with the Bishop organ on the left, the two pulpits and the altar window with various Coats of Arms. The pulpit on the right is hexagonal and was installed in 1843 (*left*).

The 'Poppy-head' pews and floor tiles were also part of the 1843 restoration (*above*).

The Curzon-Howe Coat of Arms in the east window (*right*).

St Peter's Church

The 1845 pulpit and the 'Howe standard' tiled floor (*left*) with stained glass Howe crest (*inset*). The 1845 organ gallery in the tower arch above the font (*above*).

in St James' Church Twycross.[10] However, Jennens' clock with a diamond-shaped face in Norton church was replaced in 1840 by a tower clock made by Samuel Deacon of Barton in the Beans, which is present today. Little else is known about Charles Jennens' acts of generosity to the local churches and people except that when he died in 1773, he bequeathed *"£1,000 to schools around Gopsall and £200 to the poor of adjacent townships"* and his funeral sermon preached on 4th January 1774 in St James' Church, praised his *"unbound charity and benevolence"*.[10,11] That schools were in existence "*around Gopsall*" at this time perhaps indicates that Charles Jennens had played a part in establishing and running them.

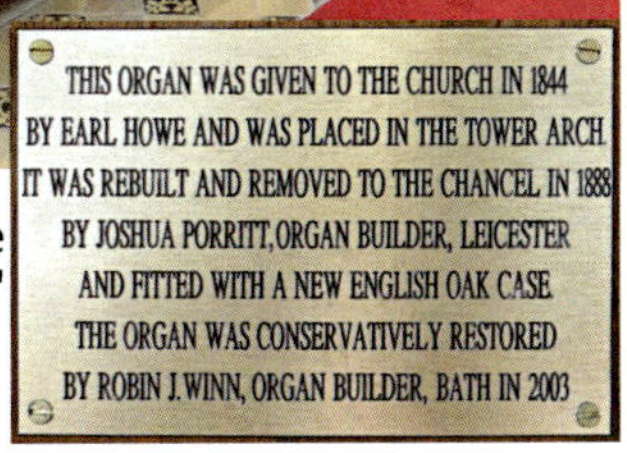

The organ in the chancel of All Saints' Church, Nailstone.

The most significant and long-lasting changes to the village churches occurred during the 19th century when the Curzon-Howe family were Lords of Gopsall (Table). The churches in Twycross and Congerstone appear to have been those most favoured by the Earls Howe and, unlike the other village churches, were renovated to include box pews for the family and servants; the family pews in both churches had the added advantage of their own fireplace. It seems clear that if it had not been for the financial intervention of the 1st and 3rd Earls, at least four of the churches would have fallen into decay and become unusable by the end of the 19th century.

It was Richard William Penn Curzon, 1st Earl Howe who instigated and paid for all the main renovation and rebuilding of the five Gopsall churches between 1834 and 1853. In addition, in 1847, he gave £500 for the renovation and enlargement of St John's Church in Heather, which was to become "*The Church of the Poor*" by "*allotting the whole nave to free-sittings*".[12] His love of music, exemplified by the fact that he had at least two organs, a harpsicord and a piano at Gopsall Hall was probably the reason why he donated pipe organs to four of the Gopsall churches and a harmonium to the fifth (Holy Trinity, Norton-Juxta-Twycross). The 4th Earl eventually replaced the harmonium with the Bishop pipe organ that was removed from Congerstone church in 1914 to make way for a larger Willis instrument, installed in memory of his sister Lady Evelyn Eyre.

Although Gopsall Hall appears to have been the major residence for the Earls Howe during the 19th and early 20th centuries, it is only the 1st Earl (d. 1870), his second wife (Anne Frances, Countess Howe; d. 1877) and two of his sons (Capt. the Hon. Frederick Curzon, d. 1882; Col. the Hon. Ernest George Curzon, d. 1885) who were buried locally in Twycross churchyard. The 2nd and 5th Earls (d. 1876 & 1964) were buried in the family vault in Holy Trinity, Penn and the 3rd (d. 1900), 4th (d. 1929) and 6th (d. 1984) Earls were buried in the churchyard of Holy Trinity, Penn Street. Surprisingly, although Georgiana, Countess Howe died at Curzon House in London, she was initially buried in Congerstone churchyard in 1906, prior to her remains and her monument being relocated to Penn Street after the 4th Earl sold Gopsall in 1918 (Chapter 9).

It was the 1st Earl who was responsible for building and subsequently supporting local village schools; the latter being helped in

The monument in memory of Georgiana, Countess Howe in Holy Trinity churchyard, Penn Street. When it was the centrepiece of St Mary's churchyard it stood alone on its three-step pedestal. The three other memorials (*from back to front*) are for Flora Curzon (Florence, Dowager Marchioness of Dufferin and Ava, d. 1925; second wife of the 4th Earl), The Hon. Frederick Graham Curzon (d. 1920; grandfather of the present 7th Earl) and Lorna Curzon (d. 1961; third wife of the 4th Earl).

part by contributions from Charles Jennens' legacy for *"schools around Gopsall"*.[1,11] National Schools[13] were built in Twycross (1822), Congerstone (1825; to serve Congerstone, Shackerstone and Bilstone, although a schoolroom and house were later built in Shackerstone in 1844), Nailstone (1828; enlarged in 1858) and Sibson (1839; Queen Adelaide laid the first stone) at the expense of Lord Howe. He also partly contributed to the building of schools in Norton-Juxta-Twycross (1839) and Heather (1845)[14]. The 1st Earl was the only or major source of running costs for the schools except for those in Sibson and Heather, which had other benefactors. The number of schools established by the Earl not only reflected the large size of the Gopsall Estate, but also his benevolence and deep religious belief, as they provided elementary education, in accordance with the teaching of the Church of England, to the children of the poor.

Congerstone Primary School (*top*) and Nailstone School House with two frontage gables, three arched bays and two date plaques: National School 1828 (*L*) & Infants School 1858 (*R*) (*bottom*). The original front gable of Congerstone school can be seen on the right, behind the 'new' double gabled front extension.

All these schools have closed except for Congerstone and Heather Primary Schools, which currently have rolls of 169 and 106 pupils respectively. Although Twycross school was demolished in 1930, it is still present as its bricks were cleaned and re-used to build the village hall! All the other school buildings have been converted to private houses, but the only one that allows its former function to be identified is in Nailstone.

Apart from providing employment and looking after the spiritual and educational needs of those living in the Gopsall villages, the Earls Howe built and maintained their village properties for their own and their workers use. Most of the house building works appear to have been performed by the 1st Earl Howe, but little information exists as to what was newly built. It is probably reasonable to assume that virtually all the village and farm properties listed in the 1912 Sibson Estate (39 cottages and farmhouses) and 1927 Gopsall Estate (179 cottages, farmhouses and public houses) sale catalogues were built, or at least renovated, by the Earls Howe. It is documented that the 1st Earl rebuilt most of the houses in the villages of Shackerstone, Sibson and Twycross and built the almshouses in Congerstone (c.1830) for four poor persons.[1,15] Almshouses in Twycross, Norton-Juxta-Twycross, Shackerstone and Nailstone are of a very similar design to those in Congerstone and date from the mid-19th century, suggesting that they were also built by the 1st Earl.

Almshouses in the Gopsall Villages

All were originally built to house four individuals or couples, but now have been converted to pairs of semi-detached cottages.

The Congerstone cottages (*top*) are still tenanted and are part of the Shackerstone Estate whereas all the others are privately owned houses. The almshouses in Twycross (*middle left*) and Norton (*bottom left*) are of very similar design although the former is rendered brick whereas the latter is now painted brick.

The almshouses in Shackerstone (*middle right*) and Nailstone (*not shown*) are constructed of red and yellow brick; their main difference being that the Nailstone cottages have 'toothed' wood bargeboards

Sibson School House

Norton-Juxta-Twycross School House

Sibson School, built by the 1st Earl in 1839, had one front gable and two arched bays and was essentially the same design as the building erected in Nailstone in 1828 (see earlier image of Nailstone school that was enlarged to have two front gables and three bays in 1858).

Norton School was also built in 1839, with some support from Lord Howe. It was built to the same design as the schools in Congerstone, Heather, Nailstone and Sibson.

The almshouses in Shackerstone are at the western end of Church Walk where six pairs of Gopsall Estate workers' cottages were built in the mid-19th century in the Arts and Craft style. The two-bedroomed cottages were built to a high standard and had steeply pitched roofs, massive chimneys, projecting gables and bay windows. One pair of cottages at the east end of Church Walk was built to serve as a schoolroom (now the village hall) and school house.[16] After the opening of the Moira West-Nuneaton railway in 1873, a lodge house, of similar design to the Church Walk cottages was built at the end of the new Shackerstone Drive to Gopsall Hall (Chapters 2 & 4).

Shackerstone school house and room - now a private house with the village hall on the right with bay window and 1844 date plaque.

There were probably only three village properties within the Gopsall Estate that could be classed as substantial residences: Twycross House, Assheton House (Twycross), and Odstone Manor house. Over the years all three were tenanted at times, but the two houses in Twycross were known to be used by the Curzon-Howe family. Little is known about how the family used Assheton House which no longer exists, except that it seemed to be used as a 'home' for some retired estate staff in about 1920. Planning permission was given (after an appeal) for the development of Assheton House and grounds to be used as a transport cafe and lorry park in 1956[17]. The property was for sale in 1960 (with associated planning permissions) but by 1963 it had become the Assheton House Country Club & Casino[18]; we doubt the 1st Earl Howe would have approved! By 1966 regular adverts were placed in papers for artists (except Beat Groups) to enter talent shows and for "*Attractive Girls*" to enter glamour contests.[19] The club closed in late 1970 or early 1971 and the house was demolished in 1979 to be replaced by ten homes with a new road called 'Assheton Lane'. In 1981, houses on the desirable 'Assheton Development' were being sold for £42,500.[20]

Assheton House, Twycross

Twycross House, dating from 1703, was substantially enlarged and renovated in the early 19th century and was used as a hunting box and, at times, the residence for members of the family (e.g. Francis, Viscount Curzon and his wife after their marriage in 1907). Today it is one of Twycross' Grade II listed buildings and part of the very successful Twycross House School.

Twycross House (c. 2004)

Excluding Gopsall Hall and Gopsall House farmhouses, the last building with a name linking it to the Gopsall Estate and the Curzon-Howe family locally was the Curzon Arms in Twycross. In the mid-19th century, it was known as the Howe or Earl Howe Arms, with the name Curzon Arms being used intermittently until the turn of the century. It was universally called the Curzon Arms throughout the 20th and early 21st centuries; sadly, today the Gopsall link has been lost and it now calls itself Turpins Bar & Grill.

The Curzon Arms (c. 1910)

The landlord of the Curzon Arms at this time was a Mr W. Peach, possibly a member of the Peach family who were gamekeepers at Gopsall from about 1880 to 1918 (Chapter 6).

The school (A) built by Earl Howe and the almshouses (B) can be seen further up the 'A444'.

Although the only remaining tangible links between the villages and their inhabitants to the Lords of Gopsall are found in churches and buildings, the memories of villagers recorded in Chapter 7 and in various 19th and early 20th century newspaper articles give some insight into how Gopsall and its Lords affected the lives of villagers. The Curzon-Howe family, who owned and occupied Gopsall Hall for 145 years, were generally fondly remembered, especially by those who were children in the early 1900s; parties with various treats being most clearly recalled. The following newspaper article[21] from December 1904 exemplifies the interaction between the 4th Earl and Countess Howe with local villagers to arrange a memorable Christmas for local children in Congerstone school, as well as providing food for poorer families and people within the area.

A CHILDREN'S DAY AT CONGERSTONE

GENEROSITY OF EARL AND COUNTESS HOWE

Holy Innocents or Children's Day, as it was called in old times, was indeed a red-letter day for Congerstone children. A number of kind friends had combined together to provide a splendid tea and entertainment for all the children of the parishes of Congerstone, Bilston (*Bilstone*) and Gopsall. As usual, The Countess Howe was to the fore with her kind generosity, and provided all the tea and a large share of the cakes and buns, etc. The Countess also sent a contribution of some of the best presents which were distributed among the children.

Mr. Barron very kindly came from Coalville and gave an entertainment with his powerful gramophone. Mr. and Mrs. Lee, of Gopsall gardens, were responsible for providing a beautiful table of good things, especially for the Band of Hope, which includes children from Congerstone, Bilston, Gopsall and Shackerstone, and numbers nearly fifty members. The tea began at half-past three, and ample justice was done to the splendid feast, and the youngsters kept going 'till nearly five o'clock.

At half-past six. The beautiful Christmas tree was lit up. It was covered in presents, and every child in the three parishes received one. Earl Howe provided the fir tree which was used for the purpose. Then came a magic lantern exhibition and over 50 comic-coloured slides, many of them moveable, were shown. Mr. Barron then caused the greatest wonder and pleasure with his gramophone. A very great deal of amusement was caused by the fact that several kind helpers dressed up in costume and paraded the whole evening to the intense delight of the children. Mr. Alfred Bates was dressed as Father Christmas and stood by the tree to give away the presents. Mr. Lee was completely disguised as a smiling Chinaman, while Mrs. Lee was an aged lady of the past century, with black poke bonnet, and Paisley shawl, and a splendid crinoline. Mr. John Dawkins was a quaker gentleman, and was most handsomely dressed. Before the children went away, they were each given an orange and a bun. Loud cheers were given for Lady Howe and the kind promoters of the feast, and the children dispersed to the tune of "'God Save the King,' played with great effect on the gramophone.

The following day the remnants of the feast in the shape of bread, milk cake, buns, tea, etc. were distributed to the poorer families in the parish and many poor old folks, received a nice reminder of the children's festival while several with large families were pleased to get a substantial help in the shape of cakes and buns towards their Christmas fare.

The prizes for the Catechism, 'Greater Catechism' and 'Little Catechism' were given away after the feast. Only those who had done the analysis fifteen times during the past year were awarded a prize. The prize winners in the Great Catechism were: H.L. Bunting, Wm. Jackson, Dorothy Garner, Ernest Jackson, Arnold Bunting, Dorothy Bunting, Mary Dawkins, Mabel Jackson and Fred Jones. The prizes for the Little Catechism were provided by Miss. M. Crowther. The system of the Catechism precisely as carried on at St. Sulspice, and as so strongly recommended by Monseigneur Donpanloup (*Dopanloup*), sometime Bishop of Orleans has been in thorough working order, and regularly used, in Congerstone parish with exceeding good results, for the last three years. The following were the subscribers to the children's feast: The Countess Howe, Rector and Mrs. Warner, Mr. George Cooke, Mr. John Dawkins, Miss Martin, Mr. W. Warner, Mr. and Mrs. Bunting, Mr. and Mrs. Lee, Mr. and Mrs. Bates, Mr. and Mrs. Parkes, Mr. and Mrs. Morris, Mrs Battye (*Battey*), Mrs. Thornton, Mr. Adenham, Mr. and Mrs. Jos. Dawkins, Mr. William Dawkins, Mrs. Lampard, Mrs. Lacey, Mrs. Dolby, Miss Mason, Mrs. Chapple, Mr. and Mrs. F. Dawkins.

Mr. Jos. Hextall officiated at the door with his usual accuracy and precision. Mr. Bunting with his usual unselfishness did the lion's share of getting the room in order both before and after the feast. Mrs. Wm. Twigg gave her valuable services as a volunteer all through the afternoon and evening.

A view of Sibson (1912)

According to the Sibson Manor sale catalogue, the School Cottages (*left*) were rented out to Mrs Thomas Berridge (£4 p.a.) and the School Trustees (1s/5p p.a.). Their appearance is virtually unchanged today except for the substitution of the hedge for a brick wall.

The pair of brick and thatched cottages in the distance, to the right of St Botolph's Church (Total rent of £12 16s/£12.80 p.a.), is now Rose Cottage.

Interestingly, the rents quoted did not include rates, which were paid by Lord Howe!

The four Earls Howe who owned the Gopsall Estate during the 19th and early 20th centuries

Left: George, Viscount Curzon (2nd Earl in 1870; *standing*) and Richard William Penn Curzon-Howe, 1st Earl Howe. They are both dressed in their Prince Albert's Own Leicestershire Yeomanry Cavalry uniforms (c. 1861).[21]

Middle: Richard William Penn Curzon-Howe, 3rd Earl Howe (1895).[21]

Right: Richard George Penn Curzon, 4th Earl Howe (photo dated 1896 when he was Viscount Curzon).[22]

Notes and References

1 *History, Gazetteer & Directory of Leicestershire & Rutland*. William White. 1846, 1863, 1877.

2 *Inventory of the Church Plate of Leicestershire with some account of The Donors (Vol. I)*. The Rev. Andrew Trolloppe. Leicester: Clarke & Hodgson, 1890, p. 396.

3 *Ibid.*, pp. 377-379.

4 IHS denotes the first three letters of the Greek name of Jesus, IHΣOYΣ.

5 *Norton. The History and Antiquities of the County of Leicester. Vol IV. Part II. containing the Sparkenhoe Hundred.* John Nichols. London 1811, p. 851.

6 According to a 1686 church register, Charles Jennens Snr had 2 pews in Holy Trinity Church for his and his servants' use. See: *A History of Norton-Juxta-Twycross*. Glynis Oakley. Barncraft Printing: Sheepy Magna, 1995, p. 30.

7 Information obtained from the following sources:

Congerstone Parish Records. The Record Office for Leicester, Leicestershire & Rutland. Doc. Ref: DE1104/31 & 32.

History, Gazetteer & Directory of Leicestershire & Rutland. William White. 1846, 1863, 1877.

Directory of Leicestershire & Rutland. C.N. Wright. London: Kelly's Directories Ltd, 1899.

A History of Norton-Juxta-Twycross. Glynis Oakley. Barncraft Printing: Sheepy Magna, 1995, pp. 29-43.

Portrait of an Estate Village: Some odd tales from Shackerstone. Aubrey Chalmers. The Graphic Print, 2014.

8 *Records of Andrew Bloxam, Naturalist and Perpetual Curate of Twycross*. Record Office for Leicester, Leicestershire & Rutland. Document Ref: DE3442.

In addition to the listed repairs and additions funded by Lord Howe, a variety of other people donated items including: the east chancel window (Sir Jonathan Wathen Waller Bt; previously Phipps and second husband of Baroness Sophia Howe; Chapter 1); a new font (Rev. A. Bloxam); The Queen's Arms (Mrs C Wright); heating stove (Robert Faux, H. Clare & others); tablets containing the Ten Commandments and rebinding the bible and prayer book (costs defrayed out of the collection made on the opening of the church on 9th July 1840).

9 The gallery organ presented by Earl Howe in 1845 was removed and replaced by a new organ, paid for by subscription and installed on the north wall of the chancel in 1898.

10 *Twycross. The History and Antiquities of the County of Leicester. Vol IV. Part II. containing the Sparkenhoe Hundred*. John Nichols. London 1811, pp. 860-861.

11 *Attested Copy of Will of Charles Jennens of Gopsall, Esq. Dated 30th April 1765; Codicil 7th Aug. 1766*. The Record Office for Leicester, Leicestershire & Rutland. Document Ref: DG22/5/8.

12 *Heather Church*. Leicester Journal, Friday 16th July 1847.

13 A National School in 19th century was a school founded in England and Wales by the National Society for Promoting Religious Education.

14 There is a date plaque on a front gable of the school, which was probably built to the same design as those in Nailstone, Norton-Juxta-Twycross and Sibson.

15 *Directory of Leicestershire & Rutland*. C.N. Wright. Leicester: Compiled by S. Barker, 1880.

16 *Shackerstone Conservation Area Appraisal*. Hinckley & Bosworth Borough Council. PDF document accessed on 3rd September 2021: https://www.hinckley-bosworth.gov.uk/downloads/file/1275/appraisal_-_shackerstone

17 *The Twycross mansion to be road cafe*. Leicester Evening Mail, Tuesday 4th December 1956.

18 *Assheton House Country Club & Casino*. Coventry Evening Telegraph, Friday 11th October 1963.

19 *Ibid.*: *Wanted Artists*, Thursday 19th May 1966; *Cabaret Queen Contest*. Friday 29th July 1966.

20 *New Instructions (Charter Surveyors, Atherstone)*. Atherstone News and Herald, Friday 11th December 1981.

21 Newspaper cutting and photos of Viscount George Curzon and the 1st and 3rd Earls Howe courtesy of The Rt Hon Frederick Richard Penn Curzon, 7th Earl Howe, GBE, PC.

22 Richard George Penn Curzon, 4th Earl Howe by Alexander Bassano (half-plate glass negative, 1896); National Portrait Gallery image NPG x574.

Gopsall Today

In 2017 the Crown Estate was realigning its portfolio which, for the Gopsall Estate, effectively meant it being broken up and offered for sale to the tenant farmers, with any parts unsold being placed on the open market. In a history going back to before the Domesday Book, this was the latest and last transfer of Gopsall Estate's or Gopsall Manor's ownership; the end of over 900 years of its existence.

Most of the tenant farmers purchased their farms which left about 1,738 acres, including two working farms (Castle Farm and Wharf Farm) and Fox Covert Farm (vacated in 2000) that were parcelled up into two, non-contiguous lots and collectively named 'The Shackerstone Estate' by Carter Jonas, the Crown's property consultants (Chapter 1). The whole of the Shackerstone Estate was finally purchased by Chris Stamper in early 2018 and Gopsall, as a cohesive entity, ceased to exist. However, most of the woods and coverts still remain and it is still possible to identify what was once the highly regarded park and gardens (Chapter 4), most of which are now within the area covered by Gopsall Hall Farm.

The Twycross lodge gate entrance to Gopsall Park with the entrance arch in place (*top*) and as seen today (*middle*). Granite setts remain in the 16ft of track where the gate once stood (*bottom*).

The main entrance to Gopsall Park was the Twycross lodge gate, which stood along the Snarestone road within Lodge Plantation. It was an imposing structure built in 1819 by Jeffry Wyatt (later Sir Jeffry Wyatville) and based on the Arch of Constantine in Rome. Although we know that the arch gates were sold in the 1951 fixtures and fittings sale (Chapter 12), the demolition of the lodge and arch may have been later, as they are still recorded on the 1955 Ordnance Survey (OS) map.[1] All that exists today are a few granite setts and a metal stud embedded in a stone block; its 130-year existence is dwarfed by that of the Arch of Constantine in Rome, which has stood for 1,706 years.

There are no visible remains of the Snarestone (Home Farm) or Bilstone entrance lodges but Shackerstone lodge (built between 1885 & 1901), together with the stone gate pillars and some of the original estate fencing, still remains at the end of Shackerstone Drive.

The site of The Kennels, just north of the Twycross entrance to the park, is

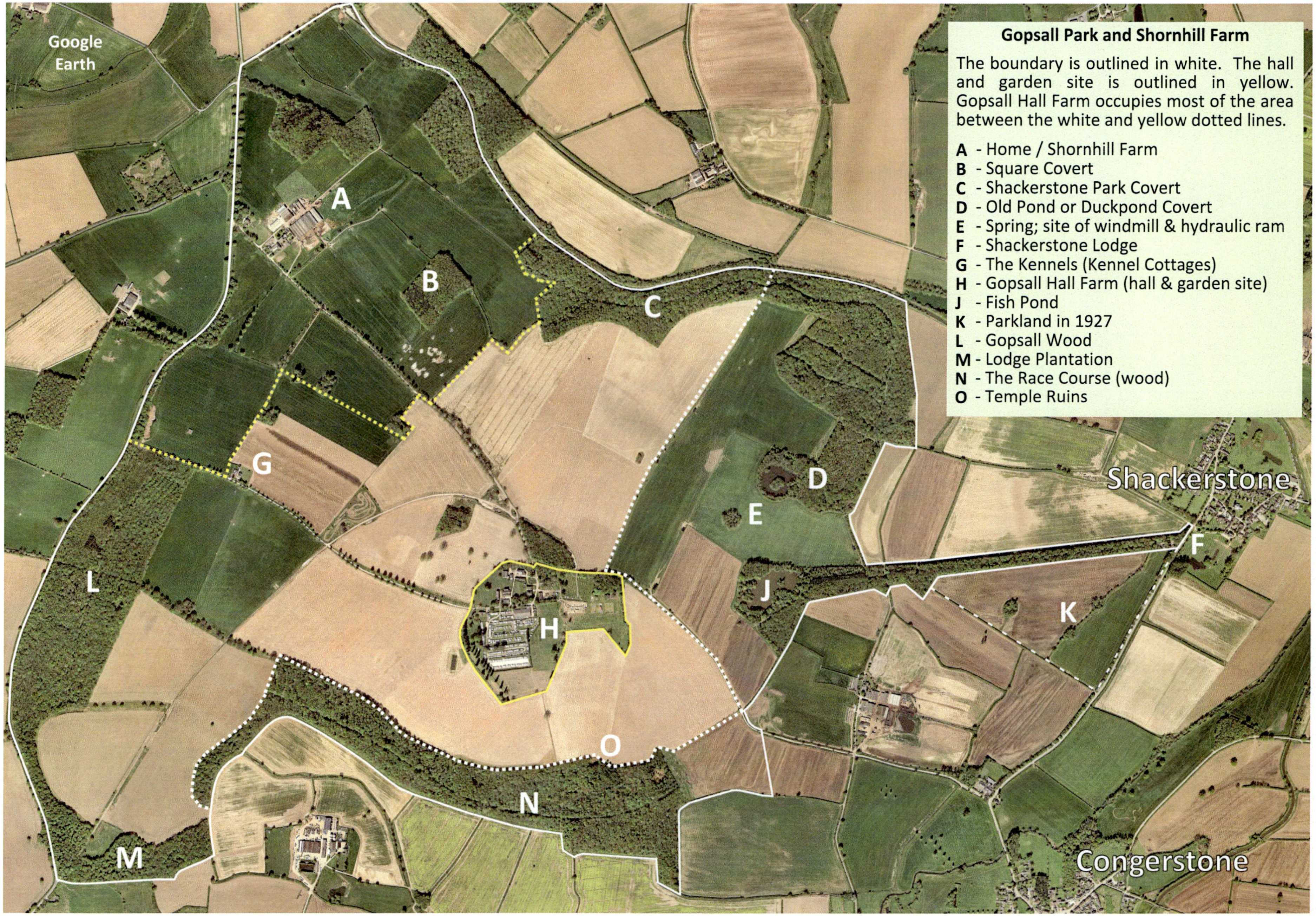
Google Earth
Gopsall Park and Shornhill Farm
The boundary is outlined in white. The hall and garden site is outlined in yellow. Gopsall Hall Farm occupies most of the area between the white and yellow dotted lines.
A - Home / Shornhill Farm
B - Square Covert
C - Shackerstone Park Covert
D - Old Pond or Duckpond Covert
E - Spring; site of windmill & hydraulic ram
F - Shackerstone Lodge
G - The Kennels (Kennel Cottages)
H - Gopsall Hall Farm (hall & garden site)
J - Fish Pond
K - Parkland in 1927
L - Gopsall Wood
M - Lodge Plantation
N - The Race Course (wood)
O - Temple Ruins
A
B
C
D
E
F
G
H
J
K
L
M
N
O
Shackerstone
Congerstone

Shackerstone lodge (*left*) and the stone gate posts at the entrance to Shackerstone Drive (*above*). The main gates have gone, but the original estate fencing and pedestrian gate are still present.

19th century outbuilding at Kennel Cottages and the 1999 Crown plaque.

now occupied by two private, detached cottages (Kennel Cottages). Parts of these cottages appear to include some of the original 19th century structures, but they have undergone several upgrades including, in 1999, by the Crown Estate.[2] A small outbuilding, now divided by the boundary between the two cottages, appears to be the only surviving intact part of the 19th century building.

Further to the north, Gopsall's farmhouse (Shornhill Farm) and its associated 19th century farm yard and buildings remain, outwardly unchanged since they were built. The farm track that passes Shornhill Farm continues for just under a mile until reaching Gopsall Hall Farm.

Shornhill farmhouse and cobbled farmyard.

Gopsall Hall farmhouse and farm buildings are sited within the area originally occupied by the hall and gardens and are a mix of some original buildings/structures and 20th century additions. The farmhouse is one of the original 19th century buildings which was the head gardener's, steward's and bailiff's house during the period between its construction (c.1850) and when the farm was leased to the Lain family in the 1960s. The other 19th century or turn of the century buildings include the walled gardens, now used for secure caravan storage, three barns/outbuildings, the power house and a pair of semi-detached cottages built in 1901. These cottages were not a completely new build, but a conversion of part of one of the original 19th century farm buildings which, in about 1870, were used for keeping pigs and ferrets.[3] The unrenovated part of this building is still used as a barn. Also present, but unseen, are the ice house and water reservoirs in the area immediately north of the walled gardens, which is still called The Nob on modern maps.

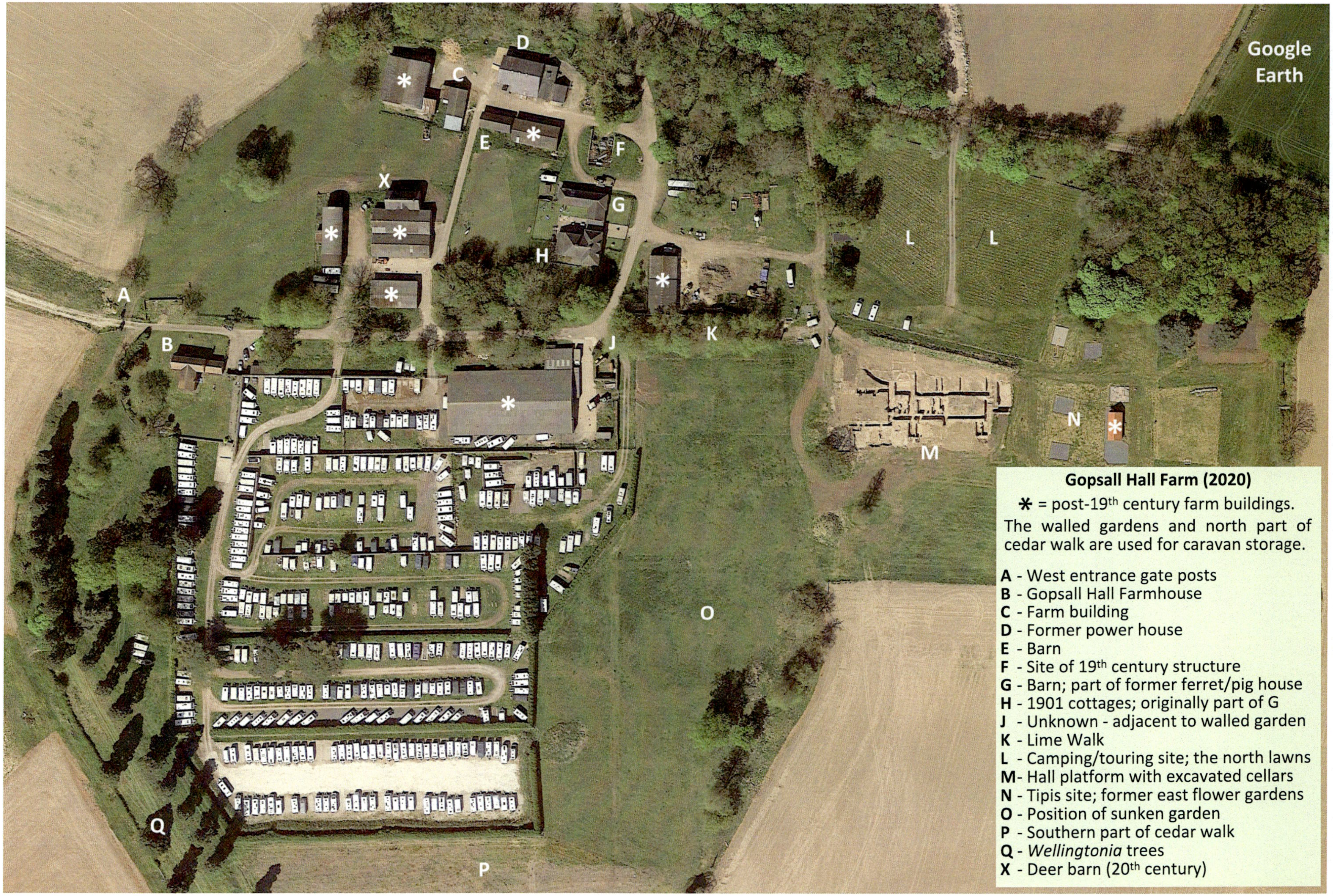

Gopsall Hall Farm (2020)

✱ = post-19th century farm buildings.

The walled gardens and north part of cedar walk are used for caravan storage.

A - West entrance gate posts
B - Gopsall Hall Farmhouse
C - Farm building
D - Former power house
E - Barn
F - Site of 19th century structure
G - Barn; part of former ferret/pig house
H - 1901 cottages; originally part of G
J - Unknown - adjacent to walled garden
K - Lime Walk
L - Camping/touring site; the north lawns
M- Hall platform with excavated cellars
N - Tipis site; former east flower gardens
O - Position of sunken garden
P - Southern part of cedar walk
Q - *Wellingtonia* trees
X - Deer barn (20th century)

The area that formed the lawns at the north entrance to the hall, now part of the 21st century Gopsall Hall Farm camping, touring and glamping site,[4] used to lead to the grassy platform on which the hall once stood. Recently, the hall area has been excavated revealing the cellars, which appear almost intact (Chapter 2). The contours of the original garden landscape still exist to the east, south and west of the hall platform, and the 19th century line of *Wellingtonia giganteum* and a few of the ancient cedars dominate the view seen from various points around what was the boundary of the park.

The west entrance (A) and Gopsall Hall farmhouse (B). The ornaments on top of the brick piers have been broken and today a track leads west past Kennel Cottages to the Snarestone road (B4116).

The power house (D; *above*); built in 1901 when the electricity supply to the hall was installed prior to the visit of King Edward VII in 1902. The two farm buildings on the left of the old photo still stand (C, *below left*; E; *below right*). Today the generators have been removed from the power house and the hall is used as the 'Old Townhall Stage' for the '110 Above' music festival.[5] Several other buildings are used for stages and as food and drink outlets.

The 110 Above Festival logo. The annual festival is so named because the Gopsall Hall site is (just) above the 110 metre contour line. Because of its elevation, the site offers excellent views of the surrounding countryside to festival goers, as it did in Gopsall Hall's heyday for the aristocratic guests of the Earls Howe. The festival forms part of Gopsall Hall Farm's successful business diversification strategy.

Pair of workers cottages built in 1901 (H; *left*)[6] and a building known as the deer barn (X; *right*). The date the barn was built is not clear. It does not appear on the 1886 (surveyed 1885) or 1903 (surveyed 1901) OS maps, but is likely to have been erected in the first years of the 20th century. It has tiled walls inside and appears to have been where game, including deer from the Gopsall Park herd, were hung and dressed.[7]

The overgrown remnants of Lime Walk (K; Chapter 4) showing surfaced area at the east end (*left*) and looking west through the avenue of the remaining lime trees (*right*). Two stone lion ornaments 'guard' the west end of the walk.

The *Wellingtonia* at the western edge of Cedar Walk and 6 ancient cedars (*arrows*) seen from the edge of The Race Course wood. Hedges, occupying what used to be the northern part of Cedar Walk, hide lines of stored caravans, in addition to those within the walled gardens.

Signpost on the track leading east from the hall site, close to where Bilstone lodge once stood, showing the way to the Gopsall Temple ruins.

Gopsall temple ruins at the northern edge of The Race Course wood. The ruins are surrounded by a ha-ha which has an entrance (fenced off) on the south side (*above*). The ruins are Grade II listed and were 'conserved' in 2003 and the structure made safe (i.e. dismantled).[8] At that time the Crown Estate agreed to establish a permissive footpath to the site. More details about the temple are given in Chapter 4.

The top of one of the temple arches displayed at the site after being taken down in 2003. It bears a fragment of the Greek inscription from the frieze around the temple (1st Corinthians XV, 57).

The walls of the kitchen gardens viewed from the temple ruins. Only 3 of the original 4 walls running east-west now remain; the southernmost wall has been demolished and replaced by a hedge (*dotted line*). The back, north wall is about 2ft thick and hollow; originally containing the flues from fires used to heat the walls and lean-to glasshouses. Detail of the north wall (*right*) now punctured with holes on its south side.

Above: The remains of the Viennese bridge at the outflow of the Fish Pond at the western end of Shackerstone Drive, uncovered by local contractors in 1997. The structure was demolished leaving only the brick bridge piers and part of the spillway; both overgrown today.
Right: View of the lake with part of a bridge pier on the left. There is no public access to the site.
Below: The overgrown spillway.

Bizarre modern remnants of Gopsall exist today thanks to Leicester County Council's Highways Department. Signs for Gopsall Park can be found proudly displayed on signposts in Bilstone (*above*) and at the T-junction by Congerstone Primary School (*left*). The signs go unnoticed and most locals would not know, or would have forgotten, that they exist. Modern Ordnance Survey maps still show Gopsall Park, and visitors to the area searching for 'the park' can be very confused now that the old wooden fingerpost pointing the way is no longer at the Castle Farm crossroads!

Interestingly, the two Gopsall Park signs direct you to two different places. The school sign directs you the ½ mile to the Bilstone lodge site and signpost to the temple. By contrast, travelling 1¼ miles from the Bilstone sign takes you to the hall site. **Note:** the track leading to Gopsall Hall Farm from the Castle Farm crossroads is not a public road.

Unnamed spinney containing the spring that used to supply water to Gopsall Hall and referred to by John Grundy in 1750 (Chapters 2 & 4). The spring is about 72ft below the hall site. In the late 19th and early 20th centuries water was supplied by a windmill and hydraulic ram. Nothing remains of the windmill, but ruins of buildings and underground structures remain (*right*).

Notes & References

1 The 1955 OS map is based on surveys performed pre-1930 to 1955, meaning that the Twycross and Gopsall Park map information may be based on pre-1951 data.

2 Kennel cottages do not appear on the 1955 OS map (see note 1) but are shown on the 1966 map which is based on surveys between 1957 and 1963.

In the late 19th and early 20th century, The Kennels was occupied by George 'Bill' Smith (Chapter 6) and his family before he became head gamekeeper: *Norton as I remember it - The reminiscences of Joan Booton* in *A History of Norton-juxta-Twycross* by Glynis Oakley (1995), p. 69. It is probable that The Kennels was generally used for housing Gopsall's underkeepers and their families.

3 *Gopsall by Arthur Sage*. Chapter 4.

4 *Gopsall Hall Farm - Camping, Touring and Glamping* (https://www.gopsallhallfarm.co.uk/).

5 The 110 Above Festival was started in 2009, when it was originally called Lainfest. Michael Lain is the principal organiser of the festival, which has been very successful over the years and attracted glowing reviews from the entertainment press, online and in print (https://www.110above.com/).

6 A photograph of these cottages, covered with ivy, is shown in Chapter 2, when they were known as the 'Gardeners' Cottages' and were still attached to the northern part of the farm building (labelled 'G' in the Google Earth image). According to Mrs Edith Leek, the two cottages were originally occupied by the electrician and the odd-man (Chapter 7).

7 It is possible that this building is the new larder built by the 4th Earl Howe just before the visit of King Edward VII to Gopsall (Chapter 8). Several newspapers describe the King visiting the 'new larder' where the total bag for his three days of shooting was stored: *Kings Visit to Gopsall - closing days*. Leicester Daily Post, 15th December 1902; *The KIng's visit to Leicestershire*. Yorkshire Post, 15th December 1902; *The King at Gopsall*. The Standard, 15th December, 1902.

8 The Gopsall temple conservation work was funded jointly by the Crown Estate, East Midlands Development Agency, Leicester County Council and Hinckley & Bosworth Borough Council (HBBC). There is an information board at the site which, like the leaflet produced by the HBBC, perpetuates the myth that Handel composed the Messiah while sitting in the temple.

INDEX

GOPSALL HALL

GOPSALL IN WWII

GOPSALL'S LORDS (SEE EARLS HOWE & CURZON-HOWE FAMILY)

GOPSALL PARK & FARM

GOPSALL SALES & HALL CONTENTS

GOPSALL VILLAGES & VILLAGERS (SEE MEMORIES)

HOUSEGUESTS

LODGES

MEMORIES

RACING CIRCUIT

SHOOTING & HUNTING (INC. GAMEKEEPERS)

STAFF